CW00702557

LINGUASIA
Borden Villa, Borden Lane
Sittingbourne, Kent ME10 1BY

ROMANIZED HINDÎ-URDÛ INTO ENGLISH DICTIONARY

VIDYÂRTHÎ'S

Romanized

HINDÎ-URDÛ

INTO

ENGLISH DICTIONARY

Compiled by

Shreerām Vidyārthî

2005

LINGUASIA

Published by
LINGUASIA
(*An imprint of* ASIA PUBLISHING HOUSE)
Borden Villa, Borden Lane,
SITTINGBOURNE,
Kent ME10 1BY [U.K.]
e-mail: linguasia@indiawise.com

First Edition: May 2005

ISBN 1 870836 15 4

A Prefatory Note

For years, while selling books from India at BOOKS FROM INDIA, in Museum Street, London, I was often asked, nay pestered, for an ENGLISH / HINDI, and HINDI / ENGLISH DICTIONARY in 'standard English script'. For years, I resisted this demand by protesting the phonetic inexact nature of this 'standard English script' in carrying and conveying the sound systems and phonetic values of Indic languages. [I still don't know as to what is so 'standard' about this thing called 'English script', except what has been presumed in the West and imposed on the rest of the world.] And for years, I have also complained that if we Indians were not taught 'this foreign tongue called English' in our own, familiar *Dévanágarî* script, why do the English people expect other tongues of the world to be transcribed in their letters?

I have also exercised the effrontery of accusing the Brits and other Europeans of perpetuating their cultural imperialism by pressing their demands for Romanisation of all foreign languages for their benefit.....

All the vitriol I could muster up and regularly showered upon these neo-learners of the 'Hindoo lingo' has nòt deterred them from pressing their demand. I have even gone to the extent of accusing them of being intellectual lethargics, but their demand has continued. They still want a 'Phonetic dictionary' of 'Indian'.

Now, I am a hard-working man and have done a bit of writing in my forty-five years of journalistic pursuits. But even I draw a line when it comes to working too hard and to being a glutton for punishment. I don't go out of my way to find difficult and cumbersome chores. So the thought of compiling such a dictionary, from scratch, definitely did not appeal to me. To meet this growing demand, I had to find a ready-made dictionary, something done by a *Raj-wallah* for the benefit of the ex-*Raj-wallahs*.

I rummaged through the remnants of the *Raj*-scholarship in search of such works of reference as were prepared by the British civil servants, with the help of their *munshis,* and by over-zealous proselytising priests to make their task of converting the natives to their 'faith of the lord' somewhat easy.

I came across quite a few: all available in third-rate facsimile reprints. I checked them for the quality of their lexicographical merits and for their linguistic currency. Most of these proved to be pieces of what I call, for want of a better phrase, 'linguistic anthropology'.

How could I, a conscientious bookseller, and a devoted teacher of languages in my earlier incarnation, put forward these bits of outdated junk in front of sincere and sound-minded learners of my native tongue? Especially when they are so uncaringly produced, badly printed on very poor quality paper, wretchedly bound and grossly over-priced?

I also came across a couple of very recent, better-produced examples of this kind of work. These too met with serious resistance at the hands of simple, tourist types who want to learn a few useful words or phrases, in their bid to be able to strike a conversation with the 'natives' when they go to India on a two-week package holiday. They found these recent works 'too bulky, too pricey and too academic' to use.

I was left with a couple of choices. One was a compilation put out by National Press, Allahabad, without any mention of or reference to the name of the compiler who could be blamed for the quality of this shoddy piece of work. The other was *The New Royal Dictionary* compiled by Rev. Thomas Craven

ADBHUT 7 ADHÚRÁ

Adbhut, *a.* Wonderful ; extraordinary ; grossly out of groove.

Addá, *n.* Rendezvous ; stand for carriages, &c. ; a perch for a tame bird caged or uncaged.

Ádhá, *a.* Half ; one of the two equal parts of a thing or measure.—*karná*, to divide into two equal parts.—*honá*, to become emaciated ; to be reduced or wasted by disease.—*sísí*, the name of a disease which affects half the head with pain ; a specific form of neuralgia.

Addhí, *n.* A species of very thin muslin ; one-sixteenth of a pice.

Adham, *a.* Base ; vile ; low.

Adhan, *n.* Hot water ; water placed on a fire to become heated for the purpose of cooking rice, *dál*, &c.

Adhangí, *a.* A person effected with paralysis so that he can move the limbs of only one-half of his body.

Ádhár, *n.* (Ahár) Food ; a support ; a patron ; a person on whom another depends for his subsistence ; a canal ; a basin round the base of a tree.

Adhar, *n.* The lip of the lower jaw ; mid air ; the firmament.—*amrit*, ambrosia of the lips ; kiss.

Adharm, *n.* Irreligiousness ; viciousness ; immorality ; unrighteousness ; sinfulness.

Adhelá, **Dhelá**, *n.* The half a pice piece.

Adhelí, **Dhelí**, *n.* The eight-anna piece.

Adher, *a.* Middle-aged ; a person who has passed the prime of life (applied most commonly to women.)

Adhik, *a.* Surpassing ; exceeding ; more ; additional.

Adhikár, *n.* An estate ; property in one's possession ; a right ; a privilege ; property acquired by inheritance.—*dená*, to invest with power or authority ; to authorize ; to appoint or commission.—*rakhná*, to hold authority.—*karná*, to exercise authority.

Ádhíntá, **Adhíntá**, *n.* Humility ; submission ; servility ; dependence.

Adhíraj, *n.* Impatience ; fickleness ; confusion ; hastiness.

Adhírtá, *n.* Perplexity ; disorder.

Ádhí rát, *n.* Midnight.

Adhkapárí, **Adhkapalí**, *n.* A pain affecting one side of the head.

Ádhonádh, *adv.* An exact half.—*karná*, to bisect.

Adhúrá, *a.* Only half done ; unfinished ; incomplete.

Fascimile page from the old
'Student's Hindi English Dictionary'

and published by Methodist Publishing House, Lucknow 1911.

The first one was blemished by too many provincialisms, and serious missives in terms of standard, India-wide, streetwise vocabulary. It appeared that the compiler (whether he was an English civil servant functioning in India, or his *munshi* doing his donkey-work under instructions, I don't know) had been taken in by highly localised vocabulary and pronunciations and had made no effort to compare and reconcile with the wider usage of the language variously called Hindî/ Hindustánî/ Urdû. 'Correcting' that one amounted to total replacement of the existing baggage.

The second work was lexicographically far far superior to the one discussed hereabove. However this was heavily laden with scholarly exposition of each entry and contained whole sentence-examples of words as they were in use at the time. Also too many entries were those of vocabulary commonly used in matters administrative, and involved with the judicial system of the day, with a suitable mixture of words required for Church business. (After all, the compiler was a Reverend of the C. of E.). Even correcting, or updating this was a very heavy task for me to undertake, having had no experience of lexicographic practice.

In any case I was looking for a work that would be of use to lay people, a handy, portable size and relatively inexpensive.

So I set about completely revamping the anonymous work. And it took some revamping (see the facsimile page opposite). After about four-and-a-half years of hard, almost blinding work on the project, what I have been able to achieve is presented here, for you to use and appreciate or otherwise.

I am a stickler for the author's legal and moral claim to a work and have fought some vigorous battles, and incurred heavy losses, in the process, protecting author's rights. I would never append my own name to another person's work. So there was no question of putting my name to an existing work, whether credited to someone by name or anonymous. But in this case, I have appended my name as the 'compiler and editor' because (1) there is no way of identifying the compiler of the original work, or even ascertaining whether this was an individual's work, or a jumble of many compilers' output; and (2) 80% to 90% of entries have been corrected, revised, updated, or been freshly created by me. And what remains of the original work in this compilation is commonly entered in all dictionaries.

To justify my claims to authorship of this work a bit further, I have gone to considerable lengths to redesign the whole work, from page layouts to the choice of typography; from creating a 'key to pronunciations' to 'correctly *Romanising*' the words which were haphazardly spelt in the original work. Therefore my claim to the authorship of this work is based on the same principle which allowed Christopher Marlowe to claim *The Jew of Malta* as his own work as different from William Shakespeare's *The Merchant of Venice*. I may not be as creative a genius as those two referred to hereabove; but my work is as original.

Another point ought to be made, in every lexicographical work in every language. However tall claims may be made for the comprehensiveness of such books, 'completeness' should neither be presumed nor claimed. I say this owing to awareness of the fact that language is not a finite, dogmatic or a dormant bunch of sounds or mere spellings, but a living entity, a vibrant, throbbing, living and growing organism. New words are coming into being and flowing into the stream of public usage.

Therefore, all works of lexicographical reference can only be as up-to-date as the date of going to press. Any 'new arrivals' in this journey, after this point in time, would have missed the train and must wait their turn till the next edition.

In my file, there are many such 'new arrivals'. I must keep them on the platform of my patience and wait the scheduled departure of the next train.

I am aware of one specific shortcoming that this compilation has and for which neo-learners of the language will not bless me: While delineating the grammatical status of each head-word and the derivatives, I have stuck to indicating the case of each word, but have ignored the need to mark their gender status or, in most cases, even their linguistic origins. This shortcoming has not crept in because I was trying to be PC (I mean 'politically correct'), but because I became aware of the need for indicating gender-markings when I was more than halfway through the work. [The original work had no such markings.] I shall have to make up for this shortcoming next time I indulge in this kind of work, or go for a revision of this one. In the meantime, I hope this 'problem' will not hinder neolearners of Hindi from achieving whatever their goal.

Without the slightest hesitation, I am happy to acknowledge my debt to the anonymous compiler, or compilers of *The Student's Romanized Practical Hindustánî-English Dictionary,* published by National Press, Allahabad, in providing me with an existing structure of such a compilation and inspiring me to do what I have been able to do.

And I'll be failing to pay my *Guru-Rin,* my debt of honour, to my teachers, in this matter if I do not acknowledge the practical guidance in the composition of lexicographical units which late Dr. Bhola Nath Tiwari and late Dr. Mahendra Chaturvedi gave me, during the short period of study which I spent with them in 1964, while I was studying for an M.A. in Hindi at Delhi University. Regrettably, I never finished that Master's in Hindi. Money, or the lack thereof, came in the way. But in the course of those few months in the company of these illustrious lexicographers I learnt a lot, and fast.

I wouldn't have dared put my name to any work of this nature while these great souls were around. They would have seen through my ignorant and non-scholarly ways right away. It is a relief, and a pity, that today's linguistics scholars (nameless though will they remain, out of my deference for them) couldn't even find time to look my work over, even cursorily, before I surrendered it to print. I would have preferred their learned input. Instead I am left with my regrets.

—*Shreeram Vidyarthi*
April 26, 2005

Borden Villa,
Borden Lane
SITTINGBOURNE,
Kent ME 10 1BY
United Kingdom

Guide to sequence of words

And a word of apology!

Owing to different alphabetical sequence of letters in Hindi and English, keeping various word-groupings, or derivatives together has not always been possible. Therefore, following my instincts and on the basis of oral values in pronunciation, I have had to devise a sequence which will make it easy for the Anglophile Indians and foreign learners to use this dictionary.

For instance, word **Do** means **Two** in English. However, derivatives of this head-word, like duganá/ duhará/ du-pahar etc. could not be grouped together.

Another point, worth taking into account while using this work is that when I came across some multiple derivatives of headwords like **Mu<u>n</u>h** and **Pánî,** I over-looked the need for listing the derivatives in their alphabetical sequence. Later on when this flaw came to my attention, the typesetting work had progressed so far that it was not practical to make the necessary changes. I guess, my own lexicographical skills were barely evolving while I was working on this dictionary. Perhaps, in the light of this realization, with successive editions of this and further works of mine in the pipeline, I will hone my skills much more. My effort, at making Indic languages accessible to script-wise illiterates, continues.

Shreeram Vidyarthi

KEY TO PRONUNCIATION

At the very outset, I wish to make it clear that the Roman script, in which English and other European languages are written, is incapable of conveying accurate pronunciations of the Indic languages like Hindi, Bengali etc. without resorting to around 200 cryptic contortions and neo-constructions of letters of the Roman alphabet. To my mind that is a task fit for professors of linguistics, and not for the tourists and occasional travellers, or lay people trying to communicate with their Asian neighbours. If one were to ask the neo-learners of an Indic language to master those hundreds of 'new' or artificially created letters, one might as well urge upon the learners to master the original scripts of these languages.

Only advantage this Roman script can boast of is that, through this, one can learn more than one language, without having to go to the extent of mastering hundreds of scripts. And it is with this in mind that I have come out with this dictionary.

I have adopted here the simplest possible method of scripting Indic words that we could devise, without contortions. However, regrettably, some new constructions, not too complicated, you will have to learn and identify to achieve a reasonable semblance of accurate pronunciation.

A	As 'U' in up, upper, utter, etc.
Á	As in 'A', class, pass, etc.
É,Í,Ó,Ú,	The right-ward tilting sign on top of these vowels, whether in upper case or lower, running case, has the effect of flattering and prolonging the vowel sounds. Like 'É' will sound like 'ay' as in 'essasy'; 'Í' will sound like 'ee' as in 'creed'. 'Ó' should sound like 'o' in 'old' and 'over'; and 'Ú' should sound as 'oo' as in 'loot'.

÷	A dot (resembling a full stop [.]) under a letter is indicative of some sounds which Hindi/ Hindustani/ Urdu have borrowed from Sanskrit and Persian: A dot under 'k' will make it a harder sound to pronounce; a dot under 'r' will produce a sound involving the rolling of your tongue (like Americans do when they utter words like 'Laboratory'— or 'labratory' as they call it—or like the Irish pronounce the name of their lush green country); a dot under 'kh' will produce a sound resembling 'h' as pronounced by Russians and Slavs, as in a town name called 'OHRID' etc.
-i-	This symbol is only used where we have to elicit the meanings of some Persianised Urdu/ Hindustani joint-words, indicating a link between the two parts, like '*Kúchá-i-yár* meaning 'the street where the loved one lives'.
-o-	This is also used to indicate a link between two entities, only this one means 'and', like in English we have started using '-n- ' indicating 'and' (Black-n-white, Rock-n-roll, etc.).

Key to abbreviations:

a./ adj.	Adjective
adv.	Adverb
n.	Noun
Pref.	Prefix
pron.	Pronoun
Prov.	Proverb
Suf.	Suffix
v.	Verb

Alphabet Chart with Roman as applied herein.

Vowels			Consonants		
अ	a	account, rural	क	k	kill, okay, seek
आ	á	alms, father	क़	q	
इ	i	in, fill, lily	ख	kh	inkhorn
ई	í	police, east, tea	ख़	kḥ	loch (Scottish)
उ	u	full	ग	g	gun, jargon, dog
ऊ	ú	rude, flu	ग़	g̣	
ऋ	ri	ripple, merrily	घ	gh	loghut
ए	e	prey	ङ	n̲	sing, sink
ऐ	ai	hand, cat	च	ch	chime, matching, church
ओ	o	oak, stone, go	छ	chh	churchhill
औ	au	awe, off	ज	j	jam, major, hedge
ं	n		ज़	z	zip, gazette, gaze
ँ	n		झ	jh	hedgehog
ः	h		ञ	n	singe
			ट	ṭ	talk, mate, last
			ठ	ṭh	anthill
			ड	d	dome, guide, mad
			ड़	ṛ	
			ढ	dh	redhaired
			ढ़	ṛh	
			ण	ṇ	
			त	t	tu (as in French or Italian)

थ	th	
द	d	madame (as in French)
ध	dh	
न	n	not, many, in
प	p	pink, caper, sip
फ	ph	uphill
फ़	f	father, telephone, half
ब	b	bark, debate, rub
भ	bh	abhor
म	m	man, seminar, jam
य	y	yet, loyal, boy
र	r	red, foray, year
ल	l	lead, overly, panel
व	v/w	vulture, ivy, have
श	sh	sure
ष	sh	shun, bush
स	s	saint, reset, gas
ह	h	hear, behave
क्ष	ksh	action
त्र	tra	extra
ज्ञ	gya	

Hindi - Urdu interface with Roman letters

A. a. a short vowel sound, equal to the Hindi letter (अ) lending pronounceability to all consonants in Hindi, and *alif* (ا) of Urdu and Persian scrpts, also used on its own, usually at the start of a word, like *Ab, Apná,* and *Adhúrá.* As a vowel sound, it equals *zabar* (َ) in Urdu, placed on top of a character, pronouncing like *Utter, upper, ulcer, &c.* In Hindi, it is also used as a prefix, implying negation to the following word, like ***a**-samán, **a**-tul, &c.*

Á, á, is a long vowel sound, equal to (आ and T) in Hindi, or *alif mamdúda* (آ) as in *Ásmán, Ágáh, &c.* On its own, it always appears at the beginning of a word, as an independent sound. For example, *Ánand, Ágaman.* In the middle of a word, or at the end of a word, it will always provide a vowel sound, as in *kamál, Lambá.*

‘A, ‘a, in this dictionary is being used to denote the Urdu sound (ع) as in *‘arq,* and ‘Á, ‘á, for the sound of ( ) as in *Áqil,* or *‘ámil.* In Hindi, Devanagari script, these sounds will be represented by (ा) and (आ). It can be used independently as vowel sound as well as tonal addition to the preceding consonant sound.

B,b, is being used to denote the Hindi letter (ब) and the Urdu letter (ب). When one-and-a-half value of this consonant is required, [which only occurs in the middle of a word or at the end and never at the beginning of one] as in *babbar* or *Abbá.* When a dilution of this consonant is desired, usually at the beginning or in the middle of the word, like *byáh,* or *Zabt,* then a single use is immediately followed by a full consonant sound as in these quoted examples **bh** represents (भ) in Hindi and (بھ) of Urdu.

C,c, in English alphabet is used variously to denote ‘s’ sound [in *place*] as well as ‘k’ sound [*class* and *commerce*]. In this dictionary, we are using it only in conjunction with ‘h’ to form a single letter ‘Ch’ to denote Hindi sound of (च) and Urdu sound of (چ). In latter part of this letter listing ‘Chh’ will also be found to denote a successive Hindi sound of (छ) and Urdu sound of (چھ). Unfortunately English sound system has no equivalent sound to indicate parallels.

D, d, is being used to denote the Hindi sound of (द) and Urdu sound of (د). When dotted at the bottom, like 'ḍ' it will indicate Hindi sound (ड) and Urdu sound of (ڈ). It will also be used in conjunction with 'h' as 'Dh' to convey the Hindi sound of (ध) and Urdu sound of (دھ). With a dot under 'D,d' and a sufix 'H,h' we obtain an aspirated sound of Hindi (ढ) and Urdu (ڈھ).

E, e, is to represent the Hindi sound (ए) and Urdu sound (ے). It can be used independently as vowel sound as well as tonal addition to the preceding consonant, represented by (े) in Hind and by (ی) in Urdu.

F, f, is to register the Persian-Urdu sound of (ف) which has for long been imported into Hindi as (फ़) which is obtained by placing a softening dot under the Hindi letter (फ).

G, g, is used here, in the first instance, to denote the Hindi sound (ग) and Urdu sound (گ); in the second place, when used with a dot (.) at the bottom, it will indicate the Persian-Urdu sound of (غ) and the imported Hindi sound of (ग़).

H, h, is equivalent to Hindi sound (ह) and Urdu sound (ہ) and (ح).

I, i, is being used for the short vowel sound of Hindi (इ) and Urdu *zer* (ِ). In the second place, with the benefit of a forward slash on top of it, like (Í, í), is being applied to denote Hindi (ई) and Urdu (ی). In the third place, the letter 'I, i' with an apostrophe coma placed before it, we have used it to denote the specific Urdu sound of *ain* (ع). It can be used independently as vowel sound as well as tonal addition to the preceding consonant which is represented by (ि) symbol in Hindi and *zér* and (اِ) in Urdu.

J, j, is a consonant sound and is used to denote the Hindi letter (ज) and Urdu letter (ج). Diluted to half value, this letter will be followed by a semi-vowel like *'Y, y'* and double value, it will precede vowels like *a,e,i,o,u.* Some times an aspirated consonant sound will be obtained by adding *'h'* to it to indicate Hindi (झ) and Urdu (جھ).

K, k, denotes (क) in Hindi and (ک) in Urdu. By adding an '*h*' to it we also obtain an aspirated sound equal to (ख) in Hindi and (کھ) in Urdu. Some times this letter, when dotted at the bottom, is used to indicate the Arabic-Urdu sound of (ق) and the imported Hindi sound (क़). With a dot (.) underneath 'K, k' and Suffix 'h' we obtain the Arabo-Persian-Urdu sound of (خ) and the imported Hindi sound of (ख़).

L, l, stands here for (ल) in Hindi and (ل) in Urdu. This consonant is also applied in half, or diluted value when it precedes semi-vowel '*y*' and in double value (or one-and-a half value, as we say in Hindi) and followed by standard vowel tones.

M, m, stands for (म) in Hindi and (م) in Urdu. In its diluted, half-value sound it also functions as a nasal tone in the middle of a word as well as at the end of one.

N, n, sounds like (न) in Hindi and (ن) in Urdu. In its diluted, half-value sound it also functions as a nasal tone in the middle of a word, or at the end of one. With a dot underneath, 'ṇ' represents Hindi (ण).

O, o, sounds like (ओ) in Hindi and (او) in Urdu. This vowel sound functions as an independent letter as well as a tonal addition to preceding consonants. In Persian-Urdu vocabulary, it also functions as an interjection, applied to equals and inferiors meaning 'and'. Also used as a form of informal address.

P, p, stands for the consonant (प) in Hindi and (پ) in Urdu. It is also used as one-and-a-half value, equal to (प्प) in Hindi and (پّ) in Urdu. When suffixed by an 'h', it equals (फ) in Hindi and (پھ) in Urdu.

Q, q, represents the letter (ق) in Urdu and the imported-from-Arabic sound of (क़) in Hindi.

R, r, is equal to (र) in Hindi and (ر) in Urdu. When used with a dot (.) at the bottom, it represents the sound (ड़) in Hindi and (ڑ) in Urdu.

S, s, stands for (स) in Hindi and all three sound of (س and ص) in Urdu. It is also used with addition of 'h' to express (श) sound in Hindi and (ش) in Urdu.

T, t, sounds like (त) in Hindi and (ت and ط) in Urdu. With a dot (.) at the bottom, it will also represent (ट) sound in Hindi and (ٹ) in Urdu. When suffixed by an 'h' it represents the aspirated sound of (थ) in Hindi and of (تھ) in Urdu. When used enjoined with a dot at the bottom, it would sound like (ठ) in Hindi and (ٹھ) in Urdu.

U, u, is a vowel equivalent of (उ) in Hindi and (اُ) in Urdu. If functions as a full letter in its own right, but also grants a tonal value to the preceding consonant, which is represented by (ु) symbol in Hindi and (ُ) in Urdu. When used with a forward slash (́) on top, this assumes a longer vowel sound of (ऊ) in Hindi and (اُو) in Urdu, or vowel tone of (ू) in Hindi and *Pésh,* in Urdu.

V, v & W, w Both of these letters represent the same consonant in Hindi (व) and Urdu (و). Subtle difference between the two sounds in Hindi and Urdu is that words spelt with 'V' would carry greater emphasis on the consonant (व) or (و) while words spelt with 'W' will tend to emphasize two vovel sounds, i.e. 'u' and 'a' in quick succession, almot bridging the two sounds, as if some old fat soul grunting while getting out of a deep pile sofa: "Oo-ah". Therefore, though we have listed words spelt with each of these letters separately, one section after the other, you should not be surprised to see same words(s) listed in both lists. For the Hindi speakers, in phonetic terms, **V** and **W** are interchangable.

X, x, is redundant in terms of transliterating any standard Hindi or Urdu words. Therefore, we have compiled no words under this heading. Hindi and Urdu vocabulary can well manage its repertoire of compound letters by combining other letters of the Roman alphabet.

Y, y, is used to denote letter (य) in Hindi and letter (ی) in Urdu. It serves no vowel function in our scheme of transliteration.

Z, z, is used for representing the imported-from persian sound of (ज़) in Hindi and (ض ز ظ ذ) all four sounds of Urdu alphabet.

HINDÎ-URDÛ into English Dictionary [In Roman Script]

A. a. a short vowel sound, equal to the Hindi letter (अ) lending pronounceability to all consonants in Hindi, and *alif* (ا) of Urdu and Persian scrpts, also used on its own, usually at the start of a word, like *Ab, Apná,* and *Adhúrá.* As a vowel sound, it equals *zabar* (َ) in Urdu, placed on top of a character, pronouncing like *Utter, upper, ulcer, &c.* In Hindi, it is also used as a prefix, implying negation to the following word, like ***a**-samán, **a**-tul, &c.*

Á, á, is a long vowel sound, equal to (आ and ा) in Hindi, or *alif mamdúda* (آ) as in *Ásmán, Ágáh, &c.* On its own, it always appears at the beginning of a word, as an independent sound. For example, *Ánand, Ágaman.* In the middle of a word, or at the end of a word, it will always provide a vowel sound, as in *kamál, Lambá.*

'A, 'a, in this dictionary is being used to denote the Urdu sound (ع) as in *'arq,* and 'Á, 'á, for the sound of (عا) as in *Áqil,* or *'ámil.* In Hindi, Devanagari script, these sounds will be represented by (ा) and (आ). It can be used independently as vowel sound as well as tonal addition to the preceding consonant sound.

Ab, *adv.* Now; just now; at the present time. *—hi,* adv. Immediately; at this very moment. *—se,* adv. Henceforth; from this moment on; from hereon; in future. *—tak,* adv. Till now; so far. *—tab,* adv. Occasionally. *—tab honá,* adv. To be nearer death.

Áb, *n.* Water; magnificence; shine; honour; sparkle (in gems); temper or rigidity (or steel); keenness of edge (of a sword). *—i-baqá,* adj. Water of life. *—i-bárán,* adj. Rain water. *—bázi,* v. Sporting in water; swimming. *—o-dáná,* means of a livelihood. *—didá,* adj. The tear-filled eyes. *—o-hawá,* n. Climate; weather conditions. *—i-hayát,* adj. Water of life; nectar; the mythical liquid that imparts immortality to those who partake it. *—i-jári,* adj. Running water; a stream; flowing tears. *—kári,* v. The business of a distiller of a spirituous liquor; a distillery. *—khorá,* adj. A vessel for drinking out of. *—i-nuqrá,* n. mercury; silver reduced to liquid state by means of a solvent. *—páshi,* v. Irrigation; the business of watering the agricultural fields. —*I-rawán,* adj. Running water; spring; cloth of very fine texture. —*shár,* n. A waterfall. —*i-shor,* adj. A brackish water. —*i-zar,* Gold-wash.

Abábil, *n.* The swallow; a petite, singing bird that appears in spring.

Abad, *n.* Time without end; the boundless ocean of time. —*ul-ábád,* adv. For ever and ever, for all time to come; till eternity.

Ábád, *a.* Cultivated and inhabited; prosperous; settled; established. —*i,* n. A settlement (of people); an inhabited spot. —*karná,* v. To make a place inhabitable; to develop land conditions to be fit for human settlement.

Abaddh, *a.* Varied; not bonded; not tied down.

Abádh, *adv.* Without hurdle, unhindered; free; without restraint.

Ábáí, *a.* Ancestral; descending to or inherited by one from his forefathers.

Abal, *a.* Feeble; wanting in bodily strength.

Ábarú, *n.* self-respect, honour. (See **Ábrú** also).

'Abas, *a.* Vain; useless; unavailing; idle.

'Abbási, *n.* Name of a flower; the colour red.

'Abbásiyán, *n.* The children of Muhammad's uncle Abb*ás*.

'Abd, *n.* A servant of God; a votary of God, hence also (*met.*) a slave.

'Abdiyat, *n.* Slavery; servitude.

Aber, *n.* Delay; lateness.

Ábguzár, *n.* An express messenger; a courier; a fordable passage across the bed of a stream or river.

Ábhá, *n.* Light radiance; magnificence; beauty.

Abhadra, *a.* Indecent; indecorous.

Abhág, *n.* Ill-luck; misfortune.

Abhágá, Abhági, *a.* Unlucky; unfortunate; ill-starred.

Abhakshya, *a.* Inedible; uneatable; forbidden food.

Ábharan, *n.* Ornaments; trinkets.

Abhibhávak, *n.* Guardian; one taking care of; one responsible for.

Abhidhán, *n.* A dictionary; a lexicon; a word-book.

Abhiját, *a.* Aristocratic; well-born; classic; of noble birth. —*tantra. n.* Aristocracy; system of rule by upper classes. —*varg. n.* Nobility; aristocratic class.

Abhilákhá, Abhiláshá, *n.* Desire; longing; wish, hankering.

Abhimán, *n.* Pride; haughtiness; vanity.

Abhimáni, *a.* Haughty; proud; vain. *—ká sar nichá,* 'pride goeth before a fall.'

Abhinandan, *n.* Greeting; reception; a ceremonious welcome; applause. *—granth, n.* Commemorative Volume. *—patra. n.* A welcome address. *—samároh, n.* A reception ceremony.

Abhinn, *n.* Intimate; note distant; close; identical.

Abhipráe, *n.* Intention; implication; purport; design.

Abhisár, *n.* Rendezvous; a meeting (of lovers). *—iká, n.* A woman going out to meet her lover; one keeping an assignation.

Abhishek, *n.* Installation on a throne as a sovereign by the ceremony of royal function; purification by sprinkling the water of the sacred Ganges on a person.

Abhrak, *n.* The mineral called talc; powdered mica.

Ábhúshaṇ, *n.* Jewellery; finery; trinkets.

Abhyágat, *n.* A guest; a visitor who is entertained by the person whom he visits.

Abhyás, *n.* Practice; habit; meditation.

Ábi, *a.* Aquatic; living in or frequenting watery regions. *—ghorá, n.* hyppopotamus or river-house.

'Ábid, *n.* A devotee; a deeply religious person.

Ábila, *n.* A blister.

Abinási, *a.* Indestructible; eternal; immortal.

'Ábir, *n.* A voyager; a traveller across land and water.

Abir, *n.* A red powder having a red colour which is sprinkled on people among the Hindus during the Holi; saturnalia.

Ábista, *a.* Pregnant (a woman or animal).

Abiswás, Avishwás, *n.* Mistrust; lack of trust; non-belief; lack of belief; untrustworthiness; unreliability; scepticism.

Abiswásí, Avishwásí, *a.* One who does not trust, one who does not believe, a non-believer; sceptic.

Abla, *a.* Wanting in bodily strength; weak. *n.* a woman.

Ablah, *a.* Wanting in bodily strength; weak. *n.* a nincompoop.

Ablahi, *n.* Folly.

Abláí, Ablápá, *n.* Debility; languor; feebleness.

Ablaq, *a.* Marked with patches of black and white; pie-bald.

Ablaqá, *n.* A starling; a bird of the *maina* species.

Abná, *n. (Plur. of Ibn).* Offspring; tribe.

Abnáe-jins, *n.* Fellow-beings; companions.

Ábnús, *n.* A heavy kind of black wood; commonly known as ebony; (proverbially) black.

Abodh, *n.* Ignorance; stupidity; wanting in understanding; lacking in sense.

Abr, *n.* A cloud. *—i-gal˜íz,* dense clouds. *—i-ázur,* clouds that pass away without raining. *—chhâná,* the sky to be overcast with clouds. *—i-murda,* a sponge.

Abra, *n.* The upper fold of a garment made of two layers of the same material.

Abrak, *n.* Talc; mica.

Abrár, *n. (Plur. of Birr).* Virtuous men; good men.

Abras, *a.* Affected with leprosy.

Abri, *a.* An alteration of sunshine and shade due to the presence of clouds in the sky. *—kágaz,* paper whose colour is variegated: marble paper.

Abrú, *n.* Eyebrow.

Ábru, *n.* Self-respect; one's honour; the name of a poet. *—barbád karná,* to deprive one of his own conduct. *—lená,* to deprive one of his good reputation. *—rakhná,* to maintain one's self-respect. *—utárá,* to disgrace one.

Áb táb, Áb-o-táb, *n.* Splendour; radiance; magnificence.

Abtar, *a.* Spoilt; ruined; vitiated; wretched; disordered.

Abú, *n.* Father (used to form the first part of a man's name), as in *Abul-bashar,* the father of the human race, Adam; *Abulfazl,* the name of the Secretary of Emperor Akbar; *Abúbakr,* the name of an *atúbak* prince to whom S'adi dedicated the *Gulistán;* also the father-in-law and immediate successor of Mohammed.

Abújh, *a.* Wanting in understanding or sense; stupid.

Abwáb, *n. (Plur. of Bab).* Doors; gates; heads of public revenue; sources of government income. *—alúfa,* payments exacted from land-owners by the government for the maintenance of schools, hospitals and the like for the benefit of public.

Abyát, *n. (Plur. of Bait).* Rhyming couplets; houses.

Abyáz, *a.* Very white; resplendent; dazzling.

Achal, *a.* Stationary; fixed; permanent; perpetual; immovable; non-movable; a mountain.

Achar, *a.* One that does not move; fixed in location; without movement.

Áchaman, *n.* Rinsing out the mouth with water sipped from the palm of the hand before engaging in a religious act, before partaking of food, or after meals.

Achambhá, *n.* A wonder; marvel; something that astounds; something incredibly extraordinary. *—karna,* to be lost in wonder.

Áchának, *adv.* Unexpectedly; all of a sudden; accidentally.

Achár, *n.* Preserves prepared with oil, vinegar, salt, spices, &c.; pickle.

Áchár, *n.* Conduct; mode of life; custom; practice; religious custom; practice; religious custom; indispensable, religious observance.

Acharaj, *n.* Wonder; surprize; amazement.

Ácháryа, *n.* Instructor in religion; a performer of religious ceremonies; one learned in Hindu philosophy or science.

Áchárí, *n.* One who strictly follows established rules and practices. *a.* having the quality of strictly following established rules and practices.

Achchhá, *a.* Very well; alright; nice; handsome; good; pioturesque; benevolent; kind; valuable; excellent. *—hond,* to be cured. *—karná,* to cure; to heal. *—lagná,* to be agree-able. *achchhe 86—,* the very best. *ackchhi tarah,* well; thoroughly. *achchhí kahí,* what next?

Achchhar, *n.* [a corruption of 'Akshar'] A letter of the alphabet, [in Urdu it is called *harf*].

Achchhat, *n.* [a corruption of 'Akshat'] Rice; grains of rice being used in Hindu ritual and ceremonials; part of the oblations to deities.

Achet, *a.* Unconscious; out of senses; one who is not aware of one's deeds or surroundings.

Achhwání, *n.* A kind of warm drink made of spiced and sugard wine or ale given to sick persons, women in child-bed or the like; something that refreshes or warms.

Achraj, *n.* Something that is wonderful or marvellous; something that is miraculous. *—karná, v.* to wonder; to marvel; to regard as a miracle; to consider to be progidious.

Ád, [See *Ádi*].

Adá, *n.* Posture; performance; discharge. **—honá,** *v.* to be paid; **—karná,** *v.* to repay; to discharge. **—dikháná,** *v.* to show off, to pretend, to put on a show, to put on an act.

Adab, *n.* The showing of due respect to superiors in consequence of good breeding and a proper bringing up; a sense of respect for persons superior to ourselves which makes us behave venerably towards them; politeness; courtesy; respect; veneration. *—karná,* to treat another with reverence or respect.

Ádáb, *n.* Greeting, good manners, etiquette, refined behaviour. **—bajá lání,** *v.* to greet a venerable one. **—arz karná,** *v.* to offer saluatations, to greet.

'Adad, *n.* A figure; a number.

'Adálat, *n.* A court of justice; a court of law. *—i-apíl,* an appellate court. *—i-diwáni,* a civil court. *—i-faujdarí,* criminal court. *—i-khafífa,* court of small causes. *—i-mál,* revenue court.

Ádam, *n.* The name of the first man created. *—khor,* a cannibal; maneater. *—zád,* the human race; mankind.

'Adam, *n.* That which does not exist; default in putting in an appearance. *—maujúdagí,* in one's absence. *—pairawí,* in default of presence of the plaintiff or complainant to press his cause against the defendant or accused. *—subút,* the absence of evidence leading to the inference of proof.

Adaq, *a.* Most subtle or abstruse; very abstract in character.

Ádar, *n.* Respect; reverence; honour; the notice that is taken of any one by the public. *—yogya,* venerable; worthy of respect.

'Ádat, *n.* Habit; way; manner. *—dálná,* to form a habit by repeated practice. *—parná,* to get into the habit of.

'Adáwat, *n.* Ill-feeling; malice; spite. *—rakhná,* to entertain ill-feeling; to keep strife alive. *—nikálná,* to take revenge.

Adbadá, *a.* Without due consideration, out of synch, uneasy, topsy-turvy.

Adbadá kar, *adv.* Without due deliberation caused by a feeling of uneasiness.

Adbhut, *a.* Wonderful; extraordinary; grossly out of groove.

Addá, *n.* Rendezvous; stand for carriages, &c.; a perch for a tame bird caged or uncaged.

Adh, *A prefix meaning, half;* generally used in a diminutive sense; as in *adh-baná,* half-done, incomplete state; *ad-galá,* half-cooked; insufficiently cooked; *ad-mará,* half-dead; so lean and emaciated as to be a mere skeleton; (as an idiom) to be so beaten as to be left half-dead.

Ádhá, *a.* Half; one of the two equal parts of a thing or measure. —*karná,* to divide into two equal parts. —*honá,* to become emaciated; to be reduced or wasted by disease. —*sísí,* the name of a disease which affects half the head with pain; a specific form of neuralgia.

Addhí, *n.* A species of very thin muslin; one-sixteenth of a pice.

Adhaṃ, *a.* Base; vile; low.

Adhan, *n.* Hot water; water placed on a fire to become heated for the purpose of cooking rice, *dál,* &c.

Adhangí, *a.* A person effected with paralysis so that he can move the limbs of only one-half of his body.

Adhar, *n.* The lip of the lower jaw; mid air; the firmament. —*amrit,* ambrosia of the lips; kiss.

Ádhár, *n.* (Ahár) Food; a support; a patron; a person on whom another depends for his subsistence; a canal; a basin round the base of a tree.

Adharm, *n.* Irreligiousness; viciousness; immorality; uarighteousness; sinfulness.

Adhelá, Dhela, *n.* The half a pice piece (now obsolete).

Adhelí, Dhelí, *n.* The eight-anna piece (now obsolete).

Adheṛ, *a.* Middle-aged; a person who has passed the prime of life (applied most commonly to women).

Ádhí, *a.* Half, 50%, incomplete, half-done. —*bat, n.* Half complete, half-made statement. —*rát, n.* Midnight.

Adhik, *a.* Surpassing; exceeding; more; additional.

Adhikár, *n.* An estate; property in one's possession; a right; a privilege; property acquired by inheritance. —*dená,* to invest with power or authority; to authorize; to appoint or commission. —*rakhná,* to hold authority. —*karná,* to exercise authority.

Ádhíntá, Adhíntá, *n.* Humility; submission; servility; dependence.

Adhíraj, *n.* Impatience, la of patience, fickleness, confusion, hastiness.

Adhiráj, *n.* The sovereign, the supreme ruler.

Adhírtá, *n.* Perplexity; disorder.

Ádhi-rát, *n.* Midnight.

Adhkapári, Adhkapálí, *n.* A pain affecting one side of the head.

Adhogati, *n.* Downfall; degradation.

Ádhon-ádh, *adv.* An exact half. —*karná,* to bisect.

Ádhunik, *a.* Modern; uptodate; current; presently in fashion; a fashion-conscious person. —*á,* a. A fashionable lady. —*tá,* n. Modernity; quality of being current and with the times. —*vichár-dhárá,* n. Modern thinking.

Adhúrá, *a.* Only half-done; unfinished; incomplete.

Adhyáe, *n.* Chapter; section; division of produce into two equal parts for the purpose of apportionment between landlord and tenant.

Adhyáná, *v.* To halve; to appropriate in equal halves.

Adhyápak, *n.* Teacher; one who gives education; trainer.

Adhyátma, *n.* Spiritual contemplation. —*gyán,* n. Spiritual knowledge; awareness of the inner self. —*Vád,* n. Spiritualism.

Ádi, *adj.* Ancient; of beginning; of start. –*ádj,* adv. Etc. etc.; so on and so forth. –*kál,* adj. Antiquity; beginning period; beginning of time; commencing stage. *Kálín,* adj. of ancient times; of an early period. –*purush,* n. The beginner of the human race; first man; the God Himself; the supremesoul; the seed entity. –*vásí,* n. Aboriginal people; the early man; the native(s); traibal(s).

Ádí, *a.* addict; habitual; hooked on. —*ho jáná,* v. To become an addict; to fall pray to a habit; to become obsessed with.

Adib, *n.* A teacher of manners and discipline.

Adig, *a.* Immovable; firm; steady. —*Vishwás,* a. Unflinching faith; firm belief.

'Ádil, *a.* Just; fair; considerate; equitable. —*áná,* fairly; justly; equitable.

Adilla, *n.* Examination; test; proof; sign; argument.

Adin, *n.* Luckless day; disastrous day.

Áditya, *n.* The Sun god; a proper name for boys.

'Adl, *n.* Rendering to everyone what is his due. —*gustarí,* the administration of justice.

Adlá badlá, Adal badal, *n.* One for an other; exchangeing one for another; the awarding of compensation; the giving up of one thing in order to receive another. —*karná,* to affect an exchange.

Ádmí, *n.* *(Lit.)* A descendant of Adam; hence the human race;

mankind; individual; person; husband; dependent; adult; fearless man; right and proper person. —*banáná,* to civilize; to make acquainted with the arts and sciences of modern knowledge. —*honá,* to be possessed of such qualities as distinguish a human being from the brute creature; hence to partake of quality of rationality, and the effects that flow therefrom. —*ho jáná,* to attain the status of manhood; to be no longer a youth or child. —*píchhe,* one after every man; per head.

Ádmíyat, *n.* The humankind, the quality of humanity which comprises generosity, benevolence and a tender regard for the good of others. —*pakarná,* to become habituated or accustomed to the ways of civilized human beings; hence to become civilized or cultured. —*sikháná,* to teach one the ways of civilization. —*se khárij hona,* to be expelled from the pale of civilization; to be a boor.

Adná, *a.* Trifling; of little consequence; mean; base; ignoble. *n.* a person of little consequence; a person without any influence; an obscure man. —*o-á'la,* the highest and the lowest.

Adrá, *n.* The name of the month in which the monsoon season in Hindustan commences.

Adrak, *n.* Ginger in its green state; the roots of the ginger plant as they are dug out of the earth, before they are cured or otherwise prepared for human use or consumption.

Adrakí, *n.* Tincture with a flavour of ginger.

Adrishya, *a.* Invisible; imperceptible; out of sight.

'Adú, *n.* Enemy; foe; one who is hostilely inclined towards another.

'Adul, *n.* *(Plur. of 'Adil).* Straightforward; honest; frank; just; upright.

Advait, *n.* Non-dualism, a system within the Hindu philosophy, part of *Vedántic* school of thought.

Adwán, Adwáyan, *n.* The ropes at the end of a bedstead intended for the purpose of keeping the texture of the bedstead in position, *i.e.,* to prevent it from moving up or down. —*kasná,* to tighten the strings fastened to the end of a bed to prevent the texture of the bed from becoming slack or loose.

Adwár, *n.* *(Plur. of Daur).* Ages that have expired in the past; bygone ages; times that have elapsed; past generations or ages.

Adwiyat, *n.* *(Plur. of Dawáí),* Different kinds of medicine;

medicines of different varieties; medicines.

Áf, *n.* The sun; the musk-deer; species of animal from which a very fragrant kind of perfume is obtained.

Af'á, Af'ai, *n.* A snake; a viper.

Af'ál, *n. (Plur. of F'el).* The acts of deeds that habitually constitute one's conduct; the ordinary or habitual conduct of one's life; deeds; conduct.

Áfáq, *n. (Plur. of Ufuq).* The horizon; the imaginary line that in ordinary sight forms the boundary between the heaven and the earth; regions of the earth.

Áfat, *n. (Plur. Áfát).* Vexation; preplexity; annoyance; cause of annoyance; trouble; distress; cause of great anxiety; misery; wretchedness. *—áná,* to be overtaken by a misfortune or calamity. *—ká márá, —zadá, —rasídá,* one overwhelmed with misfortunes or troubles. *—macháná,* to create disturbance; to kick up a hell of a row. *—ká parkálá,* a very cunning person. *—men phansná,* to be involveed or intricated in some difficulty. *—utháná,* to bear or endure some trouble or misfortune.

Afgán, *n.* Bewailing; lamentation; dweller of Afghanistan.

Afgár, *a.* Wounded. *n.* A sore on the back of any beast of burden caused by the placing of a saddle upon it or by the carrying of heavy loads.

Afím, Afyún, *n.* The juice of the poppy flower commonly known as opium. *—chí,* one addicted to opium-eating or opium-smoking. *—í chehra,* having the emaciated and pale countenance of an opiumeater or smoker.

'Áfíyat, *n.* Good health; well-being.

Afkár, *n. (Plur. of Fikr),* Thoughts; cares; opinions; meditations.

Aflák, *n. (Plur. of Falak).* The heavens. *—í,* pertaining to the heavens; heavenly; celestial.

Aflátún, *n.* The name given by the Arabs to the famous Greek philosopher Plato. *(met.)* assuming; boastful; disdainful.

Afrád, *n. (Plur. of Fard).* An individual; one; sheets of paper.

Afráz, *n. (Plural of Farz).* Duties; responsibilities; Liabilities.

Áfrín, *n.* Praise; applause; *intj.* Bravo! Well done! Here! here! *—karná,* to praise; to applaud. *Jahán—,* the Creator of the world; God.

Afríninda, *n.* The Creator.

Áfrinish, *n.* Creation.

Afrokhta, *a.* Set on fire; ablaze; inflamed.

Afroz, *a. (used in comp.).* Brightening; illuminating; enkindling.

Afsah, *n. (Plur. of Fasíh)* Exceedingly eloquent.

Afsáná, *n.* A story; any creation of the imagination not founded upon actual facts; a tale. *—khwán̲,—go,* a teller of stories; a novelist; a writer of fiction.

Afsar, *n. (Corr. of the English).* Officer; a person holding a superior appointment in the Civil or Military departments of the Government service; the head official of a department. *—á'la,* the head official of a department.

Afshán̲, *a. (used in comp.),* as *Nur-afshán̲,* &c. Scattering; spreading this side and that in a disorderly manner; diffusing. *—í kágaz,* speckled paper; paper covered with gold or silver wash.

Afshurda, *a.* Pressed or rinsed out; strained; filtered.

Afsos, *n.* Grief; sorrow; regret. *intj.* it is a matter of regret! Alas! Ah!

Afsún, *n.* A magic spell; a magic formula intended to operate as a charm. *—gar,* a magician; a wizard; a sorcerer.

Afsurda, *a.* Benumbed; withered; devoid of the power of sensation through cold; dejected; dispirited; depressed. *—khátir, —dil,* low-spirited; depressed; in state of melancholy.

Áftáb, *n.* The sun. *—parast,* a worshipper of the sun. *—gir,* a light umbrella used mostly by ladies to keep off the sun's rays from falling on them; a sunshade; any contrivance erected or constructed to keep out the sun's rays from any particular spot.

Áftába, *n.* A vessel for containing water; a pitcher.

Aftáwa, *n.* A kind of firework.

Afwáh, *n. (Plur of Fwah).* Rumour; current report.

Afwáj, *n. (Plur. of Fauj).* Troops; forces; armies. *—i-bahrí,naval troops; naval forces.*

Afzá, a suffix; (as *Hairat-afzá, sehat-afzá,* etc. meaning Augmenting; enlarging; increasing, improving.

Afzáish, *n.* The act of becoming multiplied or augmented; enlargement; multiplication; increase.

Afzal, *n. (Plur. of Fazl).* Virtues; excllencies; accomplishments; refinement; attainments; favours.

Afzal, *a.* The best of all; the most excellent.

Afzúd, *n.* Plenty; abundance; superfluity; excess.

Afzún, *a.* Greater; more.

Ág, Fire; flame; *(met.)* anger; passion; love; hatred; jealousy. *—dená,* v. To perform funeral rites. —*par pání pherná,* v. To pacify; to calm down an argument, or a fight. —*par lotná,* v. to be uneasy, or restless. —*aur pání ká rishtá,* a. innate mutual hostility. —*phánkná,* v. To boast enormously; to lie grossly. —barasná, v. (for weather) to be extremely hot. —*men kúdaná,* v. To take a deliberate risk; to endanger one's self. —*men ghí dálná,* adv. To stroke the fires; to exacerbate al already difficult situation. —*lagá kar tamáshá dekhná,* v. To excite trouble and then ejoy it. —*par kuán khodná,* adv. To prepare for emergency after it has arrived. —*babúlá honá,* v. To be furious; to blow one's top in anger; to get into a rage.

Ágá, *n.* The front of anything; the forehead; in future; in time to come. —*píchhá,* back and fron; one after another; in succession. —*píchhá dekhná,* yá *sochná,* to consider well the consequences or results of an act or undertaking before doing or launching out on it; to look before and after. —*píchhá karná, to hesitate; to waver; to be undecided.* —*píchhá sambhálná,* to act prudently.

Agahan, *n.* The name of the ninth month of the Hindu *Vikram* calender. —*í,* the name for the autumn harvest.

Agádh, *a.* Bottomless; unfathomable; exceedingly deep.

Ágáh, *a.* Deeply learned or versed in any subject; well-informed, alert. —*karná,* to inform; to forewarn; to caution.

Ágáhí, *n.* Information; knowledge; watchfulness; warning.

Agal-bagal, *adv.* By the side of one another; side by side. —*karná,* to change the position of things so that those that were in the fron are placed at the back.

Agam, *a.* Inaccessible; unattainable; incomprehensible; impassable; impenetrable; bottomless; deep; boundless.

Ágam, *n.* Futurity; the next world. —*vidyá,* the science of prophesying or foreteḷing the future events. —*gyání* a prophet; a sooth-sayer.

Agaṇit, *a.* Numberless; incalculable.

Agar, *conj.* If so; in that case; under such circumstances.

Agar, *n.* The wood of aloes *(elwa, musabbar).*

Agaṛ-bagaṛ, *n.* A jumble; rub-bish. *adj.* mixed in a confused manner.

Agarche, *conj.* Although; even if; conceding that; even granting.

Agáṛí, *adv.* In front; before. *n.* money paid in advance; a first charge on a property. —*pichháṛí lagáná,* to tie the fore and hind legs of a horse with ropes fastened to pegs.

Agast, *n.* A corruption of the English August; slightly simplified; a tree.

Ágat, *a.* One who has come; one just arrived.

Agaund, *n.* The top of the sugarcane plant cut up for seed.

Agauní, [corruption of Agawání] *n.* The going or sending forward of anyone to receive another as a mark of honour. —*karná, v.* to advance to meet the bridegroom on the occasion of the celebration of his marriage or to meet a visitor on the road.

Agawání, *n.* (see. *Aǵauni,* and *Agwani).*

Ágáz, *n.* Commencement; beginning.

Áge, *adv.* In front; before; prior; in the past; ahead. —áge, ahead; in front. —*áná,* to come into one's sight; to put oneself forward; to defy; to happen in the future; to come to pass. —*barhná,* to advance; to improve; to outdo; to progress. —*dálná,* to throw or place in front of. —*dekhná,* to look in front; to consider the future. —*karná,* to place before another; to cause a person to go ahead as a guide or leader. —*píchhe,* one after another; one succeeding another; one succeeding another; before and after; at sometime or other.

Agh, *n.* Crime; guilt; offence; sin; suffering; wickedness.

Ághá, *n.* A title meaning lord; chief; master; commonly applied to the merchants and money-lenders from Afghánistan who come to India to carry on their business.

Agháná, *v.* To be satiated; to be surfeited; to be glutted. a. filled.

Aghor, *n.* A title of Lord Shiva, the Destroyer; dreadful. —*panth,* an order of mendicants who worship Shiva; —*panthi,* followers of Shiva, those belonging to the order of; *(metaph.)* a glutton; one who has unclean eating habits.

Aghorí, *n.* Filthy; unclean; avaricious; covetous. *n.* a gormandiser. —*pan, n.* filthiness; uncleanliness.

Aginbot, *n.* A steamer; any vessel impelled by steam power; a motor boat.

Aglá, *a.* That which is before others; next; prior; former; pertaining to the past; formerly. —*janam,* the next life; the life after death.

Agní, *n.* Fire. *—hom,* a sacrifice offered on fire. *—pújak,* a fire-worshipperk a zoroaster.

Agochar, *a.* Imperceptible; invisible; used particularly to indicate this attribute of God.

Aguá, *n.* A leader; manager; head.

Agúṛh, *a.* Easy to understand; not difficult to understand; evident, frank; can-did; open.

Agwání, *n.* A person sent in advance to meet another. *—karná* to advance to greet or welcome another; to escort one to his home.

Agwárá, *n.* The front part of any place (*i.e.,* of a building or garden, &c.). *—pichhwárá,* in the front and at the back of any locality.

Ágyá, *n.* Command; order; permission; direction. *—kárí,* acting according to orders; obedient. *—karná,* to give orders; to issue instructions. *—men rakhná,* to keep under one's authority; to rule.

Agyánatá, *n.* Ignorance; inexperience; folly; foolishness.

Agyání, *adj.* Ignorant; foolish; stupid.

Ágyánusár, *adv.* In compliance with orders given.

Agyá-ghás, *n.* A species of grass possessing medicinal qualities, commonly called lemongrass.

Agyárí, *n.* The lighting of fire by Hindús at the time of taking part in religious devotion.

Áh, *n.* A sigh, a curse, a long breath (indicating sadness, or sorrow), *'Ah me! Alas!'*. *—bharná, —khínchaná.* Adv. give vent to a sigh. *—paraná,* being affected by the curse expressed through a sigh. *—márná,* v. to curse someone as retribution for one's own distresss, or sorrow.

Ahad, *n.* Unity; one; an unity pledge.

Ahádís, *n. (Plur. of Hadís).* Traditions particularly those that are attributed to Mohammedans; sayings to Muhammad and his companions handed down from generation to generation by word of mouth.

Áhak, *n.* Quicklime; mortar; cement.

Ahálí-mawálí, *n.* The populace; the inhabitants of a place generally; a party consisting of all classes and conditions of people.

Aham, *a.* important; significant; heavy.

Aham, *n.* Ego; pride; arrogance; *—kár,* n. still meaning ego; pride; arrogance.

Áhan, *n.* Iron. —*gar,* a worker in iron; an ironsmith. —*í,* made of iron. —*rubá,* magnet; loadstone *(chumbak patthar).*

Áhang, *n.* Intention; object; purpose.

Ahankár, *n.* Vanity; arrogance.

Áhár, *n.* Food; victuals; anything that is eaten as a meal.

Áhat, *n.* A sound causing alarm; any sound that causes apprehension; a noise. —*lená,* to be on the alert.

Ahbáb, *n. (Plur. of Habíb).* Friends and relations; those dear to one.

'Ahd, *n.* Mandate; order; a testamentary document; promise covenant; vow; time; reign. —*bándhná,* to make a promise. —*karwáná,* to bind by conditions. —*námah,* a document recording a treaty; a charter. —*o-paimán karná,* to make an agreement. —*shikaní,* breach of faith; unfulfilment of a promise. *Puráná* aur *Nayá—náma.* Old and New Testaments, the Bible. —*i-hukúmat,* in the reign of.

Ahdí, *a.* Indolent; lazy; slow.

Aher, *n.* Game; prey; field sport. —*iyá, n.* a sportsman; hunter.

Ahi, *n.* Serpent; snake.

Ahinsá, *n.* Non-violence; lack of violence. —*vád,* a. One following the creed of non-violence.

Ahír, *n.* One of the caste whose business is the tending of cows.

Áhista, *adv.* Slowly; softly; gradually; gently; leisurely; conveniently. *a.* slow; lazy; sluggish; slack.

Ahit, *n.* Harm; damage; injury; evil.

Ahkám, *n. (Plur. of Hukm).* Orders; commands; instructions.

Ahl, *n.* People; the inhabitants of a country or place; followers of the same religion; members of the same profession or family; the inmates of a house. *a.* fit; capable; worthy; possessed of; endowed with; gifted with *(when used in compos.),* as:—*i-'uql,* wise; orydebtl oissessed if oractucak wusdin, —*i-hirfa,* mechanic; artisan. —*i-dil,* generous; benevolent; liberaly. —*i-fazl,* good; virtuous; learned. —*i-'ilm,* erudite; deeply versed in knowledge. —*i-kár,* a subordinate employee; a clerk; a workman. —*i-kitáb,* people who follow the religion prescribed in a book which is believed to have its origin in divine revelation; used by the followers of Mohammad when speaking of the Bible; hence the Jews and Christians. —*i-mad,* a clerk in the vernacular department of an office. —*i-majlis,* a prominent member of society; one well-known in social circles. *—i-m' arifat,* possessed of the knowledge of God. *—i-mansab,* the holder of an office. *—i-qalam,* a civilian; one engaged in the civil affairs. *—i-sukhn,* eloquent litering person. *—i-shara',* the followers of some established and recognised religion. *—i-zamán,* one who acts according to the needs of the prevailing times; a time-server. *—i-zauq,* possessing a refined taste; an appreciator of beauty; discerning.

Áhlád, *n.* Delight; rapture; gladness.

Ahliya, . A wife. *saráe—,* the apartments of a dwelling-house set apart for the use of the occupant's wife, female relations and their attendants; a harem, inner count of the house.

Ahliyat, *n.* Nobility; worthiness; gallantry.

Ahmaq, *n.* An idiot; a stupid person; a fool. *—banáná,* to make a fool of one; to show one in such a ridiculous light as to make him appear to be a fool. *—pan,* silliness; stupidity; foolishness. *-ul-lazí,* a very great fool; most stupid; absolutely devoid of commonsense.

Ahsan, *a.* Exceedingly lovely; most beautiful; very splendid; most excellent.

Áhú, *n.* Deer; viciousness; shortcoming; fault. *—barra,* a fawn. *—chashm,* possessing eyes that are as bright and soft as those of a deer, gazelleeyed.

Ahwál, *n. (Plur. of Hál).* Circumstances; condition; state of things. *pursií,* an enquiry after the state of one's health.

Ai, *intj.* A vecative particle meaning lo ! hark ! here ! I say ! listen !

'Aib, *n. (Plur. 'Aiyúb.)* A defect of character; a personal shortcoming; vice bodily infirmity; defectiveness; unsoundness; moral delinquincy. *—bín yá gír,* one who is habitually given to finding faults in others. *—chhipáná, —poshí,* the act of hiding or concealing one's fault. *—goí,* slandering; calumniating; speaking evil of another. *—joí,* fault-finding; criticising. *—lagáná,* to impute some blame to another. *—í,* a person who has many defects of character; a person tainted with vices.

'Áid, *part. a.* Turning toward; happening; referring to; being restored. *—honá,* to be liable to; to be amenable to; to have preferred against one; to be charged with (legal).

Ailán, *n.* Declaration; announcement; public pledge; open commitment.

Ailániyá, *adv.* Openly; evidently; publicly; aloud.

'Ain, *a.* Precise; intrinsic; actual; just. *n.* a letter of the Urdu Alphabet; a fountain; gold; the very essence of a thing; eye. *gawáh-i-'aini,* an eye-witness. *—main,* the identical; exactly alike. *—waqt par,* in the nick of time, *i.e.,* at the most critical moment.

Áín, *n.* Constitution; statute; regulation; a more or less sanctified set of rules that must not be toyed with.

Áiná, *n.* Looking-glass; mirror. *—sáz,* maker of looking-glass. *—rú,* a person having beaming or growing countenance.

'Ainak, *n.* Spectacle; glasses to assist the eye-sight.

Ainchná, *v.* To draw; to attract.

Ainthná, *v.* To twist; to tighten; to contort; to wriggle.

Aisá, *adv.* Such; like this; similar to this. *—na ho,* may it not happen ! God forbid ! *—waisá,* insignificant; trifling; of no value or importance.

Aise, *adv.* Thus; in this manner.

'Aish, *n.* Enjoyment; pleasure; delight; luxuriousness. *—gáh,* yá*—mahal,* place of entertainment. *—o-'ishrat,* licentiousness; lewdness; moral deprevity.

Aishwarya, *n.* Splendour; pomp; divine glory and power; wealth.

Aiwán, *n.* Palace; beautiful and spacious residence.

Aiyám, *n.* *(Plur. of Yaum.)* Time; days; season; period; weather.

'Aiyár, *a.* Cunning; sly; subtle. *n.* a sensualist; a profligate; a debauchee; one utterly degraded in morals; a voluptuary. *—í,* luxury; debauchery.

Áj, *adv.* To-day; on this date. *—kal,* now-a-days; in these days; to-day or to-morrow; shortly. *—kal karná,* to procrastinate; to put off from day to day.

'Ajab, *a.* Marvellous; extraordinary; uncommon; rare.

'Ajáib, 'Ajáibát, *n.* Wonders, marvels; curiosities. *—ul makhlúqát,* wonders of the world. *—ghar,* museum; a place containing a collection of objects in natural history, or connected with literature, art or science.

Ajal, *n.* An appointed time; fate; destiny; the hour of death. *—girafta, —rasida,* at the point of death; in a condition in which no hope of life remains.

Aján, *a.* Ignorant; simple.

Ajas, *n.* Infamy; notoriety; disrepute.

Aját, *a.* one who is not born. —*shatrú,* One who has no enemies, one who's enemies are not born yet.

Ajdád, *n.* *(Plur, of Jadd).* Forefathers; ancestors.

Ajgar, *n.* The boa constrictor; one of the largest species of serpents, python.

Ajfran, *n.* Indigestion. *a.* indigestible; unwholesome.

'Ajíb, *a.* Marvellous; wonderful; extraordinary.

Ajít, *a.* Invincible; unconquerable; unsubdued; not brought into subjection.

'Ájiz, *a.* Humble; feeble; weak; fatigued; weary; helpless. —*áná, adv.* submissively; humbly. —*honá* to be rendered helpless; to render submission; to yield or submit.

'Ájizí, *n.* Submissiveness; meekness.

Ajláf, *v.* *(Plur. of Jalf).* Lowest or most degraded classes of society; people of ignoble birth; base-born creatures.

Ajmod, Ajmúd, *n.* The caraway plant, the seeds of which are used in flavouring cakes and certain kinds of sweets.

Ajnab, Ajnabí, *a.* Foreign; novel; strange. *n.* an alien.

Ajnás, *n.* *(Plur. of Jins).* Kinds; species; sorts; goods; articles of trade and commerce; chattels.

Ajrám, *n.* *(Plur. of Jarm).* In-animate bodies. —*i-falak,* celestial bodies.

Ajsám, *n.* *(Plur. of Jism).* Animate bodies (human, animal or vegetable).

Ajúr, *n.* Brick.

Ajúra, *n.* Wages; hire; fare; rent. —*dár,* a labourer for hire; hireling.

Ajwáyan, *n.* Seeds of the dill plant, used as a remedy for flatulence, caraway seeds.

Ajzá, *n.* *(Plur. of Juz).* Sections; constituent parts; portions; ingredients; component parts; the thirty sections of the *Qurán.*

Ák, *n.* A plant yielding an acrid juice, which is used in medicine; a sprout of sugarcane.

Akábir, *n.* *(Plur. of Akbar).* Noblemen; grandees; people of high rank. —*o-aságir,* high and low; rich and poor.

Akáj, *n.* [corruption of Sanskrit word *'Akárya*]. unworthy deed;

unsuitable action; improper move; Useless; wrong; injurious.

Akál, *n.* A famine; a general scarcity of food. *a.* untimely; premature. *—maut,* premature or untimely death. *—vrishtí,* rain falling out of the proper season.

Akaṛ, *n.* Crookedness; state of being contorted or misshapen; rigidity; stiffness; haughtiness; vanity; conceit; arrogance. *—bái,* spasm; the cramp. *—báz,* a vain man of feeble intellect and much ostentation; a coxcomb; a dandy. *a. akṛá,* rigid; hard; stiff; contorted.

Ákár, *n.* Shape; form; aspect; portrait; symbol; sign; taken.

Akáran, *adj.* Illogical; unjustified; without reason.

Akárath, *a.* Fruitless; vain; unsuccessful.

Akaṛná, *v.* To make contortions of the body; to writhe; to be cramped; to become stiff; to assume a proud and ostentatious bearing or demeanour; to behave conceitedly.

Ákarshak, *a.* Attractive; charming; alluring.

Ákarshaṇ, *n.* Attraction; charm; allurement.

Ákarshit, *a.* One who is attracted; charmed; one allured.

Ákás, *n.* [a corruption of *Ákásh*] The sky; the heavens. *—Vání,* divine revelation; a voice from heaven; divine inspiration. *—bel,* the air-creeper, a parasitic plant, *i.e.,* one that grows upon another plant and feeds upon its juice or sap. *—choṭí,* the zenith; the highest point in the heavens. *—gangá,* the Milky Way or Galaxy.

Ákáshvání, *n.* Oracle; a heavenly announcement; a proper name given to old 'All India Radio'.

Akasmát, *adv.* Instantly; unexpectedly; suddenly.

Akbar, *adj.* Greater; exceedingly great. *n.* the name of Moghal Emperors of India, who ruled from 1533 to 1605 A.D.

Akelá, *a.* Alone; lonely; secluded; solitary; deprived of human society or companionship

Akhaṉḍ, *adj.* Entire; intact; whole; undivided; indivisible.

Akháṛá. *n.* An arena in which wrestling contests are held; a religious fraternity, brother-hood or other; an open space of ground set apart for acrobatic performances and the display of feats of strength. *Indra ká—,* the court of the god *Indra.*

Aḳhbár, *n.* *(Plur. of Ḳhabar).* A newspaper; journal.

Áḳhir, *n.* End; termination, conclusion. *—kár, adv.* In the end; at last; finally; conclusively; eventually;

Áḳhirat, *n.* The end; last remains; bodily remains corpse.

Áḳhirí, *a.* Final; last; conclusive; the end part, the ultimate.

Aḳhláq, *n. (Plur. of Khulq).* Refined manners; politeness; the qualities or attributes that constitute nobility of character; ethics; precepts of morality.

Áḳhor, *n.* Rubbish; refuse; filth; offal. *—kí bhartí,* an assembly of coarse-minded; ill-mannered persons filled with rubbish.

Aḳhrot, *n.* Walnut, a fruit.

Aḳhtar, *n.* A star; constellation: a favourable omen; a propitious sign; good luck. *—shumár, n.* an astrologer; an astronomer. *—shumárí,* the drawing up of one's horoscope.

Ákhyán, *n.* A narrative; a tale; a legend; a fable; a story.

Akif, *a.* Diligent; industrious; assiduous; attentive to duty or business; one who passes his life in religious duties or ceremonies.

Akmal, *a.* Whole; perfect; entire; complete.

Akrám, *(Plur. of Karm).* Kindnesses; favours; generous deeds; kind actions.

'Aks, *n.* Reflection; reflected imageof any object, as in a mirror or in water; *bar.* —on the contrary in spite of; opposite to; opposed to: the reverse of.

'Aksí, *a.* Photographic. *—taswír,* a photograph, visually exact.

Aksar, *adv.* Generally, frequently, often. *—awaqát (adv.)* ordinarily, many times, in most cases.

Aksaríyat, *n.* Majority; prevalence; controlling position.

Aksír, *n.* Panacea; remedy for all diseases; specific or sovereign remedy; an elixir; a liquid for transmuting base metals into gold or for prolonging life; chemistry. *a.* of great utility; very profitable.

Ákúl, *a.* Restless, uneasy, distracted, distressed.

Akuláhaṭ, *n.* State of distress, restlessness, mental distress.

Akuláná. *v.* To be distressed, to be distracted, to be agitated, etc.

Ál, *n.* A tree yielding a red dye; children, particularly those of a daughter; descendants; dampness.

Al, *adv.* The Arabic Definite Article Corresponding to 'the'. *(used as a prefix in compos.)* as:*—'abd,* a signature. —batta, certainly; by all means; assuredly; decidedly. —*garaz,* briefly; in a few words. —*háfiz,* God preserve us !—*hamd-o-lilláhe,* praise be to God!—*widá',* last Friday of the month of Ramzán; good-bye ! fare-well ! adieu !

Álá, *a.* High; distinguished; eminent; illustrious. —*dimágh* quick-witted; intelligent; intellectually sound. —*himmat* brave; courageous; magnanimous.

Aláe-baláe, *n.* trivia; trivial or frivolous conversation; useless occupation or activity; unprofitable employment.

Alaf, *n.* Dry grass; hay. —*zár,* a meadow; a tract of land overgrown with grass; a pasture.

Alag, *a.* Separate; apart; disconnected; detached; secluded. —*alag,* separately; one at a time; individually. —*karná,* to divide; to separate: to keep apart; used to disjoin; to put asunder; to divorce. —*rahná,* to abstain from; to remain alone; to avoid; to evade.

'Alahidá, *a.* Apart; separate; distinct; excluded; set apart. —*honá,* to be separated from; to separate oneself; to disassociate one's self from.

Áláish, *n.* Defilement; pollution; corruption; contamination; corruption; contamination; refuse; offal; filth.

Alakh, *a.* Invisible; unperceiveable; without shape or form. —*purush,* the Invisible Being; the unseen God.

'Alálat, *n.* Malady; sickness; disorder; disease; ailment; aindisposition.

Alam, *n. A.* Pain; grief; anguish; affliction; agony; distress. H. A prop; a support.

'Alam, *n.* Standard; flag; mark; emblem; symbol; spear; lance. —*bardár,* standard-bearer; a staff-bearer.

'Álam, *n.* The world; universe; multitude; throng; regions; condition; state; time. —*ārá,* beautifying the world. —*i-bálá,* heaven; the dwellers in heaven. —*i-fáni,* this earth, which will some day pass away, as distinct from Heaven, which will exist throughout eternity. —*i-gaib,* the world to come the next world. —*i-siflí,*; the nether or infernal regions: the lower world. —*gír,* conquering the world, prevailing in all quarters of the world (said of diseases); universal.

'Alámat, *n.* Sign; note; symptom; token; trace; badge; brand.

Alang, *n.* Line; rank (of soldiers); row; fringe; border; margin; side.

Alaṉkár, *n.* Decoration; ornament; embellishment; rhetoric.

Aláo, Aláw, *n.* Bonfire; a flame; a fire-place.

Áláp, Áláp, *n.* A few notes of music sung as a prelude before commencing a song. —*karná,* to tune; to pitch the voice.

Álas, *n.* Idleness; aversion to work; laziness; sloth; drowsiness; indolence. —*í,* (a) lazy; indolent; idle; slothful; disinclined for work.

Álát, *(Plur. of Álá).* Tools; implements; instruments; utensils.

'Aláwá, *adv.* Besides; in addition to; as well as. —*iske,* notwithstanding; in spite of.

Álaya, *n.* An affix denoting 'the abode of', as *Himálaya,* the abode of snow; *Vidyálaya,* the abode of knowledge; &c., &c.

Albelá, *n.* pleasantly surprising; a dandy person; uniquely funny.

Alfáz, *n. (Plur. of Lafz).* Words; expression; accents.

Alganí, Arganí, *n.* A clothes line; a rope extended between two pegs or upright poles and used for hanging clothes on.

Algoza, Algoja, *n.* A wind-instrument of music somewhat resembling the flute or flageolet.

Álhá, *n.* A verse narrative eulogy to the chivalrous deeds of two young heroes, *Álhá* and *Údal;* a ballad composed in traditional metre and sung all over rural North India.

Alhaṛ, *a.* Young; untaught; inexperienced; unskilful.

'Alí, *a.* Of dignified rank; illustrious; eminent. *n.* the name of the son-in-law of the prophet Mohamed. —*band,* a charm or amulet worn in order to ward off the effects of sorcery or witchcraft.

Álí, *n.* A woman's female friend.

Álí—, used as a prefix to highlight qualities of a persona or rank. —*jáh* of dignified rank ('Your Excellency'.); —*shán,* splendid; magnificent; gorgeous; of a high decorative order.

Alif, *n.* The first letter of the Persian alphabet. —*honá,* to rear or stand on the hind legs, said of a restive horse.

'Alíl, *a.* Weak; feeble; infirm; indisposed; unwell.

'Álim, *a.* one with profound learning or knowledge; wise. —*ul-gaib,* the Omniscient (God).

Álingan, *n.* Embrace; clasp; a passionate hug.

Alláh, *n.* God. —*Alláh,* an exclamation of terror or astonishment; By God ! Good God ! My Goodness ! —*Alláh khair salláh,* thank God it is ended. —*o-Akbar*; God is Great.

Almárí, *n.* Cupboard; wardrobe; book-case; shelf.

Almás, *n.* Diamond.

Alol-kalol, *n.* Frolic; gambol; friskiness; sportiveness; playfulness.

Aloná, *a.* Without salt; insipid; tasteless.

Alop, *a.* Concealed; hidden; invisible. —*anjan,* a collyrium, or eye-salve, which renders its user invisible. —*honá,* to be hidden; to be extirpated; to become extinct; to be totally destroyed; to become invisible; to disappear from view.

Alorná, *v.* To mix by stirring; to churn.

Alp, *a.* A little; small; minute; short. —*kálik,* a. Short-lived; temporary; short term. —*buddhi,* a. An idiot; an unintelligent person. —vay, a. Under-age. —*virám.* n. Coma. a punctuation mark. —*sankhyak,* of minority group. —*áhár,* n. A short meal, a snack, or breakfast; abstemious meal.

Alqáb, *n. (Plur. of Laqab).* A title; a respectful form of address; distinctions. —*o-ádáb,* a form of address containing the titles or distinctions of the person addressed.

Alsáná, *v.* To rest; to dose off; to feel sluggish.

Alsí, *n.* Linseed. —*ká tel,* linseed oil.

Altáf, *n. (Plur. of Lutf).* Kindness; favours.

Álú, *n.* Potato. —*bukhárá,* a plum; a prune.

Álú-bukhárá. *n.* Plum; a fruit. [Literally and jestingly; *otato-fever.*]

Álúd, Álúda, *a.* Defiled; contaminated; pollnted; foul; besmeared. (Often used as a suffix), as, *gunáh-álúda,* a sinner; *khún-dlúda,* smeared with blood; blood-stained.

Álufta, *a.* Surprised; amazed; struck by astonishment.

Ám, *n.* The mango, a fruit.

Ám, *a.* Common; general; public. —*faham,* a. accessible or intelligible to common people, commonly available. *Khás-o-,* a. all and sundry. *Jalsá-I-,* a. public meeting. —*taur par,* adv. Commonly, comparatively easily.

Ámad, *n.* Arrival; approach; *—o-raft,* arrival and departure; ingress and egress; entrance and exit; inter-course. *—o-kharch,* income and expenditure; receipts and disbursements. *bálái—,* emoluments; perquisites; profits obtained from a post or office in addition to the salary or remuneration received for services rendered. *—aní,* import; income; revenue; arrival.

Ámádá, *á.* Ready; determined; prepared; alert. *—karná,* to prepare; to make ready; to excite; to awaken; to stir up; to arouse.

'Amadan, *n.* income; earnings, revenue.

Amal, *n. A. H.* Any intoxicant; any substance that induces intoxication.

'Amal, *n.* Action; operation; achievement; accomplishment; feat; execution; effect; administration; government; dominions; kingdom; territories. *—i-bejá,* misuse; abuse; misapplication. *—dar ámad,* to operate upon. *—dárí,* sovereignty; rule; sway; administration. *—karná,* v. to implement; to apply; to put into effect. *—men láaá,* to put into execution; to carry out; to give effect to. *—parhná,* to mutter an incantation, spell or charm. *(Plur. 'Amál)* Actions; conduct; behaviour; works; deed.

'Amalá, *n.* Subordinate officials employed in courts of law.

Amalí, *a.* Addict Artificial; practical. *hikmat-i—,* practical wisdom; philosophy.

Aman, *n.* Peace; quiet; absence of disturbance.

Amánat *n.* Anything given in trust; deposit; trust reliance; confidence. *—dár,* a trustee; a person with whom anything is felt or lodged in trust. *—rakhná,* to deposit; to give in trust for safe custody; to entrust. *—men khyánat,* breach of trust; breach of confidence; betrayal of one's trust.

Ámane-sámane, *adv.* Confronting; face to face; opposite; facing.

Amání, *n.* Trust; charge; safe-keeping; security.

Amar, *a.* Immortal; eternal; everlasting *—lok,* Heaven; the abiding place of God; Paradise.

'Amárí, *n.* A covered litter or *haudá* for the back of an elephant.

Amáwas, *n.* [Short, corruption of *'Amávasyá'*] The day of new moon; a conjunction of the sun and moon.

Amáwat, *n.* The dried juice of the mango.

Ambá, *n.* Mother; a female deity; a name for Durgá; the Mother goddess.

Ambár, *n.* Heap; pile accumulation; store; stock; supply. —*khána,* a granary; storehouse; barn.

Ambar, *n.* A rich perfume; ambergris; clothes; wearing apparel; the sky; the atmosphere.

Ambiya, *n. H.* A small unripe mango, *A (Plur. of Nabí), Prophets.*

Amboh, *n.* Crowd: multitude; throng; concourse.

Amchúr, *n.* Dried raw mango powder (used as a souring spice in cooking and snacks. (also known as *khatáí* in common parlance.

Ámez, *suffix.* Meaning mixed with; —*ish,* n. mixture; adulteration; sociability; conviviality.

'Ámíl, *n.* Collector of revenue; a comptroller of finances, ruler; administrator.

Ámín, *intj.* or *n.* Amen; so be it; a term occurring generally at the end of a prayer; and meaning 'So be it'.

Amín, *n.* Trustee; guardian; supervisor: bailiff.

Amír, *a.* A prince; a rich man; a chieftain; grandee. —*áná,* princely; lordly. —*ul-umará,* a paramount ruler: lord of lords. —í. nobility; sovereignty. —*ul-bahr,* the admiral of a fleet. —*ul-bahr,* the admiral of a fleet. —*ul-moninín,* Commander of the Faithful (a title accorded to the Caliphs by their followers) —*záda,* a prince; a nobleman's son. *a. of noble parentage; of aristocratic descent.*

Amiṭ, *a.* Indestructible; imperishable; indelible; ineradicable.

Amjad, *a.* Very magnificent; exceedingly splendid; extremely grand.

Amn, *n.* Safety; security; peace; tranquility.

Ámokhta, *part. a.* Learnt; taught; trained. *n.* revision by students of their week's lessons.

Amol, *a.* Invaluable; priceless; inestimable; above all price.

Ámoz, *(used in compos.).* Taught; trained (animal).

Amr, *n.* An order; command; regulation; affair; transaction: the imperative mood in Grammar. —*i-tangíh talab,* a point at issue; a question requiring to be decided.

Amráz, *n. (Plur. of Marz).*

Maladies; disorders; sickness; ailments; indisposition.

Amrit, *n.* Water of life; elixir of life; nectar.

Amrúd, *n.* A guava, fruit.

Amsál, *n. (Plur. of Masal).* Proverbs; fables; similes; parables.

Amúl, *a.* one without root, one without known origins.

An, *a prefix* meaning 'without'. Examples: *An*-padhá meaning *illiterate; an*jáná meaning *unknown. An*-kahá meaning *what remains unsaid.*

Án, *n.* Custom; honour; grace; solemn promise; elegance; commitment.

Áná, *n.* An old coin of India, one-sixteenth of a rupee.

Anádar, *n.* Disrespect; affront; insult.

Anádi, *a.* Everlasting; without beginning or end.

Anágat, *a.* Not arrived; not attained; future; unknown.

Anáj, *n.* Corn; grain; food. *—ká kírá,* a weevil (*ghun*). *—ká kothlá,* a barn; a granary; a storehouse for corn.

Anal, *n.* Fire; blaze; flame.

Anám, *a.* One without name; reference to the Supreme Being.

Anámá, *n.* The finger on which a ring is generally word.

Ánan, *n.* Mouth; countenance; face; order; command. *—fánan,* in an instant; at once.

Ána<u>n</u>d, *n.* Happiness; joy; bliss; contentment.

Anannás, *n.* A pineaple.

Ana<u>n</u>t, *a.* Infinite; boundless; endless; limitless. *n.* an attribute of the god Vishnu.

Anár, *n.* Pomegranate; a kind of firework.

Anáṛí, *a.* Awkward; unskilful; lacking in experience; uneducated; ignorant.

Anarth, *a.* Meaningless; unintelligible; improper; profitless; unfit; useless. *n.* absurdity; nonsense; calamity; injustice; oppression; offence. *—karná,* to oppress; to act unjustly; to sin; to offend.

A-nashwar, *a.* Immortal; immutable; imperishable.

Anáth, *a.* Having no master or protector; husbandless; for lorn; orphan; defenceless.

An-byáhá, *a.* Unmarried. *n.* a bachelor.

Á<u>n</u>ch, *n.* The heat of a flame; fire; (proverbially) harm; warmth; blaze of fire; glow; fervour;

inteusity; ardour. —*áná,* v. To come to harm; to suffer damage.

Áṉchal, Aṉchal, *n.* Hem; border; fringe; edge; a loose sheet worn by women as a covering for head and shoulders; women's breast.

Anchit, *adv.* Unawares; unexpectedly; without warning.

Aṉḍá, *n.* Egg. —*dená,* to lay an egg. —*sená,* to hatch eggs; to incubate. *(Colluq.)* progeny.

Aṉḍak, *a.* Little; small; diminutive; few.

Aṉdar, *prep.* Inside; within; in the interior of; in. —*karná,* to bring inside; to drive in; to place within; to conceal.

Aṉdarúni, *a.* Inmost; innermost; in the very interior. —*í,* internal; inward; in the depths of the interior.

Aṉdáz, Aṉdáza, *n.* Measure; dimension; quantity; degree; extent; mode; method; manner; proportion; symmetry; guess; inference; conjecture; grace; elegance; attractiveness; *used in compos.)* one who throws, flings or hurls; as *gol-andáz,* one who hurls (fires) balls or shells, *i.e.,* an artillery-man. *dast-aṉ-dáz,* a meddler; a meddle-some person; *barq-andáz,* a rifleman. —*karná,* to estimate; to calculate; to value; to appraise; to conjecture; to guess.

Aṉdázan, *adv.* Approximately; by inference; rought; by guess work

Aṉdeshá, *n.* Concern; anxiety; apprehension; fear; reflection; meditation; danger; peril; risk; doubt; uncertainty. —*karná,* to ponder; to deliberate; to hesitate; to be afraid. —*maṉd,* oppressed by anxiety or care.

Aṉdhá, *a.* Blind; unable to see: dim; obscure; dark; heedless; rash; thoughtless. *n.* a blind person;; *Alka-ká* who is intellectually blind, *i.e.,* stupid person. —*dhuṉd, adv.* blindly; preposterously; rashly; exorbitantly; excessively; irrationally; immediately. —*dhuṉd lutáná,* to squander; to spend wastefully; to dissipate. —*karná,* to put out one's eyes; to render one blind; to deceive; to throw dust in one's eyes. —*kuá,* a deep well, spring or source which is dried up.

Aṉdher, *n.* Injustice; oppression; tyranny; violence; anarchy; misgovernment. —*karná,* to oppress; to tyrannize over; to wrong —*khátá,* unfairness in transacting of business or dishonesty in keeping accounts.

Aṉdherá, *n.* Darkness; gloom; obscurity; cloudiness. *a.* dark; dim; obscure.

Áṉdhi, *n.* Storm; gale; tempest; hurricane; cyclone; tornado.

A<u>n</u>dhkár, *n.* Darkness; a dust storm causing partial darkness.

A<u>n</u>doh, *n.* Sorrow; grief; anxiety; care; mental distress. *—nák, —gín, á.* afflicted with grief or sorrow; oppressed with care.

Á<u>n</u>dolan, *n.* Movement; agitation. Campaign.

Anek, *a.* Several; many; much; plenty.

A<u>n</u>g, *n.* Body; a limb; member or organ of the body; part; portion; division. *—bal,* physical strength; energy. *—bha<u>n</u>g honá,* to be cut off; to be amputated; to be mutilated. *—vidyá* anotamy; the science of the internal structure of the human hody.

A<u>n</u>gá, A<u>n</u>garkhá, *n.* A long coat worn by men in India.

Á<u>n</u>gan, A<u>n</u>gnáí, *n.* A courtyard; an enclosed piece of ground in the interior of a house.

A<u>n</u>gárá, *n.* Embers; live or glowing coals; fire-brand.

A<u>n</u>gez, *prefix,* Meaning containing, or with. Examples: *hairat—,* a Full of surprize; *Wahshat—,* filled with terror;.

A<u>n</u>gíkár, n./v. Acceptance; adoption; approval (of a suggestion, or proposal).

An-gintí, *a.* Countless; in-numer-able; numberless; incalculable.

A<u>n</u>gíṭhí, *n.* A brazier; a small portable stone; a chafing dish.

A<u>n</u>giyá, *n.* (from *Anga* meaning body), a piece of clothing that clings to the body; brassiere; bodice; corset.

A<u>n</u>gochhá, *n.* Bath-towel; a cloth used for drying the body after bathing.

A<u>n</u>gṛáí, *n.* Yawning and stretching the limbs owing to drowsiness or sleepiness.

A<u>n</u>gṛáná, *v.* To yawn; to stretch the limbs.

A<u>n</u>grezí, *a.* English. *n.* the English language.

A<u>n</u>gul, *n.* A finger's breadth.

A<u>n</u>gulí, *n.* A finger; *pair ki—,* a toe.

A<u>n</u>gúr, *n.* The grape; the fruit of the vine-tree from which wine is obtained.

Angúrí, *a.* Drink made from grapes; wine; (proverbially) juicy; *Angúrí Hont,* kissable lips.

A<u>n</u>gúṭhá, *n.* The thumb; the big ote.

A<u>n</u>gúṭhí, *n.* Ring worn on the finger.

An-hit, Unfriendly; inimical; antagonistic; hostile.

An-honá, *a.* Impossible; incapable of accomplishment; impracti-cable.

Aṇí, *n.* Sharp point; the prow, bow, or stem of a vessel; the point or edge of a sharp instrument or weapon. *—dár,* sharp pointed; keen-edged.

Anishṭ, *n.* Harm; calamity. *—kári,* a. Harmful; ominous; calamitous.

Anítí, *n.* Injustice; contrary to rules; improper conduct; unbecoming behaviour.

Aṉjalí, *n.* The hollow formed by the junction of the two hands with the sides of the palm touching each other.

Aṉjám, *n.* End; conclusion; termination; result; issue. *—páná,* to be accomplished; to be executed or carried out; to carry into effect. *—dená,* to terminate; to conduct; to bring into effect; to act in compliance with; to conform to.

Aṉjan, *n.* An application to relieve inflammation of the eyes, or to darken and beautify them; antimony.

An-jáná, Anján, *a.* Unknowing; unintentional; unpremeditated; not deliberate; resulting from ignorance; an unknown person; stranger. *—e, adr* inadvertenly; unwittingly; unintentionally; without premeditaion. *—banańá* to feign ignorance; to pretend to be ignorant of a person or thing; to disclaim all knowledge of a person or thing.

Aṉjaní, *a.* Stye; a small tumour on the eyelid.

Aṉjír, *n. (Plur. of Najm).* Stars; constellations; heavenly bodies.

Aṉjuman, *n.* Assembly; meeting; gathering; society; association; a banquet; feast; repast.

Aṉk, Áṉk, *n.* A letter of the alphabet; figure; a mark; a private mark or figure denoting the sale price of articles of merchandise.

Ankabút, *n.* A spider.

Áṉkh, *n.* The eye; eyesight; power of vision; a judgment; perception; descrimination; powers of observation; sense; a tender shoot or sprout upon a joint of sugarcane which will take root and grow if it is planted. *—áná* yá *á jáná,* to suffer from inflammation of the eyes; to have sore-eyes. *—bachánà,* to depart stealthily; to steal away; to pretend not to see a person; to glance in another direction. *—badalná,* to deprive a person of one's favour or esteem; to change; one's opinion of a person. *—barábar na kar sakná,* to be unable to look a person in the face owing to shame. *—dikháná,* to look at a person in a menacing or threatening way; to glare at a person; to assume an angry look. *—o**n** me**n** charbí chháná,* to be intentionally blind; to be too pround to recognize one's old friends; to live extravagantly. *—me**n** khák áálná,* to throw dust in one's eyes; to deceive; to defraud; to impose upon. *—o**n** me**n** khatakná,* to be an eyesore to a person; to have a feeling like the pricking of a thorn in the eye; to be regarded with envy and dislike. *—me**n** phirná,* to be always present before one's eyes, *i.e.,* to be always remembered with love and affection; to be very much missed during one's absence. *—o**n** me**n** na ja**n**chná* to meet with one's disapproval or disapprobation.

Á<u>n</u>kná, *v.* To value; to estimate; to appraise; to mark.

A<u>n</u>kur, A<u>n</u>kurá, *n.* A tender shoot; a sprout.

A<u>n</u>kush, *n.* A pointed iron instrument with which elephants are goaded or driven forward.

An-mol, *adj.* Priceless; invaluable; of inestimable value.

Ann, *n.* Food; victuals; com. *—jal,* n. bread-and-butter; subsistence. *—dátá,* a. Master, patron; benefactor, provider of subsistence. *—práshan,* n. A ritual and ceremony to mark a child'first taking of non-liquid food.

Anokhá, *n.* Rare; uncommon; unusual; extraordinary; marvellous; wonderful; unique; singular.

An-paṛh, *a.* Uneducated; illiterate; ignorant; unread; untaught; uninstructed.

A<u>n</u>s, A<u>n</u>sh, *n.* Share; portion; part; division; extract; essence; pith.

A<u>n</u>sab, *a.* Advisable; suitable; proper; appropriate; convenient.

Anshan, *n.* Fast; abandonement of food.

Á<u>n</u>sú. *n.* Tear. *—bahná,* to shed tears. *—po**n**chhná,* to console or comforte *áth áth —roná,* to weep bitterly; to shed many tears. *—pí jáná,* to suppress one's tears; to abstain from weeping; to control one's grief or sorrow.

A<u>n</u>t, *n.* End; conclusion; termination; completion. *a.* last; final; conclusive. *adv.* at last; finally; after all; elsewhere. *—kál, n.* the moment of death; one's last moment.

Á<u>n</u>t, *n.* The entrails; intestines; guts; bowels.

A<u>n</u>tahkaran, *n.* The understanding; the intellect; the heart; the soul; conscience; mind; will.

A<u>n</u>tar, *n.* Difference; distinction; divergence; distance; space. *a.* internal; interior, *pre.* within; inside; amongst; between. *—bháo;* innate, inborn. *—yámí.*

omniscient; an attribute of God; knowing the inmost thoughts of the heart. *—dhán honá,* to become invisible; to vanish; to disappear.

Antaratap, *n.* Intermittent fever; malaria or fever and agne.

A͟ntaṛi, *n.* Entrails; intestines; bowels; guts. *—ká bal kholná,* to set a hearty meal after being hungry for an unusually long time. *—me͟n balparná,* to suffer from stomachache. *—jalná,* to be extremely hungry; to be famished through lack of food.

Anubhav, *n.* Exoerience. —siddh, a. Proven by experience; empirical. *—i,* a. With experience; practical; empirically wise. *—karná,* v. To feel; to go through anexperience.

Anuchar, *n.* An attendant; a follower; a hanger-on.

Anuchit, *a.* Improper; unsuitable unbecoming; inappropriate.

Anudár, *a.* Un-generous; conservative; miserly; parochial; parsimonious; stingy.

Anugrah, *n.* Favour; kindness; good-will; indulgence.

Anukaraṇ, *n.* Following; imitation; emulation.

Anukúl, *a.* In conformity with; coinciding with; corresponding to; in harmony with; favourable.

Anumán, *n.* Inference; presumption; logical conclusion; guess; conjecture; hypothesis.

Anumodan, *n.* Approval; approbation; seconding of an opinion or proposition.

Anúpam, *n.* Matchless; incomparable; peerless; immutable; unrivalled.

Anupát, *n.* Proportion

Anupayogí, *a.* Useless; unavailing; of no benefit; serving no purpose.

Anurág, *n.* Love; affection; fondness; endearment; attachment; longing; craving; ardent; desire.

Anurúp, *a.* In conformity; like; analogous; in accordance with.

Anurodh, *n.* Request; beseechment; urgung; imploring; entreaty.

Anusár, *a.* According to; in compliance with; in acquiescence with.

Anushásan, *n.* Discipline; orderliness.

Anushthán, *n.* Organised event; an undertaking; a beginning; an inception; an observance; a rite; a practice.

Anúṭhá, *a.* Rare; uncommon; singular; extraordinary; unique; wonderful; marvelous; strange.

Anuwád, *n.* Translation; reproduction from. one language into another. *—ak,* n. Translator; one who renders from one into another language.

Án͟w, *n.* Mucus, or white glutinous matter discharged from the bowels in case of dysentery.

Án͟wá, *n.* Kiln; potter's kiln; oven. *—ká án͟wá hí kharáb honá,* prov. The whole lot being rotten; to have disgusting lot.

Anwar, *n.* Radiance; glowing; sparkling; brilliant.

Anwár, *n. (Plur. of Núr).* Rays; beams; beams of light; brightness.

Anwásná, *v.* To render a new earthen pot fit for use by allowing water to remain in it for some time; to rinse.

Án͟vlá-Áon͟lá, *n.* Myrobalans; a species of dried fruit used in dyeing, tanning and for medicial purpose.

Anyáy, *n.* Injustice; tyranny; oppression.

Áp, *pron.* (used as a term of respect instead of the second personal pronoun *'tum'*). Self; selves; your self; yourselves; you; Sir. *—swárthí,* selfish; regarding one's own interest chiefly or solely. *—hí —se,* voluntarily; spontaneously, alone. *áps se báhar honá,* to be violently excited or agitated; to be imcontrollably angry; to be in a state of rapture or extreme delight; to be furious or enraged.

Apáhíj, *a.* Crippled; lame; indolent; lazy, handicappee.

Apaharaṇ, *n.* Abduction; kidnapping; usurpation.

Apamán, *n.* Scorn; contempt; derison; disrespect; ridicule.

Aparádh, *n.* Crime; fault; offence; guilt. *—í,* a. One who commits such deeds, a criminal.

Aparampár, *a.* Limitless; boundless; beyond measure.

Ápas, *pro.* One another; each other; themselves. *—dárí.* brotherhood; fraternity; kindred. *—men͟,* mutually; reciprocally.

A-pawitra, *a.* Unclean; impure; defiled; ritually unacceptable; *—tá,* n. Defilement; pollution; impurity; the state of being ritually unacceptable.

Apekshá, *n.* Expectation; requirement.

Apharná, *v.* To over-eat; to obtain inflated stomach; to feel stuffy and uneasy in stomach.

Ap-jas, *n.* Disgrace; ignominy; infamy; dishonour; disrepute.

Apná, *pron.* One's own; pertaining to oneself. *—pan,* a. Cordiality; affinity. *—paráyá,* a. kindred and alien. *—ullú sidhá karná,* adv. To have an to grind; to serve one's own ends. *—ghar badnám karná,* v. To foul one's own nest. —ghar bharn*á,* v. To feather one's own nest. &c.

Ápravás, *n.* Settling abroad; living in a country other than the country of one's birth (a modern imperial concept whereby nation-states try to reserve the land and resources for the perceived natives of their land.)

Ap-shabd, *a.* Swear words; abuse; vulgar words.

'Aqab, *adv.* Behind; in the rear; after; following after; in pursuit.

'Aqáid, *n. (Plur. of 'Aqida),* Creed; religious belief or doctrines; the tenets of any religion.

Aqálím, *n. (Plur. of Iqlím).* Countries; regions; climes; zones.

Aqárib, *n. (Plur. of Qaríb).* Relations; kin; kinsmen; kindred.

'Aqd, *n.* A knot; a marriage tie; bond of matrimony; marriage; an agreement; contract.

Aqdas, *a.* Very holy; most sacred; consecrated; or dedicated.

'Áqibat, *n.* The end; conclusion; future state; futurity. *—andesh,* having a regard for the future regardful of the consequences of one's deeds and actions.

'Áqil, *a.* Wise: prudent; discreet; sensible. *n.* a wise and prudent man.

' Aql, *n.* Sense; reason; understanding; wisdom; intellect. *—chakkar men áná,* to marvel at; to be struck by wonder. *—dauráná,* to exercise one's sense. *—khabt honá,* to be confused; perplexed, or distracted: to be at one's wit's end. *—ká dushman,* a stupid; blockhead; fool. *—men fitúr parná* to be of unsound mind; to be mentally deranged or deficient. *—par parda par jáná,* to be slow of understanding; to be slow-witted.

'Aqlmand, *a.* Wise; prudent; discreet; sensible; intelligent.

'Aqrab, *n.* A scorpion: scorpio, one of the signs of the Zodiac.

Aqsám, *n. (Plur. of Qism).* Sorts; kinds; descriptions; varieties; species.

'Aqúbat, *n.* Torture; torment; chastisement; severe bodily punishment.

Áṛ, *n.* A screen; a shelter; a protection; a defence; pretext; pretence, *áre háth lená,* to reprove; to censure; to upbraid; to reproach; to humiliate.

Áṛá, *a.* Crooked; bent; inclined; oblique; across; transverse.

Árá, *n.* A saw. —*kash,* a sawyer.

Arab, *n.* One hundred millions. —*kharab,* countless; innumerable.

Árádhak, *n.* A worshipper; one who adores (someone, or something).

Árádhaná, *n.* Worship; adoration; prayer; supplication.

Árádhya, *n.* One worthy of worship; one adorable.

'Arafá, *n.* A vigil; a wake.

Áráish, *n.* Decoration; ornamentation; embellishment; adornment.

'Aráiz, *n. (Plur. of 'Arz).* Petitions; humble request.

Árám, *n.* Rest; ease; comfort; relief. —*dená,* to give relief, to console; to comfort. —*páná,* —to obtain rest or relief; to recover from sickness; to be restored to health. —*talab,* indolent: lazy: slothful: fond of ease or comfort.

Árambh, *n.* Beginning: prologue; prelude.

Árásta, *a.* Prepared; adorned; decorated; decked out. —*gí, n.* preparation; decoration; adornment.

Arbáb, *n. (Plur. of Rabb).* Lords; masters; preservers; rulers; owners; proprietors. —*i-'adálat,* officers of a court of law. —*i-nishát,* vocalists; singers; dancers and musicians.

Arbaṛ, *n.* Nonsense; meaningless words. a nonseosical; rought; rugged; uneven; craggy. —*bakná,* to speak foolishly and unintelligibly; to talk incoherently.

Ardáwá, *n.* Coarsely ground meal.

Ardhá<u>n</u>gí, *a.* Palsied: partially paralysed.

Ardhá<u>n</u>giní, *n.* One's better half; wife; life-partner.

Argawán, Argawání, *a.* Purple; a colour formed by the mixture of red and blue.

Argh, *n.* (Corruption of Sanskrit word *Arghya)* water offered in oblation, especially to Sun god after bath. —*dená,* v. To offer water in oblation.

Aṛhái, *a.* Two and a half.

Áṛhat, *n.* Commission on sale; sale by a broker or commission agent; brokerage; commission. —*iyá.* broker: commission agent.

Árí, *n.* A small saw; a hand saw.

'Árif, *n.* A holy or pious man; a righteous person. *a.* wise; prudent; sagacious.

Aṛiyal, *a.* Stubborn; obstinate; self-willed; obdurate.

'Áriyat, *n.* A loan; anything borrowed. *—í,* borrowed; taken on loan; lent.

Áriz, *n.* The cheeks; an occurrence: and incident; an event. *—honá,* to happen; to occur; to take place; to befall, *—í* accidental; unforeseen; unexpected; casual.

Árizá, *n.* Sickness; malady; disease.

Arkán, *n. (Plur. of Rukn).* Pillars or chief supporters. *—i-daulat,* statesmen and politicians who are the pillars, or chief supporters of State.

Armán, *n.* Craving; longing; intense desire.

Aṛná, *v.* To be stubborn; to be obdurate; to become stuck; to get tangled; to stick to one's position or principles.

Árogya. *n.* Health; soundness of body or mind; freedom from sickness.

Árog. *n.* The act of belching; eructation.

Ároh, *n.* Ascent; climbing upward.

Árohaṇ, *n.* Ascent; the act of climbing; the act of ascending; ascension.

Árohí, *a.* One who is ascending; one riding; one climbing.

Aṛos-paṛos, *n.* Neighbour-hood; vicinity.

'Arq, *n.* Juice; essence; sap; spirit; sweat; perspiration. *—khínchná,* to distil.

'Arsá, *n.* A space or period of time; an interval; a plain. *—karná, lagáná,* to delay.

'Arsh, *n.* A throne; a roof; sky.

Ársí, *n.* A mirror; a thumb ring containing a mirror worn by females (Hence the proverb *Háth kangan ko ársí kyá !* What it the point of offering a mirror to a bangle on your wrist!).

Arth, *n.* Intention: motive: object: aim: purpose; meaning; interpretation. *—batáná, v.* to explain: to elucidate the meaning of.

Arthát, *adv.* Namely; that is to say; to wit.

Arthí, *n.* A bier on which a Hindu corpse is carried.

Árthik, *a.* Pertaining to economy; related to economics. *—sthiti,* n. economic condition. *—vyavasthá,* n. Economic management.

Áṛú, *n.* Peach, a fruit. *(Proverbially)* naïve; one failing to grasp the situation.

Arzán, *a.* Cheap; low in price.

'Arzí, *n.* A petition; an application; a memorial.

Árzú, *n.* Desire; wish; yearning; hankering; craving; longing.

Ás, Áshá, *n.* Hope; trust; expectation; confidence; reliance; dependance.

Asambhav, *a.* Impossible; not likely; impracticable.

Asádháraṇ, *a.* Extra-ordinary; unusual; uncommon; unique.

Asádhya, *n.* Impractical; unobtainable; not feasible.

Asaháy, *a.* One without help; helpless; lonesome.

Asahya, *a.* Intolerable; unbearable.

Ásáiash, *n.* Rest; repose; ease; comfort; enjoyment; felicity.

'Asal, *n.* Honey; real.

Asalatan, *adv.* Originally; personally; radically; altogether. —*házir honá,* v. To attend personally.

Asámí. *n. (Plur. of Ism),* Names; tenants;clients; cultivators.

Ásan, *n.* A seat; a stool or a carpet to sit on; posture; attitude; a small mat on which Hindus sit while praying.

Ásán, *a.* Easy; comfortable; convenient; not difficult of accomplishment. —*karná, v.* to render easy; to facilitate.

Asangat, *a.* Incoherent; inconsistent; absurd; irrational incompatible; anomalous; discordant.

Asankhya, *a.* Innummerable; countless.

Ásann, *adv.* Impending; immediately likely; imminent. —*mrityu.* a. One who's death is imminent; under the shadow of death.

Asantosh, *n.* Dissatisfaction; discontentment; unhappiness; resentment.

Asantushṭ, *adj.* Unhappy; discontented; Dissatisfied; resentful.

Asaphal, *a.* Unsuccessful; failure.

Asar, *n.* Impression; effect; influence; trace; result; consequence; issue. —*pirír honá,* to be effective; to affect.

Ásár, *n. (Plur. of Asar).* Marks; signs; traces; tokens; impressions; symptoms; symbols.

Ásará, Áshray, *n. Shelter; refuge; hiding place; asylum; resting place.* —*dená,* v. to offer shelter, etc. —*mánganá,* v. to beg for, to ask for shelter etc.

Asás-ul-bait, Asásá, *n.* Household furniture; property; wealth.

Asatya, *a.* Untrue; a lie; false.

Asbáb, *n. (Plur. of Sabab)* Furniture; apparatus; appliances:

baggage; cause; reasons; belongings.

Áseb, *n.* Misfortune; affliction; calamity; an evil spirit *(bhút paret).*

Asgar, *a.* Minor; less; least; nameof the younger grandson of 'Alí.

Asharaf, *a.* Exceedingly noble; dignified. *—ul-makhlúqát,* most pre-eminent of all created beings.

Asharafí, *n.* A gold coin.

Áshcharya, *n.* Surprise; astonishment; amazement.

'Áshiq, *n.* Lover; wooer. *—mizáj,* sportive; sprightly; gay.

Áshiyána, *n.* Nest.

Ashk, *n.* Tears.

Áshkárá, *a.* Evident: manifest; apparent; clear; plain.

Ashlíl, *a.* Obscene; indecent; vulgar. *—tá,* n. Obscenity; vulgarity.

Áshná, *n.* An chre acquaintance; a good friend; a very intimate friend; a bosom friend.

Ashnán, *n.* (a corruptions of sanskrit *Snán*) Bathing; religious purification by water.

Áshob, *n.* Tumult; clamour; inflammation of the eyes; misfortune; a storm; a tempest.

Áshram, *n.* Abode; ashram of man following a religious order; a place of peaceful living; a home for a focussed group, i.e. *Vidhawá—,* n. A home for widows. *Sádhú—,* n. A home for mendicants, and so on...

Ashubh, *a.* Unfavourable; unpropitious; inauspicious.

Ashuddh, *a.* Impure; polluted; contaminated; wrong; incorrect.

Áshufta, *a.* Afflicted: distressed.

Ashwa, *n.* A Horse.

Asíl, *a.* Of noble birth; of aristocratic descent; genuine.

Asír, *n.* A prisoner: a captive. *—i-áb-o-gil,* having an intense love for one's mother-country; patriotic. *—i-sultání,* a state-prisoner.

Ásírbád, *n.* [a corruption of Sanskrit *Áshírvád*] Blessing; benediction; greeting; salutation.

Ásís, *n.* Blessing; benediction; the return of a compliment or greeting by a superior.

Asl, *n.* Root; origin; basis; foundation; pedigree; capital; principal; stock-in-trade. *a.* essential; fundamental: original: integral; real. *—masúd* principal and interest. *—ul-usúl,* fundamental principle.

Ásmán, *n.* They sky; the firmament; Heaven.

Ás pás, *n.* Neighbourhood; vicinity; proximity; circumference. *adv.* around; on all sides; on all direction.

Ásram, [See *Áshram*].

Ast, *n.* Setting of the sun. *—honá,* to set (sun); to disappear.

Astabal, *n.* The place where horses, &c., are kept; a stable.

Ástána, *n.* Threshold; entrance.

Astar, *n.* Lining; priming. *—Hári,* plastering; coating.

Asthal, Asthán, *n.* (a corruption of sanskrit *sthal* and *Sthán*) Dry ground; place; spot; dwelling-palce; residence.

Astháyí, *a.* One that is not permanent; temporary; unstable; provisional.

Ástín, *n.* A sleeve; the part of a garment which covers the arm. *—ká sánp,* a domestic enemy with a mask of friendship on.

Astut, (Corruption of Sanskrit word *'Stuti'*) *n.* Praise: a joyful tribute or homage paid to the Divine Being, often expressed in song; glorification; anthem; hymn psalm.

Ásúda, *a.* Satisfied; satiated; gratified; pleased; at rest; tranquil. *—dil,* of serene mind; composed. *—hál,* contented; prosperous; well-to-do.

Asur, *n.* A sort of evil spirit; a demon.

Áswád, *n.* Taste; flavour; relish.

Aswár, *n.* A horseman; cavalry; a rider.

Aswasth, *a.* Unhealthy; not in perfect health; sickly.

'Atá, *n.* A gift; endowment; that which is given; a present; favour. *—karná,* to bestow; to confer; to endow; to give freely.

Áṭá, *n.* Floor; meal; ground grain, corn, &c., reduced into powder.

Aṭakná, *v.* To be stopped; to be prevented; to stick together; to be entangled.

Atálíq, *n.* A private tutor or instructor; a guardian; one who has the care of education of another.

Átaṉk, *n.* Terror; panic. *—vádí,* a. Terrorist; violent revolutionaries.

Átash, *a.* Fire; light; splendour; anger. *—afroz,* an incendiary. *—angez, a.* stirring up fire; *n.* fire-kindler; a seditious person. *—báz,* a maker of fire-works; a plyer or exhibitor of fireworks *—bází,* fire-works; display of fireworks. *—dán,* a fire-place; a receptacle for fire; hearth; a stove. *—fisháṉ, a.* scattering fire; *n.* volcanic eruption. *—mizáj, a.* fiery-tempered; hot-tempered. *—parast,* a fire-worshipper, a Guebre or Parsee. *—zadgí,* the firing of houses;

conflagration. —*zani,* striker of fire by means of flint and steel; incendiary. —*nák,* fiery; hot.

Atfál, *n. (Plur. of Tifl).* Children: infants. (Persian *Plur. Tiflán).*

Ath, *n.* The beginning.

Atháh, *a.* Too deep to be measured; unfathomable; of unmeasureable depth.

Áṭh, *a.* Eight. —*áth án̲sú roná,* to weep and flow tears exceedingly. —*on̲ pahar,* whole day and night; all the twenty-four hours; constantly. —*koníá,* octangular: eight-cornered.

Aṭhwáṛá, *n.* A week; the eighth day.

Athwá, *conj.* Or; even: or else.

Ati, *a.* Very much; too; *adv. more than enough; excessively;* prep beyond; *n.* excess; superabundance; that which exceeds limit; *(chiefly used as the first member of compounds),* as; *ati-sundar,* &c.

Atisár, *n.* Dysentery; griping of the bowels and requent discharges.

Atít, *n.* Past; time bygone: history. —*sápeksh,* a. Retrospective.

Atíyá, n. A grant; an assignment; a stipend; an allowance. —*kár,* a grantee; an assignee. —*i-dawámí,* perpetual grant. —*i-sarkár,* government grant.

Aṭkal, *n.* Conjecture; surmise; fancy; supposition; guess; rought estimate. —*báz,* one who judges at random; one who forms opinion on the supposed possibility or probability of a fact; an appraiser. —*pochchú, a.* uncertain; without aim, rule or method.

Aṭkáná, *v.* To obstruct: to detain; to impede; to check: to fasten; to put on; to get one entangled. *atká rakhná,* to keep back to; to withhold; to put off.

Átm, *n.* Self. [*Also used as a prefix to create adjectival phrases, like*—] —*gat,* adj. Internal; subjective. —*ghát,* n. Suicide. —*Gyán,* n. Self-knowledge. —*gláni,* n. Languor of spirit. —*kathá,* n. Autobiography. —*nin̲dá,* n. Self-criticism. —*Prashan̲sá,* n. Self-praise. etc. etc.

Átma, *n.* Self. *a.* Pertaining to self; personal. —*kathá,* n. Autobiography. —*kendrit,* a. Self-centred. —*get,* a. Subjective; inner. —*summán,* n. Self-respect. —*ghát/hatyá,* n. Suicide. —*aj,* n. Son. —*ajá,* n. Daughter. —tushṭ, a. Self-contained; contented (within oneself). —*tyág,* n. Self-sacrifice. —*dáh,* v. Self-immolation. —*nin̲dá,* n. Self-criticism; self condemnation. —*niyan̲traṇ,* v. Self-control;

self-restraint. *—niríkshan̤,* v. Self-examination; intropection. *—nirn̤ay,* n. Self-determination. *—nirbhar,* a. Self-dependent; self-reliant; self-sufficient. *—prashan̲sá,* n. Self-praise. *—rati,* n. Narcissism. *—rakshá,* n. Self-defense. *—van̲chaná,* n. Self-deception. *—vishwás,* n. Self-confidence. *—san̲yam,* n. Self-control. *—swíkriti,* n. Cofession; acceptance of one's own guilt.

Átmá, *n.* A supernatural being; the moral and emotional part of human nature; spirit; soul; mind; the intellectual power in man; the reasoning faculty; appetite. *Param—,* the Supreme Spirit; the Supreme God. *—satáná,* to cause pain to; to afflict *—t̤han̲d̤í honá,* to be gratified; to be satisfied. *—ghát karná,* to murder one's self; to kill one's self intentionally; to commit suicide.

At̤ná, *v.* To be held; to be filled; to be contained; to go or fit into.

'Atr, 'itr, *n.* Scent; fragrance; essence of sweetsmelling flowers; ottar (or otto) of rose, &c.*—dán, n.* a scent case; a perfume box. *—khín̲chná,* to extract the essence of *(Plur. 'Atriyát).*

Atráf, *n. (Plur. of Taraf).* Sides; quarters in any direction; confines; skirts; borders; boundaries; frontiers; surroundings; outlying districts.

Atript, *a.* Unsatisfied; unfulfilled; frustrated.

'Attár, *n.* A perfnme; One who sells scents and (in Urdú) an apothecary; a druggist.

Atusht̤, *a.* Unsatisfied; unhappy; unquenched.

Atwár, *n. (Plur. of Taur).* Ways; manners; behaviour; conduct; dealing; demeanours. *khush—,* courteous; polite; civil; well-mannered; of good behaviour.

Atyan̲t, *a.* Very much; exceeding; vast; utmost; *adv.* too; excessively.

Aubásh, *n.* A loose, disorderly, vicious person; one addicted to lewdness; one indulged in sensual pleasures of any kind; a scamp; a rate; a dissolute fellow; *a.* licentious; dissolute.

Auchat̤, *a.* Unexpectedly; all at once; inadvertently.

Augun, Awagun̤, *n.* Fault; blemish; defect; flaw; vice.

Auj, *n.* The top; the highest point; utmost elevation of rank, prosperity, &c.; dignity. *—i-fulack,* acquire the highest rank.

Aukhad, Ausad, *n.* [a corruption os Sansknit *Aushadhi*] That which cures a disease; medicine; a drug; relief; redress.

Auládd, *n.* Children; descendants; offspring; issue.

Auliyá, *n. (Plur. of Walí).* Saints; pious men; persons eminent for piety and virtus; the holy persons; apostles; friends and companions of the prophet Mohammed.

Aundhá, *a.* Turned upside down; turned to a contrary direction; overturned; in complete disorder; the upper part undermost; reversed. *—ná, v.* to overthrow from the foundation; to overturn; to invert; to turn upside down; to reverse.

Aune-paune, *adv.* More or less; not totally; partially.

Auntná, *r.* To boil (as milk, water, &c.); to be in a state of ebullition by the action of heat.

Auqát, *n.* Ability; capacity; position; perceived station in life or status in society.

Aur, *conj.* And; also; *a.* other; more; else; different. *—ek,* another; one beside; separate. *—hí,* quite different. *—hí koí,* other; some one else. *—kyá,* certainly; what else?*—nahín to,* and otherwise; and if not then.

'Aurat, *n.* The female of the human race; a woman; a wife.

Ausáf, *n. (Plurs of Wasf).* Qualities; properties; attributes; character; praises; commendations; qualifications; merits. *—hamída,* commendable qualifications; praiseworthy qualities; noble properties.

Ausán, *a.* Intrepidity; valour; courage; coolness and readiness of resource on pressing occasions; disposition and frame of mind; presence of mind; sensation. *-khatá honá,* to render insensible to dizzy; to be stupefied; to stand aghast; to lose one's presence of mind.

Ausár, *n.* (Corruption of Sanskrit *Awasar*) Opportunity; chance; time; occasion; leisure.

Ausat, *a.* Average; medium; mediocre; middling; moderate; common. *—nikálná,* v. to strike up an average.

Autár, awatár, *n.* An incarnation, a divine act of assuming a worldly body to perform redemption of a deteriorating world order; descent of a deity in a human form.*[Hindus firmly believe that whenever the world order descends into chaos, the divine bodies intercede, in human form, to rectify the situation].*

Aukás, Avakásh, *n.* Interval; free time; time without fruitful engagement, or employment; leisure; opportunity.

Auwal, *a.* First; principal; chief; prior; primary; beginning. *—an,* at first; in the first place.

Auzár, *n.* Tools; implements; instruments; apparatus; arms; weapons.

Avashya, *adv.* Assuredly; without fail; undoubtedly; indispensably; inevitably; essentially; necessarily; positively; precisely.

Avasthá, *n.* Condition; state; circumstance; position; stage of life; age.

Áwá-gaman, *n.* The passing of a soul into another body after death; transmigration; coming and going *(tanásukh).*

'Awám, *n. (Plur. of 'Amm).* The common people; the uneducated, uncultured class of people; plebeian; the vulgar; the commonalty; the populace. *—ul-nás,* the public; the populace at large; all persons without any distinction of rank, education or profession.

Áwára, *n.* wanderer; without settled bome or habitation; abandoned; astray; vagrant; dissolute; *n.* a wanderer; an idle, worthless stroller from place to place without having any abode and means of earning and honest livelihood; a vagabond; a profligate.

Áwáz, *n.* Voice; seund; tone; noise; cry; report. *—báz gasht,* an echo; reverberation; return of sound. *—par kán dharná,* to lend an attentive ear; to listen.

Áwáza, *n.* Clamour; noise; rumour; common fame. *—tawáza,* a sarcastic reproach; a scoff; a taunt; a gibe; derison; insulting expressions. *—phenkná, v.* to reproach with insulting words; to upbraid; to jeer at; to spesk in inuendoes.

Ayál, *n.* The long hair on the neck of a horse, lion, &c.; mane.

'Ayádat, *n.* Visiting the sick persons; making enquiries after the health of a sick person *bímárpursí).*

'Ayál-o-atfál, *n.* Family; children; family members.

Áyám, *n.* Dimention; amplitude; magnitude; regulation.

'Ayán, *a.* Clearly visible to the eye or obvious to the undestanding; evident; plain; manifest; clear.

Áyandá, *a.* Time to come; future; next; ensuing; coming; *adv.* in future; next time; hereafter.

Áyat, *n. (Plur. of Áyát).* A short division of the chapters in the Scriptures; paragraph; stanza; sentence; mark; square.

Ayógya, *a.* Unsuitable; unworthy; improper; out of place; indecorous; unqualified.

Ayogyatá, *n.* Unsuitability; lack of qualification; disqualification; inability.

Áyu, *n.* Age; the time during which an individual has lived.

Az, *prep.* from; by; with; *conj.* than. —*bas ki,* inasmuch as; neverthelss. —*khud,* of one's own accord; of himself; spontaneously. —*sar-i-nau,* afresh; anew; *de novo.*

Á'zá, *n. (Plur. of 'Azw).* Limbs; members of the body; joints.

'Azáb, *n.* Extreme pain; anguish of mind or body; torment; torture; pain.

Ázád, *a.* Free; at liberty; unrestrained; not in confinement; independent; not bound; released; *n.* a freeman; a free-thinker; a kind of devotee among Mohamedans.

Ázádí, *n.* Freedom; liberty; independence; release.

Azal, *n.* Duration without beginning or end; eternity; beginning.

Azalí, *a.* Having no beginning or end of existence; everlasting; perpetual; ceaseless.

Á'zam, *a. (Sup. of 'Azím).* greatest; very great.

Azán, *n.* The announcement of the prayer and its time thereof; summons to prayer (usually chanted from the turret of a mosque).

Ázár, *n.* Disease; sickness; malady; outrage; maltreatment; persecution; torment. —*pahunchána, v.* to inflict pain; to torture; to vex; to hurt.

Azázíl, *n.* Name of the chief of the fallen angels; the devil or prince of darkness; Satan.

Azhdahá, *n.* A great snake; a python; a dragon.

'Azím, *a.* Large; vast; enormous; huge; difficult; great; grand; high in rank. —*ul-shán,* magnificent; glorious; pompous; grand.

Azíyat, *n.* Oppression; distress; injury; affliction; torment; annoyance. —*dená,* to molest; to oppress; to trouble; to torment; to hurt.

'Aziz, *a.* dear; beloved; affectionate; loving; precious; darling; highly esteemed; *n.* a precious friend; a relative; one beloved; —*jánná,* to hold dear; to value highly. —*ul-qadr,* of great value, or high esteem.

'Azm, *n.* Firm resolution; settled purpose; design; end; aim; intention.

'Azmat, *n.* Greatness; exaltation;

elevation; grandeur; pomp; haughtiness.

Ázmáish, *n.* Trial; prove; examination; test; experiment; scrutiny; assay.

Ázmúda, *a.* Tried; tested; examined; experimented; assayed; —*kár, a.* experienced; practised; *n.* an experienced person; veteran.

Ázurda, *a.* Afflicted; depressed; dejected; cast down; disheartened; deprived of courage; weary; disgusted; sad; sorrowful; vexed. —*khátir,* troubled in mind; grieved in heart; displeased; offended; desponding.

B,b, is being used to denote the Hindi letter (ब) and the Urdu letter (ب). When one-and-a-half value of this consonant is required, [which only occurs in the middle of a word or at the end and never at the beginning of one] as in *babbar* or *Abbá.* When a dilution of this consonant is desired, usually at the beginning or in the middle of the word, like *byáh,* or *Zabt,* then a single use is immediately followed by a full consonant sound as in these quoted examples **bh** represents (भ) in Hindi and (بھ) of Urdu.

Ba, *prep.* A Persian prefix. To gether; for; from; in; to; upon, as; be *ásání,* with ease. *—har hál,* by every means. *—zidd honá,* To be importunate. *—qaul,* according to one, &.c., &.c.

Bá, *Pref.* With, by possessed of, as in *—Bá-izzat,* respectable, honourable, respectably, honourably. *—Bá-ittifáq,* with concord, in harmony. *Bá-zid;* insistent, obstinate, etc.

Báb, *n.* A chapter; a division of a book; section; heading; subject; affair; matter; case; door; *prep.* about; in respect of; with regard to.

Bábá, *n.* Father; grandfather; old man (by way of respect); sire.

Babar, *n.* A tiger; a lion.

Bábat, *adv.* On account; regarding; about; in respect of; *n. account; head; matter; item.*

Bábú, *n.* A title among Hindús equivalent to Mr., Sir, or Esq.; (term of endearment) a child; a prince; (term of respect) a lord; a master; a clerk in an office; father.

Babúl, *n.* The name of a tree of the Mimosa kind; the acacia tree.

Báchá, Váchá, *v.* To have read, to have checked.

Bachan, Vachan, *v.* Word; talk; conversation; pledge; contract; promise. *—dená,* v. To promise; to agree; to pledge. *—hárná,* v. To loose a bet, to have dishonoured a commitment. *—nibháná,* v. To honour a bet, or one's word or pledge.

Bánchaná, Váchaná, *v.* To read; to examine (a document); to palm-read.

Bachánа́, *v.* To save; to deliver; to rescue; to spare; to reserve; to preserve; to defend; to guard; to evade; to elude.

Bacháo, *n.* Defence; protection; deliverance; safety; escape; excuse.

Bachat, *n.* Remainder; savings; surplus; profit.

Bachcha, Bachchí, *n.* A baby; an infant; a child; the young of an animal, *bachkáná, bachkání,* fit for children.

Bachchhá, Bachhṛá, *n.* A calf; the young of a cow. *(fem.)* Bachhiyá, a she-calf.

Bachheṛá, *n.* Colt. *(fem.)* Bachheri; filly; foal.

Bachńá, *v.* To be safe; to evade or to avoid trouble; to be careful of.

Bachpan, *n.* Childhood; infancy; childishness.

Bád, *n.* Wind; air; breeze; a gentle gole. *—báa a.* sail of a boat. *—pá,* a swift horse; a fleet steed. *—i-simúm,* a hot pestilential wind. *—i-sabá,* morning breeze. *—numá,* a weathercock; vane.

Bad, *a.* Bad; evil; iniquitous; mischievous; wicked; addicted to vice; corrupt; inauspicious; unfortunate; (gererally. used in the formation of compounds), as; *bad akhláq;* immoral; impolite; incivil. *—'amalí',* misgovernment; misrule; mal-administration. *—andesh,* evil-minded; malicious. *—bakht,* unlucky; wretched; miserable. *—du'á,* curse; imprecation. *—dyánátí,* dishonesty; unfair dealing; corrupt practice. *—hawás,* stupefied; in consternation. *—hazmi,* indigestion*—sulúkí,* misbehaviour; ill-treatment; discourtesy. *—súrat,* ill-looking; illshaped. *—gumání,* suspicion; mistrust; distrust. *—m'áshí, n.* rascality; profligacy; loose conduct; bad way of living; &c., &c

Ba'd, *Prep.* After; subsequent; subsequently; afterwards.

Badá, *a.* Pre-ordained; decreed; appointed by God beforehand all that happens; *n.* the divine decree; fate; destiny.

Baḍá, Baṛá, *a.* big; great; large; tall; elder; of higher rank. *—ádmí,* a. A big shot; a powerful person.

Bádal, *n.* Cloud. *—phatná,* the sky to be clear or uncloudy; clouds to disperse. *—chháná,* the sky to be overcast with clouds.

Badal, *n.* Change; alteration; substitution; barter; exchange; the return of like for like; giving or taking of one thing for another. *—lená,* to change; to exchange.

Badalná, *v.* To change; to alter; to substitute; to shift; to barter; to transfer; to disguise; to transplant; to transform; to shuflle *(bát badláná).*

Badalwáná, *v.* To cause to be changed; to get changed. *badalwáí, badláí,* barter; price of exchange

Bádám, *n.* An almond. *—í,* almond-shaped; of the colour of almond.

Badan, *n. H.* Face; countenance; mouth. *A.* Bedy. *—tútná,* to feel racking pain all over the body.

Badar, *a.* Out of doors; out; without; outside. *—rau,* drain, channel; sewer. *shahr—karná;* to expel out of the city; to banish.

Badh, *n.* (corruption of Sanskrit *'Vadh'*) slaughter; murder; slaying; execution; killing. *—sthal,* n. place of slaughter, or killing.

Bádh, *n.* Cord or string of a bedstead.

Bádhá, *n.* Obstruction; interruption; hindrance; impediment. *bádhak,* one who interrupts, impedes or obstructs. *—dálná,* to interrupt; to impede; to hinder.

Badhái, Badháwa, *n.* Congratulations (on a festive occasion, or an auspicious events in one's life). *-le jáná,* v. to carry a message of congratulations (often done with sweet-meats and presents, indicative of joy).

Badhiyá, *n.* A bullock or any eastrated or gelded animal. *—baithná,* to be bankrupt.

Bádí, *a.* Generating wind in the stomach; windy; flatulent; rheumatic. *—ká badan,* corpulence; bloated body.

Badí, *n.* Evil; badness; wickedness; injury; mischief. *—par áná,* to be bent on mischief. *—karná,* to do wrong; to speak ill of; to slander; to backbite.

Badíha, *n.* Anything done without previous consideration; an improptu; an extempore.

Badlá, *n.* Revenge; compensation; retalisation; recompense; vengeance; lieu; exchange; retribution; return. *—dená,* to indemnify; to compensate; to make restitution. *—lená,* to take revenge; to wreak vengeance on. *badle men,* in lieu of; in return for; in exchange for.

Badná, *v.* to bid; to bet; to enter into a wager.

Badr, *n.* The full moon.

Bádsháh, *n.* Sovereign; king. *—at,* kingdom; the territory ruled by a king. *—i,* pertaining to kingship or government. *—í-sanad,* a grant of land by a sovereign to be held rent-free. *—záda,* the son of a sovereign; a prince. *—zádí,* a princess.

Báe, Baí, The name of a disease characterised by an accumulation of wind in the stomach; flatulency; rheumatism.

Bael, *n.* Ox; bull. (Proverbially) one who shows brute force and has no use for intelligence. *Á—mujhe már,* To provoke an unintelligent party into undesirable action, unnecessarily.

Báen, Báín, *adv.* On the left; *—háth,* left hand. *—taraf,* the left hand side.

Bag, *n.* A crane; a heron

Bág, *n.* Rein of a bridle; reins. *—ḍor,* a rope tied round the head of a horse for the purpose of leading it. *—uṭháná,* to start a horse at full gallop.

Bág, *n. (Plur. Bágát, Bághát).* Garden; park. *—bág,* immensely pleased; delighted. *—bán,* gardener *(málí). —báni, n.* the work of a gardener. *—ícha,* small garden. *—wálá,* one who owns a garden. *kampaní—,* a public park or garden which is the property of Government. *—i-'Adam,* the garden of Eden.

Bagair, *adv.* Without; except; besides.

Bagal, *n.* The armpit. *—bajáná,* to mock; to deride. *—ho jáná,* to get out of one's way. *—gír honá,* to embrace; to hug; to put one's arms round another's neck in token of affection. *—ká dushman,* a secret enemy; a person whose enmity is undisclosed. *—men dabáná,* to obtain possession of another's goods of property by means underhand, *i.e.,* fraudulently; to hide secretly under one's arms.

Bagáwat, *n.* Mutiny; rebellion; revolt; riot.

Bágh, *n.* Tiger; *—ni,* n. a female tiger; a tigress.

Baghár, *n.* Oil or ghee heated to boiling point with onions and other spices in it mixed and stirred with certain kinds of food cooked to serve as a condiment, *i.e.,* to provide a relishable taste; seasoning; flavouring. *—dená,* v. To sauté.

Bágí, *a.* Rebellious; mutinous; riotous; *n.* a rebel; a mutineer.

Bagúlá, *n.* A tornado; a whirlwind; a cyclone.

Bah jáná, *v.* To flow out; to be ruined.

Bahá dená, *v.* To throw away; to dissipate; to destroy; to spend uselessly. *—phirná,* to wander about from one place to another without any definite purpose; to be super-fluous.

Bahádur, *a.* Brave; courageous; gallant; *n.* a hero; a title expressive of distinction. *—í-jang,* unconquerable; one who does not give in. *—í.* bravery; gallantry; fearlessness.

Bahak, *n.* a. Rave; inconherent talk or behaviour; straying from the path; an aberration.

Bahakná, *v.* To be deceived; to be led astray; to wander about in search of the right course; to wander about hither and thither not knowing where one is going under the influence of liquor.

Bahál, *a.* Happy; flourishing; in the ordinary condition; the same as before, *i.e,* in *statuquo;* in good health; reinstated; restored to health or office. —*honá,* to be reinstated in a former office or to the former state of health. —*rahná,* to be affirmed on appeal. —*rakhná,* to keep or maintain *in statu quo*; to continue; to maintain.

Baháli, *n.* A cart covered with a canopy, drawn by bullocks [means of conveyance in the rural areas].

Báhan, *n.* [A corruption of Sanskrit word *Váhan*], a beast or vehicle suitable for carrying person, or burdens.

Bahána, *n.* A pretext; an excuse; a pretence. —*karná,* v. To make an excuse, to pretend; to put on an act. *Baháne-báz,* n. a maker of excuses; a habitual pretence maker.

Bahána, *v.* To throw away; to cause to flow; to throw into water; to pour out; to squander.

Bahangí, *n.* A pole placed across the shoulder with ropes fastened to either end, for supporting articles of heavy weight tied to them and balanced across the shoulder for purpose of carrying.

Baháo, *n.* A course or channel for the flow of water; current; stream.

Báhar, *adv.* Outside; abroad; out; *(met.)* disinterested; unconcerned. —*bhítar,* outside and inside. —*karná,* to turn out; to eject. —*í,* an outsider; a stranger. —*lejáná,* to take away from any place; to export; to take to another country.

Bahár, *n.* The spring season; beauty; elegance; prettiness; loveliness pleasure. —*istán,* a place made picturesque by the flowers that grow in the spring tide; the name of a Persian book by Jámí. —*paráná,* to be in lively spirits; to feel glad; to be in a light humour; to be in the prime of youth; to be in full bloom.

Ba-har-kaif, *adv.* By any possible means; by any means whatsoever; somehow or other.

Ba-har-súrat, *adv.* In any case; in every respect.

Bahas, *n.* Discussion; debate; argument; wrangling. —*karná,* v. To discuss; to debate; to enter into an argument. —*men paṛná,* v. To enter into an exchange of illogical and angry words.

Baheliyá, *n.* A fowler; one who catches wild birds for the purpose of selling them; one who is a seller of wild birds by profession.

Baheṭú, *n.* One who wanders about

from place to place aimlessly; a vagrant; a vagabond.

Bahí, *n.* An account book. —*khátá,* a ledger; a book in which daily accounts are entered. —*paṭwárí,* a paṭwárí's registers. —*rokaṛ, n.* daily cash book.

Bahilá, *n.* Barren. —*ná,* to divert; to amuse by engaging one's attention.

Bahin, *n.* A sister.

Bahírá, *n.* (properly *Buhaira*). A sea of small dimensions; a large lake.

Bahkáná, *v.* To lead astray by deception; to cause any one to do anything by deceiving or misleading him; to seduce; to mislead; to misdirect. *bahká ke le jáná,* to take one away by a resort to deception; to kidnap; to run away with.

Bahkáwá, *n.* Imposition; trick; stratagem.

Bahláná, *n.* To divert; to amuse; to turn away one's attention from melancholy thoughts.

Bahná, *v.* To flow; to blow; (wind); to float; on the surface of water.

Bahnoí, *n.* A brother-in-law (a sister's husband).

Bahr, *n.* The sea; a gulf or bay; an ocean; a rhyme; a worse; a fleet. —*í,* pertaining to the sea; maritime; naval; *n.* a. falcon.

Bahrá, *a.* Deaf; short of hearing. —*ho jáná,* to become deaf.

Bahu, *a. Prefix* Much; many; large.

Bahú, *n.* A daughter-in-law; a wife,—*betí,* the ladies of one's household.

Báhú, *n.* The arm.

Bahurúpiyá, *n.* [Literally] a maker of many faces; a performer able to put on many acts.

Bahut, *a. & pref.* Much; many; more than enough; sufficient; plenty. —*áet,* n. abundance; excess; enough. —*erá* a. very much; plenty.

Bahuvachan, *a.* Plural.

Báí, *n.* An appellation of respect applied to a lady; madam; wife; flatulency; wind in the stomach; reheumatism.

Baid, *a.* [Corruption of *'Vaidya'*]. One who practices medicine; a doctor; a physician; one versed in the science of curing deseases.

Ba'íd, *a.* Distant; absent; remote. —*ul'-aql,* devoid of sense; foolish; not amenable to reason.

Baigan, *n.* The vegetable called bringal; the fruit of the eggplant eaten as a vegetable. —*í,* a. of the colour of.

Baikun̲th, Vaikun̲th, *n.* Heaven; Paradise; elysium.

Bail, *n.* A bull; an ox; *(met.)* a stupid person.

Bainámá, *n.* A legal deed of sale.

Bainjaní, *a.* Purple; of a purple colour. (see 'Baigan').

Bair, *n.* Enmity; hostility; animosity. *—nikálná,* to be revenged; to seek vengeance. *—í, n.* an enemy; a foe *—rakhná,* to owe a grudge; to entertain animosity; to keep up a blood-feud.

Bairág, *n.* Penance; asceticism; abnigation of a worldly life; devotion. *—í,* a Hindú devotee who practices the most rigid asceticism, giving up all participation in the pleasure of this world and devoting himself exclusively to the contemplation of thing spiritual.

Baisákhí, *n.* A crutch; the support on which people who are lame rest themselves in order to enable them to walk.

Baisákhí, Vaisákhí, *n.* the first day of Vaisakh, a month in the Hindu calender, a major festival of the Hindus, the biggest event in Punjabi social and cultural life, always falls in with the 13th of April in the Roman year.

Bait, *n.* A rhymed couplet; a house; a place of worship. *—ul-haram;* the mosque at Mecca. *—ul-khalá, n.* a privy; a latrine. *—ul-muqaddas;* the holy temple at Jerusalem.

Baiṭhak, *n.* Seat; the reception room of a private dwelling-house; a drawing room; a form of physical exercise consisting in getting up and sitting down in quick succession without touching the ground with the hands or seeking any other kind of support.

Baiṭháná, Baiṭhálná, *v.* To urge on to take one's seat; to cause on to take one's seat whilst waiting; to establish; to station; to fix; to plant; to set (as a broken joint or bone).

Baiṭhná, *v.* To sit down; to be unemployed or idle; to brood (for the purpose of hatching eggs); to perch; to expend; to lay out; to fall down or sink (as a wall).

Báj, *n.* A duty; a toll; a custom duty; a tax; an octroi. *—dár,* a tax, duty or revenue collector. *—guzár,* one who pays a tax or duty or impost.

Bajá, *a.* Appropriate; relevant; in place; right; accurate; proper. *—láná,* to achieve; to accomplish.—, *á, v.* to make a sound proceed from anything; to play on a musical instrument; to test anything by the sound it gives out.*—ne wálá, bajaniyá,* a musician; one who plays a musical instrument.

Bájá, Bájan, *n.* A musical instrument.

Bajáe, *adv.* Instead; in place of; in lieu of.

Bajbajáná, *v.* To. make an effervescing noise in the act of putrefying; to ferment; to simmer; to bubble.

Bajháná, *v.* To ensnare; to entangle; to entrap.

Bajná, Bájná, *v.* To give out a sound; to have the reputation of being; to go by the name of.

Bajr, Bajjar, Vajr, *n.* A thunderbolt; a diamond; *a.* hard; very hard; impenetrable. —*angi,* a robust man; a man having a very strong frame; a man having strong bones and powerful muscles. —*pare us par,* a form of imprecation or curse meaning may be person cursed be struck by lightning.

Bajrá, *n.* A kind of small, light, river boat used mostly for passenger traffic as distinguished from the large flat-bottomed boats used for the transport of goods.

Bájrá, *n.* a baser grain; millets; staple food on poorer, rural coomunities of north India.

Bak, Bagulá, *n.* Heron; (Proverbially) a hypocrite; a simulator. —*bhagat,* v. One flying under false colours. —*vritti,* n. A Heron-like mentality; hypocrisy.

Bák, Vákya, *n.* Language; dialect; speech; sentence, statement.

Bakáwal, *n.* Chief steward; the head cook of an establishment, where there are one or more subordinate cooks.

Bakbak, Bakwád, Bakwás, *n.* Chatter; foolish talk; useless conversation; lies; falehoods; nonsense words. —*karná,* v. to indulge in.

Bakhán, *n.* An explanatory statement; an account given of another stating of his virtues and good qualities; an account given to a person of another. —*ná,* to command; to disparage.

Bakhár, Bakhárí, *n.* A granary; a store-house for stocking grain.

Bakheṛá, *n.* Complication; any vexatious business; obstacles; clog; lumber; contention; quarrel; wrangling. —*macháná,* to create a disturbance; to raise unnecessary difficulties. —*mitáná,* to settle a dispute; to terminate a vexatious business.

Bakherná, Bikhráná, *v.* To throw about in a disorderly fashion; to scatter.

Bákhí, *n.* The hollow on the underside of the arm where it joins the shoulder; the underside of the armpit.

Bakhiyá, *n.* Back stitching; —*ná,*

v. to back stitch; to quilt; to sew a second time the ends of a seam to give it additional durability.

Baḳhrá, *n.* Share; allotment; portion. —*karná,* to divide into shares; to apportion shares or portions; to distribute.

Baḳhsh, *p. n.* Giving; bestowing; forgiving; *n.* giver; bestower; forgiver; donation; portion; gift; pardon; forgiveness; *(used as last member of compounds),* as in *táj-bakhsh,* bestowing a diadem; *ráhat—,* providing or procuring rest. *naját—,* bestowing salvation. —*dená, v.* to give; to forgive. —*india,* one who bestows, gives, or forgives; God. —*í,* a paymaster. —*ísh,* a present; a gratuity. —*ná* to give; to bestow; to forgive. —*náma,* a deed of gift.

Baḳht, *n.* Lot; good fortune; prosperity; portion. —*áwar,* lucky; fortunate. —*ázmái,* trial of fortune. —*khufta,* an unlucky person. —*yárí,* good fortune.

Baḳhtar, *n.* Armour. —*band,* a. armour-plated. —*posh,* a. Clad in armour.

Bakhúr, *n.* Frankincense; scent.

Bakkí, *a.* Talkative; chatter-some; prattling.

Baklá, Bakkál, *n.* The bark of a tree; the rind or peel of a fruit.

Bakoṭná, *v.* To scratch with the nails.

Bakrá, *n. m.* A he-goat. Bakrí, *n. f.* a she-goat.

Baksuá, *n.* A buckle.

Bal, *n.* Side; direction; twisting; coil —*dár,* twisted; coiled; contorted. —*nikalná,* to become straightened; to be humbled; to have one's pride taken out of him.

Bal, *n.* Strength; power; force; potency; vigour; vitality; emphasis; stress. —*púrvak,* adv. By force; under duress. —*prayog.* adv. Coercion; exercise of force. —*vardhak,* a . Imparting energy; giving strength; nutritious (food/diet/medicine). —*ván/shálí,* a. Possessor of strength; powerful. —*hin.* a. Devoid of energy; powerless; weak.

Bal, *n.* A twist; a coil. —*kháná,* v. To twist and turn (one's lissom body as a coquettish gesture: simplestons might call it a sexy move). —*khulná,* v. To be straightened out; to be set right.

Bál, *n.* Hair; an ear of corn; an infant; a very young child; a crack in a vessel made of glass, china or clay; a wing. —*banáná,* to dress the hair of one's head; to shave. —*kí khál nikálná,* to be excessively critical.

Balá, *n.* Calamity; an affliction; misfortune; an evil spirit. —*I-*

ján, a. A life-long affliction. *—ká/kí,* a. Of the highest order; of miraculous proportions. *Jáne merí—,* prov. why on earth should I know that? *—talná,* v. To be rid of a problem/ or person. *—píchhe parná,* v. To be pestered by an undesirable. *—mol lená,* v. To deliberately subject oneself to an affliction, to get into trouble.

Bálá, *n.* A girl not arrived at the age of puberty; an earring.

Bálá, *pre.* Above; up; *n.* top. *—o-past,* above and below. *—dast,* the upperhand. *—khána,* a roon on the top storey.

Balágat, *n.* The art of expressing thoughts in such a way as to produce conviction and persuasion; oratory; eloquence; rhetoric; maturity.

Báláí, *n.* Anything extra or additional; cream; *a.* extra; additional; external; superficial. *—ámad,* emoluments; bribes. *—kám,* odd jobs. *—maze,* superficial or secret pleasures.

Bálak, *n.* An infant; a young child. *—pan,* childhood; infancy; childishness.

Bálam, *n.* A husband. *—khírá,* a sort of cucumber in the rainy season; a variety of *Cucmis saturies.*

Báláposh, *n.* A coverlet; a quilt.

Balátkár, *v.* Rape; enforced coital; ravishment; being coerced into sexual intercourse.

Bálchhar, *n.* Spikenard; dried hyacinth.

Báldár, *a.* Hairy; shaggy.

Balgam, *n.* The thick viscid matter discharged by coughing or vomiting; bronchial mucus; phlegm.

Bál-hatyá, *n.* Infanticide; child murder; killing of a very young person.

Bal-hín, *n.* Powerless; helpless; lacking strength; impotent.

Bálí, *n.* An ear-ring.

Bálídagí, *n.* Increase; growth; a gradual growth or advancement through progressive changes.

Bálig, *a.* Of mature age; attained to puberty; having arrived to full size and strength; *a.* an adult; a youth.

Bálisht, *n.* A span; the space from the point of the thumb to that of the little finger, when extended; nine inches.

Balishṭh, *Adj.* Strong; powerful.

Balki, *adv. & conj.* But; moreover; on the contrary; nay rather; on the other hand.

Ballam, *a.* A long pointed weapon used in war and hunting for thrusting or throwing; a lance; a spear; a javelin. *—bardár,* a lancer; a spearman.

Ballí, *n.* The pole or bamboo with which a boat is propelled or steered; one of the pieces; of timber which follows the slope of a roof and which supports the covering matter; a pole; a rafter; a prop.

Bálná. *v.* To burn; to make a fire; to light (a candle).

Bál-toṛ, *n.* A boil or sore caused by plucking out, or breaking a hair off one's body; a pimple.

Bálú, *n.* Sand. *—burd,* arable land covered by a deposit of sand after an inundation and so ruined. *—sáhí,* a kind of sweetmeat (so called from the sand-like appearance of the sugar sprinkled on it).

Balút, *n.* An acorn; a chestnut tree; an oak.

Balwá, *a.* Riot; insurrection; rebellion; mutiny.

Bám, *n.* The pole or shaft of a carriage; a fountain; a team used by Hindús as an ejaculation addressed to Shiva, (always with the name of *Mahadeo, e.g., bambam mahadeo);* a deep-toned drum. *—macháná,* to create a disturbance. *—ká golá,* a bomb; a shell.

Bám-panth, Vám-panth, *n.* Left wing (in politics) *—í,* a. Left-winger; leftist; radical.

Bámá, Vámá, *n.* Woman (Traditionally women sit or stand on the left hand side of their husbands, or male partners).

Báman, Váman, *n.* Vomit; the matter ejected from the stomach; emetic. *—karná,* v. To vomit, to belch forth; to emit.

Bambá, *n.* A fount; a well; a pump; the spout the let water out.

Bámdád, *n.* Morning; dawn.

Bámhan, Bráhmaṇ, *n.* a Priest, a member of the highest caste among the Hindus.

Bán, *n.* Habit; nature; manner; temper; a keeper; a guardian *(used as last member of compounds),* as *gáṛí bán,* a coachman or driver; *fíl-bán,* an elephant-keeper or driver, &c., &c.

Báṇ, Váṇ, *n.* An arrow; a missile; a piercing projectile discharged with a bow. [Hindi and Urdu poets also refer to the act of seeing as 'hurling arrows from the bows of one's eyes'].

Ban, *a.* A wood; a forest; a jungle; any extensive area densely grown over with trees that grow wild and undergrowth; a crop of cotton. *—ailá,* wild; belonging to the forest —*bás,* to dwell in a forest; an exile. —*biláo,* the civet cat. —*mánus, n.* an ourang outang, a gorila.

Báná, *a.* Dress; uniform; garments; habit; calling; woof; a sort of *patá,* with a thickedged blade and a wooden hilt.

Banafshá, *n.* A small purple-coloured sweet-odoured flower known by the name of violet a liquid obtained by bioling these flowes and used as medicine.

Banána, *v.* To make; to fabricate; to ridicule; to prepare; to build; to set right; to mend or repair; to preteud.

Banáo, Banáwaṭ, *n.* Dressing; decking (oneself); concord; composition; workmanship; pretence; appearance; form; construction.

Banát, *n.* A kind of warm woollen fabric called broad cloth.

Bá<u>n</u>chná, *v.* To read; to study.

Ba<u>n</u>d, *n.* A binding; a knot; a bandage; hindrance; captivity; an embankment. —*karná, v.* to shut; to close; to end; *(used in compos.) as ná'l-ba<u>n</u>d,* a farrier. —*o-bast,* arrangement; organization; settlement; settlement of the land revenue.

Ba<u>n</u>dá, *n.* A dependent; a bondman; a slave; a humble servant; human being. —*gí, n.* servitude; adoration; salutation; humility. —*parwar,* one who treats his servants kindly.

Ba<u>n</u>danwár, *n.* Leaves and flowers strung together in a line and suspended across gateways at marriages and other festive occasions.

Bandar, In. A monkey; (proverbially) a naughty boy. —*iyá,* female of the specie. —*wálá,* n. A street entertainer who uses monkeys to perform acrobatics and human-like activities.

Bandar, Bandargáh, *n.* Seaport, a town or city adjoining the seaport (Porbandar in Gujarat, Bandar-abbas in Iran); a harbour for ships; an anchorage.

Banderí, *n.* A ring-pole; the ridge of a house.

Bá<u>n</u>dh, *n.* The embankment raised to prevent the flowing in or the flowing out of water.

Ba<u>n</u>dhak, *n.* A pledge; an article pawned; a mortgage, a bonded labourer.

Bá<u>n</u>dhná, *n.* To tie up; to bind; to enchain; to stop (water, &c.); to bind together (in marriage); to contract; to wager.

Ba<u>n</u>dhu, *n.* Kinsman; relative; friend; *(Hindú Law)* cognate kinsmen of a remote degree, *i.e.*, kinsmen sprung from a different family but connected by funeral oblation.

Ba<u>n</u>dhuá, *n.* A prisoner; a captive; a person in chains.

Ba<u>n</u>dhyá, *a.* Barren; sterile; childless.

Bá<u>n</u>dí, *n.* A female slave, a maid servent.

Ba<u>n</u>ḍí, *n.* A sort of waist-coat having sleeves that reach to the elbow; the body of the garment itself extending as far as the waist and fitted with buttons down the front.

Ba<u>n</u>díḳháná, Ba<u>n</u>dígriaha *n.* A gaol; a prison; a concentration campl any place where the people are confined, or contained.

Ba<u>n</u>dish, *n.* The act of tying or binding; the make; structure; plan; fabrication; plot; intrigue. *—bá<u>n</u>dhná,* to form a rhyming stanza.

Ba<u>n</u>dúq, *n.* A gun fired by raising to the shoulder; a rifle; a pístol. *—chi,* a fire after taking aim; to discharge a gun.

Baneti, *n.* A club weighted at both ends and held in the midedle for the purpose of flourishing; a torch formed by cloth dipped in some inflammable substance and wound round both ends of a club and lighted for the purpose of whirling round so as to form a double cicle of fire.

Bá<u>n</u>g, *n.* Sound; cry the call to prayers among Mohamedans; the crowing of the cock.

Bá<u>n</u>gaṛ, *n.* Raised ground; elevated ground; upland.

Bángí, *n.* A pattern; a sample.

Ba<u>n</u>glá, *n.* A dwelling house built after the pattern of those inhabited by Europeans in India; a bungalow. *—pán,* a species of betel-leaf. *—zabán,* the Bengalee language.

Bá<u>n</u>h, *n.* The arm from the shoulder to the elbow; sleeve; support; help; security; guarantee. *—pakarná,* to protect and support. *—charháná,* to get ready by tucking up one's sleeves.

Bá<u>n</u>í, *n.* Builder; architect; founder; author; inventor; origin. *—kár,* expert; clever rascal.

Baní Ádam, *n.* Sons of Adam; the human race.

Baní Israel, *n.* The sons of Israel; the Israelites.

Banihár, *a.* A labourer who is paid his wages not in money but in kind.

Banij, *n.* [Corruption of Sanskrit word *Vāṇijya*] Trade; commerce; traffic in goods and commodities.

Banitá, *n.* A woman; a wife.

Baniyá, *n.* A person belonging to a sub-division of the Vaishya caste whose business is to deal in grain, to keep a shop, to trade or sell provisions; *(met.)* a mean-minded man; a timid. cringing man.

Ba<u>n</u>jar, *n.* Wasteland, unfit for cultivation; unproductive land overgrown with coarse, wild shrubs and grasses.

Ba<u>n</u>járá, *n.* A member of the now almost extinct class of people who were itinerant, gypsies.

Bá<u>n</u>ká, *a.* crooked; bent; cunning; foppish; gay; wanton; rake; bully. *—chor,* an expert thief.

Ban-mánus, *n.* The orang-utan.

Báns, *n.* The bamboo; a bamboo or rod measuring about 10 feet used for measuring land, tanks, ditches, &c. *—par charháná,* to hold another up to ridicule; to make another a laughing stock; to brand another with infamy. *—phor,* one of the caste whose business it is to split bamboos into thin strips in order to make baskets, &c.

Ba<u>n</u>s, Va<u>n</u>sh, *n.* Family pedigree; lineage; family stock; descendant. *—áwalí,* genealogical tree. *—lochan,* a secretion of a milk-white colour found in the hollow of the bamboo and popularly known by the name of bomboo-manna.

Ba<u>n</u>sí, Bá<u>n</u>surí, *n.* A. flute.

Bá<u>n</u>ṭ, *n.* Share, division; part; weights (used for measuring stuff on a weighing scale). *—ná,* v. To divide; to distribute; to share, to give away; to allocate portions.

Bánú, *n.* A lady; gentlewoman; a lady of high position.

Báo, *n.* Wind, air; flatulency; rheumatism. *—batás,* the wind-disease supposed to be due to the sufferer being possessed by an evil spirit. *—kie ghore pa̤r sawár honá,* to be as swift as the wind; to be conceited. *—golá,* the disease known as colic; flatulency with disorder of the bowels.

Báolá, Báwalá, *a.* Mad; crazy extremely stupid.

Báolí, *n.* A masonry well having a wide passage down the sides of which steps are made leading to the surface of the water; a mad woman.

Báp, *n.* Father; senior; superior. *—dádá* ancestors, forefathers. *—ká mál,* a. Unearned, or inherited wealth. *—ká ghar,* n.

[literally] father's house, [proverbially] place of unauthorised stay.

Bapautí, *n.* Patrimony; the share of paternal property inherited by a son or daughter.

Baphárá, *n.* Vapour. *—lená,* to inhale vapour or a vapour bath.

Baqá, *n.* Eternity; immortality; permanently enduring; remaining for ever.

Baqar, *a.* A bull. *—'íd,* a festival among Mohamedans held in commemoration of Abraham's offering to sacrifice his son.

Baqáyá, *n. (Plur. of Baquiya).* Arrears; balance.

Báqí, *a.* Remaining; lasting; permanent; left in arrears; still due; remnant; eternal; balance. *—ayám,* remaining or unexpired period the remainder of one's life. *—parná,* to fall into arrears. *—dár,* a defaulter; one who has fallen into arrears. *—rah jáná,* to be left over; to be left as an unpaid balance. *—nikálná,* to prepare a balance sheet; to find out by calculation what is still due.

Báqir, *a.* Learned; possessing great wealth and learning.

Baqqál, *n.* The name of a caste the members of which chiefly adopt the calling of a grain merchant or a shopkeeper.

Bar, Var, *n.* Election; choice; request; boon; bridegroom. *—dán,* the granting of a bride from her betrothed; the bestowing of a blessing.

Bar, *a.* Taking away; carrying off; *n.* one who carries off or takes away; one who seizes; a bearer, *(used as the last member of compounds),* as; *námabar,* bearer of a letter; messenger; *dilbar,* a ravisher of hearts.

Barsí, *n.* An event marking a year. mostly the annual event marking the death of an important person, or a relative.

Baṛ, *n.* The banyan tree *(bar-gad).*

Bár, *n.* Time; occasion; delay; day of the week; obstacle; (in *H.* & *U.*) gate; doorway; admittance; (in *U.* & *P.*) tribunal; leree; convention. *—bár;* repeatedly; again and again. —'*i*-ám, public audience. *—i-kháss,* privy council chamber; private audience hall. — *yábí-i-darbár,* admission to a court of leree.

Bár, *n.* Load; burden; cargo; fruit; produce; (in *P. phrases.)* dignity; God; *a.* burdensom; heavy. *—i-iláh,* Great God !*—bardár,* a carrier; beast of burden; a cart. *—bar-dárí,* transport; transit charges; freight. *—i-taraddud,* the burden of disproof*—i-jaház,* a ships's cargo. *—i-khálir,* trouble of mind. —*war,* fruitful; plentiful.

Bár, *n.* Edge; a hedge; margin.

Baṛá, *a.* Large; great; immense; exalted; elder; principal; important; *adv.* very; exceedingly.

Báṛá, *n.* An enclosure; a space enclosed round on all sides.

Barbád, *a.* spoilt; destroyed; wasted; empoverished; rendered useless. —*honá,* v. to be laid waste; to be destroyed, etc. —*karná,* v. To spoil, to destroy, etc.

Barábar, *a.* &. *pre.* Abreast; level; on a level with; up to; equal to; adjoining; even; regular; *adv.* invariably; constantly; always; regularly; conjointly. —*áná,* to come level with; to overtake. —*karná,* to make level or even; to waste; to bring to a termination; to make equal. —*kí ṭakkar ká,* of equal rank or standing; on a par. —*í, n.* equality; rivalry; exactness; insolence. —*í karná,* to emulate; to vie with; to withstand; to be presumptuous.

Baráe, *adv.* For the sake of; because of; for the purpose of; in order to. —*Khudá,* for God's sake. —*nám,* in name only; not real.

Báráh, Váráh, *n.* A hog; a boar; the third incarnation of Vishnu among Hindús.

Bárah, *a.* Twelve. —*bát karná,* to scatter; to throw into confusion; to confound; to ruin. —*patthar,* a cantonment or encampment bounded by twelve pillars. —*singhá,* a stag; au antelope. —*wafát,* the twelve days of Mohamed's illness.

Barahná, *a.* Naked; bare.

Baṛái, *n.* Greatness; bragging; position, praise.

Barjaná, Varjana, *v.* To prohibit; to forbid; to restrain; to shun; to leave.

Barkat, *n.* Blessing; good fortune; prosperity.

Baras, (Varsh), *n.* A Year. —*ná,* v. to rain; to overdo; to get very agitated.

Barat, Vrat, *n.* Fast; abstention from partaking food; a voluntary and meritorious act of austerity, an act of devotion; pledge.

Barát, Bárát, *n.* The procession accompanying a bridegroom to the house of the bride where the marriage ceremony takes place. —*í,* the persons who accompany the bridegroom to the house of the bride on the occasion of a marriage; the attendants at a marriage.

Baratná, *v.* To reflect; to use; to employ; to apply to spend.

Baṛbaṛáná, *v.* To murmur; to

grumble; to chatter nonsense; to talk in one's sleep; to speak incoherently in delirium.

Barchhá, Barchhí, *n.* A spear; a javelia. *—bardár,* a spearman.

Bardah, *n.* A prisoner of war; slave. *—farosh,* a slave dealer. *—faroshi,* the slave trade.

Báre, *adv.* At last; at length.

Bareṭhá, *n.* A laundryman; a washerman *(dhobí); fem.* Bareṭhin.

Barf, *n.* Ice; snow.

Barfí, *n.* A kind of sweetmeat made of cream, *Khoá,* and sugar in which the ingredients in their prepared state are made to assume a crystalline form which gives to the sweetmeat a crispness, and crumbling texture.

Barg, *n.* Leaf; knapsack containing provisions for a journey; a kind of musical instrument; melody. *—i-gul,* a leaf of the rose.

Báṛh, *n.* Growth; increase; promotion; flood; volley; edge; fence. *—rakhná,* to sharpen by grinding.

Baṛhaí, *n.* A carpenter.

Barham, *a.* Confused; jumbled together; topsy-turvy; angry; sullen. *—darham karná,* to throw into confusion or disorder; to complicate; to mar.

Baṛháná, *v.* To enlarge; to elongate; to increase; to augment; to multiply; to advance; to close up (shop); to put only (a lamp), *barhá láná,* to bring forward; to bring on.

Barhaqq, *a.* As a matter of right; true; rightful; proper; positive; inevitable.

Baṛháwá, *n.* Inducement or enconragement to advance; stimulus; flattery. *—dená,* to give encouragement; to excite; to spur on.

Baṛhiyá, *a.* Of good quality; high-priced; excellent.

Baṛhtí, *n.* Increase; surplus; promotion; advancement, *kamtí—,* a little more or less; about.

Barí, *a.* Free; exempt; acquitted; absolved; discharged. *—karná,* to relieve from responsibility; to discharge from liability to exonerate. *—uzzimma,* free from responsibility or liability.

Bárí, Párí, *n.* Time; turn for duty. *—bárí pári,* turn by turn; alternately; innings.

Bárík, *a.* Fine; slender; thin; slim; delicate; subtle; minute; hair-splitting. *—áwáz,* a fine sound; a high note. *—bát,* a subtle point; a hairsplitting distinction. *—bín,* possessed of quick apprehension; having a fine perception. *—miyán,* slender waist.

Báríkí, *n.* Fineness; minuteness; niceness; delicacy; keenness of insight. *—nikálná,* to discriminate; to criticise.

Bárish, *n.* Rain.

Barjasta, *a.* Betitting; right; opportune; impromptu.

Barkhá, *n.* The rainy season; rain.

Barḳhást, *n.* Dismissal; a breaking up; a dissolution.

Barḳhiláf, *adv.* Contradictory; adverse; untrue; opposed to. —*i-'áin,* contrary to law; illegal.

Barmá, *n.* A carpenter's tool, operated with a stringed bow, to drill holes in wood; a hand-operated drill.

Barmahál, *n.* &. *adv.* Fitting; suitable; opportune; in the nick of time; seasonably.

Barnan, Varṇan, *n.* A description; an explanation; a narrative. *karná* v. to describe; to extol the virtues or faults of; to explain, etc.

Barpá karná, *v.* To set on foot; to start; to cause; to raise; to establish; to incite; to pitch (a tent.).

Barq, *n.* Lightning; a watchman. *—andáz,* gunner.

Barr, *n.* Wasp.

Barr, *n.* Land. *—i-á'zam,* a continent. *—an wa baharan,* by land and water.

Barrá, *n.* A lamb or a kid.

Barrana, Barráhaṭ, *n.* Talking in one's sleep; the incoherent utterances of a person when asleep.

Barráq, *a.* Radiant; shining; splendid; *n.* splendour.

Barsát, *n.* The rainy season extending in Northeru India. (from July to September).

Barsí, *n.* an event marking a year, mostly the annual event marking the death of an important person, or a relative.

Bartan, *n.* Any utensil in general; a plate; a dish; a cup, &c.

Bartáo, Bartáv, *n.* Treatment; conduct; usage; practice. *—karná,* to act or behave towards one; to treat or use another.

Bartarafí, *n.* Dismissal; discharge.

Bartarí, *n.* Eminence; superiority excellence.

Bartmán, *a.* (a corruption of *Sanskrit Vartmán*). The present time; existing; current; abiding.

Bárúd, *n.* Gunpowder. *—khána,* powder magazine; a fire and rainproof store-room specially built for the storage of gun-powder.

Báruṭ, *n.* Whiskers; moustache.

Barwat, *n.* Spleen; a tumour in the belly.

Baryár, *a.* Strong; vigorous; violent; rich; the plant *sida rhomboides,* used for medicinal purposes.

Bás, Bása, *n.* Dwelling; lodging; residence; nest of a bird. —*karná,* to lodge or stay with; to roost (bird); to make its nest (bird).

Bás, *n.*Scent; fragrance; odour; offensive odour; stench; trace. *matí,* possessing fragrance; a fragrant kind of rice.

Bas, *a. P.* Enough; that will do; stop; *n. S.* Power; anthority; control; opportunity. —*chaláná,* to exercise one's authority or sway. —*men rakhná,* to keep under one's control or authority; to keep one under subjection.

Básan, *n.* A vessel; a dish.

Basáná, *v.* To people; to inhabit with people; to colonize; to populate.

Basant, *n.* The spring season; a Hindu festival. —*í rang,* a colour having a light yellowish tint.

Basárat, *n.* Sight; perception; discernment; knowledge.

Basar karná, *v.* To bring to an end; to pass one's time, to make do.

Basar karná, *v.* A bird's roost; a night's lodging. *Basere ká waqt,* the evening twilight; the roosting time.

Bashar, *n.* A human being, a person.

Bashara, *n.* A dream; a vision.

Bashárat, *n.* Happy news; joyons tidings.

Bá-shart, *adv.* Conditionally; on condition; provided that.

Basháshat, *n.* Liveliness; cheerfulness; buoyancy of spirit; lightheartedness.

Bá-shiddat, *adv.* Intensely; with intensity; violently; forcefully; deeply.

Báshindá, *n.* A dweller; a resident; a native.

Bashrá, *n.* Physiognomy; countenance; face; appearance.

Bashriyat, *n.* Humanity; qualities or attributes distinctive of the proper nature or constitution of man.

Básí, *a.* Stale; musty; *n.* an inhabitant.

Basná, *r.* To settle down; to commence to reside permanently; to make one's home; to be built (city or village).

Básná, [See *Vásná*].

Bastá, *n.* A cloth in which any parcel or bundle (papers, books, &c.,) is wrapped up; a wrapper. *a.* bound; closed; fastened; folded up; congealed; frozen.

Bastar, Vastra, *n.* Cloth; garment; waring apparel.

Bastí, *n.* A settlement of a number of people in one place; a village; a small town.

Basúlá, *n.* A tool shaped like an axe for pearing wood; an adze.

Batak, . *n.* A goose; a duck. *—ká bachcha,* a duckling.

Bát, *n.* Speech; conversation; talk; gossip; news; matter; circumstance; subject. *—bát men̲,* for the least thing. *—badalná,* to equivocate; to fall back upon one's word. *—banáná,* to concoct; to fabricate; to talk boastingly. *—bígáṛná,* mar; to thwart or frustrate; to ruin one's credit. *—chheṛná,* to broach a subject in the course of conversation; *—halkí honá,* to have but little esteem or credit. *—ká sachchá,* true to one's word; one whose word can be relied on. *—ki bát men̲,* suddenly; *—káṭná* to break the thread of a discourse by interrupting the speaker in the course of his conversation. *—khulná,* a matter to leak out or become known to the public. *—lagáná,* to negotiate; make arrangements for; to charge with. *—lagná,* to be impressed or offended by what is said by one. *—on̲ men á janá,* to be taken in or decided. *—pakaṛná,* to size censuriously on what is said. *—en̲ sunáná,* to censure; to reproach; to revile; to abuse. *—ṭálná,* to evade. *—on̲ men̲ farq áná,* to lose credit or repute.

Bát, *n.* A pain in the large joints of the limbs; rheumatism.

Báṭ. *n.* Weight; measure.

Báṭ, *n.* A road; a highway. *—johná,* to be on the look out for, to wait for.

Batálat, *n.* Folly; vanity; falsehood.

Batáná, *v.* To show; to point; to explain; to teach.

Batás, *n.* Wind; air; atmosphere.

Batásá, Batáshá, *n.* A small sweetmeat semi-globular in shape having a flat bottom made from dissolved sugar and having a brittle crustlike exterior, the interior being honeycombed. *—sá ghulná,* to dissolve very easily in water.

Batauri, *a.* A swelling produced by water collecting in a particular part of the human body or by flatulency.

Baṭer, *n.* The quail; small game bird.

Bátí, Battí, *n.* The wick of a candle or lamp; a candle; a lamp.

Báṭiká, Váṭiká, *a.* A garden.

Bátil, *a.* False; incorrect; spurious;

unfounded; futile; void; vain. —*karná,* to falsify; to prove to be false. —*samajhná,* to regard or treat as false. —*us-sihr,* a frustrator of an enchantment.

Baṭmár, *n.* A highwayman; a robber who attacks travellers journeying along a road.

Baṭná, *v.* To twist; to be divided in shares; to be distributed.

Baṭohí, *n.* A. traveller; a wayfarer.

Baṭor, *a.* A crowd; gathering. —*ná,* to gather; to collect.

Baṭṭebáz, *n.* A juggler; a cheat; a humbug; a swindler. —*i,* deception; swindling; cheating.

Battísí, *n.* An aggregate of 32 things; a set of teeth (32 in number). —*bajná,* to shiver with cold causing the upper and lower rows of teeth chatter. —*dikháná,* to show the teeth in the act of laughing or grinning, to feel embarrassed.

Baṭuá, *n.* A small bag opening and closi8ng by a string used to keep money, betel spices and the like; a purse.

Baṭwárá, *n.* Partition; *(leg.)* division of land among co-sharers by metes and bounds, in a joint Hinduú family governed by the *Mitákshara* law, the mere intention to effect a partition among the co-parcenters.

Bauchhár, *n.* Spray from falling rain driven in by the wing; particles of water driven by the wind from falling rain.

Bauláná, Bauráná, *v.* to become mad; to become crazy.

Bavanḏar, Bawanḏar, *n.* Cyclone; typhoon; a major crisis or trouble, *n.* A whirlwind; a cyclone; a tornado.

Báwarchí, n. A cook. —*khána,* a cookroom or house.

Bayá, *n.* A small bird, the weaver bird.

Bayábán, *n.* A desert; a wilderness.

Bayán, *n.* Statement; declaration; explanation.

Bayáná, *n.* Ernest money; a token payment against a deal made as a sign of good faith. —*dená,* v. To make such payment.

Bayár, *n.* Wind; air.

Báz, *n.* The falcon; the hawk; a species of a bird of prey.

Báz, *adv.* Without, out of —*áná v.* to leave off or give up anything. —*rakhná,* to keep aloof from any one or thing.

Bázár, *n.* A public market; a market held periodically or at regular intervals. —*karná,* to go shopping. —*í khabar,* a rumour —*lagáná,* to exhibit commodities in a public place to the public for sale. —*í,* common; ordinary.

Bazáz, *n.* A draper; a cloth merchant; a retail dealer in cloth.

Bází, *n.* Play; sport; a contest at sport. —*lagáná,* to stake at a play; to wager; to lay a bet. —*jítná,* or *le jáná,* to win; to be victorious.

Bázigar, *n.* An acrobat; a magician.

Bazm, *n.* An assembly or company of guests at a feast.

Bázu, *n.* The arm; the wings; the fold of a door; side of a bedstead. —*ba<u>n</u>d,* an armlet.

Be, A prefix denothing the meaning 'without' and equiva'ent to the English in; im-, up-, in-, ir-, or-less,-dis-, mis-, ill-; devoid of; out of, &c., as; *be-áb,* without lustre; lustreless. *be-ábrúí,* dishonour. *be-chain,* uneasy; restless. *be-dakhl karná,* to dispossess. *be-gunáh,* innocent. *be-hadd,* infinite; bound less, *be-ímán,* irreligious, *be-imtíyáz,* impertinent. *be-intizámí,* mismanagement. *be-mauqa',* ill-timed. *be-sabr,* impatient. *be-ulfat,* devoid of friendship. *be-ulfat,* devoid of friendship. *be-tál,* our of time (in music).

Be'aib, *a.* Faultless; without blemish, with no vues.

Be-asar, *a.* Ineffectual.

Be-aulád, *a.* Without offspring; childless.

Be-báq, *a* and *adv.* Paid up in full; without remainder or arrear. —*karná,* to settle; to adjust; to liquidate; cuispoken.

Be-barg-o-bar, *a.* Barren; fruitless.

Be-chára, *v.* Helpless; without remedy, means or resources; poor; *n.* a miserable wretch; poor fellow.

Be-charág, *a.* Desolate; ruined beyond hope; childless.

Bechná, *v.* To sell; to dispose of. *bechí karná,* to endorse. *bechne ke iáiq,* saleable. *bechnewálá,* a seller; a vendor.

Bedár, *a.* Awake; watchful; vigilant. —*bakht,* fortunate. —*í,* vigilance; watchfulness; wakefulness.

Be-dard, *a.* Devoid of compassion; pitiless; merciless; heartless.

Be-dastúr, *a.* Unusual; not customary.

Beḍaul, *a.* Clumay; awakward; ugly; mis-shappen.

Beḍhab, *a.* Ugly; ill-shaped; severe; untoward; awkward; grave.

Bedhaṛak, *a.* and *adv.* Without fear or dread dauntlessly; fearlessly.

Bedhná, *v.* To pierce; to bore; to perforate; to stab.

Bedí, Vedí, *n.* An Alter; a raised dais or platform consecrated for the performance of a ritual, or ceremony.

Be-dídá, *a.* One without the benefit of sight; blind; *(proverbially)* one without sense of shame; one unable to see what is obvious.

Be-fáida, *a.* Useless; futile; unavailing; profitless.

Be-fikr, *a.* Thoughtless; unconcerned; careless; free from all anxieties and misgivings.

Begam, *n.* A lady of position or rank, a nobleman's wife.

Begána, *a* Foreign; strange; not related; not a friend; allen; unknown; *n.* a stranger; a foreigner; an alien.

Begár, *n.* Compulsory labour with or without payment. *—pakarná,* to press into service of some kind with or without payment. *—tálná,* to work in a half-hearted or careless manner.

Be-hijáb, *a.* Lacking in modesty; shameless.

Behrí, *n.* Contribution; subscription; instalment.

Behtar, *a.* Better; preferable; best that can be; *—í,* n. Welfare, betterment. *—ín,* The best; most superior; do; the most advisable course to pursue. *—í,* welfare; excellence; advantage; improvement; merit. *—jánná,* to regard as superior or more excellent.

Behúda, *a.* Unmannered; senseless; foolish; stupid; obscene; irrelevant; absurd; frivolous. *—go,* a talker of nonsense; a foul-mouthed fellow.

Be-hurmat, *a.* Having no self respect; dishonourable; disgraceful.

Be-ikhtyárí, *n.* Beyond one's power; beyond one's control.

Bejá, *a.* In a wrong place; ill-timed; improper; wrong; unjust.

Bekár, *a.* Out of work; useless; idle; worthless. *—karná,* to throw out of employment; to thwart; to undo.

Beḳhabar, *a.* Uninformed; absence of suspicion; unexpecting; not cautioned.

Beḳhatar, *a.* Assured; having no misgivings; safe; out of peril or danger.

Beḳhudí, *a.* The being, beside oneself; ecstacy; rapture; insensibility; stupefaction.

Bel, *n. H.* The wood apple; a creeper; a tendent; a festoon of leaves; embroidery; the Arabian jasmine. *P.* Spade; shovel; pick-axe; pole for directing a boat. *—dár,* a digger; one who uses a spade.

Belá, *n. H.* A musical instrument resembling the violin; a species of the jasmine flower; a shallow cup; time; while; moment; season. *P.* Money to be distributed in charity.

Belan, *n.* A rolling pin; a roller.

Be-liház, *a.* Wanting in respectfulness by reason of ill-breeding; wanting in manners.

Be-mausam, *a.* Out of season.

Bemazá, *a.* Tasteless; insipid; uninteresting; dull.

Bemurauwat, *a.* Unkind; cruel; impolite; uncivil.

Bén, *n.* A reed pipe; a flute; a fife

Be-nazír, *a.* Incomparable; matchless; having no equal.

Benawá, *a.* Indigent; poor. *—í, n.* begging; mendicancy.

Be<u>n</u>dá, *a.* Crooked; across; rough; *n.* the wooden bolt to bar placed across a door to fasten it.

Be<u>n</u>dí sunáná, *v.* To speak harshly; to revile; to insult.

Beqiyás, *n.* That which is beyond comprehension; inconceivable; that which cannot be understood; mysterious.

Ber, Der, *n.* Delay; turn; while; the Indian plum.

Beṛá, *a.* Raít; float; boat; timber formed into a raft to be brought down a river; a fleet; enclosure; yard; railing. *—pár lagáná* yá *karná,* to ferry a raft or boat across a stream; *(met.)* to help on through a difficulty. *—pár honá,* to tide over a difficulty; to get through a business successfully.

Be-raham, *a.* Ruthless; without pity; merciless.

Beṛí, *n.* Iron fetters; the chains fastened to the legs of a criminal. *—parná, v.* to be in fetters; to be imprisoned. *beríyá<u>n</u> kátná,* to have one's chains or fetters taken off; to be releaseed from imprisonment.

Besh, *a.* Good; proper; excellent; more. *—bahá, —qímat,* of great value or price; valuable; precious. *kam-o—,* more or less; about.

Beshtar, *a.* Mostly; generally; as a rule.

Beṭá, *n.* A son; a child. *—banáná,* to look upon as a son; to make one a son by adoption.

Betahásha, *a.* Furiously; headlong; without consideration for anything else; regardless of everything.

Be-tamíz, *a.* Rude; unmannered wanting in discrimination.

Beṭí, *n.* A daughter.

Bewá, *n.* A widow.

Bewafá, *a.* Faithless; insincere; treacherous; disloyal; perfidious; untrustworthy. —*í,* treachery; faithlessness; insincerity; disloyalty; perfidy.

Bezár, *a.* Annoyed; angry; displeased. (*Noun* Bezárí).

Bhabak, *n.* A burst of flame; a sudden emission of obnoxious odour. —*ná, v.* to burst forth or out.

Bhabbhar, *n.* The disorder of a panic; uproar; disorder; confusion.

Bharbhaṛáná, *v.* To swell; to be inflamed.

Bhábhí, *n.* A sister-in-law; a brother's wife.

Bhabhúká, *a.* Red hot; blazing; glowing; excessively beautiful. —*honá,* to grow red in the face or lived through rage.

Bhabhút, *n.* The ashes of burnt cowdung which professional mendicants rub on their bodies. —*ramá lená,* to turn a *faqír* or *jogí.*

Bhabká, *n.* A blast from a furnace; a distilling machine.

Bhabkí, *n.* Threat; menace. *gídar*—, an empty threat. —*meṉ á jáná,* to give in being influenced by an empty threat.

Bhaddá, *a.* Awkward; dull; stupid; silly; mis-shapen; lumpish.

Bhádon, *n.* The name of the fifth month of the Hindú solar year.

Bhadra, *a.* Gentle; good; noble; auspicious. Also a form of address while dealing with upper classes (*Bhadralog* in common parlance).

Bhadrá, *a.* The female of *Bhadra.*

Bhaiṉgá, Bhengá, *n.* Squinty-eyed.

Bhaeṉs, *n.* Domestic buffallow. —*á* n. Male of the specie.

Bhág, *n.* Part; portion; allotment; apportionment; share in a partnership or of an inheritance; division (in *Arith.*); fortune. —*jágná* yá *khulná,* for one's fortune to change from indifferent or bad to good; for one to become all of a sudden lucky. —*karná,* to effect a division on apportionment. —*phútná,* to be visited with misfortune or ill-luck. —*wán,* a lucky or fortunate person.

Bhagat, *n.* A devotee; a pious man.

Bhaginí, *n.* Sister, female cousin.

Bhágná, *v.* To run; to flee; to escape; to get away.

Bhagwán, Bhagwat, *n.* God.

Bháí, Bhaiyá, *n.* Brother; friend.

chachera—, consin, *sautela*—, half brother; brother by another mother of the same father. —*band,* brothers; relations; brotherhood. —*chárá,* fraternity; people of the same caste.

Bhains, *n.* A female buffalo. —*á,* a male buffalo.

Bhairav, *n.* Lord Shiva in his enraged form. Also the name of a rhythmic morning *Rág,* performed for the purpose of waking up the world from slumber.

Bhairaví, *n.* Another morning *Rág,* gentler than *Bhairav.*

Bhajan, *n.* A hymn of adoration; prayer accompanied with the performance of religious rites —*karná, v.* to worship; to sing a religious song.

Bhájí, *n.* Vegetables; cooked vegetables; one's share of food.

Bhajná, *v.* To worship; to count the beads of a rosary.

Bhákhá, Bháshá, *n.* Speech; language; dialect.

Bhakosaná, *v.* To eat up; to devour; to stuff oneself up.

Bhaktí, *n.* Faith; devotion; religiousness.

Bhál, *n.* An arrow head; forehead; fortune.

Bhálá, *n.* A spear; a javelin; a lance. —*bardár,* a lancer; a spearman.

Bhalá, *a.* Excellent; good; all right; in good health; righteous. —*ádmí,* a gentleman; a stupid fellow. —*burá kahná,* to speak ill of one; to abuse. —*changá, a.* in the enjoyment of good health. —*mánná,* to take anything well. *í, n.* welfare; prosperity.

Bhálú, *n.* The bear.

Bhambhírí, *n.* The red butterfly; a swift runner.

Bhambhoṛná, *v.* To tear and mangle; to worry; to gnaw; to bite.

Bháná, *v.* To please; to suit; to fit.

Bhanak, *n.* A low or faint sound proceeding from a distance. —*parná,* to be heard faintly.

Bhanbhanáná, Bhinbhináná, *v.* To make a humming or a buzzing noise; to grumble in an undertone.

Bháṇḍ, *n.* A clown; a buffoon; a mimic; a comic actor.

Bháṇḍá, *n.* An earthen vessel or pot.

Bhaṇḍá phuṭná, *v.* For a secret to leack out; to be an open secret.

Bhaṇḍár, *n.* A storehouse; a godown. —*á,* a feast of jogís or *faqís.* —*í,* a steward; a butler; a treasurer.

Bháng, *n.* Hemp; a drink made from the leaves of the hemp plant reduced to the state of a paste and mixed with water, milk, spices, sugar, &c., which produces intoxication.

Bhang honá, *v.* To be broken; to be destroyed; to be vitiated.

Bhangí, *n.* One of the sweeper caste.

Bhangimá, *n.* Pose; posture; curvature; obliquity; tilt; slant.

Bhangrá, *n.* A boisterous folk dance form of Punjab, renowned throughout the world, and performed by Punjabis at almost every festive occasion.

Bhangur, *a.* Brittle, fragile; transient; perishable. *Kshan—,* a. Momentary; something that will perish in moments.

Bhánjá, *n.* A nephew.

Bhanjáná, *v.* To have a piece of money of large value changed into coins of smaller value.

Bhánji, *n.* A niece; tale-bearing; interruption; hinderance. *—márná,* to interere; to meddle.

Bhánjná, *v.* To fold; to break; to turn; to brandish; to count one's beads; rehearse.

Bhánpná, *v.* To guess; to make out.

Bhánt, *n.* Manner; mode; kind. *—ká,* of several kinds; of various sorts.

Bhanwar, *n.* A revolution; whirl; a whirlpool; an eddy; the humble bee; a creeper. *—jál,* the world and its snares. *—men parná,* to whirl round; to fall into a whirlpool. *—kalí, n.* a collar (for a dog, goat, &c.).

Bháo, Bháv, *n.* Price; rate; expression of one's meaning by signs; sentiment. *—batáná, v.* to express one's sentiments whilst dancing, by movement of the arms, head and body. *—baṛháná, v.* to raise or enhance the price of any commodity. *—utarná* yá *ghaṭná,* a fall in price.

Bháp, *n.* Steam.

Bhar, *v.* Full; as much as. *—dená,* to fill; to pay up. *—maqdúr, maqdúr—,* to the best of one's abilities.

Bhár, *n.* Burden; responsibility. *—utárná,* to relieve oneself of his burden or responsibility. *páp ká—utárná,* to make atonement for one's sins.

Bhár, *n.* A furnace; an oven; fireplace for parching grain. *—jhonkná,* to light or heat the oven; to feed the fire; to be engaged in some mean occupation.

Bháṛá, *n.* Hire; fare; freight; rent. *bháre ká tattú,* a hired pony, *(fig.)* the slave of necessity or habit.

Bhaṛak, *n.* Splendour; show; pomp; shying; starting; burst of anger; fury; flame; passion or agitation. *—dár,* refulgent; glittering; splendid; brilliant; *—ná,* to startle; to scare; to alarm; to shy; to palpitate; to blaze up.

Bharam, *a.* Error; doubt; bewilderment; labyrinth; misapprehension; suspicion; character; credit. *—gaṉwáná,* to sacrifice one's reputation; tp lose one's credit. *—khulná,* to be exposed.

Bhaṛbhaṛíyá, *a.* Open-hearted; simple; a chatter-box; one who cannot keep a secret.

Bhaṛbhúṉja, *n.* One who parches grain for sale.

Bhárí, *a.* Weighty; big; grand; great; crowded; important; costly; hard; sluggish; loud and deep (voice); hoarse; dejected. *—bharkam;* grave; sedate; patient. *—lagná,* to feel heavy; to feel tiresome.

Bhaṛkáná, *v.* To frighten; to scare; to instigate; to make one's mind irresolute; to cause a fire to burn brightly by blowing on to it.

Bharná, *v.* To fill; to satisfy; to heal (wound); to develop; to become plump; to perform; to discharge. *—bharná,* to pay off a debt; to make good a loss. *múṉh—,* to stop one's mouth by a bribe.

Bharosá, *n.* Hope; dependence; trust; reliance; confidence; faith.

Bharpái, *n.* A receipt for payment in full, to be done with.

Bharpúr, *a.* Full to the brim; as full as it can possibly be.

Bharráná, *v.* To become hoarse or husky.

Bhartá, *n.* A mash made from bolled or fried vegetables mixed with *ghee* or oil. *—kur dená,* to beat soundly; to thrash severely; to work to death.

Bhartí, *n.* Insertion; stuffing; accumulation; filling in; enrolement; enlistment; recruiting. *—karná,* v. to fill; to admit; to recruit.

Bhakosaná, *v.* To eat up; to devour; to stuff oneself up.

Blasm, *n.* Ashes. *—karná,* to reduce to ashes; to burn down; to urterly destroy or ruin. *—ramáná, v.* to rule the body over with ashes.

Bháshá, *n.* (*See under* Bhákhá).

Bhát, *n.* Cooked rice; common man's traditional diet, especially in poorer regions of India. *Dál—,* n. Rice and lentil-soup mixed meal; *Máchh—,* n. Fish-curry & Rice, mixed meal (common in Bengal).

Bháṭ, *n.* Minstrels, bards, street singers singing praises of the ruler, or the gods.

Bhaṭakná, *v.* To wander about; to go astray.

Bhátá, *n.* The ebb-tide; tide; current. *juár—,* the flow and ebb tides.

Bhatíjá, *n.* Nephew (f. *Bhatíjí*).

Bhaṭiyárá, *n.* One who provides food and lodging for travellers in a *Saráí.*

Bhaṭiyarkháná, A *saráe;* an inn.

Bhaṭká, *v.* Gone astray; lost.

Bhaṭakan, *n.* The state of being lost; state of going astray; state of loosing one's aim; aimlessness.

Bhaṭakaná, *v.* To go astray; to be lost; to be without aim; to loose sense of direction.

Bhattá, *n.* Allowance over and above one's fixed wages.

Bhaṭṭhá, *n.* An oven; a furnace; a distillery; a kiln.

Bhaunchál, Bhuíndol, Bhukamp, *n.* Earthquake.

Bhaunh, *n.* The eyebrow. *—charháná,* v. To raise one's eyebrow; to frown; *—tarerná,* n. To scowl; to show indifference.

Bhaunkna, Bhúnkná, *v. To bark; to talk* nonsense; to talk foolishly.

Bhaunrá, *n.* A large black bee which makes a buzzing noise when flying. (It is believed to be enamoured of the lotus flower and to be emblematic of marriage).

Bháví, *a.* Future; coming; would-be.

Bhavishya, *n.* The future; destiny; the time yet to come. *—darshí,* a. The seer, one who can through the future. *—vaktá,* a. One who can tell what is to come; a prediction-maker, an astrologer. *—vání.,* n. A prediction; an oracle; a prophesy. *—apne háth men honá,* adv. Being the maker of one's own destiny.

Bhawságar, *n.* The ocean of the world; existence; the world.

Bháwná, *n.* Present consciousness of past ideas; recollection; fancy; meditation; doubt; desire.

Bhawan, *n.* A house; temple; shrine; site.

Bhay, *n.* Fear; dread; apprehension. *—dikháná, v.* to frighten; to cause apprehension *—kháná, v.* To be frightened; to be afraid.

Bhayának, Bhayankar, *a.* Frightful; dreadful; formidable; terrifying.

Bhed, *n.* Difference; rupture; variety; secrety; mystery. —*kholná, v.* to unmask; to expose; to unravel. —*lená v.* to sound; to worm oneself into another's confidence. —*páná,* to find out a secret. —*dená,* to give one a clue by which to find out a secret.

Bhediyá, *n.* A scont; a spy.

Bhejá, *n.* The brain; *v.* —*kháná,* to annoy or worry one beyond endurance.]

Bhejná, *v.* To send; to despatch.

Bheká, Bhesh, Bhes, *n.* Disguise; an appearance that is assumed.

Bhelí, *n.* A lump.

Bhe<u>n</u>gá, Bhaingá, *n.* Squinty-eyed.

Bhe<u>n</u>ṭ, *n.* Visit; interview; call; meeting. —*charháná,* to offer as a present; to offer as a *Nazar.* —honá, to see or meet one; to be sacrificed.

Bheṛ, *n.* Sheep. —*ká bachchá,* a lamb. —*ká gosht,* mutton.

Bheṛiyá, *n.* A wolf.

Bhichchá, Bhikshá, Bhíkh, *n.* A Alms. —*má<u>n</u>gna,* to beg alms.

Bhichhuk, Bhikshuk, Bhíkhárí, *n.* A beggar.

Bhígá, *a.* Wet; moist; damp.

Bhígná, *v.* To get wet.

Bhinn, *a.* Separate, different, individual. —*bhinn,* a. different ones. more than one.

Bhiṛ, Barr, *a.* A hornet; a wasp. —*ká chhattá,* a wasp's or hornet's nest. —*ke chhatte me<u>n</u> háth dálná,* to raise a hornet's nest round oneself—hence to stir up mischief or evil. *sotí barro<u>n</u> ko jagáná,* to rouse a sleeping foe; to revive an old quarrel.

Bhíṛ, Bhíṛ/bháṛ, Bhíṛ/bhaṛakká, A crowd; a large gathering of people.

Bhiṛná, *v.* To quarrel with one; to assail one.

Bhiṛáná, *v.* To bring into contact with something or another; to cause to fight; to join.

Bhishtí, *n.* A water-carrier. who carries water inside a back-pack made of a whole goat-skin. common sight in Muslim communities.

Bhít, Bhitti, *n.* A wall; a parapet. —*chitra,* n. A wall-painting; a fresco.

Bhítar, *ad.* Inside; within. —*í már,* hurt or injury sustained internally.

Bhog, *n.* Experience; enjoyment; sexual pleasure; living through the result of one's good or evil deeds; also, feast; consecrated food. —*lagáná,* v. To offer food to the deity. —*lipsá.* n. Lasciviiousness; lewdness; desire for sexual pleasure. —*vád,* n. Epicureanism; hedonism. —*vilás,* n. Debauchery; sexual indulgence.

Bhoj, *n.* A feast after the death of a relation, or the performance of a ceremony.

Bhojan, *n.* Food; victuals; provisions. —*karná,* to eat one's meal.

Bholá, Bholí, *a.* Simple; artless naive —*bát,* simple artless chat.

Bhonḍáy, *a.* Ugly; ill-formed; deformed.

Bhonkná, *v.* To thrust; to stab.

Bhor, *n.* The dawn of day; the early morning. —*kar dená,* to spend all night.

Bhránt, *a.* Confused; misguided; misled; strayed; errant.

Bhránti, *n.* Confusion; error; illusion.

Bhrashṭ, *a.* Polluted; depraved; out of caste; lost; fallen. —*honá,* to be polluted or rined.

Bhrátá, *n.* Brother.

Bhrúṇ, *n.* Foetus; embryo. —*hatyá,* v. Foeticide. —*vigyán,* n. Embryology.

Bhúbal, *n.* Hot ashes.

Bhugatná, *v.* To reap as one sows.

Bhúgol, *n.* The world; the round earth, geography.

Bhugtán, *n.* Settlement in full. —*karná* yá *bhugtáná,* to effect a settlement by making a payment in full.

Bhuj, Bhujá, *n.* The arm above the elbow.

Bhúkh, *n.* Hunger; appetite; an internal feeling which creates in one a craving for food. —*on marná,* to starve; to be on the point of starvation.

Bhúl, *n.* Mistake; forgetfulness. —*bhulaiyán,* a maze; a labyrinth. —*chúk,* blunder. —*ke na karná,* do not do it even by mistake; guard against every possibility of doing it even though it be by mistake. —Iakkar, a careless, forgetful person.

Bhunáná, To get parched or fried; to have a piece of money of large value changed for pieces of money of smaller value.

Bhungá, *n.* An insect; *a.* weak; feeble.

Bhúnná, *v.* To parch; to íry.

Bhúp, *n.* King; sovereign; landlord; guardian of the earth; lord of the world.

Bhúrá, *a.* Fair; auburn; brownish.

Bhurbhurá, *a.* Sandy; in a state of dry powder. *—ná, v.* to sprinkle over with some finely powdered substance such as salt, sugar, pepper, &c. also to crumble.

Bhus, Bhúsí, Bhúsá *n.* Husk; chaff; the outer coat in which most grains are enclosed. *—bharná, v.* to stuff.

Bhúshaṇ, Bhúkhan, *n.* Jewels; adornments; embellish-ments.

Bhút, Bhutná, *n.* A ghost; an evil spirit. *—banná,* to behave like an evil spirit under the influence of intoxicating liquor; to drink till one reaches the stage of stupes. *—há haunted by ghost. —kál,* the past tense.

Bhuṭṭá, *n.* The maize; the corn-on-cub.

Bí, *a.* (Short for *Bíbí).* A vocative particle placed after the noun addressed to a respectable woman.

Bibád, Vivád, *n.* Argument; discussion; contest; altercation; lawsuit. *—karná, v.* to dispute; to litigate.

Bibek, Vivek, *n.* Discretion; discernment; judgment; sense; true knowledge.

Bibhav, Vaibhau, *n.* Power; wealth; grandeur; magnificence.

Bíbí, *n.* A respectable lady; a wife, (equivalent to *English* Madam. *French* Madame. *Germ.* frau).

Bích, *pre.* In; among; *n.* middle; centre; difference; falling out. *—bicháo karná, v.* to intervene and thereby save a quarrel. *—meṉ parná,* to interfere; to be surety or security for. *bíchoṉ—,* right in the middle; exactly in the middle; in the very midst.

Bichakná, *v.* To be frightened or alarmed; to run away through fear.

Bichálí, *n.* Straw; rice-straw.

Bichár, Vichár, *n.* Deliberation; decision; exercise of judgment.

Bichchhú, *n.* Scorpion.

Bichháná, *v.* To spread out; to scatter about.

Bichhauná, *n.* Bedding; covering for the floor.

Bichhoh, *n.* Separation; absence.

Bidá, Vidá, *n.* Departure; farewell. *—honá,* to depart. *—karná,* to grant permission; to degert; to bid farewell.

Bidesí, *n.* A foreigner; a person coming from another town a country.

Bidh, Vidhi, *n.* Precept; rule; mode; manner.

Bidhátá, Vidhátá, *n.* God.

Bidhwá, Vidhwa, *n.* A widow.

Bidyá, Vidyá, *n.* Knowledge. *—rathí* a student; a seeker after knowledge. *—wán,* a learned man; a profound scholar.

Bigána, Begáná, *a.* Strange; unknown; not one's own.

Bigáṛ, *n.* Confusion; ruin; falling out. *—ná,* to spoil; to mix in a confused manner; to change (a custom).

Bigáṛná, *v.* To be changed for the worse; to be disfigured; to be damaged; to be spoilt; to go or turn bad; to get out of order; to show one's annoyance, anger or temper; to become wicked; to revolt.

Bíghá, *n.* A square measure of land equalling in area about one-half of an English acre.

Bihár, *n.* Diversion; sport; merriment. *—í, n,* playful; gay; a name of Krishna.

Bíhaṛ, *n.* Wilderness; very rough terrain.

Bihrí, *n.* Subscription; contribution to a common fund.

Bihisht, *n.* Paradise; Heaven.

Bíj, *n.* Seed; kernel; grain; origin. *—boná, v.* to sow seed. *—ganit, n.* algebra.

Bijai, Vijai, *n.* Victory; triumph.

Bíjak, *n.* An invoice; a list; a ticket.

Bijjú, *n.* The Indian badger.

Bijlí, *a.* Lightning; a thunder-bolt. *—kaundhná* yá *chamakná,* the flashing of lightning. *—girná,* to be struck by lightning. *—ki karak, n.* a clap of thunder.

Bikaṭ, Vikaṭ, *a.* Difficult; formidable; dangerous.

Bikharná, *v.* The be scattered; to be dispersed; to be disordered; to be dishevelled (as hair).

Bikrí, *n.* Sale; demand; money realized or sales.

Bil, *n.* Hole; burrow. *—dhúndhná, v.* to look for a hole (to creep into through fear); to wish to hide oneself in order to escape. *—kul,* wholly; entirely; exactly.

Bilá, *pre.* Without. *—nága,* without any breaks. *—shakk,* without suspicion. *—takalluf,* without hindrance. *—tawaqquf,* without delay.

Bilakhaná, *v.* to cry; to wail (in sorrow, in mourning; in pain).

Bilamb, Vilamb, *n.* Delay. *—ná, v.* To delay.

Biláo, Bilár, *n.* A male cat.

Biláp, *n.* Wailing; lamentation. *—karná, v.* To lament or cry aloud.

Bilbiláná, *v.* To be tormented with pain; to whine from pain, grief or hunger, &c.; to sob or cry violently.

Bilfarz, *adv.* On the condition that; granted that; suppose.

Billaur, *n.* Crystal; crystal glass. —*sá,* crystalline.

Billí, *n.* A she-cat.

Bímá, *n.* Insurance; rate of insurance. —*karná, v.* to insure; to effect an insurance or policy.

Bímár, *a.* Sick; ill. —*dárí, n.* nursing the sick. —*pursí,* visiting the sick.

Bin, *pre.* Without; wanting; except; (the meaning may often be rendered by the English negative prefixes *un, in* or by the affix *less*), as *bin jáne,* without knowing; unwittingly. —*máre tauba karná,* to fear without a cause.

Bín, *p. a.* Seeing; beholding; looking; regarding *(used in compos.),* as; *dur-bin, n.* a telescope. *khurd-bin,* a microscope. —*á, p. a.* Seeing; clearsighted; having sight. —*á karná,* to give sight to. —*áí,* eyesight; vision.

Bín, *n.* A musical instrument, snake-charmers gourd-reed, shrill-toned but intoxicating instrument.

Biná, *n.* Basis; foundation; root; footing; source; commencement; structure. —*bar,* owing to; by reason of. —*dálná,* to found; to lay the foundation. —í-da'wa, the cause of action in a civil suit.

Binaná, Bunaná, *v.* To weave; to knit, to twine.

Binatí, Vinatí, *n.* Prayer; request.

Binaulá, *n.* The seed of the cotton plant.

Bipat, Vipadá, Vipattí, *n.* Calamity; adversity; misfortune; Poverty; suffering; disaster.

Bír, Vír, *n.* A hero; a brave gallant man; a valiant man; a brother.

Bíṛá, *n.* A betel-leaf dressed with lime, catechew, small fragrance, betelnut and other flavouring ingredients, folded up in readiness to be put into the mouth. —*utháná, v.* to accept a challenge.

Birádar, *n.* Brother. —*í,* brotherhood; members of the same group; members of an association formed for some definite purpose; brotherhood. —*í ss khárij karná* yá *huqqá páni band karná,* to ostracise one from his other group; to discard one from a caste.

Birah, Virah; *n.* Separation; absence.

Birájman, *a.* Sitting in state; sceptre in hand.

Birdh, Vriddha, *a.* Old; aged.

Birlá, *a.* Rare; uncommon; scarce.

Birodh, Virodh, *a.* Contrary; opposite; contrariwise.

Birthá, Vrithá, *a.* Useless; vain; to no purpose.

Birudh, Viruddha, *a.* Contrary to; against.

Bisarná, *a.* To be forgotten; to lose the remembrance of.

Bisátí, *n.* A pedlar; a vendor of small wares.

Bishesh, Vishesh, *a.* Special; particular; excellent; high quality.

Bismil, *a.* Sacrificed; slaughtered. —*gáh,* place of sacrifice; a slaughter-house. —*láh,* a formula, meaning 'in the name of God' pronounced by Mohamedans at the beginning of all actions and works; *intj.* God be with you ! very good ! all right ! —*láh karná,* to begin anything; to fall to

Bisrám, Vishrám, *n.* Repose; ease; cessation from labour or fatigue.

Bistár, Vistár, *n.* Extension; expansion; detail; copiousness.

Bistar, Bistrá, *n.* Bedding.

Biswá, *n.* the twentieth part of a bigha.

Biswás, Vishwás, *n.* Trust; confidence; reliance, dependence; belief. —*ghát,* breach of faith; violation of trust; treachery. —*ghátí, n.* A traitor; a treacherous friend.

Biváí, *n.* A kibe; a chilblain.

Biyábán, *n.* Desert; wilderness.

Biyáná, *v.* To give birth to.

Biyápná, Vyápná, *v.* To pervade; to penetrate; to fill; to occupy; to affect.

Bodá, *a.* Weak; low-spirited; timid; *n.* buffalo.

Bodh, *n.* Perception; sense; knowledge; understanding; comprehension; explanation. —*gamya,* a. Intelligible; comprehensible. —*ak,* a. One that would explain; one who would cause it to be understood; an indicator. —*avya,* a. Something worth knowing; knowable.

Bohni, *n.* The first business transaction of the day accompanied by a receipt of cash.

Bojh, *n.* Burden; load; cargo; incumbrance; difficulty; responsibility. —*utárná,* to relieve (oneself) of a burden. —*sir par honá,* to be under an obligation. —*ládná,* to emburden; to encumber.

Bol, *n.* Speech; word; utterance; voice; taunt. —*bálá,* prosperity; preponderance success. —*chál,* talk; conversation; idiom; dialect. —*ná,* to speak; to say; to utter. —*í,* language; speech; dialect; (auction).

Borá, *n.* A gunny bag; a sack.

Bosá, *n.* Kiss.

Bosída, *a.* Dilapidated; rotten; worn out.

Bostán, *n.* Pleasure garden; flower-garden; name of a celebrated work by the Persian poet *Sa'dí.*

Botal, *n.* Bottle. —*charbáná,* to indulge in intoxicating liquor. —*khúná,* pantry.

Boṭí, *n.* A small piece of flesh or meat. —*utár lená,* to cut off a piece of flesh. —*yá<u>n</u> kátná,* to make mincement of. *giní—napá shorbá,* to cut one's coat according to his cloth; to keep within one's means.

Brahma, *n.* The eternal spirit; the Supreme Being; Soul of the Universe. —*gyán,* n. The Divine knowledge; true understanding of the Supreme Being derived from the Vedas. —*lok,* n. A place in heaven where the departed souls of the pious ones dwell (after departing from this mortal world). —*ghát,* n. Killing of a Brahman (a member of the priestly class of the Hindus). —*drohí,* a. One who is hostile to the Supreme being; a non-believer. —*nishth,* a One completely dedicated to knowing Brahma. —*pad,* n. Salvation; liberation from the cycle of birth and death. —*bhoj,* a. a feast for Brahmans. —*muhúrt,* n. very early dawn. —*randhra,* n. The suture on top of the human skull (Hindus believe it is essential to crack open this suture after cremation of their dead, so that the soul of the deceased person is released into the greater universe).

Brahmachárí, *a.* A celibate person.

Brahmacharya, *n.* A state of celibacy; the first stage of human life for Hindus (under the *Ashrama* system) during which all efforts and energies must be directed towards the acquisition of knowledge and understanding of greater truths of life than the facts of worldly life.

Brihaspatí, *n. (Astro.)* The Jupiter; *(Myth.)* the regent of the planet Jupiter and preceptor of the gods. —*wár,* Thursday.

Brittá<u>n</u>t, Vrittá<u>n</u>t, *n.* Narrative; history; tidings; account; occurrence; condition.

Bú, *n.* Odour; scent; smell; trace.

Búá, *n.* Aunty; father's sister *(phúphí);* aunt.

Buddhi, *n.* Intellect; intelligence; wisdom; mind; sense. —*bal,* n. Mental power; keeness of intellect. —*hin,* a. intellectually dull; short on intelligence. —*kaushal,* n. Wisdom; sagacity; deftness.

—*gamya,* a. intelligible; understandable. —*jívi,* a. An intellectual; one who makes a living through his or her mental faculties or the application thereof.

Buḍḍhá, *n.* An old man. Buḍḍhí, an old woman.

Bugz, *n.* Malice; animosity; resentment; rancour; revenge.

Bujhauwal, *n.* Enigma; riddle; connundrum.

Bujháná, *v.* To put on (fire); to extinguish; to satisfy (hunger); to quench (thirst); to drive away or out.

Bukhár, *n.* Fever; vapour; steam; warmth; animosity. —*dil men̲ rakhná,* to harbour animosity against another. —*níkálná,* to give vent to one's rage.

Buláhat, *n.* Call; summons; invitation.

Buláná, *v.* To send for; to call; to summon; to invite; to give out a sound.

Buland, *a.* High; elevated; loud; tall; exalted; sublime. —*hausila, a.* ambitious; magnanimous; enterprising. —*martaba,* of high rank or dignity.

Bulbul, *n.* The nightingale.

Bún̲d, *n.* Drop. —*tapakná,* to drop down in drops; to trickle.

Buniyád, *n.* Foundation; basis; ground; origin.

Buqchá, *n.* A small bundle of clothes; a knapsack; a wallet.

Burá, *a.* Bad; evil; vicious; defective. —*bhalá kahná, v.* to speak abusively of one. —*lagná, v.* to prove disagreeable or unpleasant. —*mánaná.*

Burádá, *n.* Sawdust; filings.

Buráí, *n.* Evil; depravity; harm; calumny; evil consequence. —*par kamar kasná,* to be bent on doing harm or mischief.

Burdbar, *a.* Forbearing, to-learant; patient; gentle; meek.

Burj, *n.* Bastion; tower; turret. —*í-hamal,* the sign Aries.

Burqá, *n.* A long covering for the body used by Mohamedan ladies extending from the crown of the head to the feet and having two holes about the region of the -eyes to permit the wearer to see through.

But, *n.* Idol; image; status; *a.* speechless; dumb. —*parastí, n.* idolatory; image-worship. —*KHána,* pagoda; any building containing an image or images of heathen deities.

Búṭá, *n.* Plant (vegetation); an embroidery pattern based on floral and vegetational design.

Búṭí, *n.* Herbs used for medicinal purposes.

Butta dená, *v.* To take in; to cheat; to deceive; to evade.

Buzurg, *n.* Venerable; ages; elder; saint; senior citizen; sage. *—án,* n. Ancestors; elders. *—áná,* adv. In the manner of elders; sage-like posture;

Byádh, *n.* [Corruption of Sanskrit *Vyádhi*] Sickness; illness; ailment; pain; anguish.

Byádhá, *n.* Hunter; sportsman; fowler.

Byáh, *n. See under* Bibáh.

Byáj, *n.* Interest on money lent.

Byákaran, Vyákaraṇ, *n.* Grammar; discipline.

Byákul, Vyákul, *a.* Restless, agitated; anxious; uneasy; perplexed.

Byarth, Vyarth, *a.* In vain; useless; worthless; meaningless.

Byohár, Vyavahár, *n.* Behaviour; treatment; dealings; the way of interacting with-.

Byopár, Byápár, [Sanskrit; Vyápar], *n.* Trade; Commerce; traffic in goods and commodities; buying and selling. *—í,* n. One who indulges in such activity; a dealer, a merchant.

Byorá, *n.* Detailed account.

Byontná, *v.* Cutting out of cloth into shape for making clothes.

C,c, in English alphabet is used variously to denote 's' sound [in *place*] as well as 'k' sound [*class* and *commerce*]. In this dictionary, we are using it only in conjunction with 'h' to form a single letter 'Ch' to denote Hindi sound of (च) and Urdu sound of (چ). In latter part of this letter listing 'Chh' will also be found to denote a successive Hindi sound of (छ) and Urdu sound of (چھ). Unfortunately English sound system has no equivalent sound to indicate parallels.

Chá, Cháe, *n.* Tea. —*dání,* n. A Container holding dry tea; teapot; —*pání,* n. a tea-party; *(Proverbially)* a bribe; an under-the-table payment a 'herbal' brew that originated in India and China and has conquered the world through British merchandising enterprise.

Chabná, Chabáná, Chabená, *v.* To chew; to masticate; to Crunch.

Chabená, *n.* Parched grain (used as food), snack.

Chábí, Chábhí, *n.* Key *(táí);* an instrument for shutting or opening a lock; a guide; a key-note.

Chábuk, *n.* A horse-whip; a lash. —*márná,* to whip; to lash; to flog. —*phatkárná,* to crack a whip —*sawár,* n. a horse breaker; a jockey; *a.* quick active; nimble. —*dast,* dexterous; adroit; active in the use of hand, and, in the exercise of the mental faculties.

Chabútará, *n.* A terrace; a raised level space of earth; a platform.

Cháchá, Chachá, *n.* A paternal uncle; father's brother. —*zád bháí* yá *bahin,* cousin; son or daughter of a paternal uncle.

Chacherá / Chacherí, *adj.* One's cousin, from paternal uncle, i.e. father's younger brother's son or daughter.

Cháchí, *n.* A paternal aunt.

Chachiyá Sasur, *n.* Uncle-in-law. Chachiyá Sás, *n.* Aunt-in-law.

Chachorná, *v.* The draw something with the mouth from; to suck.

Chádar, *n.* A sheet; a coverlet; a table-cloth a cloth or sheet loosely thrown over one's shoulders. —*charháná;* v. Offering a sheet, or piece of cloth at a shrine.

Cháh, Cháhat, *n.* Desire; wish; longing; craving; liking; fondness; appetite; want; requirement; demand; affection. *P. n.* A well; a pit; a dimple. —*i-zanakh,* —*i-zaqan,* the dimple of the chin; a slight natural depression in the chin. —*kan, n.* a well-digger.

Chahár, *a.* Four. *—chand,* fourfold. *—dah,* fourteen. *—shamba,* Wednesday. *—am,* fourth.

Chahbachchá, *n.* A cistern; a small reservoir; a vat; a sinkhole.

Chahchahá, *n.* Song (of a bird); chirping; warbling; singing; chatter; merriment.

Cháé, [See *Chá*]

Cháhe, *conj.* Either; or; though. *—jitná,* howmuchsoever, *—jo,* whosoever or whichsoever.

Chahkan, *n.* Chirpy, somewhat shrill, kind of noise that happy children, or even adults in a happy children, or even adults in a happy mood, make. *—á,* v. the act of making such noise.

Chahlá, Chehlá, *n.* Mud; puddle; mire; *a.* miry; marshy; wet.

Cháhná, *v.* To wish; to desire; to want; to require; to be inclined to; to like; to love; to choose; to ask for; to crave.

Chailá, *v.* A piece of wood split for burning.

Chailí, *n.* A chip; a splinter.

Chait, *(Sansk. Chaitra), n.* The name of a month of the Hindu year corresponding to English March-April. *—í fasl,* the harvest cut in the spring season, *i.e.,* in the month of March.

Chaitan, *(sansk. Chaitanya), a.* Rational; alive; sentient; conscious; alert; awake; *n.* a living and sentient being; soul. *—honá,* to be wide awake; to be on alert; to be conscious.

Chák, *n. H.* A potter's wheel; a millstone. *P.* A narrow opening in clothes (left intentionally); slit; fissure. *—gerebán,* having the collar rent; afflicted; sad. *—karná,* to rend; to tear.

Chakáchaun̲dh, *n.* The effect on the eyes of a sudden flash of light. *—lagná,* to be dazzled.

Chákar, *n.* A servant; an attendant. *—í, n.* service.

Chaḳh-Chaḳh, *n.* Wrangling; altercation; discord.

Chakhná, *v.* To taste; to relish; to enjoy; to experience; to suffer.

Chakká, *n.* Wheel (of a cart); anything round and flat; thick curd or coagulated milk.

Chakkar, *n.* Anything revolving in a circle; circuit; round; a circle; a circular missile; giddiness; perplexity; maze. *—khání, v.* to be put into rotatory motion; to move or fly in a circle; to take a circuitous road. *—márná, v.* to revolve; to take a round about road; to wheel round. *—men̲ áná, v.* to be entangled in the meshes of. *—men̲ dálná,* to involve one in difficulty; to lead astray.

Chakkí, *n.* A pair of millstone; a grinding stone; a whirlgig.

Chaklá, *a.* Broad; wide; circular; a round and broad stale of stone or piece of a wood.

Chakmá, *n.* Cheating; trick. *—dená, v.* to practise deception; to occasion loss or damage.

Chaknáchúr, *a.* Dashed to pieces; shattered; *n.* small pieces; atoms; scraps. *—karná,* to break or dash to pieces.

Chakor, *n.* A species of partridge commonly found in Greece.

Chakotrá, *n.* Pumelo; a fruit of the lime kind of a large size.

Chakravartí, *n.* Sovereign of the world; emperor.

Chaktí, *n.* A small round patch of leather, metal, cloth, &c.

Chakwá, Chakwí, *n.* A species of water-fowl. commonly known by the name of Brahmaní duck.

Chal, *intj.* Get or go away; be off or away with you; go away from here. *—dená, v.* to secretly go away. *—jáná,* to pass away; to be loosened (as the bowels); to fall. *—parná,* to come into operation; to come into season.

Chál, *n.* Style and manner of movement; bearing; carriage; usage, custom, behaviour. *—chalan;* n. Conduct; behaviour; character.

Chálak, *n.* Driver; operator; a person in operational control of a machine; vehicle, or instrument.

Chálák, *a.* Artful; cunning; expert; experienced; quick. *—í, n.* artfulness; cunning. *—karná,* to practise artfulness or cunning. *—log,* designing or artful persons; sharpers.

Chálán, *n.* A way bill; a draft; a pass; the sending up of an accused person to be tried before a Magistrate; (technically) a form or tender used for depositing money in a goverment treasury.

Chaláná, *v.* To give impetus or motion to; to impart motion to; to set going; to stir; to fire (a gun); to use *(láthí, sword).*

Chalná, *v.* To move; to stir; to depart; to walk ; to flow; to blow; to sail; to be fired; to start; to go beyond.

Chálná, *v.* To sift; to cause to pass through a sieve.

Chaltá, *n.* Moving; in motion; running; ordinary; passable; busy; potent. *chalte chalte,* whilst going; on the way; by degrees. *—kám,* work done hurriedly; work done indifferently on account of haste. *—purzá,* a taker in; a sharper; one who practices deception on others. *Chaltí dukán,* a prospering or flourishing business.

Chám, Charm, Chamrá, *n.* Skin, leather; hide.

Chamak, *n.* Shine; brilliance; splendour. *—dár, a.* shining; resplendent. *—ná.* to shine; to flash; to glare; to startle.

Chaman, *n.* A flower-bed in a garden; any place that is decked with prolific verdure. *—zár,* a green meadow. *—istán,* a flower-bed, A place in Baluchistan, famous for its sweet, seedless grapes.

Chamar, Cháṉwar, *n.* A contrivance made generally from the hair of a horse's tail used for the purpose of whisking off flies, ritually hovered over the holy books or deities, as a sign of reverence.

Chamár, *n.* The name of one of the lowest castes among the Hindus whose principal occupation is that of working in leather. [The words is also used, sometimes, as a term of abuse to hint at the lower station of the recipient of the remark made].

Chambelí, *n.* The flower of the Jasmine plant.

Chamchá, Chammach, *n.* A spoon; a ladle. [Prover-bially sychophants, *—gírí, adv.* psychophancy; false praise; flattery.

Chamchamáhat, *n.* Brightness; splendour; radiance.

Chamkílá, *a.* Shining; radiant; glowing.

Cháṉp. *n.* The cock of a gun. *—charháná, v.* to cock a gun.

Chaṉpá, *n.* The name of a tree bearing a fragrant yellow flower. *—kalí, n.* a necklace made of pieces which resembles in form of the unblown flowers of the *champá* tree.

Chaṉpat honá, *v.* To vanish; to disappear.

Chamṛá, *n.* Leather; hide; skin. *—udherná,* to flay; to skin, to tear the hide of an animal; to tear off the skin of a human being.

Chaná, *n.* The kind of pulse known as gram; chick-peas.

Chaṉchal, *á.* Restless; changeful; uncertain; wanton; *n.* a restless person; a person who cannot remain still.

Chaṉd, *a.* Some; few.

Cháṉd, *n.* The moon; the crown of the head. *—ká tukrá, handsome person. —márí, n.* target practice; firing at a target.

Chaṉḍá, *n.* Subscription.

Cháṉḍál, *n.* One of the lowest castes amongst the Hindus; a keeper of the nacropolis, or cremation grounds; (a.) a miserly person; a wretch; an outcaste.

Cha<u>n</u>dan, *n.* Sandal; sandal-wood; fragrant; indicative of a cool sensuality.

Cha<u>n</u>darmá, *n.* The moon.

Cha<u>n</u>darmukhí, *n.* As beautiful as the moon.

Cha<u>n</u>ḍí, *n.* A female deity, with a ferocious countenance, also known as *Kálí* especially worshipped in Bengal and hailed as *Kálí Kalkatte wálí.*

Chá<u>n</u>dí, *n.* Silver; *—ká warq, n.* a leaf of silver; a thin plate of silver.

Chá<u>n</u>dní, *n.* Moonlight; a white cloth spread over a carpet or other place to sit on; a ceiling cloth; any white and shining thing which resembles the light of the moon. *—chítakná,* the moonlight to be bright; the full brightness of the moonshine.

Cha<u>n</u>dúl, *n.* The pyramid-crested lark.

Cha<u>n</u>gá, *a.* In sound health; true; pure; healed; cured.

Cha<u>n</u>gul, *n.* Talons; claws.

Chánṭá, Chapeṭá, Chapat. *n.* A blow dealt with the palm of the hand; a slap.

Chapátí, *n.* A thin cake of unleavened bread.

Chapkan, *n.* A loose outer garment.

Cháplús, *a.* A flatterer; a sycophant.

Chapṛá, *n.* Sealing wax; lac.

Chaprásí, *n.* A peon; an orderly; the lowest rank in office employees.

Chapṭá, *a.* Flat-shaped. *—ná,* to flatten; to press flat; to press even.

Cháq, *a.* Alert; active; smart; sound; healthy.

Chaqmaq, *n.* a flint; or a steel bit for striking fire.

Cháqú, *n.* A knife; a clasp-knife.

Chár, *n.* Four. *—á<u>n</u>khe<u>n</u> honá,* meeting; interview. *—bísí, four-score. —din kí bahár,* the pleasure of a few days. *—din kí zindagí,* transient life. *—ddin kí chá<u>n</u>dní,* temporary enjoyment. *—guná,* fourfold. *— jámá,* a kind of saddle made of cloth. -*o<u>n</u>-chár,* inevitably; perforce. *—páya,* quadruped. *—'anásir,* four elements *i.e.,* earth *(khák),* water *(áb),* wind *(bád)* fire *(átash). —zánú baithná,* to sit cross-legged. *—o<u>n</u>,* the four; all; four. *—o<u>n</u> sháne chit,* spread out at full length on the back.

Charágáh, *n.* Meadow; pasture; grazing land.

Chárá, *n.* Food (for cattle); fodder; forage; bait (for a fish).

Chárá, *n.* Remedy; cure; help; redress. *—pizír,* remediable. *—sází,* using means for a remedy.

Charan, *n.* The foot; base or root of a tree. *—amrit,* the water in which the feet of an idol, priest, a *Brahman,* a *gurú,* a husband or a guest have been washed. *—raj, n.* dust of the feet. *—lená,* to touch the feet of any venerable person.

Charáná, *v.* To graze; to pasture; to feed; *(met.)* to lead one by the nose; to make a fool of.

Chara<u>n</u>d, Charindá, *n.* Graminivorous; an animal that grazes; a beast.

Charas, Charsá, *n.* A large leather bucket for drawing water from the wells. *(purwat, moth.)—bhar zamín,* (*lit,* 'as much land as can be covered by a hide'; *(met.)* as much land as can be irrigated by a pair of bullocks.

Charas, *n.* The exudation of the flowers of hemp collected with the dew and prepared for use as an intoxicating drug.

Charb, *n.* Fat; greary; oily; smooth; glib; sharp; prevailing. *—í,* fat; grease; tallow. *—í-dár,* greasy; sleek. *—í kí jhillí,* caul; the fine membrane that covers the fat. *—gizá,* rich food; dainties. *—zabán,* smooth-tongued; flattering.

Charchá, *n.* Gossip; incidental mention; popular talk; talking over past events; discourse; recapitulation; rumour.

Charcharáná, *v.* To crackle (as burning wood); to make an abrupt noise; to sputter.

Charg, *n.* A kind of falcon or hawk; a hyeua *(charkh).*

Chaṛhá, *a.* Risen; high (prices, a tune); swollen (river); in practice; possessed by (as evil spirit). *—barhá,* a wealthy, or great person. *—ná,* to cause to ascend, mount, or embark; to raise; to offer up; to brace (a drum); to string (a bow); to cock; to put on or into; to apply (colour); to fix (a bayonet); to imbibe; to lead (an army). *—í* yá*—o,* ascent; rise; acclivity; elevation; ascension; promotion; innundation; loftiness; conveying; embarkation; assault; onset. *—o-utár,* rise and fall; ascent and descent; tapering at both ends; flood-tide and ebbtide. *—wá,* a religious offering; anything presented in sacrifice.

Chaṛhná, *v.* To ascend; to climb; to embark; to be conveyed; to come on (as faver), to fall in arrears (pay); to be elevated; to be offered (a sacrifice); to be strung (as a bow); to be set (bone); to be entered in (account); to take effect (poison, intoxicants, &c.,); to elapse (as time). *charh baithná,* to mount; to ride; to overcome.

Charitr, *n.* Character; behaviour; conduct; bearing; manner; deeds; wiles; adventures; biography.

Charkaṭá, *n.* The man who cuts forage for animals, elephants, &c.

Charkh, *n.* A wheel; a lathe; the celestial globe; the heavens; circular motion; fortune. *—i-akhzar,* the ethereal sphere. —i-*dawwár, n.* revolving heaven; *(mst.)* changeable fortune. *—márná, v.* to turn round; to move or soar in a circle; to circulate (blood). *—hindolá,* a merry-go-round.

Charkhá, *n.* A spinning wheel; a reel; the axis of a pulley; *a.* thin; weak; rickety (as a cart, &c.). *—poní,* spinning and carding. *—ho jáná,* to become worn out or rickety.

Charkhí, *n.* A pulley; an instrument for separating cotton from the seed; a kind of fire-works; a dumb-waiter. *—fánus,* a revolving lantern made of talc with pictures all round *(fánús-í-khiyál).*

Charní, *n.* A feeding through; manager.

Charwáhá, *n.* A tender or feeder of cattle; a grazier; a cowherd; a shepherd.

Chashm, *n.* The eye. *—i-bímár,* an eye that looks half-closed from modesty; an epithet of beauty; a drooping eye. *—numái, n.* reproof; rebuke. *—o-chiág;* dearly beloved; light of the eye. *—poshí karná,* to turn one's eyes away; to overlook; to excuse; to connive. *—í-khún-álúd,* eyes; fierce looks. *áhú—,* gazelle-eyed; soft-eyed (an epithet expressive of beauty).

Chashmá, *n.* A spring; source; fountain; spectacles.

Chashmak, *n.* A wink; misunderstanding. *—zadan,* a winking.`

Cháshní, *n.* Flavour; taste; a mixture of sweet and sour; a specimen; the viscous state of a syrup.

Chásht, *n.* The middle hours between the sunrise and the meridian; breakfast. *—namáz,* morning prayer.

Chaská, *n.* Taste; relish; zest; desire; habit, addition.

Chaspán, *n.* Adhesive; slimy; sticking to; applicable. *—karná,* to stick; to affix; *(Leg.)* to paste a summons or notice on some conspicuous part of a person's dwelling house or place of business when the person himself cannot be found for the summons or notice to be personally served on him.

Chaspída, *p. a.* Struck to; glued; adhered; attached; addicted (to).

Chaṭ, *adv.* Quickly; instantly; in a hurry; all at once. —*pathoná,* to die suddenly; *n.* the sound of breaking or cracking. —*chat,* the sound of repented cracking or of quickly repeated strokes; *adv.* wholly; altogether; clean. —*kar jácá, v.* to lick the platter clean; to make away with; to embezzle. —*patá,* a. deliciously savoury.

Cháṭ, *n.* Tasting; licking; delicacy; a spicey, savoury concoction made from fruits, vegetables and snacks, mixed with dips and relishes; roadside snack. —*ná,* to lick; to eat holes into cloth or herbage (as a worm; a locust). —*parná,* to acquire a taste or longing for.

Chaṭáí, *n.* A mat.

Chaṭakná, *v.* To crackle (as burning wood, &c,); to split; to burst; to be irritated; estrangement to take place between two persons.

Chaṭká, *n.* A parching sun; dearth; excessive thirst. —*lagná,* to be very thirsty; to desire eagerly.

Chaṭkaní, *n.* A bolt (of a door).

Chaṭkílá, *n.* Brilliant; glittering; gaudy; pungent; savoury; strong; in excess (salt, &ci, in a dish).

Chaṭní, *n.* A kind of pickle or sauce; the solid ingredients of which are bruised and retained in the vinegar. —*karná,* to reduce to pulp; to mash.

Chaṭorá, *a.* Greedy; voracious; *n.* a gormand; an epicure; one who wastes his money on delicacies. —*pan,* epicureanism; toothsomeness.

Chaṭpaṭí, Chaṭpaṭá *n.* Brisk; *a.* pungent; hot tasty *(charpará).*

Chaṭṭán, *n.* Rock; a large block of stone.

Chatur, *pref.* Four. —*bhuj,* having four arms; quadrilateral. —*dashi,* the fourteenth day of the moon's age. —*uarg,* the four objects of human pursuit collectively, *vis.,* (1) virtue, (2) pleasure, (3) wealth, (4) final beatitude. —*raru,* the four castes of Hindús, *viz.,* the *Brahman; Kshatriya, Vaishya,* and *Súdrá.* —*vedi,* one familiar with the *Vedas (chaube).*

Chatur, *a.* Active; smart; quick; clever; ingenious sharp; shrewd; asture; cunning.

Chau, *prefix.* Four; *(used as a prefix).* —*bandi,* shoeing. —*bolá,* a verse of four lines. —*pahal,* four-sides, —*pher,* all round. —*rastá,* junction of 4 roads; quadrivium. —*khúnt barábar bázú,* a rhombus. —*gird,* on all sides. *—lará,* n necklace of 4 strings or rows. *—mása,* four months of the rainy season. *—mahlá,* four-storied. *—hattá,* a square with shops on all sides;—

Chaudharí, *n.* A title; an honorific form of address; the headman of a village, tribe or caste.

Chaugán, *n.* A plain; the game of polo.

Chaugará, *n.* A rabbit; a hare.

Chauká, *n.* An aggregate of four.

Chauká, *n.* Kitchen, also the work done in the kitchen; *—bartan karná,* v. to deal with the chores of kitchen; to do the cooking, and deal with the pots and pans.

Chaukanná, *a.* Circumspect; cautious; vigilant on one's guard; on the watch.

Chaukarí, *n.* A carriage and four; bound; leap; bounce. *—bhúlná,* to lose one's elastic tread; to be confounded; to have one's senses benumbed.

Chaukasí, *n.* Vigilance; circumspection. *—rakhná,* to keep watch over; to guard; to watch.

Chaukhaṭ, Chaukhaṭá, *n.* A door-frame; sill and lintel of a door-frame. *—bázú,* the four pieces and wood forming the frame of a door.

Chaukí, *n.* A low square pedestal; a stool; a bench; a chair; a station of police, custom, octroi, &c.; an outpost; a guard; an aggregate of our. *—dár,* a watchman; a sentinel. *—már,* a smuggler. *—men rakhná,* to keep in custody; to detain a suspected person.

Chaundhyáná, *v.* To be dazzled; to be frightened out of one's senses.

Chaunk, *n.* a sudden start. *—áná,* to starte; to rouse. *—ná,* to be startled. *—uthná,* to start up; to wake up suddenly.

Chaunsar, Chausar, Chaupaṛ. *n.* A game like *pachísí,* but played with dice instead of cowries.

Chaupán, *n.* A shepherd; a cowhered.

Chaupaṭ, *a.* Wide open; flat; ruined; destroyed.

Chaupáyá, *n.* Anything having four legs; *n.* a quadruped; a beast; an animal.

Chauṛá, *a.* Broad; wide; expanded. *—í,* breadth; width; extension; expansion. *—karná,* to make broad; to enlarge; to widen.

Chauras, *a.* Even; level; plane. *—áná,* to make even or smooth; to level.

Chautará, *—tará,* n. A squarish platform; *—mukhá* a. Four-sided; one lookit four-ways.

Chauth, *n.* A tribute to the extent of one-fourth of the regular government revenue levied by the Marhattas from the neighbouring princes. *—á,* fourth. *—e,* fourthly *—áí,* a quarter. —í, a ceremony observed among Mohamedans on the fourth day after marriage when the bride and bridegroom beat each other with sticks covered with flowers. *—íyá,* a quartan ague.

Cháwal, *n.* Rice cleared of the husk and not cooked.

Chechak, *n.* Small-pox; measles *(sítlá, mátá)*. *—rú,* pock-marked.

Chehil, Chehal, *a.* Forty. *—qadamí* walk; ramble; an excursion; roving *—um,* the fortieth day of mourning after *Moharrum* festival among Mohamedans.

Chéhrá, *n.* Face; countenance; visage*—bandí,* a descriptive roll. *—likhná,* to make a descriptive roll (of).

Chélá, *n.* A pupil; a disciple; a follower; a slave brought up in the house. *—karná,* to make a disciple or convert of.

Chét, *n.* Sensation; consciousness; wits; memory; recollection; remembrance. *—an,* rational; alive; living; of sound mind. *—karná,* yá *chetná,* to remember; to recollect; to think; to consider; to recover the senses.

Chhab, Chhavi, *n.* Beauty; charm; grace; decoration; shape; structure; graceful form*—ílá,* comely; handsome; good-looking; gay; sprightly.

Chhabíl, *n.* A roadside stall mounted in summer months and on festive occasions by the rich and the charitable, by individuals as well as organisation, offering cold drinks, some times sweetened but often just cold drinking water, to people passing by. Hindus to it more often and call it a *Pyáú.* Muslims do it at *Moharram* time and call it a *Sabíl.*

Chhachhúndar, *n.* The musk-rat.

Chhágal, *n.* A leathern bottle with a spout to it.

Chhai, Kshay, *n.* Loss; diminution; crumbling; damage.

Chhai-Rog, Kshay Rog, *n.* A diseases known as consumption; tuberculosis.

Chhail, Chhailá, Chhail Chikaniyá, *a.* Handsome; comely; beautiful; dashing; foppish; *n.* a gay young spark; a beau.

Chhá jáná, *v.* To overspread.

Chhajjá, *n.* A gallery or balcony constructed along the outer wall of a building usually on the second or some higher storey;

the spreading branches of a tree which afford shade; a covered way.

Chhakáchhak, *a.* Brimful; full to repletion; full.

Chhakáná, *v.* To fully satisfy; to cloy; to pamper; to chastise; to punish; to take one in; to make a fool of one.

Chhakká, *n.* A sixer [in cricket]. *—panjá karná,* To play tricks; to practice deceipt.

Chhakké chhúkná, To become bewildered; confound; to become confounded.

Chhakṛá, *n.* A two-wheeled bullock cart; a cart for carrying goods.

Chhal, *n.* Fraud; deception; imposture; pretence; excuse; evasion; disgnise; feint. *—bal, n.* trickery; fraud and force.

Chhál, *n.* Bark; peel; rind; skin.—*utarna,* To peel; to flay.

Chhálá, *n.* A blister; a pimple *mirg—,* a deer-skin. *—parná,* a blister to rise; to be blistered.

Chhalakná, *v.* To be split; to run over; to splash; to cause liquid to be split from a vessel by reason of any sudden or abrupt movement.

Chhaláng, *n.* A leap; a bound *—márná,* to leap; to bound.

Chhaláwá, *n.* Will-o-the-wisp; Jack-o-lantern; a light seen in bogs and marshes due to the phenomenon of reflection which receives as it is approached thus, often leading travellers astray.

Chháliyá, *n.* The betel-nut.

Chhallá, *n.* A small plain ring. *—dár,* provided or fitted with rings.

Chhalní, Chalní, *n.* A strainer; a seive; an implement for separating the finer from the coarser particles of any powdered substance. *—honá,* to become perforated; to be filled with holes; to be riddled.

Chhalorí, *n.* A blister; a whitlow; a felon.

Chhamá, Khimá, Kshamá, *n.* Pardon; forgiveness.

Chhamáhí, *adv.* Half yearly; six monthly.

Chham-chham, *n.* A sound made by the falling of a heavy shower of rain; the tinkling sound made by jewels when their wearer is in the act of walking. *—áná,* to make a tinkling sound.

Chhán, *n.* A roof; the bamboo or wooden frame over which thatch is spread for constructing the roof of a house. *—á,* to roof; to cover; to spread; to shade.

Chhánaná, *v.* To sift; to strain to filter; to search minutely; to canvas; te analyse; to explore.

Chhand, *n.* A stanza in poetry; a measure in music; prosody; poetical metre.

Chhaṉgá, *n.* A man having six fingers on one or both hands.

Chhangulí, *n.* The little finger of the hand.

Chhánh, Chháṉv, Chháon, *n.* Shade; shadow; shelter.

Chhánṭ, *n.* The act of sifting through, separating, putting things in their respective categories and classes, etc. *—ná* v. to sift, to separate, to sort out; to select. *—karná,* v. To retrench; to trim; to prune, etc.

Chháon, [See *Chhánh*].

Chháoní, Chhávní. A cantonment; harracks for soliders; thatching; roofing.

Chháp, *n.* Stamp; print; impresion (of a stamp or type, &c.); a seal; signet; an official stamp in general. *—lagáná,* to seal; to stamp; to print.

Chhápá, *n.* Edition; printing; press; a night attack. *—kháná,* a printing office; a press. *—márná,* to surprise an adversary in a might attack. *patthar ká—,* Lithography.

Chhapák, *n.* A splash; a sound made when a heavy object falls in the water, or when a swimmer jumps into water from a height.

Chhappar, *n.* A shed; a hut; a sloping thatch. *—band,* a thatcher. *—par dharná,* to throw aside as worthless. *—phár ke dená.* to give in an unexpected manner; to surprise one with an unexpected gift. *—tút parvá,* a sudden calamity to befad one.

Chhaṛ, *n.* Shaft; pole; pike; an iron rod; a fishing-rod.

Chhaṛá, *a.* Single; alone; solitary; *n.* an oruament for the foot.

Chhaṛí, *a.* Stick; rod; cane; walking stick. *—bardár,* the marshal who walks before people of consequence with the mace or wand of office.

Chharrá, *n.* Small shot. *—piláná,* to load a gun with shot. *—uráná,* to smoke *madak.*

Chhat, *n.* A ceiling. *—lagáná,* to ceil; to cover the inner roof of a building. *—pátná,* to lay a floor on the roof.

Chhátá, *n.* An umbrella; a mushroom; a fungus.

Chhaṭáṉk, *n.* A sixteenth part of a seer; a Traditional Indian weight-measure which was discarded in the wake of decimalization in 1952.

Chhaṭé-chhamáhé, *adv.* Now and then; once in a while; after long intervals.

Chhaṭí, Chhaṭhí,*n.* The sixth day after the birth of a child on which day the house undergoes a thorough cleaning; the mid-wife receives her remuneration and present and the mother and child are bathed, the child being named, whilst friends are invited to partake of the joyfulness of the occasion. *—ká dúdh yád dilár* to obastise severely.

Chhátí, *n.* The breast; the chest; the bosom; spirit; courage; liberal attitude. *—bhar áná,* v. to be greatly moved emotionally. *—par patthar rakhná,* v. To bear it; to be patient. *—par sánp lotná,* v. Being envious; to be tormented by envy. *—pakaṛ ke rah jáná,* v. to grieve or mourn in silence *—píṭná,* to grieve or mourn openly; to lament in public. *—ṭhanḍí honá* to be comforted, to be solaced. *—se lagáná,* to embrace, to hug, to fondle. *—kholke milná,* to meet openly, to meet frankly. *—nikal kar chalná,* to go out proudly; to move about pompously; to confront outsiders with an air of arrogance.

Chhaṭpaṭáná, *v.* Writhing; to flounder; to wince in pain; to flutter (like fish out of water.

Chhatr, *n.* An umbrella of state held over kings. *—dhárí, n.* one entitled to have an umbrella held over him when walking abroad; a king; a noble. *—í,* the ordinary umbrella used in every day life; a canopy; the hood of a carriage; a perch fixed on the top of a long bamboo pole for pigeons to settle.

Chhattá, *n.* Honey-comb; hive.

Chhattísí, Chhattísa, *a.* Cunning; artful; crafty.

Chhauná, *n.* The young of an animal.

Chhéd, *n.* A hole. *—ná,* to bore or pierce a hole.

Chhénkná, *v.* To stop; to prevent; to obstruct; to molest; to annoy.

Chhéní, *n.* A chisel for cutting iron or stone.

Chhéṛ, *v.* The act of irritating; the act of vexing; the act of of worrying. *—chhár,* vexation; disturbance. *—ná, v.* to irritate; to annoy.

Chherí, *n.* A goat.

Chhetr, Kshetr, Khet, *n.* A field; a ground; a plot of land. *yuddh-,* battle field. *—phal,* measurement of the area/size of.

Chhichhlá, *a.* Shallow.

Chhichhorá, *n.* Vain; petty; trifing; insignificant; contemptible; tawdry

Chhichhrá, *n.* The skinny portion of a piece of meat that is discarded for eating purposes; the cellular membrane that covers the surface of the body; the slough (of a wound); the crust (of a sore).

Chhidná, *v.* To be pierced.

Chhiká, Chhín̲ká *n.* A net of strings or cords hung from a ceiling or other high place to keep food, &c., from the reach of destructive animals; such as dogs, cats, mice.

Chhilká, *n.* Crust; husk; shell; pee;; rind; skin. *—utárná, v.* remove the skin, peel, rind or shell of anything.

Chhílná, *v.* To skin; to pare; to peel; to remove the natural outer covering of any thing; to smoothe the outer surface of wood.

Chhímí, *n.* A pod; a been.

Chhin, Kshaṇ, *n.* Moment; instant. *—bhar men̲,* in a moment; in an instant; immediately.

Chhínaná, *v.* To snatch away; To take by force; to deprive the rightful owner of something.

Chhinál, *n.* An inconstant woman; a tart; a whorish woman; a woman of low moral character.

Chhín̲k, *n.* A sneeze. *—ná, v.* to sneeze.

Chhín̲ṭ, *n.* A kind of marked cloth called chintz.

Chhínṭ, Chhinṭá, *n.* Droplet, spray from water. *—márná,* v. To spray some one; to hit someone with droplets of water.

Chhipáná, To hide or conceal; to disguise.

Chhípí, *n.* A cloth printer.

Chhipná, *v.* To hide oneself; to endeavour ot evade a difficulty; to fly in the face of trouble; to lie in ambush.

Chhipkalí, *n.* A lizard.

Chhiṛakná, *v.* To sprinkle; to water by sprinkling.

Chhiṭkáná, Chhiṭkárná, *v.* To scatter, to strew; to spread about in a disorderly manner.

Chhokrá, Chhorá, *n.* A boy; a youth.

Chhokrí, Chhorí, *n.* a girl; a damsel.

Chholdárí, *n.* A decorative tent, raised at family occasions to accommodate visiting guests; a vast canopy.

Chhop, *n.* A coat of paint; plaster. *—chháp karná,* to plaster; to paint.

Chhor, *n.* Borders; margin.

Chhoṛná, *v.* To let go; to abandon; to release; to shoot; to discharge.

Chhoṭá, *a.* Little; small; mean; younger; low; base. *—bará,* of different kinds; large and small; young and old; high and low.

Chhoṭe Sáhib, *n.* A person holding a subordinate rank or position.

Chhúchhá, Chhúchhí, *a.* Empty; hollow; ears of corn from which the grain has been beaten out.

Chhuhárá, *n.* Dried date.

Chhúná, *v.* To touch; to feel; to meddle with (as papers seattered or strewn on a table).

Chhurá, *n.* A knife with a large blade; a dagger; a chopper; a razor (barber's slang). *—márna,* to stab.

Chhurí, *n.* A knife; small daggers.

Chhuṛáná, *v.* To dismiss; to free by force; to part; to have one released or liberated; to re-cue; to redeem (a pledge). *chhurá lená,* to take or snatch away.

Chhút, *n.* Touch of anything impure or base; contamination; defilement.

Chhúṭ, *n.* Relief; allowance; exemption; discount.

Chhuṭáná, *v.* To fire (a gun); to discharge (an arrow).

Chhuṭkárá, *n.* Liberation; release; acquital; emancipation; deliverance. *—dená, v.* To give one his liberty; to set one free; to acquit; to discharge from a liability. *—páná,* to obtain dehverance, release or exemption; to be got rid of.

Chhúṭná, *v.* To be liberated; to be discharged or dismissed; to be acquited; to be redeemed; to be abandoned; to be loft out; or omitted; to go off (a gun); to use the hands freely in striking; to shoot forth; to come out or from (as colour from cloth); to begin to move (train).

Chhuṭpan, Chhoṭapan, *n.* Childhood; the early years of one's life.

Chhuṭ-puṭ, *a.* Sundry; miscellaneous; petty expenses; contingencies.

Chhuṭṭí, *n.* Leave; holiday; permission; leisure. *—dená, v.* to grant leave; to dismiss *—milná,* to obtain leave from an engagement, after its conclusion; to obtain permission; to obtain leave. *karná,* To dismiss, to fire rom one's job), to declare holiday; to end the matter.

Chichiyáná, *v.* To squeak; to scream; to shriek; to bleat; to screech.

Chikwá, *n.* A butcher who slaughters only goats and sheep for the purpose of selling their meat.

Chikan, *n.* Embroidered muslin cloth; muslin on which is worked flowers, and other designs with cotton or silk thread. —*doz,* an embroiderer.

Chikárá, *n.* A kind of musical instrument constructed on the principle of the violin provided with four or five metal strings and played of with a bow strung with horse hair; the ravine deer commonly found along the banks of the Jumna in places where the ground is very much cut up.

Chíkaṭ, Chikṭa, *a.* Covered with grease and dirt; clammy; sticky; greasy and black; dirty; filthy.

Chíkh, *n.* Scream; shriek; yell. —*nárná, v.* To raise a cry; to cry out londly; to scream when crying.

Chikná, *a.* Oily; greasy; smooth; polished; shining; slippery; smooth-spoken; wanton. —*í,* Grease; oiliness; fat; lubri-cant. —*chupri,* smooth talk; flattery; gloss.

Chíl, *n.* The kite. —*jhapattá,* the downward swoop of a kite; a boy's game something like bear-baiting; also an eagle.

Chilam, *n.* An earthenware potshaped vessel either plain or ornamented placed on a *huqqá,* to hold the tobacco to be smoken, and the fire to burn it; —*bharná,* to prepare the chilam; to fill a pipe.

Chilamchí, *n.* A wash-hand bas-in made of metal; a large metal bowl of shallow capacity.

Chillá, *n. H.* The string of a bow; gold threads in the border of a turban; thread or string tied as a vow or charm on a tomb, shrine or tree. —*charháná,* to bend a bow for the purpose of shooting an arrow. *P.* The forty days of Lent during which the religious fraternities of the East seclude themselves in either cells or in the mosques, or remain at home fasting and engaging in divine worship; the period of 40 days after childbirth during which a woman remains unclean; the period of 40 days in winter when the cold is most severe; quarantine.

Chilláná, *v.* To cry out; to scream out; to give a loud shriek, to shont.

Chimgádaṛ, *n.* The flying-fox; the bat.

Chimṛá, *a.* Tough; hard; not easily pierced; inflexible; inelastic.

Chimṭá, *n.* Fire tongs; tongs; pincers; forceps.

Chimṭí káṭná, *v.* To pinch.

Chín, Chún, *a.* Picking; collecting; fold; pucker; crease; wrinkle.

Chín, *n.* Cry; squeak; chirp; chatter. —*buláná, v.* to cause one to cry. —*bolná,* to utter a cry of helplessness or humility; to admit oneself beaten.

Chi<u>n</u>gárí, *n* A spark of fire. —*dálná,* to sow dissension.

Chi<u>n</u>ghāṛ, *n.* A loud noise; a roar.

Chi<u>n</u>gṛá, *n.* A shrimp; a prawn.

Chinh, *n.* Mark; spot; scar; print; token; badge; emblem; characters.

Chíní, *n.* Sugar; as china-day.

Chí<u>n</u>ṭá, Chí<u>n</u>ṭṭí, *n.* The ant.

Chi<u>n</u>tá, *n.* Care; worry; anxiety, thought or meditation.

Chí<u>n</u>ṭá, [See *Chú<u>n</u>tá*].

Chípaṛ, *n.* Gum, or mucus of the eye.

Chipakná, Chipatná, Chimatná, *v.* To stick; to adhere; to hold fast to.

Chipchipá, a. Sticky; glutinous. —*ná,* to be sticky; to be adhesive; to be clammy.

Chipchipá, *a.* Sticky; glutinous.

Chippí, *n.* A small piece stuck on to anything; a patch, a sticker.

Chipṭáná, *a.* To paste; to cause to stick; to post.

Chiq, Chik, *n.* A folding screen made of thin straps or sticks of bamboo, bound together by string and let down in front of a door or window from the part of the wall above the doorway.

Chiṛh, Chiṛ, *n.* Offence; huff; displeasure; vexation; dis-like; provocation; mocking. —*áná,* to mock; to jeer; to provoke; to irritate.

Chírá, *n.* A slit; a cut; a wound; a split. —*dená,* v. to cut; to operate (on a wound, or cist).

Chiráetá, *n.* A kind of gentian; a decoction of thin sticks which has a bitter taste and is used medicinally to act on the liver.

Chirág, *n.* A lamp; a light. —*barháná,* to extinguish a lamp; to put out a light. —*áan,* a stand for lamp or light.

Chira<u>n</u>jív, *a.* Long-lived; *adv.* long may you live (used as a benediction).

Chirau<u>n</u>jí, *n.* The kernel of a species of small nut.

Chirauṭá, *n.* *(Mas.)* A cock-sparrow.

Chiraurí, *n.* Entreaty; prayer; begging; beseeching.

Chiṛchiṛá, *a.* Angry; annoyed; irritating; vexed; cross. —*haṭ, n.* fretfulness; irritability.

Chiṛímár, *n.* A fowler; a birdcatcher.

Chiṛiyá, *n.* A bird. —*khána,* an aviary.

Chirkín, *a.* Dirty; filthy; squalid; slovenly; *n.* ordure; dung.

Chirkuṭ, *n.* A piece; a rag; a bit; a scrap.—*iyá,* ragged; a ragamuffian.

Chírná, *v.* To rend or split; to splinter; to make an incision.

Chiṭ, *adv.* Flat on the back; *n.* mind; attention; memory. —*bátná,* the attention to be diverted. —*dená,* to pay attention. —*ho jáná,* to fall or be thrown flat on the back. —*kabrá,* speckled; spotted; piebald.

Chit, *n.* A piece; a chip; a scrape; a rag; —*lagáná, v.* to stick a small piece of paper (on); to patch.

Chitá, *n.* A pile of wood on which the Hindus burn their dead; a funeral pile; a pyre. —*piṇḍ,* an offering of cakes, rice, milk, &c., to the manes at the time of burning a corpse.

Chítá, *n.* A leopard.

Chítal, *n.* A spotted dear; a leopard; a large spotted snake; a variegated; spotted.

Chitáná, *v.* To draw attention; to inform; to remind; to warn; to caution.

Chitaoní, Chétáwaní, *n.* Warning; a timely notices; a caution; a clue; a reminder.

Chithářná, *v.* To tear to pieces or rags; to fill a paper with a scrawl; to fill a paper with a scrawl; to scrible.

Chithṛá, *n.* Tatter; rag; shred.

Chitr, *n.* A picture; a painting; delineation; writing; sketch; a surprising appearance or phenomenon; *a.* bright; spotted; wonderful. —*álaya, n.* studio. —*kárí,* portrait-painting; the art of painting. —*varn,* picture sque as a peacock.

Chiṭṭá, *a.* Clear; white; speckled; spotted; *n.* silver coin.

Chiṭṭhá, *n.* Pay roll; a roll of stipendiaries; a memorandum of money paid to servants; a pay bill; schedule. —*bántná,* to distribute pay.

Chiṭṭhí, *n.* A letter; a note.

Chittí, *n.* A scar; a bloch; a freekly; mildew or rot (in cloth, &c.) —*dár,* spotted. —*parná,* to form a scar; to scar.

Chíz, *n.* Thing; article; an item; a precious thing. —*bást,* goods; chattels; furniture; *(Phys.)* matter —*e. adv.* somewhat; something; a little.

Choáná,Chuwáná, *v.* To distil; to filter; to drain; to draw off; to cause to drop.

Chob, *n.* The pole of a tent; a drumstick; a post; of a tent; a drumstick; a post; a staff; wood; timber. —*dár,* an officer who carries a silver or gold staff announcing the arrival of visitors; an usher; a herald. —*dastí,* a walking stick.

Chochlá, *n.* Playfulness; dalliance; blandishment; humour; airs; affectations.

Chogá, *n.* A cloak; an overcoat; a long garment.

Chokar, *n.* Husk of wheat or barley; bran.

Chokhá, *a.* Pure; unadulterated; genuine; good; excellent; fine; sharp.

Cholá, *a.* Pure; unadulterated; genuine; good; excellent; fine; sharp.

Cholá, *n.* The body; frame. *—badalná,* to transmigrate. *—chhorná,* to die.

Chonch, *n.* Beak; bill (of a bird); a spout. *—márná, v.* to peck. *—miláná,* to bill and coo.

Chongá, *n.* A tube; a barrel; a funnel; a cylindrical tin case; a joint of bamboo closed at one end.

Chor, *n.* A thief; a pilferer; a robber; a secret; hidden; sly; treacherous. *—bálú,* quick-sand. *—darwáza, n.* a private door; a tap-door. *—rástá,* a secret path; a by-way, *kálá—,* a great thief; nobody; anybody.

Chorí, *n.* Theft; robbery; stealth; hiding; concealment. *—se,* stealthily; secretly; on the sly; clandestinely. *—lagáná,* to charge with theft; to accuse of stealing.

Choṭ, *n.* A blow; a stroke; hurt; wound; injury; fall; loss; shock; attempt; effort; wish; aim. *—bándhná,* to restrain or defend (by magic). *—par—,* stroke upon stroke; one misfortune after another. *—karná, v.* to make an attack; to cast a spell (on). *—kháná,* to receive a blow; to be wounded; to suffer loss. *—lagná,* to feel pain; to receive on injury.

Choṭí, *n.* Top; summit; peak; pinnacle; a lock of hair left on the top of the head (the rest being shaven off); the hair braided and hung down behind; creast (of a bird). *—dár,* crested; having a peak; tapering; pointed. *—gúndhná,* to plait or braid the hair. *—katwáná,* to be under subjection; to be a slave.

Chubháná, *v.* To pierce; to prick; to thrust into; to stab; to goad.

Chubhná, *v.* To be thrust into; to be pierced; to be stabbed.

Chugad, *n.* The small screech owl; a fool.

Chugal, *a.* A tale-bearer; a backbiter; a slanderer; one who informs (against). *—í,* telling tales; back-biting; a slander; informing (against). *—khor,* one who does the above things.

Chugná, *v.* To pick up food (with beak); to feed.

Chúlá, *n.* A rat; a mouse. *—dán.,* a rat-trap; a mouse trap. *—már,* a sparrow-hawk; a mouser; a cormorant.

Chuhal, *n.* Jollity; mirth; merriment. *—dár,* mirthful gay; amusing pleasant. *—karná,* to earol; to be cheerful; to make merry, &c.

Chúk, *n.* Omission; failure; miss; blunder; error; fault *—ná,* to err; to mistake to fail.

Chukáná, *v.* To finish; to settle to fix the price or rate of to decide; to pay (a debt or tax, &c).

Chukauṭá, *n.* Contract; bargain; agreement. *—chukáná,* to pay a sum stipulated for or agreed upon.

Chúl, *n.* The pivot of a door on which it turns in a socket in the threshold; a tenon; an axle tree arm.

Chulbuláhaṭ, Chulbulápan, *n.* Fidgetiness; restlessness; sportiveness; gaiety.

Chúlhá, *n.* An oven a fire-place; a hearth. *—jhoṉkná, v.* to heat an oven; to cook; to feed a fire.

Chullú, *n.* A hollowed palm of one's hand to hold water; a handful (of any liquid); *—bhar pání men dúb marná,* To be greatly embarrassed; to die of shame; to feel stupid.

Chummak Patthar, *n.* A magnet; a loadstone.

Chúná, *v.* To drop (as ripe fruit from a tree, &c.); to leak; to ze; to be filtered; to secrete; *n.* lime. *—lagáná,* to defame; to defeat. *—ki bhattí,* a lime-kiln. *bhuná—,* slaked lime; *kachchá—,* quicklime.

Chunaná, *v.* To pick; to choose; to select; to gather; to glean; to place in order; to lay (dishes on a table); to plait cloth.

Chunar, Chunarí, *n.* A longish scarf, or a decorous sheet of cloth lossely worn by Indian women to cover their cleavage, and some times even their head as a sign of modesty.

Chundhá, *n.* Dimsighted; purblind; *n.* a blinkard.

Chunnaṭ, *n.* Crimping; gathering.

Chúnṭá, Chiyúnṭá, *n.* A large ant.

Chup, *n.* Silence; stillness; *a.* silent; quiet. *—cháp, adv.* silently; quietly. *intj.* silence ! be quiet ! *—lagná,* to be struck dumb.

Chupṛí, *a.* oiled, greased; unctuous. *—bát,* smoothed or honeyed words; flattery. *—roṭí,* a buttered, or oiled bread.

Chupaṛná, *v.* To grease; to lubricate; to anoint; to bosmear; to varnish; to gloss over; to palliate.

Chuqandar, *n.* Beet-root; beet.

Chúr, *n.* Powder; atoms; *a.* crushed; broken to atoms; exhausted; besotted. —*á,* filings; saw-dust. —*chár,* fragments; crumbs. —*karná,* to shatter; to break into small pieces, to smash to smithereens.

Churail, *n.* A witch; a hag; a dirty woman; a slut.

Chúran, Chúrn, *n.* Dust; aromatic powder; a digestive-powder (composed of ground spices, &c.). —*man,* broken-hearted; repentant; contrite.

Churáná, *v.* To steal; to pilfer; to rob; to misappropriate. *án̲kh—,* to take a furtive glance at; not to look straight at one.

Chúrí, *n.* A bangle of lac, glass, or metal worn on the wrist; a gather; a pucker.—*yán̲ thandí karná,* to break one's bangles (as a woman does on the death of her husband).

Chuskí, *n.* A suck; a sip; a pull (at a *huqqá)* or pipe).

Chúsná, *v.* To suck; to absorb; to draw in.

Chust, *a.* Quick; active; brisk; expert; elever; smart; tight; well set. —*í,* nimbleness; alertness; agility; activity; skill. —*o-chálúk,* active; alert; fleet; agile.

Chút, *n.* Anus; back orifice of humans. [This word is often used as a part of swear-word terminolgy to insult the recipient of such 'graces'. —*maráná,* v. (literally) To have a forced intercourse with someone and cause maximum pain in the process. —*tiá,* a. (and a swear-word) One who is used to suffer the aforementioned process; one without intelligence; a block-head.

Chútar, *n.* The backside; buttock; posteriors; rump.

Chutkí, *n.* The pinch; a handful; snapping the fingers; a medicinal powder. —*bajáte men̲* in a moment; in a trice. —*bajáná,* to fillip with the fingers.—*gon̲ men̲ uráná,* to turn off in a joke; to turn into ridicule.

Chutkulá, *n.* Jest; banter; humour; wit; *bon mot;* a conundrum. —*chhorná,* to let off a squib; to put forth a playfully mischievous story. *n.* Sundry or miscellaneous expenses; petty expenditure or contingencies.

Chúza, *n.* A chicken; a young bird.

❄❄❄❄❄❄❄❄❄❄❄❄❄❄❄❄❄❄❄❄

दग़ा दिलदार ही तो देगा!

Dagá dildár hî to dégá!

(Only those close to you can betray you.)

❄❄❄❄❄❄❄❄❄❄❄❄❄❄❄❄❄❄❄❄

D, d, is being used to denote the Hindi sound of (द) and Urdu sound of (د). When dotted at the bottom, like 'd' it will indicate Hindi sound (ड) and Urdu sound of (ڈ). It will also be used in conjunction with 'h' as 'Dh' to convey the Hindi sound of (ध) and Urdu sound of (دھ). With a dot under 'D,d' and a sufix 'H,h' we obtain an aspirated sound of Hindi (ढ) and Urdu (ڈھ).

Dá, *S.* Giving; giver, *(used as last member of comp.),* as sukhdá, case giving; *janm-dá,* a father; (similar to the Persian *dih,* as *árám-dih,* giving rest).

Dáb, *n.* Pressure; authority; control. *—jamáná,* to exercise control or authority over; to subdue; to rub.

Dáb, *P. n.* Ostentation; pomp.

Dáb, *A. n.* Manner; habit; affair; state. *—i-sohba,* good manners; civilisation. *—jamáná,* to subject to one's control. *—lená,* to subdue; to withhold fraudulently.

Dabak baithná, *v.* To crouch; to skulk.

Dabáná, Dábná, *v.* To press; to squeeze; to reproach; to censure; to sub-due; to oppress; to control.

Dabáo, Dabáw, *n.* Pressure; constraint; submission.

Ḍabbá, *n.* A small box; soldier's ammunition pouch or cartridge-box; a container.

Dabbág, *n.* A tanner.

Dabdabá, *n.* Dignity; noble or majestic bearing; pomp; grandeur.

Ḍabḍabáná, *v.* To be filled with tears (said of the eyes).

Dabíz, a Thick; coarse; strong; durable.

Dabkáná, Dubakáná, *v.* To hide; to conceal.

Dabná, *v.* To be pressed down; to be crushed; to be buried; to be hidden or concealed; to be suppressed; to be put down or quelled; to be shampooed.

Dabochná, *v.* To seize; to clutch; to grasp; to press tight.

Dachhiná, Dakshiná, *v.* A ceremonial gift to a Brahman.

Dád, *n.* Ring-worm; a skin disease in which itchy pimples appear in rings. *—mardan, —már,* a plant used for the cure of ring-worm *(Cassía alata.).*

Dád, *n.* Gift; present; liberality; generosity; benevolence; munificence. (in literasy gatherings) appreçiation from fellow participants.

Dád, *n.* Justice; demanding justice; complaint. *—cháhná,* to demand justice. —*khwáh,* complainant; plaintiff.

Dádará, *n.* A musical style in India vocal classical singing.

Dádá, *n.* Paternal grandfather. *Dádí,* paternal grandmother.

Dádaní, *n.* Money advanced to agriculturists, labourers, and manufacturers for the conduct of their business.

Dadorá, *n.* An inflammation or swelling caused by the bite of a masquito.

Dádur, *n.* Frog.

Dáemí, *a.* Eternal; without beginning or end; lasting for ever.

Dáen, *n.* Threshing out corn by having it trodden by bullocks.

Dáerá, *n.* A circle; ring; circumference.

Ḍaf, *n.* A tambourine.

Dafa', *n.* Averting; warding off; removing; repulsing; thrusting; pushing.

Daf'a, *n.* One time; a section; class; item; a collective body. —*dár,* an officer in command of a small body of infantry or a troop of cavalry, *kaí—,* several times; frequently.

Ḍaf'atan, *adv.* Unexpectedly; all of a sudden.

Dafíná, *n.* Buried or hidden treasure; treasure-trove.

Ḍaflá, *n.* A small tambourine.

Dafn, *n.* Burial; interment. —*áná,* or—*karná,* to bury or inter.

Daftar, *n.* An office. —*í,* one who has charge of stationery in an office, binds books, rules, papers, &c.

Daftí, *n.* Boards forming the cover of a book; cardboard.

Dág, *n.* Stain; spot; mark; cicatrix; scar; sorrow; stigma. —*lagná,* to be damaged; to be branded. —*í,* stained; spotted; spolt. —*ná,* to be branded; to be discharged (as a gun).

Dag, *n.* A pace; a step.

Dagá, *n.* Deception; imposture; fraud; delusion; false blief. —*báz, n.* a deceiver; cheat or imposter; knave. —*karná,* to deceive; to use deceitful or treacherous means.

Ḍagar, *n.* A way; a route; a path.

Dagdagá, *n.* Anxiety; uneasiness; agitation; fear; apprehension.

Ḍagmagáná, *v.* To totter; to walk unsteadily; to stagger; to reel; to shake.

Dah, Das, *v.* Ten. —*chand,* tenfold; ten times. —*yakí,* tithes; one-tenth part. —*áí,* the figure ten; tenth part; the ten's place in numeration.

Dah, *n.* An eddy; a whirlpool; very deep water; an abyas; a deep pool.

Dáh, *n.* Fire; conflagration; burning; inflammation; ardour; zeal; envy. —*kriyá,* the burning of a dead body; cremation of a corpse. —*rakhná,* to bear ill-will; to cherish spite.

Dahal, *n.* Dread; fear; apprehension. —*ná,* to tremble or quiver with fear.

Daháná, *n.* The mouth; an opening or orifice; the mouth of a river, &c.

Daháṛ, *a.* Scream; a shriek; a shrill cry; a ṛoar.

Dahdaháná, *v.* To bloom; to blossom; to flourish; to glow.

Dahéj, *n.* Dowry; the property that a wife brings to her husband's homestead upon marriage.

Dahí, *n.* Curds; coagulated milk, yoghurt

Dáhiná, *a.* Right (hand).

Dahlíz, *n.* A threshold; the entrance of a house; a porch or portico. —*ká kuttá,* a housedog; a hanger-on.

Dahqán, *n.* A rustic; a peasant; a villager; a cultivator; an agriculturist. —*í,* rude; coarse or unrefined in manners; boorish.

Dahriyá, *n.* An atheist; one who denies the existence of God; a heretic.

Dahshat, *n.* Fear; apprehension; terror; alarm; dread. —*an-gez* or—*nák, a.* terrifying; threatening; causing fear; dreadful. —*zada,* overwhelmed with fear; terrified.

Dáí, *n.* A mid-wife; a nurse; a female servant. —*khiláí,* a dry nurse. —*piláí,* a wet nurse.

Dáim, *a.* Lasting; continuing; always; perpetual; *adv.* continually; always. —*ul-habs,* imprisonment for life. —*ul-khamar,* constantly drinking liquor; a habitual drunkard. —*ul-maraz,* continually sick.

Dair, *n.* A temple; a place of worship; a convent or monastery.

Dait, Daitya, *n.* An evil spirit; a demon; a giant.

Dáwá, *n.* Claim; complaint; petition.

Ḍák, *n.* Post (for conveyance of letters); the mail; relay of man or horses for conveyance of the post or travellers. —*gárí, n.* mail train; mail-cart. —*mahsúl,* postal-charges. —*men chitthí dálná,* to post a letter.

Ḍáká, *n.* Gang-robbery; dacoity. —*ḍálná, v.* to commit dacoity or robbery in gangas, —*zaní,* highway robbery.

Ḍakár, *n.* Belch; eructation; roaring (tiger); bellowing (ox).

Dákh, *n.* Grape; a raisin. *—latá,* a vine-tendril. *—ras,* wine; grape-juice.

Dakkan, Dakkhan, Dakshiṇ, *n.* South (as in directions); a given proper name for South India; a suffix attached to the kingdom and city of Hyderabad, in order in indicate it as being different from a city of the same name in Sindh.

Dákḥil, *a.* Entering; inserted; included. *—daftar,* filed with the record; laid aside. *—honá,* to enter; to penetrate; to be inserted. *kḥárij,* a transfer of land or property under one name to another name in a deed or register.

Dákḥila, *n.* Entrance fee; admittance.

Dakḥl, *n.* Entering (upon); ingress; access; taking possession (of); occupancy; proficiency; knowledge; competency; jurisdiction; meddling. *—páná,* to have access; to obtain possession, *be —karná, v.* to eject; to dispossess. *—bejá,* unlawful possession; trespass. *—bil jabr,* forcible possession. *—yábí,* obtaining possession; permission to enter.

Dakshiṇ, *n.* the South (as in directions).

Dakshiṇá, *n.* See *Dachhiná.*

Dal, *n.* Leaf (of a tree); thickness; a party or body of men; a large army. *—dár,* thick; solid; plumpy.

Dál, *n.* Pulse; lentils; vetches. *—daliyá,* poor diet; coarse fare. *—roṭí, (met).* livelihood; subsistence. *—galná, (met.)* to have an advantage; to succeed; to get on with. *—men̲ kuchh kálá,* something wrong or suspicious; something amiss. *patlí—ká khánewálá,* one whe lives on pulse thin and watery; a feeble person; a miser.

Ḍál, Ḍálí, Ḍár, *n.* A branch; *—ká pakká, a.* ripened on the tree. *—túṭá,* plucked from the branch; fresh.

Ḍalá, *n.* A large lump; a clod *(dhelá).*

Dálán, *n.* A hall; a country and; *pesh—,* a balcony.

Daldal, *n.* Marshy land; bog; quagmire; slough.

Ḍalí, *n.* A betel-nut; a lump of sugar a piece.

Ḍálí, *n.* A small branch; a twig; a present of fruit; sweetmeat, &c.

Daliddar, Daridra, *n.* One suffering from poverty; poor, needy, wretched, deprived. *—tá,*

State of poverty, indigence.

Dalíl, *n.* Argument; proof; demonstration. *—pesh karná,* to adduce evidence or argument. —*an,* by way of argument.

Dallál. *n.* One who brings together the seller and the buyer; a broker. —*í,* brokerage.

Dalná, *v.* To grind coarsely; to split (pulse).

Ḍálná, *v.* To throw; to drop; to pour; to inject; to lay before; to put on (a garment); to put aside; to sow; to broadcast; to thrust, *(used to form intensives by annexing to the base of another verb),* as *toṛ ḍálná,* to break to pieces, *khá ḍálná,* to eat up the whole.

Dam, *n.* Breath; air; life; a moment; blast (of a furnace); puff or pull of a *huqqa;* simmering over a slow fire; energy; vigour; strength; recreation. *—bharná,* to boast (of); to sing the praises (of). *—phúlná,* to breathe short. *—í-shamsher,* edge of a sword *—men̲ dam áná,* to recover one's breath; to recover one's senses. *nák men̲—áná,* to be greatly distressed. *—nikal jáná, to expire; —*toṛaná, to breathe one's last.

Dámád, *n.* A son-in-law.

Damág, Dimág, *n.* The brain; head; intellect; intelligence; pride. *—pareshán karná,* v. to confuse; to cause disturbance. *—chaṛhná,* to becomeproud, or conceited. *—kẖálí ho jáná,* v. To become deranged; to get confused.

Dáman, *n.* Skirt (of a garment); foot (of a mountain). *—churáná,* to shake off; te get rid of. *—pakaṛná,* to come under the protection of; to become an adherent; to cry for mercy; to seek redress from.

Damdamá, *n.* Sound of a drum; booming of a cannon, &c.; tumult; report; pomp; a mound; a raised battery *(morchá).*

Dáminí, *n.* Lightning.

Dán. *n.* Gift; present; grant; charity; alms; a dowry. *—pati,* an exceedingly munificent man. *—puṇya,* almagiving; charity.

Dán, *a.* A suffix denoting the receptiacle, place or stand for anything, as *qalam-dán,* a pencase; *shama'-dán,* a lamp-stand, &c., &c.

Dán̲, *a.* Knowing; understanding, *(used as last member of compounds),* as qadr-*dán̲,* knowing the worth or value (of).

Dáná, *n.* Grain; corn; seed; a bead; a pustule. *—dár,* granulated. *—pání,* livelihood; food.

Daṇḍ, *n.* Punishment; fine; retribution; compensation.

Ḍaṇḍ, *n.* Push-ups; a gymnastic exercise.

Daṇdán-sáz, *n.* A dentist.

Ḍáṇḍ, Dáṇr, *n.* An oar; retaliation; a measure of length.

Ḍaṇḍá, *n.* A staff; a club; a pole;

Ḍaṇḍí, *n.* Beam (of scales); a handle; stem; a path. —*márná,* to give short weight.

Daṇḍwat, *n.* Prostration; obeisance; bow.

Dang, *a.* Astonished; confounded; stupefied. —*rah jáná,* to be stupefied; to be astonished; to be confounded.

Dangá, *n.* Wrangling; hubbub; tumult; riot. —*báz,* quarrelsome; turbulent; *n.* a turbulent fellow. —*karná,* to create a hubbub.

Dangal, *n.* A wrestling bout. —*men utarná,* to appear in the arena.

Dánish, *n.* Knowledge; wisdom; science. —*mand,* learned; wise.

Dánisht, *n.* Knowledge; opinion. —*a.* knowingly; wittingly.

Ḍank, *n.* Sting (of a wasp or scorpion); nib (of a pen).—*márná,* to sting.

Ḍanká, *n.* A drum stick; a large kettle-drum. *(fig.)* notoriety; fame. —*bajáná,* to proclaim; to make public. —*ki chot par kahná,* to proclaim by beat of drum.

Dánt, *n.* A tooth; tusk. —*banánewálá,* a dentist. —*káṭí roṭí khaná,* to be an intimate friend. —*kichkicháná,* to gnash the teeth in rage.

Dánv, Dáon, *n.* Time; turn; chance; opportunity; clutch; ambush; sleight; trick (in wrestling); a stake; a throw of dice. —*pénch,* *n.* Strategem.

Ḍánwáḍol, *adv.* Unable to make-up one's mind; indecisive; unsettled. —*honá,* *v.* To be, or become so.

Dar, *n.* Door; gate; *a.* outer. *(used in comp.);* as; *dar áná,* to come out; to issue. —*bán,* a doorkeeper. —*ba-dar,* from door to door, &c., &c.

Dar, *pre.* In; into; within; on; upon; *per;* at; near; close by; under; concerning; about; of; *(used as a prefix),* as; *darámad,* a coming in entrance; income; import. —*ámad, barámad,* ingress and egress; receipts and disbursement. —*báb,* in the matter (of); relating (to). —*pas* in pursuit or quest of; intent on. —*kanár,* on one side; a part, &c., &c.

Dar, *n.* Rate; price; value; tarrif; standard.

Dar, *n.* Crack; cravice; fissure; breach; a hole.

Dár, *n.* A dwelling; house; mansion; seat; country; *(used in compos.),* as; *dár-o-madár,* dependence. *—ul-ákhirat,* the next world. *—ul-baqá;* the everlasting world. *—ul-khiláfax,* capital; seat of Government*—us-salám,* heaven. *—ush-shafá* a hospital. *—o-dasta,* house and family, &c., &c.

Ḍar, *n.* Fear; dread; awe. *—dikháná,* to frighten to terrify. *—ná;* to fear; to be frightened. *—pok,* timid; coward; chicken-hear-ted.

Darakẖt, *n.* A tree.

Darap, Darp, *n.* Arrogance; (false) pride; conceit.

Daras, Dars, *n. H.* Seeing; sight *—dikháná,* to give (one) a glimpse (of). *P.* A lecture; a lesson. *—dená* yá *kahná,* to lecture; to preach. —o-tadrís, learning and teaching.

Daráz, *a.* Long; tall; extended. *—dast, a.* oppressive; tyrannical. *—qad.* tall of stature.

Darbár, *n.* Court; hall of audience; á levee; the executive government of a state. *—i-'ám,* public audience. *—i-kẖáss,* private audience. *—karná, v.* to hold a court or levee. *—í,* courtly; courtier. *—í zabán,* court language.

Dard, *n.* Ache; pain; pity; compassion. *—álúd,* overwhelmed in grief. *—ámez,* painful; piteous; pathetic. *—angez,* pitiable; exciting compassion *—farzandí —,* parental affection. *—mand,* sympathizing. *—mauqúf karnewálá,* sedative; an anodyne.

Dareg, *n.* A sigh; sorrow; disinclination. *—karná,* to withhold; to think much; to grudge.

Dargáh, *n.* A shrine or tomb of some reputed saint; door; a palace.

Dáṛh, *n.* A jaw tooth; grinder.

Darham, *a.* Intricate; confused; jumbled; vexed; angry. *—barham karná, v.* to confound; to disorganize; to jumble; to turn topsy-turvy.

Daridra, [See *Daliddar*]

Dáṛhí, *n.* Beard. *—dhúp men̲ sufed karná,* to be wanting in experience, wisdom or judgment.

Daríbá, *n,*A stall in market.

Darindá, *a.* Rapacious; ferocious; *n.* a ravenous; animal; a bird of prey, a beast.

Darkár, *a.* Necessary; in requisition; required.

Darkẖwást, *n.* Request; demand;

petition; entreaty; appeal. —*í-sarsari,* summary application. —*kuni<u>n</u>da, n.* applicant; petitioner.

Darmiyán, *prep.* Between; among; during; in view; *adv.* in the middle; in the midst. —*áná,* to intervene, to take place between. *is—me<u>n</u>* in the meantime; in the interim; meanwhile.—*í, a.* intermediate; middling; *n.* mediator; go-between; an interpreter.

Darog, *n.* A lie; falsehood. —*e-halfi,* perjury.

Darp, *n.* [See *Darap*].

Darpaṇ, *n.* A mirror; a looking-glass.

Darshan, *n.* Interview; visiting; sight; vision; exhibition. —*dená,* to vouchsafe an interview. —*í,* worthy of seeing.

Dárú, *n.* Remedy; drug; medicine; spirituous liquor; wine.

Darwázá, *n.* A door.

Darwésh, *n.* A dervis; a mendicant; a beggar.

Daryá, *n.* The sea; a river. —*barár,* alluvial land —*burá,* diluvion. *nekí kar—me<u>n</u> dál, (lit.)* Do good and throw it in the water; *(met.)* expect not good in return. *Daryá ko kúze me<u>n</u> band karná,* to say much in a few words; to attempt the impossible.

Daryáft, *n.* Inquiry; finding out; discovery; discernment; exploration.

Darzí, *n.* A tailor; a seamster.

Dás, *n.* A slave; a servant. —*í,* a female slave.

Dast, *n.* Hand; cubit; stool; purge; *(used as a first and last member of compounds),* as; dastand*áz,* intermeddling; interfering. —*ba dast,* hand in hand; from band to hand. —*basta,* with folded hands. —*panáh,* tongs. —*kár,* artisan. —*kári,* handicraft; manufacture. —*gír,* a helper; an assistant. —y*áb;* attained; obtained.

Dastá, *n.* A handle; hilt; a bundle of 24 arrows; a quire of paper; a nosegay; a squadron. —*dár,* commander of a brigade.

Dastak, *n.* A knock at a door; a writ; a passport.

Dástán, *n.* A story; a fable; a tale. —*go,* a story-teller.

Dastarkhwán, *n.* A table-cloth on which the dishes of meal are spread. —*kí billí,* uninvited guest.

Dastúr, *n.* Custom; practice; usage; manner. —*ul-'amal,* model; rules of practice; code of law; form of Government *ba—,* according to rule or custom; *in statu quo. be—,* irregular; anamalous; unlawful.

Dátá, *a.* Giving; imparting; liberal; generous; *n.* giver; donor; God.

Ḍaul, *n.* Shape; form; make; build; way; method; device; scheme; plan. *—par láná, v.* to systematize; to regulate. *be—,* ill-shaped; ugly; performed.

Daulat, *n.* Riches; wealth; good fortune; prosperity; means. *—mand,* opulent; rich. *ba—,* by means (of); by the favour (of).

Dauṛ, *n.* Going round; revolving; circular motion; the circulating (of wine); times of—; coming round of times; circuit; orbit; turn; tour; course. *—daurá,* jurisdiction; sway.

Daur, *n.* Race; a run; endeavour; raid; *—dhúp,* exertion; labour and fatigue.

Daura, *n.* Tour; circuit; course. *—supurd,* commitment for trial before the circuit session.

Dauṛná, *v.* To run; to go quickly; to gallop.

Dawá, *n.* Medicine; a remedy. *—farosh,* a druggist. *—khána,* a dispensary; a medical hall *—karná,* to treat medically; to apply a remedy.

Da'wá, *n.* Claim; demand; plaint; charge. *—dár,* a claimant; plaintiff; a suitor. *—í-bilá-dalíl,* an unsupported claim. *—i-wirásat,* a claim to inheritance.

Dáwát, *n.* An inkpot.

Da'wat, *n.* A feast; banquet *—i-walímá,* a marriage feast.

Dayá, *n.* Compassion; pity; mercy; kindness; benevolence. *—ván, —vant,* a very compassionate or merciful person.

Dayár, Diyár, *n.* Country; province.

Dég, in. A large metal pot for cooking; a caldron *—sho,* a scullion. *—en khanakná,* preparations for a feast to be going on.

Déhát, *n.* Villages *—i-istimrárí,* villages held at a fixed rent. *—í,* rural; rustic.

Dékhná, *v.* To see; to look; to behond; to observe; to search; to watch; to feel (as pulse). *—bhálná,* to examine; to inspect. *dekhne men,* apparently; in appearance. *—dekhnehárá,* an on-looker; beholder; spectator. *dekhá dekhí,* in imitation. *dekho,* look here ! take care ! be on your guard. *dekhte rah jáná,* to gape in vain.

Dén, *n.* Giving; gift; debt; liability. *den-len,* two-way transaction commercial transactions; traffic; debt and credit.

Déná, *v.* To give; to grant; to impart; to yield; to afford; to lay (eggs); to pay (debt); to cause (pain). *de ḍálná, v.* to give away. *de márná,* to dash against. *—marná,* to bequeath.

Déo, Dév, Dewtá, *n.* A god; a demon; a giant; a deity. *—álay, a temple; a pagoda.* —lok, Heaven; Paradise. *públak,* a worshipper; a pagan.

Ḍeoṛhí, *n.* Threshold; entrance; door. *—dár,* door-keeper; porter.

Dér, Dérí *n.* Lateness; delay; tardiness; *a.* long; old; antique; *adv.* a long while; tardily. *—pá,* durable; lasting. *—lagáná,* to delay; to tarry.

Dériná, *a.* Ancient; experienced; *n.* an old or experienced person.

Dés, Desh, *n.* Country; region; territory. *—áchár,* local or country usage. *—tyág,* emigration; voluntary exile. *—nikálá,* banishment.

Dewar, *n.* The husband's younger brother.

Ḍhab, *n.* Manner; style; fashion; course; position. *—lagná,* to be caught or taken by artful management *—ḍálná,* to form a habit.

Dhabbá, *n.* A stain; a blot;a stigma; a mark.

Dháe-bhái, Dudh-bhái, *n.* Foster-brother.

Dhágá, *n.* Thread. *—pironá,* to thread a needle. *—dálná,* to quilt.

Dhaj, *n.* Mien; appearance; air; style; fashion; posture; attitude.

Dhajá, Dhwajá, *n.* Banner; flag; ensign; pennon; a slip of cloth.

Dhakká, *n.* Shove; push; jostle; shock; stroke of misfortune. *—kháná,* to receive a blow. *dinon ko dhakke dená,* to push through life somehow; to live with difficulty. *dhakkam dhakká;* shoving and jostling. *dhakke kháná,* to be kicked; to wander about, to suffe.

Ḍhakná, Ḍhakkan, *n.* A cover; a lid.

Ḍhál, *n.* Cast; mould; bent; slope; declivity; target; buckler; shield.

Ḍhálná, *v.* To pour; to shed; to cast (metal infusion); to form; to shape.

Ḍhálú, Ḍhalwán, *a.* Sloping; slant.

Dhamáká, *n.* Explosion; a massive discharge of destructive force; a huge audible sound [like something breaking the sound-barrier].

Dhamkáná, *v.* To threaten; to menace; to chide; to scold.

Dhan, *n.* Property (of any description); riches; money; wealth;

gold; good fortune. —*árjan,* acquisition of property or wealth.

Dhan, Dhanya, *intj.* How fortune! Blessings (on you) ! Thanks. —*mánná,* to express devout thanks; to be grateful (for).

Dhán, *n.* Rice in husk; paddy.

Dhanak, Dhanuk, Dhanush, *n.* A bow; a rainbow.

Dhán**chá,** *n.* Skeleton; frame; mould.

Dhándlí, *n.* Trickery; deceipt; falsehood. —*karná,* v. to practice trickery, etc.

Ḍhang, *n.* Characteristic; mode; fashion; style; manners; behaviour.

Dhanní, *n.* A beam.

Ḍhánkná, *v.* To cover; to conceal; to hide.

Dhappú, *a.* Bulky; corpulent; fat.

Dhaṛ, *n.* Trunk; the body. —*rah jáná,* the body to be paralysed.

Dhár, *n.* Edge (of a sword); sharpness; ṣtream; current. —*dharná, v.* to sharpen; to give an edge to.

Dhará, *n.* The earth; ground; one that bears the burden [of all cratures, big and small]; symbol of extreme tolerance and forbearance.

Dhárá, *n.* A channel; a water-course; a torrent.

Dhaṛá, *n.* A weight usually of 10 seers; a counterbalancing weight. —*karná* to counterpoise. *ulṭá—bándhná,* to frame or bring a counter-charge.

Ḍháṛas, *n.* Confidence; courage; fortitude; patience. —*bándhná* to keep up th spirits; to have courage or patience.

Dhárí, *a.* Bearing; holding; carrying; supporting; *n.* bearer; holder; *(used as last member of comp.),* as *júxlhárs,* having life, &c., &c.

Dhárí, *n.* Line; a stripe; a streak.

Dharm, *n.* Religious observance; piety; religion; good works; duty; innocence. —*átmá, n.* a pious man; the Holy Spirit. —*awtár,* god of justice; your holiness; embodiment of righteousness. —*i,* virtuous; just; honest; religious.

Dharná, *v.* To place; to put down; to lay down; to stake; to apply (mind or ear); to hold; to seize. —den*á, v.* to enforce payment of a debt or compliance with a demand by sitting (or seating an agent) doggedly at the debtor's door.

Dhartí, *n.* The earth; earth; ground; land. —*ká phúl,* mushroom.

Dhasan, Dhasán, *n.* A quicksand; swamp; bog; quag-mire; *a.* swampy; boggy.

Dhasná, Dhan̲sná, Dhasakná, *v.* To sink; to enter; to run (into); to pierce; to give way; to slip or fall down; to slip out of place.

Dhat, *n.* (lat) a bad habit; vice. —*parná,* to become addicted to.

Dhatúrá, *n.* The thorn-apple (a powerful narcotic).

Dhaulá, *a.* White; clean; *n.* any white thing (as milk, &c.)

Ḍhaun̲chá, *n.* The sum of four times a number or quantity added to its half; the *pahárá,* or multiplication table of 4½ times.

Dhaun̲kná, *v.* To blow (with bellows, &c.); to puff.

Dhaun̲kní, *n.* Bellows; hard breathing; panting.

Dháwá, *n.* An expeditious march; incursion; inroad; assault; running. —*karná, v.* to rush at; to fall upon; to invade.

Ḍhelá, *n.* Half of a *Paisá,* a coin of very low value today and hence extinct from use; proverbially indicating a small, negligible monetary value.

Ḍhelá, *n.* A clod (of earth); a lump (of clay, chalk, &c.); mass; the eye-ball. —*márná,* to pelt.

Ḍhér, *a.* Much; abundant; *n.* heap; stick; mound. —*kar dená,* to make a heap or pile (of); to kill.

Dhí, *n.* A daughter.

Ḍhíl, *n.* Relaxedness; slackness; laxity; slow; lazy. —*á,* losse; not tight; remiss; lazy.

Dhímá, *a.* Slow; lazy; inactive; faint; dim; dull; slight (fever); allayed; lulled. —*karná,* to soften; to mitigate. —*par jáná,* to be abated or lulled.

Dhín̲war, *n.* A fisherman.

Dhíraj, *n.* Patience; forbearance. —*bán̲dhná,* to solace; to comfort.

Ḍhíṭh, *a.* Impudent; insolent; pert; obstimate; wilful.

Dhobí, *n.* A washerman; a launderer. *Dhobin,* A washerwoman; a lundress.

Dhoká, Dhokhá, *n.* Deception; delusion; false appearance. —*dená, v.* to deceive; to mislead. —*kháná,* to be deceived; to be deluded. *dhokhe kí tattí,* a false screen. *dhokhe men̲ rakhná,* to feed with false hopes or promises.

Dhoná, *v.* To wash; to cleanse; to rinse out.

Ḍhoná, *v.* To carry; to transport; to bear up (a load).

Dhruv, *n.* Name of a *Puránic*

character; name of the Polar star; focal point. —*íkaran,* v. Focusing; centralization; bringing it all to a focal point.

Dhúá<u>n</u>, *n.* Smoke; vapour. *dhúe<u>n</u> bakherná,* to exhaust one's resources. *dhúe<u>n</u> pání ká, sharík,* a sharer in smoke and water;; next-door neighbour. —*kash;* a chimney; a funnel.

Dhúl, *n.* Dust. —*kí rassí batná, v.* to attempt an impossibility; to labour in vain.

Dhúm, *n.* Noise; tumult; uproar; celebrity; display; pomp. —*macháná,* to create an uproar.

Dhun, *n.* Longing; ardent desire; propensity; assiduity; *(also in music)* a tune.

Dhu<u>n</u>dh, *n.* Haze; mist; cloudiness; dimsightedness; purblindness. *-lá, a.* dim.

Ḍhú<u>n</u>dhná, *v.* To seek; to search for; to make strict enquiry or investigation.

Dhuni, Dhwani, *n.* sound; *(in music)* a tune.

Dhúní, *n.* Fumigation or burning of incense to purify the air or as a medical application; bonfire the smoke-fire over which a Hindú ascetic sits by way of penance.

Dhunkí, *n.* The bow with which cotton is cleaned or carded.

Dhuniyá, *n.* A carder or cleaner of cotton.

Dhúp, *n. S.* Incense; frankincense; aromatic vapour or smoke. *U.* and *H.* Sunlight; sunshing —*chhá<u>n</u>,* sunshine and shade; shot silk. —*kdl,* hot weather. —*kháná,* to bask in the sun. *badlí kí—,* clouded sun.

Dhurá, Dhurí, *n.* An axle; an axis; an axle-tree.

Dhus, *n.* Fortification; a sterile sandy eminence; a battery.

Dhyán, *n.* Contemplation; meditation; divine intuition or discernment.—*dená,* v. To pay attention; to heed.—*rakhná,* to watch; to keep guard; to keep an eye on.—*diláná,* v. To draw attention to; to point out; to indicate.

Dibáchá, *n.* Preface; exordium; introduction; preamble.

Díd, *n.* Sight; vision; spectacle. —*bán,* a watch; a guard; a sentinel. —*na shuníd,* wonderful; strange; extraordinary. —*ár,* look; interview; appearance; countenance. —*khwáh,* soliciting an interview; *n.* one who seeks an interview. —*be,* blind, without sight.

Dídá, *part.* Seen; observed; perceived; having seen; *(used in comp.)* as *jahán dída,* experienced, &c., &c. *—o-dánista,* knowingly; wittingly; intentionally; purposely.

Dídá, *n.* The eye; the sight; *(met.)* impudence. *—phár, phár kar dekhná,* to look steadfastly at; to share at. *—ká pání dhalná,* to throw away all modesty; to become shameless. *shokh—,* saucy-eyed; fearless; bod; shameless; wanton.

Dídár, sight; audience with; the sight.

Dígar, *adj.* and *adv.* Other; another; next; over again; moreover; besides.

Ḍigrí, *n. (Corr. of the English).* A decree. *—ijmálí,* joint decree. *—páná,* to obtain a decree. *—jári karná,* to enforce a decree. *—dár,* decree-holder.

Dikhána, Dikhláná, *v.* To show; to indicate; to direct; to denote; to exhibit; to display.

Dikháú, *n.* Showy; spurious; illusive.

Dikháwaṭ, *n.* Show; display; ostentation; pomp; exhibition.

Dil, *n.* Heart; mind; soul; spirit. *—ázár,* heart-tormenting. *—árá,* beloved; a sweet-heart. *—bahlná,* to be amused or diverted. *—kash, a.* heart attracting; alluring; attractive. *—gír,* heart-stricken; low-spirited; melancholy; sad. *—i-shikasta,* comfortless; sorely afflicted. *—sozí,* heart-burning; warnth of feeling; ardour. *—ké phaphole phoṛná,* to take revenge.

Dilásá, *n.* Comfort; consolation; soothing.

Dilér, *n.* Intrepid; venturesome; courageous; animated; valiant. *—í,* intrepidity; venture; courage.

Dimáġ, *n.* The brain; head; mind; intellect; conceit; pride. *—pareshán karná,* to produce a confused state of mind. *—khalí ho jáná,* to become light-head; to be worried. *—karná,* to put on airs; to be arrowgant. *uská —nahin̲ miltá,* his pride is extreme.

Dímak, *n.* White-ants, wood worm.

Din, *n.* Day (of 24 hours); day (of 12 hours) daytime; time; circumstances. *—ba din,* day by day; daily. *—paṛná,* evil days to fall. *—púre karná,* to drag out one's days. *—chaṛhe,* late in the morning. *Baṛá din,* Christmas day.

Dípak, *n.* Light; lamp; candle.

Diqq, *a.* Thin; slender; delicate; indisposed; ailing; vexed; annoyed; *n.* hectic fever. *—harná,* to tease; to irritate; to worry; to harass; to annoy.

—*honá,* to be indisposed; to be alling; to be annoyed.

Diqqat. *n.* Difficulty; delicate matter; trouble; perplexity; distress; diligence; industry.

Disáwer, *n.* A foreign country; foreign mart; emporium. —*ko bharná,* to load for exportation.

Dishá, *n.* sight. —*baná,* a conjurer who hoodwinks the lookers-on—*bandí,* closing the eyes by conjuration.

Diwálá, *n.* Bankruptcy; insolvency; pauperism.

Diwáláí, *n.* A Hindú festival at which they worship Lakshmi at night, illuminate houses and streets and gamble.

Diwán, *n.* A royal court; a tribunal; senate; a minister; a chief officer of state; a secretary; the collected writings of an author. —*kḥána,* a hall of audience; a hall; a chamber.

Díwáná, *a.* Mad; insane; lunatic; frenzied. —*pan,* madness; insanity.

Diwání, *n.* A wall. *diwár bhí kán rakhtí haí.* P. *diwár ham gosh dárad,* walls also have ears. —*í-qahqahá,* the great wall of China; great laughter.

Díyá, *n.* A light; a lamp; a lantern. —*battí karná,* to prepare the lights. —*barháná,* to extinguish a light; to put out a lamp. —*saláí,* a lucifer match.

Do, *a.* Two. —*hará,* a Double. —*haráná,* adv. To repeat. —*ráhá,* n. A fork in the road; where the paths divide and go separate ways. —*ábá,* (lit.) Two waters. (in usage) the area, or land between two riversbefore their confluence. —*pahar,* Mid-day. —*galá,* a. one who can't be trusted; one who uses double talk, a bastard; a cross-bred; an illegitimate one. —*galí báten,* a. Words with double meanings. —*muhá, rukhá,* a Two-faced. —*sálá,* a. biennial (event). —*dhárí,* a. Double-edged (sword, or knife, or dagger). —*ek,* One or two. —*Chár,* a few. —*ṭúk,* Frank; categorical; crystal clear (statements etc.); decisive. —*faslí,* a. Yielding two crops a year. —*chár sunáná,* adv. To rebuke; to reprimand. —*kí chár sunána,* adv. To rebuke; to reprimand. —*kí chár sunáná,* to give as good as one gets; to pay in the same coin with interest. —*chár honá,* adv. To confront; to have to deal with. —*háth honá,* adv. To test one's comparative strength. —*kauṛí ká,* a. Worth nothing; inconsequential. —*din ká mehmán,* a. transitory; temporary resident. —*ghoṛon kí sawárí karná,* adv. To try to ride two horses. —*roṭí* *kamáná,* a. To make both ends meat. &c. &c.

Doglá, *a.* Mixed; cross-bred; mongrel.

Do-guṇá, [See *Duguná*].

Dohná, Duhná, *v.* To milk. *Dohní,* a milk pail.

Dohráná, *v.* To fold; to double; to repeat; to revise; to suffer a relapse.

Dohráo, Dohráwá, *n.* The act of doubling or folding; reduplication; repetition; revision; an equivoque; a *doubleentendre.*

Dokh, Dosh, *n.* Fault; vice; defect; blemish; blame; calumny; wrong; sin. *—lagáná,* to impute a fault or crime; to accuse (of); to calumniate.

Ḍol, *n.* A bucket of leather or metal for drawing water.

Ḍolá, *n.* A swing; a cradle; a palanquin; a litter. *—dená,* to give a daughter to a superior by way of tribute.

Ḍolná, *v.* To swing; to reel; to sway from side to side; to move; to waver; to move to and fro.

Ḍonḍí, Ḍhonṛí, Ḍhanḍorá, *n.* Proclamation by beat of drum.

Ḍongá, *n.* A trough; a cance; a boat.

Donon, *a.* The two; both; both of them. *—waqt milte,* at dusk. *—háth tdlí bajná,* to give as good as one gets.

Ḍor, Ḍorá, Ḍorí, *n.* Thread; string; cord; line; streak. *—áálná,* to quilt.

Dosh, *n.* See *Dokh.*

Doshízá, *n.* A virgin; a daughter.

Dost, *n.* A friend; one beloved; a lover; a sweetheart. *—rakhná,* to hold dear; to like. *—nawáz,* cherisher of friends. *—áná* friendship.

Dozakh, *n.* Hell; the belly. *—í,* hellish; infernal; damned; hell deserving.

Driṛhtá, *n.* Steadiness; firmness; perseverance; confirmation.

Drishṭí, *n.* Seeing; vision; view; eyesight. *—karná,* to take a view of; to look; to behold.

Drishṭant, *n.* Example; illustration; allegory; simile.

Du, *a.* Two *(used in compounds only),* as; *duábá.* a tract of land lying between two rivers. *—arthí,* double meaning; ambiguous, &c., &c.

Du'á, *n.* Prayer; supplication (to God); a blessing; benediction; wish; congratulation. *bad—,* a curse; malediction. *—dená, v.* to give a blessing; to bless; to pay for. *—i-khair,* a prayer for one's welfare.

Dubdhá, Duvidhá, *n.* Doubt; suspense; uncertainty, dilemma.

Dúdh, *n.* milk. *dúdhon naháo, púton phalo,* a kind of benediction, may you abound in cattle and children.

Ḍugḍugí, *n.* A small kettledrum (used in making proclamation by drum and by jugglers, &c.). *—pítná,* to proclaim by drum; to make public.

Duguṇá / Do-guṇá, *adj.* Multiple of two; twice-as-much; two-fold.

Duháí, *n.* A cry for help, or mercy, or justice; appeal. *Bhagwán kí—,* By God ! God help us !

Dwíp, *n.* An island; a continent.

Dúkán, *n.* A shop; a workshop. *—barháná,* to close a shop. *—chalná,* a shop or business to flourish. *—lagáná,* to set out a shop.

Dukh, *n.* Pain; ache; suffering; distress; grief; uneasiness; oppression. *—uṭháná, v.* to suffer pain; to experience difficulty.

Dukhṛá, *n.* Suffering; calamity; distress; woe; hard labour. *—roná,* to tell one's misery. *—rote phirná,* to go about telling one's grievances or troubles.

Dukhtar, *n.* Girl; daughter; virgin; maid. *—i-rabíba,* a step-daughter.

Dulár, *n.* Affection. *—í* or*—á,* darling.

Dúlhá, *n.* A bridegroom. *Dulhin,* a bride.

Dum, *n.* Tail; end; a constant follower. *—dabá kar bhágná,* to run away; to turn the tail. *—dár tárá,* a comet.

Dumbal, *n.* A boil.

Dún, *adj.* Double. *—ki hánkná,* to be in the habit of bragging; to boast.

Duniya, *n.* The world; the people of this world; worldly; enjoyments or blessings. *—dár,* worldly; a mammonist.

Dúr, *n.* Distant; remote; far away; to a distance. *(often used in com.),* as: *dúr-andeshí,* far-sightedness; forecast. *—bín,* far-seeing; far-sighted; *n.* a telescope. *—karná.* to remove (from); to put far away; to keep at a distance. *—rahná,* to abstain; to remain apart.

Durust, *a.* Right; fit proper; just; correct accurate; precise; exact. *—rakhná,* to admit; to allow. *—'aql,* of right mind; sound of understanding. *—karná, v.* to set right; to put in order; to regulate; to adjust. *—samajhná* to *v.* apprehend rightly.

Dushman, *n.* Enemy; foe; adversary. *—i-ján,* a mortal enemy. *—zátí,* a personal foe. *'aql ká—,* a foe of knowledge; a stupid person; a fool.

Dushwárí, *n.* Difficulty.

Dushṭ, *a.* Corrupted; depraved; wicked; evil; faulty; *n.* a. bad or wicked man; a miscreant; a vile wretch.

Dúsrá, Dúsre, Dúsrí, *a.* Second; duplicate; another.

Dút, *n.* Messenger; envoy; emissary; ambassador; angel who passes between God and men.

Duvidhá, *n.* [See *Dubdhá*].

Dyánat, Dyánatdárí, *n.* Honesty; piety; virtue. *—dár,* upright; honest; just *bad—,* dishonest.

Dyút, *n.* Gambling; *-kríṛá.* A game of poker; to play for money.

E, e, is to represent the Hindi sound (ए) and Urdu sound (ے). It can be used independently as vowel sound as well as tonal addition to the preceding consonant, represented by (े) in Hind and by (یے) in Urdu.

Ehtiyáj, *n.* Necessity; want; need; urgency. —*honá, v.* to be in need of.

Ek, *a.* One; simple; alone; sole; a; an; unique; singular *(used as first and last member, of comp.)* as: *ek-bár,* once upon a time; *ek-barjí,* all at once. *eklautá,* an only son. *ekrangá, a.* of one colour. *eksán, a.* of one colour. *eksán,* similar; corresponding. *ek-musht* handful; in the lump or mass. [*See* An-ék].

Eká, *n.* Unity; union; combination; league; compact; conspiracy. —*karná,* to act simultaneously; to act in unison or concert. —*ekí,* all at once; suddenly. —í, unit; unanimity; solitude.

Ekáksh, *a.* One-eyed; blind of one eye; *n.* a crow.

Ekánt, *n.* A lonely or secret place; a seclusion *a.* secluded; lonely; secret; *adv.* apart; aside; alone. —*ho baithna,* to seclude oneself; to retire from the world.

Ekatr, *a.* In one place; together.

Ekaṭṭhá, *adv.* United; collected; together; a lump in the aggregate. —*karná, v.* to collect; to assemble; to accumulate; to sun up. —*ho jáná, v.* to come together; to assemble; to congregate; to flock.

Eksán, *adv.* Alike.

Eláichí, *ná,* cardamoms coated with sugar; comfits.

Elchí, *n.* An ambassador; envoy; delegate. —*garí.* ambassadorship; embassy.

Eṛí, *n.* Heel; spur. —*márná,* to urge a horse on with the heel; to spur.

Eṛká, *n.* A ram; a large ram or he-goat trained for fighting.

Etad, *pro. a.* This *(used at the beginning of comp.)* as *etadarth, adv.* on this account; for this reason—*kál,* the present time; now.

Ewam, *adv.* Thus so; even so (yún).

'Ewaz, *n.* ('Iwaz.) A substitute; in lieu of; in exchange for a compensation; a return. —*dená, v.* to pay compensation (to); to reimburse. —*ba-'ewaz,* in lieu of; as compensation or indemnity; *mutatis mutandis.*

फ़ुर्सत शरारत की माँ होती है।

Fursat sharát kí mán hotí hai

(Free time breeds mischief.)

F, f, is to register the Persian-Urdu sound of (ف) which has for long been imported into Hindi as (फ़) which is obtained by placing a softening dot under the Hindi letter (फ).

Fahím, Fahímá, *a.* Of great understanding or intellect; very intelligent; learned.

Fahish, *a.* Foul; evil; abominable; nefarious; immodest; indecent; obscene.

Fahm, *n.* Understanding; sense; conception; Intellect; intelligence. *ám—,* adj. Common sense; commonly known; popular. *—dár,* adj. Intelligent; sharp. *Galat—í,* n. Misunderstanding; confusion. *Khush—í,* n. A happy illusion.

Fáidá, *n.* Profit; advantage; benefit; good; used; gain; moral (of a story); inference. *—utháná, v.* to reap benefit from; to utilise; to make the most (of.) *—maná,* profitable; useful; benefited. *be—,* profitless, useless; unavailing; *adv.* in vain; uselessly; to no purpose.

Fá'il, *n.* Doer; operator; maker; *(Gram.)* the subject of a verbal sentence. *—i-haqíqí,* God. *—i-mukhtár,* a free agent.

Failsúf, *a.* Wise; intelligent; shrewd; cunning; artful; *n.* a philosopher; a cunning or artful person; an impostor. *—í, n.* sophistry; hypocrisy; artfulness; trickery.

Faislá, *n.* Separation; decision; adjudication; judgment; decree; settlement; arbitration.

Faiyáz, *a.* Most bountiful; munificent; liberal; generous; copious; abundant.

Faiz, *n.* Abundance; beneficence; bounty; favour; grace; charity; benefit. *—bakhsh,* bountiful; beneficent. *—pahunchání,* to bestow favours (on); to give alms to. *—i-'ám,* general abundance; to public good. *—yáb,* favoured; blessed.

Fajr, *n.* Daybreak; dawn; *barí—,* early in the morning.

Fakhr, *n.* Glory; just or proper pride; egotism; boasting. *—samajhná, v.* to consider as a thing to be proud of, or to glory in; to take a just pride in.

Fákhtá, *n.* Dove; a pigeon-like bird. *-uráná.* prov. To relax and have a good time whatever might be happening around; to be free from anxiety. *—ho jáná,* v. to swoon; to loose one's senses. *kulla—,* the ash-coloured turtle dove. *serotí—,* the red turtle-dove.

Falak, *n.* Heaven; sky; the celestial sphere. *—ul-afták,* the highest heaven; the *preimum mobile.* —*zadá,* heaven-stricken; oppressed by fate.

Falákhun, *n.* A sling for throwing stones.

Fálij, *n.* Palsy; paralysis. —*girná* yá *honá,* to be stricken with palsy.

Falítá, *n.* A wick; a match; a torch. —*dár,* matchlock. —*dená* to apply a match (to); to set light (to).

Fáltú, *a.* Spare; surplus; what is over and above unemployed.

Fám, *n.* Like; resembling; of the colour of *(affixed to noune denoting colour),* as sy*áhfám,* blackish, *la'l-fám,* ruby-coloured.

Faná, *n.* Motality; perdition; death. —*pizír,* destructible; perishable. —*fil-láh honá,* to be lost in contemplation of God and insensible to all else. —*ho jáná,* to vanish; to perish; to pass away.

Fání, *a.* Passing away; mortal; transitory; inconstant. *jahán-i-fání.* this transitory world.

Fánn, *n.* A Species; kind; way. *P.* and U. an art; a craft; artifice; wile; stratagem. —*fitúr,* —fareb; art and cunning; wiles.

Fánús, *n.* A pharos; a lantern; a glass shade of a candle-tick.

Fáqá, *n.* Starvation; hunger; fasting; poverty; destitution. —*kashí,* fasting; endurance of hunger. —*mast,* one who is cheerful and jolly in the midst of poverty; a poor starvelling who affects the airs of a wealthy man.

Faqat, *adv.* Only; merely; simply; no more.

Faqír, *n.* A beggar; a derwish; an ascetic. —*dost,* friendly to the poor. —*karná,* to impoverish; to reduce to beggary. —*í, beggary;* poverty; the life of a dervis. —*í laṭká,* a cheap medicine or remedy.

Faqq, *a.* Lost; gone; flown (colour from the face, &c.); faded; pallid; disnayed. —*ho jáná,* to fly from the face; to turn white or pale with fear; to look blank.

Fara', *n.* The uppermost part of anything; a branch; a bough.

Farágat, *n.* Freedom (from business, &c.); disengagedness; leisure; rest; repose; convenience; comfort; easy circumstances; a call of nature. —*jáná,* to go to ease oneself; to go to the rear.

Faráham, *a.* Brought together; collected; assembled, —*karná, v.* to gather together; to accumulate.

Faráiz, *n. (Plur. of Farz).* Duties;

obligations; laws; divine precepts.

Farámosh, *a.* Forgotten. *—í,* forgetfulness; oblivion; unmindfulness.

Farár, *n.* Absconding; fight; running away. *—honá, v.* to flee; to take to fight; to abscond. *—í,* The state of being a fugitive, an abscondee or having escaped. *—mujrim,* an escaped convict.

Farbah, *a.* Plump; fat; corpulent (*moṭá. —i,* corpulence; fatness (*muṭápá*).

Fard, *a.* One; sole; single; odd; unique; *n.* a single individual; a single article; a unit; the outer fold of a quilt; account sheet; list; catalogue. *—i-jamabandí,* rent-roll; rental. *—i-jurm,* a calendar of crime. *—men nám charcháná,* to register the name of; to enlist; to enroll. *fardan fardan,* one by one; severally; single.

Fardá, *a.* To-morrow. *—i-qiyámat,* the resurrection morn.

Fareb, *n.* Deciving; alluring; seducing; deceipt; fraud; delusion; allurement. *Dil—,* One that enchants the heart; *Mardum—,* one who deceives or betrays human being.

Fareftá, *a.* Fascinated; infatuated; charmed; enamoured. *—honá,* to be fascinated by; to be anamoured of.

Fárgúl, *n.* A wrapper; a cloak *(labádá).*

Farhang, *n.* A dictionary; a lexicon; a vocabulary; excellence; understanding; wisdom.

Farhat, *n.* Pleasure; joy; cheerfulness; amusement; recreation. *—afza, a.* increasing delight; entertaining. *—bakhsh, a.* pleasure-giving; amusing; refreshing.

Fárig, *a.* Free; at leisure; disengaged. *—ul-bál,* free from care or anxiety; in easy circumstances. *—khatí,* a deed of release of discharge; deed of dissolution of partnership; acquittance.

Faríq, *n.* Party; body; company. *—i-awwal,* the principal party in a lawsuit. *—i-sání,* the opposite party, the defendants. *—ain,* the two parties in a lawsuit; both parties.

Farmáish, *n.* Order; commands; commission. *—í, a.* made to order; excellent; good. *—karná,* to give an order for goods.

Farmán, *n.* Order; command; mandate; decree; a royal letter; a grant; charter *—bardár,* obedient; compliant. *—bardárí karná,* to yield obedience to the commands (of). *—rawá,* sway; authority; a sovereign.

Farmáná, *v.* To order; to say; to affirm; to do; to commit to; to grant.

Farod, *n.* Alighting; stopping; the arrival and deposit of goods within certain defined limits. —*gáh,* a camping-ground; a halting-place.

Farokḥt, *n.* Selling; sale.

Farokḥta, *a.* Kindled; inflamed; burn; shining; radiant *(afrokhta).*

Faromáyá, *a.* Ignoble; low; mean; abject; base; humble.

Farosh, *a.* Selling; seller *(used as last member of compounds);* as; *mewa-farosh,* fruit-seller.

Faroshindá, *n.* Seller; vendor. —*i-majází,* a licensed vendor.

Farotan, *a.* Humble; lowly; submissive. —*í,* humility; submissiveness.

Farq, *n.* Separation; interval; partition; difference; distinction; *a.* separate; distinct. —*á jáná,* deterioration ot occur (in); a difference or misunderstanding to arise (in or between). —*parná,* a discrepancy to occur (in account.) —*karná,* to distinguish; to make a difference in; to alter.

Farr, *n.* Glory; pomp; state; dignity; magnificence; splendour; lustre.

Farrásh, *n.* Bed-maker; chamberlain; sweeper.

Farráṭá, *n.* The sound of anything rushing or fluttering in the air. —*lená* or *bharná,* to rush or fly along; to run swiftly; to read fast.

Farrukḥ, *a.* Happy; fortunate.

Farsh, *n.* Paving; carpeting; a carpet; a mattress; a bed; a floor-cloth; a pavement; a floor; earth *(e.g. az'arsh tá farsh)* ásmán se zamín tak.

Farshí, *n.* A huqqá with a flat bottom. —*júíá,* a slipper. —salám, a very low bow.

Farsúdá, *v.* Obliterated; worn; rubbed; torn; decayed.

Faryád, *n.* Complaint; cry for help; redress. —*ras,* a dispenser of justice. —*í,* a complainant.

Farz, *a.* Obligatory; encumbent; *n.* an indispensable duty; a moral obligation; onus; supposition; hypotehesis. —*utárná* yá *adá karná,* to fulfil an obligation; to discharge a duty. —*karná,* to fulfil an obligation; to discharge a duty. —*karná, v.* to take for granted; to suppose; to grant. *bil-farz,* on the supposition or hypothesis that. —*í,* not real or essential; fictitious; obligatory.

Farzand, *n.* Offspring; child; a son. —*i-ḳhalaf,* a favourite son; a dutiful son. —*rashíá,* a good child.

Fasád, *n.* Disturbance; dissension;

quarrelling; brawl; mutiny; rebellion. —*macháná,* to create or excite a disturbance. —*i-kḥún,* bad state of the blood.

Fasáhat, *n.* Fluency of speech; eloquence; perspicuousness of speech.

Fasáná, *n.* A fiction; a romance; a story; a fable.

Fásh, *a.* Divulged; spread abroad; manifest.

Fásid, *n.* Corrupt; unlawful; wicked; mischievous; noxious. —*níyat;* criminal intention.

Fasíh, *a.* Polished (language); eloquent; fluent (of speech).

Fásil, *a.* Superfluous; excessive; extra; deeply learned; accomplished; virtuous; *n.* superfluity; surplus. —*honá,* to become learned; to attain to proficiency or perfection.

Fasíl, *n.* Rampart; wall of defence.

Fásilá, *n.* Space; distance; interval; gap; apart.

Fasl, *n.* Harvest; crops; chapter; article. —*i-stáda,* a standing crop. —*i-kḥaríf,* the autumn crop. —*i-rabí,* the winter crop.

Fatah, *n.* Victory; conquest; triumph. —*páná,* to gain a victory over. —*karná,* v. to conquer.

Fátihá, *n.* Commencement; exordium; prayers for the dead; oblations and offerings to the saints. —*dená,* to invoke blessings on a deceased relative.

Fatílá, *n.* A wick; a match; a fuse. —*soz,* a candlestick; a metal lamp.

Fatwá, *n.* Judgment; decree; decision or sentence in a judicial proceeding. —*dená,* to deliver a judgment in a civil suit or criminal case.

Fauj, *n.* An army; a throng; a multitude; a huge concourse of people. —*bhartí karná,* to assemble or mobilise an army; to enrol recruits. —*bahrí,* naval forces; a fleet or navy. —*dárí karná,* to commit a crime; to be guilty of a breach of the peace. —*kashi,* —*charháná,* to take an inroad or invasion; to attack.

Fauládá, *n.* Steel. —*ká'arq,* tincture of steel. *kushta*—, calcined steel—*i.e.,* steel reduced to powder by the action of heat.

Fauqíyat, *n.* Superiority; excellence; pre-eminence. —*páná,* to excel; to surpass, or be pre-eminent. —*lejáná,* to bear away the palm, *i.e.,* to prove superior to all rivals or competitors.

Fauran, *n.* Immediately; at once; straightway; instantly.

Faut, *n.* Death; decease. *—honá,* to die; to pass away.

Fawáid, *n. (Plur. of Fáidá).* Profits; gains; benefits; advantages.

Fawwára, *n.* Fountain; a natural or artifical jet or spout of water.

Fazihat, *n.* Shame; ignominy; disgrace. *—honá,* to be dishonoured; to be exposed to reproach or ignominy.

Fazílat, *n.* Superiority; excellence; proficiency; erudition; virtue.

Fazl, *n.* Grace; bounty; benevolence; favour. *—i-Iláhi,* the grace of God.

Fihrist, *n.* An index; a catalogue; a list; a schedule. *—fautí, —farárí,* a list containing the names of dead persons and absentees. *—i-mardum shumárí,* a census roll.

Fi, *prep.* In; into; during; regarding; owing to; with; along with; by; each; per (as: *fí sadí,* per cent., &c., &c.), *n.* blemish; flaw or defect; an intrigue. *—l-badihá,* promptly; without previous deliberation or preparation, *prima facie. —l-jumla,* in short; on the whole. *fí ma bain-i-faríqain,* between the parties; *inter partes. —nikálná,* to detect any error or defect; to find fault. *—zamána,* at, or up to, the present time.

Fi'l, (fe'l), *n.* Deed; action; operation. *fi'l-záminí,* security to be of good conduct, *bil fi'l* indeed; really; actually. *fi'lan aur qaulan,* in word and deed.

Fidá, *n.* Sacrifice; devotion; dedication. *—honá,* to be sacrificed; giving up one's life to save another's.

Fidiyá, *n.* Ransom; atonement; redemption.

Fidwí, *n.* Your devoted servant (a term of respect and humility used by inferiors in place of the pronoun "I").

Fikr. *n.* Thought; meditation; anxiety; care; sorrow. *—karná,* to think upon; to to ponder; to meditate or reflect upon; to devise plans or schemes; to feel regret. *be—,* freedom from anxiety; easiness of mind; heedlessness.

Fíl, Píl, *n.* An elephant. *—murg,* a turkey. *—pá,* elephantiasis. *—páyá,* a pillar; a column; a post.

Filfil, *n.* Pepper.

Fiqrá, *n.* A sentence; a phrase. *—bandí,* composition; formation of a sentence.

Fiqrébází, *n.* Taunts; hurtful, slanted, utterances.

Firangí, *a.* A European; a foreigner; an Englishman.

—*istán.* The country of-, England, Europe.

Firáq, *n.* Expectancy; looking for; waiting for; hoping for; angling for.

Farásat, *n.* Keenness of perception; discernment; sagacity; acuteness; sound judgement.

Firdaus, *n.* Paradise; a garden.

Firishtá, *n.* An angel; a heavenly being.

Fíroz, *a.* Victorious; trumphant; successful; prosperous.

Fírozá, *n.* A turpoise; a precious stone of a blue colour.

Firqá, *n.* A sect; a community; a communal group. —*parastí,* Communalism; sectarianism.

Fishán, Fisháni, *a.* Spreading; strewing scattering; sprinkling; diffusing *(used as a last member of compounds),* as *átish-fishán;* scattering fire, &c.

Fítá, *n.* Ribbon; tape.

Fitná, *n.* Crooked; shrewd; wily.

Fitrat, *n.* Disposition; nature; wiliness; cunninness; temperament.

Fitúr, *n.* Craze; infirmity; unsound state of mind. —*sawár honá,* v. to go crazy; to be obsessed.

Fizúl, *a.* Superfluous; redundant; excessive; unncessary; useless. —*kharch,* a extravagant; prodigal; wasteful.

❄❄❄❄❄❄❄❄❄❄❄❄❄❄❄❄❄❄❄❄

गीता सभी धर्मों की गुरुगीता है।

Gita sabhí dharmo<u>n</u> kí guru-gítá hai.

(Gita is the song of all divines.)

❄❄❄❄❄❄❄❄❄❄❄❄❄❄❄❄❄❄❄❄

G, g, is used here, in the first instance, to denote the Hindi sound (ग) and Urdu sound (گ); in the second place, when used with a dot (.) at the bottom, it will indicate the Persian-Urdu sound of (غ) and the imported Hindi sound of (ग़).

Gá, *a.* The sign of the future tense as *shall, will;* and also used as a mark of respect. *—Cf. kijíyegá* and *karo.*

Gab, *a.* Stupid; dull of intellect; slow-witted.

Ġaban, *n.* Embezzlement; misappropriation of money.

Gabí, *a.* Dull-witted; lacking in intellect; weak-minded.

Gach, *n.* Mortar; cement.

Gáchh, *n.* A tree. *—mirch,* cayenne pepper.

Gachpach, *a.* Crowded; packed or stuffed closely together; jumbled; muddy; slushy or miry; producing a squashing sound when trodden upon.

Gadá, *n.* A Mace; a bulbous kind of weapon with a arm-long handle which can be used to pulverse an opponent; monkey-faced Hindu deity Hanumán and many others are other shown carrying such a weapon.

Gadálá, *n.* A crowbar.

Ġadar, *n.* Mutiny; insurrection; revolution. *—karná* yá *macháná, v.* to raise a revolt or mutiny.

Gaḍariyá, *n.* A shepherd.

Gaḍbaḍ, Gaṛbaṛ, Gaṭ paṭ, Gaḍmaḍ, *n.* Disorder; confusion; tumult; an uproar; irregular intermixture; a state of absolute disorder and confusion; *a.* higgledy-piggledy; topsy-turvy; confused; in perfect disorder.

Gadd, Gadya, *n.* A soft quilted bedding stuffed with cotton, cushion.

Gaddar, Gadri, *a.* Unripe; half ripe.

Gaddí, *n.* A cushion; a padded seat; a royal cushion or throne. *—par baithná,* to ascend the throne.

Gaḍḍí, *n.* A small bundle of anything.

Gaḍh, Gaṛh, *n.* A castle; a fortress; a den of.

Gadhá, *n.* An ass. *Gadhí,* a she-ass.

Gadká, *n.* A club or cudgel; a blunt wooden sword.

Gadlá, Gandlá, *a.* Foul; dirty or muddy (water or other liquid).

Gáe, Gaú, Gow, *n.* Cow. This is the most popular domestic beast in Hindu families in India. Hindus consider cows to be sacred, owing to multifarious religious and mythological connections. In common parlance, people often refer to cow as *Gaú mátá*. 'The cow mother!' *—ká gosht,* beef.

Ḉáeb, Ḉáib, *a.* Absent; vanished; invisible; *n.* the future; the Invisible Being (God.) *—áná,* during one's absence; invisibly. *—karná, v.* to conceal; to secrete; to make away with.

Gáek, Gáyak, *n.* A Singer. *—i,* n. The art of singing; singing skill.

Gáeká, Gáyiká, *n.* A female singer. *—yen,* Female singers.

Gáen Gáyan, *n.* The act of singing; the art of singing.

Gaf, *a.* Closely woven.

Gaffár, Gaffúr, *n.* The forgiver of sins (God).

Ḉáfil, *a.* Negligent; careless; heedless.

Ḉaflat, *n.* Carelessness; inattention; unmindfulness; negligence; a swoon; stupor; insensibility.

Gafá, *n.* Forgiveness; pardon; absolution.

Gagan, *n.* The firmament; the sky; the heavens.

Gagrá, Gagrí, Gágar, Gagariyá, *n.* A pitcher; an earthen or metal water pot.

Gáh, *n.* Place *(used in compos. as; shikárgáh,* a hunting-ground. *'ibádat gáh,* a place of worship); time; turn; *adv.* during some time. *—o-be-gáh,* in or out of season; occasionally. *—e ba gáhe,* sometimes; now and then.

Gáhak, Gráhak, *n.* A customer; a purchaser a customer. *ján ká gáhak,* one who seeks to take the life of another.

Gahgír, *n.* An untrained or unbroken horse.

Gahná, *n.* Jewellery; gold and silver ornaments; a pledge or security.

Gahrá, *a.* Deep; profound; intimate or familiar. *—áo,* depth; profundity.

Gahrí bát, Gahrá khiyál, *n.* An important remark; a ser-ious affair. *—gahrí nínd,* sound sleep; deep slumber.

Gahwárá, *n.* A swing; a cradle.

Ḉaib, *n.* Absence; concealment; invisibility; a secret or mystery. *'álam-i—,* the invisible world, or the future existence. *—dán,* possessing a knowledge of hidden things; *n.* a prophet; a soothsayer.

Gaibat, *n.* Absence; invisibility; concealment. *—men,* during one's absence, *i.e.* behind his back.

Gail, *n.* Road; thoroughfare; highway; pathway; track; a bunch of plantains [See *Gáen*].

Ġai<u>n</u>ḍá, Ge<u>n</u>ḍá, *n.* A rhinoceros *(ge<u>n</u>ṛá).* a thick-skinned person; one who is not easily influenced.

Gai<u>n</u>dá, Ge<u>n</u>dá, *n.* Name of a flower; the Indian marigold.

Ġair, *n.* A foreigner; an alien; a stranger; a competitor; *a.* strange; foreign; deteriorated; other; altered; (used as *prep., adv.* and a negative prefix equivalent to not; non-un-, in-, ir-, &c. and meaning without; except; but; contrary to as in *ġair-insáf,* not just. *—háziri,* non-attendance. *—matlab,* undesirable. *—mu'atbar,* incredible. *—mumkin-al-wusúl,* irrecoverable, &c., &c.).

Ġairat, *n.* Pride; sense of honour; self-respect; *—mand,* a. one with a sense of self-respect. *—be-ġhairat,* devoid of any sense of honour; without a sense of self-respect.

Gaj, *n.* An elephant. *—ráj,* a huge elephant.

Gajar, *n.* Striking of a gong, after the hours 4, 8 and 12. *—dam,* before daybreak.

Gájar, *n.* A carrot.*—gattá,* a oppgun (a child's toy)

Gájrá, *n.*A garland; a gold; necklace.

Gal, Gar, *n.* The throat; neck. *—bahiyá<u>n</u> ḍálná,* to place the arms round the neck (of a person): to embrace. *—muchchhá,* turned-up whiskers; a curled moustache. *—phaṭákí,* bragging; boastfulness. [See *Galá*].

Gál, *v.* The cheek. *gál bajáná, v.* to talk nonsensically; to speak foolishly; to give insolent replies when rebuked or reproved by a superior. *—phuláná,* to be in sulky humour.

Galá, *n.* The neck; the throat; voice. *—pháṛ ke bolná, (lit.)* to rend or tear the throat; to snout or bawl very loudly. *—ṭípná,* to strangle or throttle a person by squeezing or compressing the throat. *—paṛ jáná,* (lit.) To grab one by the throat; (proverbially) to pick a fight with. *—gale par chhurí phernä, (lit.)* to pass a knife across the throat (of); *(fig.)* to oppress or harass.

Gálá, *n.* Carded cotton.

Galahí, *n.* The forecastle or forcepart of a ship; to prow or part of a ship.

Galáná, *v.* To melt; to dissolve; to become liquid, to make soft by cooking.

Galáo, Galáwaṭ, *n.* Solution; act of solution; in a liquid, act of softening by cooking.

Ġalat, *a.* Wrong; incrorrect; erroneous; mistake. *—fahmí, n.* misunderstanding; misconception; incorrect notion or idea. *—goí, n.* telling of lies. *—náma,* list of *errata,* (errors) in a book, &c. *—ṭhahráná,* to prove to be incorrect or inaccurate, or wrong.

Ġalatí, *n.* A mistake; an error; a miscalculation; an oversight. *—karná,* to commit a mistake.

Ġalbá, *n.* Victory; triumph; success in battle. *—páná,* to gain a victory; to triumph over an enemy.

Galgal, *n.* A citron.

Gálí, Gál, *n.* Abuse; abusive language; insulting expression. *—galauj,* reciprocal abuse; abusing and being abused in return.

Galí, *n.* A narrow lane; an alley.

Ġálib, *a.* Victorious; predominant; most likely. *—honá,* v. to overpower; to surmount. [This word also is the pen-name of the most famous and gifted poet of Urdu and Persian languages, **Mirzá Asadullá Khán** *Ġálib.*

Ġáliban, *adv.* In all likelihood; very probably.

Ġalíchá, *n.* Carpet.

Ġalíz, *a.* Foul; dirty; filthy; thick; coarse.

Gallá, *n.* A flock; a herd. *—bán,* shepherd; a cowherd; (*fig.*) a pastor.

Ġallá, *n.* Corn; grain. *—farosh,* a grain-merchant.

Galná, *v.* To melt; to dissolve; to become liquid; to be cooked; to rot; to decay or decompos.

Galpharạ́, *n.* The jaw; the angle of the mouth; the gills (of a fish).

Galtán, *a.* Rolling; moving.

Gám, *n. P.* A. foot; a pace. *H.* A village.

Ġam, *n.* Grief, woe, sorrow; morning; anxiety. *—kḥwár,* a. One who shares the grief, a sympathiser; a comforter. *—zadá,* a. One caught by grief; one overwhelmed by sorrow. *—galat karná,* adv. To drown one's sorrows; to suppress, or forget one's pains. *—gusár,* An intimate friend; a sharer of sorrows; one who offers consolation in moments of sorrow. *—gín,* a. one gripped by sorrow, one depressed by grief, etc.

Gamak, *n.* The rolling (beating) of a kettle-drum; smell; fragrance.

Gaman, *n.* Act of going, departure, exit.

Gambbír, *a.* Deep; profound; serious; grave.

Gamlá, *n.* Flower-pot.

Gammat, *n.* A pastime; recreation; amusement.

Gammáz, *n.* A back-biter; a tale-bearer.

Gamzá, *n.* Ogling; an amorous glance; a wink; flirtation.

Gáná, *v.* To sing; to celebrate; to extol or laud. —*bajáná,* song and music.

Ga<u>n</u>d, *n.* Stink; stench; offensive smell. —*á,* stinking; rotten; putrid; foul; obscene. —*karná,* to render foul or unclean; to pollute.

Gá<u>n</u>ḍ, *n.* Anus; rear orifice of the human body; bum; arse. *Me<u>n</u> dená,* v. To push 'it' up someone's arse.—*márná,* v. The act of having anal intercourse; (*proverbially)* to cause damage to.—*ú,* adj. Sodomite; bugger; a sexual pervert.—*ú-pan,* n. sodomy; buggery; a sexual perversion.

Ga<u>n</u>dá, *n.* A knotted string tied round the neck of a child as a charm against enhancement; the number 4.

Ga<u>n</u>dásá, *n.* A chopper for cutting fodder, machete.

Ga<u>n</u>dh, *n.* Smell; fragrance; essence. —*i,* n. one who deals in fragramces, scents and essences or perfumes.

Ga<u>n</u>dhak, *n.* Sulphur. —*ká tel,* n. Sulphuric acid; oil of vitriol.

Ga<u>n</u>dhraj, *n.* nickname for Sandalwood.

Ga<u>n</u>dum, *n.* Wheat. —*i-kirmání,* vermicelli (*si<u>n</u>wai*). —*rang,* tawny; light brown; swarthy.

Ga<u>n</u>gá, *a.* The river Ganges. —*jalí úṭháná,* to swear by the water of the Ganges.

Ga<u>n</u>gotrí, *n.* The source of the Ganges.

Ġaní, *a.* Rich; wealthy.

Ġaním, *n.* A robber; an enemy.

Ġanímat, *n.* Booty; plunder; blessing; abundance. —*samajhaná,* v. To appreciate what is at hand; to value status quo.

Gaṇit, *n.* Arithmetic.

Ga<u>n</u>j, *n.* Treasure; hidden treasure; hoard in wealth; a granary; a storehouse or mart for grain; a heap or pile. —*i-shahídá<u>n</u>,* burial place of martyrs.

Ga<u>n</u>j, *n.* Baldness. —*á,* bald-headed; bald.

Gá<u>n</u>já, *n.* An intoxicating drug obtained from hemp.

Ga<u>n</u>júr, *n.* Treasurer.

Ga<u>n</u>ná, *n.* Sugarcane

Gá<u>n</u>th, *n.* A knot; a fastening; a bond; an engagement; joint; a purse; entanglement; difficulty. —*joṛná,* to tie the nuptial, knot, *i.e.,* to perform the marriage ceremony. —*ká púrá,* having a well-filled purse, *i.e.,* wealthy. —*ukhaṛná,* dislocation.

Ganth-kaṭá, *n.* A "cut-purpose"; a pickpocket.

Gánṭhná, *v.* To tie; to fasten; to stitch; to cobble.

Gáṇw, Gáon, *n.* A village; a hamlet. —*kí bolí,* a. The rustic speech; the local dialect. —*kí gorí,* The village belle.

Ganwáná, *v.* To lose; to waste; to dissipate.

Ganwár, *n.* A villager; a rustic; a peasant; *a.* stupid; clownish; boorsih.

Gáo, *n. m.* A bull; an ox; *n. f.* a cow; a heifer. —*dum,* thicker at one end than at the other; tapering. —*mesh,* a buffalo. —*palang*; a giraffe; a cameleopard.

Gap, *n.* Gossip; idle or frivolous talk; rumours. —*chhántná,* to be fond of gossiping.

Gapakná, *v.* To swallow; to catch (as a ball).

Ġár, *n.* A cave; a cavern; a hollow or pit. —*paṛ jáná,* to become deep (as a wound or sore).

Gárá, *n.* Mud moistened with water and used as substitute for mortar.

Garáchá, *n.* A eunuch.

Garaj, *n.* Thunder; roar.

Garán, Girán, *a.* Heavy; grievous; calamitous; dear. —*bahá, a.* costly. —*honá,* to be grievous or burdensome; to rise or increase in price. —*karná,* to make heavy; to enhance or raise the price of *-khátir,* disagreeable; sad.

Garání, Girání, *n.* Scarcity; dearness; dearth; rise (in price); dejection; depression.

Garárá, *n.* A gargle; a gurgling sound. —*dár paijáma,* loose or baggy trouser.

Gaṛariyá, *n.* A shepherd; a herdsman.

Ġárat, *n.* Plunder; pillage; devastation; rapine. —*gar,* a plunderer; a freebooter.

Ġaraz, *n.* Aim; end; object in view; intention; business; interest; concern; spite. *adv. in short; briefly.* —*rakhná,* to aim (at); to feel an interest or concern (in.) —*mandí,* selfishness; self-interest.

Garchi, *conj.* Although.

Ġard, Ġardá, *n.* Dust; going round; turning round and round; rotating (*used as a last member* *of compounds)* as; *jahángard,* one who has travelled all over or round, the world *—áluda, a.* covered with dust. *—áwara gard,* vagrant.

Gardan, *n.* The neck. *—kash,* proud; conceited; haughty; insolvent; mutinous; stubborn. *—jhukáná, (lit.)* to bow or bend the neck; *i.e.,* to yield or submit. *—par sawár honá, (lit.)* to mount or ride upon the neck (of); *i.e.,* to oppress; to tyrannise (over). *—uṛáná,* to behead; to decapitate.

Gardán, *n.* Conjugation of verbs.

Ģardish, *n.* Revolution; changes and vicissitudes of life; adversity; vagrancy. *—men̲ áná,* to fall into misfortune; to be in a state of revolution.

Gardún, *n.* A wheel; heavens; firmament; a windless. *—himmat,* noble-minded.

Gaṛh, Gaṛhí, *n.* A castle; a fortress.

Gaṛhá, *n.* A pit; a cavity; a deep hole or hollow.

Gáṛhá, *n.* A coarse Indian cloth; *a.* thick; strong (as coffee).

Gaṛhat, *n.* Shape; form; make; mode.

Gaṛhan̲t, *adj.* Forged; false; contraband. *man—,* adj. Imaginary; lies; false.

Gaṛhná, *v.* To shape by hammering; to mould or form into shape.

Garí, *n.* The kernel of any nut, as the cocoanut, &c.; *(used in compos.)* acting; operating making, as *zargarí,* the trade or occupation of goldsmith, &c.

Gáṛí, *n.* A cart; a carriage; a conveyance. *rel—,* a railway, train. *hawá—,* a motor car. *—wan,* a coachman; a driver of a carriage.

Ģaríb, Poor; needy; destitute; meek; humble; submissive. *n.* a poor person; who is meek or humble; a stranger; a foreigner. *—í,* poverty; humility. *—kḥána, n.* one's own humble house or dwelling-place. *—nawáz,* polite and hospitable to strangers; kind to the poor. *—parwar,* cherisher or protector of the poor (a term of respect used in addressing a superior).

Ģaríq, *a.* Sunk; submerged; immersed.

Garm, *a.* Hot; warm; burning; eager; ardent; zealous; intent; angry; ill-tempered. *—á-garm, (lit.)* hot and hot, *i.e.,* freshly cooked and steaming hot; spontaneous. *—bazárí,* brisk or active buying and selling in a market. *—joshí,* ardent or warm affection; enthusiasm; fervour. *—kḥabar,* the latest news. *—mizáj, a.* of a violent temper; irritable; excitable.

Garmá, *n.* Summer. *—í, n.* stimulant; incitement; encouragement.

Garmí, *n.* Heat; warmth; the summer season; ardour; zeal; briskness; passion; excitment; anger; ardent affection.

Gaṛná, *v.* To pierce; to penetrate; to be thrust into; to be buried to be uncomfortable (as a bed or seat) owing to roughness or unevenness of its surface.

Gáṛná, *v.* To bury; to inter; to drive into (as a nail into wood, or a stake in the ground); to plant.

Garuṛ, *n.* A specie of large heron; a powerful bird; mythologically, Lord *Vishnú's* mount. Proper name of the Indonesian national airline.

Ġarur, *n.* Pride; vanity; arrogance.

Ġash, *n.* A swoon; a fainting fit; stupor or insensibility.

Gasht, *n.* The beat or round of a public officer. *—í,* a watchman; a patrol.

Gat, Gati, *n.* Plight; condition; state; motion; progress; attainment; issue; fate; destiny; mode of procedure; an air of tune. *—banáná,* to reduce to a condition of misery.

Gát, *n.* Body; colour; dress.

Gaṭhílá, *a.* Knotty; strong; well developed; robust.

Gaṭhiyá, *n.* Rheumatism; arthritis.

Gaṭhrí, *n.* bundle; a package; a parcel; a bale. *—báṉdhná,* to pack up. *—márná,* to plunder.

Gati, [See *Gat*].

Gaṭṭá, *n.* A joint; the ankle; a sweetmeat; a corn (as on the foot); the portion of a tube which fits into the bottom of a *huqqá, gaṭṭe paṛná,* to suffer from corns on the feet.

Gattá, *n.* Cardboard.

Gaṭṭhá, *n.* A bundle; a package; the twentieth part of a survey or's chain.

Gauhar, *n.* A pearl; a jewel, gem or precious stone; essence; origin; intellect. *—i-shab-chirág,* the carbuncle (a kind of gem); an elegant speech or composition.

Ġaur, *n.* Meditation; reflection; profound deliberation. *—talab,* demanding earnest consideration.

Gaurá, *n.* The goddess Párwatí; a cock-sparrow.

Gauraiyá, *n.* A Sparrow; a small, though noisy bird.

Gautam, *n. prop.* The name of Buddha or Sakya-muní, the founder of Buddhism.

Gawáh, *n.* A witness; an evidence; proof testimony. *—í,* evidence;

testimony; the deposition of a witness. —*í dená,* to bear witness; to give evidence; to testify. —*likhná, v.* to attend or witness a document (by signing it). —*i-ta'límí,* a tutored witness. —*i-mudda'í,* a prosecution witness. —*i mudd'á-alaih,* a witness for the defence. —*i-chashmdíd or ruiyat,* an eyewitness. —*i-samá'í,* a witness who gives hearsay evidence.

Gawaiyá, Gáyak, *n.* A singer.

Gawárá, *a.* Agreeable; pleasant; acceptable; palatable; digestible; putting with; enduring. —*karná, v.* to bear or endure; to submit to. *ná*—, unpleasent; offensive; disagreeable; impalatable.

Gáwdí, *n.* A fool; a stupid; a blockhead.

Ģáyat, *n.* The utmost extent, limit or degree; the very extreme; a flag or banner; *a.* extreme; excessive; consummate; *adv.* excessively; extremely; utterly. *'ilm-i*—, Mathematics.

Gáyatrí, *n.* A sacred verse from the Rigveda, recited by Brahmans at their morning and evening prayers.

Gaz, *n.* A yard; a rod for measuring cloth; a ram-rod (for a gun) *desi*—, an Indian measure of cloth equivalent to 33 inches. *lambarí*—a statute yard, *i.e.*, 36 inches.

Gazab, *n.* Anger; wrath; vengeance; wrong; injustice; oppression; woe; disaster; *a.* angry; vexed; annoyed; fearless; excessive; injurious—*nák, a.*enraged; furiously angry. —*tút parná,* to be overtaken by the wrath or vengeance of God; to be over-whelmed by misfortune.

Gazak, *n.* A relish taken after wine and intoxicating drugs.

Ģazal, *n.* An ode; a ballad; a short poem or song.

Gazál, *n.* A fawn; a young deer.

Gazála, *a.* fawn-like, after used to compare a woman's large, dark innocent-looking eyes. *(Gazála-chashm).*

Gazand, *n.* Harm; misfortune; sorrow. —*gí,* bite; sting. —*a. n.* biter; stinger; a venomous reptile, &c.; *a.* injurious, venomous.

Ģází, *n.* One who takes part in a warlike expedition (especially against infidels); a warrior; a hero.

Gazí, *n.* A thin coarse cotton cloth.

Gehún, *n.* Wheat.

Gend, *n.* A ball.

Genda, *n.* The Indian marigold.

Gerú, *n.* Red earth or ochre.

Gerú, *n.* Red orchre; raddle; russett coloured soil [often found in lumps and ground sometimes to mixed with honey and used in medication].

Geruá, *adj.* Russett coloured; a variation on the usual saffron clothes worn by *sádhúsm* i.e. medicants in India.

Gesú, *n.* A ringlet; a curl; *—dár,* curly.

Ghabráhat, *n.* Confusion; perplexity; bewilderment; alarm.

Ghág, Ghágh, *a.* Old; aged; experienced astute; shrewd.

Gháil, Gháyal, *n.* Injured; wounded; casualty in combat; war-wounded; emotionally hurt.

Ghám, *n.* Heat; intense warmth; sultriness; sunbeams; sunshine. *—lená,* to bask in the sun.

Ghama<u>n</u>d, *n.* Pride; haughtiness; overbearing demeanour. *—karná,* to be pround. *—í, proud; hanghty.*

Ghámar, *a.* Slow; stupid.

Ghamorí, *n.* Prickly heat.

Ghamásán, *n.* A closely contested battle; a sharp encounter.

Ghan, *n.* Cluds; a sledge hammer. *—ghor,* a dense or heavy cloud; a peal or clap of thunder.

Ghaná, *a.* Thick; close; dense; numerous; much.

Gha<u>n</u>gholná, *v.* To stir water in order to mix or dissolve any substance in it.

Gha<u>n</u>ṭá, *n.* A bell; a gong; a clock; an hour. *—bajáná,* to strike the time on a gong.

Gha<u>n</u>ṭí, *n.* A small bell; a small brass pot.

Ghá<u>n</u>tí, *n.* Larynx.

Gháo, Gháv, *n.* A wound; a sore. *—bharná,* to cure or heal a sore. *—karná,* to inflict a wound.

Ghar, *n.* House; dwelling; abode; home; a den; a nest; case or holder; native place. *—ábád karná,* to marry a wife; to beget children. *—bárí, grihasti,* a family man; domestic affairs. *—baiṭhná, v.* (*lit.*) to sit at home; to be out of employment; a shouse to collapse, or fall in *—ká nám ḍuboná,* to bring dishonour on the family. *—wálí,* the mistress of a house; a wife.

Ghaṛá, *n.* A pitcher; a jar; a water pot.

Gharámí, *n.* A thatcher.

Ghará<u>n</u>á, *n.* Family; household; (in music) tradition.

Gharau<u>n</u>dá, *n.* A nest; a dwelling; a shelter; a home.

Gharelú, *a.* Domestic; household; tame; domesticated.

Ghaṛí, *n.* Time; hour; moment; a watch; a clock or timepiece; a gong. *—bhar men̲,* in a short time; in an instant. *—ghaṛí,* every now and then; repeatedly; at frequent intervals. *—men̲ tola —men̲ másha,* fickle in character or disposition. *dhúp—,* a sundial. *ret ghaṛí,* an hour-glass.

Ghaṛíyá, *n.* A melting-pot; a crucible; a wasp's nest.

Ghaṛiyál, *n.* A gong; a crocodile.

Gharrá, *n.* The death-rattle. *—lagná,* to have 'the rattles' (in the throat) when at the point of death.

Ghás, *n.* Grass; hay; straw.

Ghasíṭná, *v.* To pull; to haul; to drag.

Ghasiyárá, *n.* A grass-cutter.

Ghát, *n.* Slaughter; killing; massacre; opportunity; wish or desire. *—men̲ baithná,* to lie in ambush; to lie in wait.

Ghaṭ, *n.* Mind; heart; soul; thought. *—ghaṭ niwásí,* dwelling or abiding in the heart (applied to God). *—men̲ baiṭhná,* to dwell in the heart.

Gháṭ, *n.* A landing-place; a quay or wharf; a ferry; a bathing-place on the bank of a river; reduction; a decrease; failure; a shortcoming; a mountain-pass or a place on the bank of a river where tolls and cutoms duties are collected. *—már,* a smuggler. *—mán̲jhí,* a ferry-man.*—ghát, ká paní píná,* prov. To frequently change sides; to sleep around; to hop from bed to bed.

Gháṭá, *n.* Deficiency; decrease; insufficiency; loss. *—baiṭhná,* to pay compensation for losses or damages. *—paṛná,* to bear a loss; to sustain damages.

Ghátak, *n.* Murderous; fatal; blood-thirsty.

Ghaṭáná, *v.* To decrease; to diminish; to alleviate; to lessen; to degrade; to subtract.

Ghaṭáo, *n.* Decrease; diminution; abatement; reduction; falling-off-*barháo, increase and decrease.*

Gháṭí, *n.* A mountain pass; a valley or vale; larynx.

Ghaṭiyá, *a.* Low-priced; of small value.

Ghen̲ṭá, *n.* A pig; a swine; a hog.

Gher, *n.* Circumference; circuit. *—e men̲ paṛná,* to be encompassed or surrounded.

Gherá, *n.* Circumference; run; measure round; compass; a circle; a fence or enclosure;

siege; blockade. —*ḍálná,* to lay siege to; to besiege or blockade. —*uṭháná,* to raise a siege.

Gherná, *v.* To surround; to enclose; to fence; to invest; to besiege or blockade.

Ghí, *n.* Clarified butter. —*ká chirág jaláná,* to achieve or attain one's object; to celebrate; —*ke kuppe se já lagná,* to discover a source of unlimited wealth.

Ghichpich, *a.* Close; thick; compact; crowded.

Ghighí, *a.* To become tongue-tied owing to fear; excitement, emotion, &c.

Ghighiyáná, *v.* To falter or stammer in speech; to seem very meek or submissive; to coax, to cajole; to wheedle.

Ghin, *n.* Disgust; abhorrence; loathing; intense dislike.

Ghinauná, *a.* Disgusting; one provoking intense dislike; loathsome; detestable; one eliciting abhorrence.

Ghirná, *v.* To be surrounded to enclosed; to be encompassed or encircled; to gather (as clouds, &c.).

Ghirní, *n.* A pulley; an instrument for twisting or twining ropes. —*kháná, v.* to revolve or rotate.

Ghisáo, Ghisáwaṭ, *n.* Friction; rubbing.

Ghisná, *v.* To rub; to scour.

Ghokná, *v.* To recite of learn it by heart.

Gholná, *v.* To melt; to dissolve; to mix with a liquid; to form into a solution.

Ghongá, *n.* A cockle or cockle-shell; a snail or snail-shell; any spiral shell.

Ghonslá, *n.* A bird's nest.

Ghonṭná, *v.* To rub; to grind; to pulverize (medicine, &c.); to press; to throttle or strangle; to choke or suffocate; to polish by rubbing; to shave; to read repeatedly.

Ghoṛá, *n.* Horse; a clothes-horse; hammer (of a gun).

Ghoṛí, *n.* A mare.

Ghughú, *n.* An owl (*ullú*); (*metaphorically*), a stupid; or blockhead.

Ghulá, *adv.* Melted; desolved; mellow; soft. —*milá,* adj. Close; familiar; intimate.

Ghumáná, *v.* To turn or whirl round; to cause to revolve or rotate; to roll; to brandish or flourish (as a sword); to circulate; to lead away. —*phiráná,* to prevaricate; to give evasive replies.

Ghumṛí, *n.* Vertigo; giddiness; dizziness.

Ghun, *n.* A weevil; to name of insects destructive to wood and grain.

Ghúṉghar, *n.* A curl. —*wále bál,* currly hair.

Ghúṉghaṭ, *n.* A veil or covering for the face. —*káṛhná,* to wear a veil. —*wálí,* a veiled *(pardah)* woman who does not appear in the presence of strangers.

Ghúṉs, Ghús *n.* A bribe; an illegal gratification.

Ghúṉsá, *n.* A blow with the fist; a punch. —*bází* boxing; fighting with the fists; fisticuffs.

Ghúṉṭ, *n.* A gulp; a draught; quantity swallowed at one time; a pull or draw (at a pipe, &c.). *lahú ká*—, *(lit.)* a gulp of blood; *(met.)* for-bearance.

Ghúrá, *n.* Sweepings; rubbish; a dust-heap; a dung-hill; manure.

Ghúrá, —*n.* Rubbish leap; dumping ground for garbage; pile of refuse material.

Ghuṛakná, *v.* To scowl; to reprove; to rebuke; to threaten or menace.

Ghuṛdauṛ, *n.* A race-course; a horse race.

Ghuṛkí, *n.* Rebuke; reprimand; censure.

Ghúrná, *v.* To state; to gaze intently or flxedly (at); to look angrily (at).

Ghuṛsál, *n.* A stable.

Ghusáná, Ghuseṛná, *n.* To thrust; to cause to enter or penetrate.

Ghusná, *v.* To enter; to penetrate; to interfere. or fixedly (at); to look angrily (at).

Ghuṛsál, *n.* The knee; *v.* to be pounded, bruised or crushed (as grain); to be choked or suffocated. *ghutnoṉ chalnná,* to crawl on all fours (as a child).

Gídaṛ, *n.* Jackal, —*bhabkí,* bravado; boasting or vaunting.

Giddh, *n.* A vulture, (proverbially) one who pounces on the unsus-pecting, or helpless ones, like those ravenous birds gathering around a wounded or a dying animal.

Gídhná, *v.* To be tamed; to become familiar.

Gidí, *a.* Timid; faint-hearted; cowardly; lacking in physical or moral courage.

Ģilá, *n.* Complaint; accusation; blame. —*guzárí karná,* to lodge or prefer a complaint; to complain.

Gílá, *a.* Damp; moist; humid; wet; soft—*pan,* wetness; dampness; moisture; humidity.

Gíláf, *n.* A covering; a case; a sheath or scabbard; a pillowcase.

Gilahrí, *n.* A squirrel.

Gilázat, Ģalázat, *n.* Dirt; filth.

Gin, A suffix (denoting "full of" affected with, or possessed of) added to nouns to form possessive adjectives—as; *andoh-gín,* sorrowful, &c.

Ginaná, *v.* To count; to calculate; to compute; to reckon.

Ginání, *v.* To cause to be counted; to count as an assurance to the recipient; to count as a matter of emphasis; to enumerate.

Gínjná, Ginjolná, *v.* To rub and crush with the hands; to mash with the hands.

Gintí, *n.* Counting; reckoning; calculating; the rule of addition in Arithmetic; muster-roll; consideration; esteem; regard. *—kí,* a small number; a few. *—lená,* to muster.

Gír, *p.a.* Taking by force; seizing; conquering; *n.* a taker; a capturer; a conqueror (*used as a last member of compounds),* as; *jahán-gír,* overcome (conquered or subdued) by sorrow *Panáhgír,* n. seeker of refuge; asylum-seeker.

Giraft, Girift, *n.* Seizure; capture; handle; grasp; clutch; grip; criticism. *—karná,* to make an objection to; to take exception to.*—ár,* arrested; seized; taken captive. *—karná,* to arrest or apprehend; to take captive. *árí,* arrest; seizure; capture; imprisonment; captivity.

Girah, *n.* a knot; a knob; a joint; one sixteenth of a *gaj* or 'yard' of 36 inches; a gland; a purse; a difficulty; bias or prejudice. *—men rakhná,* to put in one's pocket or purse.

Giráná, *v.* To drop; to let fall; to throw down; to spill.

Giran, *n.* A pledge; a pawn; anything deposited as security for the payment of a debt.

Gird, *n.* Round; circumference; circuit; orbit; *pre.* and *adv.* around; near; in proximity to. *—áb, n.* whirlpool; eddy. *—áwar,* a patrolling officer.

Girdá, *n.* A round cake of bread; wafer; anything that is round or circular in shape a ring or circle.

Girdgán, *n.* A walnut.

Girebán, *n.* The collar of a garment.

Girgiráná, *v.* To beseech; to implore; to entreat; to grovel.

Girgaț, Girgiț, *n.* A chameleon.

Giri, *n.* Mountain; a heavy article; a massive rock.

Girijá, *n.* [Giri+já] A mountain girl; one born of a mountain; daughter of a mountain; an epithet of *Párvatí,* Lord *Shiva's* consort.

Giriya-o-zárí, *n.* Lamentation; mourning.

Girjá, *n.* A church or chapel.

Girná, *v.* To fall; to drop; to sink; to subside.

Giroh, *n.* A party; a mob; a crowd; a class.

Girte-parte, *adv.* With difficulty; with much trouble or exertion.

Girwí, *n.* Anything pledged, pawned or mortgaged. *—rakhnewálá,* a pawnbroker; a mortgagee. *—see chhuráná,* redeeming a pledge or mortgage.

Gít, *n.* A song; a melody; a tune; a lyric.

Gítá, *n.* One that is sung. [Also a shorter but proper name for a specific book, **Srimad-Bhagavadgítá** considered a divine sermon delivered by Lord Krishna himself on the battle-field of Kurukshetra in the course of the *Mahábhárata* war and now-a-days a part of daily reading in Hindu households.]

Gizá, *n.* Food; victuals; diet.

Gobar, *n.* Cattle dung; excreta or faeces of animals. *—ganesh,* a dimwitted person; an intellectual dummy; a gullible person.

Gobhí (ká phúl), *n.* Cauliflower. *Pattá—, Band—,* n. Cabbage.

Gochar, *a.* Known; perceived; *n.* knowledge; perception; a pasture ground.

God, Godí, *n.* The lap; bosom.*—lená,* to adopt a child.

Godám, *n. (Corr. of the English).* Godown; a store; warehouse.

Godí, *n.* Berth (as in port, for ships to park and load-unload.

Godná, *n.* To prick; to pierce; to tattoo; to puncture.

Goh, *n.* The iguana.

Gohráná, *v.* To shout; to bawl; to vociferate.

Gojar, *n.* A centepede.

Gol, *a.* Round; spherical; circular. *—mál karná,* to mix; to misappropriate or embezzle.

Golá, *n.* A large ball; a cannonball; a cocoanut; *—márná,* to bombard.

Golandáz, *n.* An artillery-man; a gunner; a bombardier*—í,* gunnery; the science of artillery, or the art of managing guns.

Golí, *n.* A ball; a bullet; a pill; a marble; a shot. *—khelná,* to play marbles. *—márná,* to shoot.

Golmirch, *n.* Pepper.

Gond, *n.* Gum.

Gop, *n.* a cowhered; a herdsman. *—í,* a milk-maid; a dairy-maid.

Gop, *adv.* Secret; hidden; concealed; confidential. *—níya,* a. to be kept secret; deserving confidentiality; required to be concealed.

Gophan, *n.* A sling.

Goṛ, *n.* A leg; a foot. *—paṛná, v.* to touch one's feet as a token of respect and humility.

Gorá, *a.* Having a fair complexion; handsome; beautiful; *n.* a European soldier.

Gorait, *n.* A watchman; guardian; a custodian.

Goras, *n.* Milk; butter-milk.

Gosáín, *n.* A devotee; a pious or religious man.

Gosh, *n.* The ear. *—guzár karná, v.* to communicate; to report. *—málí,* ringing or twisting the ears as a punishment; chastisement; reproof.

Goshá, *n.* A corner; a nook; an angle; privacy; seclusion; side or quarter. *—nishín, n.* a recluse; a hermit.

Gosht, *n.* Meat; flesh; *—kḥor, a.* flesh-eating; carnivorous.

Goshwárá, *n.* An earring; boring or piercing the ears; abstract of an account.

Gospand, *n.* a sheep; a goat.

Got, Gotra, *n.* Lineage; descent; genealogy; pedigree; parent-age.

Goṭá, *n.* Gold or silver lace.

Gotá, *n.* A dive; a plunge; immersion. *—báz, —kḥor,* a diver. *—márná,* to dive or plunge; to be deeply engrossed or absorbed in.

Gotiyá, *n.* A kinsman; a relative; a caste-brother; from the same clan [on the basis of *Got, gotra*].

Grah, *a.* planet. *—dekhná,* to refer to or consult one's horoscope.

Grahaṇ, *n.* In Hindu mythology, the seizure of the sun or moon by *Rahú*—hence, an eclipse of the sun or moon; seizing; arrest; apprehension; acceptance. *—karná,* to accept; to admit; to acknowledge.

Grahasth, *n.* A household; the head; or senior member of a family. *—í,* domestic affairs; worldly affairs.

Grám, *n.* A village; a hamlet.

Granth, *n.* A book or treatise; a composition in prose or verse; the religious book in sacred writings of the Sikhs.

Gú, *n.* Faeces; shit; dung. *—mút,* human excreta. *—men ghasíṭaná,* adv. To subject someone to utter humiliation. *men dhelá phenkaná,* To provoke a wily tongue.

Guálá, Guwál, *n.* A cowherd; a milkman. *—in,* a milk-maid.

Ġubár, *n.* Dust; a dust-storm; fog; annoyance; rancour; malice; perplexity. *—nikálná, v.* to give vent to one's feelings of spite and ill-will; to exact vengeance.

Ġubárá, *n.* A balloon; a fire-balloon; a mortar for throwing shells; a bomb.

Guchchhá, *n.* A bunch; cluster.

Gudá, *n.* Anus; rear passage of human body.

Gúdá, *n.* Brain; marrow; kernel; pith.

Gúdaṛ, *n.* Old cotton; rags; torn and tattered clothes; a quilt.

Gudáz, *n.* Thick; stout; corpulent; plump; soft.

Guḍḍá, Guṛiyá, A doll: a puppet; an effigy; an object of contempt or derision.

Gudgudá, *a.* Plump; soft.

Gudgudí, *n.* Tickling. *—karná* v. To tickle.

Gudṛí, *n.* Ragged or tattered clothes; rags.

Gufá, *n.* A cave; a cavern; a lair; a den. *—men band rahaná,* adv. To lead a life of seclusion.

Guft-o-gú, Guftár, Guft-o-shuníd, *n.* Speech; locution; discourse; conversation; controversy.

Gul, *n.* A rose; a flower; snuff (of a lamp or candle); the scar left by burn. *—gul-andám* or *gul-badan,* slender; graceful. *—chharre uṛáná,* to scatter flowers; to live extravagantly. *—istán, n.* rose-garden; the name of of a celebrated work by the Persian poet Sa'adí. *—gír, n.* snuffers used for trimming candles. *—honá,* to be extinguished.

Gul, *n.* Noise; uproar; tumult.

Guláb, *n.* (lit.) Rose-water; (in usage) a red rose. *—í,* a. Rosy; rose-coloured. *—í gál,* a. rosy cheeks; cheeks with a pinkish hue. *—í hont'a* a. lips as delicate and curly as rose-scented water (sprinkled on foods and people at festive occasions). *—jámun,* n. A sweetmeat, a dried-milk ball soaked in sugary syrup.

Gulám, *n.* A slave; a bondsman. *—gardish, n.* the enclosed verandah of a tent; a covered passage round a mosque or other building, &c.*—í,* slavery; servitude; bondage. *—on̲ ki kḥaríd farokḥt,* buying and selling of slaves; slave-trading.

Guldastá, *n.* A nosegay; a bouquet.

Gulel, *n.* A bow for shooting pellets; *a.* boy's catapult.

Gulguliyá, *n.* A jackdaw.

Gulú, *n.* The neck; the throat. *khush—,* having a sweet or melodious voice. *—band,* a comforter; a neck cloth; a muffler.

Gum, *a.* Lost; missing; absent; confused; perplexed; distractive. *—ráh, n.* one who has lost his way; one who has gone astray. *—nám, a.* nameless; anonymous; ignoble; *Gum-shudá,* one that is lost, or gone astray.

Gumán, *n.* Doubt; suspicion; mistrust; surmise; opinion; idea; pride; vanity. *—hai,* it is probable or likely.

Gumáshta, *n.* An agent.

Gumbaz, Gumbad, *n.* A dome; a cupola.

Gumṛa, *n.* A swelling; an inflammation; a protuberance.

Gumṛí, *n.* A pimple.

Guṇ, *n.* Quality; attribute; property; virtue; virtue. *Tri—,* n. Three essential attributes of all things and all beings *(Sattva, Rajas, Tamas,* i.e. The Virtuous, the indulgent and the demonic, according to Hindu tradition). *—kárí, —kárak,* Effective; beneficial. *—gáná,* v. To sing the praises of; to eulogise; to extol the virtues of. *—gráhak,* n. A connoisseur; one who appreciates; one who values. *—í, —wán,* a. Meritorious; virtuous; possessor of qualities. *—hín,* a. devoid of virtues.

Guṇá, *a.* (used as suffix) Compounds of; times multiplied. *Do—,* twice as much, or twice as many. *Chau—*Four-times. *Ti—,* Three-times.

Guṇáḍhya, *a.* gifted; virtuous; posesser of qualities.

Guṇáguṇ, *a.* Various; diverse; warts and virtues alike; of many colours and kinds.

Gunáh, *n.* Sin; wickedness; iniquity; vice.*—gár,* a sinner; a culprit; one guilty of any sin or offence. *be—,* sinless; innocent.

Guncha, *n.* A bud; a blossom.

Gunḍá, *n.* A fop; a knave; a licentious or dissolute fellow; *a.* dissolute; depraved; rakish.

Gúndhná, *v.* To knead; to plait; to braid; to twist.

Gúngá, *a.* Dumb; mute; speechless; silent.

Gunguná, *a.* Lukewarm; tepid; slightly warm.

Gun-gunáná, *v.* To hum (a song or a tune); bathroom singing; to render a tune without instrumental accompaniment.

Guniyá, *n.* A mason's or carpenter's square.

Gúnj, *n.* Echo; humming; buzzing; resonance.

Gunjáish, *n.* Room; space; margin; capacity.

Gupt, *a.* Hidden; concealed; invisible. —*dán,* a present given privately as an act of charity.

Guptí, *n.* A sword-stick; a walking-stick containing a sword.

Guṛ, *n.* Molasses; treacle; jaggery. —*ambá,* mangoes boiled with meal and sugar.

Gur, *n.* A formula; a prescribed form; a general expression for solving problems. —*duárá, n.* a monastery.

Gurbá, *n.* A cat. —*i-miskín, (lit.)* a meek cat; (*fig.*) a wicked and cunning person.

Ġurbat, *n.* Meekness; humility; submissiveness; emigration; exile. —*zada,* wretched; miserable.

Ġurdá, *n.* A kidney; courage; bravery. *bare—ká ádmí,* a courageous man.

Gurez, *n.* Escape; flight. —*karná,* to shun; to avoid; to ward off (danger).

Gurg, *n.* A wolf (*bheṛiyá*).

Gurgá, *n.* A servant boy; a scullion.

Gúṛh, *a.* Mysterious; abtruse; obscure.

Gurú, *n.* A religious teacher; a spiritual guide. —*ghanṭál* a confirmed scoundrel.

Gurúb, *n.* Sunset.

Gurúr, *n.* Pride; haughtiness; vanity; conceit.

Gurz, *n.* Mace; an iron club. —*bardár,* a mace-bearer.

Ġusl, *a.* A bath. —*karná,* to bathe.

Ġussá, *n.* Anger; wrath; rage; vexation. —*diláná,* to put out of temper; to enrage. —*píná,* to suppress one's anger; to subdue one's temper.

Ġustáḳh, *a.* Impertinent; impudent; audacious; rude. —*í,* insolence; impudence; impertinence; andacity.

Guṭakna, *v.* To gulp; to swallow to coo (as a pigeon).

Guṭhlí, *n.* Seed or stone to fruit.

Gúthná, *v.* To string (as beads, &c.); to thread.

Guzar, *n.* A path; a passage; a way; a road; ingress and egress; a pass; a ferry; living; a passing; elapsing. —*áb,* a ford; a canal. —*gáh-i-'ám,* a public road, a thoroughfare. —*náma,* a passport. *haq-i—,* right of way. —*jáná,* to pass away; to die; to expire.

Guzárá, *n.* A passage; a crossing;

livelihood; means of subsistence. —*karná,* to effect a crossing; to eke out a miserable existence.

Guzárish, *n.* Explanation; representation; petition; application; request.

Guzarná, *v.* To pass; to come to pass; to happen; to elapse; to befall; to excel; to die. *dar-guzar karná, v.* to overlook; to excuse; to refrain or abstain from; to avoid.

Guzasht, Guzashtá, *n.* The past.

Guzrán, *n.* Course of life; subsistence; livelihood. —*karná,* to subsist with difficulty.

Guzráná, *v.* To present; to offer; to proffer.

Gyán, *n.* Knowledge; wisdom; intellect; perspicuousness. *dharm*—, religious knowledge. —*wán* or *gyání,* intelligent.

Gyát, *adj.* Known; apparent. —*á,* n. One who knows; knowledgeable. —*avya,* n. one worthy of knowing; something worth knowing.

H, h, is equivalent to Hindi sound (ह) and Urdu sound (ہ) and (ح).

Há, *intj.* Ah ! alas ! —*há karná, v.* to implore; to beseech. —*há kár,* sounds of lamentation.

Habas, Havis, *n.* Passion, desire, greed.

Habíb, *n.* A lover a sweetheart; a special favourite; an intimate friend.

Habs, *n.* Confinement; imprisonment. —*i-dawám,* transportation for life—*un-nafs,* choking; suffocation.

Habshí, *n.* An Abyssinian. (In imperial parlance of the Arabs as well as in the Western slave-trading days, the word was commonly translated as —Negro, a black slave, an animal, beast.

Habúra, *n.* A free-booter; a plunderer; a highway robber.

Hechkolá, *n.* A jolt; a shaking. Hadaf, *n.* A mark; a butt; a target. —*márná* to strike a mark or target.

Hadarat, *n.* An earthquake.

Hadáyá, *n. (Plur. of Hadiyá).* Gifts; offerings.

Hadd, *n.* Boundary; extremity; extent; a separations; the utmost point or degree; a starting point. *az—, adv.* at most; at least; extremely; utterly. —*bándhná, v.* to define; to mark the limits or boundaries of. —*i-siyásat men,* under the jurisdiction of, *be—,* limitless; boundless; infinite.

Haḍḍí, *n.* A bone. —*ṭúṭná,* a bone to be broken or fractured.

Hádí, *n.* A director; a guide; a leader.

Hadís, *n.* Traditions; the traditional sayings of Mohammed.

Hádisá, *n.* A new thing; a novelty; a mishap; an accident; calamity; disaster.

Hadiyá, *n.* Gift; offering. —*karná* to make an offering.

Háfiz, *n.* A custodian; a protector; a guardian; a keeper; one who knows the whole *Qur'an* by heart; one who has a good retentive memory.

Háfizá, *n.* A retentive memory.

Haft, *a.* Seven. —*aqlím,* the seven regions; the world. —*hazárí,* commander of seven thousand. —*zabán,* master of seven languages; an expert linguist.

Haftá, *n.* A week; seven days; the seventh day—*i.e.,* Saturday.

Haftáwár, *adv.* Weekly; per week.

Haibat, *n.* Fear; apprehension; terror; horror. —*nák,* terrible; awful.

Haidar, *n.* A lion; name of Ali, son-in-law of Mohammed.

Haif, *n.* Justice; affliction; sorrow; a pity; a shame. *Intj.* Ah ! alas !

Háik, *n.* A weaver.

Haikal, *n.* Figure; form; personal appearance; a temple; a palace; a stately mansion.

Háil, *n.* Hindering; impeding; obstructing; intervening; obstacle. *—honá,* to obstruct; to hinder.

Hairán, *a.* Confused; distracted; perplexed; surprised; amazed. *—í, n.* perplexity; confusion; astonishment.

Hairat, *n.* Amazement; astonishment. *—angez,* adj. Amazing; astonishing.

Haisiyat, *n.* Ability; capacity; faculty; means; state or condition. *—kḥaráb honá, v.* to deface; to disfigure*—i'urfí,* reputation; good name.

Haiwán, *n.* Animal, abrute; a beast; a blockhead. *—i-mutlaq,* a brute. *—i-nátiq,* a. A sensible being; human. *—iyat,* Bestiality; animal nature; animal passions.

Hajámat, *n.* The craft practised by a *Hajjám* (barber); Shaving and haircutting. *—baná, dená,* v. (proverbially—) To clean one out; to deprive one of all possessions cunningly.

Hajar, *n.* A stone; prohibition; interdiction (in law); annulment. *—ul-aswád,* the black stone in the *Ka'aba* or temple at Macca.

Hájat, *n.* Want; need; requirement; poverty; a call of nature; a place of detention for prisoners under trial. *—rafa' karná,* to supply a want; to ease nature. *—rawái,* the act of furnishing anything that is needful.

Hájí, *n.* One who has performed the pilgrimage to Mecca *—ul-kharámain,* one who has performed the pilgrimage to the sacred places at Mecca and Medína.

Hájib, *n.* A door-keeper; a porter; a minister of state; screen.

Hajiz, *n.* A barrier; an obstruction; an obstacle.

Hajj, *n.* Pilgrimage to Mecca.

Hajjám, *n.* Thickness; bulk; girth; size.

Hajo, Haju, *n.* A satire; ignominy; censure. *—malíh,* seeming praise but satire; irony.

Hajr, *n.* Separation; distinction.

Hajrát, *n.* One year.

Hajúm, *n.* A crowd; a random gathering.

Hákam, *n.* An arbitrator; a mediator.

Hakíkat, Haqíqat, *n.* The truth; factually; reality. *—an,* adv. In real terms; as a matter of fact. *Haq-o—,* Moral and real.

Hakím, *n.* A doctor; a physician; a sage; a philosopher; a deeply learned man *ním—,* an unexperienced physician. *—í,* the practice of medicine.

Hákim, *n.* A judge; a magistrate; a ruler; a commander; a master; the Supreme Judge (God). *—i-'álá,* the paramount power; the supreme authority. *—waqt,* the government of the day *—í,* authority; dominion; jurisdiction; sway.

Hakkák, *n.* One who cuts and polishes precious stone.

Haklá, *n.* A stammerer; one who has an impediment in his speech. *—ná, v.* to stammer; to stutter.

Hal, *n.* A plough. *—bandí,* assessment based on the number of ploughs used.

Hal, *n.* Solution (to a problem); answer (to a question). *—karná,* v. To solve. *—nikálná,* v. To find a solution to.

Hál, *n.* Circumstance; state; case; the present time; business; affair; history; account. *adj.* and *adv.* present; current; at present. *—ánki, adv.* since; although; however; even. *—behál honá,* to be reduced from a good to a bad condition; to become deteriorated. *tabáh—,* in financial difficulties.

Hálá, *n.* The circle or ring sometimes seen round the moon.

Hálá, *n.* Drink (alcoholic); intoxicant.

Haláhal, *n.* Venom; Lethal poison; according to Hindu legend, when gods and demons churned the great ocean together, among other things, a massive container of lethal poison emerged from the bottom of the sea and in order to save the creatures of the world from its dangerous effects, Lord *Shiva* swallowed it. Hence one of his pseudonyms *Haláhal dhárí.*

Halák, *a.* Dead, lost; killed in battle; murdered. *—honá,* v. to be killed, to be murdered. To become casualty of war. *—karná,* v. To kill, to murder; to kill in combat, &c.

Halákat, *n.* Destruction; ruin; execution; manslaughter. *—i-lázim-malzúm,* justifiable homicide.

Halál, *n.* Legal; lawful; permissible. *—khor,* a sweeper; a scavenger; one who eats what is lawful.

Halaq, *n.* The throat; the gullet; the wind pipe. *—band karná,* v. to throttle; to suffocate (with a view to kill); to strangle. (Proverbially) to enforce silence.

Hálat, *n.* State; condition; nature; temperament.—*men*, in the event of. —*ba hálat,* under the influence (of). *(Plur. Hálát).*

Haláwat, *n.* Sweetness; pleasure; taste.

Halchal, *n.* Bustle; tumult and confusion; hurry-scurry. —*paṛná,* to be confused or perplexed; to be panic-stricken.

Haldí, *n.* Turmeric.

Halím, *a.* Gentle; mild; for bearing; docile; tractable. —*í, n.* forbearance; meekness; docility.

Habsá, *n.* An oar.

Halká, *a.* Light (in weight, character, &c.); unimportant; insignificant; mean; fatigue; silly; mild or gentle (as: applied for weather); trifling; trivial; easy to digest; lowpriced; moderate; cheap.

Hall, *n.* Melting; dissolved.

Halorá, *n.* A wave; a billow.

Halorná, *v.* To shake; to oscillate; to be agitated or ruffled (sea); to collect; to accumulate.

Halqá, *n.* A circle; a ring; a hoop; a horse's collar; a circuit (of a village, &c.); an assembly. —*bándhná,* to encompass; to invest; to besiege. —*be gosh, n.* a slave.

Halwá, Haluá, Heluá, *n.* Pudding; sweet dish; traditionally made with semolina, but many other concoctions are made in the same way with different materials, like Carrots; *Gájar-Halwá.*

Halwáhá, *n.* A ploughman; a tiller of the soil.

Halwáhí, *n.* Tillage; ploughing.

Halwán, *n.* A kid; a lamb.

Ham, *pro.* We; *adv.* and *conj.* also; even; likewise; as well as; together with other; mutually; whether; either; fellow; co-*(used in compounds),* as; *ham-áwází,* harmony; concord. —*peshá,* a fellow-craftsman, or artisan. —*sáyá,* neighbouring; contiguous. —*watan,* a fellow countryman; a compatriot, &c., &c.

Hamá, *a.* Equal; equivalent; alike; similar; *n.* a contemporary; a friend; a companion.

Hamal, *n.* Pregnancy; conception.

Hamárá, *pro.* Our; ours.

Hamáshuma, *n.* We two; both of us; the common people.

Hamd, *n.* Praise (of God). —*karná,* to praise or bless (God).

Hamen, *pr. pl.* Us; to us.

Hameshá, *adv.* Always; ever; perpetually; continually; uninterruptedly.

Hámí, *n.* Protector; defender; patron; supporter; helper; assurance. *—bharná,* to be responsible; to give an assurance.

Hámid, *n.* One who praises God.

Hamídá, *a.* Praiseworthy; meritorious.

Hámilá, *n.* Pregnant; with a baby in the womb.

Hamín, *n.* Anxiety; uneasiness; sorrow; grief.

Hamiyat, *n.* Zeal; fervour; ardour; enthusiasm.

Hamíz, *a.* Sharp; keen.

Hamlá, *n.* Attack; assault; onslaught. *—áwar,* an aggressor; an assailant; an attacker.

Hammám, *n.* A bath; a warm bath.

Hámphná, Hámpná, *v.* To be out of breath; to pant.

Hamwár, *a.* Level; even; smooth.

Hán, *adv.* Yes; indeed; certainly; verily.

Háni, *n.* Loss; detriment; damage; injury; deficiency.

Hándá, *n.* A large cooking pot; a cauldron.

Hánḍí, Hanḍiyá, Hánrí, Hanriyá, *n.* A small, domestic sized cooking pot.

Hang, *n.* Understanding; intellect; wisdom.

Hangámá, *n.* Season; period; time; an assemblage. *—á,* a multitude; tumult; disorder. *—karná,* to riot; to create a disturbance.

Hángí, *n.* A sieve made of cloth.

Hánk, *n.* Howling; screaming; shouting. *—pukár ke kahná, v.* to state loudly in public.

Hankárí, *a.* Haughty; proud; conceited; self-opinionated.

Hánkná, *v.* To say; to tell; to boast; to fan; to drive.

Hanoz, *adv.* Yet; still; up to now; not yet.

Hans, *n.* A swan; (in Hindu mythology this bird is the mount of goddess Saraswati, the deity of learning, and fine arts.

Hansáná, *v.* To excite laughing; to turn to ridicule; to expose; to ridicule.

Hansí, *n.* Laughter; fun; ridicule; joking; jesting, *—men uṛáná,* to turn aside with a joke. *—ṭhaṭṭhá karná,* to make game of; to ridicule.

Hansiyá, Hansua, *n.* A sickle; a scythe.

Hansulí, *n.* The collar-bone; a collar of gold or silver.

Hansmukh, *n.* Cheerful; jovil; merry; jolly; gay.

Hansná, *v.* To be merry; to be jovial; to snile; to laugh at; to ridicule.

Hansoṛpan, Hansoṛpaná, *n.* Mirth; gaiety; joviality.

Hant, *n.* [An interjection] expressing sorrow; grief.

Hantavya, *adj.* Worth killing; object of slaying; fit to be killed.

Hantá, *n.* A slayer; one who commits murder.

Haqíqat, *n.* Essence; path; subject matter; reality; the actual facts or circumstances of a case; account; story; description. —*khulná, v.* to be discovered. *fil—,* as a matter of fact; virtually. (also see 'Hakíkat').

Haqíqí, *a.* Essential; real; actual; own.

Haqír, *a.* Despicable; contemptible; mean; base.

Haqq, *a.* Just; proper; correct; true; in conformity with fact or reality; *n.* justness; propriety; truth; justice; equity; title; claim; share; duty; benefit; the truth —*i.e.,* the true God. —*adá karná, v.* to give one his dues; to act justly or eqnitably. —*talafi, n.* violation of one's rights or privileges. —*i-shufá,* right of pre-emption. —*ta'ála,* the Most High God —*i-wirsá,* right of inheritance.

Haqqiyat, *n.* Claim; title; ownership; property; share.

Har, *n.* Each; every; any; all —*án,* always; constantly; continuously; —*chand,* notwithstanding; in spite of; however. —*che bád-ábád,* no matter what the consequences may be. —*dil'aríz,* universally beloved. —*fan moulá,* a jack of all trades; one who claims to have a theoretical and practical knowledge of every trade and profession.

Hár, *n.* A necklace; a garland or wreath; a flock or herd of cattle. —*gúndhná,* to thread or string a garland of of flowers. *gale ká —honá, (lit.)* to hang round a person's neck (as a necklace) —*i.e.,* to love a person very dearly; to be closely attached to a person.

Hár, *n.* Cultivated land in the vicinity of a village; a plot of land; a pasture-ground.

Hár, *n.* Fatigue; exhaustion; defeat; rout; overthrow; loss. —*jít,* loss and gain; gambling. —*mán lená,* to acknowledge defeat.

Hár kar, *adv.* Forcibly; compulsarily; reluctantly; under stress of circumstances; at last; finally; conclusively.

Hará, *a.* Green; fresh. —*bhará,* fruitful; productive; luxuriant fertile; flourishing; prosperous.

Harakh, [See *Harsh*].

Haram, *n.* Holy; sacred; consecrated; the temple *(K'aba)* of Mecca; a wife; a concubine; a female slave; a harem; a seraglio.

Harám, *a.* Forbidden; unlawful; illegal; prescribed. —*kḥor,* one who accepts bribes; a dishonest person. —*záda,* a wicked fellow; a scoundrel; a bastard.

Haran, Hiran, *n.* A deer; an antelope; stealing; thieving.

Haráná, *v.* To defeat; to overthrow.

Harárat, *n.* Heat; warmth; anger; rage; enthusiasm; ardour; zeal.

Haráwal, *n.* The vanguard. or advanced guard of an army.

Haṛbaṛí, *n.* Bustle; hurry; haste; confusion; disorder. —*paṛná,* to be agitated or flurried.

Haṛbong, *n.* Anarchy; misgovernment.

Harf, *n.* A letter of the alphabet; blame; censure; infamy; changing; edge; border; brink. —*áshná,* one who has a rudimentary knowledge of reading and writing —*par unglí rakhná, v.* to find fault with. —*shinas,* attentive to what is said; one who accepts, and is guided by, the advice he receives—*o-hikáyat,* conversation; discussion; disputation.

Hargiz, *adv.* Ever. —*nahin̲,* never.

Haṛhaṛáná, *v.* To tremble; to shiver; to quiver.

Haríf, *n.* an enemy; an adversary; a competitor; a rival; a fellow-workman; a partner; *a.* clever; artful; cunning; impertinent; audacious; cheeky.

Hárij, *n.* A disturber; a hindrance; an obstacle.

Harís, *a.* Greedy; avaricious; coverous.

Hariyal, *n.* a green pigeon.

Hariyálí, *n.* Greenery.

Harj, *n.* Obstacle; hindrance; interruption; confusion; loss; injury; damage. —*a.* damurrage.

Harkárá, *n.* A messenger; bearer of news; a footman.

Harkat, *n.* Motion; action; procedure; deed; fault; hindrance; loss; damage; a short vowel. —*dená,* to set in motion.

Harkát, *n. (Plur. of Harkat).* Motions; actions; proceedings. —*i-sálisá,* the three short vowels. —*o-saknát,* gestures; postures.

Hárná, *v.* To be defeated; to be vanquished; to be exhausted; to lose (in play).

Harná/Hirná, *n.* A stag; a buck; a male deer or antelope.

Harní, Hirní, *n. f.* A doe; a hind; a female deer.

Harr, *n.* Heat; warmth.

Harráf, *a.* Clever; ingenious; talkative; loquacious; garrulous.

Harráj, *a.* Running rapidly; *n.* an auction.

Harsh, *n.* Joy; jubilation; mirth; delight; happiness. —*kárak,* exhilarating; cause of happiness; delightful. —*dhwani*/-*nád*/n. A cry of joy; a shriek of delight. —*vihwal,* adj. Overwhelmed by joy. —*átirek,* n. Excessive joy; ecstasy; rapturous state. —*it,* adj. Happy; delighted; in a joyous mood. —*onmád,* n. Ecstasy of joy; a rapturous state of mind.

Harwáhá Halwáhá, *n.* A ploughman; a tiller; an agricultural labourer.

Harzá, *a.* Haughty; vain; proud; conceited. —*gardí,* vain and frivolous conversation.

Hasab-o-nasab, *n.* Pedigree; genecology; descent; lineage.

Hasad, *n.* Envy; jealousy; enmity; ambition. —*rakhná,* to bear malice.

Hasan, *a.* Good; beautiful; name of Alí's son.

Hasb, *n.* Calculating; computing; considering; *adv.* in accordance with; agreeable to; conformably to; in conformity with; *(used as first member of compound),* as *hasb-ul-irshád,* in accordance with orders. —*i-dilkḥwáh,* agreeably to the wishes of. —*i-zábtá,* according to rule or custom. —*manshá,* in conformity with the purport or intention of.

Háshiyá, *n.* Side; border; edge; margin; comments; annotations. —*chaṛháná, v.* to make comments; to make notes in margin. —*chhoṛná, v.* to leave a margin on paper. —*gawáh,* a witness who attests a document by signing it.

Hashmat, *n.* Dignity; pomp; riches; wealth; retinue; train of followers.

Hashr, *n.* Meeting; congregation; the resurrection; tumult; uproar; noise; weeping and wailing; lamentation. —*barpá karná,* to raise an uproar; to lament.

Hasht, *a.* Eight. —*pahlú,* octangular. —*ád,* eighty. —*ádsála,* an octogenarian.

Hásid, *n.* A jealous or envious person; an enemy; an antagonist; an adversary; a rival.

Hásil, *(Plur. Hásilát)*. Product; produce; result; inference; revenue; advantage; profit; gain; acquiring; purport; object. *—i-kalám,* shortly; in brief.

Hasín, *a.* Beautiful; graceful; comply; attractive.

Hasr, *n.* Surrounding; besieging; limit; siege; blockade; dependence; reliance. *—karná,* to surround; to besiege; to rely or depend upon.

Hasrat, *n.* Grief; sorrow; regret; craving; desire. *—áluda,* over-burdened with grief.

Hast, *n.* Hand. *—kalá,* n. Handicraft.*—kaushal/lághav,* n. Dexterity of hand.

Hastí, *n.* Life; existence; being; the world; wealth; merit.

Hasti, *n.* An elephant. *—dáṉt,* an elephant's tusks; ivory. *—ní,* a female elephant. *—pál,* an elephant driver *(maháwat).*

Háṭ, Haṭiyá, *n.* Shop; stall. *—bázár,* n. Market.

Hátá, *n.* Premises; courtyard.

Hatak, *n.* Disgrace; disgracing; defamation; slander; libel; affront; insult.

Haṭáná, *v.* To remove; to set back; to repel; to defer; to postpone.

Hath, *n.* (based on **Háth,** a hand) it means a *hand* being used as a prefix. i.e. *—kaṛí,* Hand-cuffs; manacles. *—pher karná,* v. To perform a sleight of hand; to play trickery on those who trust you.

Haṭh, *n.* Pertinacity; stubbornness; obstinacy; perseverance; peevishness.

Háth, *n.* The hand; an arm; paw; a cubit (measure); a hand (a work-man); hand (at cards); a blow; a slap; a smack. *—iáná,* to come into the possession of; to fall into the power of. *—baiṭhná v.* to become expert by practice in any art or profession *pasárná, v.* *—pasáre jáná,* to depart this life empty-handed. *—chhoṛná, v.* to strike a blow at. *—dená,* to lend a hand, *i.e.,* to render assistance. *—sáf karná,* to beat; to thrash; to kill; to plunder. *—kangan ko ársí kyá?, (Prov.)* the thing is self-evident. *—meṉ lená,* to get into one's power or clutches; to bring into subjection.

Hathauṛá, *n.* A sledge hammer.

Hathauṛí, *n.* A small hammer.

Hathelí, *n.* The palm of the hand. *—par sarsoṉ jamáná, v.* to perform any thing quickly; to perform marvellous feats.

Haṭhí, *a.* Stubborn; perverse, peevish.

Háthí, *n.* An elephant (also see 'Hastí').

Hathiyár, *n.* Tool; implements;

instrument; weapon. —*band,* armed; equipped with weapon.

Hath-kanḍa, *n.* Cleverness; astuteness; skill; art, trick.

Háthon̲ *adv.* By the hands. —*háth karná,* to act in harmony. —*háth lená,* to receive one with every mark of respect, to deal with dexterity.

Hátif, *n.* One who cries aloud; one who applauds or praises.

Hátim, *n.* A judge; a judicial officer; the name of a very liberal man; a generous; liberal; benevolent.

Haṭná, *v.* To withdraw; to retire; to move aside; to be driven back (also see Haṭáná).

Hatt-ul-imkán, *adv.* To the utmost of one's power' to the best of one's power; to the best of one's ability.

Hatyá, *n.* killing; murder; Massacre; slaughter; destruction. —*rá,* wicked; evil, sinful; *n.* a murderer; a scoundrel.

Haudá, *n.* A saddle mounted on an elephant.

Hauká, *n.* Greediness; covetousness; avarice. —*karná,* to be greedy.

Haul, *n.* Fright; terror; extreme fear. —*dil,* sadness; melancholy. —*baiṭhn̲á,* to be overwhelmed with fear. —*nák,* adj. Stunning; frightening; shocking.

Haule, *adv.* By degrees; gradually; slowly. [often used twice, i.e. *Haule-Haule*].

Haun̲s, *n.* Craving; desire; lust; ambition; malice; jealousy. —*karná,* to desire ardently

Hausilá, Hauslá, *n.* Bravery; courage; aspiration; ambition; aspiration; ambition. —*mand,* a. brave, courageous, etc. —*karná,* n. To make a courageous move; to take grip of the situation.

Hauz, *n.* Pond; cistern; reservoir.

Hawá, *n.* Atmosphere; air; breeze; wind; rumour; hearsay; reputation. —*uṛná,* to be reported or announced —*bán̲dhná, v.* to gain a reputation; to become celebrated, or renowned —*bigaṛná, v.* the air to become poisoned; to lose one's reputation. —*karná, v. (lit.)* to breathe the air; to take an airing. —*ke ghoṛe par sawár honá,* to move with great speed or rapidity; to be in great haste.

Hawádis, *n. (Plur. of Hádisa,)* Disasters; misfortunes; calamities.

Hawáí, *a.* Of the air; of the sky; a piece of firework that rockets upward. —*jaház,* n. Aeroplane.

Hawálá, *n.* Transfer; charge; trust; custody; possession; reference; *adv.* in the care or custody of. —*dená, v.* to make a reference.

Hawálát, *n.* A lock-up; custody; a place of detention for prisoners under trial. *—men rakhná,* to place in custody.

Havaldár, Havildar, *n.* A non-commissioned military officer, a junior level police officer.

Hawále, *adv.* In the charge of; in the care or custody of. *—karná, v.* to deposit in trust; to enrust to the keeping of.

Hawas, *n.* Desire; lust; ambition; curiosity.

Hawás, *n.* The (five) senses. *—bákhta,* bereft of one's senses; insane. *—thikáne honá,* to be in full possession of one's senses.

Hawelí, *n.* A house built of brick or stone; a mansion; a dwelling house.

Hayá, *n.* Modesty; bashfulness; sense of shame. *be—,* devoid of shame; shameless; impudent.

Hayát, *n.* Life; existence. *—táza,* a new life; a new lease of life (used to express recovery from serious illness).

Hazár, *a.* A thousand *—dástán,* —a thousand tales, *—pá,* a centepede; a millepede; a myriapod.

Hazar, *n.* Caution; vigilance; prudence; fear; apprehension.

Házimá, Házmá, *n.* Digestive system; power to digest; capacity to absorb.

Házir, *a.* Present; in attendance; at hand; ready; willing; satisfied. *—jawábí, n.* readiness in answering; repartee. *—karná,* to conduct a person into the presence of another; to introduce a person. *—zámin, n. m.* one who acts as surety for the attendance or appearance of any person in a court of law. *—o-názir,* omnipresent and omniscient (attributes of the Deity). *gair—,* absent; not in accordance.

Háziri, *n.* Breakfast; presence; attendance; a gift presented to a saint. *—Bharná,* To attend; to mark one's presence; to receive (a dignitary).

Házirín, *n.* Persons in attendance; audience; assembly; congregation.

Hazl. *n. (Plur. Hazliyát).* a jest; a joke. *—go, n.* a gossip; an idle talker.

Hazm, *n.* Routing; putting to flight; digestion; embezzlement; misappropriation.

Hazrat, *n.* Presence; attendance; dignity; a term of respect used in addressing any great man. *Hazrat-i-Ísá,* n. Lord Jesus Christ.

Hech, *a.* Some; any; good for nothing; useless and worthless. *—jánaná, v.* to regard as absolutely worthless and unworthy of consideration. —*puch,* of no account; insignificant.

Hekaṛ, *n.* Sturdy; well-developed and muscular; robust; burly. —*i, n.* physical strength; power; authority; -*í se,* by sheer strength; by main force. —*karná,* to threaten; to exert physical force; to brag; to boast.

Hel-mel, *n.* Close friendship intimacy; familiarity.

Hem, *n.* Gold. —*kánti,* n. golden glitter. —*ábh,* n. Lustre of gold.

Hemant, *n.* The winter season.

Herná, *v.* To observe closely; to peer into; to seek for; to hunt; to catch.

Heṭhá, *n.* Low; inferior; mean; base; abject; lazy; idle; cowardly.

Hetu, Het, *n.* Cause; reason; purpose; motive.

Hetwábhás, *n.* [A derivative of *Hetu*] A fallacy; a sophism.

Hichakná, Hichkicháná, *v.* To shrink from; to draw back from; to waver; to hesitate; to turn from, in disgust or aversion; jerk; to jolt.

Hichkí, *n.* The hiccough. —*lagná, v.* to gasp for breath when at the point of death.

Hidáyat, *n.* Guidance, direction; good advice. —*e-tákídí, karná,* to enjoin strictly. —*náma,* a book of instructions.

Hiddat, *n.* Sharpness (of a weapon); the edge (of a sword, &c.); keenness; acuteness; vehemence; strength.

Hifázat, *n.* Guarding; keeping; care; protection; safety. —*kḥud, n.* self-defence. —*meṉ rakhná.* —*karná v.* to place in safety, or in custody; to guard or defend.

Hifz, *n.* Preservation; care; custody; protection; memory; *adv.* from memory; by heart. —*karná, v.* to commit to memory; to learn by heart. —*paṛhná,* to repeat from memory. —*e-marátib,* observance of the rules of etiquette.

Hijáb, *n.* A veil; concealment; modesty; sense of shame; night. —*kháná, v.* to feel ashamed. —*uṭháná,* to lose all sense of shame; to become utterly shameless; the covering worn by Muslim women (Burqá).

Hijje, *n.* Spellings.

Hijṛá, *n.* A Eunuch; an impotent man. —*banáná,* v. To castrate; to emasculate.

Hijrí, *a.* Pertaining to, or according to, the Mohammedan era.

Hikáyat, *n.* Narrative; narration; tale; story; history. —*karná,* to recount; to relate.

Hikmat, *n.* Wisdom; knowledge; mystery; cleverness; skill; frugality; thrift. *—e-'amalí,* practical skill. *—í, a.* clever; ingenious; artful; cunning; frugal; economical.

Híla, *n.* Artifice; stratagem; deceit; deception; fraud. *—báz, a.* artful; deceitful; fraudulent; *n.* a deceitful fellow; a knave; an impostor.

Hilál, *n.* The new moon.

Hiláná, *v.* To cause to shake; to agitate; to tame; to domesticate; to cause to swim.

Himáqat, *n.* Folly; foolishness; stupidity.

Himáyat, *n.* Protection; defence; support; patronage. *—í, n.* guardian; protector; supporter.

Himmat, *n.* Mind; thought; attention; inclination; desire; determination; intention; ambition; generosity; courage; power; favour. *—bá<u>n</u>dhná,* to pluck up courage. *—hárná, n.* to become discouraged, or dispirited.

Hi<u>n</u>dsá, *n.* A digit; a number [as in mathematics].

Hi<u>n</u>duwáná, *n.* A water-melon; a pumpkin.

Hi<u>n</u>dú, *n.* A dweller of Hindustán; a follower of Hindu faith. *—í,* of the Hindus; a medieval name for the Hindi language. *—stání,* n. Another name for the common language of North India. *—stán,* n. The land of Hindus.

Hí<u>n</u>g, *n.* Assafoetida.

Hinhináná, *v.* To neigh (as a horse).

Hi<u>n</u>sá, *n.* Violence; use of force. *Hinsak,* adj. One committing violence.

Hiqárat, *n.* Contempt; scorn; baseness; disgrace; insult. *—kí nazar se dekhná,* v. to despise; to regard with contempt.

Híra, *n.* A diamond; adamant; *a.* worthy; virtuous.

Hírásá<u>n</u>, *a.* Terrifying; frightening; alarmed; afraid; frightened.

Hirásat, *n.* Watching; care; custody; charge.

Hirdá, Hirday, *n.* (See *Hridaya*).

Hirfa, Hirfat, *n.* Craft: trade; profession; skill; art; villainy; wickedness.

Hirs, *n.* Greediness; avarice; ambition; cupidity; avidity.

Hisáb, *n.* Counting; calculation; computation; reckoning; account; a bill (of charges); rate; price; measure; proportion. *—navís,* a. A book-keeper; an accountant. *—í-kitábí,* a. a shrewd, calculating person, a sharp one.

Hísár, *n.* A fort; a castle; ramparts; enclosure; fence; surrounding; besieging; a place name in Haryáná.

Hiska, *n.* Rivalry; competition; contention; imitation.

Hiss, *n.* Feeling; sense; imagination; sympathy.

Hissá, *n.* Part; portion; lot; share; division.

Hit, *n.* Love; affection; friendship, interest.

Hiyá, *n.* The heart; the mind; the soul; life.

Hiyáo, *n.* Courage; bravery; heart; manliness. *—khulná,* to take courage. *—paṛná,* to have the courage (to).

Ho, *a.* Being. *—chukná,* to terminate; to come to an evil. *—jáná,* to become. *—so—,* no matter what may happen.

Holá, *n.* Green or unripe gram.

Holí, Holiká, *n.* Hindu festival of colours. celebrated on the last day of the month of *Phágun,* in the Vikram calendar.

Hom, Homa, *n.* Among the Hinddus, the casting of clarified butter *(ghí),* &c., into a fire as an offering to the gods, accompanied by prayers. *—karná, v.* to cast into fire.

Honá, *v.* To be; to exist; to become; to come; to be effected or accomplished; to come to pass; to happen; to occur; to prove to be; to serve; to succeed; to terminate; to cease; *n.* being; existence; possibility; *a.* possible; lifely,*—ho jáná, v.* to become; to be born. *hone jog, a.* likely to be or to happen; possible. *—honehárá,* or *honewálá, a.* about to be, or to occur; imminent.

Honahár, *adj.* Promising; the inevitable; destiny.

Honí, *n.* Destiny; predestination; inevitable.

Hoṉṭh, Hoṭ, *n.* The lip *—hiláná, v.* to move the lips; to speak. *— káṭná,* or *—chabáná,* to bite the lips (in anger, regret, &c.); to be penitent; to be apprehensive.

Hosh, *n.* Understanding; intellect; sense; mind; soul. *—pá-karná, v.* to reach the age of discretion. *—meṉ áná,* to come to one's senses; to be restored to one's senses (after intoxication, swooning, &c.) *o-hawás.*

Hoshiyár/Hoshyár, *a.* Intelligent; sensible; clever; wise; prudent; cautious. *—í,* intelligence; wisdom; prudence; shrewdness;

caution; carefulness. —*karná, v.* to warn one.

Hotá, (Imperfect part. of *honá).* Being; becoming; occurring; coming to pass. —*chalá áná,* to be a custom from the earliest times. —*jáná,* to be going on.

Hrás, *n.* Decay; fall; diminution. —*mán,* adj. Decaying; falling; suffering a downfall. —*onmukh,* adj. One heading for a fall; in the process of decay; heading for diminution.

Hridaya, *n.* Heart; bosom; core; the best part. —*kamp,* n. Palpitation; heart-throb. —*gat,* adj. What is in one's heart; of the heart. —*gráhí,* adj. One captivating the heart; charming. —*vidárak,* adj. Heat rending; one that breaks the heart. —*í,* adj. One that pierces the heart. —*sparshí,* adj. One that touches the heart; moving. —*hín,* adj. One without a heart; cruel; unfeeling. —*esh,* n. Lord of one's heart; darling. —*rog,* n. Heart disease.

Hrishṭ, *adj.* Glad; delighted; pleased. —*pushṭ,* n. Stout; robust.

Huá so huá, *(lit.)* What is passed is past; *(met.)* let bygones be bygones; let the dead past bury the dead.

Hú-ba-húá, *adv.* Quite; exactly; precisely *(bi-'ain-hí).*

Hubáb, *n.* Bubble.

Hubb, *n.* Love; affection; friendship; wish. —*ul-watani,* patriotism; love of one's mother-country.

Hujjat, *n.* Argument; plea; proof; reason; excuse; contention; discussion. —*i-'lá-tá'il,* a frivolous excuse —*í,* one who advances sound reasons or arguments; a disputer; one who is fond of arguing and disputing.

Hujrá, *n.* A room; an apartment; a chamber.

Hujúm, *n.* A crowd; a multitude; a throng; a mob; an assault.

Hukamá, *n. (Plur. of Hakím).* Sages; philosophers; learned men; physicians.

Hukkám, *n. (Plur. of Hákim, q.v.).* administrator, ruler, the boss.

Hukm, *n.* Order; instruction, judgment; sentence; decree; judicial decision; jurisdiction; government; control; order; command; law; statute; rule; sanction; permission. —*chaláná,* to wield or exercise authority; to rule or govern. —*qat'ai,* a decisive or peremptory order. —*i-mauqufí,* order of dismissal (of a person); stay of judgment.

Hukúmat, *n.* Judicial authority; jurisdiction; sway; rule; sovereignty. —*i-jamhúri,* a republic;

a democratic form of government. —*i-skakḥsí,* despotic government; monarchy.

Hullaṛ, *a.* Noise; uproar; tumult; disturbance.

Huliyá, *n.* Face; countenance; features; a description of one's person appearance —*náma,* a descriptive roll.

Hunar, *n.* Proficiency in any art; skill; art; dexterity.

Hunḍí, *n.* A bill of exchange; a draft; a cheque. —*darsání,* a bill of exchange payable at sight, *i.e.,* on presentation. —*mi'ádi,* a bill payable after the expiry of stipulated period.

Huqúq, *n. (Plur. of Haqq, q.v.)* Rights; claims; demands.

Húr, Húrí, *n.* A virgin of Paradise; a black-eyed nymph. —*ká bachchá,* a very beautiful maiden or youth.

Hurmat, *n.* Respect; dignity; honour; chastity. —*rakhná, v.* to maintain one's honour or dignity. —*lená,* to defame one's honour or reputation.

Hurúf, *n. (Plur. of Harf, q. v.)* letters of alphabet.

Husn, *n.* Goodness; beauty; comeliness. —*ittifáq,* a lucky chance; a favourable opportunity. —*intizám,* wise management or administration. —*i-tadbír,* judicious or wise policy. —*i-za̲n̲n,* a good opinion; a favourable judgment.

Husúl, *n.* Gain; profit; benefit; advantage.

Huzúr, *n.* Present; also used as a term of respect in place of the 2nd personal pronoun. —*í, n.* presence.

Huzzár, *n. (Plur. of Házir, q.v.)*

I, i, is being used for the short vowel sound of Hindi (इ) and Urdu *zer* (ِ). In the second place, with the benefit of a forward slash on top of it, like (Í, í), is being applied to denote Hindi (ई) and Urdu (ی). In the third place, the letter 'I, i' with an apostrophe coma placed before it, we have used it to denote the specific Urdu sound of *ain* (ع). It can be used independently as vowel sound as well as tonal addition to the preceding consonant which is represented by (ि) symbol in Hindi and *zér* and (اِ) in Urdu.

I'adat, *n.* Visiting the sick. *—karná,* to enquire regarding the health (of one who is sick).

I'anat, *n.* Aid; help; assistance; favour; support.

Ibá, *n.* Denial; refusal; negation.

'Ibádat, *n.* Relgious service; divine worship; adoration; humble obedience. *—gáh, n.* place of divine worship; a temple; a mosque; a church.

'Ibárat, *n.* Speech; a word; phrase; expression, or passage (in a book); an explanation; style; mode of expression; composition. *—árái, n.* an ornamental style of writing. *púch—,* a loose style of writing.

Ibdá', *n.* Invention; production of something new.

Ib-hám, *n.* Confusion; doubt; uncertainty; suspicion; the thumb; the toe; *a.* covered; hidden; unknown.

Iblís, *n.* Satan; the devil.

Ibn, *n.* Son; child; offspring. *(used in compounds only in its nominative form),* as *ibn-ul-amír,* of noble birth. *—ul-ġaraz,* a selfish person. *—ul-waqt,* a timeserver.

Ibrár, *n.* Victory; triumph; success.

'Ibrat, *n.* Admonition; aversion warning; caution; *(met.)* fear. *—angez,* serving as an example or a warning; cautionary. *—pakaṛná, v.* to take warning (from).

Ibríq. *n.* An ewer.

Ibtidá, *n.* Beginning; commencement; birth; source; origin. *—se,* from the commencement; *ab initio. —men,* originally. *—í,* preliminary; introductory; primary.

Ibtilá, *n.* Suffering; affliction; misfortune.

Ibtisám, *n.* Smile; cheerfulness; gaiety.

Ichchhá, *a.* Desire; wish. (Also used as a prefix) *—patra,* n. A will. *—mrityú,* n. Death at will (A feat achieved by ancients in India, like Bhíshma in the

Mahábhárata). —*púrti,* n. Fulfilment of a desire.

Ichchhit, *a.* Desired one.

Ichchhuk, *a. One who desires; desirous of.*

'Íd, *n.* Festival; a feast day. —*uz-zuhá,* the festival of sacrifices, held on the 10th of the month *zul-hijjá,* in commemoration of Abraham's offering up his son Isaac. —*ul-fitr,* the festival of the breaking of the fast (after Ramzán).

Idhar, *adv.* This way; this side. —*udhar,* adv. Around here; hither-thither; nearby.

Idkḥál, *n.* (from *dakhl*) Insertion; entry; putting in.

Idráj, *n.* Folding up, or together; inclosing.

Idrák, *n.* Understanding; comprehension; perception; apprehension.

Ifáqá, *a.* Convalescence; restoration to health; recovery (from sickness).

'Iffat, *n.* Abstinence; continence; chastity; purity; virtue; modesty.

Iflás, *n.* Poverty; destitution; indigence.

Ifrát, *n.* Excess; superahundance; superfluity; plentifulness.

Ifshá, *n.* Disclosing divulging; publishing. —*i-ráz.* disclosure of a secret; the detection or discovery of a secret.

Iftár, *n.* Breaking a fast. —*í,* things suitable to be eaten when breaking a fast.

Iftikḥár, *n.* Glory; honour; distinction; elegance. —*náma,* a complimentary or cong-ratulatory letter.

Iftirá, *n.* Slander; calumny; false accusation; fiction.

Igar-digar, *a.* Disordered; disarranged; damaged; spoilt; injured.

Igmáz, *n.* Connivance; neglect; dis-imulating; coquetry. —*karná,* to connive at; to overlook.

Ih, *a.* Here; in this world; of this world. —*lílá,* mundane play; life in this world.

Ihánat, *n.* Contempt scorn; disdain; affront; insult.

Iháta, *n.* Enclosure; premises; precincts. —*gherná, v.* to enclose within a fence; to fix the limits or boundaries (of).

Ihlák, *n.* Destruction; ruin; perdition.

Ihsán, Ehsán, *n. (Plur. Ihsánát).* Beneficence; favour; kindness; obligation. —*farámosh, a.* ungrateful; forgetful or unmindful of favours received. —*mand,* grateful; thankful.

Ihtimál, *n.* Doubt; uncertainty; probability; supposition. *—karná, v.* to doubt; to be uncertain. *—an, adv.* probably; most likely. *—í,* doubtful; probably questionable; suspicious.

Ihtimám, *n.* Management; control; supervision; care; deligence. *—men̲ rakhná,* to entrust (to); to place in the care or charge (of).

Ihtirámí, *n.* Respect; reverence; difference; veneration.

Ihtiráz, *n.* Guarding (against); abstinence; forbearance; sub duing the passions and appetites.

Ihtisáb, *n.* Drawing up accounts; calculating; estimating; superintendence of police, and of the weights and measures used in a market.

Ihtishám, *n.* Pomp; grandeur; retinue, or train.

Ihtiyáj, *n. (Plur. Ihtiyá, át).* Necessity; need; occasion.

Ihtiyát, *n.* Caution; care; vigilance; circumspection. *—an; adv.* cautiously; prudently; circumspectly.

Ihzár, *n.* Causing to be present; securing the attendance of; summons.

Ijábat, *n.* Answering; granting a favourable reply; acceptance approval; sanction; assent.

Íjád, *n.* Creation; production invention.

Ijálat, *n.* Speed; haste; anticipation.

Ijára, *n.* Leasing a house, land, &c.; contract; tent; hire; monopoly. *—dár,* a tenant; a lessee; a proprietor.

Ijázat, *n.* Permission; authority; sanction; license; passport *—k̲hwáh, n.* a petitioner; an applicant; a supplicant.

Ijlás, *n.* Sitting of a court of justice.

Ijmá', *n.* Assembly; council; throng; crowd; amount.

Ijmál, *n.* Collecting; epitome; summary. *—í,* abridged; brief.

Ijrá, *n.* Circulation; issuing; carrying into effect; putting in execution.

Ijtináb, *n.* Keeping aloof from; avoiding; shunning; refraining or abstaining (from); selfdenial; self-control; moderation.

'Ijz, *n.* Humiliation; powerlessness; submission.

Ik, *a.* One. Frequently used as a prefix, i.e. *—áí,* a. Unit. *—tárá,* n. A mono-stringed musical instrument, often used by street singers and bards to keep time-scales. *—allá,* a. Alone, solitary. *—ká-dukká,* adv. A person or two; not crowded; not rushed off one's feet.

Ikaṭṭhá, *a.* United; collected; gathered together; in the aggregate; simultaneously. *—karná,* to amass; to accumulate; to convene.

Íkh, Ukh, *n.* Sugar-cane.

Ikḥfá, *n.* Concealment; rendering invisible.

Ikḥlás, *n.* Purity; sincere affection; loyalty; agility; familiarity. *—joṛná,* to form an intimate friendship. *—rakhná.* to entertain a sincere regard (for).

Ikḥráj, *n. (Plur. Ikḥráját).* Expulsion; ejection; exclusion; expenditure.

Ikḥtiláf, *n.* Disagreement; difference; dissension; breach or rupture (of friendship). *—ráe,* difference or divergence of opinion.

Ikḥtilát, *n.* Mixture; union; intercourse; intimacy; friendship; ardent affection.

Ikḥtirá', *n.* Invention; discovery; devising; contriving.

Ikḥtisár, *n.* Abridgement; curtailment; summary. *—karná, v.* to abbreiviate; to abridge; (in *Arith.)* to reduce; to simplify.

Ikḥtitám, *n.* End; termination; conclusion; fulfilment.

Ikḥtiyár, *n.* Choice; option; control; right; privilege; jurisdiction. *—í-jáiz,* lawful; power right or authority. *—karná v.* to choose; to adopt; to resort to. *—í,* optional; descretionary.

Ikḥwán, Ikḥwat, *n.* Brothers; friends. *—uz-zamán,* a contemporary.

Iklautá, *a.* The only one; unique; single.

Ikrám, *n.* Generosity; benevolence; liberality; respect.

Iksír, Aksír, *n.* The philosopher's stone; a powder or mixture believed by the alchemists to possess the power of transmuting the baser metals into gold; an elixir; a sovereign remedy; a remedy to cure every disease.

Iláchí, Iláechí, *n.* Cardamoms, *dáná,* n. seeds of cardamoms.

Iláh, *n.* God. *—í,* pertaining to God; divine *—íyát,* divinity; theology.

'Iláj, *n.* Remedy; medicine; cure; medical treatment. *—pizír,* curable. *lá—,* incurable; irremediable.

'Iláqa, *n.* Connection; affinity; concern; reference; relevancy; intercourse; a dependency; a district. *—dár, a.* connected; related; *n.* a relative; a dependant; one who undertakes to pay the rates or taxes of a district, village, &c.*—se báhar,* beyond the limits or jurisdiction (of). —*men*, within the limits or jurisdiction of.

Ilhád, *n.* Idolatory; religious unbelief; scepticism; atheism.

Ilhám, *n.* Inspiration; divine revelation.

Ilhán, *n. (Plur. of Lahan).* Notes (in music); tune; airs; a musical voice.

Ilháq, *n.* Annexation; addition; union.

'Illat, *n.* Disease: sickness; malady; weakness; infirmity; a vice; defeat; rubbish; an excuse; pretext; an accusation. —*i-gái,* final cause. —*lagáná, v.* to rebuke; to censure; to accuse. —*a-ma'lúl,* cause to affect.

'Ilm, *n.* Knowledge; learning; science. —*i, a.* scientific; literary. —*i-adab,* literature; the science of morality; etiquette. —*i-akhláq,* moral philosophy. —*i-bahs, n.* the science of logic. —*i-riyází,* mathematics. —*i-kalám, n.* eloquence. —*i-kímiya,* chemistry; alchemy.

Ilmás, *n.* A diamond; adamant.

Iltifát, *n.* Regard; attention; respect; politeness; kindness.

Iltijá, Iltimás, *n.* Petition request; application.

Iltiwá, *n.* Deferring; putting off; postponing; delaying. —*jang,* a truce.

Ilzám, *n.* Blame; reproach; censure; accusation; impeachment, —*lagáná,* —*dená,* to accuse; to charge; to indict; to impeach.

Imá, *n.* Sign; type; wink.

Imád, *n.* Pillar; column; support; proper confidence; reliance.

Imám, *n.* Spiritual leader, or guide; priest; patriarch.

Ímán, *n.* Religion; creed; faith; belief; conscience; probity; integrity; trustworthiness. —*dárí, n.* honesty; fidelity. —*láná,* to be converted. —*men khalal yá farq áná* to prove faithless or dishonest.

Imárat, *n.* A building; a house; a structure; edifice;

Imdád, *n.* [from *'Madad'*] assistance; aid; help; succour; gift; endowment.

Imkán, *n.* Possibility; power.

Imlá, *n.* Orthography; correct writing; dictation.

Imlí, *n.* The tamarind tree or its fruit.

Imrat, Amrit, *a.* Ambrosia; nectar; water or elixir of life.

Imratí, *n.* A syrupy sweetmeat, greatly cherished by North Indians.

Imroz, *n.* To-day. *—farda,* to-day or to-morrow.

Imtihán, *n.* Trial; test; experiment; temptation. *—dená, v.* to be a candidate at; or to pass an examination. *—karná,* to subject to a test or an examination.

Imtiyáz, *n.* Separation; distinction; discernment; judgment.

In'ám, *n.* Reward; gift; prize.

'Ináyat, *n. (Plur. 'Ináyát).* Favour; gift; bounty; assistance; support; patronage; kindness. *—rakhná, v.* to regard with kindness or favour.

Inch, *n.* a measurement of length, 1/12th of a foot; 1/36th of a yard; 2.5 times the length of a centimetre.

Índhan, *n.* Fuel; twigs gathered in the wild for burning; any other form of material used for burning to obtain energy or heat

Indívar, *n.* Blue lotus.

Indra, *n.* The leader of gods-in-heaven, a deity credited with causing rains. *—lok;* n. The dwelling place of Indra. *—jál,* n. magic; illusion. *—ká akhárá,* n. The court of Indra wherein beautiful damsels entertain the prĕsent assemply.

Indradhanush, *n.* The Rainbow. [Since Indra is credited with causing rains, this phenomenon of the rainy season is also named after him].

Indráyan, *n.* A wild gourd; a beautiful fruit having a bitter taste.

Indrí, Indriya, *n.* Organs in the human body (There are operational organs like hands, feet, skin etc. and there are sensory organs like nose for smell, tongue for taste, ears for hearing, eyes for seeting, etc.) Control and management —commonly thought of as 'conquest over the senses' —of these organs is considered a worthy pursuit in Hindu way of thinking.

Indu, *n.* Moon; also a proper name given to boys as well as girls.

Infisál, *n.* Separation; adjustment; settlement or decision of a law suit.

Ingit, *n.* Signal; pointing out; indication; method of conveying information.

Inglish, *n.* The English language; a person from England; (commonly) any European.

Inglistán, *n.* a. country known as England; the land of the English people.

Inhidám, *n.* Demolition; destruction; annihilation; extinction; extermination.

Injan, Injin, *n.* Engine; the main power unit, providing locomotion in any vehicle or piece of machinery. *—iar,* n. Engineer; one who runs, makes and mends the engine.

Injíl, *n.* The Evangel; the Gospel; the New Testament of the Bible.

Injoriya, *n.* Moonlight.

Inkár, *n.* Denial; refusal; negstion; rejection.

Inkisáf, *n.* Solar eclipse.

Inkisár, Inkisárí, *n.* Humility; meekness submissiveness; abjectness; despondency.

Inqiláb, *n.* Revolution; alteration; subversion.

Inqisám, *n.* Division; distribution; sharing.

Insáf, *n.* Justice; equity; impartial decision; equitable settlement. *—talab, a.* demanding justice or redress; a supplicant for justice. *—karná, v.* to administer justice.

Insán, *n.* A man; a human being; a mortal; mankind; the human race.

Inshá, *n.* Writing; composition; mode of expression. *—pardází, n.* composition; elegance of style in writing.

Ins-o-jinn, *n.* Human beings and spirits.

Ínt, Íntá, *n.* Brick; *deṛh íṇṭ ki masjid chunaná,* to have one's own way; to follow one's own way; to follow one's own inclination, or to adopt one's own plan, however limited or half-baked may it be.

Intihá, *n.* Conclusion termination; end.

Intikháb, *n.* Choice; selection; extract.

Intiqál, *n.* Transporting; trans-mission; removal; death; decease. *—az daryá-e-shor,* transportation beyond the sea. *—náma,* (in *Law*), deed of transfer or conveyance of the effects of a deceased person to his legal heirs or assigns.

Intiqám, *n.* Vengeance; revenge; reprisal; retaliation. *—lená,* to wreak or exact vengeance; to take revenge.

Intisáb, *n.* Relationship; lineage; pedigree; descent.

Intishár, *n.* Disorder; conclusion; irregularity; explanation.

Intizám, *n.* Arrangement; order; system; regulation; management; scheme. *—rakhná, v.* to maintain discipline; to keep order. *—karná, v.* to make arrangements; to set in order.

Intizár, Intizárí, *n.* Waiting; expecting *—dekhná,* to be on the look out. —*khin̲chná,* to look out (for); to wait anxiously.

Iqbál, *n.* Prosperity; auspices; confession; assent. —*í-da'wa,* admission of a claim. —*man̲dí, n.* good fortune; prosperity.

Iqrár, *n.* Confession; avoid; agreement; acknowledgement; bond.

Iqtibás, *n.* Acquiring; procuring; gaining begging; quotation.

Iqtidár, *n.* Authority; control; ability; dignity.

Iqtisám, *n.* Division; partition.

Irádá, *n.* Desire; inclination; aim; object; plan; purport. *irádse se,* with the design or intention (of); with a view (to).

Irádatan, *adv.* Willingly; deliberately; intentionally.

'Iráz, *n.* Avoiding; shunning; fleeing, or escaping from.

Ird-gird, *a.* Nearby; not too far; in close vicinity; in.

'Irfá, 'Irfán, *n.* Knowledge; science; philosophy; wisdom.

Írkhá, *n.* Envy; jealousy; spite; antagonism; rivalry; malice. *[Also see Írshyá]*

Irsál, Arsál, *n.* Despatch; transmission; remittance. —*náma,* invoice of goods, rents, &c., despatched or forwarded.

Irshád, *n.* Order; command; instruction; injunction; directions; will.

Írshyá, *n.* Jealousy. —*lu,* a. One who is jealous.*[Also see Írshyá]*

Irtikáb, *n.* Engaging in an enterprise or adventure; conamission of a sin; crime or offence.

Is, *dem, pro.* This. —*par,* for this reason; hence; hereupon. —*hálat men,* inasmuch as; under these circumstances. —*shart se,* on this condition or stipulation. —*g̣araz se,* with this purpose or intention; with this end or object in view.

Ísá, *n.* Jesus Christ.

Ísabgol, *n.* Seeds of a medicnal plant; plantago ovate; Psyllium.

Ísái, *a.* One who follows the path of Jesus *(Ísá).*

Isbát, *n.* Confirmation; proof; corroboration; certain kn̲owledge.

Ísh, *n.* Lord God, Master.

Íshál, *n.* Purging; diarrhoea.

Ishára, *n.* Sign; beck; nod; wink; hint; mark; trace.

'Ishq, *n.* Excessive love; ardent affection; passion.

'Ishrat, *n.* Pleasure; enjoyment; mirth.

Isht̤, *a.* Desired; wished for; prayed for; cherished

Ishtihá, *n.* Hunger; appetite; desire; craving.

Ishtihár, *n.* Proclamation; public announcement or notice; fame; celebrity. *—dená,* to proclaim; to notify.

Ishtiqáq, *n.* Derivation; root; etymology.

Ishtiyáq, *n.* Ardent desire; strong inclination; longing; craving; love.

Íshvar, *n.* God. *—á* n. Blasphemy; *—nishṭh,* a. A theist. *—na kare,* prov. God forbid.

Isláh, *n.* Correction; rectification; adjustment. *—pizír, a.* curable; remediable.

Islám, *n.* Mohamedan religion. *—í,* a follower of the Mahomedan religion. (literally the word means 'Peace')

Ism, *n.* Naṃe; a noun. *—bá musammá,* a name suitably denoting the qualities of the person or thing named. *—nawisí,* a muster-roll; sharíf, good name.

Ispát, *n.* Steel.

Isráf, *n.* Expenditure; expenses; disbursements; extravagance; waste.

Isrár, *n.* Secret; secrecy; mystery; influence of an evil spirit.

Istádá, *n.* Erected; set up; standing.

Istarí, *n.* A smoothing-iron.

Isthir, Sthir, *a.* Standing; stagnant; fixed; firm; immovable.

Isti'adád, *n.* Preparation; proficiency; capability; mental ability or capacity; talents.

Isti'afá, *n.* Resignation (of employment).

Isti'árá, *n.* Requesting a loan; borrowing; a metaphor; a figure of speech.

Istidu'á, *n.* Asking; entreating; beseeching; supplication; demand; claim.

Istifrág, *n.* Vomiting; belching; rejecting.

Istigásá, *n.* Requesting help; demanding justice; a complaint; a plaint.

Istihqáq, *n.* Claiming as a right or due; demanding justice or redress; claim; demand; title; merit. *—i-tarka bilá-wasiyat,* title to the property of a person who dies intestate. *—i-taqdím-i-kharídári,* right of pre-emption. *—í-infikák-i-rahn,* equity of redemption of a mortgage.

Istiláh, *n.* Idiom; phrase; technical term. *—í, a.* idiomatical; technical.

Istimrárí, *n.* Continuous; perpetual; ceaseless; permanent. *—paṭṭa,* a lease in perpetuity. *—paṭṭedár,* one holding a lease or tenure at a fixed rent.

Istiqbál, *n.* Encountering; meeting; reception or welcome of a visitor; the future; the future tense.

Istiqlál, *n.* Steadiness; resoluteness; perseverance.

Istiráhat, *n.* Rest; repose; cease.

Istrí, Stri, *n.* A woman; a wife.

Ísví, *a.* Year of the lord; Calendrical marking of the year based on the birthdate of Jesus.

Itar, *a.* The other; different; beyond.

Itaráná, *v.* To assume an air of exaltation; to behave in a conceited manner.

Itaráz, Aitaráz, *n.* Opposition; objection; criticism; fault-finding.

Itavár, *n.* Sunday [also known as **Ravivár.**

Iṭhláná, *v.* To act affectedly; to gain airs; to assume a swaggering posture.

Iti, *n.* The epilogue.

Iti-siddham, *v.* Q.E.D; whatever we set out to prove, has been proved.

Itihás, *n.* History; story of what has gone by. *—kár,* n. Historian(s). *—vettá,* n. A scholar of history. *—agya,* n. Historiographer.

Iti-vritta, *n.* A narrative (which has logical conclusion; a story).

Itihás, *n.* History; record; stories; fables.

Itmínán, *n.* Rest; repose; peace; contentment; confidence; trust; security.

Itná, *a.* This much; so much; this far. *—sá,* a. This bit; so little.

'Itr, *n.* Perfume; odour; fragrance; essence. *—khínchná,* to extract an essence.

Ittifáq, *n. (Plur. Ittifáqát).* Agreement; accord; union; friendship; consent; combination; affair; chance; opportunity. *—an,* accidentally; by chance. *—í,* accidental; casual; unexpected.

Ittilá, *n.* Information; knowledge; notice. Proclamation; announcement; cognizance; acquaintance.

Ittyádi, *adv.* Etc. etc. (literally) This and others.

'Iwaz, Ewaz, *n.* Compensation; reward; *prop.* instead; for. *—í,* a substitute; *a. locum tenens;* a proxy.

Ízá, *n.* Pain; affliction; distress; trouble; oppression.

Izár, *n.* Drawers; trousers; *pyjámás.*

Izárband, Ijárband, *n.* A fastener; a string, or lace used as a belt to hold Indian pyjamas, or trousers up.

Izdiwáj, *n.* Marriage; wedding; nuptials.

Izhár, *n.* Manifestation; show; declaration; statement; deposition; evidence.

Izdihám, *n.* Throng; concourse; crowd; multitude.

Iztiráb, Iztirábí, *n.* Anxiety; perturbation; restlessness; impatience.

'Izzat, *n.* Honour; respect; reputation; glory.

जब प्यार की गुफ़्तगू होने लगी,
आप से तुम, तुम से तू होने लगी।

Jab pyár kî gufta-gû honé lagî,
Âp sé tum, tum sé tû hone lagî.

(Familiarity breeds contempt.)

J, j, is a consonant sound and is used to denote the Hindi letter (ज) and Urdu letter (ج). Diluted to half value, this letter will be followed by a semi-vowel like *'Y, y'* and double value, it will precede vowels like *a,e,i,o,u.* Some times an aspirated consonant sound will be obtained by adding *'h'* to it to indicate Hindi (झ) and Urdu (جھ).

Já, *n.* Place; locality; spot; site. *—ba—, adv.* everywhere; here and there. *be—, a.* wrong; improper.

Jab, *abv.* When, on condition that-, provided that-.

Jabaran, Jabardastí, *adv.* By force; under duress; by exertion of pressure; against one's will or desire.

Jabbár, *n.* Omnipotent; an oppressor.

Jábar, *n.* Force; compulsion; coercion; oppression. *—an, adv.* compulsorily; forcibly. *—an-o-qahran,* willingly or unwillingly.

Jabín, *n.* The forehead; the brows.

Jabṛá, *n.* Jaw, (proverbially) the vice-grip.

Jadíd, *n.* New; recent; modern.

Jádú, *n.* Magic; witchcraft; the black art; sorcery. *—gar,* margician; wizard; sorcerer. *fem. —garní,* a sorceress; a witch.

Jáe, *n.* A place; locality; spot. *—namáz, n.* a carpet; mat or cloth on which prayers are offered up. *—ibádat,* a. place of worship.

Jáedád, Jáydád, *n.* Property, wealth; possessions; belongings.

Jáephal, *n.* Nutmeg.

Jáe-zarúr, *n.* Latrine; privy; water-closet.

Jafá, *n.* Violence; tyranny; oppression; high-handedness. *—kash,* hardworking; dillgent.

Jáfrí, *n.* Lattice work; bamboo screen.

Jag, *n.* The world; the universe; the earth. *—pálak,* the Supreme Being. *—trátá,* the Saviour or Redeemer of the world. *—mohan,* a. One who enchants the world (an attribute of God in incarnation).

Jagadambá, *n.* The mother of the world; the mother goddess; another name for goddess Durgá.

Jagadísh, *n.* A proper name; (literally) Lord of the world (*Sanskrit;* Jagat+Ísh).

Jagah, *n.* Place; locality; quarter; room; stead; vacancy; appointment. *—dená, v.* to confer or bestow a post or an appointment (upon); to provide room or space for; to lodge.

Jagáná, *v.* To waken; to rouse from sleep.

Jágaraṇ, *n.* A wake, ritual all-night prayer-meetings.

Jagarátá, *n.* An all-night hymn singing in praise of *Durgá,* also known as *Vaishno Deví,* the mother goddess who's mount is a lion.

Jágarúk, *a.* (Literally) One who is awake, alert, aware. *—tá,* State of alertness, awareness.

Jagat, *n.* The world; the spread of beings; surrounding environment.

Jaghaṇya, *a.* Awful; abominable; detestable; heinous.

Jágir *n.* Land and villages given by government.

Jagmagáná, *v.* Glistening; glittering; shining brightly; sparkling.

Jágná, *v.* To wake up from sleep; to remain awake; to recover one's senses.

Jágrit, *a.* Awake; aware; not-asleep.

Jágriti, *n.* Awakening; awareness.

Jáh, *n.* Ránk. *—o-jalál,* pomp and splendour.

Jahálat, *n.* Ignorance; limited knowledge; letharges.

Jahán, *n.* The world. *—áfrín, n.* Creator of the world. *—dída,* a great traveller; a man of the world, i.e., an experienced person. *—panáh, n.* protector of the world; his majesty; your majesty.

Jahán̲, *adv.* Where; wherever; wheresoever. *—tak ho sake,* as far as possible.

Jahannam, Jahannum, *n.* Hell. *—í,* hellish.

Jaház, *n.* Ship; vessel. *Hawái—*n. aeroplane. *—í, n.* Sailor.

Jahez, Dahez, Dahej, *n.* A dowry; a bride's portion.

Jáhil, *n.* Boorish; illiterate; uncivil.

Jai, *n.* Victory; triumph; cōnquest.*—jai kar karna, v.* to shout in honour of triumph or victory; to rejoice.*—málá,* necklace or garland of victory; laurels.

Jaisá, *adv.* As; such as; according as. *—cháhiye,* as it ought to be; properly. *jaise taise,* somehow or other. *jaise ko taisá,* tit for tat.

Jáiz, *a.* Permissible; lawful; right; good or valid (in Law); authorised.

Jakaṛná, *v.* To tighten; to tie tightly; to fasten.

Jal, *n.* Water; aqua. *—ad,* n. Clud. *—kar,* a. Water tax. *—vibhág,* n.

Water Department. —*kúp,* n. Water-well. —*char,* —*chárí,* n. Aquatic animals, ones who live and breathe in water. —*thal ek honá,* v. state of deluge; heavy flooding. —*sená,* n. Navy. —*yán,* n. A ship. —*yátrá,* n. A sea voyage. —*praváh,* a. Flow of water. —*prapát,* n. Water fall. —*magna,* a. Submerged. —*srot,* n. Source of water. —*hín,* a. Without water; dry. —*nidhi,* n. Ocean. —*pán,* n. A light meal.

Ja'l, *n.* A fabrication; counterfeit; a forgery. —*í,* fabricated; forged. —*sáz, n.* a counterfeiter; a forger.

Jál, *n.* Net; snare; trellis-work; magic; illusion; deception. —*siláhi, n.* armour; coat-of-mail. —*men láná,* to ensnare; to entrap.

Jalná, *v.* To burn; to feel jealous; to get angry about.

Jálá, Jálí, *n.* A cobweb; a spider's web; a net; a cataract (in the eye); a large jar.

Jalá, *a.* Burnt; scorched. —*bhuná,* enraged; angry. —*tan,* choleric.

Jalál, *n.* Glory; eminence; dignity; power. —*í, a.* glorious; illustrious; majestic.

Jalan, *n.* Burning; heat; inflammation; passion; rage; envy; hatred.

Jaláná, *v.* To burn; to ignite; to kindle; to inflame; to irritate; to excite jealousy; to grieve; to smart (pain).

Jalá-watan, *n.* Leaving one's country; emigration; banishment; exile.

Jald, *a.* Swift; quick; fleet; active; nimble; hasty; rash. —*mizáj,* hasty; sharp-tempered.

Jaldí, *n.* Quickness; speed; celerity; impetuosity. —*karná,* to hasten; to hurry; to be rash or impetuous.

Jalíl, *a.* Glorious; illustrious. —*ul-qadr,* high in dignity or rank.

Jalís, *n.* A companion; an associate; a chum; a close friend.

Jallád, *n.* An executioner; a hangman; a cruel person

Jalná, *v.* To burn; to be burnt; to be lighted, ignited, or kindled; to be inflamed or consumed (with passion).

Jalsá, *n.* A public event; public meeting; celebration.

Jalús, *n.* A procession; public display; mostly a large group of people marching together and shouting slogans, some times to protest and some times to celebrate.

Jal-Váyu, *n.* (Literally: Air and

water, referring to-) Climate. Living-conditions.

Jalwá, *n.* Conspiouousness; lutsre; splendour. —*gar,* splendid; conspicuous.

Jám, *n.* A cup; a drinking-vessel; a goblet; a wine-glass; a mirror. —*i-labrez, n.* a bumper; a glass or cup filled to the brim (with wine).

Jámá, *n.* A garment; a robe; a gown; a vest. —*se báhar honá, v.* to be in an ungovernable rage. —*men̲ phúle na samáná,* to be transported (with joy).

Jama', *n.* A collection; an assembly; a congregation; an accumulation; amount; sum; total; the plural number; capital principal; stock; the credit side of an account. v. *ki—bandi karná.* v. to assess the revenue (of). —*kharch miláná,* v. to balance accounts. —*kharch navís,* a book-keeper; an accountant. —*wásil báqí,* payments and arrears.

Jamá'at, *n.* A meeting; an assembly; a society.

Jamádar, *n.* A petty ranking minion in the army; the scavenger, street-cleaner etc. in Indian civilian life.

Jamái, Jámátá, Jan̲wái, *n.* A son-in-law.

Jamál, *n.* Beauty; grace; elegance; prettiness. —*í, n.* lovable; amiable.

Jáman, *n.* Rennet; a live sour culture used to coagulate milk into yoghurt (commonly known in India as curd).

Jamáo, *n.* A crowd; multitude; a collection.

Jamát, *n.* Class; grouping; organisation.

Jambhái, *n.* Yawn. —*lená,* v. To Yawn.

Jambúr, Jamúr, *n.* A tool; a swivel; a pair of pliers.

Jam-ghaṭ, *n.* Crowd, gathering.

Jámi', *a.* All; universal; whole; entire. —*masjid,* the principal mosque.

Jamikand, Jimikand, *n.* A yam; a kind of vegetable.

Jamílá, *a.* Beautiful; pretty; graceful.

Jamná, *v.* To freeze; to coagulate; to stabilise in a location or position.

Jámun, *n.* A purple, summer fruit, a black plum. —*i,* a. a colour of this fruit.

Jamuná, Yamuná, *n.* Proper name of the river that flows alongside Delhi, Agra and then merges with Ganga at Allahabad (*Pryágráj).*

Jamuháí [See *Jambháí*].

Jan, *n.* People; public; folk. —*ándolan,* n. a popular movement. —*gaṇaná,* n. Census. —*jágaraṇ,* n. Renaissance; popular awakening. —*Jívan,* n. Public life. —*tantra,* n. Democracy. —*tantríya,* a. Democratic. —*dhan,* n. Public-wealth. —*priya,* a. Popular amongst the people. —*mat,* n. Public opinion. —*mat sangrah,* n. A referendum. —*man/mánas,* n. public mind; populat thinking. —*ranjan,* n. Gratification of public; pleasing to the people. —*shakti,* n. man-power; collective public strength. —*shruti,* n. tradition; common-knowledge. —*sankhyá,* n. Population. —*samáj,* n. Community. —*samudáy,* n. A gathered crowd. —*sádháran,* n. Common man. —*sevá,* n. Public service; social work. —*hit,* n. Public interest. —*hín,* a. Desolate; deserted; no-one around; lonely.

Ján. *n.* Life; soul; spirit; mind; animation; the essence (of a thing). —*áfrín,* Creator of life (an epithet of the Deity). —*báz,* *a.* risking life; *n.* a daring or intrepid man. —*ba haqq taslím karná,* to die; to expire. —*bakḥshí,* forgiveness; pardon (of a capital crime). —*ba-lab,* at the point of death. —*par khelná,* to put (one's) life at stake. —*fisháni,* hard labour; extreme diligence. —*kandaní,* the agonies of death. —*nisárí,* readiness to sacrifice (one's life for another).

Ján, *n.* Knowledge; apprehension; information —*bújh kar,* knowingly; wittingly; intentionally. —*pahchán,* an acquaintance; a familiar friend.

Jáná, *v.* To go; to depart; to pass away; to die. *já parná,* to chance; to befall. *já lená,* to catch up; to outstrip. *jáne dená,* to overlook; to excuse, to let go.

Janáb, *n.* A place to which one repairs for refuge, &c., (hence a title of respect in addressing a great man); your honour; your majesty. —*i'álí.* Exalted Sir. —*i-man,* My Dear sir.

Janak, *n.* Father; name of a just and wise king in Indian antiquity; father of princess Sítá who later married lord Rám of Ayodhyá.

Jánakí, *n.* (Literally) born of Janak, a second name for princess Sítá.

Janam, Janm, *n.* Birth; origin; life. —*bhúm, n.* birthplace; fatherland. —*din,* birthday. —*kundalí,* a short horoscope; a genealogical table.

Jánaná, *v.* To know; to find out; to discover.

Janani, *n.* Mother; one who gives birth.

Jánashín, *n.* A successor; an inheritor.

Janárdan, *n.* A proper name; an epithet of Lord vishnu; the ruler of mankind.

Janatá, *n.* People; public; common folk.

Janázá, *n.* A bier, particularly one with a corpse laid upon it; a funeral.

Jáṉch, *n.* Trial; test; experiment; examination; proof; estimate; valuation.

Jang, *n.* War; warfare; hostilities; battle; contest. —*í, n.* warrior; combatant; *a.* war-like; martial. *jangi-jaház,* a man-of-war; a warship.

Jaṉgal, *n.* A dense wood or forest; unfertile or uncultivated land. —*í,* barbarous; uncivilised; wild.

Jaṉgalá, *n.* Parting; palisade; fence; railing; grating.

Janghá, Jáṉgh, *n.* Thigh.

Jánib, *adv.* In the direction of; towards.

Jaṉjál, *n.* Riddle; complexity; maze; problem. *Ji ká,* Deep-rooted irritant.

Jannat, *n.* Paradise; heaven.

Jaṉtar, Yaṉtra, *n.* Machine; engine; appliance; instrument; a charm. —*mantr,* jugglery; conjuring.

Jaṉtrí, *n.* An almanac; a calendar.

Jaṉtu, *n.* A living being, (literally) one who is born.

Janúb, *n.* South. —*í, a.* southern. —*ki taraf, adv.* southward.

Janún, Junún, *a.* Madness; lunacy; insanity.

Jánwar, *n.* Animal; beast.

Jap, *n.* A silent repetition of a name or *mantra* as an act of devotion and dedication.

Japná, *v.* The act of reciting a name or *mantra.*

Jap-málá, *n.* A rosary of beads.

Jaṛ, *a.* Root; stationary; insert; stupid; senseless. —*tá,* n. stupidity; inertness.

Jar-jar, *a.* Falling to pieces; torn to shreds; worn out; crumbling.

Jará, *n.* Old age. —*grast,* a. A victim of old age.

Jáṛá, *n.* Winter; the cold season; cold weather. —*chaṛhná, v.* to suffer from ague.

Jaṛáú, *a.* Embedded with, embellished with; studed with (gems etc.).

Jaṛáwal, *n.* Winter clothing; warm clothing, worn during winter.

Jaṛí, *n.* Herb; medicinal vegetation. —*jarí búti,* n. Herbal medicine obtained from roots and folliage of plants.

Jári, *a.* Flowing; running; current; permanent; prevalent; rife; continuous; in force (a law).

Jaríb, *n.* A surveyor's measuring chain (of 20 gathás or 66 feet). —*kash,* a surveyor.

Jarráh, *n.* A surgeon. —*í, n.* surgery; *a.* surgical.

Jashn, *n.* Feast; banquet; festival; jubilee; rejoicing.

Jasím, *a.* Fat; stout; corpulent.

Jast,Jastá, *n.* Zinc. *rúp*—, *n.* pewter.

Jásús, *n.* A spy; an emissary.

Jatan, Yatn, *n.* Exertion; endeavour; perseverance; diligence; carefulness; remedy effort.

Ját, Játi, *n.* Caste; class grouping; specie.

Ját, *n.* A proper name for an ethnic group of people who dwell in Western India.

Jatan, Yatn, *n.* Effort, attempt. —*karná,* v. To make an effort; to attempt.

Jaṭil, *a.* Difficult; complex; involved; elaborate.

Jathá, Yathá, *adv.* As; in the manner of; like; according to.

Jaṭká, *adj.* Inarticulate; naïve; rough; simplistic.

Jatthá, *n.* A group; a gang; a band of people; a flock; a mass.

Jau, *n.* Barley; a barley-corn (a measure); a jot; an atom; a tittle.

Jauhar, *n.* Amazing deeds; astonishing performance; outstanding skill. —*dikháná,* v. To perform to the amazement of.

Jauharí, *n.* A jeweller; a gem dealer; one who has a true understanding and appreciation of gems and precious metals.

Jauz, *n.* Nutmeg.

Jawá, *n.* A clove of garlic, &c.

Jawáb, *n.* Answer; reply; response. —*deh,* a. Answerable; accountable. —*dehí,* n. Accountability; responsibility to answer for ones deeds and actions.

Jawán, *n.* A young man or woman; youth; an adult; a soldier; *a.* young; youthful; in the prime of life; in the flower of youth; vigorous. —*í,* youth; age of discretion.

Jáwatri, *n.* Mace (a kind of spice); the bark of nutmeg.

Jay, Jai, *n.* Victory; triumph. *—kí jay,* exc. A victory salute; a triumphal shout, mostly offered to the public leaders, venerables and deities. *—jay kár,* sloganeering.

Jayanti, *n.* Day or date marking some one's date of birth, a kind of jubilee celebration (hence *rajat jayanti:* silver jubilee, or *swarn jayanti: golden* jubilee, etc.).

Jazb, *adv.* Absorption. *—karná,* v. To absorb. *—honá,* v. To be absorbed.

Jazbá, *n.* A sentiment; a feeling; sensitivity.

Jázib, *a.* Attractive; enticing; absorbing. *—kágaz,* blotting paper. *quwat-i-jázibá,* power of attraction.

Jazírá, *v.* An island. *—numá,* peninsula.

Jeb, *n.* Pocket. *—i-kháss,* privy purse. *—katará,* pick-pocket.

Jel, *n. (Corr. from the English).* A jail; prison. *—kháne ká dároga, n.* a jailor.

Jeṭh, *n.* Husband's elder brother.

Jeṭhá, *n.* Elder; senior.

Jhabba, In. A tassel.

Jhabṛá, *a.* Long-haired; shaggy.

Jháen-Jháen, *n.* A fierce rustle of strong-billowing wind; a sound produced by violent flow of air through a desolate landscape.—*karná,* v. To altercate; to initiate a fierce argument for no apparent reason.

Jhagaṛná, *v.* To dispute; to argue; to wrangle.

Jhág, *n.* Foam; lather; scum; froth.

Jhaggá, *n.* A baggy top; a loose wearing gown.

Jhagṛá, *n.* Dispute; quarrel squable; brawl. *—lú, a.* Quarrelsome; disputatious; irascible.

Jhajhar, *n.* A goblet; a pitcher.

Jhakh, *n.* Craze; whim; an obsession.

Jhakkaṛ, *n.* A storm; a tempest; a cyclone; a hurricane; a tornado.

Jhakkí, *a.* Crazy; whimsical; whacky; a pratt. *—í pan,* The state of craziness, &c.

Jhalak, *n.* Glitter; sparkle; brightness; brilliance; radiance.

Jhálar, *n.* A frill; a fringe; an ornamental border.

Jhámp, *n.* A weather-shed; a covering.*—ná,* v. To cover; to shade.

Jhanak, *n.* Ringing; jingling; tinkling.

Jhanak-bái, *n.* Acute rheumatism.

Jhanḍá, *n.* A flag; a banner; a standard; an ensign; flagstaff. *—par charhánâ,* to defame; to stigmatize; to render infamous.

Jhánjh, *n.* Cymbals.

Jhanjhat, *n.* Perplexity; wrangling; disputing. *—í, —iyá, a.* quarrelsome; contentious; difficult; complicated; *n.* a wrangler; a quarrelsome person.

Jhankár, *n.* Bushes; shrubs; underwood.

Jhánk, Jhánkí, *n.* A glimpse; a scene from the life of-, a sneak preview. *Tánk—,* adv. Taking a peep at; spying on.

Jhánkí, *n.* A glimpse; a shot; a trailor of bigger sequence.

Jhánkná, *v.* To take a peep at; to glance at; to cursorily look at.

Jhánsá, *n.* Deceit; deception; double-dealing; cheating.

Jhánṭ, *n.* Body of hair around genitals; pubes; public hair.

Jhapaṭ, Jhapaṭṭá, *n.* A leap: a bound; a spring; a jump; a pounce; a snatch; a snap.

Jhapkí, *a.* Drowsiness; sleepiness; inclination for sleep.

Jháṛ, *n.* A bush; a shrub; brambles; brushwood; a lustre or chandelier.

Jháṛá, *n.* A search; a stool. *—dená, v.* to submit to a search.

Jháṛan, *n.* A duster; a coarse cloth for cleaning furniture, &c.

Jhaṛí, *n.* Continuous rain; showers of rain.

Jháṛí, Jháṛná, *v.* To sweep; to brush; to dust. *jháṛ-pachháṛ kar dekhná, v.* to examine minutely. *—phúnkná, v.* to exercise; to recite charms or spells over (a sick person).

Jháṛú, *n.* A broom; a comet. *—dená, v.* to sweep. *—phir jáná, v.* make a clean sweep of everything in a house.

Jhaṭká, *n.* a shock; a jolt; a concussion. *—dená,* v. To give a shock, or jolt etc. [The term is also used for a method of slaughtering the animals whereby the creature is beheaded in a single swipe of the weapon].

Jhíl, *n.* A lake.

Jhillí, *n.* A thin skin; a membrane; the caul.

Jhilmil, *n.* Shimmer; twinkle; flickering (lightwise). *—áná,* v. To shimmer, &c.

Jhilmílí, *n.* A shutter; a venetian blind.

Jhíngá, *n.* A shrimp; a prawn.

Jhíngur, *n.* A cricket.

Jhiṛak, *n.* Reprimand; snub; scolding. *—ná,* v. To reprimand, to rebuke.

Jhísí, *n.* Drizzling rain, in small drops.

Jhoká, *a.* Breeze; a current; puff, gust, or blast, (of wind); shock; swinging; a fraudulent turn (of scales in weighing).

Jhol, *n.* Rumple; pucker; crease; brood; birth; litter; soup.

Jholá, Jholí, *n.* A bag; a wallet; a knapsack; palsy; paralysis

Jhon̲pṛá, Jhon̲pṛí *n.* A hut; a cottage.

Jhukáná, *v.* To bend downwards; to tilt; to incline; to nod; to bow.

Jhukná, *v.* To bend; to bow; to succumb; to surrender; to accept a rival's argument or proposition; to lean; to tilt; to yield; to show respect for.

Jhukáo, Jhukáwaṭ, *n.* The state of being bent down-wards; bend; curve; inclination.

Jhúlá, *n.* A swing; a cradle.

Jhuláná, *v.* To swing; to push a swing; to rock a cradle; to dangle.

Jhulsáná, *v.* To cause scorching; to cause scalding; To cause searing.

Jhulasná, *n.* To sear; to scorch; to scald.

Jhúmná, *v.* To shake; to sway from side to side; to stagger; to roll; to nod (through sleep); to lower (as clouds).

Jhun̲ḍ, *n.* A multitude; a crowd; a flock; a swarm. *—ke—,* dense crowds; whole flocks.

Jhun̲jhaláhaṭ, *n.* Irritation; anger; rage.

Jhun̲jhláná, *v.* To be irritable; to rage; to be peevish.

Jhunjhuaná, *n.* Rattle; Baby's simple toy that makes a rattling noise.

Jhurrí, *n.* A wrinkle; a pucker; a fold.

Jhúṭh, *n.* Leavings of food; (*jhúthá, jhúthan);* defilement; a lie; a falsehood *—pakarná, v.* to detect a lie.

Jhúṭhá, *a.* Lying; insincere; counterfeit; base (as coin). *—dastáwez,* a false or forged document.

Jhuṭpuṭá, *n.* Dawn; day-break; twilight.

Jí, *n.* soul; spirit; mind; disposition. *—á jáná,* v. To have the heart set on. *—bhar áná,* adv. To be emotionally overwhelmed. *—se utar jáná,* adv. To forfeit the good opinion of.

Jíban, *n.* Life; life span; living style.

Jíbh, *n.* (*Sanskrit* **Jihwá**). Tongue. *—lap-lapáná,* v. to hang one's tongue out to grab what one has been hankering after.

Jigar, *n.* The heart; the liver; vital organs; courage; kernel; *(mst.)* a son. *—figár,* heart-broken; stricken with grief. *—ká ṭukṛá, lakḥt-i-jigar*—(lit.). a piece of the liver or heart; *(met.)* a son.

Jihád, *n.* A religious war.

Jihálat, *n.* Ignorance; lack of knowledge; barbarism.

Jiláná, *v.* To restore to life; to reanimate.

Jild, *n.* The skin; hide; binding of a book; a volume. *sáz a* book-binder, *amráz-i-jildí,* skin disease.

Jíná, *v.* To live; to exist.

Jinn, *n.* A genie; a male fairy. (*Fem. pari*) a spirit; a demon.

Jins, *n.* Kind; species; class; gender; stock; good; commodities; grain crop. *abnás—,* those of the same class.

Jism, *n.* The body (with the limbs and members). *—ání, a.* corporeal; carnal; material; pertaining to body.

Jít, *n.* Winning; victory; gain; advantage; success.

Jítá, *n.* Over and above; extra; alive; living; existent.

Jite jí, *a.* In the lifetime; living.

Jítná, *v.* To win; to conquer; to subdue; to succeed.

Jitná, *adv.* So much; so many; as much as.

Jíváṇu, *n.* Germs, microbes; small creatures.

Jíw, *n.* Life; soul; animal; living creature.

Jíwiká, *n.* Pension; livelibood; means of subsistence.

Jo, *Rel. pro.* Who; which; what. *—ho so ho,* no matter what may happen.

Joban, Yauvan, *n.* Youth; young age.

Joddha, Yoddhá, *n.* A warrior; combatant; a hero.

Jog, Yog, *n.* (Literally) The sum total; Yoga.

Jogí, *a.* A yogi; one who has renounced the world and worldly pursuits; (Commonly) any saffron-clad mendicant.

Jogiyá, *a.* An alternative name for saffron colour; also a common name for the saffron robes worn by yogis.

Jokhon, Jokhim, *n.* adversity; danger; risk; hazard. *—ká kám,* a perilous undertaking. *—men* *parná,* to run a risk; to incur danger.

Joláhá, Juláha, *n.* A weaver.

Jon̲k, *n.* A leech.

Joṛ, *n.* Joint; junction; union; soldering; combination; total; a pir; a match. *—toṛ,* device; contrivance.

Joṛá, *n.* A pair; a couple; a suit (of clothes).

Joṛí, *n.* A pair of horses; a carriage and pair. *—han̲káná,* to drive a pair of horses.

Joṛná, *v.* To join; to mend; to bind; to stitch together; to set (a bone); to add together.

Joṛú, *n.* Wife. *—ká, Bhái,* brother-in-law (wife's brother).

Josh, *n.* Boiling; effervescence; excitement; passion; zeal; enthusiasm. *—í-kḥún,* maternal or paternal affection. *—men̲ áná,* to boil; to overcome with emotion.

Joshí, Jotshí, Jyotishí, *n.* Astrologer; predictor of future events by calculating the position of heavenly bodies.

Joshán̲da, *n.* A decoction *(káṛhá)* of herbs.

Jot, Jyoti, *n.* A sunbeam; light; the faculty of seeing; brilliancy.

Jot, *n.* A cord that fastens the yoke of a plough, &c., cultivation; the rent paid by a cultivatorl cultivated land. *—á, n.* cultivator; an agriculturist; farmer.

Jotish, Jyotish, *n.* Astronomy; astrology.

Júá, *n.* Gambling; playing with dice, cards, &c.; gaming. *—báz,—rí, n.* a gambler; a gamester.

Juálá, Jwála, *n.* Flame; blaze; fire; heat; passion.*—mukhí, n.* a volcano.

Juár, Jawár *n.* Millet; maize.

Judá, *a.* Separate; apart; absent; away. *—í, n.* separation; parting; discord; estrangement. *—í ḍálná, —í ḍál dená, v.* to effect a separation; to sow discord.

Jug, Yug, *n.* An era; a long span of time; a named period in history. *—ánt,* a. End of an era, &c.

Jugálí, *n.* Chewing the cud; something that farm animals do when they are not actually grazing.

Jugat, Yukti, *n.* Method, means; mode; dexterity; skill.

Jugnún̲, *n.* A firefly a; glow-worm.

Jugráfiyá, *n.* Geography; location.

Júhí, *n.* Name of a flower; Jasmine; name of the fragrance drawn from or based on this flower.

Juláb, *n.* (As medicine) Purgative; (as ailment) Dysentery, or loose motions.

Jum'a, *n.* Friday.

Jum'arát, *n.* Movement; motion; vibration; agitation.

Jumlá, *n.* Whole; total; aggregate; sentence; clause. *fi'l,—adv.* in short; on the whole.

Jú<u>n</u>, *n.* A louse; anything as small as a louse; a jot; a tittle. *—kí chál chálná, v.* to creep along; to move very slowly.

Jún, Yoni, *n.* Birth; transmigration; the body (as the casket of the soul).

Júná, *n.* Old; worn out; decayed.

Junaiyá, *n.* Moonlight; the moon.

Junún, *n.* Madness; lunacy; insanity.

Júṛá, *n.* A trees of hair; a tuft of hair; often a woman's hair-do in the shape of a big bun on top, at the back of the head.

Jurm, *n.* A crime; an offence; a misdeameanour; a sin. *—í-sangin, n.* a capital offence.

Jurmáná, *n.* Fine; forfeit; penalty*—karná, v.* to inflict a fine. *—mu'áf karná,* to remit a penalty or fine.

Juráb, *n.* A sock; a stocking.

Jussá, *n.* The body; the physical form or figure.

Jútá, Jútí, *n.* A shoe; a slipper;

Juva, Yuva, *a.* Young; youthful; juvenile; in the prime of youth.

Juz, *n.* Part; portion; particle; ingredient; a section of a book (consisting of 8 leaves). *—dan, n.* a portfolio.

Juzám, *n.* Leprosy. *—khána, n.* a lazaretto*—í,* a leper.

Jwálá, *n.* Fire; heat; (proverbially) hunger. *—Jwálá-mukhí,* n. A Volcano; A fierce fire.

Jwala<u>n</u>t, *a.* Shining; sparkling (example of-); glaring.

Jwar, *n.* Fever

Jyámiti, *n.* Geometry; linear layout; [also known as *Rekhá-ganit*].

Jyotish, *n.* Astrology; the science of prediction based on the relative position of the heavenly bodies.

कर्म-भानु ही बुद्धि-कमल विकसित करता है।

Karma bhánu hi buddhi-kamal vikasit kartá hai.

(Only deeds will help the lotus of wisdom bloom.)

K, k, denotes (क) in Hindi and (ک) in Urdu. By adding an '*h*' to it we also obtain an aspirated sound equal to (ख) in Hindi and (کھ) in Urdu. Some times this letter, when dotted at the bottom, is used to indicate the Arabic-Urdu sound of (ق) and the imported Hindi sound (क़). With a dot (.) underneath 'K, k' and Suffix 'h' we obtain the Arabo-Persian-Urdu sound of (خ) and the imported Hindi sound of (ख़).

Ká, *pre.* Of; pertaining or belonging to; regarding or concerning; made or composed of.

Kab, *adv.* When; since. —*kab,* sometimes; now and then. —*tak o talak,* up to what time? how long? till when?—*se,* since when? from what date?

Ka'bá, *n.* The square temple at Mecca.

Kabáb, *n.* Roasted meat; roast; small pieces of meat roasted or boiled on a skewer or spike.

Kabáṛ, *n.* Rubbish; refuse; old broken articles, as furniture, &c. —*í,* a dealer in old and broken furniture; rag & bone men.

Kabar, Kabr, *n.* Grave; burial place.

Kabhí, *adv.* At some time or other; ever. —*kabhí,* occasionally. —*nahín,* never.

Kabír, *a.* Great; eminent; illustrious; *n.* the name of a renowned and revered Hindi saint poet who eloquently spoke of universal values and one-ness of God and the foolishness of ritual. —*pan̲thí,* followers of Kabír.

Kabúl, *adj.* Acceptance; consent; agreement; recognition; sanction; acknowledgement; admission; approval; choice.—*karná,* v. To accept; to approve; to confess.

Kabúliyat, *n.* Acceptance; a document of acceptance.

Kabútar, *n.* Pigeon. —*í,* n. Female pigeion. —*bází,* n. Pigeon fancying; pigeon racing. —*kḥáná,* n. A pigeon House.

Kabútarbáz, *n.* Pigeon-fancier —í, n. Hobby of Pigeon-fancying.

Kachehrí, *n.* A court of justice; a tribunal; a public office. —*barkḥwást karná,* to close, adjourn or dismiss a court. —*lagáná,* to collect a crowd; to raise a tumult or uproar.

Kachchhap, Kachhuá, Kachhwá, *n.* A turtle; tortoise; a hard-skinned, slow-moving functionary who is unaffected by demands being made and expediency being urged upon [*proverbially called*—] bureaucrats and comfortable politicians.

Kachchá, Kachchí, *a.* Green; unripe; raw; uncooked; imperfect; inexperienced; built of mud (a house). *—dil.* timid *—'umr,* childhood; infancy, immaturity.

Kachchhá/Kachchhí *n.* underpants; underwear

Kachhár, *n.* Moist or marshy land lying at the side of a river.

Kachiyáná, *v.* to be afraid; to shrink or recoil in fear.

Kachrá, *n.* Rubbish; refuse; dirt; filth.

Kachúmar, *n.* pulp; resultant of crushing; pulverised material; finely chopped up vegetables or foodstuffs; thoroughly pounded stuff. *—nikálná,* v. To render something unserviceable, or a person seriously hurt by giving either of them a thorough crushing or pounding.

Kad, *a.* Height (of people) from head-to-toe. *—dávar,* a. One rather tall; well-built.

Kadáchit, *adv.* Perhaps; probably; if (with a negative).

Kadálí, *n.* A plantain tree.

Kadápi, *adv.* Sometimes; occasionally; never; on no account; not in any case.

Kaddú, *n.* A pumpkin; a gourd *(sitáphal, kubrá) —dána,* the name of a disease; tapeworms.

Kadlí-phal, *n.* Banana.

Kadúrat, Kudúrat, *n.* Malice; ill-will; dust.

Kaf, *n.* Froth; foam; spittle; saliva; phlegm; scum or slime. *—gír.* spoon; perforated ladle.

Kafáf, *n.* Competency; pittance; daily bread; *a.* adequate; equal to.

Kafálat, *n.* Surety; security; a pledge; bail. *—bín-nafs,* personal bail or security. *—náma* bail-bond.

Kafan, *n.* Winding-sheet; shroud; grave clothes. *—dafan,* funeral; burial.

Kafára, *n.* Atonement; expiration; penitence.

Kaff, *n.* Hand; palm of the hand. *—i-afsos malná,* to wring the hands in grief. *—i-pá,* sole of the foot.

Káfí, *a.* Enough; sufficient. *—o-wáfí,* ample; enough and to spare.

Kafíl, *n.* A security; a surety.

Káfir, *a.* Infidel; impious; ungodly; an infidel; a non-believer; an atheist.

Kafsh, *n.* A slipper; a sandal; a shoe. *—gar* or*-doz;* a shoemaker or dealer in shoes.

Káfúr, *n.* Camphor. *—honá, v.* to disappear; to abscond. *—í shama',* a camphor candle.

Kág, Kágá, *n.* Crow; considered rather unclean bird and Hindus try their best to keep them out of the kitchen and dining areas.

Kagár, *n.* Edge; margin; side; border; cornice.

Kágáz, *n. (Plur. Kágazát).* Paper; writing or document; account; newspaper. *—sarkárí,* government paper; a government currency or promissory note; a registered or stamped paper.

Kahálat, *n.* Indolence; laziness; idleness.

Kahán, *adv.* Where; whither. *—ká—,* from where to where. *—par,* to what degree or extent; to what place.

Kahání, *n.* A story; a fable; a tale.

Kaháwat, *n.* Proverb; saying; adage.

Káhil, *a.* Lax; idle; lazy; negligent. *—wujúd, n.* an indolent fellow.

Kahín, *adv.* Somewhere; some place; wherever; perhaps. *—nahín,* adv. Nowhere; never anywhere. *Jahán—* wherever possible.

Kahláná, *v.* To send a message; to intimate; to inform.

Kahná, *v.* To say; to speak to utter; to declare; to state; to bid; to order; to call; to name. *—mánná,* to render obedience; to obey.

Kai, *n.* How many? *—bár?,* How many times?

Kaí, *n.* Many; multiples. *—prakar,* Many types. *—tarike,* Many ways, &c.

Káí, *n.* Green scum or slime on stagnant water; moss; rust. *logná,* to become rusty.

Kaifiyat, *n.* Quality; nature; state; news; story. *—i-kámil,* full particulars. *—talab karná,* to request information. *—likhná, v.* to draw up a report or schedule.

Káinát, *n.* All existent things; the world; or universe.

Kainchí, *n.* A pair of scissors; clippers. *—márná,* v. To swipe; to cleverly take possession of what is not yours. *—sí zubán,* a. A sharp tongue; one given to angry outbursts.

Kainchul, Kainchulí, *n.* The slough, or cast skin of a snake.

Kaisá, *adv.* Like what? how? what sort or manner? in what way? by what means? why? *—hí,* of whatsoever sort; howsoever. *kaise ho,* how are you? *—hi ho,* whatever may it be.

Káj, Kárj, Kárya, *n.* Work; business; occupation.

Kajak, *n.* A goad for an elephant.

Kájal, *n.* Soot; lamp-black.

Kajáwá, *n.* A camel's saddle.

Kák, [see kág].

Káká, *n.* A paternal uncle. *kákí, n.* a paternal aunt.

Kakol, *n.* A raven.

Kakoṛná, *v.* To scratch; to scrape.

Kakrez, *n.* Dark purple colour.

Kakṛí, *n.* A kind of cucumber.

Kákul, *n.* A curl; ringlet. *kákulen chhorná,* to let one's curls hang down.

Kal, *n.* &. *adv.* The morrow; tomorrow; yesterday. —*ká ádmí, (lit.)* a man of yesterday; a man recently risen into prominence; an upstart.

Kal, *n.* A machine, or a part of one; a trimmer or hammer (of a gun) an instrument.

Kal, *n.* Peace; tranquillity; rest. —*bekal honá,* to be disturbed or disquieted; to be uneasy.

Kál, *n.* Time; (in *Gram.*) tense; season; period; death; destiny. —*chakra,* an epoch.

Kál, Akál, *n.* Famine; dearth; calamity; *a.* bad; inauspicious; calamitous. —*ká tútá yá márá,* famine-stricken, destitute.

Kalá, *n.* Art; skill; expertise; mastery; ability. —*kár,* a. Artist. —*kriti,* n. A work of art. —*kaushal,* a. Artistic skill. —*midhi,* a. Artistic; appreciator of arts. —*báz,* a. Acrobat. —*bází,* n. Acrobatics. —*vilásí,* a. A dilettante.

Kálá, *a.* Black; dark; awful; terrible; *n.* the black and most venomous species of cobra. —*páni, (lit.)* black water; transportation across the sea; deportation, *múnh kálá karná, (lit.)* to blacken the face (of); to disgrace or dishonour. *káli pílí áṉkheṉ karná,* to assume an angry and menacing look.

Kalábázi, *n.* Tumbling; making somersault.

Kalág, *n.* A crow; a raven.

Kalah, *n.* Strife; contention; quarrel.

Kaláí, *n.* The wrist; forearm.

Kálak, Kálikh, *n.* Blackness. —*ká ṭiká lagáná,* to stain; to stigmatize; to disgrace.

Kalál, Kalár, Kalwár, *n.* A distiller; a dealer in spirits, liquors; a caste among Hindus. —*khána, kalárí,* a liquor-shop; a distillery.

Kalám, *n.* Word; speech; a complete sentence.

Kalaṉk, *n.* Spot; stain; reproach; disgrace; guilt; calumny.

—lagáná, to calumniate; to bring disgrace (upon); to brand with infamy *—i, —it,* a. disgraced; reduced to ignominy; calumniated.

Kalapná, *v.* To grieve; to lament; to be in distress or pain.

Kalas, Kalash, *n.* A pinnacle; a dome.

Kalejá, *n.* The (human) liver; the vital organs; *(met.)* courage; magnanimity or noble-mindedness. *—uchhalná, v.* to be over joyed; to be transported with joy. *—par sánp lotná,* to be affected with envy or jealousy. *—phatná,* to be touched with pity or compassion. *—thandá karná, v.* to haze one's wishes fulfilled; to obtain ease. *—se lagá rakhná,* to love very dearly; to feel intense affection for.

Kalejí, *n.* The liver of an animal as part of meatarian food.

Kaleu, Kalewa, *n.* Breakfast.

Kalgí, *n.* A spire or pinnacle above a dome; crest; comb (or a cock); cockscomb (a flower).

Kalí, *n.* A bud or blossom; new feather of a bird; quicklime; a kind of tobacco pipe or huqqa. *—ká chúná,* limestone.

Kálí, *n.* (Literally means black) A female goddess, rather fierce and ferocious in countenance, worshipped in Nepal and Bengal in a big way. Highwaymen —*Thugs* —of medievel period were her worshippers.

Kalíd, *n.* A key; an index.

Kalijug, Kaliyug, *n.* The fourth Hindu era; the present or iron age.

Kalím, *n.* One who addresses another. *—Ullah,* one who speaks to God; an epithet of Moses.

Kálimá, *n.* Blackness; blemish; darkness.

Kalima, *n.* Mohammedan confession of faith. *—paṛháná, v.* to convert one to Mohammedanism. *—paṛhná,* to repent; the Muslim confession of faith.

Káliyá, *n.* (On the street, just a word for teasing, means —black.) In *Bhágavat-Purán,* this is a mammoth aquatic python with many heads who tried to terrorise the poor cowherds of Dwárká and was vanquished by Krishna, their friend and protector.

Kalláná, *v.* To smart or tingle, as skin when any pungent substance is applied to it.

Kalol, Kilol, *n.* Play; sport; frolic; enjoyment.

Kalpaná, *n.* Assumption; fiction; imagination; supposition. *—chitra,* n. Imaginary picture. —lok, n. World of fantasy; imaginary world. —pravan, adj.

Creative; master of imagination. —prasút, adj. Fictional; imaginary. —*shakti,* n. Capacity to imagine; faculty of imagination. —*taru/ vriksha,* n. A mythical tree that grants all boons to those who sit under itand pray to. —*tít,* adj. Beyond imagination; unimaginable.

Kalpáná, *v.* To grieve; to inflict sorrow or grief.

Kálpanik, *adj.* Fictitious; imaginary; untrue.

Kalsá, Kalsí, *n.* An earthen or metal water-pot.

Kalush, *n.* Impurity; sin; stain; turbidity. —*it,* adj. Impure; profane; sinful; turbid; wicket.

Kalyán, *n.* Welfare; prosperity; happiness.

Kam, *a.* Deficient; less; small; *adv.* seldom; rarely; (*used as first member of comps. to express lack,* negation or inferiority), *e.g., —'aqlí,* want or lack of understanding —*himmat,* spiritless. —*tarín,* least; meanest.

Kám, H. *n.* Action; work; duty; employment; affair; service; use; need (of). —*chaláú,* serving as a make-shift. —*chor,* a shirker; a lazy workman —*se kám rakhná,* to mind one's own business.

Kám, H. *n.* Inclination; desire; passion; love of pleasure; the Hindu Cupid, or god of love.

Kamáí, *n.* Earnings; gain; profits; work.

Kamal, *n.* The lotus.

Kamál, *n.* Wonder; perfection; termination; excellence; *a.* complete; entire; perfect; extreme. —*dikháná,* to display wonderful powers. —*rakhná,* to be master of. —*karná* to work wonders.

Kamán, *n.* A bow; a spring; an arch; a curve; command. *a.* curved; arched; bowed; flexible *(used in comp.),* as; —*abrú,* arched eye-brows. —*charháná, v.* to bend a bow.

Kamáná, *v.* To earn; to work; to perform; to save; to cure or curry leather; to clean (a latrine, &c.); to prepare land for cultivation; to diminish.

Kama<u>n</u>ḍal, *n.* A vessel, sometimes the only vessel carried and used by mendicants—*sádhús* —of India.

Kamar, *n.* The waist; the loins. —*band, n.* waisthand; girdle.

Kamí, *a.* Dearth; scarcity; loss. —*bashí,* fluctuation.

Kámil, *a.* Complete; perfect; skilled.

Kamíná, *a.* Low; mean; base.

Kammal, Kambal, *n.* A blanket.

Ká<u>m</u>pná, *v.* To tremble; to shake.

Kaṇ, *n.* Minute bit; particle; grain.

Kán, *n.* Ear(s); heed; regard. *—dená,* v. to pay attention to. *—bharná,* v. to back-bite; to incite some one against. *—men kahná,* v. to whisper; to say things discretely; to have a quite word. *—á phúsí,* n. Whisper; gossip.

Káṇá, *a.* Blind of one eye.

Kanak, *n.* Gold.

Kanárá, Kinárá, *n.* Seashore; river-bank; side; edge; margin.

Ká<u>n</u>ch, *n.* Glass; crystal.

Ka<u>n</u>chan, *n.* Gold.

Ka<u>n</u>chukí, *n.* Brassiere; bikini type of feminine wear

Ka<u>n</u>ḍá, *n.* Dried cow-dung cakes used as fuel.

Ka<u>n</u>dhá, Ká<u>n</u>dhá, *n.* Shoulder; assistance; help; a hand in carrying someone's coffin.

Ka<u>n</u>gál, Ka<u>n</u>glá, *a.* Poor; destitute; friendless. *—kar dená,* to reduce to poverty; to impoverish.

Ka<u>n</u>ghá, *n.* a small, wooden comb, specially used by Sikhs, a part of their five sacred symbols.

Ka<u>n</u>ghí, *n.* A Comb.

Ka<u>n</u>gúra, *n.* A pinnacle; a spire; a turret.

Kanjús, *n.* A miser; a niggard; *a.* miserly; niggardly.

Ka<u>n</u>kar, *n.* Gravel; limestone.

Ká<u>n</u>sá, *n.* Bell-metal; bronze.

Ká<u>n</u>ṭá, *n.* A thorn; spur; the tongue of a balance; a fishbone; fishing-hook; fork; quill (of a porcupine). *—khaṭakná, v.* to imbue with envy and hatred, *ká<u>n</u>ṭe boná, v.* to sow troubles or dissensions.

Ka<u>n</u>ṭh, *n.* Windpipe; throat; voice. *—karná, v.* to learn by heart. *—málá,* scrofula *(Khanázír).*

Kanṭhá, Kanṭhí, *n.* A necklace or rosary (of gold or silver beads, pearls, crystal, flowers, &c.).

Ka<u>n</u>wal, *n.* The lotus.

Kannyá, *n.* A young girl; a maiden; a virgin; a daughter.

Kapál, *n.* The forehead; the brows; the skull; the upper portion of the head; destiny; fate. *—khulná, v.* to have a favourable turn of fortune.

Kapás, *n.* The cotton plant.

Kapaṭ, *n.* Deceit; fraud; ruse; guile; trickery; hyprocrisy. *—karná,* v. To indulge in deceit, &c. *—chál,* a. Deceitful moves, &c. *—í, a.* insincere; treacherous; scheming.

Kapáṭ, *n.* Door, two panes of a door. *—kholná,* v. To open the door.

Kapkapí, *n.* Shivering; trembling; quaking.

Kapol, *n.* The cheek.

Kapṛá, *n.* Cloth; chothing; garments.

Kapúr, *n.* Camphor.

Kár, P. *n.* Business; affair; work. *—ámad,* useful; serviceable. *—ázmúda,* experienced. *—pardáz,* a manager; an agent.

Kar, *n.* The hand; tax; tribute. *—lagáná,* to levy a tax.

Kaṛá, *a.* Hard; stiff; tough; harsh; cruel. *n.* a bracelet; a ring of any kind.

Kaṛáh, *n.* A cauldron; a large metal Vak. *—í,* a frying-pan.

Karáhná, *v.* To sigh; to groan; to moan.

Kárak, *n. (in Gram.)* Case.

Kaṛak, *n.* A crash; a crack; a clap of thunder.

Kaṛáká, *n.* Crash made by breaking anything; a fast. *—guzarná,* to abstain from all food owing to poverty. *kaṛáke ká jáṛá,* intense or piercing cold.

Karam, *a.* Kindness; generosity; benevolence.

Karámat, *n. (Plur. Karámát).* Munificence; liberality; dignity; reverence; a miracle; miraculous or supernatural power.

Karámát, *n.* A miraculous deed; magical performance; feat.

Káraṇ, *n.* Cause; reason; means; motive.

Karárá, *a.* Hard; firm; rigid; sturdy; crisp; well-baked (bread, &c.).

Kaṛchhí, *n.* A big, serving spoon. A scoop.

Karchhul, *n.* An iron spoon or ladle.

Káṛhá, *n.* A decoction; a medicinal extract.

Kaṛháí, *n.* Embroidery; needlework.

Káṛhná, *v.* To draw (a sword, &c.); to draw (a sketch, &c.); to delineate; to paint; to work or embroider flowers on cloth; to discover; to detect; to infer.

Karíb, *adv.* Near; close; intimate. *—an,* adv. Almost, approximately; nearly.

Kárígar, *n.* An artisan; a mechanic; an artificer.

Karím, *a.* Gracious; compassionate; bountiful; an epithet of the Deity. *—í, n.* bounty; mercy; grace.

Káristání, *n.* Cleverness; doing; work.

Kárkháná, *n.* Workshop; manufactory. *—dár, n.* a manufacture; the manager of a workshop.

Karm-chárí/ Karam-chárí, *n.* Worker; workman; employee.

Karmaṭh, *adj.* Hard-working.

Karma-hín, *adj.* Unlucky; unfortunate; one with no divine credit for good deeds performed in the past.

Karṇ *v.* To do; to make; to perform; to execute; to act; to cause to be or become; to take (in marriage).

Karoṛ, *a.* Ten millions. *—patí,* possessor of a *karoṛ* (of rupees).

Kartá, Kartár, *n.* Maker; Creator; do-ev; one who is guilty of—.

Kartab, *n.* Deed; action; business; the palm of the hand.

Karwaṭ, *n.* The position of lying or sleeping on one side; turning from one side to the other. *karwaṭen̲ badalná,* or*—lená,* to change sides; to joint the opposite (or enemy's) side; to act traitorously.

Karz, *n.* Debt; loan; obligation. *—chukáná,* v. To pay off the debt; to discharge one's obligation(s). *—dár,* adj. Debtor; obligated; beholden; one owing.

Kasak, *n.* Pain; agony; ache; affliction. *—miṭáná, —nikálná,* to relieve pain.

Kasaná, *v.* To cause to try; to prove; to cause to tighten; to spoil (as milk, &c.) by standing.

Kasar, *n.* Fraction; loss; shortage damage; indigestation. *—nikálná,* to take revenge; to exact vengeance.

Kasauṭí, *n.* Touchstone; test; proof; criterion.

Kashf, *n.* An opening; manifestation; revealation; divine inspiration; solution; performance of a miracle.

Kashídá, *n.* A kind of needlework; *a.* sullen; sulky; reserved.

Kashish, *n.* Attraction; enticement; gravitation; trial; difficulty; writing; penmanship. *—i-saql, n.* the law of gravity.

Kashṭ, *n.* Distress; affliction; destitution; poverty; violence.

Kásht, *n.* Cultivation; agriculture. *—kár, n.* farmer; cultivator.

Kasná, *v.* To tighten; to fasten; to test; to assay. *kamar—,* to gird up the loins; to prepare; to resolve.

Kasrat, *n.* Excess; abundance; surplus; exercise; usage. *—i-ráe,* majority of votes.

Kastúrí, *n.* Musk.

Káṭ, *n.* A cut; incision; execution; wound; piece; fraction; plot (of ground); sharpness. *—chhán̲t,* cutting and clipping; curatiling. *—kabálá,* a conditional engagement.

Kaṭahal, *a.* Jack fruit; a vegetable.

Kaṭahrá, *n.* Railing; palisade; a wooden cage.

Kaṭár, *n.* (*Dim.* Katárí). A dagger; a dirk. —*márná,* to stab with a dagger; a dirk. —*márná,* to stab with a dagger.

Katarná, *v.* To clip; to cut; to pare.

Katarní, *n.* Scissors; clippers.

Káṭh, *n.* Wood; timber; the stocks. —*ká kiṛá,* woodworm.

Kathá, *n.* A tale; an anecdote; a story; a sermon; readings from sacred books.

Káṭhi, *n.* A saddle; body; scabbard.

Kaṭhin, *a.* Difficult; hard; harsh; abstruse.

Kaṭhor, *adj.* Hard; tough; strong; sturdy, relentless; callous; rigid. —*hridaya,* adj. Hard-hearted; cruel; uncaring. —*tá,* n. Cruelty; severity; callousness; hardship; unrelenting.

Kátib, *n.* A clerk; a writer; a scribe; a calligrapher.

Kaṭílá, *n.* Thorny; charming; land overgrown with brushwood. *katíli án̲kh,* captivating eyes.

Kátná, *v.* To spin.

Káṭná, *v.* To cut; to clip; to slash; to sever; to dissect; to saw; to mow; to reap; to bite; to sting; to corrode; to erode; to cancel; to pass (time); to deduct; to earn (money).

Kaṭní, *n.* Harvest time.

Kaṭorá, *n.* A cup; a bowl.

Kaun, *pro.* Who? —*sá,* which? what?

Kaun̲d, Kaun̲dh, *n.* Lightning.

Kaur, *n.* Morsel; mouthful.

Kauṛí, *n.* A shell (sometimes used as coin); money. —*kauṛí ko tan̲g honá,* to be reduced to poverty. —*kauṛí joṛná,* to save every farthing. —*ko na púchhná,* to esteem one at less than the value of one *cowrie, i.e.,* to regard one with great contempt.

Kausar, *n.* Name of a fountain in Paradise.

Kautuk, *n.* Festivity; a show; enojoyment; sport; trick; artifice.

Kauvá, Kawwá, *n.* A crow; a raven; an ugly-looking and rather raucous-sounding bird [Also see **Kág, Kágá**].

Kavi, *n.* Poet; lyricist. —*tá,* n. Poem; lyric. —*sangrah,* n. An anthology of poems. —*ráj,* n. An honorific title attached to highly qualified doctors (*Vaidyas*) in traditional Hindu system.

Kedár, *n.* meadow; a mountain; a proper Name amongst the Hindus, owing to one their places of pilgrimage, called *Kedárnáth,* located up in the Himalays, very close to chinese border.

Kehar, Keharí, *n.* A lion.

Kehi, *n.* A peacock.

Kekṛá, *n.* A crab; the sign of Cancer.

Kelá, *n.* A plantain; a banana.

Kes, Kesh, *n.* The hair of the head; a cock's comb.

Kesar, *n.* Saffron.

Kewal, *adv.* Only; solely; merely.

Ḳhabar, *n.* News; intelligence; information; report; care. *—dár, a.* well-informed; careful; cautious. *—dihindá,* an informant; a spy. *—gír, n.* protector; guardian.

Ḳhabásat, *n.* Badness; depravity.

Ḳhabbáz, *n.* A baker.

Ḳhabís, *a.* Wicked; depraved; *n.* an evil spirit.

Ḳhabt, *n.* Madness; lunacy; insanity.

Khachchar, *n.* A mule.

Khaḍḍ, *n.* A ditch; pot hole.

Khád, *n.* Dung; manure; fertiliser.

Khaḍḍá, Gaḍḍhá, *n.* A pit; a ditch; a hollow. *—khodaná,* v. To create pitfalls.

Khaddar, *n.* A coarse cotton cloth, usually made of hand-spun and hand-woven material.

Ḳhádim, *n. (Plur. Khádam or Khádimán);* (Fem. *Khádimá*). A servant; an attendant.

Ḳhadshá, *n.* Doubt; anxiety; uneasiness; fear.

Ḳhafá, *adv.* Angry; cross; unhappy; displeased.

Ḳhafif, *a.* Light; slight; trivial; of no weight or importance.

Ḳhafifá, *a.* Petty; trivial; trifling. 'ad*álat-i—,* a small cause court.

Khagahá, *n.* A rhinoceros.

Khagol, *n.* The vault or circle of the heavens; the firmament; solar-system.

Khagrás, *n.* A full eclipse of the sun (literally meaning that the demon *Ráhu* has made a morsel *—grás* —of the Sun and swallowed it whole).

Khái, S. *n.* A ditch; a most; a trench.

Ḳháif, *A. a.* Afraid; timorous; timid.

Khailá, *n.* A calf.

Khaile, *n.* Many; several; much; very.

Ḳhaimá, *n.* A tent; pavilion. *—gáh,* camping ground.

Ḳhainch, *n.* Pulling; bauling; drawing; scarcity; attraction. *khainchá-khainchí,* pulling and tugging; struggle; contention.

Ḳhair, *n.* Good; prosperity; *a.* and *adv.* good; well; best; no matter.

Ḳhairát, A. *n.* Good works; acts

of charity. —*khána, n.* almshouse. —*i, a.* Charitable.

Kḥairiyat, *n.* Safety; well-being; out of harm's way.

Kháj, *n.* The itch.

Khajálat, *n.* Modesty; bashfulness; shame.

Khajúr, *n.* The date palm and its fruit.

Kḥák, *n.* Dust; earth; ashes. —*uráná, v.* to make a stir or commotion. —Chh*ánaná, v. (lit.)* to sift or strain dust; *(met.)* to labour in vain.

Kḥáká, *n.* Plan; sketch; outline.

Khakhár, Khangár, *n.* Phlegm; discharge from the throat in case of cough; mucous.

Khákí, *adj.* Earthy; dusty; terrestrial; the colour of earth or dust; cloth of the colour of earth or dust (much used for making military and other uniforms).

Khal, *n.* A villain; a demon; a person of anti-social attitudes.

Khál, *n.* Skin; hide; bellows. —*khín̲chná,* to flay; to skin. —*upár, n.* A skinflint; one who is very exacting in money affairs.

Kḥálá, *n.* maternal aunt; mother's sister. —*ká ghar,* a. an easy undertaking; a place of utterly no-demands [Also see **Kḥálú**].

Kḥalá, *n.* Empty space; vacuum.

Kḥalaf, *n.* An beir; successor; son. —*us-sidq,* a legitimate or dutiful son. *ná—,* an undutiful son.

Kḥaláeq, *n. (Plur. of Khalq).* All created things; the creation; men; people.

Kḥalal, *n.* Break; interruption; disturbance; disorder; ruin; defect; harm. *an̲dáz, a.* giving rise to confusion; intermeddling; *n.* a disturber of the peace; a meddlesome person. —*damág,* mad; having the mental faculties deranged.

Khalás, *a.* Redeemed; delivered; liberated; saved; rescued; set free. —*í,* redemption; liberation; salvation; deliverance.

Kḥálí, *a.* Empty; vacant; hollow; unoccupied; blank; destitute (of); pure; sole; *adv.* alone; singly.

Kḥalíj, *n.* A gulf; bay; inlet.

Kḥalíl, *n.* A friend. —*ulláh,* a friend of God, *i.e.,* a God-fearing or pious person.

Kḥalíq, *a.* Good-natured; kindly disposed; polite; courteous.

Kḥáliq, *n.* The Creator.

Kḥális, *n.* Unadulterated; unalloyed; pure; unmixed; genuine.

Kḥalish, *n.* Pain; care; affliction; anxiety.

Khalíyán, *n.* A threshing-floor; a barn; granary.

Khalt, *n.* Mixture; medley; confused. *—malt,* mingled; confused; jumbled.

Ḳhálú, *n.* A maternal uncle; mother's brother; mother's sister's husband.

Khalwat, *n.* Loneliness; solitude; privacy.

Ḳham, *a.* Curved; bent; twisted; coiled; *n.* bent; curve; twist; curl; ringlet. *—thonkná,* to strike the hands against the arms when engaging in a wrestling contest; to challenge.

Ḳhám, *a.* Raw; unripe; green; immature; inexperienced. *—ámadaní,* gross income. *—ḳhyálí,* vain imaginations; crude ideas.

Khámá, *n.* A reed used as a pen.

Khambá, Khambhá, *n.* A pole, a piller, a post; a marker. *Bijlí ká—,* a. A lamp post, &c.

Ḳhamír, *n.* A souring agent, yeast; a fermenting additive. *—í rotí,* a. Leavened bread.

Ḳhamiyázá, *n.* Result; punishment; retribution.

Ḳhamir, *n.* Covering; concealing; fermenting; leavening; alcoholic or spirituous liquor; spirits.

Ḳhámosh, *a.* Silent; mute; speechless; dumb. *—í, n.* silence.

Ḳhams, Ḳhamasa, *a.* Five; a verse containing five lines.

Ḳhamyázá, *n.* Stretching; extending; yawning.

Ḳhán, *n.* Master; chief; chieftain; a title used by Pathán rulers. *—khánán,* lord of lords; prime minister.

Khán, Kán, *n.* Mine; quarry; abundance.

Khána, *v.* To eat; to drink; to consume; to take (as medicine, &c.); to embezzle; *(met.)* to feel; to endure; to harass or pester (as in *ján khána); n.* food; meal; victuals.

Ḳhána, *n.* Dwelling; abode; residence; house; compartment; receptacle; column (of a schedule, &c.). *—badosh, a.* having no fixed abode; nomadic; wandering from place to place; *n.* one who has no permanent and settled home; vagrant; gypsy. *—i-siyásat,* house of correction; reformatory; penetentiary. *—shumárí,* census.

Ḳhánagí, *a.* Domestic; relating to a house or family.

Ḳhánam, *n.* Lady; a woman of high rank; the title of the wife of a *Khán.*

Khaṉḍ, *n.* Piece; portion; part; chapter; share. *—khand karná* v. To smash to pieces.

Kháṉḍ, *n.* Sugar; sweet.

Khaṉḍahar, *n.* Ruins; a dilapidated building or structure; a run-down property. Leftovers of a monument.

Khandak, *n.* Ditch; moat; trench.

Khanḍan, *n.* Refutation; rebuttal; repudiation; denial. *—mandan,* v. reopudiation and vindication; to-ing and fro-ing of rumours, especially in politics and private scandals.

Kḥándán, *n.* Family; lineage. *—í, a.* ancestral; hereditary.

Khanḍit, *a.* Broken; shattered; disrupted; scattered.

Khangálná, *v.* To wash; to rinse; to scour.

Kḥanjar, *n.* A Dagger; a poniard.

Khanjaṛí, *n.* A basic music-making instrument, barely meant to provide some rhythm and time-keeping, favourite of streetsingers; timbrel.

Khánqá, Khánqáh, *n.* Convent; nunnery

Kḥánsámá, *n.* A domestic who has charge of household stores; a butler; a steward.

Khánsná, *a.* To cough.

Khánsí, *n.* A cough.

Khapná, *v.* To be destroyed; to be killed; to be consumed; to be exhausted.

Khappar, *n.* A cupel; a begging bowl; sometimes even the upturned hollow of a human, skull, used by *Aghorí* mendicants.

Khaprá, *n.* A tile.

Kḥáqán, *n.* Emperor; king.

Kḥar, *n.* An ass; a donkey; a stupid person; a fool. *—dimág,* a. One with the brains of an ass; a foolish being; a dullard.

Kḥár, *n.* Thorn; prickle; spine; fish-bone; thistle. *—pusht,* porcupine. *—khánú,* to feed envy or jealousy.

Khará, *a.* Correct; in true form; pure; genuine; upright; honest; straightforward; plainspeaking. *—ásámí,* a. good paymaster. *—utarná,* adv. To be proven true to expectations. *—khotá,* a. good-and-bad together; useful and useless together. *—sikká,* a. good coin; a good person.

Khaṛá, *a.* Erect; upright; perpendicular; steep; precipitous. *—khet,* standing crops.

Khárá, *a.* Salty; brackish; savoury.

Kḥaráb, *a.* Bad; evil; wicked; depraved; ruined; destroved; damaged; waste. *—át, (Plur. of Kḥarába),* ruins; desolate places; a tavern; an inn. *—í,* badness; depravity; evil; trouble.

Kharád, *n.* Lathe.

Kharaiṛa, *n.* A curry comb.

Kharal, *n.* A mortar. *—karná,* to pound in a mortar.

Ḳharásh, *n.* Irritation; itch; scratch; soarness in the throat.

Khaṛáún, *n.* Wooden slipper, worn by holymen in India everywhere and by the devotees inside sacred premises as leather-made footwear are considered unclean.

Ḳharbúzá, *n.* Musk-melon.

Ḳharch, Ḳharchá, *n.* Expenditure:

disbursements; re-sources; cost; debit side of an account. *—uṭhánā, v.* to undertake the expense of. *—honá,* to be spent; to be exhausted.

Khardal, *n.* Mustard seed.

Khaṛg, *n.* Sword; sabre; cutlass; scimitar.

Kharhá, *n.* A hare; a rabbit.

Kháṛí, *n.* Creek; bay; inlet; gulf.

Khaṛiá, [See *Khariyá*].

Ḳharíd, *n.* Purchase; buying. *—farokht,* buying and selling. *—ká mol,* cost price; prime cost. *—ná, v.* to buy; to purchase; to invest in.

Ḳharíf, *n.* Autumn; the autumnal harvest.

Ḳharij , Kheríj, *n.* Small change; coins of small dnominations; retail.

Ḳhárij, *a.* External; outside; outcast; exempt; expelled rejected.

Ḳhárish, *n.* Itch; mange.

Kharíta, *n.* Pouch; purse; a receptacle.

Khaṛiyá, *n.* Chalk; soft white mineral with which mineral with which we write on coarse surfaces.

Ḳharosh, *n.* Uproar; tumult; loud noise; clamour.

Ḳharráṭá, *n.* Snore. *—lená,* v. To snore; to sleep without care. *—lete rahná,* adv. Being lazy and useless while other around are doing their bit.

Khartum, *n.* Trunk of an elephant.

Khas, *n.* Name of a fragrant grass of which *tatties* are made.

Ḳhás, *a.* Special; specific; rare; matching, *—ul-ḳhás,* a. A very special thing. *—kar,* Adv. Especially. *—iyat,* a. Specialty, significant feature.

Ḳhásá, Ḳhássá, *a.* Pure; noble; good; pretty; virtuous; *n.* characteristic; peculiar; disposition; dinner (of kings and noblemen); a kind of fine cloth; muslin. *—chunná, v.* to lay dinner on the table.

Khasáil, *n. (Plur. of Khisál).* Habits; good qualities; virtues; talents.

Ḳhasam, *n.* Husband; mate.

Ḳhasásat, *n.* Sordidness; stinginess.

Khashkhásh, Khashkhash, *n.* Poppy-seed.

Ḳhasís, *a.* Stingy; miserly; ignoble.

Ḳhaslat, *n.* Disposition; habit; nature.

Khasrá, *n.* A list of fields in a village. *—i-taqsím,* register of shares in a field.

Khass, *a.* Lettuce.

Khastá, *a.* Wounded; afflicted; sick. *—dil.* heart-broken.

Ḳhat, *n.* A letter; aa line; handwriting. *Ḳhush—,* a. Good hand-writing writing, line. *—nas-ta'liq,* plain round Persian handwriting. *—i-shikasta,* running handwriting.

Ḳhatá, *n.* Mistake; misdeed; offence; fault; guilt; error. *—karná,* v. To commit an error, &c. *—vár,* n. One who commits a mistake, &c.

Khátá, *n.* Account; ledger; narrative.

Khatáí, *n.* a puffed up biscuit; cookie. *Khastá—,* a. softer biscuit.

Khaṭáí, *n.* Sour taste; sour-tasting dip (used with snacks); (in some regions) dry raw mango slices, ground and used as spice.

Khaṭakná, *v.* To sound; to rattle; to doubt; to disgust. To click; to pinch; to offend; to raise apprehensions; to be an eye-sore.

Ḳhatar, Ḳhatará, *n.* Danger; hazard; peril. *—nák, a.* dangerous; risky.

Ḳhátib, *a.* Public speaker; orator; preacher.

Ḳhátim, *n.* A finger-ring; seal; end; conclusion. *—ul-ambiyá, —ul-mursalín,* the last of the prophets or apostles.

Ḳhátimá, *n.* End; termination; issue. *—bil-khair,* a happy end or issue. —tak *pahuncháná,* to carry to a conclusion; to bring to an end.

Ḳhátir, *n.* Heart; mind; sake; behalf; account; thought; memory; inclination; affection; favour; regard; choice. *—nishán, a.* impressed; on the mind. *—an, adv.* for the sake of; as a favour.

Khaṭiyá, *n.* A small bedstead; a bier, a col.

Khaṭká, *n.* Fear; apprehension; suspicion; sound of footsteps; knocking; tapping. *—lagná, v.* to dread; to fear.

Khaṭ-khaṭáná, *v.* To tap; to knock; to keep on reminding.

Khaṭlá, *n.* A breach; dissension; strife; encumbrance; possessions; wife and family; heap;

multitude; household effects; business; occupation.

Kḥatm, *n.* Seal; end; conclusion; recitation or perusal of the *Qurán; a* done; completed; terminated.

Khaṭ-mal, *n.* A bed bug; (metaphorically) blood-sucker parasite.

Khaṭolá, *n.* Baby cot; a gondola; a basket hanging under a balloon.

Kḥatra, *n.* Danger; fear; apprehension. *khatre me<u>n</u> dálná,* to expose to danger; to imperil.

Khatrí, *n.* Name of a caste among the Hindus. (*Sanskrit:* Kshatriya).

Khaṭṭá, *a.* Sour. *Khaṭṭe angúr,* a. Unaffordable; unobtainable; beyond reach.

Khaṭṭik, Khaṭík, *n.* A hunter; one who lives by killing and selling game, or by keeping pigs and poultry; a tanner.

Kḥátún, *n.* A noble woman; a lady.

Kháú, *a.* Voracious; gluttonous; obeise; (proverbially 'one who accepts bribes'). *—yár,* a. Selfish friend; a fair weather friend.

Kḥauf, *n.* Fear; terror; dread.

Khauláná, *v.* To cause to boil.

Khaulná, *v.* To boil; to be agitated by heat.

Kḥáwar, *n.* The west (but often used poetically for the east, and for the sun) *—an, n.* the east and west.

Kḥawása, *n. (Plur. of Kḥáss,* and of *Kḥássa).* Grandees; ministers of state; attendants; properties; attributes. *—o-'awámm, n.* high and low.

Kḥáwátín, *n.* Ladies.

Kḥáwind, *n.* Lord; master; husband.

Kḥayál, *n.* *(Plur. Kḥayálát).* Thought; opinion; suspicion; idea; whim; fancy; regard; deference; concern; care; vision; spectre; shadow; delusion. *—bá<u>n</u>dhná, v.* to build castles in the air.

Kḥayálá, *n.* Apparition; spectre.

Kḥazáná, *n.* Wealth; riches; opulence; treasury. *khazánchí,* cashier; treasurer.

Khed, *n.* Depression; dejection; sorrow; regret; pain.

Khedná, *v.* To pursue; to chase; to persecute; to expel.

Khel, *n.* Play; game; activity indulged in light-heartedly, or with little concern for wining or loosing. sport; pastime. *—ná, v.* to play; to gambol; to frolic. *—samajhná,* to regard as very easy, or as child's play.

Khelauná, [See *Khilauná*].

Khená, *n.* To row; to paddle; to propel a boat by means of oars.

Kheṛá, *n.* Village; hamlet.

Khet, *n.* Field; ground; land; soil; battle-field. *—í,* husbandry; cultivation; farming. *—niráná, v.* to weed a field.

Khewaṭ, *n.* A rower; an oarsman; a boatman; a fisherman; assigned share of revenue.

Ḳhibrat, *n.* Wisdom; profound knowledge and experience.

Khichná, *v.* To be pulled; to be drawn; to be hauled; to be stretched to hold or stand sloof from.

Khichṛí, Khichaṛí, *n.* Kedgery; a dish prepared by cooking rice and lentils together; a diet fit for a person with week digestion; a low-calorie diet for a sick person recovering; a medley; hotch-potch. *Apní—alag pakáná;* To do one's own thing; without regard to relevance with what is going on around; being out of synch with the rest of the group.

Ḳhidmat, *n.* Service; duty; office; function; ministry; attendance. *—gár,* a servant; an attendant. The English being in India could not pronounce *—Khid-mut-gár,* so they used to call them *'Khit-magar'.*

Ḳhiffat, *n.* Lightness; lack of dignity; degradation; disgrace.

Khijálat, *n.* Modesty; shame; bashfulness.

Khíjh, *n.* Irritation; tease. *—ná,* to be irritated; to get angry.

Khijláná, *v.* To vex; to get angry; to become annoyed; to be irritated.

Ḳhiláf, *n.* Opposition; contrariety; lie; falsehood; *a.* contrary to; opposite; against; adverse. *—qánún,* illegal. *—qi-yás,* ridiculous; absurd; inconceiveable.

Ḳhiláfat, *n.* The office of a Caliph; deputyship.

Ḳhilál, *n.* A pin; tooth-pick; a long thorn, prickle, straw, &c., (such being frequently used as a pin and tooth-pick).

Khiláná, *v.* To feed; to provide food. Ghar baithe —prov., To provide for some one who is lethargic, or not pulling his or her weaight; to look after a habitual idler. *—piláná,* met., To bribe; to grease palms; to give sweetners to those in authority.

Khilárí, *a.* Playful; fond of play; over-found of any kind of amusements; *n.* juggler; conjuror; gamester.

Ḳhil'at, *n.* A dress; a robe of honour.

Khilkhiláná, *v.* To giggle; to burst into peels of laughter.

Khilauná, *n.* A toy; a plaything; something you take lightly.

Khillí, *n.* Jest; joke; humour; fun. —*báz,* playful; humorous.

Khilná, *v.* To bloom; to blow; to open, as a flower; to burst (as parched gram); to be delighted; to present a suitable or charming appearance.

Ḳhilqat, *n.* The creation; the universe and its inhabitants. *'ajib-ul—,* a monster; a prodigious creature.

Ḳhilqí, *a.* Natural; innate; inherent; constitutional.

Ḳhilt, *n.* One of the four humours of the human body as blood, bile, phlegm and spleen, on the conditions and proportions of which bodily and mental health was formerly supposed to depend.

Khilwáṛ, *v.* Playful mood; *—men,* adv. In a playful spirit.

Ḳhilwat, *n.* Privacy; solitude retirement; a private conference; closet. *—o-jalwat men̲,* in private and in public; secretly and openly.

Khír, *n.* Rice-pudding. Colloquially, also 'milk', from Sanskrit *Kshír.*

Khírá, *n.* Cucumber.

Ḳhirad, *n.* Understanding; intellect; wisdom. *—mand, a.* wise; intelligent.

Ḳhiráj, *n.* Tax; duty; tribute; revenue. *—guzár, n.* a tributary; *a.* feudatory. *—lagná,* to levy a tax or tribute; to impose a tax.

Ḳhirám, *n.* Walking in a dignified manner; stately; gait. *ḳhush—, a.* walking gracefully.

Khírí, *n.* Udder; breast; teat; pap.

Khiṛkí, *n.* Window, an opening.

Ḳhirman, *n.* Harvest; a barn; heap.

Ḳhirs, *n.* A bear.

Khís, *n.* The first milk given by a cow after calving; grin.

Ḳhisál, *(Plur. of Ḳhaslat)*

Khisárá, *n.* Loss; damage; injury.

Ḳhisht, *n.* Brick.

Khisyáná, *v.* To put to shame; to grin; to grind or gnash the teeth.

Khiskáná, Khaskáná, *v.* To move; to remove; to shift or move the position of.

Ḳhissat, *n.* Meanness; sordidness; stinginess.

Ḳhitáb, *n.* Conversation; discourse; a title. *—e'táb,* censures; rebukes.

Ḳhitta, *n.* Plot of land; region; country; district.

Khiyál, *n.* See *Khayál.*

Ḳhiyánat, *n.* Infidelity; unfaithfulness; breach of confidence; misappropriation; embezzlement.

Kḥizáb, *n.* Dyeing of the hair; a black tincture or dye for the hair.

Kḥizán, *á* Falling of the leaves; autumn; decay; old age.

Kḥo, Kḥú, *n.* Habit; custom; tem perament; disposition; nature.

Khod, *n.* Helmet; armour for the head.

Khodná, *v.* To dig; to excavate; to delve; to hollow; to carve; to engrave. *Khod-khod kar púchhaná,* prov. To question closely; to dig deeper for information.

Khoh, *n.* A cave; a cavern; abyss; pit; chasm.

Khoj, *n.* Enquiry; investigation; search; quest; trace; clue. *—ná,* to search; to investigate; to explore (*also see* **Khojí**).

Khojá, *n.* A eunuch.

Khojí, *n.* Searcher; investigator; dowser; One who find out what is not apparent; exploner.

Khokhalá, *a.* Hollow; without substance; empty; boastful.

Kholná, *v.* To open; to loose; to unfasten; to reveal; to disclose.

Khomchá, Khonchá, *n.* A street-side stall; a mobile vending facility; a non-permanent trading post; an unstable business.

Khoná, *v.* To lose; to waste; to squander. *kho kar síkhná,* to buy experience.

Khonchná, *v.* To scratch; to rend; to tear; to rip open; to thrust.

Khontá, *n.* Bird's nest.

Khopṛá, Khoprá *n.* The kernel of a cocoanut; the skull.

Khopṛí, *n.* Skull; cranium; head. *—khá jáná,* to worry; to harass.

Kḥoshá, *n.* An ear of corn; a bunch or cluster of fruit. *—chín,* a gleaner.

Khot, *n.* Falsehood; lying; deceipt; vice; adulteration; alloy; blemish; defect. *—á, a.* defective; adulterated; fraudulent; base (coin); forged document). *—ái, n.* blemish; defect; impiety; vice; forgery.

Kḥúb, *a.* Very good; excellent; magnificent. *—súrat, a.* beautiful; charming. *—í,* beauty; gracefulness; excellence.

Kḥud, *pro.* Self (my-, thy-, &c.); own; private; personal. *—ikhtiyárí,* self-control, self reliance, self-restraint. *—ba-kḥud,* voluntarily; spontaneously. *—rái, n.* self-conceit. *—garazí,* selfishness. *—mukḥtárí,* independence. *—kushí,* self-destruction; suicide.

Kḥudá, *n.* God; The Supreme Being; the Creator; lord; master; ruler; *(used chiefly in comps.)* as *Kḥudá dád,* granted by God. *—kare,* would to God; God grant. —*ná kḥwásta,* God forbid. —*tars,* God-fearing; pious. —*ta'ala,* the Most High God.

Kḥudáí, *a.* Divine; a divinity; Godhead; providence; omnipotence; omniscience.

Khudáwand, *n.* Lord; master; husband. —*í,* lordship; sovereignty; majesty; divinity.

Khuff, A. *n.* Boot.

Kḥufta, *n.* Sleeping; asleep; dormant.

Kḥufiya, *a.* Concealed; hidden; secret; unrevealed.

Khujalí, *n.* Scratching; skin irritation, itch, scabbies. —*honá,* n. To feel scratchy, to feel itchy; (proverbially) to get a randam urge for doing something.

Khujáná, Khujláná, *v.* To scratch; to itch; to cause to itch. *Khoprí*—, v. To scratch one's head (in search for answers, to revive losr memory, as an excuse for lack of retention).

Khujasta, Khujista, *a.* Happy; fortu Nate; blessed; auspicious.

Khúk, *n.* Boar; swine; pig; hog.

Khukrí, Khukhrí, *n.* A curved dagger; a typical Gorkhá weapon, ritually worn by Gorkhá soldiers all over the world.

Khulá, *a.* Open; not shut; not enclosed; exposed; bare; unconfined; loose; manifest; frank. —*khule khazáne, khullam khullá,* openly; publicly.

Khulása, *n.* Essence; extract; abstract; abridgement; epitome.

Kḥuld, *n.* Eternity; the world to come; paradise.

Kḥulf, *n.* Breach of promise.

Kḥullat, *n.* True or sincere friendship.

Khulná, *v.* To open; to expand; to be untied; to be loosed; to be exposed; to become clear; to be freed from restraint; to clear up (as clouds).

Khulj, *n.* Nature; temperament; inherent; disposition; courteousness.

Kḥulús, *n.* Purity; sincerity; frendship; affection.

Kḥumár, *n.* Intoxication; drunkenness; effects of drunkenness; as headache. *kḥammár, n.* a confirmed drunkard.

Kḥún, *n.* Blood; killing; slaughter; murder; bloodshed; massacre. —*áluda, a.* bloodstained; bloody. —*bahána,* to shed blood. —*i-jigar píná,* to control one's feelings or emotions. —*kḥwár, a.* blood-thirsty; murderous—*ká'ewaz, n.* compensation or fine for bloodshed; blood-money. —*í, n.* murderer.

Khunkí, *n.* Coldness; temperateness; prosperity.

Khúnṭá, *n.* A stake; peg; a tent-peg; *(met.)* support; protection.

Khúnṭí, *n.* peg; a pin; root of the hair.

Khunyá, *n.* Modulation; melody; harmony. *—gar,* musician; minstrel. *—gar,* musician; minstrel. *—garí,* minstrelsy.

Khur, *n.* Hoof; cloven-hoof.

Khur, *n.* Eating. *—o-nosh,* meat and drink. *—o-posh,* food and raiment.

Khurachná, *v.* To scratch; to scrape.

Kḥuráfát, *n.* Mischief; trouble; indecent act; evil deed. *—tí,* a. One who commits mischief, &c.

Kḥurák, *n.* Food; victuals; estables; rations.

Khuránt, *a.* Old; aged; experienced.

Kḥurd, *a.* Small; little; minute; young. *—bín,* microscope. *—burd karná,* to consume; to embezzle. *—sál,* of tender age; young. *—sálí,* childhood; youth; minority; infancy.

Kḥurdá, *(Perf. part. of Khurdan).* Eaten; consumed; made away with; *part. a.* afflicted; corroded.

Khurdan, *v.* Eating; drinking; consuming; suffering. *—í, n.* provisions; eatables.

Kḥurdiyáh, *n.* Money-changer.

Kḥurish, *n.* Eating and drinking; food; fare; victuals.

Kḥurmá, *n.* A date; a kind of sweetmeat.

Kḥurram, *a.* Glad; pleased; cheerful; happy. *—í,* Gladness; cheerfulness.

Kḥursand, *a.* Contended; satisfied; pleased. *—í,* contentment; satisfaction.

Kḥurshaid, Khurshíd, *n.* The sun

Kḥurúj, *n.* Going out; egress; exit; issue; exodus.

Kḥush, *a.* Happy; joyful; contented; satisfied. *—numá,* a. Appears to happy, etc. *—ámad,* n. Flattery; undue praise; *—ámadí,* a. One who indulges in flattery; sycophantic. *—gawaár,* a. conducive to being Happy; making for atmosphere, setting, circumstances, etc. *—hál,* a. Happy; content; economically well off. *—tabiyat;* a. Of happy countenance. *—fahamí,* n. A happy illusion; a false hope. *—bú,* perfume; Scent. *—dáman,* mother-in-law. *—kḥabrí,* glad tidings; good news. *—m'ásh,* well-off; well-fed. *—waqt,* happy; delighted; pleased. *—zabán,* eloquent; fluent.

Kḥush-hál, *n.* Happy; in good cheer; in good shape; prosperous; in comfortable living conditions. *—í,* n. Prosperity; good living conditions.

Kḥushí, *n.* Happiness; felicity; gladness; joly. *—manáná,* to make merry; to rejoice.

Kḥushk, *a.* Dry; parched; withered; shrivelled. *—sálí,* drought.

Kḥusúsan, *adv.* Particularly; especially; expressly.

Kḥusúsiyat, *n.* Peculiarity; speciality.

Kḥutbá, *n.* A sermon; a religious discourse.

Kḥutút, *n. (Plur. of Khatt).* Lines; stripes; letters; epistles.

Kḥuzú, *n.* Sleep; slumber; dream; vision. *—áwar,* any substance producing sleep; a soporofic. *—ída,* sleep; drowsy. *kḥyál,* phantom; delusion.

Kḥwáh, Kḥuáha, *n. conj.* Either; whether; *a.* wishing; desiring *(used in comp.)* as: *—ma—,* willing or unwilling; *nolens volens.*

Kḥwáhish, *n.* Wish; desire; inclination; tendency; bent. *—mand, a.* desirous; inclined.

Kḥwájá, *n.* Lord; master; gentleman; person of distinction. *—sará,* a eunuch in the service of a prince.

Kḥwán, *a.* Reading; reciting; *n.* reader; reciter; tray. *—posh,* a tray-cloth.

Khwándá, *a.* Read; recited; repeated; chanted; having the knowledge of reading and writing. *ná—, a.* illiterate; ignorant; *n.* one who cannot read or write; an illiterate person. *—gí,* reading.

Kḥwár, *a.* Wretched; contemptible; ruined; miserable. *—í, n.* meannes; vileness.

Kḥwást, *n.* Wish; desire. *—gár, n.* applicant; suitor; petitioner.

Ki, *con.* As; because; since; that; *pro.* who; what.

Kibr, *n.* Pride; haughtiness; dignity.

Kibriyá, *n.* Grandeur; splendour; pomp; magnificence; an attribute of the Deity.

Kíchaṛ, Slush; slime; mattery discharge that collects in the corners of the eyes.

Kidhar, *adv.* Where? whither? in what direction. *—se,* whence? from what quarter or direction?

Kifáyat, *n.* Enough; sufficiency; abundance; thrift; economy; prudence. *—sha'árí, n.* frugality; economy.

Kíl, *n.* A nail; tack; peg; the core (of a boil).

Kilkárí, *n.* Shouting; cut-cry. *—márná, n.* to shout with joy.

Kímíyá, *n.* Alchemy; chemistry; a specific. *—banáná,* to convert base metals into silver or gold; to earn or obtain money very easily. *—gar,* alchemist.

Kína, *n.* Animosity; enmity; rancour; malice; ill-will. *—war, a.* malicious; spiteful; inimical.

Kinár, *n.* Margin; edge; border; bosom; embrace.

Kinárá, *a.* Margin; shore; seaside; coast. *—ho jáná,* to stand aloof; to withdraw.

Kínch, *n.* Dirt; mire.

Kinká, *n.* Slave; poor person.

Kinnárat, *n. (Plur.)* Harps.

Kír, *n.* A parrot.

Kířá, *n.* Worm; maggot; insect. *—makorá,* insects; reptiles; creeping things; vermin.

Kiráyá, *n.* Rent; fare; hire. *—par chaláná,* to let; to give one hire; to lease. *—dár,* tenant; hirer; lessee. *—náma,* a deed of lease; a lease.

Kirch, Kirich, *n.* A sword (esp. a straight one for thrusting with); a splinter.

Kirdár, *n.* Action; labour; employment; business; conduct; character; habit.

Kirdigár, *n.* The Creator; God.

Kíří, *n.* Ant.

Kiríţ, *n.* Wreath; garland; crown; goodness; piety; virtue.

Kirpál, Kripál, *a.* Compassionate; pitiful; merciful; tender; kind.

Kírti, S. Praise; renown; celebrity; fame; virtue.

Kis, *pro.* To whom, what, or which.

Kisán, *n.* Ploughman; tiller; cultivator.

Kisbat, Kiswat, *n.* A barber's toolbag

Kishmísh, *n.* Raisins; dry grapes.

Kishmiz, *n.* Coriander.

Kisht, *n.* Instalment; part.

Kishtí, *n.* A boat; a vessel; a ship; a bark, or barque. *—bán,* boatman; sailor; mariner.

Kisí, *pron.* Some; any. *—tarah,* anyhow; somehow; by hook or by crook.

Kitáb, *n.* Book. *—i-Iláhí* or *ásmání,* a holy or sacred book; scripture. *—farosh,* a bookseller.

Kitábá, Kitábat, *n.* Writing; inscription; epitaph; motto. *kitábat, n.* the profession of a copyist.

Kitná, *adv.* How much; how many; some; several. *—hí, adv.* howsoever; however much or many.

Kivář, Kivářiá, *n.* Door; gate.

Klesh, *n.* Pain; trouble; affliction; anxiety.

Klikh, *n.* Darkess; soot; stain; stigma.

Koelá, *n.* Charcoal. *patthar ká, —,* coke.

Koft, *n.* Anger; irritation, unhappiness. [Not too overt].

Koftá, *n.* A food preparation obtained by crushing vegetables, or mincing meats, turning them into spherical dough-balls, lightly frying them and then cooking them in gravy.

Koh, *n.* Mountain; hill. *—átish fishán,* volcano; a mountain of volcanic origin. *—i-paikar,* like a mountain; enormous; gigantic.

Kohán, *n.* The hump of a camel, bullock, &c.

Koháná, *n.* To be angry.

Kohistán, *n.* A mountainous country; forest. *—í,* mountainous; hilly; *n.* a mountaineer.

Kohní, *n.* The elbow.

Kohrá,Kuhrá, *n.* Fog; mist; haze.

Koí, *pro.* Anybody; somebody; some. *—bhí,* whoever; whosoever. *—na koí,* some one or other.

Koel, *n.* The Indian cuckoo.

Kokh, *n.* The belly; the womb.

Koláhal, *n.* Confused noise; uproar; tumult.

Kolhú, *n.* An oil-press; a sugar-mill.

Komal, *a.* Soft; tender; mild. *—tá, n.* softness; placidity; mildness.

Kompal, Konpal, *n.* Fresh, tender leaf [of a plant, or a tree].

Koná, S. *n.* A corner; an angle; a side.

Kop, *n.* Anger; rage; indignation.

Kor, *n.* Edge; border; side; margin; tip; trifle. *—bakhtí, n.* calamity; disaster. *—bátin,* ignorant.

Korá, *a.* Clean, unspoilt; coarse; unbleached; blunt (speach); less-than-friendly. Unused; new; fresh.

Koṛá, *n.* whip. *—márná, v.* to flog; to whip.

Koṛh, *n.* Leprosy. *—men kháj,* one calamity succeeding another. *—í, n.* a leper. *—in, n.* a female leper.

Koṛí, *n.* A score; twenty.

Kornish, *n.* Salutation; greeting; adoration; prostration.

Kos, H. *n.* A distance of about two miles; a league. *kále—, n.* a considerable distance.

Kosh, S. *n.* A dictionary; a vocabulary; treasure; treasury; store.

Koshak, *n.* An egg.

Koshish, *n.* Striving; endeavour; effort; exertion; labour; attempt; study. *—i-behúda, n.* a fruitless attempt; a vain effort.

Kosná, *v.* To curse; to vituperate; to abuse.

Koṭhá, S. *n.* Granary; barn; storehouse; a large room; an upper story; a floor; the upper part of the body; the stomach; the womb.

Koṭhá, *n.* A prostitute's work-place; a house of illrepute. *Koṭhe par já baiṭhná,* v. To become a prostitute.

Koṭhí, H. *n.* Granary; barn; warehouse; factory; treasury; a mercantile house or firm; a house built of brick or stone; residence.

Koṭhrí, *n.* A small closet; a room; a chamber.

Koṭi, *n.* End; top; tip; point; crore; ten millions.

Kotwál, *n. (lit.)* The keeper of a castle; the chief police officer of a city or town; a city magistrate.

Koyá, *n.* The eye-ball; corner of the eye; pulp of the jackfruit; cocoon of the silkworm.

Kram, *n.* A step; degree; proceeding; bound; manner; sequence.

Kripá, *n.* Favour; kindness; compassion; grace; mercy. *—nidhán.* compassionate; merciful.

Kripaṇ, *n.* Miser; stingey; non-generous; pitiable; sordid; avaricious; *n.* a niggard. *—tá,* n. Miserly nature; lack of generosity, etc.

Krishí, *n.* Agriculture; husbandry.

Krishṇ, Krishna, *a.* Black; dark; the god Krishna (the Apollo of the Hindus), the eighth and most celebrated of the ten incarnations of the god Vishnu. *—paksh,* the dark half of a month during which the moon is on the wane.

Kristán, *n.* A Christian.

Kritaghna, *adj.* Betrayer; disloyal; one who disowns favors bestowed; onw who forgets obligations(s); traitor. *—tá,* n. Betrayal; disloyalty; treachery.

Kritagya, *adj.* One who is aware of favors/obligations received; one who acknowledges these favors/obligations. *—tá,* n. Acknowledging favors; loyalty; sense of obligation.

Kriti, *n.* Creation; composition; work.

Krititva, *n.* Creativity; skill.

Kriyá, *n.* Performance; action; deed; business; labour (in *Gram.)* a verb. *—karm,* religious duty; funeral ceremonies; obsequies.

Krodh, *n.* Anger; rage; passion; resentment. *—it,* angry; wrathful.

Krúratá, *n.* Cruelty; fierceness.

Kshamá, *n.* Patience; forbearance; pardon; forgiveness; the earth.

Kshamatá, *n.* Ability; capacity; skill.

Kshaṇ, *n.* An instant; moment twinkling of an eye; leisure; opportunity.

Kshay, *n.* Loss; destruction; decay; wasting away. —*rog,* consumption; phthisis.

Kshetr, *n.* Land; field; country; a wife; a sacred spot; a place of pilgrimage; (in *Geom.)* figure, diagram, triangle, &c.

Kshipra, *adj.* Sharp; fast, speedy. —*hast,* adj. Fast worker; efficient.

Kshír, *n.* Milk; milky juice of sap of plants; water.

Kshudra, *a.* Small; minute; insignificant; poor; contemptible; *n.* a mean person.

Ku, *n.* A prefix implying use lessness, badness, deterioration, depreciation, defectiveness, &c., as *kuchál,* misconduct, *kudashá,* miserable condition. —*thaur,* bad place.

Kuá̲n̲, Kúá, *n.* A well; A pit.

Kuárá, Kuá̲n̲rá, *n.* A bachelor.

Kuá̲n̲ri, Kuárí *n.* Virgin; Spinster; unmarried woman.

Kub, Kúbaṛ, *n.* A hump. —*ja,* humpbacked; deformed.

Kuch, *n.* Breast of a woman; bosom.

Kúch, *n.* March; journey; departure; decamping.

Kúchá, *n.* A narrow street; a lane; an alley. —*gadá,* a street-beggar. —*gard,* a vagrant; vagabond.

Kúchakí, *v.* Purple colour.

Kuchalná, *v.* To crush; to squash; to subdue (a rebellion or a mutiny).

Kuchh, *pro.* and *adv.* Something; somewhat; anything; some; any; a few; little; whatever. —*ho,* happen or come what may; no matter what happens. —*parwá nahí̲n̲,* it is of no consequence. —*nahí̲n̲,* nothing; none.

Kúchí, *n.* A brush.

Kudálí, *n.* Pickaxe; small mattock.

Kúdná, *v.* To leap; to spring; to bound; to jump; to rejoice.

Kudarat, *n.* Nature; countenance; attitude; self-motivated; not subject to external prompting. —*í,* a. Natural; spontaneous; unprompted, &c.

Kudúrat, *n.* Muddiness; impurity (in water &c.); foulness; *(met.)* perturbation; affliction; resentment; malice. —*rakhná* to bear malice.

Kufr, *n.* Unbelief; scepticism; paganism; ingratitude; blasphemy.

Kufrán, *n.* Unbelief; ingratitude. —*i-ni'amat,* unthankfulness for favour received; ingratitude.

Kuhásá, *n.* Vapour; mist; fog; haze.

Kuhní, *n.* The elbow.

Kuhrám, *v.* Weeping and lamentation; loud cries of sorrow.

Kujá, *adv.* Where; whither; whence; from where.

Kújá, *n.* A small baked earthen vessel.—*misrí/mishrí,* n. Sugar candy, crystallised in one of these earthen vessels.

Ku-játi, *adj.* Bad grouping; bad sort (of people); low caste; criminal community/ tribe.

Kúkar, Kukur, *n.* A dog; a mongrel *(fem.) kúkri,* a bitch.

Kukkuṭ, *n.* A cock; a male bird; a claw.

Kukkuṭí, *n.* A hen.

Kukurmuttá, *n.* Mushroom; self-growing.

Kul, *n.* Herd; flock; multitude; caste; tribe; family; lineage; pedigree; noble race or descent. —*ván, n.* an aristocrat; a person of high birth.

Kulbulána, *v.* To flutter; to toss about in pain; to writhe or wriggle (as a worm, snake, &c.); to itch; to rumble (the bowels).

Kulél, *n.* Friskiness; capering; restiveness (of a horse).

Kúlhá, *n.* Hip; the prominent part below waist. —*matkáná;* v. To wiggle one's waist and bum.

Kulhaṛ, *n.* A country-made, baked earthen cup, commonly used in Northern India as a disposable drinking vessel.

Kulháṛá, Ḳulháṛi, *n.* Axe; hatchet

Kulín, *a.* Of good family; of noble descent; of high birth.

Kulish, *n.* A weapon; the thunderbolt of Indra, the ruler of heavens.

Kull, *n.* The whole; total; sum. —*jama, n.* full amount; *adv.* in the total; in all.

Kulish, *n.* A weapon; the thunderbolt of India.

Kumak, *n.* Aid; assistance; help; succour.

Kumár, *n.* A youth; a boy; a son; heir-apparent; prince. *(fem.) kumárí,* maid; virgin; daughter; princess.

Kumhár, *n.* A potter.

Kumhláná, *v.* To fade; to wither; to become dejected.

Kumud, *n.* Water-lily; lotus.

Kunain, *n.* Quinine; a medicine dispense for malaria in olden days; (proverbially) a bitter pill given to a dear one with the best of motives.

Kunbá, *n.* Family; tribe.

Ku<u>n</u>d, *a.* Blunt; dull; slow-witted; obtuse; stupid. —*zahn,* dull in intellect; thick-headed.

Kuṉḍ, *n.* A basin; a pitcher; a pit for sacrifice; a hole; an abyss; a pool; a reservoir.

Kuṉḍá, Kuṉḍí, *n.* A door chain; a clasp. *—kharkáná,* v. To knock at the door.

Kuṉḍalí, *n.* Horoscope. *—khínchná,* to draw up a horoscope.

Kuṉdan, *n.* Pure gold; a pure; bright.

Kunisht, *n.* A temple; a Jewish synagogue.

Kuṉj, *n.* An arbour; a grove; a lane; an alley; a cave.

Kuṉjar, *n.* An elephant.

Kuṉjí, *n.* A key.

Kuṉjṛá, *n.* Greengrocer; fruiterer; vegetable seller. *(fem.) kuṉjaṛin.*

Kuṉtal, *n.* Hair; lock, curl, or ringlet of hair.

Kuṉwar, *n.* The son of a Raja; a prince.

Kúp, *n.* A well, a waterhole. *—mandúk,* a. A frog trapped inside a water-hole; one going nowhere; one who's access to wider world has been cut off; one condemned to limited experience.

Kuppá, *n.* A large leathern vessel for holding oil, &c. *—honá,* to become very fat or corpulent.

Kúṛá, *n.* Refuse; sweepings; filth; rubbish.

Kuṛak, *n.* Clucking of a hen; a clucking hen.

Kuraṉg, *n.* A species of deer.

Kuṛhan, *n.* Sulking; grudge carried within.

Kuṛhná, *v.* To sulk; to whimper within; to grieve; to mourn; to lament.

Kurkurá, *adj.* Crunchy; crumbly [description of sweets, etc.].

Kuṛkuṛáná, *v.* To speak angrily; to cluck (a hen).

Kurm, Kúrm, *n.* Tortoise; turtle.

Kurmurá, *n.* Puffed rice.

Kurra, *n.* A foal.

Kurri, *n.* Cartilage; gristle.

Kursí, *n.* Chair; seat; stool; chair of state; throne; bench (of a judge); base of a pillar; pedestal; a raised foundation; genealogy. *—náma,* genealogical tree; pedigree.

Kursuf, *n.* Cotton, &c., put into an inkstand.

Kurtá, *n.* A simpleton's tunic in olden days that became a national uniform for the politicians after independence, and is a fashionable rag in today's India, and has qualified *haute couture* on the Paris catwalks.

Kurúp, *a.* Ill-formed; deformed; misshapen; ugly.

Kush, *n.* Killer; slayer.

Kushá, *n.* Straw. —*ásan,* n. Straw mat; floor mat for sitting on (made of straw).

Kushádá, *a.* Opened; uncovered; discovered; displayed; frank; happy; clear.

Kushágra, *n.* The sharp-end of stra; sharp.—*buddhi,* n. One exceptionally intelligent.

Kushal, *n.* Health; welfare; properity; happiness; *a.* right; suitable; healthy; prosperous; able; clever.

Ku-shásan, *adj.* Bad management of affairs; maladministration.

Kushkí, *n.* Mansion; castle.

Kusht, *n.* Slaughter. —*o-kḥún,* massacre; slaughter.

Kushṭ, *n.* Leprosy; debilitating disability.

Kushtí, *n.* Wrestling. —*báz,* a wrestler.

Kusúf, *n.* Eclipse of the sun.

Kút. *n.* Survey; guess; a rough estimate.—*ná, v.* To measure; to assess; to estimate; to evaluate; to put a value on.

Kúṭ, *adj.* Secret; hidden; underhand.—*níti,* n. Diplomacy. —*nítigya,* n. Diplomat(s)

Kutarná, *v.* To bite; to gnaw.

Kuṭhiyá, Kuṭhiyár, *n.* Storehouse; granary; barn. —*í,* store-keeper.

Kuṭí, *v.* Hut; hovel.

Kuṭil, *a.* Crooked; distorted; bent; twisted; wicked; vicious; sinful; cruel.

Kutiyá, *n.* Bitch.

Kuṭná, *n.* A pimp; a pander; a go-

Kútná, *v.* To assess; to estimate; to evaluate; to measure; to put a value on.

Kuttá, *n.* Dog; mongrel. —*kḥána,* a kennel.

Kuṭṭaní, *n.* A madam; pimp (lady) of a house of prostitution.

Kutub, *n. (Plur. of Kitáb).* Books. —*farosh,* bookseller. —*kḥána,* library.

Kuṭumb, *n.* Family; kindred; kinsmen.

Kúzá, *n.* An earthen goblet or drinking vessel; a pitcher.

Kyá, *pro.* What; how; why. —*kḥúb,* well done! bravo!—*hai,* what do you say? what is the matter?

Kyú<u>n</u>, *adv.* Why; how; wherefore. —*ki,* because; since; for. —*nahí<u>n</u>,* why not? certainly; surely. —*na ho,* undoubtedly; indubitably.

L, l, stands here for (ल) in Hindi and (ل) in Urdu. This consonant is also applied in half, or diluted value when it precedes semi-vowel *'y'* and in double value (or one-and-a half value, as we say in Hindi) and followed by standard vowel tones.

Lá, (A negative *adv.* privative); no; not; by no means; there is not; without. It occurs in combination with Arabic and Persian words, and may sometimes be rendered by the English negative prefixes *un-, in-, ir-, im-,* or the affix *less. lásání, adj.* without a second; incomparable. *—chár,* without remedy; irremediable. *—hásil, a.* unproductive; barren.

Lab, *n.* Lips; edge; brim. *—e shírím,* a. Sweet lips; alluring lips; one who speaks sweetly. *—á lab,* a. Full to the brim. *—on par ján áná,* adv. Being in the death throws; dying; on the death-bed.

Labádá, *n.* A waterproof; a mackintosh; a cloak.

Lábat, *n.* A doll; puppet; plaything.

Lábh, *n.* Gain; profit; benefit; produce.

Labrez, *a.* Brimful; overflowing.

Lachak, *n.* Elasticity; flexibility; bending; resilience; springy quality. *—ilá,* a. One with the quality of elasticity; flexible; &c.

Láchár, *a.* Helpless; poor; destitute. *—karná, v.* to compel; to coerce; to disable.

Lachar, *n.* A simpleton; an ignoramus.

Lachchhan, *n.* Sign; mark; trace; token; feature; description; manner, symptoms.

Luchhmí, Lachchhamí, Lakshmí, *n.* Goddess of wealth and the spouse of Lord Vishnú; prosperity; good fortune; a proper name for boys (with suffixes like 'Lal' 'Das' 'Mal' etc.) and for girls (with suffixes like 'Devi', 'Bala', 'Bai' etc.); *—pati,* n. (literally) the husband of—; wealthy. *—pújá,* n. Ceremonial worship of the goddess; the festival of *Dípávalí,* which literally means 'the festival of lights'. *Griha—,* n. a courteous epithet for one's 'better-half'.

Laddú, *n.* A beast of burden.

Laḍḍú, *n.* A kind of sweetmeat; *man ke laddú kháná,* to eat imaginary *laddús;* hence, to build castles in the air.

Láḍlá, *adj.* Dear; darling; one brought-up afectionately; pampered (child); favourite one. *—í,* adj. Female of the same.

Ládná, *v.* To load; to burden; to freight.

Lae, Laya, *n.* Tune; air; taste; desire.

Lafangá, *n.* A vagrant; a person moving about without a purpose or mission; a useless hanger-on.

Lafangiyá, *n.* Coxcomb; a vain fellow given to boasting.

Laffáz, *a.* Eloquent; talkative; loquacious. *—í,* n. Word play; loquacious speech; clever use of words; verbose talk.

Lafif, *a.* Wrapped; folded; complex; *n.* a mixed crowd; an assembling of various tribes; a friend.

Lafz, *n.* Word; saying; term; expression. *—ba—,* word for word; verbatim. *—í,* verbal; literal.

Lág, *n.* Affinity; affection; love; attempt; enmity; grudge; rivalry; plot; secret; charm; jugglery; sleight of hand. *—rakhná, v.* to har-hour ill-will.

Lagá, *a.* Attached; united; connected; joined. *—dená,* to apply; to hoard. *lagái bujhái karná,* to sow dissension.

Lagám, *n.* Bridle; bit and reins. *be lagám, a.* unrestrained; unbridled.

Lagan, *n.* Obsessive desire; determined pursuit; (colloquially) also Marriage.

Lagán, *n.* Rent; land revenue.

Lagáná, *v.* To apply; to close; to shut; to attach; to put to work; to employ; to ascribe; to impute; to attribute; to join; to connect; to add on; to fix; to put on; to set in; to fasten; to install; to stick on; to moor; to close; to apply; to set (fire); to spread (a carpet): to strike (a slap); to put in; to plant—*bujháná,* to sow dissension; to excite quarrels.

Lagáo, *a.* Relating; connection; intercourse; adherence. *be—,* separate; impartial; unbiassed.

Lágar, *a.* Lean; thin; emaciated.

Lágat, *n.* Cost; expense; outlay.

Lagátar, *adv.* To the end; inclusive.

Lagbhag, *adv.* Close; near; almost; nearly; about.

Lage-háth, *adv.* Simultaneously; together; at the same time.

Lághav, *n.* Dexterity; smartness; finesse; skill precision; proficiency.

Laghu, *a.* Quick; swift; fleet; little; small; young; weak; low; frivolous.

Lagná, *v.* To be joined; to become fixed; to be planted or set (trees, &c.); to feel or have a desire; to cost; to be imposed.

Lagzish, *n.* Slipping; stumbling; tottering; prevarication; equivocation.

Lahakná, *v.* To glitter; to sparkle; to glisten; to be kindled; to ignite.

Lahangá, *n.* A Loose, long skirt worn by rural women around the waist, flowing downward. In villages this is a colourful and decorative garment on its own. In cities, it is a comparatively simpler affair as it forms the base for a sárí worn around and on top of it.

Lahar, Lahr, *n.* Wave; billow; emotion; fit of passion; ecstasy; frenzy; effect of snake-bite. *—uṭhná, v.* to rise (waves, emotions, &c.) emotion to surge; *—áná,* to be delightful (to the eye); to undulate; to raise delusive hopes. *—dár,* adj. Wavy (water, line, pattern, hair): whimsical; crotchety; flashing; fine.

Láhiq, *n.* Appendage; supplement; reach. *—honá, v.* to be reached; to overtake.

Lahajá, *n.* Accent; posture; manner of delivery; attitude.

Lahlahána, *v.* To bloom; to flourish; to be verdant.

Lahrí, *n.* Fanciful; capricious; merry; jovial; *n.* a whimsical person; a merry-andrew; a clown.

Lahriyá, *a.* Wavy; waved or watered, as silk, &c.; serpentine; *n.* waved or watered silk.

Lahsan, Lahsun, *n.* Garlic; a freckle; a blotch.

Lahú, *n.* Blood—*ke ghúnt píná, (lit.)* to drink, as it were drops of blood; to endure patiently and meekly.

Lahzá, *n.* A moment; an instant; a second; a glance.

Lail, *n.* Night. *—o-nihár,* night and day.

Láiq, *n.* Fit; proper; becoming; decent; worthy; deserving; capable; competent; convenient.

Láj, Lajjá, *n.* Bashfulness; modesty; shame; honour; reputation. *—rakhná,* to protect the honour (of). *—wantí* coy; bashful; modest; chaste.

Lajílá, *adj.* Shy; bashful; modest.

Lakaṛ-bagghá, *n.* Wood-pecker; heyna.

Lakaṛ-hárá, *n.* Wood-cutter; lumberjack.

Lákh, *n.* Gum; lac; a hundred thousand. *—kí battí,* a stick of sealing-wax. *—on men, adv.* in public.

Lakherá, *n.* A dealer in articles made of lac.

Lakhlakh, *a.* Weak; feeble; lean.

Lakḥlakḥá, *n.* A strong perfume; a censer; a lamp.

Lakhná, *v.* To see; to perceive; to observe; to look at.

Lakhpatí, *n.* A millionaire.

Lakḥt, *n.* Piece; bit; fragment; portion; some; a little. *yak—, adv.* all at once; suddenly. *—i-jigar,* son or daughter.

Lakír, *n.* A line; trail; streak; pattern. *—ká fakír,* a. A traditionalist; one stuck to a set pattern of behaviour; *—pítaná,* v. To tread the beaten path. *—par chalná,* v. To follow the conventional path.

Lakkaṛ, *n.* Timber; hard-dried; stiff.

Lakṛí, *n.* A stick; staff; wood; timber; firewood; fuel; *a.* stiff; rigid; thin; emaciated. *ek—se sab ko há<u>n</u>kná, (lit.)* to drive everyone with the same stick; to treat all alike; to act impartially.

Lakshaṇ, *n.* Mark; symptom; token; characteristic; quality.

Lakshmí, *n.* The goddess of wealth (also see **Lachhmí**).

Lakshya, *n.* Aim; goal; target. *—púrti,* n. Fulfilment of a target; achievement of a goal. *—siddhi,* n. Attainment of an object/target.

Lakwá, *a.* Paralysis; palsy. *—marná,* v. To suffer an attack of.

La'l, *n.* A ruby.

Lál, *a.* Red; scarlet; ruddy; red-hot; inflamed; enraged; beloved; darling; precious. *n.* an infant boy; a son; a darling; a pat. *—pílí á<u>n</u>khe<u>n</u> nikálná,* to be flush with passion; to be inflamed with anger.

Lálá, *n.* Sir; master; a respectable Hindu; a banker; a title given to persons of the Vaisya class, &c.; clerk; a respectful term of address to a father; a father-in-law; a dear boy; darling, (in *pers.*) a major-domo; a slave; a prattler; a babbler.

Lálá, *a.* Bright; shining; resplendent (pearls).

Lála, *n.* A tulip; (in India) the red-poppy. *—rukh, a.* tulip-cheeked; red cheeked; rosy-cheeked. *—zár,* a bed or garden of tulips.

Lálach, *n.* Covetousness; greed; avarice. *—dená, v.* to tempt; to allure. *—me<u>n</u> áná,* to be moved by covetousness.

Lalát, Lilát, *n.* Forehead; brow; fortune; fate.

Lalit, *a.* Beautiful; lovely; charming.

Lalkárná, *v.* To call out; to shout; to vociferate; to halloo; to hail.

Lallí, *n.* A girl.

Lallo, *n.* Tongue; desire; longing. *—patto,* flattery; coaxing.

Lallú, Lallá, *n.* A boy.

Lálsá, *n.* Longing; craving; hankering; ardent desire.

Lám, *n.* Army; brigade; a Persian letter; *a.* crooked; curved. *—qáf kahná,* to abuse.

Lambá, *n.* Long; tall; expanded; great; large; spacious; capacious. *—honá,* to make off; to take to one's heels. *lambí chaurí háṉkná,* to tell a long story; to brag, or boast.

Lambaṛ, *n.* A fox.

Lambar, *n. (Corr. from the English Number)* Rank; turn. *—dár,* headman of a village who is responsible for collecting and paying Government revenue. *—wár, adv.* in order; by turns.

Lamhá, *n.* A moment; a minute; an istant.

Lampaṭ, *a.* Lewd; lascivious; debauch; wanton; lecherous. *—tá,* n. The habit of wantonness; lewdness; lasciviousness.

Lambotará, *a.* Tall; overlong.

Lams, *n.* The sense of touch.

La'n, *n.* Abuse; rebuke; censure; vituperation. *—t'an,* cursing; imprecating.

Láná, *v.* To bring; to fetch; to introduce; to import.

La'nat, *n.* Abuse; curse; imprecation; malediction. *—í,* accursed; execrable.

Laṉgar, *n.* A communal feast; a system of offering food to those visiting a place of (Sikh) worship. *—lagáná,* v. To distribute free.

Laṉgar, *n.* Anchor (of a ship or a boat). *—dálná,* v. to cast anchor; to come to anchor. *—Uṭháná,* v. To set sail.

Laṉgaṛ, *n.* (see **laṉgaṛá**); A condition causing limping; a pebble tied to a string or rope as ballast when the string is flung to bring down something distant or flying in the air (like a kite). *—dín,* a. One who is limping. [a phrase used as a tease-word].

Laṉgaṛá, *a.* Lame; limp. This is also a variety of mangoes found in India. *—ná,* v. To limp; to hobble.

Laṉgaṛí, *n.* Ostensibly the female of a limping person; actually a leg-trick by which one trips an opponent, or even a friend in jest. *—márná,* v. To apply the fore-mentioned leg-trick.

Laṉghan, *n.* Starvation; abstinence from food. *—karná,* to fast; to go without food.

Langoṭ, Langoṭá, *n.* A strip of cloth tucked around to cover one's private parts; traditionally referred to by the English as loin-cloth. *—ká kachchá,* a. Lewd; lustful; one with a weakness for sex; 'socially active' or promiscuous. *—ká sachchá,* a. Sexually righteous; one who is not given to instant sexual gratification. *—band,* a. Celibate. *—ṭiyá yár,* a. Close friend; a chum. *—bandhwáná,* v. To render penniless; to make destitute *—bikwáná,* v. To deprive some one of the barest minimum; to render indigent. *—í men mast,* a. Happy and carefree in abject poverty, or even adversity.

Langṛá, *a.* Lame; halt. *—haṭ, n.* lameness. *—áná,* to limp.

Langúr, *n.* A baboon.

Lanká, *n.* An Island at the Southern tip of Indian peninsula; modern Sri Lanka. *sone kí—* (literally) a city built of gold that was burnt down by the monkey-messenger of Lord Ráma called Hanuman. (proverbially) an edifice constructed on arrogance that could be brought down by the slightest determined effort by a worthy opponant.

Lamtaráni, *n.* Boasting; bragging; conceitedness.

Lap, *n.* A handful.

Lapak, *n.* Bound; spring; leap; flash. *—ná,* to catch; to seize; to hurry; to flash.

Lapaṭ, *n.* A Flame; flash.

Lapeṭ, *n.* Fold; bandage; girth; circumference. *—ná,* to fold; to wrap up; to pack; to roll; to enclose. *—dár,* adj. Wrap-around; fit for wrapping. *—men áná,* v. to become entangled with; to get trapped.

Laqab, *n.* Title; appellation of honour; nickname.

Laqat, *a.* Weak; feeble; decrepit; infirm.

Laqlaq, *n.* A stork.

Laqwa, *n.* Paralysis.

Laṛ, *n.* String; cord; twine; thread; chain; series; row; line; company.

Lár, *n.* Saliva; spittle.

Láṛ *n.* Caress; coaxing; playfulness of a child.

Laṛáí, *n.* War; battle; quarrel; fight; combat; hostility; enmity. *—ká sámán,* ammunition; munitions. *andaráni—,* civil war.

Laṛait, *n.* A fighter; combatant; one who possesses a fighting skills.

Laṛáká, *a.* Quarrclsome; riotous; pugnacious; warlike; marital.

Laṛakpan, *n.* Boyish behaviour; childishness; puerility.

Larazná, *v.* To shake to tremble; to shiver; to quiver.

Laṛbaṛáná, *v.* To stammer; to stutter; to falter to stagger.

Laṛhiya, *n.* A small cart.

Laṛká, *n.* Boy; younman; son; male child; (proverbially) bridegroom.

Laṛkí, *n.* A girl; maid; lass; daughter.

Láṛlá, *a.* Darling; beloved.

Laṛná, *v.* To fight; to wage war. *lar parná, v.* to fall out.

Larzish, *n.* Shaking; trembling; earthquake; ague.

Las, *n.* Clamminess; stickiness. *—dár, a.* viscous; glutinous; clammy.

Lásá, *n.* Glue; bird-lime; anything glutinous or clammy.

Lásh, *n.* A dead body; a corpse; a carcass. *—dálná, (lit.)* to throw (one) down the corpse; to knock down dead; to kill on the spot.

Lashkar, *n.* Army camp. *—kashi,* mobilising an army. *pesh*—an advance guard of an army.

Lassan/ Lahsun/ Lassun, *n.* Garlic.

Lassán, *a.* Eloquent; fluent; garrulous; loquacious. *—í,* eloquence; garrulity; loquaciousness.

Lassí, *n.* a cooling drink, sweet or salty (depending on your choice) prepared by liquidising yoghurt/ curd. Often taken with breakfast, or lunch, occasionally on its own.

Lat, *n.* Bad habit; vice; evil practice; whim; faultiness; defectiveness.

Laṭ, S. *n.* A fool; a stupid fellow; a lock of hair; tangled silk.

Lát, *n.* Leg, kick. *—on ke bhút báton se nahín mánte,* (proverb): Some people only understand the language of brute force; Rod is the only logic of fools. *—márná,* v. To kick; to spurn; to give up with contempt.

Láṭ, *n. (Corr. from the English).* Lord; lot (in a sale); pillar; obelisk; minaret; old or worn-out clothes.

Latáfat, *n.* Elegance; deliciousness; delicacy; pleasantness; purity; handsomeness; gracefulness.

Laṭakná, *v.* To hang; to suspend; to droop; to depend on.

Lathāṭná, *v.* To pursue; to insult; to revile; to besmear; to daub.

Láṭhí, Laṭhiyá, *n.* Stick; staff; endgel; club; baton.

Latíf, *n.* Elegant; graceful; beautiful; agreeable; courteous;

fine; delicate —*gizá,* light food. —*taba', a.* of gentle disposition.

Latífá, *n.* Joke; witticism; anecdote. —*go/báz,* n. A stand-up joker.

Laṭká, *n.* Charm; fascination; spell; incantation; a simple remedy; *a.* hung; suspended; pendant; dangling.

Laṭkan, *n.* Anything hanging; an ear-drop; a nose-ring; a pendant; a hanging-lamp; a pendulum.

Laṭkáná, *v.* To cause to hang or dangle; to hang; to suspend; to append; to attach (to); to put off; to postpone.

Laṭpaṭáná, *v.* To rock; to totter to stagger; to trip; to walk affectedly; to loiter; to stammer or falter (in) speech.

Laṭṭhá, *a.* A log; a raft; a long bamboo pole used for land measurement. Also, a tradename for awhite bleached cotton cloth.

Laṭṭú, *a.* A spinning top; a toy; (also means) a light bulb; knob. *par —honá,* v. To fall head over heals for—; to be bewitched by; to be enamoured with to be dazzled by.

Lau, *n.* Flame (of fire); any pointed flame.

Lau, *n.* Deep meditation; attention; devotion; ardent desire; longing; craving.

Lauh, *n.* A table; a tablet; a plank or board for writing on.

Laukí, *n.* A gourd a pampkin.

Laukik, S. and H. *a.* Worldly; popular; familiar; ordinary; usual; common; customary.

Laukná, *v.* To shine; to glitter; to sparkle; to flash.

Laukná, Lokná, *v.* To catch (a ball, &c.).

Laulín, Lavlín, *a.* Engrossed in; absorbed in; immersed in [relevant to pleasurable activities]; deep in thought.

Launá, *v.* To cut; to move; to reap; *n.* cutting; reaping —*kál, n.* reaping-time; harvest.

Launḍá, *n.* A boy; a lad; a son; a page; *(Fem.), laundí,* a girl; a daughter; a slave-girl; a servant-girl; a bond-maid.

Launjí, *n.* Pickle.

Lauṛá, *n.* Penus; male genital organ.

Laus, A, *n.* Contamination; pollution; defilement; impurity.

Lauṭáná, *n.* To turn over; to invert; to send back; to return; to reject.

Lauṭná, *v.* To turn over; to turn back; to return; to retreat; to play false; to be false (to). *lauṭ pauṭ chhápná,* to print on both sides.

Lauz, *n.* An almond; a kind of sweetment containing almonds or made in the shape of almonds.

Lává, *n.* Reaper; a harvest-hand; bringer. (proverb) —*lutrá,* adj. A tale-bearer; a slanderer.

Lavaṇ, *n.* Salt. —*kachchh,* n. salt marsh. —*bhaskar,* n. a mixture of various salts, used for medicinal purposes. —*ságar,* a. salt sea; salty sea.

Lavang, Laung, *n.* Clove; also a decorative piece of jewellery worn on the pierced nose, often made of precious matal, often studded with small gems and shaped like a clove.

Lávanya, *n.* Beauty, charm, loveable quality. (see *Lunáí* also).

Lavázimá, Lavázmá, *n.* Accoutrement; paraphernelia; perceived necessities (like pickles and preserves with basic meals); hence the plural use—*Lavázmát.*

Láwá, *n.* A kind of quail.

Lawáhiq, *n. Plur. of Láhiq or Láhíqá)* Relations; kindred; followers; dependants; servants.

Láwáris, *a.* Heirless; childless; *n.* an orphan.

Lázíb, *a. (Plur. of Lazb.)* Hard; difficult; solid.

Lázim, *n.* Anything that is necessary or requisite; *a.* necessary; essential; incumbent; important; suitable; proper; inseparable. —*malzúm,* reciprocated; reciprocal; correlative.

Lazíz, *a.* Sweet delicious; pleasant; savoury; tasteful.

Lazzat, *n. (Plur. of Lazzát),* Pleasure; deliciousness; flavour; relish.

Lehí, *n.* Paste.

Lekh, *n.* Signature; a writing; a document; an epistle; a letter.

Lekhá, *n.* A written document; an account; a ledger; regard; estimation; state; condition; style. —*púrá karná, v.* to settle or close an account. *lekhe,* in the estimation; from the point of view of.

Lekhak, *n.* A writer; a scribe; a clerk; an author; an accountant.

Lekhaní, *n.* A writing reed; a reed-pen; a pen.

Lekin, *conj.* But; still; however; notwithstanding; in spite of.

Lená, *v.* To take; to accept; to receive; to buy; to borrow; to consume; to seize; to conquer; to extort. *le dálná, v.* to master completely. *lená ek na dená do, (Lit.)* neither one to receive nor two to give; having nothing to gain or lose; having no concern whatever with. *lene ke dene* *parná, (Lit.)* to be compelled to pay instead of receiving; to be involved in a difficulty; to be or become a loser (by); to be on the point of death.

Len-den, *n. (Lit.)* Taking and giving; buying and selling; trade; barter; business.

Lep, *n.* Plaster; ointment; mortar; chunam; whitewash; smearing; daubing.

Lepálak, *n.* An adopted child; a foster-child.

Lesná, *v.* To plaster; to smear; to daub.

Leṭná, *v.* To lie down; to rest. *Letwán,* a. One lying flat; horizontal; horizontally placed.

Lezam, *n.* A bow with an iron chain instead of a string, used by athletes.

Libás, *n.* Dress; costume; apparel.

Lifáfa, *n.* An envelope; a wrapper; outer case; *(fig.)* gilding; whitewash; outward show; anything frail or fragile. *tikatdár—,* a stamped envelope.

Lifáfiya, *a.* Having a gaudy outer cover; showy; ostentatious.

Liháf, *n.* A coverlet; quilt; a counterpane; a quilted garment; *(met.)* a wife.

Liház, *n.* Observation; view; attention; regard; consideration; respect; reference; look; glance; notice; shame; importance; weight; *ba—,* in consideration of; with reference to. *—na karná,* to pay no attention or regard to; to lose all sense of shame.

Lihází, *adv.* Consequently; for this reason; therefore.

Lík, *n.* Track-mark; line; tradition; convention. *—par chalná,* v. To follow a set of guiding rules, or patterns.

Líkh, *n.* A nit; the egg of a louse.

Likhná, *v.* To write; to copy; to compose (a work, &c.); to register; to portray; *n.* writing; handwriting.

Lílá, *n.* Play; sport; pastime; diversion. *—watí, a.* playful; sportive; frolicsome; beautiful.

Lilná, *v.* To swallow; to gulp.

Lípná, *v.* To plaster (especially with clay and cowdung); to whitewash.

Lipaṭaná, *v.* To stick; to cling; to wrap; to wind around; to join; to unite with; to embrace; to get entangled with; to get involved with.

Lipṭáná, *v.* To fold; to wrap; to embrace.

Liyáqat, *n.* Fitness; suitability; worth; merit; skill; ability;

sptitude; prudence; judgment *hasb-i—*, according to the merit or ability (of).

Liye, *pre.* For; on account (of); in behalf (of); for the sake of.

Lobán, Lubán, *n.* A kind of incense; frankincense; benzoin. *—dání,* a censer.

Lobh, *n.* Greed; avarice; handering. *—í,* a. greedy; one who is liable to hanker for.

Loch, *n.* Starch; stickiness.

Lochan, *n.* The eye.

Log, *n.* Mankind; people; folk; family; tribe.

Lohá, *n.* Iron; a weapon; a sword. *lohe ke chane chabáná, v. (lit.)* to chew iron grams; to accomplish a very difficult task. *lohár,* a worker in iron; blacksmith. *lohárkḥána,* n. black-smith's workshop or forge; a smithy.

Loí, *n.* A blanket; flannel.

Lok, *n.* The world; universe; region; mankind; people; sight; regard. *swarg—,* heaven, *pátál—,* hell. *—prasidh,* famous or notorious.

Lok-aishaṇá, *n.* Desire for popularity; hankering after public recognition.

Lomaṛ, *n.* He-fox. [Commonly known in India as **Bheṛiyá**].

Lomṛí, *n.* She-fox [Also see **Lomar**].

Lon, *n.* Salt. *—iyá, a.* saline; brackish; saltish; *n.* a maker or vendor of salt.

Lop, *n.* Cutting off; mutilation; disappearance; annulling; *a.* vanished; hidden.

Loṛhá, *n.* A stone pestle.

Loṭ, *n.* Wallowing; rolling *—pot honá,* to roll and toss rest-lessly; to die suddenly.

Loṭá, *n.* A small metal pot.

Loṭan, *n.* Rolling; tumbling; a tumbler pigeon.

Loth, *n.* Corpse; dead body; carcass.

Loṭná, *v.* To roll; to toss about; to wallow; to sprawl.

Lú'áb, *n.* Spittle; saliva; mucus.

Lubáb, *n.* Pith; essence; the best part of a thing; *a.* pure; unmixed; unsullied.

Lubháná, *v.* To charm; to fascinate; to allure.

Luchchá, *n.* A vagabond; a reprobate; a dissolute or profligate fellow; *a.* low; mean; base; wicked; dissolute.

Lugat, *n. (Plur. Lugát).* Tongue; dictionary; glossary.

Lugwí, *a.* Verbal; literal.

Lukáná, *v.* To hide; to conceal.

Lukná, *v.* To hide oneself; to lie hidden.

Lúlú, *n. (Plur. La'áli.)* A peal.

Lungí, *n.* Long loose sheet, wrapped around one's waist, flowing downward, to make a sort of skirt.

Lunj, Lunjá, *a.* Without hands and (or) feet; crippled lame; *a.* one who has lost the use of his hands and (or) feet; a cripple.

Lúṭ, *n.* Plunder; pillage; spoil; booty. *—luterá,* a plunder; marauder; freebooter. *—ká mál,* plunder; booty.

Lúṭaná, *v.* To loot; to plunder; to rob; to extort; to overcharge; to misappropriate; to ravel; to delight in [*as in* Mazá lúṭaná= to enjoy; to have fun with, &c].

Luṭáná, *v.* To cause to plunder; to squander; to roll about.

Lutf, *n.* Courtesy; favour; kindness; elegance; pleasure; enjoyment. *—yeh hai,* the principal thing is.

Lutí, *n.* An adopted child; *a.* adopted; brought up in the family; by choice.

M, m, stands for (म) in Hindi and (م) in Urdu. In its diluted, half-value sound it also functions as a nasal tone in the middle of a word as well as at the end of one.

Má, *n.* A mother; a term of respect applied to an elderly woman; *bin má báp ká, n.* an orphan; *a.* orphan; fatherless and motherless.

Machalná, *v.* To be wayward/ perverse/ obstinate; to be cross; to go on isisting; to sulk. *Ji-,* v. To feel nausea; to feel sick; to feel like vomiting.

Machán, *n.* A stage; a platform; a scaffold.

Machherá, *n.* A fisherman; a fish-catcher. *—í/Machheran,* n. A fisher-woman. [Also called *Machhuárá/Machhwárá*].

Máchchh/Matsya, *n.* Fish the tenth incarnation of Lord Vishnu, known as *Matsyávatár.*

Machchhar, *n.* A mosquito; a gnat.

Machchhí/Machhlí/Machhrí, *n.* A fish. *—ká par,* n. The fin of fish. *—wálá,* n. A fishmonger.

Machhuá/ Machhwá, *n.* A fisher-man; a fish catcher.

Machláná, *v.* To be wayward; to pretend ignorance; to feel nausea.

Mad/ Madd, *n.* Extension; protraction; entry; article; columns; heading. *—I-nazar,* adv. Within sight; in view; taking account of.

Mad/ Madya, *n.* Intoxicant; alcoholicdrinks; opiates; arro-gance; vanity. *—bharí,* a. Passionate; in a fit of passion. *—chúr karná,* v. To deflate a swollen head; to knowck out one's pride; to cut some one to size; toput some one in his/her place.

Mádá, *n.* Female of a specie [*Nar* being the male]. In Urdu and persian, the same word means 'scope' room' allowance etc.'.

Madad, *n.* help; assistance; aid; succour; support.

Mádak, *a.* Intoxicating; fascinat-ing; bewitching; charming.

Madákhil, *a.* Income; revenue; inward flow.

Madár, *n.* Axis; pivot; centre; the turning point; an orbit.

Mádar, *n.* Mother. *—zád,* a. innate; congenial. *—í,* a. Maternal; motherly. *Mádarí Zabán,* n. Mother tongue; native language. *—I-watan,* n. Mother country; native land. *—chod,* a. A swear word [meaning *mother-fucker*].

Madárí, *n.* A juggler'a conjurer; a tumbler; an acrobat; a street-side entertainer (often accompanied by a minor animal show).

Madarsá/ Madrassá, *n.* school; educational institutions run by Muslim communities on strict religious lines.

Maddáh, *n.* One who praises; an admirer; a fan; one who eulogises.

Madfan, *a.* a cemetery; a burial place.

Madfún, *a.* Buried; interred; hidden; underground.

Madh/ Madhya, *a.* Centre; middle; within; inside. *—kál,* a. Medieval period [in history]. *—sthatá,* n. Mediation. *—márg,* n. The middle path [in buddhist faith]; a centrist policy. *—rátri,* n. Midnight. *—vay,* a. Middle age. *—varg/vitt,* Middle class; bourgeois.

Madhu, *n.* Honey; the juice or nectar of flowers; the grape wine; any intoxicating liquor or drug; pride; the season of spring; prime; or bloom of youth.

Madhur, *n.* Sweetness; syrup; *a.* sweet; pleasant; agreeable; soft; tender; melodious.

Mágh, *n.* Name of a month in the Hindú calender. *—melá,* n. An annual gathering of devotees on the confluence of Gangá and Jamuná, at Prayág-ráj lasting the whole month.

Maghá, *n.* The tenth constellation; an astrological mark in Hindu calculations.

Mag̣lúb, *a.* Conquered; subdued; subjugated.

Mag̣múm, *a.* Grieved; sad; melancholy; sorrowful.

Mag̣ríb, *n.* The west. *—í,* western.

Mag̣rúr, *v.* Proud; haughty; arrogant; overbearing.

Mag̣z, *n.* The brain; narrow; kernel; pith; essence; the best part of anything.

Mag̣zí, *n.* Edge; hem; seam; border.

Máh, Más, *n.* Month.

Mahá, *a.* Great; big one; immense; mammoth. *—kál,* n. The great equaliser; the annihilator; the Time Indefinite. *—dev,* n. a name for Lord Shiva. *—nagar,* n. A big city; a metropolis. *—pralay,* n. the Great Deluge. *—prasthán/ prayán,* n. The final journey; the death. *—purush,* a. A great person; a venerated one. *—balí,* a. A very powerful person. *—mátya,* n. The Prime Minister. *—mati,* a. A great genius; a highly intelligent person. *—múrkh,* a. A blithering idiot. *—rathí,* a. A great warrior; a leading person in his chosen field of work. *—ságar,* a. An ocean (as bigger than mere 'sea'). *—prasád,* (euphemism for) meat, meat obtained from a sacrificed beast. &c.

Mahabbat, [See *Muhabbat*].

Mahájan, *n.* The man with money; the money-lender, the trader. (literally means; great man).

Mahak, *n.* Fragrance; odour; scent; perfume. —*ná,* to diffuse an agreeable odour or perfume.

Mahakmá, *a.* A tribunal; department; section.

Mahal, *n.* House; place; palace; abode; mansion; opportunity; queen. —*saráe,* private apartment (of a king or a nobleman); seraglio; *bar—,* suitable; appropriate.

Mahallá [See *Muhallá*].

Mahán, *a.* Great; grand; eminent. —*tá,* n. Nobility; eminence; Quality of greatness.

Mahangá, High-priced; dear; costly; expensive.

Mahangái, Mahangí, *a.* Dearness; High cost; expensiveness. —*bhattá,* a. Dearness allowance; an income suppliment given to employees to keep them apace with the rising cost of living.

Mahant, *n.* A monk; an abbot; a religious devotee.

Mahar, *n.* Property settled upon a wife at the time of marriage (amongst the Muslims).

Mahár, Mihar, *n.* A piece of wood with a string attached to it, put through the nose of a camel (to guide him by); rein; bridle; *be—,* or *shutr-i-bemahár, a.* unbridled; unrestrained.

Máhar, Máhir, *n.* Expert; specialist; skilled; adept; a dab hand. —*Mahárat,* n. Expertise; speciality; &c.

Mahátam, Máhátmya, *a.* Importance; glory; praise of qualities of—. [In India, very often a chapter is added to most holy texts, like *Gítá* and *Rámáyan,* simply offering a narrative of qualities and importance and impact of the actual text. This chapter is titled *Máhátmya*].

Mahátmá, *n.* Literally, a great soul; revered one; venerated one; a commonly used nick-name for M.K. Gandhi, referred to as 'the father of the nation' in India.

Maháwat, Mahaut, *n.* Elephant-driver.

Mahbúb, *n.* One who is beloved; a sweetheart; a beautiful or lovely woman.

Mahfil, *n.* A place of meeting or assembly; an assembly; a congregation.

Muhfúz, *adj.* Safe; protected.

Mahfúz, *a.* Guarded; preserved; protected; kept in safety; exempted; committed to memory.

Mahimá, *n.* Greatness; magnitude; glory; majesty; power; high rank.

Mahín, *n.* Fine; thin. *—áwáz, n.* shrill sound; a high note.

Mahíná, *n.* A month; monthly pay, salary, or wages.

Máhir, *n.* A master (of any art or craft); an adept; an expert; *a.* acute; ingenious; skilful; expert; well-versed (in); familiar (with).

Máhiyat, *n.* Essence; quality; nature; intrinsic worth; condition; matter of fact.

Mahjúr, *a.* Separated; cut off; forsaken.

Mahoday, *n.* Sir; an honorific form of address. *Mahodayá,* n. Madam; the feminine version of the same as above.

Mahram, *n.* A spouse; an intimate friend; bodice.

Mahrúm, *a.* Forbidden; prohibited; debarred; excluded; disappointed; unfortunate; wretched.

Mahshaṛ, *n.* A place of assembly; the Day of Judgment.

Mahshúr, *a.* Congregated; assembled; raised from the dead.

Mahsúl, *n.* Produce; profit; advantage; revenue; tax *a.* produced; extracted; acquired; collected. *—chor,* a smuggler. *—lagáná,* to levy or impose a tax.

Mahsús, *a.* Felt; perceived; perceptible; sensible.

Mahur, *n.* Poison.

Mahz, *a.* Pure; unmixed; unalloyed; mere; simple; *adv.* purely; simply; merely; solely utterly; quite. *—náchír, n.* a mere nothing; a mere trifle. *—qaid, n.* simple imprisonment.

Mahzar, *n.* Assembly; a place of assembly; a public attestation.

Mahzúz, *a.* Fortunate; blessed; wealthy; contended; pleased; glad; happy.

Maidá, *n.* An open field; a plain; a racecourse; a parade ground; a battlefield; war. *—chhorná,* to flee from the battle-field. *—márná,* to win a battle.

Mail, *n.* Dirt; filth; pollution; rust; scum; *(Met.)* sadness; vexation; displeasure. *—chhántná,* to refine; to clarify. *—láná,* to be sad; to take offence.

Mailá, *a.* Dirty; filthy; foul; unclean; soiled; polluted.

Mainá, *n.* Starling; a talkative bird; superior mynah bird. [In Indian folklore, *Kissá Totá-Mainá* is a very popular series of narrative tales wherein a parrot and a mynah bird tell a succession of tales of male and female infidelity and betrayal of true love.

Maithun, *n.* Copulation; sexual intercourse.

Maitrí, *n.* Friendship; liaison.

Maiyat, *n.* Corpse, wrapped up in cloth and carried to burial grounds.

Majál, *n.* Place; room; scope; opportunity; power; authority; ability.

Majális, *n. (Plur. of Majlis).* Sessions; conferences; assemblies.

Májará, *n.* An incident; event; accident; circumstances.

Majbúr, *part.* Compelled; constrained; helpless; oppressed. *—an, adv.* compulsarily; of necessity; necessarily. *—í, n.* compulsion; coercion; constrained; helplessnes.

Majhalá, Majhlá, *a.* Middle, intermediate; *adv. majhile,* in the middle; *a.* in the midst.

Majhár, Majhdhár, H. *n.* The middle; centre; *a.* in middle; in the midst (of).

Majhúlí, P. *n.* Ignorance; indolence; laziness.

Majíd, A. *a.* Glorious; noble; exalted; high. *Kalám majíd, n.* the glorious word of God; the Qurán.

Majíth, *n.* A drug, the root of which yields a red dye.

Majlis, A. *n.* Assembly; congregation; council; a convivial meeting. *—e-raqs, n.* a. dancing-party; a ball. *—í,* a person invited to an assembly.

Majma', A. *n.* Place of assembly; congregation; assembly collection; heap. *—ul-bahrain, n.* place where two seas meet.

Majmú'a, *n.* The whole; the aggregate; crowd; assembly; a form (in printing); a magazine. *—i-qawánín, n.* a body or code of laws.

Majnún, *n.* A maniac; a fanatic; *part.* insane; mad; demanted.

Majrúh, *a.* Wounded; smitten.

Majúr/ Mazdúr, *n.* Labourer; worker; hired hand. *—í,* n. wages; remuneration for work performed.

Majús, *n.* A fire-worshipper; Guebre; follower of Zoroaster.

Makaí, [See Makká].

Makán, *n.* Place; station; house; home; abode; residence.

Makar, *n.* The tenth sign of the zodiac, capricorn; a crocodile. *—rekhá,* a. tropic of Capricorn;

—*sankránti,* a. A day of transition in the month of *Mágh* when the sun crosses over to the mansion of Capricornus.

Makarand, *n.* Nactar of the fragrant flowers that the honey-bees draw.

Makháná, *n.* A plant; the parched seed of the lotus.

Makḥfí, *a.* Hidden; secret; occult. —*na rahe,* be it known.

Makḥlasí, *n.* Safety; security; deliverance; liberation; liberty.

Makḥlúq, *n. (Plur. Makhlúqát.)* Created things, creature.

Makhlút, *a.* Mixed; mingled; blended; confused.

Makḥmal, *n.* Velvet.

Makḥmúr, *a.* Drunk; inebriated; intoxicated.

Makḥná, *n.* An elephant without tusks; a cock without spurs.

Makḥrúj, *n.* Exit; point of egress; outlet; utterance; source; origin; issue.

Makḥsús, *a.* Particular; peculiar; specific; private.

Makḥtún, *a.* Circumcised.

Makḥzan, *n.* A storehouse; granary; barn.

Makká, *n.* Indian corn; maze.

Makkár, *n.* A cheat; an impostor; a knave; *a.* false; deceitful; cunning; crafty.

Makkhan, *n.* Butter.

Makkhí, Mákhí, *n.* A fly; sight of a gun. —*chús,* a miser; a skinflint. (See **'Makshiká**).

Makṛí, *n.* A spider.

Makrúh, *a.* pated; abhorred; odious; detestable; loathsome; disgusting; obscene.

Makshiká, *n.* A fly. —*stháne makshiká,* adv. copying blindly; imitating without thought or relevance.

Maktá, *n.* First couplet of a *Ghazal.* [In this Persian poetic form it is only the first two lines which rhyme with each other. All the following couplets will have the first line not rhyming and the latter line rhyming with the ending syllable of this *Maktá*] [Also see *Matlá*].

Maktab, *n.* A school.

Maktúb, *n.* A writing; a letter; an epistle; *a.* written; sewn or pasted together. —*i'laih,* an addressee.

Mal, *n.* Dirt; filth; dust; rust; dregs; excrement.

Mál, *n.* Riches; wealth; property; merchandise; goods; effects; estate; rent; or revenue (from land).

—*dár-i-amámat, n.* a trustee. —*i-matrúka,* a bequest; a legacy. *naqdi*—, a dainty; a delicacy.

Málá, *n.* A wreath; a garland; a chaplet (of flowers); a row; a chain; a string (of beads, &c.) necklace; a rosary; a collection; a vocabulary; a book. —*pherná yá japná,* to recite a prayer on beads.

Maláhat, Goodness; elegance; beauty; delieacy; a rich brown complexion.

Malái, *n.* Cream; scum.

Malál, *n.* Compunction; regret; remorse; sadness; displeasure.

Málámál, *a.* Full; replete; brimful; abundant.

Malámat, *n.* Reproach; censure; rebuke; blame.

Malbús, *n.* Clothes; wearing apparel; *a.* clothed; clad; dressed. (From 'Libas').

Malichchh, Mlechchh, *n.* A sinner; a foreigner; a wicked being; of an unclean race, or caste; an infidel.

Málí, *n.* A gardener; a florist. (*Fem.* Málin).

Málik, *n.* King; master; owner; husband; the Supreme Being.

Malik, *n.* A king.

Maliká, *n.* A queen. —*i-mu'azzima,* an empress.

Malín, *a.* Sad; vexed; troubled; dirty; polluted.

Málísh, *n.* Rubbing; friction; massage; shampooing; polishing; burnishing.

Málíyat, *n.* Wealth; opulence; value; worth; revenue.

Malla, *n.* A wrestler; fighter; a professional boxer; a bodybuilder.

Malláh, *n.* A sailor; a seaman; mariner; a boatman.

Málkham, Malkhamb, *v.* An upright dumbell or post [used in gymnastic exercising]; also an upright post in a sugar mill.

Mal-más, *n.* An intercalary (thirteenth) month (in which no religious ceremonies shoudl be performed).

Malná, *v.* To rub; to scrub; to anoint; to tread on, to massage.

Mál-shri, *n.* Name of a *raginí.*

Ma'lúm, *a.* Known; distinguished; renowned; famous; evident; manifest; clear; certain; obvious.

Ma'lúmát, *n.* Things known; sciences; information.

Mámá, *n.* Maternal uncle.

Mamerá/ Mamerí, *adj.* Offspring [male and female] of one's maternal uncle (mother's brother).

Mámí, *n.* Maternal aunt.

Mamnún, *a.* Thankful; grateful.

Mámúl, *n.* Custom; habit; the norm. *-í,* a Ordinary; customary; normal; usual. *Hasb-i-,* adv. In the normal manner; as usual; in the customary way; as a matter of routine.

M'amúr, *a.* Inhabited; populated; cultivated; flourishing; full; replete; ample. *—í, n.* population; cultivation; flourishing condition; fulness.

Man, *n.* A maund in weight; a measurement of commodities equal to almost 90 lbs./ 36 Kilograms/ 40 seers. [No more in usage].

Man, *n.* The mind; intelligence; heart; soul; spirit; inclination; purpose; character; mood; temper. *—bahláná,* to divert the mind. *—maují,* conceited; capricious; jovial. *—uktáná, v.* to be tired or sick of; to be disgusted with.

Má<u>n</u>, *n.* Mother, mother-figure earth-mother. *—báp,* n. Mother-and-father; parents. *—jáyá,* a. Born of the same mother; real brother/sister.

Mán, *n.* Esteem; respect; prestige; dignity; value; measure; scale; (in a negative sense) arrogance; conseit; amorous sulking [*Mán karná, rúthaná*] *—chitra,* n. Map; site plan. *—dand,* n. A standard, a criterion. *—patra,* n. A citation; an address of honour. *—bhang,* n. Disillusionmnt; discomfiture. *—mardan,* adv. being put inone's proper place; giving or receiving a knock to one's arrogance. *—rakhná,* adv. To act in deference to; to show respect to.

Maná, *n.* Forbidding; prohibiting; refusing; hindrance; obstacle.

Manádí, Munádí, *n.* Proclamation (especially by beat of drum); preaching.

Manáhí, *adv.* Denial; forbidden; prohibition; restriction; hindrance; impediment; opposition [also see *Nishedh*].

Mánaná, *v.* To agree to; to accept; to be conciliated; to respect; to obey; to allow; to believe; to submit; to grant; to acknowledge; to consider; to feel; to experience.

Manáná, *v.* To cause to mind; to reason with; to persuade; to conciliate; to propitiate.

Manaswí, *adj.* Intelligent; wise; intellectual; self-willed; spiritual.

Manaswitá, *n.* Intelligence; wisdom; spirituality.

Mánav, *n.* Of human specie. *—tá,* n. Humanity; quality of being a human; compassion; intelligence, &c.

Manch, *n.* Stage, dais; platform; forum. *—an, v.* staging; presentation on the stage.

Mand, *a.* A suffix joined to substantives to form adjectives denoting possession, &c., *e.g., daulat—,* wealthy; rich; *'aql—,* sensible.

Mand, Manda, *a.* Slow; inactive; tedious; dull; stupid; cheap; slack; weak; trifling; small; sick; bad; wicked; *n.* the planet Saturn; *adv.* slowly; softly. *—par jáná,* to become abated; to decline; to fall (as a market).

Mánḍ, *n.*Ricewater; gruel; starch.

Mánd, *n.* Den; lair; *a.* dim; faint.

Mánda, *a.* Tired; weary; fatigued; ailing; indisposed; left; remaining.

Mandágni, *a.* (literally means 'slowing fire'), actually, indigestion; dyspepsia.

Mandákiní, *n.* An alternative name for the holy river Gangá; celestial river, Ganges.

Mandal, *n.* Disc of the sun or moon; circle; ring; orbit; halo (round the sun or moon); the sky; circumference; compass; wheel; globe; sphere; arena; *a.* round circular; spherical; zone; *rás—, n.* the zodiacal circle.

Manḍalí, Manḍli, *n.* Company; as sembly; association; sect.

Manḍap, *n.* An open hall; a pavilion; a shed; arbour; a bower. *—i-atlasí,* the lower; heaven, or crystalline sphere.

Manḍí, *n.* Market; mart; warehouse.

Manḍir, *n.* A temple; a home; a housing.

Máng, *n.* Want; request; demand. *—honá, v.* to be in request or demand.

Máng, *n.* Road; path; division; parting of the hair. *—jalí,* a widow.

Mangal, *n.* planet Mars; Tuesday; well-being; auspicious. *—kalash/ ghat,* a. a container (symbolic) of benediction; *—kárí,* a. Harbinger of good fortune; *—kámná,* a. good wishes; benediction; *káraj/ kárya,* a. a festive occasion; a cermonial; *—gán/gít,* a. tumult of auspicious singing; *—dáyak/ prad,* a bestower of good fotune; *—samáchár,* a good news; *—súchak,* a auguring good luck; *—sútra,* n. (literally) the lucky thread; a sanctified necklace worn by married women as a guarantor of their spouse's well-being.

Mangalácharan, *n.* Auspicious chants, ritually and ceremoniaously performed to bless an occasion; also, the initial verses of a work of literature (a kinf of preferatory apology and acknolwedgement of other contributors to the work).

Mangalí, *a.* A boy or a girl whose horoscope shows Mars in 4th, 8th or 12th house, and thus renders that boy or that girl as somewhat unlucky.

Mángná, *v.* To ask for; to request; to demand; to beg; to solicit; to entreat; to want; to desire; to borrow; to ask in marriage.

Mangetar, *n.* One to whom a man or woman is betrothed or affianced.

Mangní, *n.* Asking in marriage; betrothal; a loan.

Mangol, *n.* A proper name for dwellers of Mongolia; also a proper name for tribes that came from Central Asia and spread through out Southern and South-Western Asia. Mughals, who established an empire in India later on, descended from these ferocious conquerers.

Manhús, *n.* Unfortunate; inauspicious; wretched; ill-omened; abominable; *n.* an unfortunate person.

Maṇi, *n.* A jewel; legend has it that some snakes have a jewel in their crowns and that this is an antidote for all venoms. Such snakes are called *'Mani-dhar'*.

Manihár, *n.* The caste who make or sell bracelets and bangles.

Má'ní, *n.* Meaning; signification; substance; intrinsic quality; interpretation; exploration. *—khez,* adj. Meaningful; purposeful.

Mánind, *a.* Like; resembling; similar (to).

Maniyár, *n.* Merchandise of adornment. *—í,* n. Merchandiser of adornment goods.

Manjan, *n.* Tooth-powder; dentifrice.

Mánjhí, *n.* Master of a vessel; steersman; helmsman; sailor; boatman.

Manjíra, *n.* A kind of cymbal.

Mankúha, *n.* A lawful wife; a married woman.

Mannat, *n.* Assent; promise; vow; desire.

Manohar, *a.* Captivating; fascinating; charming; beautiful.

Manorath, *n.* Desire; aim; object; good; benefit; pleasure. *—suphal honá, v.* to attain one's desire; to accomplish one's object.

Máns, *n.* Flesh; meat.

Mansá, *n.* Wish; desire design; mind; thought. *—púran karná,* to gratify a desire.

Mansab, *n.* Post; office; dignity; ministry. *—dár.* an officer; the holder of a post.

Mansúb, *a.* Connected; related; allied; betrothed; constituted; appointed; attributed.

Mansúba, *n.* Resolution; determination; intention; plan; project; scheme; plot.

Ma<u>n</u>súbá, *n.* Intention; ambition; plan; resolve; scheme. —*karná/ thánaná,* v. To form an ambition; to make a firm plan.

Mansúkh, *a.* Cancelled; abolished; repealed; annulled; effaced.

Mantaq, Mantiq, *n.* Logic; reasoning eloquence. —*iya,* a logician; a litigious person.

Ma<u>n</u>tr, Ma<u>n</u>tra, *n.* Charm; spell; incantation; a passage from the Vedas; a sacred text; spiritual instruction. —*phú<u>n</u>kná,* to cast a spell.

Mánus, Manushya, *n.* A man; a human being. *Manushyatá,* n. Humanity; human race; human beings.

Mánús, *a.* Associated; sociable; friendly; familiar; cheering; comfortable; *n.* a companion; an intimate friend.

Ma<u>n</u>zar, Ma<u>n</u>zir, *n.* Countenance; features; face; sight; spectacle; scene; landscape.

Ma<u>n</u>zil, *n.* A caravansary; an inn; house; dwelling; storey; a stage; destination; boundary; end; limit. —*i-maqsúd,* goal of desire or ambition.

Ma<u>n</u>zilá, Ma<u>n</u>zilát, *n.* Stage; step; station; post of honour; dignity; condition. —*do*—, two-storyed. *ba mánzile,* in the degree or position (of); instead (of).

Ma<u>n</u>zúm, *n.* Anything arranged in a series, line or row; verse; rhyme; poetry; *a.* arranged in order; in verse poetic.

Ma<u>n</u>zúr, *a.* Seen; visible; admired; approved of; sanctioned; granted; acceptable; intended. —*i-nazar,* a favourite; an object of special favour or regard.

Ma<u>n</u>zúrí, *n.* Approval; choice; admission; consent; sanction.

Máp, *n.* Measure.

Mápak, *adj.* Means or tools or measurement.

Maqám, Muqám, *n.* A halt (in the course of a journey); a place of encampment; site; situation; residence. —*karná,* v. To make camp; to make a halt, &c.

Maqbará, *n.* A burial place; a grave; a tomb; a mausoleum.

Maqbúl, *a.* Chosen; approved; accepted; agreed on; agreeable; pleasing.

Maqdúr, *n.* Power; ability; capacity; means; resources;

hasbul.—, adv. according to (one's) power of ability.

Maqnátís, Miqnátís, *n.* A magnet; a loadstone. *—í,* a. Magnetic; attractive; one that draws you to itself. *—í shakhsiyat;* a. Attarctive personality.

Maqrúr, A. *a.* Cut; lent; oppressed with debt; in debt. *—í, n.* one who is in debt.

Maqsad, A. *n.* Meaning; purport; intention; design; desire; object; aim; scope.

Maqsúd, A Intention; purpose; object; scope.

Maqtá, *n.* Cutting; severing; amputation; interruption.

Maqtal, *n.* Place of slaughter; a spot designated for the beheading [of prisoners given a death sentence.

Maqtúl, *a.* One going for beheading; one going to be killed; the object of killing; one chosen for slaughter.

M'aqúl, *a. (Plur. Ma'qúlát).* Perceived by the intellect; intellectual; intelligible; perceptible; reasonable; probable; just; right; liberal; sufficient; nice; choice; *n.* any branch of science or knowledge; philosophy, etc.

Mar, *n.* Dying, *a.* having died, etc. *—jáná, v.* to die; to fade; to swoon. *—jiwná, v.* to recover from death; to escape from the jaws of death. *—pachná, v.* to work oneself to death; to endure pain and sorrow. *Mar-mitná,* adv. To fall head-over-heels for.

Már, *n.* Name given to God of love, *Kámdev.*

Már, P. *n.* A snake; a serpent.

Már, *n.* Beating; striking; thrashing; assaulting; a blow; punishment; affliction; battle; fight; plunder; cure; remedy. *—katyá, a.* quarrelsome; turbulent; *n.* a brawler; a quarrelsome fellow.

Márá, *a.* Beaten; stricken; smitten; killed; slain; destroyed; spilt; *n.* one who is beaten or smitten; a victim; *—márá phirná, v.* to wander about.

Márag, Márg, *n.* Way, route; path; road; course.

Márak, *adj.* Killer; Suppresser; Combatant; antidote.

Ma-rahmat, *n.* Mercy; pity; favour; clemency; pardon; a present.

Maram, Marm, *n.* Secret; mystery; the inner reality. true picture.

Marammat, *n.* Repairing; rectifying; mending; repairing. *—talab, a.* in need of repairs; out of order.

Maraṇ, *n.* Dying; death; decease; dying with shame; ruin; destruction. —*samay, a.* the dying moment; time of death.

Maraz, Marz, A. *n.* Sickness; illness; disease; malady; indisposition. —*e-ashadd, n.* severe illness. —*ul-maut, n.* mortal disease.

Mar-bhúkká, *a.* Famished; starved; greedy; voracious; ravenously hungry.

Mard, P. *n. (Plur. Mardán).* A man; a male; a husband; a hero.

Mardáná, *a.* Manly; brave; courageous; *adv.* Manfully; bravely; courageously; vigorously.

Mardánagí, *n.* Manliness; virility; manhood; valour.

Mardání, *n.* A brave woman; a heroine.

Mardúd, P. *a.* Returned; rejected; repulsed; reprobated; outcast; *n.* a reprobate; an outcast; a wretch.

Mardum, P. *n.* A man; men; people; a polite man; *a.* civil; humane. —*ázár, n.* an oppressor. —*e-chashm, n.* pupil of the eye. —*shumárí, n.* a census.

Mardumak, *n.* Pupil of the eye.

Márfat, [See *Márifat*].

Marg, P. *n.* Death. —*e-nágahání, n.* sudden death. —*e-taba'í, n.* natural death.

Márg, Márag, *n.* The path; way; method; creed; following cult; tradition, &c.

Marghat, *n.* A place where the dead bodies of Hindús are burnt or created; a crematory.

Margúb, *a.* Desired, desirable; agreeable; amiable; lovely; estimable.

Marhabá, *intj.* Hail ! Welcome; Bravo ! Well done !

Marhalá, *n.* Stage (of a journey); halting-place; a battery.

Marham, *n.* Ointment; unguent; plaster; salve.

Marhúm, *n.* One on whom God has had mercy; the deceased; the late; *a.* deceased; defunct; dead.

Márí, *n.* Plague; pestilence; epidemic. —*parná,* plague or pestilence to break out.

Ma'rifá, *n.* A proper noun.

Ma'rifat, *n.* Knowledge; science; learning; erudition; cognizance; acquaintance; means; cause; *prep.* by means of; through the medium of; through the instrumentality of.

Mariyal, *a.* Weak; lean; emaciated; lacking in physical strength and energy; lazy; slow.

Maríz, *a.* Sick; ill; indisposed; infirm; *n.* a patient; a sick person.

Marjád, Marjádá, *n.* [Corruption of sanskrit word *Maryádá*] Station; social status; rank; dignity; honour; credibility. *Marjádat, a.* [Sanskrit *Maryádit*] Disciplined; controlled; rationed; contained; under control.

M'arká, *n.* Fight; war; battle-field. *ma'rke ká,* martial; war-like; important; momentous.

Markab, *n.* Anything upon which one rides, or upon or in which one is carried or conveyed; a horse; a camel; a boat; a saddle; vehicle; carriage; conveyance *(sawárí).*

Markaṭ, *n.* Monkey.

Markaz, *n.* Centre; focal point.

Markaz, *n.* A fixed station; centre (esp of a circle); upper stroke of the letters *káf* and *gáf.* *—i-siql, n.* centre of gravity.

Marm, *n.* Inner-self; innermost; essence; real meaning. *—ántak,* adj. Fatal; terminal; life-threatening.

Marmar, *n.* Marble.

Marná, *v.* To die; to expire; to fade; to set the heart (upon); to desire vehemently; to labour or toil hard; *n.* dying; death; decease; expiry. *marne* or *marne par, a.* about to die; at the point of death. *bin áimarná, v.* to die a premature or violent death.

Márná, *v.* To beat; to strike; to smite; to hit; to kill; to destroy; to plunder; to embezzle; to subdue; to overcome; to quench; to alloy; to suppress; to shoot; to pitch (a tent).

Maroṛ, *n.* Turn; bend; twist; contortion.

Maroṛá, *n.* Gripe; severe pain in the bowels.

Maroṛná, *v.* To turn; to twist; to writhe; to contort; to gripe.

Marsiyá, *n.* An elegy; a dirge.

Martabá, *n.* Degree; dignity; office; turn; times.

Martabán, *n.* A glazed earthen ware or porcelain; jar.

Mártaul, *n.* A hammer.

Martúb, *a.* Moist; humid; damp; wet.

Ma'rúf, *a.* Well-known; famous; renowned; celebrated; notorious.

Ma'rúz, Ma'ruza, *a.* Presented; offered; submitted; related; written; dated; *a.* explanation; presentation; petition.

Marwáríd, *n.* Pearl.

Maryádá, *n.* [See *Marjádá*].

Marz, *n.* Ailment; malady; sickness.

Marzí, *n.* Pleasure; assent;

consent; choice. —*ke muwáfiq,* satisfactory. *apní—se,* voluntarily.

Más, Máns, *n.* Meat; flesh. —*áhárí,* a. One who eats flesh; a meat-eater. —*bhakshí, n.* carnivoye.

Más, Máh, *n.* Month. —*ik,* a. Monthly; every month; *Máhwárí,* adv; Month by month.

Masahrí, Musahrí, *n.* A mosquito curtain.

Masábi, *n. (Plur. of Musíbat).* Misfortunes; calamities; afflictions.

Masal, *n.* Fable; parable; proverb; adage; example; instance; sample; simile metaphor; station; department.

Masalá, *n.* Affairs; occupation; honour; glory; materials; ingredients; necessaries (for cooking; building, &c.); spices; condiments; drugs.

Masalná, *v.* To crush between the palms; to bruise; to pulverize; to squeeze.

Masáná, *n.* The bladder.

Masárif, *n. (Plur. of Sarfá).* Expenses; disbursements. —*i-bejá,* unnecessary expenses; extravagance.

Masarrat, *n.* Happiness; rejoicing; rapture.

Máshá, *n.* A weight of eight *rattís.*

—*tolá honá, v.* to be very changeable, fickle or inconstant.

Mash'al, *n.* Torch; flambeau; lantern.

Mashakkat, *n.* Hard work; hard labour; punishing toil.

Mashgúl, *a.* Occupied; employed; engaged; engrossed; absorbed.

Mashahúr, *a.* Famous, renowned; well-known; celebrated; proclaimed; apparent. (negatively —notorious).

Máshiyat, *n.* Will; pleasure; choice; will of God.

Mashk, *n.* A leather bag for carrying water; an inflated buffalo-hide, used as a float in crossing a river. *(Dim. Mashkíza).*

Mashkúk, *a.* Doubtful; ambiguous.

Mashkúr, *a.* Thanked; praised; worthy of thanks or praise; grateful; thankful.

Mashq, *n.* Striking; tearing; writing; a model (for imitation); exercise; practice; usage; use; *a.* tall; slender.

Mashrab, *n.* Drinking; imbibing; drinking-place.

Mashriq, *n.* The east. —*í,* eastern. —*í nisf kura,* the eastern hemisphere.

Mashrú, *a.* Begun; commeneed; legal; lawful.

Mashrúb, *a.* Drunk; imbibed; fit for drinking.

Mashrúb, *a.* Explained; above-mentioned; aforesaid.

Mashrút, *a.* Stipulated; conditional; limited; qualified.

Mashsháq, *a.* Well-parctised; expert; experienced; *n.* an expert; an adept; a practiser.

Mashúr, *a.* Enchanted; charmed; fascinated; under the power of a magic spell.

Mashwará, *n.* Counsel; consultation; conference; advice. *—mujrimána, n.* a plot or conspiracy.

Masíh, *n.* The anointed; Jesus Christ; Messiah. *—Masíhi,* Christian.

Ma'síyat, *n.* Disobedience; rebellion; sin.

Masjid, *n.* A mosque.

Masjúd, *a.* Adored; worshipped.

Maská, *n.* Butter.

Maskan, *n.* A dwelling; habitation; residence; abode.

Maskín, (See Miskín).

Maskhará, *n.* Buffoon; jester; clown.

Maslá, *n.* Proposition; problem; an intricated question or matter requiring decision; maxim; tenet; precept.

Maslahat, *n.* A thing or affair conducive to good; welfare; sound or good policy; convenience; advice; business; *muqtaza-i-masahat, a.* advisable; expedient.

Maslúb, *a.* Crucified; suspended or hanged (on a cross); gibbeted.

Maslúb, *a.* Seized; carried away by force; robbed; despoiled; deprived (of). *—ul-hawás,* robbed of the senses; having the senses weakened by age, &c.

Maslúl, *a.* Consumptive; suffering from phthisis.

Masmú'a, *a.* Heard; audible.

Masmúm, *a.* Poisoned; venomous.

Masnad, *n.* Couch; cushion; throne; chair. *—nashín,* enthroned; *n.* a ruling sovereign.

Masnaví, *n.* A kind of verse in which the couplets rhyme regularly.

Masnu's, *(Plur. Masnu'át).* Formed; made; created; invented; artificial; false; counterfeit; *n.* a work of art or skill; an invention; a contrivance. *—í,* artificial; fictitious; fabricated.

Masnún, *a.* Sharpened; polished;

circumcised; legalized; adopted into use.

Masraf, *n.* Expenditure; outlay; coast.

Masrúf, *a.* Turned; charged; declined (a noun); conjugated (a verb); expended; used; occupied; engaged; busy.

Masrúq, *a.* Stolen; robbed; plundered.

Masrúr, *a.* Happy; glad; joyful.

Massá, *n.* A wart.

Mast, *a.* Intoxicated; inebriated; drunk; insane; proud; arrogant; lascivious. *—mál-i—,* a purse-proud.

Mastak, *n.* Head; skull; cranium; forehead; top; crest; summit.

Mastúl, *n.* Mast of a ship.

Mastúr, P. *n.* Modesty; chastity.

Masturát, *n. (Plur. of Mastúrát).* Women; veiled or chaste women.

Ma'súm, *a.* Innocent; guileless; simple; protected; preserved; *n.* an innocent; an infant; a child. *—iyat,* innocence.

Masúrá, *n.* The gums (of the teeth).

Mat, *n.* An opinion a viewpoint; belief; tenet; doctrine; sect; creed; faith; vote. *—ganańá,* a. counting of votes; referendum. —; *dán,* v. Poll; polling; casting of votes. *—kendra,* n. Polling centre. *—dátá,* n. A voter; an elector. *—dátá súchí,* n. The electoral roll. *—patra,* n. A ballot paper. *—petí,* n. Ballot box. *—prachárak,* *n.* A propogandist. *—parivartan,* v. A change of doctrine/ creed/ viewpoint. *—ántar,* n. Divergent and diverse views. —v. Plebscite, &c.

Mát, *a.* Astonished; confounded; conquered; subdued; defeated. *—dená,* to checkmate; to outdo.

Mátá, *n.* Mother; a turn of respect to any woman. *—pitá,* parents; mother and father.

Mátá, *n.* Small-pox. *—dhalná,* small-box to dry up.

Mátam, *n.* Bereavement; mourning; observances at the occasion of a death in the family or neighbourhood. grief; sorrow; mourning; lamentation. *—pursí,* condolence. *—i-libás,* mourning garments.

Mátam-pursí, *n.* Condolence(s); expression of sadness and sorrow for the loss of the departed soul.

Matánat, *n.* Firmness; resoluteness; constancy; castle; fortress; stronghold.

Matang, *n.* An elephant.

Matar, *n.* Apea.

Matbá, *n.* Printing press.

Matbakh, *n.* Kitchen; cook-house.

Matbú'a, *a.* Printed; published; stamped; agreeable; acceptable.

Matbúkh, *a.* Cooked; dressed (food).

Maṭh, *n.* A hut (esp. of a devotee or ascetic); a pagan temple. *—dhárí, n.* an abbot; the senior priest of a pagan temple.

Máthá, *n.* The forehead; Frontage; visible side of things. *—sikoṛná,* v. To frown at; to look down upon. *—dukhná,* v. To suffer from headache. *—phoṛná,* v. To have to explain repeatedly; to struggle with a problem; to have to deal with an idiot, or someone who refuses to understand. *—píṭná,* v. To lament; to mourn the loss of. *—ghisná,* v. To show humility; to make repeated entreaties. *—ṭekná/naváná,* v. To bow ones head to express reverence, or respect for (a deity, or a holy personage). *—ṭhanakná,* v. To get a sudden inkling of an imminent danger. *—ṭhokná,* v. To curse one's misfortune. *—dhunaná/píṭaná,* v. To curse one's helplessness in the face of a dificulty or misfortune. *—pachchí karná,* v. To hack one's brains; to struggle in serach of a solution to problem in hand.

Mathan, Manthan, *n.* Churning; stirring; exploring thoroughly; seriously researching into evidence.

Mathná, *v.* To churn; to beat up; to knead.

Máṭí, *n.* Earth; clay. *maṭílá, a.* made of earth or clay; good for nothing; useless; *Maṭ-mailá,* a. Dusty-looking; *Maṭiyálá,* a. Dusty-coloured.

Mati, *n.* Intellect; understanding; opinion; view-point. *—bhram,* adv. hallucination; confusion. *—bhransh,* a. psychosis; derangement. *—bhrashṭ,* a. mentally derailed; deranged person. *—mand,* a. An idiot; low-witted; nincompoop. *—hín,* a. Foolish; stupid. *—phirná,* v. to undergo a change; degeneration of one's thoughts/ opinions/thoughts. *—har lená,* v. To turn someone into a moron. *—ván/mán,* a. Intelligent; wise; prudent.

Maṭká, *n.* A large earthen waterpot.

Maṭkáná, *v.* To wink; to ogle; to shake.

Matlá, *n.* Each couplet, except the first, opening one, of the *Ghazal* [a Persian poetic form [Also see *Maktá*].

Matlab, *n.* A question; request; petition; wish; object; aim; motive; *adv.* in short. —*nikálná,* to accomplish one's object. —*rakhná,* to have some motive. —*ká yár,* a self-interested friend. —*ho jáná,* to be at the end of one's resources; to be in a desperate plight.

Matláhaṭ, *n.* Nausea.

Matláná, *v.* To feel sick; to suffer from nausea.

Matlí, *n.* Nausea; vomit-like sickness.

Matlúb, *a.* Sought; desired; longed for; necessary.

Mátrá, *n.* Measure; quantity; amount; a little; a trifle.

Mátrí, *Pref.* Mother. —*ghát, n.* matricide.

Matrúb, *a.* Thrown; cast away; removed to a distance; rejected, *n.* an infidel; a remainder.

Matt, *a.* Drunk; inebriated; intoxicated (with liquor; passion; pride, &c.); maddened; furious; delighted; *n.* a drunken person; a madman; a lunatic; an infuriated elephant.

Maṭṭhá, *n.* Butter-milk; Churned up curd/yoghurt after all the cream or butter has been extracted. Also known as *Chháchh.* Also a. Slow; slack; dull; idle; lazy; heavy.

Maṭṭhí, *n.* a savoury biscuit, obtained by deep-frying hardened dough. Popular in northern India. [*Plur.* **Maṭṭhiyán**].

Maṭṭí, *n.* Earth; clay; land; ground. —*par larná, v.* to dispute or quarrel regarding land. —*yá, a.* made of earth; frail; fragile; weak; infirm.

Ma'túf, *a.* Inclined (to); having a natural bent or tendency (to).

Mátul, Mámá, *n.* Maternal uncle; mother's brother' euphemism for the nearst relative.

Matwálá, *a.* Intoxicated; inebriated; drunk.

Mauj, *n.* Wave; emotion; ecstasy; whim; caprice; abundance; plenty.

Maujúd, *a.* Existing; extent; present; ready; at hand; available. —*gí,* no. Presence; existence.

Maujúdát, *n. (Plur. of Maujúd).* Existing things; created beings; creatures; nature; effects; cash; a review or muster of troops.

Maulá, *n.* Master; lord; God.

Maulúd, *a.* Generated; born; *n.* a son; birth; nativity; birthday. —*sharíf, n.* celebration of the anniversary of the prophet. Mohammad's birth.

Maulví, Maulawí, *n.* A learned man; a professor.

Maun, *a.* Silent; taciturn; reserved (in speech); *n.* silence; taciturnity.

Mauní, *a.* One who is pledged to keeping silent; proper name for a cult of *Sádhús* in India.

Mauqá, *n.* Place; locality; opportunity; accident; *a.* opportune; fit; suitable.

Mauqúf, *a.* Stopped; delayed; abolished; ceased; fixed; bound; dependent upon; *n.* legacy; bequest.

Maurid, *n.* Place of arrival; descending.

Mausá, *n.* Mother's sister's husband, a near relative. *Mausí,* n. Mother's sister. *Mauserá,* a. Belonging to or related to *Mausí* or *Mausá.* A popular proverb: *Chorchor Mausere Bháí*— Two villains (or wrong-doers) joining hands.

Mausam, Mausím, *n.* Time; season. *—i-bahár, n.* spring. *—i-garmá, n.* summer. *—i-khizán, n.* autumn. *—i-sarmá, n.* winter.

Mauserá/ Mauserí, *adj.* Offspring [male and female] of a maternal aunt (mother's sister).

Mausúf, *n.* Described; named; praised; celebrated.

Mausúl, *a.* Joined; connected; related; (in *Gram.*) the anteedent of a relative pronoun.

Mausúm, *a.* Marked; signed; impressed, named.

Maut, *n.* Death; mortality. *—patr, n.* dying testament; will. *apni maut marná,* to die a natural death.

Mautád, Matád, *n.* Custom; habit; use; a fixed quantity or allowance (of food, &c.); a dose (of medicine); due quantity; *a.* accustomed; habituated; usual.

Mauzá, *n.* Village; hamlet; district; place; site; plot of land; occasion; occurrence; conjecture.

Mauzú, *a.* Placed; situated; established; assigned; taken for granted; *n.* site; position.

Mauzún, *a.* Weighed; balanced; well-adjusted; symmetrical; rhythmical; excellent.

Máwá, *n.* Substance; essence; starch; yolk (of an egg); leaven; curd.

Mawád, *n.* *(Plur. of Mádda).* matters; articles; females; humours (of the body); matter; pus.

Mawáshí, Maweshí, *n.* A herd of oxen; cattle; sheep; goats.

Máyá, S. *n.* Supernatural or magical power; illusion; deception; the external world; a woman; property; riches. —may, *a.* possessing magical powers;

illusory; *n.* a magician; a conjuror.

Máyá, P. *n.* Source; origin; essence; substance; wealth *—jorná,* to amass wealth; to hoard money.

Máyáví, *adj.* Illusionist; spell-master.

Ma'yúb, *a.* Wicked; vicious; defective.

Máyús, *adv.* Disappointed; one who has lost hope.

Máyús, *a.* Disappointed; hopeless; desperate. *—í, n.* hopelessness; despair; desparation.

Mazá, *n.* Taste; relish; pleasure; enjoyment; joke.

Mazák/Mazahká, *n.* Joke; jest; poking fun; humour.

Mazammat, *n.* Censure; scorn; satire, reprimand.

Mazár, *n.* Tomb; shrine; grave.

Mazbút, *a.* Strong; immoveable; stable; durable; resolute; restrained; disciplined; *adv.* firmly; tightly. *—í, n.* strength force; durability.

Mazdúr, *n.* Labourer; carrier.

Mazhab, *n.* Religion; creed; religious belief; secret.

Mází, *n.* Past time; the past; (in *Gram.*) the preterite or past tense.

Mazíd, *n.* Increase; advantage.

Mazkúr, *a.* *(Plur. Mazkúrát).* Remembered; mentioned; aforesaid: *n.* mention; relation; discourse.

Mazlúm, *a.* Treated wrongly or unjustly; oppressed; injured; meek; modest; *a.* victim of oppression; one who is wrongfully treated.

Mazmún, *n.* Sense; meaning; purport; tenor.

Ma'zúl, *n.* Deposed; degraded; dismissed.

Ma'zúr, *a.* Excused; excusable; dispensed with; unserviceable; helpless; disappointed.

Medá, *n.* A root resembling ginger, used as a drug.

Medh, *n.* Offering; oblation; sacrifice. *Ashwamedh,* a. A ritual ceremony during which a horse would be sacrificed.

Medhá, *n.* Brain-power; genius.

Mediní, *n.* The earth; land; soil; ground; a body of pilgrims going to visit the tomb or shrine of a saint.

Megh, *n.* A clud; rain. *—dhanush, n.* the rainbow.

Mehmán, *n.* A stronger; a guest; a lodger. *—í, n.* entertainment; hospitality; a banquest.

Mehnat, *n.* Labour; toil; trouble pains; diligence; travail; —*í, a.* laborious; painstaking; *n.* a labourer; a working man.

Mehráb, *n.* Place where kings and great men sit; a king's private apartment; an arch. —*i-teg,* the curve or arch of a scimitar.

Mehtar, *n.* Asweeper. (*Fem. Mehtrání*).

Mehwar, *n.* Axis; axle. —*i-zamín,* the axis of the earth.

Mekh, Mesh, *n.* A ram; the sign Aries.

Mekh, *n.* An iron or wooden pin; a peg; a nail; a wedge. —*chú, n.* a mallet; a hammer.

Mel, *n.* Connexion; agreement; combination; reconciliation; mixture; concord; union. *helmel,* close intimacy.

Melá, *a.* Assemblage; concourse of people for religious or commercial purpose; a fair.

Memná, *n.* A kid; a lamb.

Men̲, *pre.* In; into; between; with.

Men̲dak, Men̲ḍhak, *n.* A frog; a toad.

Menḍhá, Meṛhá, *n.* A ram.

Men̲h, *n.* Rain.

Men̲hdí, *n.* The name of a hedge-plant, the leaves of which are used for dyeing the hands, feet and hair; the Henna plant.

Men̲ṛ, Men̲ḍ, *n.* Limit; boundary.

Merá, *pro.* Mine; my.

Mesh, *n.* A sheep; a ram. (*Fem. Meshí*).

Methí, *n.* The plant fenugreek.

Mewá, *n. (Plur. Mewaját).* Fruit.

Mez, *n.* A table. —*bán, n.* host; master of a house. —*báni,* hospitality.

Mi'ád, *n.* Term; period; duration.

Mi'adá, *n.* Stomach; belly.

Miftáb, *n.* A key.

Mihr, *n.* Sun; love; friendship; affection; kindness.

Milá, *a.* United; combined; mixed; found. —*julá,* united; in accord.

Milan, *n.* A meeting; a rendezvous; a get together; a (romantic) union; a coming together.

Milán, *n.* Contract; union; encounter; harmony; adjust-ment; comparison.

Miláná, *v.* To unite to mix; to reconcile; to compare; to introduce one person to another.

Milansár, *a.* Sociable; amicable; polite.

Milanní, Miláo, Miláwat, *n.* Mixture; adulteration; alloy; union; annexation.

Milkiyat, *n.* Right; property; possession.

Millat, *n.* Religion; creed; sect.

Milná, *v.* To be mixed or united; to coincide; to interview; to assemble; to come into possession; to be reconciled. *mile jule rahná,* to live together or amicably.

Milní, *n.* A ritual, or custom wherein parallels and equals in both families meet each other at the occasion of weddings; pairing of relatives in the course of marital ceremonies.

Milwáì, *n.* Ceremonial gifts exchanged between paired relatives at the time of weddings; fee or reward paid to those who cause business meetings.

Mímánsá, *n.* Analysis; investigation; a school of Hindu philosophy,divided into two sections, *Púrva* [meaning 'earlier'] and *Uttar* [meaning 'latter].

Mín, *n.* A fish.

Mína, Mínú, *n.* Heaven; paradise; sky; enamel; a goblet; a decanter. —*bázár,* a fancy fair. —*kárí chhántná,* to make nice distinctions.

Minár, *n.* Minaret; obelisk.

Mínjná, *v.* To rub with the hands; to crush; to scrub; to scour.

Minṭhár, *n.* Nostril.

Minnat, *n.* Entreaty; supplication; obligation.

Minqár, *n.* Beak; bill.

Mîmánsá, *n.* Investigation; analysis; a school of Hindu Philosophy, divided into two sections, *Púrva,* [meaning 'earlier'] and *Uttar* [meaning 'latter'].

Mímansak, *n.* Investigator; nalyst.

Miutí, *n.* Apology; solicitation; entreaty.

Miqdár, *n.* Quantity; measure; rath.

Miqráz, *n.* A pair of scissors; shears.

Miqyás, *n.* The hand of a watch; a measuring instrument; a probe. —*miqyás-ul-harárat,* a thermometer; *miqyás ul-má,* a hydrameter; *miqyás-ul-mausim,* a barometer.

Mír, *n.* Chief; leader; the king in cards. —*mir-'adl,* chief justice—*majlis,* president; chairman; master of ceremonies. —*munshí,* chief secretary; head cleark.

Mírás, *n.* Inheritance; patrimony; hereditary estate or property; bequest; legacy. —*í,* hereditary.

Mírásí, *n.* A professional singer.

Mirch, *n.* Pepper; *a.* hot; pungent.

Mirchá, *n.* A chilly; a capsicum.

Mirgí, *n.* Epilepsy.

Mirríkḥ, *n.* The planet Mars.

Mirzá, *n.* A prince; a Persian or Moghal title.

Mirza'í, *n.* A sleeveless jacket, made of woolen or cotton material.

Misál, *n.* Likeness; resemblance; similarity; similitude; metaphor; simile; example; instance.

Misará, *n.* Couplet of a poem.

Misbáh, *n.* A lamp.

Misdáq, *n.* Proof of veracity; verification.

Mísh, *n.* Rivalry; competition; envy deceit; fraud; pretence; apology.

Mishra, *n.* Mixed; compound; composite; name of a community of *Brahmins;* also the name of a country, i.e. Egypt, in Arabic, the native language of that land, called *Al Misr.*

Mishrabá, *n.* A drinking vessel.

Mishraṇ, *n.* Misture; adulteration; intermingling; compound; alloy.

Misí, *a.* Made of copper.

Miskín, *a.* Meek; humble; lowly; submissive; not-so-well endowed.

Miskíní, *n.* Poverty; indigence; humility.

Misl, *a.* Like; similar; resembling; equal; *n.* likeness; similarity; similitude; resemblance; record of proceedings in a civil or criminal case; the file of a case.

Misqál, *n.* A weight equal to four *máshas,* and three and a half *rattís.*

Misrí, *n.* Sugar-candy; an Egyptian, or a native of Misr (Egypt).

Misrí/ Mishrí, *n.* Crystallized lumps of sugar.

Missí, *n.* A tooth-powder or dentifrice which relieves toothache but blackens the teeth and gums.

Mistirí, *n.* An artisan; a mason; a bricklayer; a carpenter.

Miswák, *n.* Tooth-brush; a stick used for cleaning the teeth.

Mit, *adj.* Bit; very-small. [Used as a prefix to qualify nowns, like] —*bháshan,* adv. Brief talk; to the-point conversation. —*bháshí,* adj. One not given to loose talk; one who says little and to-the-point. —*vyayí,* adj. Prudent with spending; not extravagant. —*vyayitá,* n. Quality of conservation; frugal nature.

Mít, *n.* Friend; lover.

Mitáná, *v.* To efface; to erase; to blot out; to obliterate; to abolish.

Míṭhá, *a.* Sweet; delicious; savoury; slow; idle; *n.* a general name for sweetmeats.

Mitháí, *n.* Sweetmeat. *—wálá,* a maker or vendor of sweetmeats a confectioner.

Miṭháí, *n.* Sweet-meat; confectionary.

Mithak, *n.* Legends; myths; stories from classic literature.

Miṭhás, *n.* Sweetness; endearing quality of behaviour and of speech.

Mithun, *n.* A pair; a couple; twins; the zodiacal sign Gemini (the twins).

Mithyá, *a.* False; untrue; fraudulent; counterfeit. *—pújak,* an idolator. *—rádi,* a lair.

Mití, *n.* A specified day; a fixed date; interest; discount.

Miṭná, *v.* To be effaced; to be erased; to be obliterated; to be abolished; to cease to exist; to expire.

Mitr, *n.* Friend; name of the Sun God [according to the *Vedas*].

Mitratá, *n.* Friendship.

Mitra, *n.* A friend. *—ghát,* breach of friendship.

Miṭṭí, *n.* Earth; soil; clay; land; dirt; filth; rubbish; corpse; carcase; flesh; meat; temperament; constitution. *—dená,* to bury; to inter. *—kí múrat,* figure of clay; the mortal frame, the human body.

Miyán, *n.* The middle; the waist; the loins; a scabbard.

Míyán̲, *n.* Sir; master; husband; father. *—ádmí,* a good-natured man; a gentleman.

Miyána, *a.* Middling; of medium size; moderate; *n.* the middle; the pole or shaft of a carriage; a kind of Sedan chair, or *pálkí, —qadd,* of medium height or stature.

Mizáj, *n. (Lit.)* A mixture; nature; temperament; constitution; disposition; health; pride; haughtiness; arrogance. *—ke máre, adv.* through temper or pride. *bad—, a.* ill-tempered; irritable. *khush—, a.* good-humoured. *gaa̲da—, a.* peevish; cross.

Mizájí, *a.* Constitutional; habitual; fastidious; proud; haughty; *n.* a fastidious or proud man; one who gives himself airs.

Mízán, *n.* A balance; a pair of scale; the sign Libra; measure metre; rhyme; verse; quantity; (in *Arith.*) addition; total. *—e-kull, n.* the grand total.

Mlán, *adj.* Faded; withered; Languid; weak; dirty.

Mláni, *n.* Dejection; withering; dirt.

Moch, *n.* A sprain; a strain; a twist; a twitch.

Mochak, *n.* Liberator; deliverer; saviour.

Mochan, *n.* Release; acquittal; discharge.

Mochí, *n.* The name of a caste who are workers in leather; a member of this caste; a cobbler; a shoemaker; a harness-maker.

Mod, *n.* Joy; happiness; entertainment; delight. *—ak,* a. Literally, one that provided joy, happiness, etc. Actually a name given to very popular sweet balls in India renowned as *laddoos.*

Modí, *n.* A merchant; a grocer; a shopkeeper; a grain merchant.

Moh, *n.* Attachment; infatuation; illusion; affection; fascination; spell. love for *—bhang,* n. shattering of illusion; demolition of infatuation. *—nidrá,* n. a slumber steeped in ignorance. *—pásh,* n. The snare of attachment to worldly things or beings.

Mohan, *a.* Stupefying; bewildering; deceiving; infatuating; charming; *n.* an enchanter; a sweetheart; an epithet of Krishna.

Mohar, *n.* A coins, usually made of precious metals and bearing the seal of the ruler of the day, in common usage in medieval period.

Mohará, *n.* A chess-piece; a person being moved about as a part of manipulation by some other person in authority. *Háth ká—,* a. A pawn in the hands of—. (Plural: *Muhare*).

Mohiní, *n.* A temptress; one who can cast a spell; in Hindu mythology, Lord *Vishnu* incarnated in the form of a temptress called *Mohiní* in order to distract the demons away from where the immortalising nectar was being served to heavenly deities: *Mohiní Awatár.*

Mohit, *a.* Fainted, unconscious; fascinated; deluded; enamoured.

Mohná, *v.* The allure; to tempt; to delude; to fascinate; to enchant.

Moksh, *n.* Liberation; a faith-concept whereby the soul in released from cycle of transmigration from one specie-body to another, thus the ultimate goal of every Hindu's sacraments and sacrifices and righteous endeavours.

Mol, *n.* Price; purchase; purchase money. *—barháná,* to raise the price. *—ghatáná,* to lower or reduce the price.

Mom, *n.* Wax; *—jámá,* n. oil-cloth; oil-skins; tarpaulin. *—dil;* a. a softhearted person; a compassionate one. *—battí,* n. candle-stick. *—kí Mariam,* a. A soft-hearted woman; a tender woman. *—í kágaz,* n. Tracing paper. *—ká putlá,* a. A wax dummy; a statue made out of wax.

Mor, *n.* A peacock; an exotic bird. *—pankh,* n. Feathers of a peacock. *—chhal,* n. A whisk made of peacock feathers. *—mukut;* a. A crown made from peacock feathers. *—ní,* n. A peahen.

Moṛ, *n.* Turn; bend [in the road, or a river]; a twist; a coil; a sprain; fold; deflection; direction; new departure.

Morí, Muhrí, Drain; gutter; a sewer; an opening.

Moṛná, *v.* To turn; to bend; to twist; to sprain; to screw; to plait; to pervert (one's meaning or words).

Moṭá, *a.* Fat; stout corpulent; thick; dense; coarse; gross; inferior.

Motí, *n.* A pearl.

Moṭí, *adj.* A fat one [feminine]. **Motí Bát,** Salient feature; Essence of something.

Mozá, *n.* Stocking; sock.

Mirdul, Mridul, *a.* Soft; mild; gentle; tender; *n.* water. *—subháo,* tender-hearted; of a mild or gentle disposition.

Mirga, Mrig, *a.* A deer; a gazelle; an antelope. (*Fem. Mirgí,* a doc).

Mrit, *n.* Dead; past; out of function; out of currency; no more valid; deceased; defunct

Mritak, S. *n.* A dead body; a corpse; a carcass; the dead.

Mrityu, *n.* Death; passing away; going out of function.

Muaddab, *a.* Courteous; polite; civil.

Mu'af, *n.* Forgiveness; polite; civil.

Mu'af, *n.* Forgiveness; pardon; absolution; *a.* forgiven; pardoned; exempt.

Mu'áfí, *n.* Pardon forgiveness; remission; a rent-free grant of land. *—námá,* an order or exemption from revenue of taxes.

Mu'áhidá, *n.* Contract; agreement.

Mu'ajiza, *n.* A miracle.

Muákhaza, *n.* Accountability; responsibility; punishment; damages; amends; compensation. *—se barí honá,* to be relieved of responsibility.

Mu'álaja, *n.* Curing; healing; remedy; medical attendance and treatment.

Mu'allá, *a.* Elevated; exalted; sublime; high.

Muallif, *n.* Compiler; editor; author.

Mu'allim, *n.* *(Fem. Mu'allima).* Teacher; tutor; knowledgeable.

Mu'ámalá, *n.* Business; trade; transaction; bargain; behaviour; matter; affair; concern; cause or suit (in law); jurisdiction. —*pakká karná,* to settlo or decide a matter definitely; to confirm a barain.

Muammá, *n.* Riddle; maze; puzzle.

Mu'ammah, *n.* What is unapparent, obscure, or difficult; a riddle; an enigma; a puzzle.

Muannas; *a.* Feminine; effeminate.

Muarraḳha, *a.* Dated; written.

Muarriḳh, *n.* A chronicle; a recorder; a historian.

Muassar, *a.* Influential; one who leaves an impression; one with impact.

Mu'attal, *a.* Suspended; unemployed; in abeyance; vacant; uninhabited; obsolete.

Mu'attar, *a.* Perfumed; odoriferous; fragrant; scented.

Mu'áwaza, *n.* Compensation; exchange; barter; remuneration.

Mu'áyaná, *n.* Inspection; supervision.

Mu'azzam, *a.* Honoured; exalted; great.

Muazzan, Muazzin, *n.* A Muslim priest; one who calls the faithful to prayer; one who performs *Azán* [call to prayer].

Mu'azzaz, *a.* Revered; highly esteemed.

Mubádká, *n.* Exchange; barter.

Mubádla, *n.* Exchange; barter; retaliation; recompense.

Mubáhisá, *n.* Debate; argument; discussion; dispute.

Mubáligá, *n.* Diligence; assiduity; utmost; effort; exaggeration; hyperbole.

Mubárak, *a.* Blessed; happy; fortunate; *intj.* hail ! welcome !

Mubarrá, *a.* Acquitted; exempted; innocent; guiltless.

Mubham, *a.* ocult; unknown; ambiguous; quivocal.

Mubtadí, *n.* A beginner, founder; originator; a novice.

Muchalká, *n.* Bond; agreement. —*i-hifz-i-aman,* a bond to keep the peace.

Múchh/ Múnchh, *n.* Moustache.

Muchhandar/ Machhendar, *adj.* [literally] One with highly visible or prominent mustache. *n.* [actually, a corrption of the name of a venerable one of the *Náth sampradáya* i.e. the Nátha sect known as —] Matsyendra*náth.*

Mudabbir, *n.* Manager; administrator; governor; minister.

Mudákhilat, *n.* Interference; access; entrance; ingress.

Mudám, *adv.* To continue; continuously; always.

Mudámí, *adj.* Continuous; everlasting.

Mudámí, *a.* Perpetual; continual; ceaseless.

Mudarris, *n.* Teacher; tutor; preceptor.

Mudd'á, *n.* Object; intention; wish; meanings; issue or matter under discussion.

Mudda'a, *n.* Desire; wish; object; aim. *—'alaih,* defendant or respondent in a lawsuit.

Mudda'í, *n.* Claimant; plaintiff; enemy. *(Fem. Mudda'íá).*

Muddat, *n.* A time period; a length of time. *—ká,* adj. Of long standing; ancient. *—se,* adv. For some time; for a long time. *—tak,* adv. For some time; for a long time (into the future). *—huí,* adv. A long time ago.

Muddatí, *adj.* Periodical; of a fixed period/duration; ancient.

Mudgar, *n.* A wooden mallet; a gymnasts club; dumbell; a mace.

Mudit, *a.* Happy; pleased; one who has enjoyed.

Mudrá, *n.* Seal; coin; currency; stamp; impression; a signet-ring; facial countenance; body posture; aspect; a position; a stylised, adopted position (as in dance and in play-acting). *Antar-ráshṭriya —kosh,* n. International Monetary Fund (IMF). *—shástra,* n. Numismatics; study of coins. *—sphíti,* n. Currency-inflation.

Mudriká, *n.* A ring; *kushá—,* a ring contrived out of *kushá*-grass worn on one's fourth finger while making a sacrifical offering to one's ancestors, i.e. *pinḍ-dán.*

Mudrit, *adj.* Imprinted; printed; sealed; closed; struck with an impression [like a coin or a stamp].

Mufáim, *a.* Tender; gentle; soft; mild.

Mufáriqat, *n.* Separation; parting.

Mufarráh, *a.* Invigorating; refreshing.

Mufassal, *adj.* Detailed; subordinate or outlying regions of a kingdom or territory; countryside [as different from urban areas]; istinct; clear; full; detailed; minute; *n.* the mofussil; the country districts as distinguished from towns and cities.

Mufíd, *a.* Profitable; beneficial; advantageous; serviceable.

Muflis, *a.* Poor; indigent; insolvent; bankrupt; pauper; wretched.

Mufrad, *a.* Solitary; single, alone; singular.

Mufsid, *a.* Mischievous; facetious; pernicious; *n.* an incendiary; a sedition-monger; mischief-maker.

Muft, *adj.* Free; gratis; without cost *adv.* In vain; without cause or justification. —*ḳhor,* adj. A freeloader; a sponger; a parasite.

Muftí, *n.* An official expounder of the Muslim Law; plain clothes [as opposed to one's official uniform, in case of soldiers or policemen].

Mugaiyar, *a.* Altered; changed.

Mugal, *n.* Moghal, or native of Tartary. *(Fem. Muqláni).*

Mugálata, *n.* Fraud; deception; delusion; error.

Muhabbat, *n.* Love; affection; friendship; *Matlab ki—,* a. Affection shown for selfish motive; cupboard love. *Bachpan ki—,* a. Puppy love.

Muháfiz, *adj.* Custodian; protector; guardian; defender; keeper. —*ḳháná,* n. Records room [in an establishment] —*e-daftar,* n. A keeper of records.

Muháfiz, *n.* Guardian; protector; watchman; sentry; sentinel.

Muhaiyá, *a.* Arranged; prepared; ready.

Muhájarat, *a.* Separation; parting.

Muhájir, *n.* Refugee; a particular community of people assembled mainly in Sindh, in Pakistan who migrated from India in their bid to settle in their cherished Muslim homeland and are still considered outsiders.

Muhál, *a.* Impossible; impracticable; absurd.

Muhallá, *n.* District; division; locality; quarter or community within a big town; ward; parish.

Muháná, *n.* The mouth of a river; an estuary; confluence (of two rivers); a strait; an inlet or outlet.

Muhandis, *n.* A geometrician; a mathematecian.

Muhá<u>n</u>s(á/e), *n.* Pi<u>m</u>ple(s) on the face.

Muhar, *n.* Seal; stamp (not postage stamp); imprint of authority. —*lagáná,* v. To imprint a document, or object with a stamp.

Muhárba, *n.* Fight; combat; cattle; encounter; war.

Muharram, *a.* Forbidden; unlawful; excluded sacred; *n.* the sacred month,' the month of Muharram; the first month of the Muhammadan year, held sacred on account of the death of Husain, son of Ali, who was killed by Yazíd, near Kúfa; mourning and lamentation; weeping and wailing.

Muharrik, *a.* Moving; stirring; incentive; *n.* mover; instigator; adviser; persuader.

Muharrir, *n.* A clerk; a writer; a scribe.

Muhásiba, *n.* Calculation; reckoning; computation; account.

Muhásara, *n.* Siege; blockade.

Muháwara, *n.* Conversation; idiom; phraseology; common or current speech; practice; usage.

Muhíb, *a.* Formidable; dreadful; awful; terrible.

Muhibb, *n.* Friend; lover.

Muhimm, *n.* Great; momentous; important; serious.

Muhít, *n.* Circumference; the ocean; one who knows or comprehends. *a.* surrounding; encircling; containing; knowing; acquainted (with).

Muhkam, *a.* Strengthened; fenced; walled; fortified.

Muhlat, *n.* Delay; procrastination; dilatoriness; eessation; armistice; leisure; respite.

Muhlik, *a.* Fatal; mortal; deadly.

Muhmal, *a.* Obsolete; in disuse; meaningless (a word); *n.* a buffoon; a clown.

Muhr, *n.* Seal; signet ring; a gold coin *(mohur).*

Muhrá, *n.* Glossiness; lustre; a piece or man in chess, backgammon, &c.; a counter (for playing any game); a shell; a pebble; a stone found in the head of a serpent.

Muhsin, *a.* Generous; liberal; benevolent; *n.* A benefactor.

Muhtáj, *a.* Poor; needy necessitous; indigent; *n.* a pauper; a beggar. *—khána, n.* poor-house; almshouse.

Muktamil, *a.* Suspected; suspicious; doubtful; bearing; enduring; capable (of); liable (to); *n.* bearer; endurer; sufferer.

Muhtamim, *n.* Manager; superintendent; agent; overseer; *a.* anxious (about); taking upon oneself the concerns of others. *—e-akhbár, n.* editor of a newspaper. *—e-band-o-bast, n.* a settlement officer. *—e-matba', n.* manager of a printing press.

Muhtarim / Muhtaram, *adj.*

Honoured; respected; venerable one.

Muhtarimá / Muhtarmá, n. [*Female*] Honoured; respected; venerable one.

Muhtashim, *a.* Great; powerful; having many followers or dependants.

Muhtasib, *n.* Calculator; reckoner; inspector of market and of weights and measures, &c.; a censor.

Muhúrt, Muhúrat, *n.* The thirtieth part of a day, equal to 48 minutes; a moment; an instant; an auspicious moment.

Mujalla, *a.* Polished; burnished; bright; apparent; manifest.

Mujallad, *a.* Bound; *n.* a bound volume or book. *mujallid,* a bookbinder.

Mujarrab, *a.* Tried; tested; assayed; proved experienced.

Mujarrad, *a.* Single; alone; unmarried.

Mujassam, *a.* Corporeal; physical; bodily.

Mujáwar, *n.* An attendant at a mosque.

Mújib, *n. (Plur. Mújibát).* Cause; reason; motive.

Mújid, *n.* Inventor; author; originator.

Mujmal, *n.* Summary; abstract; abridgment; brief; abridged.

Mujra, *n.* Obeisance; respect; deduction; premium; discount.

Mujrim, *a.* Criminal; culpable; guilty; *n.* a sinner; a criminal; a felon.

Mujtahid, *n. (Plur. Mujtahidín).* A religious preceptor or instructor; a spiritual guide; a theologian; a jurist; *a.* striving; laborious; waging war (esp. against infidels).

Muk'ab, *a.* Square or cubic in form.

Mukaddar, *a.* Turbid; muddy; sullen; gloomy; displeased.

Mukáfát, *n.* Recompense; compensation; retaliation; retribution.

Mukallaf, *a.* Elaborate; elegant; occupied with care; carefully executed.

Mukámí, *adj.* Local; based; resident.

Mukammal, *a.* Perfect; complete; consummate; accomplished.

Mukan̲d / Mukun̲d, *n.* A title of *Vishnu* and of *Krishna.*

Mukarram, *a.* Honoured; respect; revered; noble; august; illustrious.

Mukarrar, *a.* Repeated; reiterated; *adv.* repeatedly; again; a second time.

Mukáshafa, *n.* Revelation; manifestation; displaying.

Mukh, *n.* Mouth; face; countenance; beak or bill of a bird; snout or muzzle of an animal; bow or prow of a boat; commencement; entrance.

Mukh, Mukhya, *a.* Principal; chief; primary, first.

Muḳhaffaf, *a.* Contracted; abbreviated; light; contemptible; *n.* a contraction.

Muḳhálafat, Muḳhálifat, *n.* Opposition; dis-obedience; rebellion; dissension; hostility.

Muḳhálif, *a.* Contrary; adverse; repugnant; *n.* enemy; for; adversary.

Muḳhammas, *a.* Quintupled; pentangular; *n.* a pentagon; a verse of five lines.

Muḳhannas, *a.* Effeminate; abject.

Muḳhátab, Muḳhátib, *a.* Conversing (with); address-ing; speaking to; titled; named; spoken to; *n.* one. who converses with, or addresses another; a speaker; (in *Gram.*) the second person.

Muḳhbir, *a.* Announcing news; signifying; *n.* bearer of news; informer; spy; reporter.

Mukhiya, *n.* A principal chief, or leading personage; leader; head; commander or chief mate (officer) of a ship.

Muḳhlis, *a.* Pure; sincere; candid; frank; loyal; *n.* a sincere friend.

Muḳhtalif, *a.* Different; unlike dissimilar incongruous; diverse. —*auqát men̲,* at various times.

Muḳhtalit, *a.* Mixed; perplexed; confused.

Muḳhtár, *a.* Selected; preferred; invested with power or authority; independent; *n.* an agent an attorney; a solicitor; an assignee; a representative.

Muḳhtárí, *n.* Independence; authority; freedom of action; office or practice of an attorney; agency.

Muḳhtasar, *a.* Abbreviated; abridged; *n.* an abstract; a compendium; an epitome; an abridgment.

Mukláwá, *n.* A ceremony [on the Indian subcontinent] involving despatch or departure of a bride to her new, wedded home.

Mukt, Mukti, *a.* Set free; release; liberated; absolved; *n.* release; salvation; pardon; absolution.

Muktá, *a.* A pearl.

Mukul, *n.* A bud; a blossom.

Mukur, *n.* A mirror.

Mukuṭ/ Mukaṭ, *n.* A crown; a diadem; a tiara; a coronot; a crest.

Múl, *n.* Root; basis; origin; source; the lower part of anything; generation; race; capital; principal; (in *Arith.*) the square root.

Mulabbab, *a.* Brimful; overflowing.

Mulabbas, *a.* Dressed; clad; clothed; perplexed.

Muláhizá, *n.* Looking attentively at; notice; consideration; regard; minute inspection.

Mulaiṭhí, *n.* Liquorice.

Mulamma', *a.* Plated; covered with gold or silver gilt; gilded; electroplated.

Muláqát, *n.* Meeting; interview; rendezvous; visit. *—karwáná, v.* to introduce one person to another.

Mulaqqab, *a.* Titled; styled; surnamed.

Mulázimat, Malázmat, *n.* Assiduity; industry; diligence; service; duty.

Mulázim, *a.* Diligent; attentive; *n.* servant; attendant.

Mulazzaz, *a.* Delicious; savoury; tasty (foods).

Mulham, *a.* Inspired.

Mulhid, *n. (Plur. Mulhidán).* An infidel; a heretic; an unbeliever.

Mulhim, *a.* Inspiring; *n.* inspirer.

Múlí, *n.* A radish.

Mulk, *n.* Country; region realm; kingdom; dominion; territory. *—í, a.* of or relating to empire or government; political; national.

Mullá, *n.* A learned man; a muslim Lohyman.

Multafit, *a.* Attentive; paying regard to); courteous.

Multamis, *a.* Supplicating; entreating; begging; beseeching; *n.* a petitioner; a supplicant.

Multawí, *a.* Bent; oblique; delayed; postponed; pending. *—rakhná, v.* to postpone; to adjourn.

Múlya, *n.* Price; wages; value *(mol).*

Mulzim, *a.* Convicted; charged (with); accused (of); condemned.

Mumáni'at, *n.* Prohibition; hindrance; prevention; forbidding.

Múmin, Momin, *a. (Plur. Múminín).* Believing in God; orthodox; faithful; *n.* a believer.

Mumkin, *a.* Possible; practicable; feasible; liable, likely; what is to happen *(honhár).*

Mumtahan, *n.* An examinee; one who has been examined. (from 'Imtihán').

Mumtahin, *n.* Examiner; tester; auditor.

Mumtáz, *a.* Chosen or selected from; exalted; eminent; distinguished. *—honá, v.* to be preeminent among.

Munádí, *n.* Proclamation; preaching; publication. *—karná, v.* to proclaim; to promulgate.

Munáfa', *n. (Plur. of Múnafa'at).* Gains; profits; advantages; benefits. *—i-khám,* gross profits.

Munáját, *n.* Prayer; supplication.

Mun'akkis, *a.* Reflected (as a figure in a mirror or in water); reversed; inverted.

Mun'aqid, *a.* Held; celebrated; confirmed; organized; established.

Munaqqash, *a.* Printed; coloured; variegated; embroidered; engraved.

Munásib, *a.* Proper; suitable; becoming; analogous; congruous; applicable.

Munawwar, *a.* Illustrated; explained; illuminated; clear lucid.

Munázara, *a.* Disputation; argument; debate; discussion.

Munḍá, *n.* Name of a tribe in Central India.

Munḍan, *n.* Shaving the head; the Hindu ceremony of shaving a child's head for the first time.

Mundarj, Mundarjá, A. *a.* Contained; comprised; included; inserted. *—záil, adv.* as follows; as stated below.

Muṇḍer, *n.* A parapet; a coping (as of a wall); A ridge (of a roof).

Munder, *n.* The curb or coping of a well.

Múnḍná, *v.* To shave; to shear (a fleece); to cheat; to rob flagrantly.

Munfakk, *a.* Separated; disunited; severed.

Munfarija, *a.* Open; wide apart; obtuse (an angle). *munfarijatuz-záwiyá, a.* obtuse-angled (triangle, &c.).

Múngá, *n.* Coral.

Mungaurí, *n.* A lump of spiced pulse-flour dough, deep-fried, and often eaten either dipped into churned yoghurt, or other kind of sour, or sweet-n-sour dips.

Munh, *n.* Mouth; muzzle; beak; esteem; opening; source. [*proverbially*] Regard; consideration; standing; prestige; pretension. —*andhere,* adv. Before daybreak; at dawn. —*áná,* v. the mouth to become ulcerated; to utter taunts; to incur censure. —*bharná,* Prov. To buy someone's silence; to bribe sumptuously. —*band karná,* v. To gag, or silence (an Opponent); to reprimand severely. —*chaláná,* Prov. to indulge in loose talk; to utter meaningless words. —*charhná,* Prov. To become familiar with; to play on familiarity. —*churáná,* Prov. To hide from someone; to be bashful; to skulk. —*johná,* Prov. To wait on someone; to depemd onsomeone's pleasure. *kí or— karná,* adv. to head for; to go in the direction of. —*utarná,* v. To become sad; to become withdrawn. —*kálá* karná, v. To blacken (one's own or someone else's) face; to cause disgrace to; to punish; to break off with. —*kí kháná,* adv. To suffer a severe reversal; to suffer rebuke, or disgrace. —*kì bát chhínaná,* prov. To snatch one's words; to anticipate what the other was going to say. —*dekhte raj jáná,* Prov. To be stunned; to be gaze in astonishment; to be shock, horror surprised. —*ko lahú lagná,* prov. To taste blood; to get addicted to. —*kholná* v. To become abusive; to utter rash words; to dare to speak. —*par thúkná,* To insult someone; to dishonour. —*phuláná/ sujáná, Prov.* To sulk; to get upset about something. —*se lár tapakná,* Prov. To salivate about something; to lust for; to feel greed about. —*tor jawáb dená,* Prov. To give a fitting reply; to match opponent's sperformance. —*ujlá honá,* v. To succedd with credit; to pass gracefully.

Munhadim, *a.* Destroyed; ruined; demolished; razed to the ground.

Munharif, *a.* Changed; altered; crooked; oblique; disloyal; *n.* a rebel; an apostate; a renegade.

Munhassir, *a.* Restrained; confined; surrounded; besieged; contained; dependent.

Muni, *n. (Fem. Muní).* A saint; a holy man; a sage; an ascetic; a devotee; a hermit.

Munj, *n.* Jute.

Muním, *n.* Book-keeper; in-house accountant.

Muním, *n.* A clerk or accountant; a patron; a client; an agent; a headman.

Múnis, *n.* A sociable companion; an intimate friend; a consoler; *a.* consoling; cheering; comforting.

Munjamid, *a.* Frozen; congealed; solid.

Munkir, *n.* One who denies; an atheist; *a.* denying; rejecting; averse (to).

Munná, *n.* Baby (male); a word of endearment for young one(s).

Munní, *n.* Baby (female); a word of endearment for young one(s).

Munqasim, *a.* Divided; apportioned; distributed.

Munqat'a, *a.* Cut off; disjoined; interrupted; finished; exterminated; decided.

Mun̲ráí, *n.* Shaving (of one's head); wages for shaving.

Munsalik, *a.* Appended; added; annexed.

Munsarim, *n.* Manager; administrator; a subordinate settlement officer; head clerk (of a court); substitute; proxy.

Munshí, *n.* Author; composer; writer; scribe; clerk; secretary; tutor; a teacher of Persian or Urdu. *—e-falak, n.* the planet Mercury.

Mun̲shí, *n.* Clerk; teacker; tutor; a title of respect for an educated person.

Mun̲shiyáná, *n.* Clerical; pertaining to a *Mun̲shí.*

Munsif, *n.* A judge; an arbitrator; (in India) a subordinate judge; *a.* just; fair; equitable. *—mizáj, a.* just-minded. *—áná, adv.* justly; candidly.

Mun̲tahí, *adj.* Terminated; concluded; completed.

Muntaj, *a.* Deduced; inferred; concluded; *n.* conclusion; inference; consequence.

Muntaḳhab, *a.* Chosen; elected; selected; choice; rare; *n.* selection; extract; abstract.

Muntaqal, *a.* Transferred; transported; moved.

Muntaqil, *a.* Moveable; transferable; migratory.

Muntashir, *a.* Spread; diffused; published; explained.

Muntazim, *a.* Ordered; arranged; adjusted; joined; *n.* arranger; manager; economist.

Muntazir, *a.* Awaiting with anxiety; impatiently expecting; looking forward to.

Muqábala, *a.* Facing; confronting; opposing; comparison; contrast; encounter.

Muqaddam, *a.* Preferred; prior; superior; chief; preceding; *n.*

advanced guard, or vanguard, of an army; chief; leader.

Muqaddama, *n. (Plur. Muqaddamát).* The first part; preamble; preface; introduction; affair; case; lawsuit; cause; prosecution.

Muqaddar, *a.* Decreed or ordered by God; destined; *n.* late; destiny.

Muqaddas, *a.* Holy; sacred; Revered. *Kitáb-I—,* The Holy Book (Bible or Qur'án). *já-i-,* a. A Holy place; a sacred spot; a point of pilgrimage.

Muqaiyad, *a.* Shackled; in chains; imprisoned; devoted; (to); recorded.

Muqárabat, *n.* Drawing; near; approaching; proximity.

Muqarrab, *n.* Admitted; closely related; *n.* an intimate friend; a related.

Muqqaish, *n.* Brocade; decorative silver and gold embroidery.

Muqqarrara, *a.* Settled; established; fixed; prescribed; usual; certain.

Muqatta', *a.* Cut into pieces; short; beautiful; serious.

Muqattar, *a.* Distilled.

Muqawwí, *a.* Strengthening; bracing; invigorating.

Muqí, *n.* An emetic.

Muqirr, *a.* Settling; confirming; asserting; confessing.

Muqím, *a.* Remaining; residing; constant; *n.* resident; inhabitant; broker.

Muqtazá, *a.* Required; called for; *n.* requisition; demand; the ends of justice; the nick of time.

Murabba', *n.* A square; a quadrangle.

Murabba, *a.* Preserve fruit; jam.

Murabbí, *n.* Guardian; protector; patron.

Murád, *n.* Will desire; intention; tendency; vow.

Muráfa', *n.* Preferring a complaint (against); a lawsuit an appeal; an accusation.

Murája'at, *n.* Return; repetition.

Múrakh, *a.* Ignorant; stupid.

Murakkab, *a.* Mixed; compounded; composed; *n.* a compound; a sentence; a mixture.

Murálá, *n.* A peacock.

Muraqqa', *a.* Clothed in rags.

Murásilát, *n.* Correspondence; messages.

Murassa', *a.* Studded with gems; inlaid with jewels.

Múrat, Múrtí, *n.* A statue; an idol.

Murattab, *a.* Regulated; arranged; classified.

Murattib, *a.* Setting in order; director; disposer.

Murawwat, *n.* Generosity; kindness; politeness; manliness.

Murchhit, Múrchhit, *n.* Unconscious; insensible; in a swoon or faint.

Murda, *n.* A corpse; a dead body; a carcass; *a.* dead; defunct.

Murdaní, *n.* Deathly pallor; rigour mortis.

Murdár, *n.* A dead body; a corpse; a carcass; carrion; *a.* dead; impure; *intj.* Wretch ! Vile creature !

Murg, *n. (Plur. Murgán).* A bird; a fowl; a cock.

Murgí, *n.* A hen.

Muríd, *a.* Willing; desirous; *n.* disciple; scholar; hermit.

Murjháná, *v.* To fade; to wither; to pine.

Murk, *v.* To bend; to twist; to urn; to writhe.

Murkí, *n.* An earing; a nose-ring.

Murlí, *n.* Fiddle; flute. *—dhar/ wálá,* n. Nicknames for Krishna, meaning that he always carries a fiddle. *—Manohar,* n. Another nickname for Krishna, alluding to enchantment that he spreads through playing his fiddle.

Murlí, *n.* Fife; flute; pipe. *—dhar, n.* an epithet of Krishna.

Mursala, *n.* A letter; an epistle.

Mursalín, *n.* Apostles and prophets.

Murshid, *n.* A spiritual guide; a 'friend, philosopher and guide' type of person; head of an Islamic religious order; [perversely] a rascal.

Murtahan, *a.* Mortgaged; pledged; pawned.

Murtahin, *n.* Mortgagee; pawnbroker.

Múrti, Múrat, *n.* Statue; carving; (colloqially, even pictures are referred to as *Múrat*) the human frame; body; image; idol; figure; form.

Murtib, *a.* Most; humid; wet; damp; juicy.

Muruwwat, *n.* Manhood; human nature; generosity; politeness.

Musabbab, Musabbib, *n.* Appointer; pre parer; the First Cause (God). *—i-haqíqí,* the true cause, *i.e.,* God.

Musabbar, *n.* Aloes.

Musaddaq, *a.* Verified; attested.

Musaddas, *a.* Composed of six; *n.* a hexagon; a verse of six lines.

Musaffa, *a.* Clear; refined; purified; transparent.

Musaffi, *n.* Purifier; cleanser.

Musáfir, *n.* Traveller; passenger; voyager; tourist.

Musáhib, *n.* Aide-de-camp; companion; courtier.

Musallah, *a.* Armed; protected with armour; clad in coat-of-mail.

Musallam, *a.* Preserved; entire; accepted.

Musallas, *a.* Triangular; having three angles or corners.

Musalsal, *a.* Linked; successive; forming a chain or series.

Musammá, *a.* Named; called.

Musamman, *a.* Fixed; concluded; determined.

Musamman, *a.* Octangular; having eight angles.

Musammát, *n.* A title prefixed to the name of a woman; a lady.

Musanná, *n.* A copy; a duplicate; *a.* double.

Musannaf, *n.* What is composed; a book.

Musannif, *a.* An author; an editor.

Musáwát, *n.* Equation; equality; evenness; an every day affair or occurrence.

Musáwí, *a.* Equal; equivalent; neutral.

Musawwir, *n.* Printer; sculptor.

Músh, *n.* A rat; a mouse.

Mushábaha, Mushábahat, *n.* Likeness; resemblance; similitude; comparison. (See *Mushábeh*).

Mushábeh, *a.* Like; resembling; analogous; *n.* resemblance; similarity; probability.

Mushaf, *n.* A book; a volume; a page; the Quran.

Musháhara, *n.* Monthly salary; wages.

Mushákarat, *n.* Community; association, partnership.

Musharik, *n.* A partner.

Musharraf, *a.* Honoured; exalted; ennobled; decorated or ornamented (as a building).

Mushawwash, *a.* Confused; perplexed; distracted.

Mushfiq, *a.* Loving; affectionate; dear; *n.* friend.

Mushíl, *n.* A purgative; a purge; an aperient.

Mushír, *n.* Counsellor; adviser; senator. —*i-khás,* a privy councillor.

Mushk, *n.* Musk.

Mushkil, *a.* Difficult; hard; painful; intricate; doubtful; *n.* difficulty; hardship; per-plexity. *(Plur. Mushkilát).*

Musht̤, *n.* The fist a blow with the clenched fist; handful; a few.

Musht, *n.* The closed hand; the fist. *—á-mushtí, n.* boxing; fisticuffs. *—már, n.* thief; robber; plunderer.

Mushtahar, *n.* Notable; celebrated; published.

Mushtamal, Mushtamil, *a.* Comprising; containing; inclusive (of); common.

Mushtáq, *a.* Derived (as one word from another). *mushtaq* or *ism-i-mushtaq, n.* a derivative noun.

Mushtáq, *a.* Desirous; ardent; *n.* a lover.

Mushtarí, *n.* Buyer; purchaser; the planet Jupiter.

Musíbat, *n.* Misfortune; calamity; disaster.

Muskán, *n.* A smile.

Muskarahat, Muskuráhat̤, *n.* A smile; smiling; grinning.

Musmir, *a.* Fruitful.

Musrif, *a.* Extravagant; prodigal; *n.* a spendthrift; a prodigal.

Mustafid, *a.* Anxious to profit in study, &c.; advantageous; *n.* a student; a gainer.

Mustagfir, *a.* Asking pardon; penient; repentant.

Mustagís, *n.* Complainant; plaintiff; prosecutor.

Mustagní, *a.* Free from want; rich; satisfied; independent.

Mustagraq, *a.* Immersed; engrossed; occupied; hypothecated (as property).

Mustahaqq, *a.* Entitled (to); deserving (of); *n.* a just claimant; a deserving person.

Mustahkam, *a.* Firmly established; stable; fixed.

Mustahsan, *a.* Esteemed; praiseworthy; virtuous; beautiful.

Musta'idí, *n.* Readiness; promptitude; aptness.

Mustaját, *a.* Heard; acceptable; agreeable.

Mustakhrij, *a.* Drawing out; extracting; eliciting.

Musta'mal, *a.* Employed (in work); in use; common.

Mustanad, *a.* Supported; authenticated; genuine.

Mustanid, *a.* Relying on; supporting oneself upon; *n.* one who relies, &c.

Mustaqbil, *a.* Future; *n.* (in *Gram.*) the future tense.

Mustaqil, *a.* Peculiar; despotic; fixed; resolute.

Mustaqím, *a.* Erect; upright; loyal; faithful.

Must'ar, *a.* Borrow; taken on loan.

Mustasná, *a.* Excepted; excellent; praised.

Mustawí, *a.* Equal; uniform; level; straight; moderate.

Muta'addid, *a.* Many; numerous; prepared.

Muta'affin, *a.* Rotten; fetid; putrid; corrupted.

Muta'aiyin, *a.* Appointed; deputed; certain; *n.* a deputed; *a.* a *locum tenens.*

Muta'ajjib, *a.* Amazed; full of admiration (for); strange.

Muta'allim, *a.* Suspended; dependent (upon); attached (to); relative (to); *n.* kinsman; dependant; appendage.

Muta'alliqín, *n. (Plur of muta'alliq).* Children; family; dependants.

Muta'arif, *a.* Making oneself acquainted with; prying into the secrets of another; making confession.

Muta'ssib, *a.* Partial; biassed; prejudiced.

Mutabanna, *a.* Adopted (as a child).

Mutabarrak, *a.* Holy; consecrated; fortunate.

Mu'tabbar, *a.* Reliable; respectable; trustworthy.

Mu'tadil, *a.* Equal; uniform; temperate; moderate.

Mutábiq, *a.* Conformable; adaptable; suitable.

Mutafakkir, *a.* Anxious; uneasy; pensive.

Mutafanní, *a.* Artful; cunning; crafty.

Mutafarriq, *a.* Separated; Miscellaneous.

Mutagaiyar, *a.* Changed; altered; confused; perplexed.

Mutahaiyar, *a.* amazed; astounded; confounded.

Mutahammil, *a.* Patient; enduring.

Mutahaqqaq, *a.* Proved; attested; true.

Mutaharrik, *a.* Moveable; accented with vowel points.

Mutakabbir, *a.* Proud; arrogant.

Mutakallim, *n.* Speaker; (in *Gram.)* the first person.

Mutakhaiyala, *n.* Fancy; imagination.

Mutál'a, *n.* Consideration; meditation; study.

Mutaláshí, *n.* An enquirer; a searcher.

Mutalawwin, *a.* Whimsical; capricious; fickle.

Mutálí, *n.* Urine-hole; urinal.

Mutamawwal, *a.* Rich; wealth.

Mutáná, *v.* To cause to urinate.

Mutanaffir, *a.* Abhorrent; detestable.

Mutaqaddammín, *n.* Predecessors; ancestors; the ancients.

Mu'taqid, *n.* A believer; a follower of any religion; *a.* sure; certain.

Mutarajjim, *n.* Translator; interpreter.

Mu'tariz, *n.* Opposing; obstructing; resisting; *n.* an opponent; an objector; a hindrance.

Mutás, *n.* The urge to urinate. —*lagná,* v. To want to urinate.

Mutasarrif, *a.* Possessing; occupying; embezzling; extravagant; *n.* possessor; occupant; one who embezzles.

Mutawaffi, *a.* Dead; deceased; defunct.

Mutawajjih, *a.* Attentive; intent.

Mutawallid, *a.* Born; begotten; generated; propagated.

Mutawátir, *adv.* Successively; in rotation; *a.* successive; continuous; consecutive.

Mutazakkara, *a.* Mentioned; referred to; stated; named.

Mutazarrib, *a.* Beaten; agitated; disturbed.

Mutfanní, *adj.* Crafty; clever; trickster.

Mutlaq, *a.* Free; unrestricted; independent; supreme; *adv.* wholly; entirely; at all; not in the least; never.

Mutmaín, *adj.* Assured.

Mutnáza', *a.* Disputed; contested.

Mutní, *n.* (*Colloq.*) Penis.

Mutrib, *n.* Singer; minstrel; musician.

Muttafiq, *a.* Agreeing; consenting; unanimous.

Muttahid, *a.* United. *azlá'i muttahida,* united states.

Muttahidá, *adj.* United; unified.

Muttaqí, *a.* Abstemious; pious; God-fearing.

Muṭṭhí, *a.* The fist; a handful. —*garm karná,* to give a bribe.

Muwáfaqat, *n.* Conformity; accord; agreement.

Muwákhazá, *a.* Calling to account; taking satisfaction; retaliating.

Muwakkal, *n.* Guardian; protector; substitute; client.

Muzaffar, *a.* Victoriious; successful; august; *n.* victor; conqueror.

Muzáhmat, *n.* Obstacle; hindrance; impediment.

Muzáhim, *a.* Hindering; obstructing; preventing; *n.* a hinderer; obstruction; obstacle; preventive.

Múzí, *a.* Troublesome; vexatious; pernicious.

Muzirr, *a.* Hurtful; harmful; injurious.

Muzmar, *a.* Hidden; concealed; *n.* (in *Gram.*) the antecedent.

Muztarib, *a.* Agitated; anxious; afflicted.

Muztir, *a.* Reduced to want or necessity; restless; afflicted.

N, n, sounds like (न) in Hindi and (ن) in Urdu. In its diluted, half-value sound it also functions as a nasal tone in the middle of a word, or at the end of one. With a dot underneath, 'ṇ' represents Hindi (ण).

Ná, *adv.* Nay; no; not. *ná-to* or *ná-tau, conj.* If not; or else; otherwise.

Ná, *adr. Ná* is prefixed to nouns or participles, and is equivalent to the English prefixes *non, in-, in-, un-, dis-,* and the affix *less,* as:—*áshná, a.* unknown. —*manzúr, a.* disapproved; inadmissible. —*ham-wár, a.* irregular; uneven. —*kám,* useless; hopeless; unsuccessful.

Na/ Ná, *Pref.* [Indicates a negative sense in the word that it attaches to.] —*ittifaki,* adj. Disunity; lack of unanimity. —*insáfí,* adj. Injustice. —*ummíd,* adj. One without hope; disappointed. —*ummídí,* n. Hopelessness; despair. &c.

Nabát, *n. (Plur. Nabátát).* Vegetation; herb; vegetable; plant; sugarcandy; crystallized sugar.

Nabbásh, *n.* A plunderer of the dead.

Nabbáz, *n.* A physician; a doctor; a medical practitioner.

Nabbe, *a.* Ninety.

Nabh, *n.* Sky; firmament; ether. —*char/chárí/gámí,* a sky-faring; one who can fly; one who can move in the sky.

Nábhí, *n.* Navel; centre.

Nabí, *n.* A prophet; a seer.

Nabúwat, *n.* Prophesying; foretelling; predicting.

Nabz, *n.* The pulse.

Nách, *n.* Dance.

Nád, *n.* Sound; loud noise.

Naddáf, *n.* A cotton dresser; a carder.

Nadámat, *n.* Regret; repentance; penitence.

Nádán, *n.* Ignorance; simple.

Nádánista, *adv.* Unwittingly; unconsciously; ignorantly.

Nadím, *a.* Companion; intimate friend; courtier; confidant.

Nádim, *a.* Abashed; ashamed; contrite; repentant.

Nádir, *a.* Rare; uncommon; choice.

Nádira, *n.* A rarity; a curiosity; a prodigy.

Náe-o-nosh, *n.* Music and wine; revelry.

Nafa', *n.* Profit; gain; benefit; advantage.

Nafar, *n.* Servant; groom; ostler; the person, or an individual.

Nafásat, *n.* Exquisiteness; purity; refinement.

Nafí, *n.* Deduction; prohibition; refusal; rejection; annihilation; forbidden.

Nafír, Nafírí, *n.* Pipe; clarionet.

Nafís, *a.* Precious; delicate; exquisite.

Nafrat, *n.* Flight: dread; fear; aversion; disgust. *—angez, a.* disgusting.

Nafrí, *n.* Daily labour; daily wages.

Nafrín, *n.* Detestation; abhorrence; curse.

Nafs, *n.* Breath (of life): soul; spirit; person; substance; essence; mind; will; body; fact; inordinate desire; pride; pomp; envy; defect. *—kushí, n.* self-denial. *—i-nátiqa,* the rational soul. *nafsánafsí,* each one for himself.

Nafsániyat, *n.* Sensuality; pomp conceit; anger.

Nafúr, *n.* Fleeing; excelling; inflammation or swelling of the skin.

Nag, *n.* Anything immoveable; a mountain; a rock; a tree; jem; jewel.

Nág, S. *n.* Snake; serpent; the *cobra de capello,* or hooded snake; a Nága, or fabulous serpent demon so called, having a human face with the tail of a serpent; an elephant; the name of several plants; tin; lead.

Nágá, *n.* A class of Hindu mendicants who go naked and carry arms; a tribe dwelling in the hills along the southern borders of Assam.

Nágá, *a.* Vacant; absent; *n.* a blank; absence; adjournment; postponement.

Nágáh, Nágahán, *adv.* suddenly; unexpectedly.

Nágahání, *n.* Chance, *a.* unexpected; sudden. *balá-i—, n.* a sudden misfortune.

Nagar, *n.* City; a major residential community. *—nigam,* n. City-council; municipal corporation. *—páliká,* n. Municipality. *—vadhú,* n. A prostitute (literally, a wife to everyone in the city). *—wásí,* a. Dweller of the city; a citizen; townsfolk.

Nagar-pál, *n.* [Literally] Keeper of the town; town mayor.

Nagar-páliká, *n.* Municipality; town-council.

Nágin, *n.* A she-snake; a villanous woman. *—kí tarah phunkárná,* v. To hiss like a female snake; to be furiously angry.

Nagín, Nagíná, *n.* A gem, or precious stone; set in a ring; a ring. *—sar, n.* a lapidary.

Nagmá, *n.* Melody; harmony; musical note or sound; song; a sweet voice.

Nagn, *a.* Naked; bare; without folliage; without cover or clothes. *—nrity,* A brazen performance; ashow of shamelessness.

Nágrí, *n.* The most common Hindi character of writing; also called Deva Nágri; city dialect.

Nagz, *a.* Beautiful; excellent; sincere; swift; agile; nimble.

Naháfat, *n.* Leanness; emaciation; thinness.

Nahán, *n.* Bathing; ablution.

Naháná, *v.* To bathe; to wash (the body).

Nahanní, *n.* An instrument for paring the nails.

Náhar, *n.* Lion; tiger.

Nahárí, *n.* Breakfast; a kind of bridle.

Nahíf, *n.* Lean; thin; weak.

Nahín, *adv.* No; nay; not. *—to,* if not; else; otherwise.

Nahr, *n.* Stream; brook; canal; channel.

Nahs, *a.* Inauspicious; unlucky. *n.* an evil omen; misfortune.

Nai, *n.* A reed; flute; pipe; fife; tube.

Naí, *a.* New; fresh; recent.

Náí, *n.* Barber; one who's profession is grooming your hair; (in social rituals) he is the one carrying messages of betrothal etc.

Náib, *n.* substitute; deputy; delegate; victory.

Naihar, *n.* A woman's paternal home/ village/town.

Na'ím, *n.* Comfort; ease; benefit; pleasure; God.

Nain, Nainá, *n.* The eye.

Nairang, *n.* Fascination; enchantment; magic; sorcery; witchcraft; deceit; evasion; a miracle.

Naistán, *n.* Bed of reeds; field of sugarcane.

Naivedya, *n.* Oblation; ritual offerings to deity.

Naiyáyik, *n.* Logician; debator; dispenser of justice.

Náj (*corruption of* **Anáj**), *n.* Grain; corn; food.

Najásat, *n.* Uncleanness; impurity; dirtiness.

Naját, *n.* Liberty; freedom; deliverance; absolution; forgiveness; flight.

Najíb, *a.* Generous; benevolent; excellent; praiseworthy; *n.* hero; volunteer.

Najis, *a.* Dirty; filthy; impure.

Najm, *n.* A star; a planet; a horoscope.

Najúmí, *n.* Astrologer; a prediction-maker.

Nák, *n.* The nose; a prominent person or thing; honour.

Náká, *n.* Extremity (of a road, &c.); entrance (to a pass or road, &c.); eye of a needle; a toll station; a subordinate police station.

Nákárá, *a.* Worthless; useless; unserviceable; invalid.

Nakel, *n.* An animal's bridle or halter.

Nakh, *n.* Nail; claw; talon.

Naḳhás, *n.* A slave market; a horse or cattle market.

Nakhat, *n.* A star; a constellation.

Naḳhchír, *n.* The chase; hunting.

Naḳhl, *n.* A data-tree; a palmtree.

Naḳhrá, *n.* Trick; artifice; pretence; joke; conquetry; proud or haughty bearing.

Náḳhún, *n.* Nail; talon; claw.

Naḳhwat, *n.* Pride; haughtiness; arrogance; pomp.

Nakkál, *n.* An actor; a mimic; a forger; an imitater; a counterfeiter.

Nakkárá, *n.* A kettle drum [beaten to make public announcements, of official, or the ruler's dictats]. *—pítná,* v. To announce publicly. *Nakkár kh^áná,* n. A noisy debating chamber; a hall full of din. *Nakkáre kí chot par,* prov. To declare something in public, without fear.

Nakohish, Nikohish, *a.* Spurning; despising; reproach; scorn.

Nakkásh, *n.* Artist; a carver; a gilder; an engraver; a fine craftsman; a cartographper. *—í,* n. The art of fine carving (like in jewellery, ivory-work, or even carving in marble).

Naksh, *n.* A painting; drawing; embroidery; engaving; design; mark; features; impression; body lines. *—i-kadam,* adv. In the footsteps of; emulating. *Nák-,* n. Features (describable parts of human body).

Nakshá, *n.* Map; chart; site plan; delineation; sketch. *-navís,* n. A cartographer; a draftsman. *Nakshe-bází,* n. Pomp and show.

Naksír, *n.* Spistaxix; nose-bleed. *-phútná,* v. Nose to start bleeding.

Nakṭá, *n.* Nose-clipt; noseless; shameless; disgraced *a.* one whose nose has been cut off; a rogue; a class of obscene songs.

Nakul, *n.* The mongoose.

Nal, *n.* A tube; a spout; a joint of a bamboo; a read; a cylindrical case.

Nál, *n.* A horse shoe; a hoof; a wife. —*band, n.* a farrier.

Nálá, *n.* Complaint; wailing; lamentation.

Nálán, *n.* Lamentation; wailing; groaning.

Nálí, *n.* A hollow reed; tube; pipe; drain; barrel or bore (of a gun).

Nalin, *n.* Lotus flower; water-lily. —*í,* n. A bed of lotus flowers; a pond of water-lilies.

Nálish, *a.* Groan; complaint; accusation; charge; statement of a plaintiff's case; legal suit or action. —*i-zar-i-harja,* a suit or action for damages. —*ke máne' honá,* or *ho-jáná,* to be or become a bar to a complaint or action; to bar a suit.

Nam, *a.* Moist; humid; damp; wet.

Nám, *n.* Name; fame, renown, reputation. *Nám kamáná,* v. (*prov.*) To become famous; to make a name; to build a reputation; title; appellation. —*karaṇ,* n. baptism; naming ceremony. —*kírtan,* n. Constant, musical rendition of Lord's name, usually in a congregation. —*grám,* n. Whereabouts; one's name and address, etc. —*ánkit/ —zad,* a. Nominated. *Ánkan/ zadgí,* v. Nomination. —*í/ dár/ var,* a Renowned; wellknown. —*o-nishán,* n. trace vestige. —*paṭṭ/ paṭṭí,* n. Name plate; sign-board. —*mátr ke liye/ bhar ke liye,* adv. Nominally; in name only. —*levá,* a. Survivor; one to carry the name forward; one responsible for continuing the lineage. —*hín,* a. Nameless; an unknown. —*uchhálná,* adv. To bandy one's name; to bring disgrace upon; to tarnish some one's name. —*ujágar karná,* v. To bring credit to one's name. —*uṭh/ mit jáná, v.* Even the memory being lost; to have no survivor. —*kamáná,* v. Ṭo make a name for oneself; to become famous. —*ká ḍanká piṭná/ dhúm machná,* v. To become known far and wide; to beheld in high esteem all over; one's name to become a byword. —*kí bhúkh,* n. Yearning for fame/ renown. —*kí málá japná,* v. To remember every living moment; to have someone in your thoughts all the time. —*ke liye,* adv. For the sake of one's name; a question of credibility. —*par thúkná,* v. To spit at some one's name; to treat some one's name with ignominy or contempt. —*ko roná,* v. To repine for another's misdeeds. —*ḍubáná,* v. To tarnish some one's name. —*miṭá dená,* v. To wipe out one's name; to obliterate the last vestiges of some one's name. —*ná lená,* v. Not even to mention someone's name &c.

Náma, *n.* Letter; record; book; history; a deed.

Namad, Namda, *n.* A coarse woollen cloth.

Namah, *Suf.* Salutations; [at the end of all prayers to their deities, Hindus utter this word as their offering].

Namak, *n.* Salt. —*khwár,* a Loyal. —*harám,* a. Disloyal; traitor; ungratefu. —*Halál,* a. Loyal; grateful; faithful. —*ká haq adá karná,* v. To repay one's debt of gratitude. *Jale par/gháv par —chhiṛakná,* prov. (literally: to rub salt into one's wounds). To add insult to injury. —*mirch lagáná,* v. To exaggerate.

Naman, Namas, *n.* Making a bow; salutation; obeisauce. — *yit, a.* reverenced; worshipped.

Namaskár, *n.* Salutation; a term of greeting; adieu; so long. *Dúr se—karná,* prov. To keep away from; not to have anything to do with.

Namaste, *n.* Greetings to you, salutations.

Namat, *n.* Resemblance; similarity; likeness; mode; manner.

Namáz, *n.* Prayers (esp. the prayers prescribed by the Muhammadan law, which are said five times a day); adoration; worship; divine service.

Namází, *a.* In the constant habit of praying; devout; *n.* a person who prays.

Namíl, *a.* Nimble; quick; brisk; spirited (as a horse).

Námiya, *n.* Vegetation; growth; a stalk or stem of a plant; a creature.

Namkín, *a.* Savoury; salty; taining salt; saline; loquially; pretty; beautiful; witty; savcastic.

Naml, *n.* An ant.

Namná, *n.* To bow down; to make obesiance (to).

Namra, *a.* Bending; bowing down; inclined; curved; meek, submissive; courteous; polite.

Namúd, *n.* Visibility; appearance; prominence; show; pomp; honour; an index; a guide; *a.* apparent; visible; conspicuous; famous.

Namúdár, *a.* Apparent; visible; conspicuous. *n.* example; model; proof; copy. *adv.* like; after the manner.

Namúdiya, *n.* One who is fond of

show or disply; a braggart; a boaster.

Namúna, *n.* Specimen; sample; example; type; form; model.

Namús, *n.* Reputation; fame; celebrity; esteem; honour; dignity; disgrace; ignominy; shame.

Ná<u>n</u>, *adv.* No; not; nay.

Nán, *n.* Bread; a cake of bread; a loaf.

Náná, *n.* Maternal grandfather.

Náná, *a.* Different; various; diverse; many.

Nanad, *n.* Husband's sister. *Nandoí,* n. Husband's sister's husband.

Nának, Nának-sháh, *n.* The name of the founder of the Sikh sect. *Nának,-pa<u>n</u>th, n.* the religion of Nának, or of the Sikhs.

Nánárth, *a.* Having different meanings (as a word).

Ná<u>n</u>d, *n.* A large wide-mouthed earthen jar or water-pot.

Na<u>n</u>dan, *n.* Born of; the son of; the offspring of. *Nandini,* n. Female child of; the daughter of.

Ná<u>n</u>dhná, *v.* To begin; to take in hand.

Na<u>n</u>dí, *n.* The name of Lord Shiva's bull, worshipped on his own as a deity; often used (as an endearment) for a common bull, as also (mockingly) for a brainless bully man.

Na<u>n</u>gá, *adj.* Nacked; bare; without covering of any sort. *-pan,* n. Nakedness; brazen attitude. -*nách,* n. Brazen behaviour; a shameless performance.

Na<u>n</u>g-dhaṛa<u>n</u>g, *adj.* Stark naked; completely nude; shamless.

Ná<u>n</u>ghaná, lá<u>n</u>ghná, *v.* To leap over; to jump across.

Nání, *n.* A maternal grandmother.

Nannhá, *n.* Small; diminutive; tiny; neat; petty; low; *n.* a mere child; a pet; darling.

Náo, Náv, *n.* A boat; a ship; a vessel.

Náp, *n.* Measure; measurement; survey. —*bidyá,* mensuration.

Ná-páedár, *a.* Unstable; inconstant; fickle.

Nápák, *a.* Foul; dirty; impure; defiled.

Ná-pasand, *a.* Rejected; disapproved of; unacceptable.

Nápit, *n.* A barder; a shaver; a surgeon—*sálá, n.* a barber's shop; a hair cutting saloon.

Napu<u>n</u>sak, *a.* Impotent; spineless; weak personality; a coward; a eunch; Destitute of virility; of neither sex; unmanly (in *Gram*).

Naqá, *n.* Purity; cleanness; virtue; *a.* pure; clean; virtuous.

Náqá, *n.* A camel; especially a female camel.

Naqab, Naqb, *n.* A subterraneous excavation; burrow (of a rabbit); a gallery; a mine; digging through a wall; house-breaking, or burglary; a crowbar or other implement used by miners, burglars, &c.

Naqáb, Niqáb, *n.* A veil; a hood; a covering for the face.

Naqáhat, *n.* Recovery from illness; convalescence; weakness; debility.

Naqd, *a.* Prompt or ready (payment); good or choice (articles); sterling (coin); of standard value; *n.* coin; money.

Naqíb, *n.* A chief; a leader; a person gifted with intelligence; an adjutant; an aidede-camp; an agent.

Naqíh, *n.* Weak; feeble; debilitated; faint.

Náqil, *n.* Reported; recorded; narrator; copyist; painter.

Náqis, *n.* Defective; imperfect; incomplete; bad; wicked.

Naqíz, *a.* Adverse; contrary; opposite; hostile; *n.* an enemy; opposition; enmity.

Naql, *v.* Transportation; removal, translation; transfer or alienation (of property); transcribing; copying. *n.* Imitation (of a copy); a copy; a duplicate; a history; report; table. *—mutábiq-i-asl,* a true copy. *—i-khiláf,* a false copy; a misquotation.

Naqlí, *a.* Handed down; fabricated; artificial; false; *n.* a mimic (see *Nakkál*)..

Naqqára, *n.* See *Nakkárá.*

Naqqásh, See *Nakkásh.*

Naqsh, *n.* Painting; drawing; embroidery; a picture; portrait; engraving; map or plan; design; stamp; mark.

Naqshá, *n.* Delineation; picture; sketch; design; plan; model; map; chart; register; a blank form or schedule.

Nar, *n.* Man; male. *—kapál,* n. Human skull. *—kesarí,* n. Lion-hearted; brave. *—pashu,* a. A beastly man; a cruel person; an uncouth, ill-behaved, utterly selfish person. *—bali/medh,* n. Human sacrifice. *—bhakshí* a. A cannibal; a man-eater.

Nár, *n.* The pulse; the gullet; the throat; the neck.

Náṛ, *n.* A contraction of *Náṛí,* woman, *q. v.*

Narak, Nark, *n.* Hell; inferno; A place of agony and unbearable suffering. *—wásí,* a. A dweller of hell. *—gámí,* a. One destined for hell. *—ká kírá,* a. a lowly, sinful being. *—bhogan,* v. To suffer agonies and pains of hell; to undergo intense suffering.

Nárí, *n. (Plur. Nárin̲).* A woman; a female; a wife.

Nárị́, *a.* A stalk (of a plant); any tabular organ of the body; the pulse.

Náriyal, *n.* The cocoanut-tree; *(Met.),* the head; the skull.

Narkal, Narkat, *n.* A large species of reed; a bulrush.

Narm, Naram, *a.* Soft; smooth; mild; tender; simple; silly; low or subdued (in tone); moderate; *adv.* softly; gently; slowly, &c.

Narmí, Narmiyat, *n.* Softness; plipliancy; tenderness.

Narsingá, *n.* A trumpet; a bugle; a (musical) horn.

Narso̲n̲, *n.* The fourth day, past, or to come; four days ago or four days hence.

Nartak, *n.* Dancer(s) *—í,* n. A female dancer. *Ráj—* a. A royal dancer.

Nas, *a.* Sinew; vein; nerve. *—bandí,* n. Vasectomy. *-dhílí honá,* v. To be unnerved; to feel demoralised. *—nas pahchánaná/se wákif honá,* v. To know some one thoroughly. *—phaṛak uṭhná,* v. To get excited; to be thrilled. *—nas men samáná,* To permeate one's whole being. *—nas men honá,* v. To be bred in the bone.

Nasab, *n.* Genealogy; race; lineage; caste.

Nasáeh, *n. (Plur. of Nasihat).* Connects; advices; admonitions.

Nasáim, *n. (Plur. of Nasím).* Gentle breezes; zephyr; spicy gales.

Nasáná, *v.* To destroy; to efface; to exterminate; to squander; to be lost; to be destroyed; to perish.

Nasaq, *n.* Order; series; method; system; arrangement; style or mode of writing.

Nasb, *n.* Erecting; setting up; establishing.

Náseh/ Násih, *n.* Preceptor; one giving good or sound advice; *n.* adviser; counsellor; faithful minister; one who delivers sermons; a priest; one who reprimands or admonishes.

Násh, *n.* Destruction; annihilation; wiping out the existence of.

Na'sh, *n.* A bier; a cofin; a litter.

Nashá, *n.* Intoxication; inebriation; (also) intoxicant; inebriative. —*khor,* adj. An inebriate; an addict. —*Páni,* a Intoxicating substances. —*bandí,* n. Prohibition; banishment of intoxicants. —*utarná,* v. To be detoxicated; to be brought down to earth (by way of knocking one's pride off). —*hiran honá,* v. To be stunned; to be brought back to senses. *Nashe men dhutt honá,* adv. To be punch drunk.

Ná-sháistagí, *n.* Unbecoming behaviour; impropriety.

Náshak, *n.* Destructive; *n.* an antidote.

Nashástá/Nishástá, *n.* Starch; paste.

Nashát, *n.* Growing; being produced; creation; a creature.

Nasheb, Nisheb, *n.* Descent; slope; lowness (of ground); a hollow; *a.* sloping; low; hollow.

Nashébáz, *n.* An addict; a person habituated to seek intoxication; one given to intoxicants; a drunkard.

Nashílá, Nashílí, *adj.* Intoxicating; consumables that induce state of intoxication.

Náshir, *n.* Publisher; one who announces it; one who brings a piece of work to public notice.

Náshpátí, *n.* A pear.

Nashr, *n.* Spreading (as a carpet); publishing (news).

Nasht, *a.* Lost; ruined; destroyed.

Nashtar, *n.* A lancet.

Náshwán, *a.* Perishable; transient; one subject to degrade and die.

Nashwar, *a.* Destructible; transient; mortal.

Nasíb, *n.* Fortune, fate; luck; destiny. —*ázmáná,* v. To try one's luck. —*ká khel,* a. A matter of luck; destiny; out of one's hands; beyond one's control. —*ká márá,* a. Struck by bad luck. *khote*—, a. bad luck; misfortune. —*ká likhá,* a. One's lot; dictates of destiny. —*jágná,* v. For the fortune to smile at one. —*men honá,* a. To be bestowed by dame luck, &c.

Nasíhat, *n.* A sermon; precept; words of wisdom; sound advice; explanation of right and wrong.

Násij, A. *n.* A weaver; a composer.

Násiká, *n.* Nose; trunk of an elephant; a proboscis.

Násikh, *n.* Copyist; amanuensis; erasing.

Nasír, *n.* Succourer; helper; ally; friend.

Naskh, *n.* Abolition; abrogation; repeal.

Nasl, *n.* Offspring; progeny; race; genealogy; family.

Nasr, *n.* Prose; a genre of writing. *—nigár,* n. A prose-writer.

Nassár, *n.* A writer of prose.

Nástik, *n.* An infidel; an atheist.

Násúr, *n.* An ulcer; a running or suppurating sore; a fistula.

Nasut, *n.* Humanity; human nature.

Naswár, *n.* Snuff.

Násya, *a.* Pertaining to the nose; nasal; *n.* snuff.

Naṭ, *n.* Performer; entertainer; actor; dancer. *—Bhairav,* n. Name of a *Rág* in Indian classical music. *—ráj,* n. Name given to Lord *Shiv* when he is visualised as performing his Cosmic dance; a rope-dancer; a tumbler; an acrobat or gymnast; a juggler.

Na't, *n.* Praise; applause; eulogy (Muslim tradition).

Nát, *n.* Pillar; beam; log.

Nátá, *n.* Relationship; alliance.

Náṭá, *n.* Short; dwarfish; dapper; vile; wicked; vicious. *—pan, n.* shortness of stature.

Náṭak, *n.* Play; drama; stage presentation of a narrative. *—kár,* n. a playwright; a dramatist. *—karná,* v. To stage a play; to play act; to put on an act; to pretend. *—íy,* a. Dramatic; histrionic.

Nátamgár, *n.* A great merchant; a respectable man.

Naṭan, *n.* Denial; negation; refusal.

Natáns, *n.* Zenith distance.

Nátedár, *n.* A relative; a kinsman.

Nath, *n.* A piece of jewellery worn on a pierced nose; a nose-ring; a nose rope (in case of beasts of burden, like bullocks). *—utárná,* v. de-flowering of a virgin. (Amongst the prostitutes. in feudal societies. it was great ceremony where a new girl was inducted into the business, by a rich client, in return for a substantial reward to the keeper of the house).

Náth, *n.* Master; lord; husband; a title used by *jogís.*

Nathná, *n.* A nostril; nosering.

Nátí, *n.* Daughter's sons.

Natíyá, *n.* Offspring; birth; result; issue; reward.

Nátiq, *n.* Speaker; a rational animal; *a.* speaking; rational (animal); postive; final.

Nátiqa, *n.* The faculty of speech; *a.* speaking. &c. (see *Nátiq*).

Naṭkhaṭ, *a.* Naughty; wicked; roguish; artful; *n.* a naughty or mischievous child; an imp; a cheat.

Natthí, *adj.* A file or bundle of papers; enclosed; attached by a string or a paperclip.

Náṭy-shástr, *n.* The science of dramatics; the proper name of a classic Sanskrit work on performing arts, written by *Bharata Muni.*

Nau, *a.* Nine.

Nau', *n.* Kind; species; genus; mode; style.

Náú, *n.* A barber; a hair-dresser.

Naubat, *n.* A period; a turn; fit; occasion; vicissitude; degree; weight; plight; state; accident; beating of large kettle-drum.

Nauha, *n.* Mourning; lamentation.

Nauká, *n.* A boat; a ferry. *—pár lagáná,* v. to complete a project in hand.

Naukar, *n.* A servant; a domestic. *—í, n.* service; attendance; a situation; employment.

Naul, *n.* Passage-money (by a ship) hire of boats or ships.

Ná-ummed, *a.* Hopeless; desperate.

Nausádar, Naushádar, *n.* Sal ammoniac.

Na'uz, *intj.* We pray for the protection of God; God forbid. *n.* fleeing to any person for refuge or protection.

Nav, *a.* Nine. (Also used as a prefix in many instances, like—) *—grah,* n. Nine planets [according to Hindu astrology]; *—dhá bhakti,* n. Nine forms of devotion *(bhakti). —nidhi,* n. Nine treasures obtained from the (mythical) churning of the Ocean *(Samudra manthan). —ratn,* a. Nine gems; nine wise men in the kings court [Emperor Vikramáditya and Akbar are credited with having such 'nine wise men' in their respective courts]. *—ras,* n. Nine sources of enjoyment in any art forms, &c.

Náv/Nauká, *n.* Boat; yach; small ship.

Nav/Naya, *adj.* New; fresh; young; freshly arrived.

Navín, *a.* New; fresh; original; modern; recent; (and as a prefix-) neo. *—yug,* a. New era. *—yuvak,* a. A fresh young man. *—yuvatí,* a. A fresh young woman. *—mánav vád,* a. Neo-humanism. *—vadhú,* a. Newly wed bride. *—sákshar,* a. Neo-literate, &c.

Navmí/Naumí, *n.* Ninth day of each lunar month (of the Hindu calender). *Rám—,* n. A specific ḍate in the annual festivals calender, celebrated as a festival by Hindus, to comemorate *Ram's* victory over the demon king *Rávam*).

Nawá, *n.* Vice; sound; song; tune; musical tone; riches; prosperity.

Nawáb, Nawwáb, *n.* A 'nabob'; a governor of a town or province; a viceroy; a lord; a prince.

Nawad, *a.* Ninety.

Nawáh, *(Plur. of Náhiya);* environs; suburbs; territories; tracts.

Nawáḳhta, *a.* Protected; reared; cherished.

Nawálá, Niwálá, *n.* A mouthful; a morsel. *sone-ká nawalá,* a costly banquet; a delicious morsel.

Naward, *n.* A twist; a fold; traversing.

Nawásá, *n.* A daughter's son.

Nawásí, *n.* A daughter's daughter.

Nawáz, *adj.* Giver; bestower. *—ná* v. To give; to bestow. *Ḡharíb—,* adj. Patron of the poor; one who is considerate to the needy and the poor.

Nawázish, *n.* Caress; kindness; politeness; favour.

Nawázná, *v.* To bless (with); to give (to); to grant; to favour (with).

Nawed, *n.* Glad tidings; good news.

Nawín, See *Nav/Navín.*

Nawís, *n.* Writer; scribe; clerk; copyist.

Nawná, *v.* To bow; to stoop; to yield; to submit.

Nayá, *a.* New; fresh; recent; modern.

Náyak, *n.* Chief; leader; guide; headman.

Náz, *n.* Blandishment; coquetry; flirtation; pride; haughty airs.

Nazá, *a.* The pangs or agonies of death.

Nazákat, *n.* Delicacy; elegance; politeness.

Nazám, Nizám, *n.* Rule; regime; administration; also a system of government. Formal title of the former ruler of Hyderabad Deccan in India; *Nizám of Haidarábád.*

Nazar, *n.* Sight; eyesight; vision; look; glance; attention. *—áná,* a A present; a gift; an offering; a tribute; (in modern times, a euphemism for a bribe). *—band,* a. In detention; in custody; an internee. *—ḍálná,* v. To cast an eye on; to glance at. *—andáz karná,* v. To ignore; to brush aside; to overlook; to disregard. *—áná,* v. To come into view; to appear; to become visible. *—bacháná/churáná,* v. To evade being sighted; to avoid meeting some one. *—dauṛáná,* v. To glance at; to look around; to have hurried scan of things. *—na uṭháná,* v. To feel ashamed; not to look straight in the eye. *—paṛná,* v. To spot; to sight; to suddenly come across. *—par chaṛhná,* v. To catch the fancy of; to develop a liking for. *—fisalná,* v. To be dazzled. *—badalná,* v. To be deprived of one's favours; to undergo a change of attitude. *—lagná,* v. To be struck by an evil glance; to suffer someone's jealousy. *—se girná,* v. To fall out of favour.

Nazárá, *n.* Glance; look; sight; vision; scene.

Nazariyá, *n.* Point of view; attitude; opinion.

Nazdík, *adv.* Close at hand; near by; adjacent; adjoining; neighbouring. *—í, n.* nearness; propinquity; proximity; neighbourhood; vicinity.

Názil, *a.* Descending; dismounting; alighting; reaching.

Názim, *n.* Poet; composer; organizer; governor.

Nazír, *a.* Like; resembling; equal (to); *n.* a similitude; a parallel; an example; a precedent.

Názir, *n.* Eye-witness; one who has seen. [*Házir-názir:* an epithet of God Almighty: Omnipresent, all-knowing].

Názirín, *n.* Beholders; onlookers; witnesses; spectators.

Nazlá, *n.* Common cold; a runny nose; catarrh and cold.

Nazm, *n.* Order; Poetry; verse. *—o-nasq, n.* organization.

Náznín, *a.* A delicate beauty; a fondly love woman; a mistress.

Nazr, *n.* Vow; offering; gift. *—ána,* gift; present.

Názuk, *a.* Thin; light; delicate; frail; tender.

Neg, *n.* Custom; usage; pracrice; presents given on festive occasions.

Nek, *a.* Good; virtuous. *—khayál,* a. Well-meaning. *—chalan* a. Of good conduct. *—zát,* a. Of good breeding. *—dil,* a. A gentle soul; a good person. *—nám,* a. Of good repute. *—níyat,* a. Well-intentioned; honest; genuine. *—bakht,* a. Fortunate; lucky; blessed one.

Nekí, *n.* A good deed; virtue; piety. *—badí,* Good and bad (hand-in-hand); *—kar kuen men dál,* prov.

To perform a good deed and forget it; not to publicise one's beneficience

Nem, (See **Niyam**).

Neotá, Newtá, *n.* Invitation, (also Nyotá).

Nest, *a.* Non-existence; annihilation; extermination; *a.* non-existent; null; void. *—o-nábúd kar dená,* v. To wipe out the existence of.

Netá, *a.* Leader; person who speaks for the group. *—jí,* n. A nickname for a very popular nationalist leader, Subhas Chandra Bose. *—gírí,* (Derogatory) Pretence of leadership.

Nettar, Netra, *n.* An eye; eyes. *—vigyán,* a. Ophthalmology. *—hín,* a. One without eyes; blind; (colloquially) one who proceeds without seeing whither he/she is going and what is in the way.

Nezá, *n.* A reed used for making pens; a lance; spear; javelin; pike. *—báz,* a spearman; a lancer.

Nibal/Nirbal, *adj.* Weak; feeble; infirm.

Nibaṭná/ Nipaṭná, *v.* To deal with; to complete; to terminate.

Nibedan, Nivedan, *n.* Petition; request; memorial.

Nibhná, *v.* To succeed; to pass; to exist; to live; to last.

Nibháná, *v.* To cope with; to make do; to manage with.

Nibtáná, *v.* To decide; to settle; to conclude.

Níbú, *n.* A lime; a lemon.

Ních, *a.* Low; short; base; vile; low caste; an evil doer. *Únch—,* a. The high and low; distinction between high and low caste.

Nichháwar, *n.* Sacrifice; Victim; money.

Nichi<u>n</u>t, Nishchi<u>n</u>t *a.* Unconcerned; free from care or anxiety; heedless; at leisure.

Nichoṛná, *v.* To wring; to squeeze; to extort.

Nidá, *n.* Sound; voice; calling; summoning to prayer; proclamation.

Nidán, *n.* Weeding; cleaning (of weeds, &c.).

Nidán, *n.* A primary or original cause; the cause of disease; pathology; end; *adv.* in the end; at last; finally.

Nidrá, *n.* Sleep; slumber. *Chir—,* the long sleep, death; departure from this mortal world. *—rog,* n. Narcolepsy. *—vigyán,* Hypnology.

Nifáq, *n.* Duplicity; hypocrisy;

double-dealing; disagreement; hostility.

Nigáh, *n.* Look; view; aspect; attention; care. *—bán, n.* watchman; guard; custodian. *—laráná,* to ogle; to cast amatory glances.

Nigainá, *v.* To swallow; to gulp down.

Nigár, *n.* Painting; picture; portrait. *—istán, n.* a picture gallery.

Nigrání, *n.* Watchfulness; supervision; superintendence. *—karná,* to keep an eye on; to exercise supervision over.

Nigún, *a.* Inverted; upside-down; topsy-turvey.

Nihád, *n.* Nature; temperament; stature; quality; mind.

Nihái, *n.* An anvil.

Nihákà, *n.* An iguana; an enormous alligator.

Nihál, *a.* Prosperous; happy; pleased.

Nihán, Nihání, *a.* Concealed; hidden; latent; secret.

Nihárná, *v.* To look (at); to stare or gaze (at).

Niháyat, *n.* End; limit; extremity; *a.* excess; extreme; utmost.

Nihuftagí, *n.* Concealment; secrecy; obscurity.

Nij, Niji, *a.* Own; personal; individual; particular.

Nijjhar, Nirjhar, *n.* Waterfall; cataract; mountain torrent.

Nikáh, *n.* Matrimony; wedding; marriage; nuptials.

Nikál, *n.* Outlet; discharge; issue. *—dená, v.* to expel; to drive out. *—láná,* to bring off or away; to elope with. *—ná,* to take or draw out; to distil; to issue; to expel; to utter; to discover; to display; to hatch.

Nikalná, *v.* To be taken or drawn out; to be invented; to rise (as the sun); to appear; to spring; to germinate or shoot; to result; to escape. *nikal bhágná,* to make of; to run away.

Nikammá, *a.* Idle; useless; inert; indolent; good for nothing; (in some cases) unemplyed. *—pan,* n. Uselessness; worthlessness.

Nikás, *n.* Spring; source; outlet; sale; environs; suburbs.

Nikásí, *n.* Outturn; income; transit duty. *—ki chitthí, n.* a permit; a passport.

Nikaṭ, *a.* Near; close; proximate. *—púrv,* a. Near-East. *—vartí,* a. Adjacent; nearby; close by; in the vicinity; in proximity. *—drishṭi,* n. Myopia; short-sightedness.

Niketan, *n.* A temple; an abode; a dwelling place.

Nikhaṭṭu, *a.* Laxy; idle; spendthrift; worthless.

Nikhrá, *a.* Clean; clear; pure.

Nikrishṭ, *a.* Low; mean; base; *n.* a miser.

Níl, *n.* Indigo (plant); blue. *—gagan,* n. Blue sky. *—kamal,* a. Blue lotus. *—kanṭh,* n. An epithet of Lord Shiva, on account of him having swallowed a potion of lethal venom to save the world from suffering the effects thereof, and thus having obtained a blue throat: *Níl kanṭh.*

Nilá, *a.* Dark-blue; blue; livid. *—thotha,* bluestone; sulphate of copper.

Nilajjatá, Nirlajjatá, *n.* Shamelessness; depravity.

Nílám, *n.* Auction.

Nílofar, *n.* The lotus; waterlily.

Ním, *a.* Half; *n.* a half; a moiety. *—ján, a.* half-dead. *—pukhta,* half-cooked; parboiled *—roz,* midday; noon. *—shab,* midnight.

Ni'mat, *n.* Comfort; affluence; boon; favour; a delicacy

Nimit, Nimitt *n.* Mark; token; sign; cause; motive; share; for-tune; *pre.* for the sake of because of; by reason of.

Nínd, *n.* Sleep; slumber. *Sukh kí —soná,* v. To die peacefully

Nindá, *n.* Criticism; condemnation; defamation; decrying; Rebuke; reprimand; blame; censure; slander.

Ninnánawe (99), *n.* Ninety-nine; one-short-of-a-hundred. *—ká chakkar,* prov. Concerns of making a living.

Nipaṭ, *adv.* Totally; entirely; completely; exceedingly.

Nipṭárá, *n.* Adjustment; settlement; termination; conclusion.

Nipuṇ, *a.* Dexterous; clever; skilful; experienced.

Niqát, *n. (Plur. of Nuqta).* Points and dots (used in writing and printing).

Nirá, *a.* Pure; genuine; unalloyed; unadulterated.

Nirála, *a.* Secluded; solitary; lonely; rare; scarcely; separated.

Nirámish, *a.* Non-meat (diet); food with no fish/meat/poultry content.

Nira<u>n</u>jan, *a.* Pure; untainted; free from the stain of guilt; *n.* the Supreme Being.

Nira<u>n</u>kál, Nira<u>n</u>kár, *a.* Incorporeal; with form or sub-stance; *n.* the Supreme Being.

Nira<u>n</u>tar, *a.* Without interval: with no gap; continuous; non-stop.

Nirás, Nirásh, *n.* Hopeless; desperate.

Nirás/ Nirásh, *adj.* Pessimistic; one without hope; heart-broken; one who has given up hope; desperate.

Nirásá/ Niráshá, *n.* Pessimism; hopelessness; abandonment of hope.

Nirbal, (See **Nibal**).

Nirbans, Nirvansh *a.* Childless; without offspring.

Nirbhar, *a.* Dependant; Reliant; based on; subject to; subordinate of; relying on. *—tá,* n. dependance; relaince.

Nirbhík, *a.* Fearless; undaunted; unafraid.

Niríh, *a.* Innocent; harmless; simple; asking for nothing; making no demands.

Nirjan, *a.* Lonely; solitary; desolate; deserted; unihabited.

Nirkh, *n.* Price current; tariff; market price.

Nirlajj, *a.* Shamelss; brazen; impudent; immodest; lost to sense of honour or propriety. *—atá,* n. The state of impudence; immodesty, &c.

Nirog, *a.* Healthy; sound in mind and (or) body.

Nirpeksh, *a.* One who does not expect (any favour or reward for doing the right thing); non-aligned (in politics).

Nirupam, *adj.* Incomparable; without equal.

Nirván, *n.* Salvation; release; liberation (from the cycle of birth-death-and birth...). This is firmly rooted in Buddhist philosophy of release from the cycle of suffering.

Nirvasan, *a.* One without clothese; nude; bare; naked. *—á,* a. feminine form of—.

Nirvásan, *n.* Exile; deportation; banishment from one's homeland, or one's native post; expulsion; expatriation.

Nisá, *n.* Stock; principal; capital; stock-in-trade.

Nisbat, *n.* Relation; reference; relationship; comparison; espousal. *—tanásub,* ratio; proportion; percentage.

Nisf, *a.* Half, *n.* a half; one of two equal parts; a moiety. *—dáirá,* semi-circle. *—qutr,* radius of a circle. *—un-nihár,* midday; noon.

Nishá, *n.* Night; *—char,* a. Nightly creatures; demons. *—charí vritti,* a. Demonic tendencies *—kar,* n. The moon (as it marks its presence only at night).

Nishát, *n.* Joy; cheerful; liveliness; Happiness.

Nishán, *a.* Seating; setting; establishing; marking; allaying. *n.* sign; mark; seal; stamp; trace; clue; target; emblem; flag; coat-of-arms. —*bardár,* standard-bearer.

Nisháni, *n.* Mark; sign; indication; memento; token of remembrance.

Nishast, *n.* Sitting; posture; attitude.

Nishásta, *n.* Porridge; thick gruel; starch; paste.

Nishchai, *n.* Certainty; assurance; belief; trust.

Nishchal, *a.* Fixed; stable; immovable.

Nishchint, (*see* **Nichint**).

Nishchit, *a.* Ascertained; assured.

Nishedh, *n.* A taboo prohibition; ban; negation. Refusal. —*ágyá,* a. An injunction; a banning order.

Nishkalaṉk, *adj.* Spotlett; faultless; innocent of all sins; non-guilty.

Nishkám, *adj.* Selfless; unselfish; without an ulterior motive.

Nishpáp, *a.* Guiltless; innocent; sinless.

Nishṭhur/Niṭhur, *adj.* cruel; hard-hearted; inconsiderate; harsh; relentless; merciless.

Nissandeh, *a.* Undoubted; doubtless; unquestionable.

Nisyá, *n.* A thing not worthy of remembrance.

Nisyán, *n.* A thing not worthy of remembrance.

Nisyán, *n.* Forgetfulness.

Nit, Nitya, *adv.* Always; continually; perpetually.

Nít, Nítí, *n.* Policy; ethics; sense of right and wrong; guidelines; Conduct; behaviour; manners.

Niṭhallá, *a.* Bone-idle; lazy; lolling around; workshirker. —*pan,* n. Indolence; laziness; habit of being good-for-nothing. (proverbially) essentials of daily life.

Nitharná, *v.* To be cleansed or purified.

Nitya, *a.* Unceasing; continual; perpetual.

Nityánand, *n.* Eternal bliss, or happiness; a happy person.

Nivás, *n.* Residence; lodging; abode; house—*í,* n. An inhabitant; a dweller; a resident.

Nivritt, *adv.* Discharged; disposed off; dealt With; seen off. -*i,* n. The act of-; the state of-.

Niwálá, *n.* See *Nawálá.*

Niwáṛ, *n.* Coarse; broad tape used for knitting beds.

Niwásí, *n.* (See *Nivás*).

Niyam, *n.* Restraint; check; hindrance; limitation. vow; religious observance; principle. [Colloquially spoken of as **Nem**].

Niyárá, (See **Nyárá**).

Níyat, *n.* Will; purpose; design; aim; object in view. *—ke sáth,* wilfully; deliberately; intentionally.

Niyáz, *n.* Petition; prayer; supplication.

Niza', *n.* Contention; disputation; altercation; controversy; the matter in dispute.

Nizám, (See **Nazám**).

Nizár, *n.* Thin; slim; slender.

Noch, *n.* Pinch; scratch.

Nok, *n.* Point; angle; beak; bill. *—i-zabáa,* on the lip of the tongue; by heart.

Non, *n.* Common salt; colloquial name for salt. *—tel lakrí kí firáq,* prov. Concern about scraping a living.

Non-tel-lakrí, *n.* Essentials of life, [*lit.* Food and fuel etc.].

Nosh, *n.* A drink; a draught; anything that is drunk; beverage. *—i-ján farmáná,* to eat; to drink.

Nrip, Nirp, *n.* King; ruler; monarch. *—ochit,* a. Worthy of a king; becoming the status of a ruler.

Nripátmá, Nripatmaj, *n.* A prince; a king's son; *a.* of royal descent.

Nrishans, *a.* Cruel; savage; atrocious. *—atá,* n. Savagery; cruelty.

Nuhúsat, *n.* A bad omen; a foreboding of evil; a bad presage.

Nujúm, *n. (Plur. of Najam).* Stars. *—í,* an astronomer; an astrologer.

Nuktá, *n.* A point; a dot. *—bín,* or *chín, n.* a critic. *—dání,* discernment; acute perception.

Numáish, *n.* A show; display; exhibition; appearance. *—gáh, n.* a. museum an exhibition.

Numáyán, *a.* Apparent; manifest; visible.

Nuqrá, *n.* Silver; money (rupees; a white of cream colour).

Nuqs, *n.* Defect; fault; flaw; deficiency. *—nikálná,* v. To find faults with—.

Nuqsán, *n.* Loss; damage; injury; defect; deficiency.

Nuqúl, *n. Plur. of Naql, q.v.*

Núr, *n.* Light; brilliance; radiance; lustre. *—afshán,* diffusing light; lustrous. *—chashm,* a son.

Nurání, *a.* Lustrous; luminous; light; serene; angelic.

Nuskhá, *n.* Copy; model; example; recipe; prescription; a book; a writing.

Nusrat, *n.* Victory; assistance; triumph.

Nútan, *a.* New; fresh; uptodate. Also a proper name for children of either sex, with appropriate suffix.

Nuzúl, *n.* Descending; dismounting; alighting; a cataract in the eye.

Nyáé/ Nyáya, *n.* Justice; mediation fairness; integrity. —*karná,* v. To dispense justice; to mediate; to adjudicate; —*shástr,* logic.

Nyárá, *a.* Separate; living apart; unique; novel; distinct.

Nyáya, *n.* Justice; fairness; one of the six schools of Hindu philosophy.

Nyáyádhísh, *n.* Judge; an official dispensing justice according to the evidence presented.

Nyáy-páliká, *n.* Judiciary.

Nyáyálay, *n.* Court of justice.

Nyotá, *n.* An invitation (to a party, celebration, feast, or festivity.

Nyún, *a.* Short; less; lacking; deficient; low; inferior; small. —*tar,* a. lower; lesser; smaller &c. —*tam,* a. Minimum; smallest; lowest, &c.

Nyúntá, *n.* Deficiency; inferiority.

आँख ओझल, पहाड़ ओझल।

Áankh ojhal, pahár ojhal.

(Out of sight, out of mind.)

O, o, sounds like (ओ) in Hindi and (و ا) in Urdu. This vowel sound functions as an independent letter as well as a tonal addition to preceding consonants. In Persian-Urdu vocabulary, it also functions as an interjection, applied to equals and inferiors meaning 'and'. Also used as a form of informal address.

Ochhá, *a.* Empty; light; shallow; small; trifling; silly; base; bad; poor; disgraceful.

Ogh, *n.* Aggregate; multitude; gathering; collection; assembly.

Ohdá, *n.* Rank; post; designation; status. *Ohdedár,* a. One holding a position, or rank.

Oj, *n.* Vigour; virility; lustre; splendour. *—aswí,* adj. Vigorous; virile; brilliant.

Ojhá, *n.* A sooth-sayer; a sorcerer; a wizard; a magician; an exorcist; one who claims the power of casting out evil spirits, of curing snake-bite, &c., by means of charms and incantatious.

Ojhal, *a.* Invisible; hidden; private; *n.* screen; partition; concealment; privacy; retirement; *pre.* under the shelter of; from behind.

Ojharí, *n.* Bowels; intestines; guts.

Ok, *n.* The hollow of one's palm(s), formed to receive a poured cold drink for immediate consumption. [In India, higher caste people will not allow lower caste to drink from their utensils and will oblige them to drink from their own *Ok;* Also in out-door situations, like picnics and mid-journeying, people will pour and drink via *Ok* in order to avoid soiling/use of utensils].

Okáí, *n.* Nausea; vomit.

Okhlí, *n.* A mortar (a cylindrical stone/ wood vessel for pounding grain in).*—men sir dená,* v. To be ready/ willing to take a risk; to take up a difficult task. *—men sir diyá to múslon se kyá darná,* proverb. If you plunge into the flames, you are bound to get hot.

Okná, *v.* To vomit; to suffer nausea.

Olá, *n.* Hail; hailstone. *Ole parná,* v. Hail-storm happening. *—ho jáná,* v. To freeze; to get old.

Oltí, *n.* Eaves of a house.

Om, S. *n.* The mystic name for the Hindu triad, representing the union of the three gods, Vishnu, Siva and Brahma; *om,* is used as a preface to any prayer, and also as an auspicious greeting; *adv.* yes; yea; verily; so be it; amen.

O<u>n</u>kár, *n.* The sacred and mystical syllable; **Om** in written form. (Europeans mistakenly are transliterating as *Aum*).

Or, *n.* Side; direction; beginning. —*Chor,* n. Both ends of a situation; the beginning and the end of a territory, or estate.

Oṛhná, *v.* To cover; *n.* covering; quilt.

Oṛhní, *n.* A small sheet worn by women upon the head and shoulders *(chaddar)*.

Ormá, *n.* Seam; hem; felling.

Os, *n.* Dew. —*ká motí,* n. A pearl of dew; something transitory, or short-lived. —*chátne se pyás nahín bujhtí,* prov. Dew drops cannot quench one's thirst; indicating insufficiency of supply of essentials.

Osar, *n.* A heifer; young cow.

Osárá, *n.* Porch; portico.

Oshadhi, *n.* Medicine; medicinal herb.

Oshṭh, [See *Oth*].

Osrá, *n.* Time; turn; vicissitude. —*osrí.* time after time; repeatedly.

Oṭ, *n.* Covering; veil; screen; shelter; concealment.

Oṭ, *n.* A scotch; a lump of mud, or a stone or a piece of wood, &c., place under any circular object to keep it from rolling; preventive.

Oṭh, *n.* Lip(s). —*chabáná,* v. To be furious/ in rage. —*pharakná,* To be in a state of suppressed rage. —*dabáná,* v. To feel shy.

Oṭná, *v.* To boil (liquid); to sift; to gin.

Oṭní, *n.* An instrument for separating the seeds from cotton.

P, p, stands for the consonant (प) in Hindi and (پ) in Urdu. It is also used as one-and-a-half value, equal to (प्प) in Hindi and (پّ) in Urdu. When suffixed by an 'h', it equals (फ) in Hindi and (پھ) in Urdu.

Pá, *n.* An affix used in informing abstract nouns from adjectives and nouns as *burhápá,* old age; *mutá—,* fatness.

Pá, *n.* Foot; leg; foot or root of a tree *(used as first member of compounds),* as:—*bazanjir,* fettered; in chains. —*dar rikáb, a. (Lit.)* having the foot in the stirrup; *(Met.) ready.* —*mál,* trodden under foot; crushed.

Pábandí, *n.* Check; restraint; control; restriction; limitation, prohibition.

Pach/panch, Adj. Used as a prefix to indicate 'five' of the suffixed noun, i.e. —*dhátu,* n. An alloy of five metals; bell metal; kind of bronze. —*lará,* adj. Of five strings [necklace]. —*tarfá,* adj. Pantagonal; a shape with five sides to it. —*kon,* adj. (A star with—) five cones/angles. -*tattva,* n. Five elements [Air, water, earth, fire, sky]. -*bhút,* adj. Made of five elements, i.e. Our body; all things worldly. &c.

Páchak, *a.* Cooking; digestive; stomachic; causing to ripen; *n.* a digestive; a solvent.

Pacháná, *v.* To digest; to assimilate; to ferment.

Pachauní, *a.* The entrails; the digestive organs.

Pachchar, *n.* A wedge; a slip of wood used to fill up a crevice or opening. —*thokná, v.* to put a spoke in the wheel (of); to tease; to distress.

Pachchham, Pachchhim, Pachhán *n.* The West. —*í, a.* western.

Pachhár, *n.* A fall on the back; a throw. —*ná, v.* to give (one) a fall; to dash down; to overpower. —*en kháná,* to throw oneself down repeatedly in grief or pain; to writhe in agony.

Pachhorná, *v.* To winnow.

Pachhtáná, *v.* To regret; to repent; to grieve.

Pachhtáo, Pachhtáwá, *n.* Regret; remorse; repencon-trition; grief; sorrow.

Pad, *n.* Position; office; status; rank; —*adhikárí,* a. Holder of a position; an official. —*chyut karná,* v. To dismiss; to deprive some one of his/her rank or position. —*tyág,* v. Resignation from a position; abandonment of a post.

Pad, *n.* Feet (as body parts).

—kanj/kamal, a. Feet like a lotus (delicate and beautiful); feet of a deity or other venerable ones. *—gati,* n. gait; manner of movement. *—chárí,* a. A pedestrian; one who moves about on foot. *—trán,* n. Footwear. *—dalit,* a. One who is trodden under feet; down trodden; oppressed. *—chihnon par chalná,* v. To follow in the footsteps, v. To follow in the footsteps of; to emulate.

Padak, *n.* Medal; a badge; a marker in recognition of merit/ service.

Padárth, *n.* Thing(s); substance(s); object(s).

Padhárná, *v.* To go or come; to arrive; to sit; to take a seat.

Pádí, *n.* Rice in the husks; paddy *(áhán).*

Padíd, *a.* Open; clear; evident; conspicuous.

Padma, *n.* The lotus flower; a mole on the human body; ten billions.

Pádrí, *n.* A Christians priest.

Pádsháh, *n.* King; sovereign. *—áná,* royal; imperial; kingly. *—záda,* a prince. *—zádí,* a princess.

Pádsháhat, Padsháhí, *n.* Kingdom; empire; monarchy.

Páduka, *n.* A wooden shoe; a sandal; a slipper.

Padwí, *n.* Rank; dignity; title.

Páedár, *n.* Lasting; durable; permanent; strong; firm.

Páejámá, *a.* Drawers; trousers.

Páekháná, *n.* Latrine; privy *(jáe-zarúr).*

Páemálí, *a.* Destruction; ruin.

Paemáish, *n.* Measurement; assessment; size; quantity.

Paemáná, *n.* Measure; measurement ruler; *(in the context of Urdu & Persian poetry)* one peg of drink.

Páetábá, *n.* Socks; hose; stocking.

Páetakht, *n.* The capital; royal residence; seat of government.

Pag, *n.* The foot. *—dandí, n.* a Pathway; footpath; a track; by-way.

Pagáh, *n.* Dawn of day; morning.

Pagahá, *n.* A base; a tether; family roots. *Áge náth na píchhe—,* Prov. Being. without roots; having neither home nor hearth; having no way of being traced or tracked about.

Págal, *a.* Mad; insane; foolish; *n.* a madman; an idiot. *—khána,* a lunatic asylum.

Págná, *v.* To dip in or cover with syrup; to form a cake of crystallized sugar.

Pagaṛí, *n.* A turban. (In business terms), a premium paid/ payable in addition to regular rental charges, for long-terms renting of a house or a shop or offices. —*uchhálná,* v. To insult some one; to humiliate somebody. —*utárná,* v. To rob some one of his/her possessions; to fleece some one. —*badalná,* v. To change one's public stance; to change one's known opinions. —*pairon par rakhná,* v. To beg for protection/ mercy/ pardon/ support.

Pahar, Pahr, *n.* A division of time consisting of eight *gharís,* or 3 hours.

Paháṛ, *n.* A mountain; hill; rock; anything very hard; burdensome, or strong. —*sí ráten̲,* long and tedious nights (esp. of sorrow). —*í, a.* mountainous; hilly; *n.* a mountaineer; a hillman.

Pahárá, *n.* Multiplication table.

Pahchán, *n.* Acquaintance; knowledge; familiarity; distinguished sign, or mark; identification. —*ná, v.* to identify; to recognise; to know.

Pahelí, *n.* A riddle; a puzzle; an enigma.

Pahelí, *n.* Riddle; puzzle; problem.

Pahil, Pahal, *n.* Priority; defence; initiative.

Pahilá, Pahalá, *a.* The first; one at the head of thrqueue; original; primary; earliest.

Pahilauṭa, Pahilauṭha, *a.* First-born; eldest.

Pahile, *adv.* Firstly; at first; as a matter of priority; in the first place.

Pahinaná, Pahirná, *v.* To put on (clothes) to wear; to dress (in).

Pahiyá, *n.* A wheel.

Pahlú, *n.* Side; flank; wing.

Pahlú, *n.* Aspect; beside.

Pahlwán, *n.* Hero; champion; pugilist; wrestler; athlete.

Pahrá, *n.* A watch; a guard; a sentry. —*dená,* to mount guard; to keep watch. *pahre men̲ rakhná,* to keep in custody; to confine.

Páhun, *n.* A guest; a visitor. —*áí, n.* hospitality; entertainment of guests.

Pahun̲ch, *n.* Reach; access; admission; arrival; power or scope; receipt.

Pahun̲chá, *n.* The wrist.

Pahun̲cháná, *v.* To transmit; to convey; to cause to send, or to arrive.

Pahun̲chná, *v.* To reach; to arrive; to befall; to be received (by).

Páí, *n.* One-twelfth of an anna (a pie, a coin now extinct.

Paidá, *a.* Born; created; *n.* produce; earnings; profits; gain.

Paidáish, *n.* Birth; nativity; creation; produce; the first book of the Bible; Genesis. *—í, a.* natural; original.

Paidal, *a.* and *adv.* Walking; on foot; *n.* a foot-soldier; an infantryman; infantry.

Paidáwár, Paidáwárí, *n.* Produce of land; profits of trade; income.

Paigám/ Paighám, *a.* Mission; message; an embassy.

Paigár, *n.* Ditch; trench; furrow.

Paikár, *n.* Battle; war.

Paikár, *n.* A hawker; a pedlar; a retail dealer.

Paimáish, *n.* Measuring; measurement; survey. *—kuninda,* a surveyor.

Paimáná, *n.* A measure; a goblet. *—i-bárish,* a rain-gauge.

Painá, *a.* Sharp; properly honed; accurate; acute; pointed.

Paináná, *v.* To sharpen; to whet; to give a keen edge to.

Pai<u>n</u>dh, Pai<u>n</u>dhá, *n.* Road; route; highway.

Pair, *n.* The foot; footprint; footstep.

Pairái, *n.* Swimming.

Pairák, *n.* A swimmer.

Paiṛí, *n.* Ladder; flight of steps; staircase; an ankle.

Pairná, *v.* To swim; to float.

Paisá, *n.* One hundredth of a rupee (in India Bangladesh and Pakistan); (idiomatically) wealth; money; propserity.

Paiṭháo, *n.* Entrance; penetration; access; ingress; admission.

Paiṭhná, *v.* To enter; to penetrate.

Paitrik, *adj.* Ancestral; paternal; traditional.

Paiwa<u>n</u>d/ Paiba<u>n</u>d, *a.* Joined; connected; *n.* junction; connection; relation; joint; piece; patch. *—í, a.* patched; pieced; *n.* an engrafted tree; a hybrid; a mongrel.

Paizár, *n.* A slipper; a shoe.

Pajaurá, *a.* Low; base; mean.

Pájí, *a.* Wicked; vile; depraved; mean; base.

Pák, *a.* Clean; pure; upright; holy; virtuous; innocent. *—dáman, a.* chaste. *—sáfí, n.* sanctity; holiness.

Pakáná, *v.* To cook; to bake; to ripen.

Pakaṛ, *n.* Hold; grip; catch-up; seizure; grasp; understanding. *—dhakaṛ,* n. arrests; apprehensions; seizures. *—dhílí honá,* v. The hold/grip being loosened. *—mazbút honá,* v. the hold/ grip being tightened. *—men áná,* v. To fall into the hands of; to come into the clutches of.

Pakaṛná, *v.* To catch; to seize; to arrest.

Pakauṛá/í, *n.* A savoury preparation obtained by dunking pieces of vegetables in a thick paste of gram flour and then deep-fried.

Pákh/ Pakhwáṛá, *n.* A lunar fortnight.

Pákhand, *n.* Blasphemy; hypocrisy; heretical behaviour; pretence. *-í,* adj. One who pretends; a hypocrite; a heretic.

Pakháwaj, *n.* A hand-held percussion instrument. A folk musical instrument.

Pakhwáṛá, [See *Pákh*].

Pákíza, *a.* Clean; pure; chaste; virtuous.

Pakká, *a.* Cooked; boiled; baked; ripe; grey or white (hair, &c.); strong; firm; perfect; adept.

Pakná, *v.* To be cooked; to be boiled, &c.; to ripen; to turn grey (as hair).

Paksh, *n.* Side; party; flank, aspect; wing; (in terms of a calendar) a fortnight. *—pát,* adv. Partiality; favouritism. *—dhar,* A supporter; one on the side of. *—poshaṇ,* n. Advocacy; championing of a cause. *—vipaksh,* n. Pros and cons; both sides of an argument/debate/contest. *—ágháṭ,* n. Hemiparesis; partial paralysis.

Pakshí, *n.* A bird; an arrow.

Pal, *n.* Moment; instant.

Pál, *n.* Dam; embankment; dyke.

Pál, *n.* sail; tent; hanging curtain [aboard a vehicle]. *—charháná,* v. To hoist sail; [*also*] a layers of straw in which raw fruit is buried to ripen.

Pál, *n. A suffix meaning—* Protector; guardian; one who rears; one who cherishes.

Pálá, *n.* Frost; snow; protection.

Palak, *n.* An eyelid; a twinkle of an eye; a moment; an instant.

Pálak, *n.* Protector; supporter; bedstead; spinach.

Pálakí, *n.* A palanquin; a litter; a kind of sedan chair.

Palán, *n.* A pack-saddle.

Paláná, *v.* To Thatch; the task of thatching.

Palang, *n.* Bedstead; a couch or sofa for sleeping on. *—posh, n.* counterpane; coverlet; quilt.

Paláni, *a.* Carrying a pack-saddle; *n.* a maker of pack-saddles. *aspi—,* pack-horse.

Palaṭná, *v.* To turn over; to return; to change; to revert.

Palítá, *n.* A wick; candle; match of a gun; fuse in a gun.

Pallá, *n.* Side; a scale-pan; space; distance; bag (for grain); edge of a garment; a fold or shutter of a door. —*dár,* a porter; one who carries bags of grain.

Pallava, *n.* A shoot; a spray of foliage; a bud; a flower.

Pálná, *v.* To rear; to bring up; to breed; to protect; *n.* cradle.

Palṭan, *n.* [Corruption of English word *Platoon*] Troops; soldiers; organised group. Regiment; battalion.

Páltú, *a.* Domesticated; tame; kept by humans; (mockingly) sycophants; hangers-on; favourite one.

Palwáṛ, *n.* A small boat.

Pan, *n.* An affix used for forming abstract nouns from adjective and nouns and corresponding to the English affixes -hood, -ship, -ness, as *laṛakpan,* childhood; *miṭhápan* sweetness, &c.

Pan, *adj.* Pertaining to water (used as a prefix) *-chakkí,* n. Water mill. *-ḍubbí,* n. Submarine [one that dives underwater].

Pán, *n.* Betel-leaf.

Páná, *v.* To get; to receive; to acquire; to reach; to meet with; to find; to enjoy; to suffer.

Panáh, *n.* Refuge; shelter; asylum. —*gír,* a. A seeker of refuge/ asylum. —*gáh,* n. A place of shelter/ refuge/ asylum.

Panálá, Panálí, *n.* A drain; a sewer.

Panapná, *v.* To be refreshed; to be reinvigorated; to take root; to grow; to flourish; to thrive.

Pa<u>n</u>ch, *a.* Five, the number five; an arbitrator, or a body of arbiters. —*ak,* A set or aggregation of five. —*karm,* n. The five attributes, or functions of the body according to *Ayurveda,* the Indian system of medicine. —*kon,* a. A pantagon; a shape with five angles. —*kosh,* n. (According to *Vedántic* school of thought, there are five shells providing a cover/ or housing for the soul. —*guṇ,* n. Five sensations in the body (i.e. sound, touch, form, taste and smell). —*bhút*/ *tattva,* n. Five elements which comprise a body, i.e. earth, water, wind, fire and sky. —*attva ko páná, v.* (literally) Elements going back to their original form, i.e. death. —*nad,* n. (Literally) Five rivers; a name for the land of five rivers; old name for the territory today known as Punjab. —*námá,* n. A document drawn by mutual agreement to settle a dispute, or establish a trust. —*vaṭí,* n. A grove made of five tree-species: *peepal, bel, baṛ, har* and *ashok.*

Rama's place of dwelling in the famous forest of *Dandakáraṇya* in the course of his exile. —*shíl,* n. Five guiding principles of human behaviour as set out by the Buddha. [In modern history, five principles of international relations established by the propounders of the Non-Aligned Movement.

Pa<u>n</u>cham, *a.* (Literally) fifth; the fifth note of a musical scale in Indian music systems. —*ángí,* a. A fifth columnist; a traitor; one who is likely to betray the trust imposed in him/her.

Panchámrit, *n.* A ritual/medicinal preparation obtained by mixing five elixirs of life, i.e. milk, sugar, curd (yoghurt), ghee (clarified butter) and honey.

Pancháng, *n.* An almanac; an annual book giving all sorts of astrological and calendrical calculations (auspicious days, festival markers, positions of planets, their linkage with different parts of the zodiac, etc.) for the lay people.

Pancháyat, *n.* A court of arbitration; council; jury.

Pa<u>n</u>ḍá, *n.* A Hindu priest helping the pilgrims to holy places to perform their rituals; a facilitator of passage of rites. —*gírí,* n. The profession of a *Panḍá.* [In a negative sense, the word *panḍágírí* is also used to describe phoney practitioners of priestly profession, or even politicians claiming to facilitate what needs to be done in public life].

Pangu, *n.* Lame; one with a defective foot or leg.

Pání, *n.* Water; aqua; rain; liquid substance. (Also) Lustre; valour; brightness; breed; honour; sense of self-respect. —*dár* bright; tempered (steel); manly. —*phérná* v. To coat; to gild; to polish. *Purkho<u>n</u> ko —dená* to offer libations to ancestors. Respectable; honourable; lustrous; of god breeding. —*devá,* a. A son or heir who is obliged to offer libation for the deceased. —*áná,* v. To commence raining; to flood. *Munh men —áná,* v. For one's mouth to water; for one to lust after. —*utárná,* v. To humiliate; to subject some one to disgrace; to put some one down. —*ká bulbulá,* a. Transient; temporary; unstable; one with a momentary existence (like a water bubble). —*kí tarah baháná,* adv. To be extravagant with; to squander away; to spend without care or concern. —*ke mol,* adv. On the cheap. —*na púchhaná;* v.

(literally) Not even to offer a mere glass of water to a visitor/ guest; (actually) To neglect, or to treat with contempt, a guest or a visitor. *Ankhon ká —jáná,* v. To become shamless; to fail to show due regard. *—na mánganá,* v. To die instantly; to succumb on the spot. *—dená,* v. To irrigate (plants, vegetation, fileds, &c). *—par nínv rakhná,* adv. To lay foundation on (literally) water; to initiate a plan without solid base. *—pí kar ját púchhná;* adv. To discuss pros and cons after committing an act. *—pí pí kar kosná,* adv. To heap insults and curses on someone in torrent of rage. *—phir jáná,* v. All efforts going waste; all work inputs coming to nothing. *—pherná,* To dissipate; to destroy; to completely undo. *Ke áge — bharnaá,* adv. To be far inferior to; not fit to hold a candle to... &c.

Páṇi-grahaṇ, *n.* Betrothal; wedding ceremoney; ritual of groom accepting or taking the hand of the bride.

Páṇiní, *n.* Name of a Grammarian and a philosopher of ancient times in India.

Panír, *n.* Cheese.

Pa<u>n</u>já, *n.* An aggregate of five, the hand (of foot) with the fingers (or toes) extended; a paw; a claw. *Panjáb,* five rivers; name of a province in India. *—márná, v.* to attack with hands, paws or claws. *—me<u>n</u> láná,* to get into one's clutches.

Pa<u>n</u>jar, *n.* A skeleton; a bare frame; a mere outline.

Pa<u>n</u>jí, *n.* A Register; a ledger. *—karaṇ,* v. Registration. *—krit/ yit,* a. Registered.

Pa<u>n</u>jírí, *n.* Powder; a sweet powdery preparation of wheat flour, sugar and ghee, with addition of some aromatics, used as a sweet dish in the homes as well as offered as consecrated food to the members of a religious congregation (called *Prasád*).

Pa<u>n</u>k, *n.* Mud; slush; mire; bog; quagmire.

Pa<u>n</u>kaj, *n.* (literally) One born of mud/slush; lotus flower. (Proverbially) an honest being surrounded by corrupt and wicked ones.

Pa<u>n</u>kh, *n.* Feather; wing; pinion.

Pa<u>n</u>khá, *n.* Fan.

Pa<u>n</u>khuṛí, *n.* Petal; leaf of a flower.

Pa<u>n</u>kti, *n.* A Line; a row; a file; a rank; a queue. *—baddha,* a. Arranged in a row; formed in a queue. —*banáná,* v. To form a queue.

Panná, *n.* Leaf; a page; an emerald; fruit juice.

Panni, *n.* Tinfoil.

Pánṛe, Pánde, *n.* A title among Brahmans; a learned man; a sage or savant.

Pán̲s, *n.* Manure; dung.

Pán̲sá, *n.* A die; dice; throw of dice.

Pansárí, *n.* Crocer.

Pán̲t, Pán̲tí, *n.* A row; a line; a rank of soldiers.

Pan̲th, *n.* Path; road; track; way; a religious sect or order.

Pánv/paer, *n.* Foot; feet; leg(s); footing; footprints. —*gáṛí,* n. A bicycle; velocipede. —*aṛáná,* v. To interrupt; to interfere. —*ukharná,* v. To be routed; to be swept off one's determined position (in compat). —*kí jútí,* a. Utterly contemptible; of no importance; [MCPs in India consider women to be so]. —*kí dhúl,* a. Utterly cheap; of no consequence. —*jamná,* adv. To find one's feet; to get established; to consolidate one's position. —*pakaṛná,* v. To implore; to show humility; to beseech. —*píchhe na rakhná,* adv. Not to withdraw from the held position under any circumstances. —*baṛháná,* v. To step forward; to go ahead; to proceed with the mission in hand. —*bhárí honá,* adv. (said of a woman) To be pregnant; to be in the family way. —*men nehndí lagí honá,* adv. To be hesitant in walking; to be walk-shy. —*men̲ Saníchar honá,* v. To be restless; to be always on the move. —*kí jagah na honá,* adv. To be overcrowded; to be overfull; not to have even room to stand. —*so jáná,* v. To feel loss of sensation in one's legs or feet, &c.

Páp, *n.* Sin; vice; evil deed. —*kaṭná,* v. To be finished with; to be shot of; to be over with. —*kamáná/baṭorná,* v. To commit sinful/evil deeds. —*ká ghaṛá bharná,* adv. Reaching the peak of one's sinful deeds; touching the limit of evil nature. —*mol lená,* v. To knowingly indulge in wrong-doing.

Pápá, *n.* Father.

Papíhá, *n.* A species of cuckoo; a child's whistle.

Papoṭá, *n.* Eyelid.

Par, *a. (Used as a prefix).* Distant; remote; opposite; further; other; another; foreign; alien; next; great; chief. —*ádhin,* dependent; subject. —*dádá,* great-grandfather. —*des,* foreign country. —*lok, n.* the world to come.

Par, *pre.* On; upon; up to; till; in consequence of; not-withstanding; *conj.* but; still; yet; nevertheless; unless; however.

Par, Pankh, *n.* Wing(s); feather(s); pinion. —*katarná,* v. To clip one's wings; to render ineffective; to make inefficacious; to incapacitate. —*nital ániá,* v. To take to risky ways; to give oneself airs. —*lag jániá,* adv. To move at too fast a pace.

Pár, *adv.* Across; on the otherside/bank of a stream/river; extremity; limit; end; conclusion. —v. Transmission; transmigration. —*pániá,* adv. To finish off with; to get through; to get rid of.

Párá, *n.* Mercury; quicksilver. —*chaṛhná,* v. Temperature (in the thermometer) to rise; to become angry.

Parádhín, *adj.* Under an outsider's control; enslaved; not free. —*tá,* n. The state of slavery; dependence; the state of being under an outsider's control.

Parakh, *n.* Test; examination; judgement; distinguishing faculty.

Párakhí, *a.* One with a sense of judgement; connoisseur; one who can appreciate the merits of.

Parákram, *n.* Bravery; courage; Prowess; vigour.

Param, *n.* Extreme; ultimate; absolute; supreme; best; utmost. —*gat,* a. Liberation; salvation. —n. The essential element; the Supreme Being. —*pad,* n. The highest seat; heavenly abode. —*pitá, n.* Heavenly Father; God Almighty. —*haṉs,* a. Atitle, or indicatorer of rank amongs the *Sanyásís* of India.

Paramáṇu, *n.* Atom; nuclei. —*bam,* a. A Nuclear Bomb. —*bhaṭṭí,* n. Nuclear furnace; an atomic reactor

Parámarsh, *n.* Advice, counsel, consultation. —*dátá,* a. Advisor, counsel. —*dátrí samiti,* a. Advisory Committee.

Paraṉtu, *conj.* But; yet; still.

Páras, *n.* Philosopher's stone; touchstone.

Paraspar, *pro.* Each other; one another; *adv.* mutually; reciprocally.

Parast, *a.* Adoring; worshipping; *n.* worshippers, *átash—,* fire-worshipper; a zoroastrian. *but—, n.* an idolator. *khud—, a.* self-conceited.

Parastish, *n.* Worship; adoration; devotion.

Parat, *n.* Fold; layer; wrinkle; furrow; stratum.

Paráyá, *a.* Of or belonging to other; foreign; alien.

Parbat, *n.* Hill; mountain.

Parbhú, (see *'Prabhu'*).

Pár-Brahm, *n.* The Supreme God.

Parchá, *n.* A slip of paper; a newspaper.

Parchháin, *n.* Image; reflection; shadow.

Pardá, *n.* Veil; curtain; screen; secrecy; privacy; tapestry; drum (of the ear); lid (of the eye); frets (of a guitar, &c.); *—men zarda logáná,* to indulge in secret amoura (love-making) with strange men (said of a parda-nishín). *—nashín,* a woman who is kept concealed behind a screen or curtain, and who does not unveil, herself in the presence of strange men.

Pardáḳht, Pardází, *n.* Accomplish ment; completion; performance; execution.

Pár-darshì, *adj.* Transparent.

Pardes, *a.* Foreign country; away from home; not one's home country. *—í, a.* Foreigner, an outsider; an alien.

Pare, *adv.* Beyond; yonder at a distance; apart.

Pareshán, *a.* Perplexed; distracted; confused; distressed.

Parganá, *n.* A sub-division of a district.

Parimáṇ, *n.* Quantity; measure; dimension; capacity; extent; scope.

Paripúrṇ, *adj.* Filled to the brim; complete in all aspects; replete. *—atá,* n. The state of fullness; state of being complete; state of being fulfilled.

Parkár, *n.* A pair of compasses.

Paṛhá, *a.* Read; perused. *—guná,* educated; learned; *n.* an educated man.

Paṛháná, *v.* To teach; to educate; to instruct.

Parhez, *n.* Abstinence; continence; sobriety; temperance. *—gár,* chaste; sober; temperate; abstiment.

Paṛhná, *v.* To read; to peruse; to study; to learn; to recite; to repeat.

Parí, *n.* A fairy; a beautiful woman. *—stán,* fairy-land.

Párí, *n.* Turn; time; shift.

Paricharak, *n.* An attendant; a male nurse. *Parichárikà,* n. A frmale attendant; a stewardess (in the course of an air or sea voyage).

Parichay, *n.* Introduction; acquaintance; familiarity. *—patr,* a. A letter of introduction; identity card.

Pariksha, *n.* Investigation; search; examination; trial; test.

Paríkshak, *n.* Examiner; assessor; tester.

Paríkshaṇ, *n.* Experiment(s); test(s); trial(s).

Parimáṇ, *n.* Measure; standard; proof; verification; authority; cause; motive.

Páríná, *a.* Past; elapsed; expired; ancient. *—daftar,* ancient records.

Pariṇám, *n.* Result; outcome; consequence; effect; conclusion. *—swarúp,* a As a result of; consequently. *—bhugatná,* v. To suffer the consequences of...

Parinda, *n.* A bird.

Paripakva, *a.* Mature; fully developed; ripe; upto standard.

Parishkár, *n.* Refinement; polishing of an idea or aperson; fine tuning of a mentality, or attitude.

Parishram, *n.* Fatigue; exhaustion; effort; exertion; endeavour; toil; pains; labour.

Parityág, *n.* Giving up; abandonement; sacrifice; renunciation.

Pariwár, *n.* Relatives; kindred; family; friend; attendants.

Parlai, Pralaya, *n.* Annihilation; the destruction of the whole world (as at the Flood, or on the Day of Judgment); death; *(Met.)* vexation; weariness.

Parlok, *a.* The other world; next world; heavenly abode; *—gaman,* v. Death; departure from this mortal earth. *—vásí,* a. One who dwells in the other world; the dear departed. *—banáná,* adv. To perform good deeds in order to improve one's prospects in the next world. *—bigáṛná,* adv. To spoil one's shances in the after-world. *—sidhárná,* adv. To depart for the heavenly abode; to expire from this life.

Parmaṭ, *n.* [Corruption of the English word *Permit*] A written permission; a document allowing;authorising some activity.

Paṛná, *v.* To fall; to drop; to lie down; to happen; to befall.

Paranám, Praṇám, *n.* Greeting; salutattion.

Paṛnáná, *n.* Maternal great-grandfather. *(Fem. Parnáni).*

Parojan, Prayojan, *n.* Purpose; use; end; object.

Paṛos, *n.* Neighbourhood; vicinity. *—í,* a neighbour. *(Fem. Parosin).*

Parotá, Paṛpotá, *n.* Great-grandson.

Pársá, *n.* Chaste; abstemious; holy; pure.

Párshva, *n.* Aspect; behind; rear.

Parson, *adv.* The day before yesterday, or the day after to-morrow.

Parṭál, *n.* Revision; measurement; survey; test.

Partalá, *n.* A belt; strap; sword-belt; shoulder-belt. *—o-toshdán,* shoulder-belt and cartouche; a soldier's accoutrements.

Partít, Pratíti, *n.* Faith; trust; confidence; reliance.

Parwá, Parwáh, *n.* Care; anxiety; inclination; desire; affection; fear; terror.

Parwáná, *n.* A moth; *(Poet.)* a lover; an order; a pass or permit. *—i-ráh,* passport.

Parwar, *n.* Protector; patron; nourisher; cherisher. *—digár,* providence; God. *—ish,* nourishing; cherishing; patronage.

Pas, *adv.* After; behind; at length; at last; therefore; then. *—andáz,* economy; thrift. *pá karná, v.* to repulse; to repel. *—o-pesh,* shuffling; prevarication.

Pás, *n.* Watching; guarding; observance; a watch of three hours. *—bán,* watchman; guard; sentry; pastor.

Pás, *adv.* Near; close to; alongside; adjacent, in the possession of in the neighbourhood of.

Pasand, *n.* Choice; approbation; approval; acceptance; *a.* agreeable; acceptable; approved.

Pasandída, *a.* Approved; liked; agreed to; desirable.

Pásang, *n.* Makeweight; anything added to the contents of a scalepan in order to complete the weight thereof.

Pasárná, *v.* To spread; to extend; to stretch; to expand; to distend.

Pásh, *n.* A bond; tie; noose; snare; trap; fetter; chain.

Pashchátáp, *n.* Regret; remorse; repentance; contrition.

Pashchát, *adv.* After; afterwards.

Pashemání, *n.* Regret; repentance; remorse; shame; disgrace.

Pashm, *n.* Hair; down; wool.

Pashmíná, *n.* A special kind of wool [Raw wool brought from Western Tibet, ginned, spun and woven in Kashmir into an-] exceptionally fine wool cloth.

Pashná, *n.* Heel; the pastern of a horse.

Pashu, *n.* Cattle; a brute; a blockhead*—pál,* herdsman.

Pasíjná, *v.* To perspire; to sweat; to dissolve; to feel pity.

Pasíná, *n.* Sweat; perspiration. *—áná,* v. (literally) To perspire; (proverbially) to have cold feet. *—baháná,* v. To labour at; to work hard at. *Pasíne kí kamáí,* prov. Hard-earned money. *Khún —ek karná,* prov. To work really hard at something; to make a determined effort.

Paslí, *n.* A rib.

Past, *a.* Low; mean; base; degraded; vile. *—himmat,* meanspirited; devoid of courage. *—karná, v.* to vanquish; to defeat. *—qad, a.* low in stature.

Pat, *n.* Leaf. *—jhar, n.* autumn.

Pat, *n.* Honour; dignity; credibility. *—uṭh jáná,* v. To loose one's honour/ credibility; to be disgraced. *—rakhná,* v. To preserve one's honour.

Paṭ, *n.* A leaf or fold of a door.

Paṭ, *a.* Lying faced downwards; upside-down; topsy turvey.

Páṭ, *n.* Breadth; width; expanse; extent.

Páṭ, A plank; board; leaf or fold of a door.

Patá, *n.* Sign; mark; symptom; trace; clue; direction; a person's address.

Patáká, *n.* Flag; banner; standard; ensign; emblem.

Paṭáká/ Paṭáḳhá, *n.* Explosion; fireworks.

Paṭakná, *v.* To dash or throw down.

Pátál, *n.* One of the seven infernal regions, inhabited by a serpentine race; hell.

Patan, *n.* Fall; decline; diminution.

Pata<u>n</u>g, *n.* A paper kite.

Pata<u>n</u>gá, *n.* A moth; wind insect; a spark.

Paṭel, *n.* The headman of a village; fencing with *patá, q. v.* cudgelling a caste-name amongst Gujaratis.

Path, *n.* A pathway; track; road; course to follow. *—pradarshak,* a. A guide.

Páṭh, *n.* Reading; perusal; study; lesson, *—shála, n.* a school; a college.

Páṭhak, *n.* Reader; teacher; preceptor; tutor; instructor; schoolmaster.

Paṭhán, *n.* An Afghan. a dweller of Pakhtoonistan, North-West Frontier of Indo-Pak subcontinent. (Proverbially) a sharp usurer; a loan-shark. (Politically incorrect, but popularly known and accepted meaning).

Pathik, *n.* Traveller; voyager; tourist; wayfarer; a guide.

Pathráo, Pathráv, *n.* Stoning.

Pathrail, Pathrílá, *n.* Stony; rocky; rugged; gravelly.

Pathrí, *n.* The flint of a gun; grit; gravel; stone in the bladder.

Pathya, *n.* Medicine; medically prescribed diet; salubrious;

wholesome diet.

Patí, *n.* Lord; master; husband. —*ghní,* a woman who murders her husband. —*vratái,* a wife who strictly observes her marriage vows.

Patíl, *n.* A lamp wick; a linstock; a fuse.

Patlá, *a.* Thin; slender; lean; tapering; delicate. —*hál,* straitened circumstances; financial difficulties. —*karná, v.* to liquefy; to rarfy. —*pan,* thinness; emaciation; weakness.

Páṭná, *v.* To roof; to make a flooring of planks or boards; to fill up; to close; to heap; to pile.

Patní, *n.* A wife. —*bhág,* division of property among widows.

Paṭní, *n.* A ferryman; a boatman.

Patohú, *n.* A daughter-in-law.

Patolá, *n.* Piece of cloth-material; doll's clothing. *Guddí—,* doll's Clothing, dresses etc.

Pátr, *n.* A plate; a vessel; a cup; a jar.

Patra, *n.* Letter; document. *Pramáṇ-patra,* n. Certificate; authenticating document. *Prem-*, n. Love letter. *Ávedan-*, n. Letter of application; request-letter.

Patrakár, *n.* A journalist; a pressman. —*itá,* n. Journalism.

Patrí, *n.* A narrow strip of wood or metal; a payment; a bangle; wristlet; a bracelet.

Patriká, *n.* A journal; a magazine; (sometimes) also horoscope.

Pattá, *n.* Leaf of a tree; a card; a trinket.

Paṭṭá, *n.* The collor of a dog; a lock of hair; a curl; a title-deed. —*dár,* a lease-holder.

Pattal, *n.* A natural, bio-degradable platter made up by tagging broad tree-leaves together (for serving food on). —*ek pattal men kháne wále,* prov. Intimate; close friends. —*cháṭná,* adv. To live on left-overs; to be living in abject poverty; to be servile to some one. —*paṛná,* v. Platters to be laid out. —*parosná,* v. To serve food to the congregation. —*men chhed karná,* v. To be imprudently ungrateful.

Paṭṭhá, *n.* A youth; muscle; tendon; a full-grown animal; a kind of lace.

Patthar, *n.* Stone; hail-stone; *a.* hard; heavy; burdensome. —*barasná,* to hail. —*honá,* to be petrified; to be hard hearted; to be unmerciful. —*ká chhápá, n.* lithography. —*ká farsh,* pavement. —*kí lakír honá,* to be ineffacable; to be unalterable.

Paṭṭí, *n.* A bandage; a batten; strap;

strip; belt; fillet; (idiomatically) misguidance; co-share (in landed property. —*dár,* n. Partner; co-share-holder. —*paṛháná,* v. To tutor (often for mischief); to coach someone for selfish motives; to persuade some one to veer your way.

Pattrí, *n.* Annual calender; almanac; a reference book that astrologers consult.

Patwár, *n.* A helm; a rudder.

Paṭwarí, *n.* One who keeps land-records.

Pau, *n.* A good throw (in dice); the one or ace of dice. —*bárah honá, v.* to come off well; to have a good luck. —*phatná,* to dawn.

Paudá, Paudha, *n.* A plant; a young tree.

Paun, *a.* Three-quarters.

Paun/ Pavan, *n.* Wind; breeze; name of a deity. —*putra,* n. Nickname of Lord Hanuman, the monkey-faced and very venerable deity in Hindu households, and known in legends for his agility and prowess for achieving the impossible.

Paurukh, Paurush, *n.* Manhood; strength; power. manliness; virility.

Pauwá, *n.* A quarter; one-fourth of a seer; a weight of four *chhataks.*

Pavan, *n.* Wind; breeze. —*chakkí,* n. A wind mill. —*putra.* n. Name of the monkey-faced deity, *Hanumán.*

Pavitr, *a.* Holy; sacred; pure. —*atá,* n. Sanctity; purity; holiness. —*í-karan,* v. Sanctification.

Páyá, *n.* The foot of a table; bedstead, &c.; foundation; root; rank.

Páyáb, *n.* A ford; *a.* fordable. —*utarná,* to ford a river.

Payám, *n.* News; message; intelligence. —*bar, n.* a messenger; a courier; a prophet.

Payodhar, *n.* Clud; an udder.

Pazáwá, *n.* A brick-kiln.

Pazmurda, *a.* Faded; withered; decayed.

Pazír, Pazírá, *a.* Acceptable; received; agreeable; acceptable; liable.

Pech, *n.* A screw; twist; plaitfold; revolution; perplexity; deceit. —*kash, n.* a corkscrew. —*o-táb,* anxiety; uneasiness.

Pechak, *n.* A louse; a bed; a ball or skein of thread.

Pechán, *a.* Winding; tortuous; circuitous; serpentine; twisting.

Pechish, *n.* Dysentery; running 'tummy' (stomach); liquid discharge from the bowels (owing to disorders of the digestive system).

Pehchán, *n.* Indentity; familiarity; acquaintance; recognition.

Pekhná, *n.* A toy; a puppet; play.

Pel, *n.* A shave; push; nudge thrust; crowd.

Pelná, *v.* To push; to shave; to thrust; to drive in; to insert forcibly.

Peṉdá, Peṉdí, *n.* The bottom; the lowest part.

Peṉṭh, *n.* A small markert; markert-day.

Peṛ, *n.* A tree ; a plant; a shrub.

Perná, *a.* To press; to squeeze; to rack; to wring.

Pesh, *n.* Front; front; forepart; (in *Gram*). the vowel point ('); *adv.* and *prep.* in front (of); before (in time or place); *adj.* advanced; respecred; influential. *—áná, v.* to behave ; to deal with. *—bín,* a provident; prudent. *—kár,* a subordinate court offcial. *—qadeamí,* leadership; command.

Peshá, *n.* Trade; profession; calling; business; occupation; custom; habit; art; craft. *—war.* tradesman; artisan; craftsman.

Pesháb, *n.* Urine. *—karná,* v. To urinate.

Peshagí, *n.* An advance of money; earnest-money.

Pesháni, *n.* The forehead; brow; fate.

Peshi, *n.* Appearance (in court); attendance; preswnce; lead.

Peshin, *a.* Ancient; former; previous; prior; preceding.

Peshíngoí, *n.* Prophecy; prediction; foretelling.

Peshtar, *a.* and *adv.* Before; anterior; prior; formerly; previously.

Peshwá, *n.* Leader (esp. in politics); guide; a high priest; an instructor in religion or morals; the chief executive officer (among the Marhattas).

Peshwái, *n.* Leadership; guidance; the meeting and reception of a guest or visitor.

Peṭ, *n.* Stomach; belly; abdomen; (proverbially), womb. *—ká gahrá,* a. One who can keep a secret. *—káṭná,* adv. To save money by cutting down on food bill. *—ka chakkar/dhandá,* a. business of earning a livelihood. *—ká halká,* a. One incapable of keeping confidences. *—kí ág,* v. Irresistible pangs of hunger. *—se honá,* v. To be pregnant. *—giráná,* v. to abort. *—par lát márná,* v. To deprive some one of a means of making a living. *—aur píṭh ek ho jáná,* prov. To be emaciated; being reduced to a skeleton. *—pújá karná,* prov.

To enjoy a meal. —*men chúhe kúdná,* v. To feel extremely hungry.

Peṭí, *n.* Belt; a portmanteau; a trunk.

Peṭú, *a.* Gluttonous; epcurean; n. a gormandiser; a glutton; a voracious eater;

Phaban, *n.* Ornament; embellishment; decoration; elegance; grace; beauty.

Phabtí, *n.* A taunt; jest; fun.

Phág, *n.* A typical folk song, sung in Northern India at the time of Holi festival (which falls in the month of *Phágun*).

Phágun, *n.* The twelfth month of the Hindus (Feb. March; the full moon of which is near *Púrva-phálgun*).

Pháhá, Pháyá, *n.* A flake of cotton.

Phahráná, *v.* To unfurl; to flutter (a flag or a banner).

Phailáná, *v.* To stretch; to extend; to expand; to lengthen; to draw out; to scatter; to diffuse; to spread abroad; to propagate; to spread over.

Phailná, *v.* To be spread; to be extended; to grow; to increase in size; to become public.

Phal, *n.* Fruit; produce; off-spring; result; gain; consequence; the iron head of a spear; the blade of (a knife, sword, &c.). —*dár, a.* fruitful; fruit-producing. —*dená,* to yield fruit.

Phaláng, *n.* A jump; a leap; a bound.

Phalná, *v.* To bear fruit; to produce; to have issue; to prosper; to break into blisters. *phúlná, v.* to bud and blossom; to flourish.

Phaṇ, *n.* The expanded hood of a snake.

Phandá, *n.* Net; noose; trap; snare; grasp; clutches.

Phansáo, *n.* Entanglement; a narrow place; a sticking place (as a muddy road; march, &c.).

Phánsí, *n.* Noose; loop; halter; hanging; capital punishment by hanging; strangulation.

Pháoṛá/ Pháwṛá, *n.* A spade; a mattock; a tool for digging earth.

Pháoṛí/ Pháwṛí, *n.* Smaller version of the same digging tool; a rake; a hoe; a shovel.

Phapakná, *v.* To shoot forth; to sprout.

Phapholá, *n.* A blister; a bubble.

Phaphúndí, *n.* Mildew; mould.

Phaphas, *a.* Fat; flabby; corpulent; swollen; weak.

Phár̤, *n.* Rent; fissure; creak.

Phar̤akná, *v.* To flit; to flutter; to throb; to quiver; to palpitate.

Phár̤ná, *v.* To tear; to rent; to rip; to lacerate.

Phar̤phar̤áná, *v.* To shake; to shiver; to flutter; to flap (wings); to welter or wallow in blood, to writhe in pain.

Pharsá, *n.* An axe; a hatchet; a chopper.

Phar̤, *n.* Crack; sound of a slap; smack, &c. *—kárná, v.* to whip; to reprimand.

Pháṭak, *n.* Gate; door; entrance; pound (for cattle, &c.). *—dár,* a gate-keeper; a door-keeper; a pound-keeper.

Phaṭakná, *v.* To winnow; to sift.

Phaṭáo, *n.* Gap; rent; crack; separation.

Phaṭik, Sphaṭick, *n.* Crystal;

Phaṭkan, *n.* Chaff; husk.

Phaṭkarí, Phiṭkarí, *n.* Alum.

Phaṭkí, *n.* A fowler's net or share.

Phaṭná, *v.* To crack; to split; to rend; to burst; to be scattered or dispersed (as clouds); to be separated.

Phen, *n.* Foam; froth; lather; scum.

Pheni, *n.* A wormocelli kind of Indian sweatmeat, eaten after soaking in boiling milk.

Phenil, *adj.* Foamy; frothy; full of lather.

Phe<u>n</u>k, *n.* Throw; cast; fling. *—ná, v.* to throw to fling; to cast; to hurl; to dart; to let fly, (as a hawk &c.); to put a horse, &c., to full gallop; to spill; to pour out; to squander.

Phe<u>n</u>ṭí, *n.* A skein (of thread); a hank (of cord or rope).

Phe<u>n</u>ṭná, *v.* To mix; to beat up (as eggs).

Phephar̤á, *n.* The lungs.

Pher. *n.* Turn; twist; fold; bend; maze; circumference; equivocation; change; difference; loss; revolution; misfortune; difficulty. *—paṭná,* a difference of, discrepancy to arise. *—kháná, v.* to go round about way; to meet with misfortunes. *—me<u>n</u> ḍálná,* to place one in a difficulty or dilemma.

Pherí, *n.* Circuit; hawking; begging. *—wálá,* a hawker; a pedlar.

Pherná, *v.* To turn; to return; to twist; to restore; to exercise a horse. *háth—,* to caress; to fondle.

Phíká, *a.* Faded; indistinct; tasteless; insipid; dull; light (in colour); cheerless.

Phín̲chná, *v.* To squeeze; to wring; to rinse; to wash.

Phir, *adv.* Again; then; afterwards; in that case. *—bhí,* yet; still; even then.

Phiráo, *n.* Circuit; round; rotation; turning; revolution.

Phirná, *v.* To roam; to wander; to walk about; to return.

Phisalná, *v.* To slip; to slide; to glide; to err; *a.* slipper; smooth.

Phiṭkár, Phaṭkár, *n.* Curse; malediction.

Phokal, *a.* Refuse; sediment; dregs; hollowness.

Phokaṭ, *n.* A thing given gratis; worthless thing or person.

Phoṛá, *n.* A boil; abscess; tumour; ulcer. *—phunsí,* eruptions.

Phoṛná, *v.* To break; to break or burst open; to shatter; to smash to bits; to disclose or divulge (a secret).

Phuár, Phuhár, *n.* Drizzle; rain falling in small drops.

Phuárá/Phuhárá, *n.* A fountain; a jet; a pressurised emission of water (or any other fluid).

Phudakná, *v.* To jump; to leap; to spring; to hop.

Phúhaṛ, Phuhaṛ, *a.* Uneducated; undisciplined; rude; stupid; shameless; *n.* a slattern; a fool.

Phukná, *n.* A bladder; a bag.

Phúl, *n.* A flower; a blossom; a bud; bell-metal; swelling. *—charháná, v.* to offer flowers at a shrine of tomb. *—jharná,* to speak eloquently.

Phúlá, *a.* Swollen; inflamed; blossomed; bloomed. *phúle na samáná,* to be overjoyed; to be overcome or transported with joy.

Phúlná, *v.* To flower; to blossom; to bloom; to flourish; to be in good health; to swell; to be puffed up.

Phungí, *n.* A sprout; the topmost leaf of a tree.

Phun̲dhná, *n.* A tassel; a fringe.

Phún̲k, *n.* Breath; blow; puff; charm. *—phún̲k kar qadam rakhná,* to walk or act cautiously. *—dená, v.* to set fire (to); to blow up; to squander. *—ná,* to blow; to puff; to ignite; to breathe spells over.

Phúpá, Phúphá, *n.* Father's sister's husband.

Phupherá/ Phupherí, *adj.* Cousins, male/ female, from Father's side [children of father's sister].

Phúphí, *n.* Father's sister.

Phuphkarná, *n.* To hiss (as a snake).

Phurairí, Phurphurí, *n.* Silver; shudder; quiver; treambling.

Phurtí, *n.* Activity; energy; quickness; promptitude. *—lá,* quick; active; agile; nimble.

Phús, *n.* Old dry grass or straw.

Phusláná, *v.* To coax; to wheedle; to cajole; to seduce; to entice. *phuslá ke le jáná, v.* to kidnap; to elope with.

Phusphusáná, *v.* To whisper.

Phuṭ, *n.* Single; old; without a pair.

Phúṭ, *n.* A ripe cucumber; gap; breach; opening; divergence of opinion; discord. *—phút ke roná, v.* to weep bitterly; to lament.

Phúṭá, *a.* Broken; cracked; split; burst.

Píp, *n.* Matter; pus. *—parná,* to discharge pus or matter; to suppurate.

Pích, *n.* Rice-water; gruel.

Píchhá, *n.* The hinder part; stern; the rear; pursuit. *—chhuráná, v.* to rid oneself of.

Pichhárí, *n.* The rear; the ropes by which a horse's hind legs are fastened; *adv.* in the rear; behind.

Píchhe, *adv.* In the rear; behind; afterwards. *—lagná, v.* to pursue.

Pichhlá, *a.* Latter; last; past; recent; rear.

Pichkáná, *v.* To squeeze; to press.

Pickhárí, *n.* Enema; syrings. *—dená,* to give an injection.

Pidar, *n.* Father. *—kushí,* patricide. *—í,* paternal.

Pidrí, *n.* A tomitit.

Pigalná, Pighalná, *v.* To melt; to dissolve; to become soft or tender.

Pigláná/ Pighláná, *v.* To melt; to fuse; to soften; to pacify; to assuage; to coax; to flatter.

Pik, *n.* Cuckoo, *(Fem. Pikí).*

Píl, *n.* Elephant. *—bán,* elephant-keeper or driver. *—dandán,* ivory; elephant's tusks. *—murg.,* a turkey. *—pá, —páyá,* elephantiasis; a pillar; a column. *—tan,* enormous; gigantic.

Pílá, *a.* Yellow; pale.

Pilaí, *n.* The spleen; enlargement of the spleen.

Piláná, *v.* To give or cause to drink; to nurse; to suckle.

Pillá, *n.* A pup; a cub; a whelp.

Pilná, *v.* To attack; to rush against; to assault.

Pilpilá, *a.* Smooth; soft; flabby.

Píná, *v.* To drink; to imbibe; to suck; to lap; to absorb; to smoke (tobacco, &c.).

Píṇak, *n.* Stupefaction; intoxicating effects of opium.

Pinas, *n.* Cold; catarrh; a disease of the nose.

Pínas, *n.* A palanquin; a litter.

Pinḍ, Pinḍá, *n.* A round mass; heap; lump; ball; the body; the person; food; mouthful; cake or ball of meal or flour offered to the manes.

Pinḍálu, *n.* Sweet potato.

Pinḍár, *n.* Thought; idea; opinion; conceit.

Pinḍlí, *n.* The calf of the leg; the shin.

Pinhán, *a.* Secret; hidden; concealed. *—í, n.* secrecy; concealment.

Pinjará, Pinjaṛá, *n.* A cage.

Pípá, *n.* A cask; a barrel.

Pípal, Pípar, *n.* The sacred fig-tree of the Hindus; long pepper.

Pipantí, *n.* The fruit of the Pípal tree.

Píṛ, *n.* Pain; compassion; pity.

Pír, *n. (Plur. Pírán).* Monday; a saint; a spiritual guide.

Píṛá, *n.* Pain; sickness; affliction.

Píṛak, *a.* Afflicting; agonising. *n.* a tormentor; a persecutor.

Pirich, *n.* A saucer.

Pironá, *v.* To pierce; to penetrate; to thread (a needle); to string (beads, pearls, &c.).

Pirthí, *n.* The earth; ground.

Pirthmá, Pratimá, *n.* Idol; image.

Pisar, *n.* Child; son; boy; lad; youth. *—i-akhyáfí,* a step-son. *—záda,* a son's son; a grandson.

Pisách, Pishách, *n.* Demon; evil spirit; vision; apparition.

Píṣná, *v.* To grind; to bruise; to powder; to pulverize; to gnash (teeth).

Pistá, *n.* Pistachio nut.

Pissú, *n.* A flea.

Pistán, *n.* Breasts.

Pitt, Pittá, *n.* Bile; anger; passion. *—jwar, n.* bilious fever. *—níkálná, v.* to chastise severely.

Pitá, *n.* Father. *—ghát,* patricide.

Pítal, *n.* Brass.

Pítambar, *n.* A yellow silk cloth; *a.* dressed in yellow clothes.

Piṭárá, *n.* A larger basket fitted with a cover.

Píṭh, *n.* The back; spine. *—ṭhonkná,* v. To appreciate one's work or achievement; to give a pat on the back. *—dikháná,* v. to turn and run; to show the white feather; to flee from the battle field. —*par háth rakhná*, v. To support. —*píchhe*, adv, behind one's back; in the absence of. —*me<u>n</u> chhurá bho<u>n</u>kná*, v. To betray one's friendship and trust; to stab one in the back.

Píṭná, *v.* To beat up; to thrash; to strike; to give a pounding; to hammer. *Chhátí*—, v. TO lament; to mourn; to deeply regret. [Alternative form: *Pitáí karná*].

Pitr, Pittar, Pitra, *n.* Father; fore fathers;ancestors. —*paksha*, the first or dark fortnight of the lunar month Asín.

Piyá/ Priya, *n.* Husband; lover; paramour; a sweetheart. *Soí suhágan jo* —*man bháve*, prov. A marriage without love is no marriage.

Pochhná, *v.* To wipe; to rub dry; to clean.

Pod-dàr, *n.* A cashier; an examiner of coins.

Podíná/ Pudíná, *n.* Mint.

Pokhar, *n.* A pond; a pool; a tank.

Pol, *n.* Emptiness; hollowness; vacuity.

Polád/ Pholád/ Phaulád, *n.* Steel; refined iron; *(as an adj.)* strong.

Poplá, *a.* Poothless.

Por, *n.* A joint (as of the human body or a bamboo, &c.).

Poṛh, Poṛhá, *a.* Strong; robust;

Posh, *n.* Covering; apparel; clothing; garment. *Pá*—, n. shoe(s); slipper(s). *Mez*—, n. Table-cloth. *Palang*—, n. Bed-cover.

Poshak, *adj.* One providing nurture; one giving nourishment; one who fosters.

Poshák, *n.* Dress; garments; raiment; clothing.

Poshaṇ, *n.* Nurturing; feeding; providing nourishment; encouragement.

Poshída, *a.* Concealed; secret; hidden; covered; veiled.

Post, *n.* Skin; hide; crust; husk; rind; bark; shell; poppy-head. —*a. ká dána,* (khaskhas) poppy-seed.

Postín, *n.* A fur or leathern garment; fault; defect.

Pot, *a.* A bead; assessment; revenue.

Potá, *n.* Grandson; *(Fem. Potí).*

Potná, *v.* To besmear; to bedaub; to plaster; to white-wash.

Pozba<u>n</u>d, *n.* A muzzle.

Pozish, *n.* Apology.

Prabaltá, *n.* Strength; power; might; predominance.

Áá : P<u>a</u>rker   Éé : <u>E</u>ducation   Íí : <u>E</u>ager   Úú : C<u>oo</u>per

Prabandh, *n.* Bond; tie; connected narrative; discourse; &c.; a discussion; composition; literary style; a kind of song.

Prabhát, *n.* Daybreak; dawn; morning.

Prabháv, *n.* Effect; influence; impression. Impact. —*kárí,* a. Influential; —*hín,* a. Useless; ineffective; devoid of influence. —*shálí,* a. Influential; opinion-makers.

Prabhu, Parbhú, *n.* Lord Master; God.

Prabodh, *n.* Vigilance; activity; wisdom; persuasion; consolation.

Prachalan, *n.* Circulation; custom; commonality; popularity.

Prachalit, *a.* Customary; usual; circulating.

Prachanḍ, *a.* Wrathful; furious; passionate; fierce.

Práchín, *a.* Old; ancient; antique.

Práchír, *n.* Parapet; ramparts; surrounding wall (of acity or fort).

Pradesh, *n.* Region; foreign country.

Pradhán, *n.* Leader; chief; a trusted counsellor; courtier; village headman. —*mantrí,* prime minister.

Pragaṭ, Prakaṭ, *n.* Visible; apparent; public; notorious.

Prahlád, Pleasure; gladness; felicity; happiness.

Prajá, *n.* Subject; tenant; lessee. —*pálak,* the protector of his subjects, *i.e.,* a king or ruler.

Prakár, *n.* Kind; species; sort; style; manner.

Prakaraṇ, *n.* Topic; subject; chapter; explanation; book; opportunity; event.

Prakásh, *n.* Brilliance; day-light; pomp; manifestation; revelation; *a.* visible; apparent; public; bright.

Prakáshak, *n.* Publisher; one who brings to public attention.

Praláp, *n.* Chatter; delirium; incoherent conversation; lamentation; raving; warbling. —*í*/—*pak,* adj. Chatter-box; an idle chatterer; delirious; talkative.

Pralaya/ Parlai, *n.* Flood; deluge; inundation; death and destruction at a vast scale; annihilation.

Pramáṇ, *n.* Evidence; proof.

Prámáṇik, *adj.* Approved; authentic.

Prámáṇiktá, *n.* Authenticity; true quality.

Pramáṇit, *adj.* Authenticated; proven.

Pramod, *n.* Joy; pleasure; happiness.

Praṇ, *n.* Promise; pledge; vow; determination.

Práṇ, *n.* Life; soul; breath. —*ridya,* psychology.

Praṇám, *n.* Greeting; salutation; adoration.

Prapa__**n**__**ch,** *n.* Illusion; illusory creation; manifestation; delusion.

Praphullatá, *n.* Radiance; lustre; brightness; cheerfulness.

Prápt, *n.* Produce; profit; gain; benefit.

Prárabdh, *n.* Fate; destiny; predestination.

Prárthaná, *n.* Petition; prayer; entreaty; request; supplication.

Prárúp, *n.* Draft; outline.

Prasanna, *a.* Bright; pure; pleased; gracious; villing.

Prasáraṇ, *v.* Broadcast; spreading; scattering; publicly announced. —*sewá,* n. Broadcasting Service. —*kendra,* n. Broadcasting Centre; a radio station.

Prasha__**n**__**sá,** *n.* Praise; eulogy; flattery; fame.

Prashn, *n.* Question; a problem requiring solution; inquiry. —*dúti,* *n.* riddle; enigma; puzzling question. —*ottar, n.* catechism; controversy.

Prasiddh, *a.* Famous; well-known; notorious.

Prasthán, *n.* March; setting out on a journey.

Prastut, *adj.* Present; attending; ready (to serve or to function).

Prastuti, *n.* Presentation; offering.

Prasúti, *n.* Child-birth; delivery; maternity. *Kaksh,* n. Maternity room. —*griha,* n. Maternity Home.

Prátah, *n.* Morning; dawn; daybreak.

Pratáp, *n.* Splendour; glory; majesty; ardour; power; courage.

Pratham, *a.* First; primary; leading; principal.

Prati, *n. pre.* or prefix (used in comps. and signifying) again; against; towards; about; near; each; every, &c., as *pratidin,* every day; daily. —*bimb,* shadow; reflection, &c.

Pratigyá, *n.* Pledge; vow; promise; enunciation. —*patr,* n. A covenant; a written pledge; bond. —*pálan,* n. Honouring a pledge; adherence to a vow. —*bhang,* adv. Violation of a pledge; going back on a commitment; breach of a promise.

Pratík, *n.* Symbol; conceptual representation; token.

Pratirodh, *n.* Resistance; obstruction; contest; counter action.

Pratishodh, *n.* Revenge; retribution; punishment; vendetta; reprisal. *—lená,* v. To take/or to seek revenge.

Pratishṭhá, n. Prestige; status; dignity; honour. *—karná,* v. To install; to establish; to consecrate (like idols in the temples). *—ván,* n. A person with prestige; a person of some standing or status.

Pratít, *adv.* Appeared; known; acquaintance. *—honá,* v. To feel; to become aware of.

Pratítí, *n.* Confidence; trust; knowledge; understanding.

Prativád, *n.* Argument; contradiction; counter-argument; objection; protest; rejoinder.

Pratyaksh, *n.* Tangible; visible; evident; apparent; obvious. *—gyán,* a. Direct knowledge; a personal comprehension. *—darshí,* a. An eye witness. *—pramáṇ,* a. Direct evidence.

Pratyáláp, *adj.* Counter-wailing; argumentative discussion.

Praváh/ Prabáh, *n.* Flow; stream.

Prawín, *a.* Skilful; intelligent; clever; conversant with; *n.* an able person; an adept.

Práyashchit, *n.* Atonement; penance; expiation. *—karná,* v. To atone; to expiate; to offer retribution for one's wrongdoing.

Prayojan, *n.* Exigence; demand; cause; purpose; object; aim; profit.

Prem, *n.* Love; affection.

Preraṇá, *n.* Inspiration; instigation; urge; egging on.

Prerit, *n.* Sent; despatched; *n.* apostle; messenger; missionary.

Prítam, *a.* Most beloved; dearest; *n.* a. favourite friend; husband; lover.

Príti, *n.* Love; affection; attachment. *—bhoj,* n. A feast; a banquet.

Priya, *a.* Dear; beloved; darling; pleasing; pleasant one. *—jan,* a. Near and dear ones. *—tam,* a. Dearest; husband. *—darshí,* a. Dear to behold. *—bháshí,* a Sweet-spoken.

Puá, *n.* A pan-cake.

Púch, *a.* Empty; worthless; vain; absurd; petty; trial; insignificant; base; low; *n.* a thing of no consequence; absurdity; nonsense.

Púchhná, *v.* To ask (of); to question; to consult; to ask after; to invite; to help; to value.

Puchhwáná, *v.* To have enquiries made; to cause to ask; to cause to wipe or clean.

Puchkárná, *v.* To pat; to caress; to sooth.

Púd, *n.* Warp; woof.

Pújá, *n.* Worship; respect; homage; reverence; adoration (of the gods); idol-worship; devotion. *pújak,* a worshipper; an idolator; an adorer. *—rí, n.* a priest who officiates at a shrine and lives upon the offerings.

Pújná, *v.* To be filled; to be accomplished; to be perfected.

Pukár, *n.* Call; about; bowl; outcry; summons; invitation; petition; plant. *—ná,* to call; to invoke; to invite; to summon; to publish; to proclaim; to shout; to cry out; to complain.

Pukhráj, *n.* A topaz.

Puḳhtá, *a.* Cooked; baked; ripe; mature; expert; strong; built.

Pul, *n.* A bridge; a causeway; an embankment.

Pulak, *n.* Joy; delight; happiness. *—it,* adj. Pleased; delighted; joyful.

Pula<u>n</u>dá, Puli<u>n</u>dá, *n.* Bundle; parcel; package.

Pulling, *n.* The masculine gender.

Pu<u>m</u>bá, *n.* Cotton. *—bagosh,* deaf. *—dahan,* silent in company; taciturn.

Pú<u>n</u>chh, *n.* A tail; *(proverbially)* the tail-end of an episode; a hanger-on; a sycophant.

Pú<u>n</u>jí, *n.* Capital; investment. *Sájhe kí—,* a. Joint-stock. *—kar,* a. Capital levy. *—gat mál,* a. capital goods. *—gat lágat,* a. Capital costs. *—nivesh,* v. Investment. *—pati,* n. A capitalist. *—vád,* n. Capitalism.

Puṇya, *n.* Virtue; a good action; good; religious merit; welfare. *—átmá, a.* virtuous; righteous; religious; charitable.

Pur. *a.* Full; complete; laden, *(generally used as a first member of compounds)* as:*—fitná,* full of sedition and mischief. *—hunar,* very skilful or accomplished. *—zor,* powerful.

Pur, Purá, *n.* A city; town; village. *—bási,* citizen.

Púrá, *a.* Full; complete; entire; whole; accomplished; exact; precise; enough; up to the mark; skilled in; true. *—parná, v.* to be enough; to suffice. *—karná, v.* to fulfil; to carry out; to keep (a promise); to make up a deficiency.

Puráṇ, *n.* Narratives of the ancients; books of Hindu antiquity; Tales of Hindu mythology.

Puráná, *a.* Old; ancient; antiquated; aged; out of date; worn out.

Purkhá, (*Plur.* **Purkhe**), *n.* Ancestor; forefather. —*kí láj,* prov. Honour of one's forefathers.

Púrṇ, Púran, *a.* Filled. —*brahma,* the all-pervading spirit. —*mású,* the full moon.

Purohit, *n.* A family priest.

Purs, *a.* Asking; enquiring. questioning *(used at the end of comp.),* as *bázpurs; mizájpurs.*

Pursá, *a.* Of a man's height; *n.* a fathom; four cubits.

Pursish, *n.* Inquiry; asking; questioning.

Purush, *n.* A man; human being; a person; Supreme Being; God. —*kár,* a manly act.

Purushárth, *n.* An object of human endeavour; (according to Hindu tradition of thought) four basic aims of human life, i.e. *Dharma,* discharge of duty towards others; *artha,* acquisition of rightfully earned wealth; *káma,* fulfilment of just and moral desires; and *Moksha,* to achieve final emancipation of soul from this cycle of life and death. —*hín,* a. One devoid of endeavour, or will to work.

Púrv/ Púrab, *n.* East; prior; before; previous; preceding; afore. —*kathan,* a. prediction. —*kathá,* a. The story so far. —*karm,* a. Antecedents; prior deeds. —*ágraha,* n. Prejudice; bias. —*kál,* a. The past; prior period. —*janma,* n. Previous life (according to Hindu belief of trans-migration of soul and cycle of birth-and-rebirth). —*gyán,* a. Prior knowledge; fore-sight; inkling. —*niyati,* n. Destiny. —*bhút,* a. Existing previously; former. —*vartí,* a. Previous; preceding. —*ábhás,* a. A premonition. —*gámí;* adj. one(s) that have been or gone before; earlier. —*aj,* adj. Ancester(s).

Purwá/ Purwáí, *n.* The Eastern wind.

Purwaṭ, *n.* Large leathern bucket for drawing water.

Purzá, *n.* A scrap (of paper). piece; bit; rag. *purze purze urá dená,* to cut to pieces; to make mincement.

Pushp, *n.* Flower; blossom; speaks on the eye.

Pushṭ, *a.* Well-fed; nourished; fat; strong; vigorous; restorative.

Pusht, *n.* The back; support; prop; assistance; progenitors. —*ba—,* from generation to generation. —*par honá,* to back; to support. —*panáh,* refuge; asylum. —*dená,* to flee; to turn tail.

Pushtá, *n.* Buttress; prop; embankment; quay.

Pushtainí, *a.* Ancestral; hereditary.

Pushtak, *n.* Kicking out with the hind legs (a horse).

Pustak, *n.* A book. —*álay,* n. [literally] A home of books; a library; a bibliotheque. —*vikretá,* n. A bookseller. —*prakáshak,* n. A book-publisher. kít, n. A bookworm; a bookish person. —*íya gyán,* adj. Bookish knowledge. —*vyasaní,* adj. A bibliophile; a bookaholic.

Puṭhá, *n.* Paste-board; the cover of a book.

Putlá, *n.* Doll; puppet; effigy.

Putlí, *n.* The pupil of the eye. —*ká tamáshá,* a puppet show.

Putr, *n.* A son.

Putrí, *n.* A daughter.

Puṭṭhá, *n.* Rump; buttocks.

Puzá, Poza, *n.* Lip; mouth.

Pyádá/ Piyádá, *n.* A footman; messenger; peon; orderly.

Pyálá/ Piyálá, *n.* A cup; a wine cup; a glass. —*bharná,* prov. One's days being numbered; one's life span nearing end.

Pyár/ Piyár, *n.* Love; affection; fondness; care. —*karná,* v. To fondle; to caress; to love; to be in love.

Pyás/ Piyás, *n.* Thirst; desire; longing; craving. —*bujháná,* v. To quench one's thirst; to satisfy one's craving or desire. —*á,* adj. Thirsty; ardently desiring; craving for.

Pyáú, *n.* A roadside stall, mounted at festive times, as also in high summer months, by rich and charitable, individuals and/or establishment, to offer cold, drinking water, sometimes sweetened to the travellers. All communities make this charitable gesture in hot countries, but especially gesture in hot countries, but especially in India and Pakistan,

Pyáz/ Piyáz, *n.* Onion(s); leak.

क़साई पसीज जाता है, पर
कंजूस नहीं।

Qasái pasíj játá hai,
par kanjús nahi<u>n</u>.

(An assassin might show compassion,
but a miser won't.)

Q, q, represents the letter (ق) in Urdu and the imported-from-Arabic sound of (क़) in Hindi.

Qáb, *n.* A vessel; a case; a large dish.

Qa'b, *n.* A cavern; a pit; a cup.

Qabá, *n.* A long gown; a tunic.

Qabáhat, *n.* Baseness; rascality; evil; crime; harm; defect.

Qábá, *n.* A square building at Mecca, in Saudi Arabia, where millions of Muslims from all over the world congregate annually as a matter of pilgrimage.

Qabáil, *n.* (*Plu. of* **Qabílá**), Tribes; primitive social groups infused with medieval sense of simplistic loyalities. —*í,* a. Tribal.

Qabálá, *n.* A contract embodying a bargain and sale-deed; title-deed; bond; bill of sale; conveyance.

Qabas, *n.* A spark; firebrand; match.

Qabh, Qubh, *n.* Baseness; foulness; ugliness.

Qábil, *a.* Capable; skillful; qualified; worthy; admitting (of); *n.* a fit or capable person. —*e-báz-purs, a.* responsible; accountable. —*iyat,* n. Ability.

Qabíla, *n.* Family; race; progency; species; kind.

Qábila, *n.* a clever or skillful woman; a midwife; a male screw; a bolt.

Qábiz, *a.* One in control; one in possession; Astringent; one who has seized; occupier.

Qabl, *n.* The anterior or forepart; the front; *a.* prior; anterior; first; preparatory; *prep.* and *adv.* prior or previous (to); before.

Qabr, *n.* Tomb; grave. —*istán, n.* graveyard; cemetery; burial ground; sepulchre.

Qábú, *n.* Opportunity; possession; hold; control; command; power; will.—*parastí,* tyranny. *be*—, a. Out of control; without discipline.

Qabúl, *n.* Acceptance; compliance; consent; acknowledgment; *a.* accepted; approved; sanctioned. —*súrat, a.* heautiful; comely; handsome.

Qabúliyat, *n.* Acceptance; acceptance or hearing (of prayer by God); receipt; consent; counterpart of a lease.

Qabz, *n.* Constipation; a form of digestive system disorder.

Qabzá, *n.* Grasp; clutch; possession; tenure; *also* hilt of a sword; handle; hinge; i.e. something that aloows the owner/possessor to keep a hold or control on.

Qad, *n.* Height; stature; size. (See also **Kadd**). —*I-ádam,* a. Full man-size; height of a grown up man.

Qadah, *n.* Cup; glass; goblet.

Qadam, *n.* The foot; footstep; step; pace. *—báz. a.* nimbie-footed; flect. *—bos honá, v.* to kiss the feet (of) in token of humility. *—nikálná,* to break in (a horse). *sabz—, a.* unlucky; inauspicious.

Qadámat, *n.* Precedence (in point of time); priority; antiquity; age.

Qadím, *a.* Ancient; antique; archaic; antiquated. *—ulaiyám,* ancient times.

Qádir, *a.* Powerful; having legal power or authority; capable. *al—,* the Almighty *—i-mutaq,* the Omnipotent; Omnipotence.

Qadr, Qadar, *n.* Honour; power; merit; price; size; part; fate; destiny. *—dán,* one who can estimate and appreciate the true value of anything; a judge; a patron. *be—,* worth-less; disgraced. *be—i,* adv. Lack of appreciation; non-appreciation. *—karná,* adv. To appreciate; to attach value to.

Qadre, *adv.* Somewhat; some extent; partially; *n.* small quantity; a little. adv. comparatively; relatively.

Qáedá, See *Qáidá.*

Qafas, *n.* A cage; *(Met.)* the body.

Qáfilá, *n.* A caravan; a body of traders or travellers.

Qáfiya, *n.* Rhyme; metre. *—tang honá,* to be in great poverty or distress; to be involved in difficulties.

Qahhár, *a.* Very powerful; boundless (as a sea); conquering; avenging; of great force or impetuosity; *n.* conqueror; avenger; tyrant.

Qahqahá, *n.* A loud laugh; a burst of laughter; a horse-laugh; a hearty laugh.

Qahr, *n.* Power; violence; severity; rage; wrath; vengeance; punishment; a mischievous person; an incendiary. *—i-Iláhí,* divine retribution.

Qahat, *n.* Famine; death; scarcity. *—zadá,* famine-stricken; starving.

Qahwá, *n.* Coffee.

Qai, *n.* Vomit; nausea. *—láne wálí, a.* emetic.

Qaid, *n.* An imprisonment; confinement; a fetter; restraint; a bond; an obligation. *—bámashaqqat,* rigorous imprisonment. *—khána,* prison; jail. *—í,* prisoner; convict; convict; captive.

Qáid, *n.* A law-maker; a law-giver; a leader commanding unquestioned loyalty from his followers. —*i-Ázam,* a. An epithet of late Muhammad Ali Jinnah, the founding father of Pakistan.

Qá'idá, *n.* Rule; regulation; law; maxim; custom; practice; a primer; basis; (in *Geom.*) the base of a figure or column. —*jári karná, v.* to enforce a law.

Qáil, *adv.* Convinced; impressed.

Qáil, *a.* Saying; acknowledging; agreeing; convinced; confuted; *n.* an assertor; a confessor; a declarant.

Qáim, Qáyam, *adj.* Fixed; stable; Permanent.

Qáim, Qáyam, *a.* Standing; erect; per-pendicular; durable; firm; stable; in force; vigilant; persevering. —*rakhná, v.* to support; to keep up. —*muqám, n.* a deputy; *a locum tenens;* a viceroy; a proxy; *a.* acting or officiating.

Qainchí, *n.* Pair of scissors; x-shaped tool; shears; truss; the joists of a roof.

Qaisar, *n.* Caeser; the emperor; an empress; potentae; sovereign. Kaiser; the general name of Emperors of Greece. Turkey and Germany.

Qaitúl, *n.* Siesta; an afternoon nap.

Qaitúla, *n.* A midday nap or sleep; a siesta.

Qaiyúm, *n.* Everlasting; eternal; an epithet of the deity.

Qál, *n.* Theoretical knowledge; lacking in the intimacy of experience.

Qál, *n.* A saying; a word; loquaciousness; egotism.

Qalá, *n.* Soreness of the mouth.

Qalá, Qilá, *n.* Fort; fortress; castle; citadel. —*shikan top,* a siege-gun; a very large cannon.

Qaláb, *n.* One who makes fake coins; counterfeiter; swindler.

Qaláí, *n.* Wrist; pulse; fetlock of a horse.

Qala'í, *n.* Tin; a coating of tin applied to cooking utensils, &c.; whitewashing; gilding; plating. —*khulná, v.* to be discovered or disposed.

Qalam, *n.* Pen; fountain pen; a writing instrument; reed-pen; [*in botany and agriculture*] graft; cutting; trimmed moustache; whisker. —*dán,* n. Pen-holder. —*zan karná,* v. To delete; to strike off. —*kárí,* n. painting; engraving on calico; figure-work on textiles. *Sar—karná,* v. To cut off [some one's head]; to prune. —*lagáná,* v. To graft plant cuttings.

Qalam, *n.* A reed; reed-pen; pen; pencil; handwriting; —*dán,* an inkstand. —*rau,* dominion; sovereignty; jurisdiction. *yak—*, with a single stroke of the pen; at once.

Qalam, *n.* (In agriculture) A cutting; a graft. *—í ám,* a. A specie of mango fruit. *—shorá,* a. Crystallized saltpetre.

Qalám, *n.* Word; speech; discourse; a complete sentence; a proposition; a composition; a (literary) work. *Takiyá—*, prov. Prop for speech; a habitually used word or phrase [like 'y' 'know', 'actually', 'to be honest'...and so on.

Qalám, *n.* Writing; creative work(s) [i.e. *Qalám* of so-and-so].

Qalamí, *adj.* Grafted; a variety of mango; crystalline.

Qalandar, *n.* A wandering Mohamedan monk; a bear-dancer; a monkey dancer.

Qalb, *n.* Inversion; mind; intellect; main body of an army; the best part of anything; essence; counterfeit; coin; *a.* inverted; counterfeit. *—sáz,* a maker of counterfeit coin. *—í,* hearty; cordial; spurious.

Qalíl, *a.* Small; little; scanty; few. *—o-kasír,* more or less.

Qálín, *n.* Broiled meat; flesh cooked with spices, &c.; curry.

Qamar, *n.* The moon. *—i,* lunar.

Qámat, *n.* 'Stature; height; figure; form; body.

Qamchí, *n.* A whip; a twig; a cane; a switch; a lash.

Qamíz, *n.* A shirt.

Qámús, *n.* The ocean; the name of an Arabic dictionary.

Qaná'at, *n.* Contentment; resignation; abstinence.

Qanát, *n.* The wall of a tent; a canvas screen; a canvas enclosure round a tent or in a camp.

Qand, *n.* White crystallized sugar; loaf sugar. *Shakar—*, sweet potato.

Qandíl, *n. (Plur. Qanádíl).* Candle; lamp stand; candle stick.

Qanít, *n.* Obedient to God; God-fearing; devout.

Qánún, *n.* Rule; law; statue; ordinance. *—dán, n.* lawyer; jurist. *—dání,* jurisprudence. *—go,* a superintendent of the village accounts.

Qaqulá, *n.* A large cardamum *(barí iláchí).*

Qa'r, *n.* Depth or bottom of a well; gulf; cavity.

Qarábá, *n.* A large glass bottle; a decanter.

Qarábalin, *n.* An antidote; a panacea.

Qarábat, *n.* Nearness; connection; kin; kindred.

Qaráin, *n. (Plur. of Qarína).* Connections; circumstances; the conjectures; the context. *—i-'ain,* legal presumptions.

Qarár, *n.* Agreement; tranquillity; rest; peace; tenacity; (of purpose); firmness; residence. *—karná, v.* to confirm a bargain; to ratify a treaty. *—námá,* n. Deed of agreement; document indicating consent; treaty document.

Qarnulí, *n.* A picquet hunting the chase; a hunting-knife.

Qaráwal, *n.* Vanguard; the advanced guard of an army; sentinel; hunter. *—í,* skirmishing (of outposts); a running fight.

Qarhá, *n.* A wound; an ulcer; a sore.

Qárí, *n.* A reader (esp. of the Qurán).

Qaríb, *a.* Near; close; adjacent. *—íkhtitám,* nearing completion. *marg,* at the point of death.

Qarín, *a.* Connected; adjoining; annexed (to)*—i-maslahat* advisible; expedient.

Qaríná, *n.* Way; mode; manner; order; contest; symmetry; similarity.

Qarná, *n.* A trumpet; a clarionet.

Qarrád, *n.* A keeper or trainer of monkeys.

Qaryá, *n.* Village; hamlet; town.

Qarz, Qaraz, Qarzá, *n.* Debt; loan; credit. *—i-hasaná,* money lent, or a loan obtain-ed, without interest, and repay-able at the pleasure of the borrower.

Qasáí, *n.* A butcher; *a. (Met.)* hard-hearted; merciless.

Qasáid, *n. (Plur. of Qasída).* Odes.

Qasam, *n.* An oath. *—dilásá, v.* to administer an oath, *—khána,* to take an oath; to swear. *—torná,* to violate an oath. *—iyá,* sworn; on oath.

Qasbá, *n.* A smaller town.

Qasd, *n.* Intention; object; aim; wish; inclination. *—i-musammam,* fixed resolution; firm determination. *—an, adv.* purposely; wilfully; deliberately.

Qashqá, *n.* The mark (of sandal &c.) made by Hindus on the forehead to indicate their sect.

Qásid, *n.* Messenger; courtier; runner; postman; harbinger.

Qasídá, *n.* A eulogy; ode in praise of; a recitation for the appeasement of the powers that be. [An old tradition in Persian-Urdu poetry].

Qásim, *n.* A distributor; one who allots; *a.* dividing; apportioning;

allotting. —*ul-arzáq,* Distributor of daily bread, *i.e.,* God.

Qásir, *a.* Lacking; falling short; defective; unable; important. —*ul-lisán,* deficient in speech.

Qasar, *n.* Diminution; defect; evening twilight; citadel; a place; an edifice.

Qasr, *n.* Compulsion; violence; revenge.

Qassáb, *n.* A butcher.

Qat, *n.* Cutting transversely; the nib of a pen. —*zen,* a flat piece of bone or stick, one which writing-reeds or pens are cut or formed into shape.

Qata', *n.* Cutting; intersection; portion; division; a breaking off; cut; shape; fashion. —*i-ta'lluq,* separation from; abandonment. —*kalám karná,* to interrupt the speech of; to put in a word —*i-nazar,* averting the regard or attention from; without reference to.

Qata'an, *adv.* Conclusively; definitely; never; not at all.

Qatár, *n.* A line; row; rank; series; train. —*bándhná,* to put or place in a row or order.

Qátil, *n.* Murderer; assassin; *a.* mortal; deadly; fatal.

Qátilaná, *adj.* Murderous; intent upon; or with the intention of murder.

Qátir, *n.* A mule.

Qatl, *n.* Murder; killing; slaying. —*i-'ám,* general massacre. —*'am,* wilfully murder. —*i-insán,* homicide. —*i-pidar,* parricide.

Qatrá, *n.* A drop; (in *Med.*) a minim.

Qaul, *n.* Word; saying; dictum; promise; agreement; stipulation; vow; resolve. —*dená,* to pledge one's word (to). —*toṛná, v.* to break one's word or promise. —*karár karná,* to make an agreement or contract with; to make terms with. *ba—,* according to the saying or dictum of.

Qaum, *n.* Nation; a people; race; sect; caste. —*iyat, n.* nationality; clanship.

Qaus, *n.* A bow; an are of a circle. —*i-qazáh,* the rainbow.

Qawá'id, *n. (Plur. of Qá'eda).* Rules; regulations; principles; canons; grammar; parade; drill.

Qawí, *a.* Firm; powerful; strong. —*haikal,* robust; of huge or mighty size.

Qawwál, *n.* A professional singer.

Qayám, *n.* Residence; stay; encampment. —*karná,* v. To stay; to reside, &c.

Qazá, *n.* Predestination; divine decree; fate; destiny; charge; judicature; performing (of a duty). —*i-haját,* attending. to the calls of nature. —*rá,* by the action of fate; providentially; by chance.

Qází, *n.* A Muhammedan Judge or Magistrate who passes sentence in all cases of law, religions, moral, civil and criminal. —*ul-háját, (Lit.)* supplier of needs; God; *(fig.)* money.

Qaziyá, *n.* A freebooter; a robber; a plunderer. —*ajal,* the angel of death.

Qiblá, *n.* The temple of the Ka'ba in Mecca; an object of veneration or reverence; a faither; king, &c., (by way of respectful address)—*álam,* his Majesty; your Majesty. —numa, a mariner's compass.

Qíl, *n.* Word; speech; saying (in answer). —*o-qál,* dialogue; conversation; chit-chat; altercation.

Qilá, Qalá, *n.* A fort; fortress; castle; citadel.

Qillat, *n.* Littleness; smallness; scarcity; paucity; insufficiency; want.

Qímá, *n.* Pounded or minced meat. —*karná, v.* to make mince-meat of.

Qimár, *n.* Dice; any game of hazard. —*báz,* a gamester; a gambler. —*khána,* a gaming house.

Qimásh, *n.* What is collected hence and thence; merchandise; breeding; manners.

Qímat, *n.* Price; worth; value. —*lagáná,* to fix the price of; to make an offer. —*í,* valuable; costly, expensive.

Qirán, *n.* Conjunction of planets; propinquity; an auspicious conjuncture, or season.

Qirmiz, *n.* Crimson; cochineal.

Qirtás, *n.* Paper.

Qism, *n.* Kind; sort; type; variations; class. —*wár,* a. classified.

Qismat, *n.* Fortune; fate; divine decree. —*ulaṭ jáná,* one's fortune to take an adverse turn; to come under an unlucky star. —*khulná,* one's fortune to take a favourable turn. —*laṛná,* to have a good run of luck.

Qissá, *n.* Tale; story; fable often narrated in popular verse metre and interwoven with philosophical thought of the people. [Plural; *Qissáját*]. —*kotáh,* in short; briefly.

Qist, *n.* Instalment; portion, dividend; a tax. —*wár,* by instalments.

Qita', *n.* Section; division; fragment; piece; scrap.

Qittál, *n.* Battle; fighting; slaughter.

Qiwám, *n.* Essence; syrup; gradients.

Qiyáfá, *n.* Appearance; semblance; countenance; mien look; air; physiognomy *—shinás,* physiognamist.

Qiyám, *n.* Stability; permanence; stay; halt; existence; being; uprising; insurrection; keeping; preservation. *—pazir,* stationary; table; permanent.

Qiyámat, *n.* The resurrection; the last day; commotion; a great calamity. *—ṭúṭná,* great calamity to befall.

Qiyás, *n.* Judgment; opinion thought; conception; supposition; conjecture; guess. *—se báhar,* inconceiveable. *be —*above measure; enormous.

Qiyásí, *a.* Analogical; hypothetical; conjectural; presumptive (proof).

Qor, *n.* A new rope of fine cotton; tape; riband; edge; border; train; retinue; armour. *—ḳháná,* armoury; arsenal.

Qormá, *n.* A brown stew of meat or chicken, seasoned with a thick spicy sauce, mixed with ground almonds and other exotic condiments. A favourite kind of dish for the Europeans visiting their nearest Indian restaurant in their part of the world.

Qubbá, *n.* A dome; vault; cupola.

Qubl, *n.* The front part.

Qubúr, *n. (Plur. of Qabr).* Tombs; graves.

Quddús, *a.* Pure; holy; blessed; an epithet of the Deity.

Qudrat, *n.* Power; ability; vigour; force; divine power; nature; the universe. *—í,* divine; constitutional; natural; innate.

Quds, *a.* Holy; pure; *n.* sanctity; holiness.

Qudúm, *n.* Arrival; approach; advert.

Qufl, *n.* Lock.

qulába, *n.* A small curved piece of a huqqa snake; a cup with a cover (in which ice is moulded).

Qulí, *n.* A labourer; a quarter.

Qulláb, *n.* A hook; a fish-hook; an iron goad, hooked at one end.

Qulláh, *n.* A peak; summit; top of anything.

Qumqumá, *n.* A bowl; a jug; a pitcher.

Qumrí, *n.* A turtle-dove; a ring-dove.

Qunaen, *n.* Quinine; the most favoured medication for Malaria in imperial India and that neighbour-hood; (proverbially) any bitter pill.

Qur'a, *n.* Drawing lots; a wager; a bet; a cast or throw of dice; a raffle a; ballot.

Qur'án, *n.* The Holy book of the Muslims [also spelt in Roman script as *Korán* or *Al Qurán*].

Qurb, Qurbat, *n.* Nearness; proximity; adjacency; neighbourhood. *—o-jwár,* vicinity; environs; suburbs.

Qurbán, *n.* A sacrifice; an offering; an oblation *(sadqá, bali-hárí). —gáh, n.* an alter. *—í, a.* sacrificed; devoted; *n.* a sacrifice; victim.

Qurq, *n.* Seizure; confiscation; an attachment; prohibition; prevention. *—amin,* a bailiff.

Qurrat, *n.* Cheerfulness; joy; gladness. *—ul'ain,* brightness of the eye; tranquility.

Qurs, *n.* A pellet; an orb; disc, (of the sun or moon); a wafer; a lozenge.

Qusúr, *n.* A failing (of or in); deficiency; failure; defect; error; fault; sin. *—bataláná,* to find fault with. *be—,* guiltless; innocent.

Qutb, *n.* The polar star; the north pole; a centre round which anything revolves; an axis; a pivot. *—numa,* a magnetic compass.

Qutr, *n.* Diameter (of a circle); *nisf—,* radius (of a circle).

Qúwat, *n.* Strength; power; virtue; energy; faculty; authority. *—áḳhizá,* strength of mind. *—i-básirá,* faculty of vision; sight. *—i-mudriká,* the intellectual faculty.

Quzát, *n. (Plur. of Qází).* Justices; judges.

राजनीति भले लोगों का धन्धा
नहीं है।

Rajnítí bhalé logón ká
dhandhá nahín hai.

(Politics is not a business for
good people.)

R, r, is equal to (र) in Hindi and (ر) in Urdu. When used with a dot (.) at the bottom, it represents the sound (ड़) in Hindi and (ڑ) in Urdu.

Ráb, *n.* Syrup; treacle; molasses.

Rabaṛ, *n.* Rubber; elastic. —*sá,* a. Flexible; pliable. a. Flexible; pliable.

Rabb, *n.* Lord; master; protector; preserver; an epithet of the Deity. —*ul'alamín,* Lord of the universe. —*ul-'ibád,* God, the protector of his servants.

Rabbání, *a.* Divine; godly.

Rabí, *n.* Spring; the spring harvest. —*ul-auwal,* the third Mohammadan month. —*ul-ákhir.* —*ul-sání,* the fourth Mohammadan month.

Rabíb, *n.* A step-son.

Rábita, *n.* Tie; bond of union or relationship; connection; conjunction.

Rabṛí, Rábṛí, *n.* Milk thickened by boiling.

Rabt, *n.* Connexion; bond; relation; friendship; practice; habit; (in *Gram.*) construction.

Rach, *v.* To make; to shape; to create; to compose. —*ná,* v. to soak in; to sink in. [also as a *n.*-] a creative work; invention; poem; coposition. —*ayitá,* n. Creator; author; composer.

Rachaná, *n.* Make; form; workmanship; invention; creation; *v. t.* to make; to create; to invent; to plan; to decorate; to frustrate.

Radd, *a.* A reject; one repulsed; one repudiated. —*o-badal.* n. Alteration; changeover. —*I-qarz.* n. Liquidation of a debt. —*karná,* v. To reject; to turn down; to cancel, &c.

Raddá, *n.* A stratum; a layer of (of bricks). —*jamáná,* v. To instigate; to provoke; to cast an aspersion.

Raddí, *a.* Rejected; waste; worthless; hurtful; *n.* anything rejected; waste; remnants; scraps; refuse.

Raen, *n.* Night. —*baserá,* n. A night-shelter; a temporary domicile; a place of encampment.

Rafa', *n.* Elevation; exaltation; removing; repelling; settlement. —*náma, n.* a deed of settlement or compromise. —*dafa' karná, v.* to settle; to dispose of; to remove.

Rafáqat, *n.* Companionship friendship; society; communion.

Rafí', *a.* Elevating; exalting; *n.* raiser; exalter.

Rafíq, *n. (Plur. Rafiqán).* Friend; associate; comrade; ally; confederate; an adherent.

Raftár, *n.* Pace; speed. *Zamáne kí—,* prov. Way of the world; mood of the times.

Rafú, *n.* Darning. *—gar,* n. Darner.

Rafú-chakkar, *—honá.* V. To escape; to run away; to turn heels; to abscond.

Rag, *n.* Vein; fibre. *—dár,* n. Fibrous. *—pahchánaná,* v. To recognise the facts; to be thoroughly familiar with the innards of a person. *—men dauṛ jáná,* v. To have a profound effect on. *—phaṛak uṭhná,* v. One's innermost to get excited about something. *—on men bijlí dauṛná,* v. To get into high spirits. *—pakaṛ lená,* v. To take control of vitals.

Rág, *n.* Melodic mode, or a fixed structure of notes in Indian classicial music; *also* attachment; attraction; passion; emotion; love. *—dwesh,* n. The spectrum of attachment and malevolence; human nature. *—virág,* n. attachment and revulsion. *—alápná,* v. To go on harping the same tune. *—rang,* n. Revelry; merry-making.

Ragaṛ, *n.* Rubbing; friction; attrition. *—kháná, v.* to come into contact with; to collide with.

Ragbat, *n.* Longing; desire; inclination; wish. *—diláná, v.* to incite; to induce.

Ragedná, *v.* To chase; to pursue; to hunt.

Rágib, *a.* Wishing (for); desirous; eager; curious.

Rah, *pref.* (from Ráh: Way, path). *—guzar,* n. Highway. *—zan,* n. A highway man; a brigand. *—numá,* n. A guide; a pathfinder.

Ráh, *n.* Way; path; access; manner; fashion. *—nikálná, v.* To find a way; to devise a mode of conduct.

Raham, *n.* Compassion; mercy; pity; consideration. *—dil,* a. Compassionate; kind; merciful. *Be—,* a. Unrelenting; pitiless; unkind; inconsideration.

Ráhat, n. Rest; repose; case; tranquility; relief; gladness.

Rahím, *a.* Merciful or compassionate (i.e., God).

Rahasya, *n.* Secret; mystery; confidential. *—may,* a. Mysterious; secretive. *—vád,* n. A literary movement in Hindi poetry; *—odgháṭan,* v. Revelation; announcement of what was secret; (a kind of) coming out.

Rahmán, *a.* Merciful; attribute of God.

Rahná, *v.* To live; to remain; to stay; to continue. *Rah-rah-kar,* adv. intermittently; spasmodically.

Ráhu, *n.* Name of a demon who is believed to seize the sun and moon and thus cause eclipses.

Ráe, *n.* Relief; judgment; opinion; wisdom; advice.

Ráí, *n.* Mustard seed; anything very small.

Ráij, *a.* Customary; common; in vogue; current; fashionable.

Raís, *n.* A nobleman; a rich person; a grandee; a leading citizen (*also used as an adjective*). *—zádá,* a. son of-. [In Islamic state system this word implies an official rank. Therefore—] *—é-qánún,* a. Chief Law-Officer. *—e-khazáná,* a. Chief Treasurer. &c.

Ra'iyat, *n.* A subject; tenant; peasant; cultivator; dependant. *—ázár, n.* an oppressor; a tyrant. *—parwar.* benevolent ruler or landlord.

Ráj, *n.* A kingdom; realm; state; reign. *—kathá,* n. A narrative of King's deeds. *—kanyá,* n. A princess. *—káj,* n. Affairs of state; task of goernance. *—kumár,* n. A prince. *—kumárí,* n. A princess. *—kul,* n. A dynasty; a ruling family. *Kosh,* n. The state excehquer; state treasury. *—gaddí,* n. The royal throne. *—mahal,* n. The royal palace. *—tantra,* n. Monarchy. *—tilak,* n. Coronation. *—dút,* n. An Ambassador. —n. Sedition; treason. *—bhakti,* n. Loyalty to the throne; loyalism. *—bhattá,* n. Privy-purse. *—manḍal,* n. Satellite states; a chamber of princes. *—mudrá,* a. A signet; the royal seal. *—rog,* n. An incurable ailment; a chronic disease. *—vidroh,* n. Rebellion; mutiny. *—sabhá,* n. The royal court. *—sattá,* n. Royal authority. *—dháni,* n. The capital city.

Raj, *n.* Dust; dirt; pollen; farina (of flowers).

Ráj, Rájgír, *n.* A mason; a bricklayer; a builder. *—gírí,* n. The profession of brick-laying; the job of byuilding.

Rájá, *n.* King; sovereign; monarch; ruler; prince; *(fig.)* an extravagant person.

Rajab, *n.* The seventh Mohamedan month.

Rajní, *n.* Night. *—gandhá,* a. a fragrant flower that blooms at night. [Also known as **Rát kí rání**].

Rajwáṛá, *n.* A country ruled by a Raja; a native State.

Rájya, *n.* Stae; kingdom; polity; rule; reign. *—kál,* n. tenure in power; period of rule. *—tyág,* n. Abdication. *—kshetra,* n. Territory of the state; expanse of one's domain. *—vyavasthá,* n. stae policy; systems of state.

Rakáb, *n.* A stirrup; train; retinue. —*diwál, n.* a stirrup of leather.

Rakábí, Rakeb, *n.* A flat dish; a plate; a saucer.

Rákesh, *n.* (literally) The lord of the night; Moon.

Rákh, *n.* Ash(es). —*dání,* n. Ashtray. —*ḍálná,* v. To hush up the matter; to suppress (a controversy). —*men milá dená,* v. To lay waste; to devastate. —*ho jáná,* v. To be ruined; to be turned to ashes.

Rakhael, *a.* A kept woman; a concubine; a mistress; a woman cohabiting with a man, out of wedlock.

Rakhaiyá, *n.* Protector; guardian; keeper; custodian.

Rákhí, Rakshá-bandhan, *n.* A sacred coloured thread that women, especially sisters, tie on to men's, especially brothers' wrists to consecrate a bond between the two which obliges the men-folk to protect the women's honour and help them in moments of adversity. [A historic anecdote tells us that a Rájpút princess sent a *Rákhí* to Humayun, the second Mughal emperor, obliging him to rush to the aid of her husband's kingdom which was being ravaged by another Muslim invader. Tragically, Humayun arrived too late to do anything worthwhile].

Raḳhsh, *n.* Light; luminance; brilliance; the name of Rustam's horse.

Raḳhshán *n.* Dazzling; resplendent.

Raḳht, *n.* Goods and chattels; personal effects; property; raiment. —*bándhná,* to pack up; to depart.

Rakhwál, Rakhwálá, Rakhwár, *n.* Guard; watchman; keeper.

Rakhwálí, Rakhwárí, *n.* Guardianship; care; custody.

Rákib, *n.* A rider; a horseman.

Rakshá, *n.* Protection; preservation; care; guardianship. —*bandhan,* an armlet; the name of a Hindu festival, on which day Hindus bind pieces of coloured thread on their wrists.

Rakshak, *n.* Preserver; protector; guardian.

Rákshas, *n.* A demon; a monster; a cruel man. —*í,* n. Female of the specie. —*í vritti,* n. Demonic tendency. —*í viváh,* a. (literally) A demonic marriage; a marriage entered into as a result of abduction and rape. [Hindu thinkers have categorised eight kinds of marriage. This kind of marriage is the lowest in those eight].

Rakt, *n.* Blood; red; saffron;

attached. —*ábh,* adj. Red-tinged. —*im,* adj. Reddish in colour. —*kshíṇatá,* n. Anaemia. —*cháp,* n. Blood pressure. —*dán,* n. Blood-donation. —*otpal,* n. Red Lotus. —*maṇi,* n. A ruby. —*pát,* n. blood-shed. —*páyí,* adj. Blood-sucker; blood-sucking. —*pipásá,* n. Blood-thirst. —*pipású,* adj. Blood-thristy. —*ranjit,* adj. Blood-soaked. *Sambandh,* adj. Consanguinity; blood-relation(s). —*shoshak,* adj. Exploiter(s); blood-suckers. —*shoshaṇ,* n. Exploitation (to the level of extreme). —*sráv,* n. Haemorrhage. —*varṇa,* adj. Blood-red; crimson. —*vasan,* adj. Robed in red; saffron-clad; an ascetic.

Rál, *a.* Resin; pitch.

Rál, *n.* Saliva; spittle.

Rálá, *a.* Stirred; bruised; mixed.

Ralá, *n.* Mixture; union; disagreement; difference.

Raláná, *v.* To pound together; to pulverise; to grind; to mix.

Rám, *n.* (Short for-) Rámachandra, the hero of epic *Rámáyana,* the most popular character in Hindu mythology and tradition, considered to be the seventh incarnation of Lord *Vishnu,* and often referred to as *Maryádápurushottm,* "the setter of behavioural norms, or examples'. —*rám!,* n. Greetings. —*kahání* n. One's tale of woe; a narration of one's life and times. —*dhám,* a. (literally) the dwelling place of **Rám,** i.e. the city of Ayodhyá; (proverbially-) paradise. —*báṇ aushadh,* a. A panacea; an unfailing remedy; a sure-cure. —*raj,* n. The yellow ochre. —*ras,* n. Plain salt. —*kuṭiyá,* n. A humble abode. —*Rájya,* a. An ideal domain; an ideal administration/ government; Utopia. —*bharose,* adv. Hostage to fortune; to let things go as they may. —*rám karke,* adv. Somehow; with great difficulty; one way or another.

Ramaṇ, *n.* Sporting; amorous dalliance; erotic playfulness; merriment *(also as an adjective)* Dear; wooer; lover.

Rámánandí, *n.* A sect of Hindu ascetics who are followers of Rám.

Ramaṇí, *n.* A pretty woman; a desirable damsel.

Ramaṇík, *a.* Beautiful; pleasant; charming; delightful; winsome; attractive.

Rambá, *n.* The plainer; a carpenter's tool.

Rambhá, *n.* A heavenly voluptuous temptress; a nick-name used for an earthly voluptuous beauty.

Rámí, *n.* Thrower; hurler (of javelins, stones, &c.); archer; scoffer; the constellation Sagittarius.

Ramídá, *a.* Terrified; alarmed.

Rámish, *n.* Repose; gladness; joy; harmony. —*gar, n.* a musician.

Rammál, *n.* A soothsayer; a prophet; a fortune-teller; a juror.

Rammáz, *n.* One who speaks mysterious; an enigmatist; *a.* speaking mysteriously, or by signs.

Rammún, *n.* A kind of goat.

Ramaṇíy, *a.* One in possession of the qualities of *Ramaník.*

Ramná, *v.* See *Raman.*

Rá<u>m</u>pi, *n.* A knife for paring or scraping leather.

Ramtá, *a.* Wandering; roving; roaming. —*jogí,* a. A wandering mendicant; one who does not stay in one place.

Ramzán, Ramádán, *n.* The ninth month of the Muslim calender; traditionally the month during which the devout Muslims fast all day and break the fast when moon is sighted in the sky.

Rán, *n.* The thigh. —*tale dabáná, v.* to have (one) in complete subjection; to mount or ride (a horse).

Raṇ, *n.* Battle; fighting; war; combat. —*kshetr,* a. Battle-field; theatre of war. —*chandí,* n. The war-goddess; the female deity waging war on demons and evil forces. —*bherí,* a. Bugles of war; a battle-cry; war-trumpets. —*níti,* n. Strategy; war-policy. —*sajjá,* a. Livery of war; preparations of war; battle-equipment.

Ráṇá, *n.* Title of a Hindu prince or Raja; name of a Rajput tribe.

Rá<u>n</u>ḍ, *n.* A widow. —*ká sá<u>n</u>ḍ, n.* a mean despicable fellow; a spoilt child. —*ápá, n.* widow-hood.

Ra<u>n</u>ḍá, *n.* Barren; unfruitful or unproductive (as a tree); *n.* widower.

Ra<u>n</u>dá, *n.* A joiner's or carpenter's plane; a grater; a scraper.

Rándá, *a.* Driven out; expelled; forsaken; *n.* one who is expelled or rejected.

Rá<u>n</u>dh, *n.* Quarrel; dispute; contention; strife. —*kátná,* to settle a quarrel.

Rá<u>n</u>duá, *v.* To cook; to prepare food.

Rá<u>n</u>dhaniyá, *n.* A cook; a baker.

Ra<u>n</u>ḍwá/ Ra<u>n</u>ḍuá, *n.* A widower; [*proverbially*] a dirty old man; a randy, promiscuous male; cheap and worthless person; riff-raff.

Ra<u>n</u>g, *n.* Colour, Dye; complexion; paint; trump (in playcard games); grandeur; beauty; ways; influence; bloom; fashion; whim; kind; category; gaiety. —*ámez.* a. One who applies colour; a painter. —*bira<u>n</u>gá,* a. Colourful; variegated; multicoloured. —*karmi,* n. An actor; one practising stage-craft. —*ma<u>n</u>ch,* n. Stage; theatre. —*mahal,* n. A playhouse; an arena. —*bhúmi,* n. A place of amusement. —*uṛná/ utarná,* v. To fade; to loose facial lustre; to turn pale; to loose one's wits. —*ukhaṛná,* v. To loose influence; to fall on hard times. —*khulná,* v. For complexion to brighten up; to become clearer. —*chaṛhná,* v. To be influenced; to come into full bloom. —*chhoṛná,* v. For colour to run; to give up colour. —*jamná,* v. To attain a position of influence; to gain esteem; to come into full swing. —*jamáná,* v. To hold (others) under a spell/sway; to attain influence. —*dekhná,* v. To watch the ways of; to examine the state or condition of. —*nikharná,* v. For colour to brighten up; to become fairer; for one's essential self to emerge. —*par áná,* v. To assume true colour. —*phíká paṛná,* v. To fade out; to loose one's lustre; to loose influence. —*badalná,* v. To change colours; to shift opinions; to jump sides; to assume a different stance. —*me<u>n</u> ḍhalná,* v. To come under the influence of; to fall under the sway of. —*men bha<u>n</u>g karná,* To become a skeleton at a feast; to be a fly in the ointment; to mar a happy occasion; to be a wet blanket. —*racháná,* v. To celebrate with gay abandon.

Rá<u>n</u>gá, *n.* Pewter; tin.

Rangat, *v.* Colour; shade; plight; condition; relish; delight.

Ra<u>n</u>gílá, *a.* Gaudy; gay; showy; jovil; buxom; *n.* a man of pleasure.

Ra<u>n</u>gín, *a.* Variegated; coloured; ornamented; florid. —*i-'ibárat,* florid style.

Ra<u>n</u>gtará, *a.* Citron *(chakotra, sangtará).*

Rání, *n.* A queen or princess.

Ranivás, *n.* A palace where *Ránís* live; a seraglioof a prince; a harem; a *zenáná.*

Ra<u>n</u>j, *n.* Grief; sorrow; affliction. —*karná,* to grieve; to take offence; to be vexed.

Ra<u>n</u>jak, *n.* A pigment; dye stuff;

dyer. *Adj.* Recreative; entertaining.

Ranjídá, *a.* Sorrowful; sad; displeased; offended. *—khátir,* grieved.

Ranjit, *adj.* Coloured; dyed; delighted.

Ranjish, *n.* Animus; animosity; estrangement; ill-feeling.

Ranjúr, *a.* Sick; infirm; afflicted.

Rank, *a.* Avaricious; mean; pauper; wretched; *n.* a poor man; a miser.

Ráo, *n.* King; prince; chief; a title among Hindus.

Rapaṭná, *v.* To walk rapidly; to slide; to slip.

Raqbá, *n.* Area; grounds pertaining to a village or district. *—i-arází,* area of the land. *—makálá,* to calculate the area of.

Raqíb, *n.* A rival; a watcher.

Ráqíb, *n.* A competitor; an enemy.

Ráqim, *n.* A writer; a correspondent.

Raqímá, *n.* Epistle; letter; note. *—i-niyáz,* yours faithfully.

Raqíq, *a.* Thin; fine; flimsy; minute; subtile; unsubstantial.

Raqm, Raqam, *n.* Mark; figure; sign; notation of numerals; sum; total; amount; writing; kind; sort. *—karná,* to record; to enter.

Raqs, *n.* A dance; a ball. *—o-sarod,* dancing and music.

Rás, A. *n.* The head; head (of cattle); top; summit; vertex; end; cape; promontory. *rás-us-sartán,* the summer solstice. *rás-ul-jadí,* the winter solstice.

Rás, S. *n.* Sound, confused noise; din; festive amusement; speech; a chain. *—yátrá, n.* a festival in honour of Krishna and his dances with the Gopis held on the full moon of the month *Kártik.*

Ras, *n.* Sap; juice; extract; syrup; liquid; fluid; the best part of something; marrow; pith; taste; flavour. (idiomatically—) feeling; love; character. *—áyan,* alchemy; chemistry. *—pán,* v. partaking of *'Ras' agya,* a. One with the necessary aesthetic sense; a connoisseur. *—bhang,* v. Interruption in the aesthertic enjoyment of something. *—bhíná,* a. Full of flavour; steeped in sentiment. *—ráj,* a. The peak of experience; the erotic sentiment.

Rasá, *part.* and *a.* Arriving; attaining; skilful; clever; *(with compe.)* causing to arrive.

Rásabh, *a.* An ass.

Rasad, *n.* Import; revenue; income; grain; provision; ration;

share; store of grain (for an army. &c.).

Rasáí, *n.* Approach; access; contact; association.

Rasáil, *(Plur. of Risála, or Risálat).* Messages; letters; essays; books; writings.

Rasá<u>n</u>, *a.* Causing to arrive; conveying; bearing; *n.* one who conveys; bearer (used as last member of comps. *e.g., chitthí—,* letter-carrier; bearer of letters).

Rasan, *n.* Rope; cord. *—sáz, n.* a rope-maker.

Rasátal, *n.* The netherworld; hell; bottom of existence.

Ra'sha, *n.* A tremor; trembling; quivering; the shaking palsy.

Ráshan, *n.* Ration; essential supplies for any situation (War, or expedition, training course, etc.).

Ráshi, *n.* A sum; an amount; quantity; heap; (in astrology) sign of the zodiac. *—miláná,* v. To match, or compare the horoscopes (for weddings, partnerships etc.).

Rashíd, *a.* Taking or following a right way or course; orthodox; pious; *n.* one who takes or follows a right way; an orthodox or pious person.

Rashk, *n.* Malice; spite; envy; jealousy.

Rasíd, *n.* Acknowledgement of arrival or receipt; receipt; *(in comps.)* arrived; received.

Rasídá, *a.* Arrived; at hand; received; mature; ripe.

Rasik, *a.* A person with taste; one with aesthetic sense; (sometimes) frivolous; full of feeling or passion; witty; elegant; *n.* a sensualist; a libertine.

Rásiḳh, *a.* Firm; steady; standfast; established; learned; well-versed (in).

Rasm, *n. (Plur. Rasúm, q. v.).* sketch; plan; manner; custom; usage; receipt; law.

Rasílá, *a.* Full of juice; brimming with sap; enjoyable. *—pan,* n. Knack of being *Rasílá.*

Rasiyá, *a.* One who likes juicy talk; frivolous; also a proper name for a romantic folk-narrative sung with great gusto in the month of *Phágun* in many parts of Uttar Pradesh.

Rasoí, *n.* Cook-room; kitchen, cooking; dressed; food. *—yá,* a cook.

Rasná, *n.* Tongue; the bodily instrument that receives and interprets *Ras;* language.

Rasrá, Rassá, *n.* A cable; a thick rope.

Rassí, *n.* Rope; line; string; cord; reins.

Rást, *a.* Right; good; upright; honest; straight; seven; level; *adv.* actually; certainly; surely; truly.

Rástá, *n.* Road; way; path; street; lane; *(fig.)* way; manner. —*pakro,* go your way! be off!

Rastagár, *a.* Liberated; fręe; virtuous; generous.

Rashṭr, *n.* Nation; community; a mass of people with specific, land-based identity and a distinctive cultural mode. —*gán/ gít,* n. National anthem; patriotic song(s). —*dhwaj,* n. National flag; national ensign. —*chihn,* n. National emblem. —*bháshá,* n. Lingua franca. —*vád,* n. Nationalism. —*íya-karan,* v. Nationalisation. —*íyatá,* n. Nationality. —*prem/ bhakti,* n. Patriotism. *Andhí-ráshṭíyatá,* n. Xenophobia.

Rasúḳh, *n.* Access; influence; favourable relationship; credibility.

Rasúl, *n.* A messenger; an apostle. —*Al-láh,* the apostle Mohammad.

Rasúm, *n. (Plur. of Rasm, q.v.).* Customs; usages.

Rát, Rátri, *n.* Night; Dark period. —*ká rájá,* n. King of the night; owl. —*din,* adv. Day and Night; at all times; for ever; always. —*kí ráni,* n. A fragrant flower that blooms at night, also known as *Rajní-gandhá.* —*ánkhon men káṭná.* adv. To saty wide awake with worry; being unable to sleep out of concern. —*ḍhalná,* v. A substantial part of night to pass. —*aur din ká antar,* prov. Difference between day and night; a vast difference.

Ratálú, *n.* A kind of yam.

Ratn, Ratan, Ratná, *n.* Jewel; gem; pearl; the pupil of the eye. —*jarit,* studded with jewels, *nau*—, nine eminent men in the court of Vikramaditya.

Rataundhí, *n.* Partial blindness; night blindness.

Ratb, *a.* Moist; humid; succulent; juicy; soft; verdant.

Rath, *a.* Carriage; vehicle; war-chariot; the castle (in chess). —*ván,* —*bán, n.* carriage-driver; coachman. —*yátrá, n. (Lit.)* car-procession; festive procession of an idol on a car (esp. the procession of the car of Jagannáth).

Rathí, *n.* A bier.

Rati, *n.* Love; enjoyment; sexual pleasure; oestrus; copulation; proper name of the wife of *Kámadev,* the god of desire; (hence) a very pretty and desirable woman. —*unmád,* n. Erotomania. —*kriyá,* n. Copulation; sexual intercourse. —*janya rog,* n. Diseases born of sexual intercourse. —*dán,* v. Allowing Sexual intercourse to take place; to be seduced. —*priya,* a. Erotic; sexy. —*bandh,* n. Erotic posture(s). —*bháv,* a. Amorous sentiment; desire. —*ras,* n. The sexual relish. —*ranjan,* n. Coital enjoyment; sexual dalliance. —*shástra,* n. The science of love-making; erotology; sexology.

Rátib, *n.* Pension; salary; allowance; daily allowance of food; ration; allowance of food for dogs or elephants. —*khor, n.* a pensioner.

Rátrí, *n.* [See **Rát**].

Rattí, *n.* The seed of *Abrus precatorine,* used as a weight; a weight equal to eight barleycorns. —*bhar,* of the weight of a rattí; *(fig.)* very little.

Raúf, *a.* Kind; merciful; for-giving; benign.

Raugan, *a.* Fat; grease; oil; butter; clarified butter or *ghí;* varnish; smoothness.

Rannaq, *n.* Lustre; brightness; beauty; flourishing state or condition; *(Met.)* order; symmetry.

Raundná, *v.* To trample on; to tread down; to ride over; to lay waste; to destroy.

Raupya, *adj.* Made of silver; silver-coloured; silver-coinage.

Raushan, Roshan, *n.* Light; illuminated; splendid; luminous; clear; evident.

Raushní, *n.* Light; brightness; splendour; brightness or clearness (of vision); eyesight.

Rauzá, *n.* A beautiful; garden; a mausoleum.

Rávaṇ, *n.* A proper noun, a main character in the epic *Rámáyaṇa,* the chief demonic adversary of the hero, Lord Rám who defeats and slays him in battle on account of having abducted *Sítá.*

Raváyat/ Raváyát, *n.* Tradition(s); narrative; narration; legend; story.

Ravish, *n.* Walk; motion; gait; practice; custom; rule; law; mode; way; a garden-walk; an avenue.

Rawá, *n.* A grain (of sand, dust, &c.); a granule (of precious metal, congealed honey, &c.); grit (as in meal, &c.); a particle (of gold or silver); filings (of precious metals); a piece; a little.

Rawaiyá, *n.* Custom; rule; fashion.

Rawáj, Riváj, *n.* Custom; fashion; rule; prevalance; sale; *a.* current; customary.

Rawán, *a.* Going; running,

flowing; active; dexterous; *n.* text; reading; *adv.* fluently; quickly; briskly.

Rawáná, *a.* Departed; despatched; sent; *n.* a pass; permit.

Ráz, *n.* Secret; mystery. *—dár,* a confidant; a trustee.

Razá, *n.* Will; pleasure; consent; acquiescence; permission.

Razáí, *n.* Quilt; a coloured coverlet.

Rází, *a.* Contended; satisfied; agreed; willing. *—náma,* acknowledgement of the settlement or compromise of a case.

Ráziq, *n.* Cherisher; sustainer; a title of the Deity.

Razm, *n.* War; battle; combat; encounter. *—gáh,* a battlefield.

Razzáq, *n.* The supplier of the mean of subsistence; the Giver of daily bread; Providence (an epithet applied only to God). *—í, n.* Providence; an attribute of God.

Re, *intj.* O ! Hullo ! Alas ! Bravo. (*Re* is used for males, and *rí* for females).

Reg, *n.* Sand. *—e-rawáṉ. —rawán n.* quicksand. *—zár, —istán, n.* sandy desert.

Rehná, *v.* To mark with stripes or lines; to streak.

Rehṛí, *n.* Sandy or barren soil.

Rekh, Rekhá, *n.* Line; streak; stripe; row; series; furrow; fate; destiny; (in *Astron.*) the first meridian *—uthán, a.* marked with lines; streaked; striped. *—ganit, n.* geometry.

Reḳhtá, *a.* Poured out; scattered; mixed; *n. (Lit.)* the mixed dialect; the Hindustaní or Urdú language; a Hindustaní ode; mortar; plaster.

Rel, *n.* Rail*way*; train; abundance of people; continuous flow of people in a queue. *—pel,* n. Crowd; people rubbing shoulders.

Relá, *n.* A row or string of animals; a torrent; a flood shove.

Relná, *n.* To push; to shove; to hustle; to jostle.

Renḍ, Renḍí, Renṛ, *n.* Palma Christi or castor oil; *n.* plant.

Reṉgná, Riṉgná, Ríṉgná, *v.* To crecp; to crawl; to move on all fours (as a child); to plod.

Reṉ́gṭá, *n.* A young ass; the foal of an ass.

Reṉk, *n.* Braying of an ass

Reṉkná, *v.* To bray (as an ass); to low or bellow (as a buffalo, &c.).

Reṉ-reṉ, *n.* Crying or whimpering of a child; scraping or discordant sound (of a stringed instrument).

Reṉṛhú, *n.* Vehicle; carriage; cart.

Reṇu, *n.* Dust; sand; powder; atom; grit; pollen (of flowers).

Resh, *n.* Wound; sore; scar; pus; matter.

Reshá, *n.* Fibre; filament; nerve; stringiness (of fruit).

Resham, *n.* Silk.

Ret, *n.* Sand; filings. —*íla,* sandy; gritty; gravelly. —*ná,* to file; to rasp.

Rez, *n.* Pouring; scattering; shedding, *ashk*—, shedding tears. *rang*—, a painter.

Rezá, *n.* A minute fragment; atom; bit; piece. —*rez'a karná,* to break into pieces; to shatter.

Rezagí, Rezgárí, *n.* A scrap; morsel; piece; small coin.

Ri'áyá, *n.* Dependant; tenant; subjects; peasantry.

Ri'áyat, *n.* Protecting; kindness; concession; favour; pity; clemency; respect. —*í, a.* favoured; privileged; *n.* a protege; a privileged person.

Ríchh, *n.* A bear.

Rifáh, *n.* Ease; comfort; affluence.

Rifáqat, Rafáqat, *n.* Companionship; society; friendship.

Rig-Véda, *n.* The Rig-Veda, the first and most important of the four Vedas (so called because it consists chiefly of hymns or sacred verses in praise of the Hindu deities).

Ríh, *n.* Wind; air; flatulence; odour; exhalation. —*ká-dard, n.* rheumatism.

Ríhá, *a.* Released; freed; liberated; discharged.

Riháí, *n.* Liberation; release; deliverance; discharge; acquittal.

Rihlat, *n.* Removal; departure; death; decease; expiry.

Rijháná, *v.* To please; to charm; to excite; to annoy; to perplex.

Ríjhná, *v.* To be delighted; to be pleased; to be gratified.

Rikáb, *n.* A stirrup; train; retinue; goblet; bowl; plate.

Rikh, Rikhi, *n.* A saint; a sage.

Riṇ, *n.* Obligation; debt.

Rind, *n.* A sceptic; a free-thinker; debauchee; rogue; drunkard.

Ripu, *n.* An enemy; an adversary; an antagonist; a foe. —*tá,* enmity; antagonism; hostility.

Riqqat, *n.* Thinness; leanness; pity; compassion; affection.

Ríṛh, *n.* The backbone; spine; vertebra.

Ris, *n.* Anger; passion; vexation; annoyance.

Risálá, *n.* Message; mission; tract; short treatise; essay; book; a troop or squadron of eavalry. *risaldár, n.* commander of a troop of horse or squadron of cavalry.

Risálat, *n.* Mission; divine mission; apostleship.

Rishtá, *n.* Thread; string; series; relation; kinship; affinity. *—dár,* kinsman; relative.

Rishwat, *n.* Bribe. *—khorí,* v. To give or take bribe. *—bází,* n. The system of bribery.

Risná, *v.* To leak; to ooze; to drip; to fall in drops; to be vexed; to be angry.

Rít, Ríti, *n.* Method; manner; mode; custom; way; practice; vogue; tradition; style. *—baddh,* a. stylised; tied down to tradition. *—mukt,* Free from tradition; destylised. *—riváj,* n. customs; traditions; norms. *—kál,* n. A period in literary history, equal to classicial period in English literature, when poetry was highly ornate, amorous and stylised and the subject often was either moral sermons or the beauty of the loved ones and classification of human (particularly female) body. *—kávya,* a. The aforementioned type of poetry.

Ritu, *n.* Season; time of the year; a segment in the weather cycle.

Ritu-chakra, *n.* The weather cycle; the cycle of seasons; rotation of seasons.

Rituráj, *n.* [literally] The king of seasons; spring season; also a nickname for *Káma,* the Indian equivalent of the Western Cupid.

Riváj/ Riváz/ Riwáj, [See *Rawáj*].

Riyá, *n.* Acting ostentatiously; affectation; pretence; hypocrisy; dissimulation.

Riyáh, *n.* Flatulence; wind in the bowels.

Riyásat, *n.* Government; dominion; rule; nobility. *—e-jam-húri, n.* a republic; a democracy.

Riyáz, *n.* Practice; rehearsal; preparaton.

Riyáz, *n.* Rehearsal; practice (in music and drama); preparation.

Riyázat, *n.* Exercise; devotion; religious exercise; austerity; abstinence, *—í, n.* an industrious person; a devotee; an ascetic.

Riyází, *n.* Mathematics; the exact; sciences. *—dán, n.* A mathematician.

Rizálá, *a.* Low; mean; contemptible; *n.* the refuse or dregs of anything; a mean, low, or base person.

Rizq, *n.* Means of subsistence; food; sustenance; allowance; pension.

Rizáwán, *a.* Paradise; the treasurer, keeper, or guardian of Paradise; pleasure; content.

Roán, Ruán, *n.* Hair of the body; wool; fur; bristle; down.

Rob, *a.* Sweeping *(used as last member of comps.) khák—, n.* sweeper.

Robáh, Rúbáh, *n.* A fox. *—bázi, n.* foxiness; artfulness; craftiness; deceit.

Rog, *n.* Disease; an illness; an ailment; a sickness; malady; affliction. *—kárak/kárí,* a. Infectious; sickening. *—grast,* a. Ailing; diseased; sick. *—náshak,* a. Cure; curative. *—nirodhak,* a. Something that prevents disease; prophylactic. *—bhram,* n. Hypochondria. *—lakshaṇ,* n. Symptom(s). *—váhak,* a. Disease-carrier(s). *—pálná,* v. To nurthure a disease; to adopt an unhealthy habit.

Rogí, *n.* An invalid; a sick person; *a.* sick; unwell; ailing. *—sogí, a.* sick and sorry.

Rohíṇí, Rauhiṇi, Rohṇí *n.* A red cow; a cow; the name of the fourth of the nine lunar mansions.

Rohitá, *a.* Red. *n.* the red colour; a kind of deer; a species of fish, *cyprenus,* rohita commonly called *rohí,* or rohú.

Rohú, Rohí, *n.* A species of fish; *—cyrinus rohita.*

Roídagí, *n.* Growth (of plants); production; vegetation.

Rok, *n.* Restraint; hindrance; let; prohibition; bar; support; screen; shelter. *—thánb, n.* check; restraint; expedient; patching up (of a quarrel, &c.) *—tok, n.* let and hindrance; obstacle; challenge, (of a sentry).

Rokaṛ, Rokṛá, *n.* Cash; ready money; *—bahí, n.* cash-book. *—bikri, n.* cash sale or transaction.

Rokaṛí, *n.* Cashier; treasurer; banker.

Rokná, *v.* To stop; to check; to arrest; to challenge (as a sentry); to prohibit; to with hold; to detain; to avert; to protect; to besiege; to bind (as by contract).

Rolná, *n.* To roll; to plane; to smooth; to rub; to skin; to select; to rake up.

Rom, *n.* Hair; down; fur; wool; bristle; moss. *—kúp, n.* a pore of the skin.

Roná, *n.* To cry; to weep; to wail; to lament; to complain; to be sad or displeased.

Ront, Raunt, *n.* Wrangling; disputing; denying; deceit; trickery.

Rontná, Rauntná, *v.* To resist; to dispute; to deny; to deceive.

Ropá, *n.* A sapling.

Ropná, *v.* To plant; to sow; to raise; to undertake; to hinder; to defend.

Ropná, *n.* Marriage procession; betrothal.

Roshan, Raushan, *a.* Light; bright; luminous; splendid; clear; manifest. *—dán, n.* an opening to admit light; a skylight. *—'aql, n.* of enlightened mind.

Roshnáí, *n.* Light; brightness, luminance; splendour; ink.

Roshní, Raushní, *n.* Light; splendour; brightness or clearness of vision; eyesight.

Rosná, *v.* To be angry; to be vexed or irritated; to be offended.

Roṭí, *n.* Bread; meals; food; livelihood. *—kaprá aur makán,* prov. Essentials of life; means of subsistence. *—kamáná,* v. To earn a living. *—ká sawál.* prov. The problem of livelihood. *—dál,* n. simple basic food, nothing pretentious. *—dál chaláná,* v. To make two ends meet; to manage one's livelihood somehow. *—ke liye mohtáj honá,* prov. To fall short of two square meals. *—iyán torná,* v. To be out of work and idle.

Royín, *n.* Brass.

Roz, *n.* A day; daily wages; *adv.* daily; a day; per diem; every day. *—e-jazá, n.* the Judgment Day. *—e-qiyámat, n.* the day of resurrection. *—marra, a.* daily; customary; idiomatic; *adv.* daily; always; *n.* daily conversation; idiom; daily food.

Rozá, *n.* Fasting; a fast; Lent. *—torná, v.* to break a fast be fore the proper time. *—khor, n.* one who avoids observing a fast. *—kholná,* to break a fast; to partake of food after fasting.

Rozgár, *n.* Service employment; livelihood; the world; fortune; age; season. *—í, a.* serving; earning; *n.* a servant; one who earns a livelihood.

Rozí, *n.* Daily food; sustenance; means of subsistence. *—deh, n.* the Giver of daily bread (God).

Rú, *n.* Face; countenance; frontage. *—posh,* a. veiled; hidden; absconder. *—ba-rú,* a. Face-to-face; in public. *—riyáyat,* n. Consideration; concession; leniency.

Rub', *n.* A fourth part; a quarter. *—e-maskúr, n.* the inhabited quarter (portion) of the earth.

Rubá'í, *n.* A quatrain; stanza of four lines.

Ruchí, *n.* Light; lustre; beauty; liking; taste; desire; passion; desire of, or pleasure obtained from eating.

Ruchná, *v.* To be tasty or delicious to the palate; to feel appetite (for) to desire; to excite a desire or craving (in).

Rúd, *n.* Stream; river; torrent; string of a musical instrument.

Rúdhi, *n.* Convention; tradition; superstitiion; blind habit. —*vád,* n. Conventionalism. —*vádí,* a. Superstitious. —*gat,* a. Conventional; stereotypical. —*grast,* a. Convention-bound.

Rudhir, *n.* Blood.

Rúh, *n.* The soul; spirit; life; the breath of life; inspiration; divine revelation. —*ul-quds,* the angel Gabriel; (among Christians) the Holy Spirit.

Rúhání, *a.* Having a soul or spirit; spiritual *n.* spiritual being; an angel; a jinn.

Rúí, *n.* Cotton. —*dhunná,* to card cotton.

Rujú', *n.* Return; inclination; tendency; reference; appeal; bringing (into court; as a suit).

Rukáo, *n.* Hindrance; prohibition; prevention; impediment.

Rukh, *n.* Face; countenance; cheek; aspect; direction. —*pherná, v.* to become displeased.

Rukh, *n.* A tree.

Rukh, *n.* Outward part; corner; support; prop; pillar; aid; a noble; grandee.

Rúkhá, *a.* Dry; plain (as; bread, food, &c.); simple; insipid; rough; unkind; cross; cool; indifferent. —*súkhá,* plain or simple food; humble fare.

Rukhání, *n.* An auger; a chisel.

Rukhsat, *n.* Leave; permission to depart; leave of absence; dismissal, —*honá,* to depart; to bid adieu (to).

Rukná, *v.* To stop; to rest to falter (in speech); to be closed; to be prohibited.

Rukú, *n.* Bowing the head in humility and reference, as in prayer; reverential prostration.

Rumál, Rúmál, *n.* Handkerchief.

Rungṭá, Rongṭá, *n.* Hair of the body; wool.

Rúṇhná, *v.* To take offence; to have a misunderstanding (with a friend); to be offended.

Rúp, *n.* Beauty; shape; form; appearance; (good) looks; image; mould. —*sajjá,* v. Make-up; formation; decoration.

Rúpá, *n.* Silver. —*ahrá/ahlá,* a. Silver-coloured; silvery.

Rúpak, *n.* Metaphor; an allegory; a play; a feature; a literary instrument for enhancing the impact of speech or writing.

Rúpántar, *adv.* Metamorphosis; transformation; modification; adaptation.

Rupayá, *n.* (iterally) rupee; money; wealth. —*wálá,* a. Opulent; prosperous; wealthy; rich, etc. —*uṛáná,* adv. To squander; to spend in an extravagant manner, (one's wealth). —*aenṭhaná,* v. To extort; to fleece. —*joṛná,* v. To accumulate wealth; to save up one's earnings. —*márná,* v. To embezzle; to misappropriate; to fail to pay one's dues. *Rupaye kí garmí honá,* Prov. To be purse-proud; to have a swollen head on account of one's wealth.

Ruqqá, *n.* A bit; piece; a scrap (of paper, &c.); a note; an epistle; a receipt.

Rúsí, *n.* Scruff; dandruff, Russian.

Rust, *n.* Growth; *a.* strong; courageous; valiant.

Rustá, *a.* Grown; spring up (vegetation).

Rustgár, *n.* Deliverer; a saviour. —*i.* deliverance; salvation; bounty; generosity.

Rustam, *n.* The son of Zál, the most renowned of Persian heroes; *(fig.)* a hero; a brave man.

Rusúkh, *n.* [See *Rasúkh*].

Rusúm, *n. (Plur. of Rasm).* Customs; usages; established fees; dues; taxes. —*i-sarkár,* stamp duties *(Plur. Rusúmát).*

Ruswá, *a.* Disgraced; dishonoured; infamous *(rúsiyáh)* —*i-'álam,* of world-wide infamy. —*i,* irnominy; infamy.

Rutbá, *n.* A step; stair; honor; rank; degree; dignity. —*dár,* of high rank or station; distinguished; eminent. —*kam*—. of low rank.

Rúṭhá, *n.* Offended; displeased. —*rúthí,* mutual misunderstanding.

Rúthná, *v.* To sulk; to be sulky; to be displeased; to get upset.

Rutúbat, *n.* Moisture; humidity; freshness; dampness; saliva.

S, s, stands for (स) in Hindi and all three sound of (س and ص) in Urdu. It is also used with addition of 'h' to express (श) sound in Hindi and (ش) in Urdu.

Sa, *a.* A prefix signifying, with; together with; along with; having; possession; accompanied by; (it is combined) with nouns to form adjectives and adverbs).

Sá, *a.* Like (A suffix added to a substantive to denote similitude) as; *kálá—,* blackish. *larká—,* boyish; *tujh—,* like three.

Sá, *a.* Very; intensely (it is annexed to adjectives, and forms an intensive significant); as; *bahut sá,* a great deal of a great many, &c.

Sa'ádat, *n.* Good fortune; happiness; felicity. *—mand,* happy; of goodness.

Sab, *a.* All; whole; entire; total; every. *—koí,* everybody; every thing.

Sabá, *n.* Gentle breeze; morning breeze; easterly wind; a zephyr.

Sabab, *n.* Cause; reason; motive; incentive; means; instrument.

Sabad, [See *Shabda*].

Sabáhat, *n.* Beauty; grace; comeliness; elegance.

Sában,/Sábun, *n.* Soap.

Sabaq, *n.* Lesson; lecture; reading.

Sabar, Sabr, *n.* Patience; tolerance; forbearance.

Sabar, *n.* A. large species of stag; a kind of elk; chamois leather.

Sabát, *n.* Stability; durability; firmness; validity.

Sabbábá, *n.* The forefinger; the index finger.

Sabbág, *n.* A dyer.

Saberá, Sawerá, *n.* Morning; the dawn; daybreak.

Sabhá, *n.* Assembly; meeting; gathering. *—pati,* Apresident; a chair-person.

Sabíh, *a.* Beautiful; lovely; graceful.

Sabíl, *n.* A roadside stall, offering cold drinks, sherbat or just cold drinking water to travellers at festive occasions in hot countries of the Middle East and the Indian subcontinent. *—karná,* v. To arrange to raise money by begging, or borrowing. [Also See *Chhabíl*].

Sábiq, *a.* Former; preceding; previous; prior; foregoings; aforesaid; *n.* past time. *—dastúr,* as before; as usual.

Sábiqá, *a.* Past; an ancient rite or

custom; pre-eminence; superiority; intimacy; close friendship; transaction. *—paṛná, v.* to become acquainted with.

Sábir, *a.* Patient; long-suffering; enduring.

Sábit, *a.* Lasting; enduring; permanent; steady; established; real; proper; proved. *—rahná, v.* to adhere firmly (to).

Sabíya, *n.* A daughter.

Sabqat, *n.* Preceding; surpassing; excelling; precedence; superiority. *—lejáná, v.* to bear away the palm (from); to surpass.

Sabr, *n.* patience; self-restraint; endurance; suffering. *—paṛná, v.* to fall under a curse. *be—,* impatient; fidgety; avaricious.

Sabt, *n.* Firmness; permanency; stability. *—karná, v.* to inscribe; to write.

Sabt, *n.* Sunday; the Sabbath Day; the Lord's Day.

Sábú, *n.* Sago.

Sabúb, *n.* A morning draught; wine which is drunk in the morning.

Sabúrí, *n.* Patience.

Sabz, *a.* Green; verdant; fresh; unripe; raw. *—baḳhtí, n.* prosperity. *—qadam,* unfortunate; ill-omened.

Sabzá, *n.* Verdure; herbage; an iron-grey horse; sweet basil; the hemp plant. *—zar,* meadow; lawn.

Sabzí, *n.* Verdure; pot-herbs; vegetables. *—farosh,* a greengrocer. *—mandí,* vegetable market.

Sach, *n.* Truth; reality; genuineness. *a.* True; real; genuine. *adv.* Truthfully; actually; indeed; really.

Sachchá, *a.* True; genuine; pure; unalloyed; honest. *qaul ká—,* faithful to one's word.

Sachcháí, *n.* Truth; honesty.

Sachet, *a.* Conscious; attentive; cautious; watchful. *—rahná,* to be on one's guard.

Sachiv, *n.* Secretary; assistant; aide. *—álay,* n. Secretariat; an office where secretaries are based; (also) the establishment, or institutional set up that handles secretaries. Nijí—, Private secretary.

Sad, *a.* One hundred. *—barg,* Indian marigold *(gendá). —pá,* a centepede.

Sa'd, *n.* Prosperity; felicity; auspiciousness.

Sadá, *adv.* Always; perpetually; continually. *—bahár,* evergreen. *—guláb,* the China rose. *—sarvadá, a.* eternal; for ever and ever.

Sadá, *n.* Sound; tone; echo; voice; noise.

Sádá, *a.* Blank; plain; white; simple; sincere. *—lauh,* a simpleton. *sádi wazah,* a plain fashion. *—gí,* simplicity.

Sadáqat, *n.* Sincerity; loyalty; fidelity; truth.

Sadárat, *n.* Premiership.

Sadd, *n.* Obstruction; obstacle; hindrance; impediment; a ditch. *—i-ráh,* a stumbling block.

Sad'há, *a.* Hundreds; many; multitudes great many.

Sa-dhanyavád, *adv.* Gratefully; with gratitude with thanks.

Sádháraṇ, *a.* Common; usual; lawful; *adv.* commonly; generally; universally.

Sádhú, *a.* Pious; devout; virtuous; holy. *n.* a devotee; an ascetic.

Sadí, *n.* Century, *fí sadí,* per cent.

Sádiq, *a.* True; sincere; just; faithful. *—áná,* to be verified; to prove to be true. *—ul-qaul,* true to one's word.

Sádir, *a.* Issuing; emanating (from); produced; derived. *—honá,* to be issued or passed (as an order); to occur; to happen.

Sadmá, *n.* Shock; blow; concussion; collision; mis-fortune; accident. *—jismání,* physical violence. *—utháná, v.* to experience a shock; to meet with misfortune.

Sadqá, *n.* Alms; gift; a propitiatory offering or sacrifice; devotion; kindness; a person or thing devoted or sacrificed.

Sadr, Sadar, *n.* Chest; breast; the upper-most part or end (of anything); seat of Government; headquarter of a district; military cantonment; exaltation; *adv.* at the top; above.

Sadr, Sadar, *a.* Chief; top man (or woman); highest official in any part of administration/ organisation. *i-riyásat,* n. Governor; chief of state. *—i-adálat,* n. Chief; judicial officer, &c.

Sadrí, *n.* Waist-coat; jacket.

Sadrishṭ, *a.* Like (something or someone); similar to; resembling.

Sadrishṭi, *n.* the state of, or quality of likeness; similarity; resemblance.

Sadrishya, *a.* Looking like; visually similar; resembling.

Saf, Saff, *n.* Line; rank; row; series; order. *—árái,* marshalling of troops in battle array. *—i-jang,* a battlefield. *—dar,* a valiant warrior.

Sáf, *a.* Pure; clean; clean or unclouded (sky); simple; frank; innocent; distinct; thorough; complete; smooth; exact.—*dil,* open-hearted; candid; pure in mind. —*nikal jáná,* to get off scot-free.

Sáfá, *n.* A turban.

Sáfá, *n.* A fine piece of cotton cloth, mostly used as a turban, but also adapted to other uses when needed, i.e. towel, a floor-spread, or even as a container of things to be carried on one's person.

Safá, *n.* Clearness; polish; brightness; cleanness; purity; happiness; *a.* pure; clean; clear. —*chaṭkarná,* to shave clean; to swipe.

Safáí, *n.* Clearness; cleanness; purity; candour; innocence; settlement of account; destruction; ruin; conservancy. —*náma,* a deed of release given by the defendant in a suit at law.

Safaid, Sufaid, Sufed, *a.* White; clean; blank; a person dressed in white; a well-to-do person.

Safaidá, *n.* White lead; whiting chalk.

Safaidí, *n.* Whiteness; whiting white-wash; white of an egg; morning light; dawn.

Safar, *n.* Journey; travel; voyage; compaign; tour; expedition. —*námá,* description of a journey. *bahrí*—sea-voyage.

Saffák, *n.* Cruel; merciless; murderous, *n.* a murderer; an assassin.

Sáfí, *a.* Pure; just; pious; righteous.

Sáfí, P. *n.* A strainer; a filter; a duster.

Safír, *n.* Messenger; envoy; ambassador; arbitrator.

Safrá, *n.* Bile; gall; yellow colour. —*wí,* bilious.

Ság, *n.* A dish cooked from green leaves of edible plants (like spinach, mustard, etc.) and used as accompaniment of the staple food, like bread; any simple dish cooked for accompaniment of main food item. —*pát,* n. Green edible foliage. —*bhájí/ sabzí,* n. Vegetables, salads etc.

Sagá, *a.* Born of the same parents; own; kin; *n.* blood relation; relative.

Sagar, *a.* Poisonous.

Ságar, *n.* Ocean; sea; a kind of deer.

Sagam, *n.* Teak tree; teak wood.

Sarír, *a.* Small; little; minor. —*sin,* *a.* of tender age; young; *n.* child.

Ságu, *n.* A species of palm tree. —*dáná,* sago.

Sagun, *n.* [See *'Shagun'*].

Saháb, *n.* Clouds.

Sahái, Saháetá, Saháyatá, *n.* Help; assistance; aid. [also-] helper; assistant; labour-force.

Saháíf, *n. (Plur. of Sahifa).* Pages; leaves; books; volumes.

Sahaj, *a.* Easy; simple.

Sahálag, *n.* (Among Hindus); the marriage season.

Sahamná, Saham jáná, *v.* To be frightened; dread; to fear; to be in terror.

Sahan, *a.* Bearing; enduring. *n.* Endurance; patience; tolerance; forbearance. *—karná,* v. To endure; to tolerate, etc. *—shíl,* a. A person of patient nature; one with the quality of forbearance.

Sahná, Sahan karná, Sahan kar jáná, *v.* To bear; to tolerate; to endure; to suffer; to live with.

Sahar, Sahr, *n.* Morning; dawn; daybreak; early part of the day.

Sahará, n. Desert; waste; wilderness. *—nawardí,* traversing; or wandering in; a desert.

Sahárá, *n.* Rid; help; assistance; succour; dependance; concord.

Sahargáhí, *n.* Food eaten by Mohamedans before daybreak during Ramzán.

Sa-harsh, *adv.* With pleasure; happily.

Sáhas, *n.* Valour; courage; bravery.

Sahasra, *a.* Thousand.

Sahasrábdi, *n.* Millennium, a period of a thousand years

Sahbat, Sohbat, Suhbat, *n.* Company; companionship; society; social environment; social circle.

Sahelí, *n.* A woman's female companion; a handmaid.

Sahí, *n.* Signatures. *a.* Correct; right; proper. *—karná,* v. To append ones' signatures (to a document, validating the same). *—karár dená,* v. To declare (something, some statement) to be right, correct, proper. [*Also see* **Sahíh**]..

Sáhí, *n.* A porcupine.

Sáhib, *n. (Plur. Sáhibán).* Companion; comrade; lord; owner; a European gentleman; a title of courtesy, corresponding to Master; Mr. Sir; *a.* possessed of, or endowed with *(used in comps.),* as:*—i-takht,* possessor of a throne; a king or emperor. *—i-haisiyat,* a man of property or substance. *—záda,* a son; a young gentleman. *—salámat,* salutation; compliments. *—i-nasíb,* lucky; fortunate; *n.* a fortunate man.

Sáhibá, *n. (Fem. of Sáhib).* Lady; mistress; dame; wife.

Sájobí, *n.* Rule; sway; domination; influence.

Sahífá, *n.* A book; a letter; a leaf; a page.

Sahíh, *a.* Sound; valid; genuine; just; accurate; authentic; *n.* signature; sign or mark. *sahíh sálim,* safe and sound; healthy. —*ul-'aql, a.* of sound mind.

Sáhil, *n.* Bank (of a river or stream); sea-shore; beach; coast; (metaphorically) destination

Sáhir, *n.* Enchanter; magician; conjuror; sorcerer; wizard.

Sahl, *a.* Easy; simple; facile; soft. —*karná,* to make easy; to simplify.

Sahláná, v. To rub gently; to caress; to tickle; to titillate.

Sahmat, *adj.* Consenting; agreeable; of synchronous views; one who concurs.

Sahmati, *n.* Consent; approval; simila opinion; synchronised views; agreement concurrence.

Sahodar, *n.* Born of one mother.

Sáhú, *a.* Upright; honest; respectable; a merchant; a banker. —*kár,* a banker; a wealthy person; a trader *(maháján).*

Sái, *n.* Earnest money; pledge; retainer;

Sa'íd, *a.* Auspicious; lucky; fortunate.

Saif, *n.* A sword.

Saikṛá, *a.* One hundred; *fí—,* per cent.

Sail, *n.* Flowing a current; a flood.

Sailáb, *n.* Flood; torrent; deluge; inundation.

Sailání, *a.* Fond of walking or going about for amusement; strolling; wandering.

Sain, *n.* A signal; hint; wink. —*saini,* mutual signalling; mutual winks.

Sainik, *n.* Soldier; trooper; a fighting man/woman.

Sai<u>n</u>tná, *v.* To take care of; to lay by.

Sáiqá, *n.* Thunderbolt; lightning.

Saiqal, *n.* Polish; furbishing. —*gar,* an armourer; a polisher; a furbisher (of arms or tools) *(sikligar).*

Sair, *n.* Walk; excursion; recreation; amusement. —*gáh* place of recreation.

Sajan, Sájan, Sajná, *n.* Husband; lover; darling; dear one.

Sáís, *n.* Groom; horsekeeper.

Saiyád, *n.* A fowler; a hunter.

Saiyad, *n.* A lord; a prince.

Saiyáh, *n.* An itinerant; a pilgrim; a travelled man.

Sajáná, *v.* To adorn; to decorate; to prepare.

Sajdá, Sijdá, *n.* Salutation; bowing before some one in admiration. —*karná,* v. To salute; to bow before some one in admiration.

Sájhá, *n.* Partnership. *sájhe men,* jointly.

Sajílá, *a.* Well-shaped; graceful; handsome; decorated.

Sajjád, *n.* One who bows in adoration, &c.

Sajjádá, *n.* Place of adoration; mosque. —*nashin,* any religious ascetic of the Mahammadan faith.

Sajjan, *a.* [a combination of *Sanskrit* words; Sad=good + jan=person] A good person; a gentleman; an honest person; a benevolent person; a virtuous one.

Saka, Shaka, *n.* Hindu era; an epoch (called *Samvat,* on the lines of Christian era of the Roman calander).

Sakal, *a.* All; whole; entire.

Sakár, *n.* Acceptance (of a *hundi,* or bill); endorsement (of a bill noting acceptance).

Sákár, *adj.* One with a shape; one with a form; one who is visible.

Sakat, Saktí, *n.* [See *Shakti*].

Sákh, *n.* Credibility; goodwill; reputation; trust. —*dúbaná,* v. To ruinone's credibility/ goodwill. —*jamná,* v. To establish one's goodwill

Sakhá, *n.* Friend; associate; companion. *(Fem. Sakhí).*

Sakháwat, *n.* Generosity; liberality; munificence.

Sakhí, *a.* Liberal; bountiful; generous.

Sakht, *a.* Hard; harsh; strong; stiff; strict; rigorous (imprisonment); serious (illness); rude (words); dire (need). —*ján,* a. Hardy; thick-skinned; tough. —*Mízáj,* a. Hot-headed; short-tempered. —*sust kahná,* v. To rebuke; to give a dressing down.

Sákin, *a.* Tranquil; quiet; calm; quiescent (letter); an inhabitant; a resident.

Sákit, *a.* Silent; quiet; at rest.

Sakná, *v.* To be able.

Saknát, *n. (Plur. Sakanát).* A rest; a pause.

Sa-kop, *adv.* With anger; angrily.

Sakrá, Sankrá, *a.* Narrow; congested; tight (like a passage, a bazaar, etc. —*í,* a. Feminine version/ or smaller version of the same. (like a lane; a street; etc.

Sákshát, *a.* In sight; in the presence (of); before; manifestly; evidently; visible; apparent; exact; identical; *n.* meeting; interview.

Sákshí, *n.* Testimony; evidence; attestation; witness; observer; eye-witness. *—dená,* to bear witness; to produce the evidence of witnesses.

Sakúnat, *n.* Residing; dwelling; *n.* residence; abode.

Sál, *n.* The soul tree; *shorea robusta,* and its wood; the plane-tree; a wall.

Sál, *n.* A thorn; *(fig.)* pain; trouble; bore; a hole made by dividing a pin or peg into the ground, &c.

Sál, *n.* A year. *—ba-sál, adv.* annually. *—hásil, n.* annual produce. *—e-hisábí, n.* official or accounting year.

Sálá, *n.* Wife's brother; brother-in-law (often used as a term of abuse).

Salábat, *n.* Firmness; hardness; strength.

Salaf, *n.* The past; past times.

Sálagrám, Sáligrám, *n.* A species of black stone, found in the Gundak (Kathmandu, Nepal) and worshipped as an emblem of shiva.

Saláh, *n.* Advice; counsel; honesty; virtue.

Saláhiyat, *n.* Virtue; goodness; chastity; integrity.

Saláḳh, *n.* An iron bar; an ingot of gold or silver; a line, a streak.

Salám, *n.* Salutation; greeting; compliments; farewell; good-bye; safety; peace. *—'alai-kum,* peace be with you; good morning to you. *—lená,* to accept and return a salutation. *—o-payám, n.* salutations and kind messages.

Salámat, *n.* Safety; tranquillity; peace; liberty; health; *a.* safe; sound; healthy; *adv.* safely; securely. *—rahná,* to be or remain safe and sound; to prosper.

Salámí, *n.* Salutation; salute (as by "presenting arms", or firing of cannon); a present offered to a superior on being introduced to him/a guard of honour (offered by armed forces to visiting dignitaries).

Sálan, *n.* Curry of meat, fish, or vegetables.

Sáláná, *a.* and *adv.* Yearly; annual; annually; per year; per annum.

Sálár, *n.* Chieftain; head; leader. *—jang,* a. Leader on the battlefield; field commander. *Sipah—,* a. A General; a comander-in-chielf. *—e-qaum,* a. Chief of the tribe; leader of a nation. [Mockingly, one who is always willing to initiate a fight and then withdraws to personal safety, leaving partners, friends and underlings to deal with the blood-bath/consequences].

Salásat, *n.* Facility; easiness; simplicity; gentleness; clearness.

Salásil, *n. (Plur. of Silsila).* Chains; series; links. sequences

Salát, *n. (Plur. Salwát).* Prayer; benediction.

Salátín, *a.* [plural of Sultán] Kings; rulers; emperors; monarchs.

Sál-há, *n.* Years; *adv.* for many years.

Sálí, *n.* Sister-in-law; wife's sister.

Salíb, *a.* Hard; strong; three-cornered; *n.* cross; crucifix. *—par chaṛháná,* to crucify.

Salíb, *a.* Good; virtuous; righteous; fit; proper; *n.* a man of probity and honour.

Sálik, *a.* Going; travelling; *n.* traveller; *(Met.)* devotee.

Sálim, *a.* Safe; secure; perfect; complete; one whole.

Salíqa, *n.* Nature; natural disposition; manners; etiquette; respect for quorum; consideration of protocol temperament; genius; taste; knowledge; skill; *salíqe kí guft-gú,* polite conversation. *salíqa-e-majlis,* good breeding.

Salís, *a.* Easy; simple; plain.

Sális, *a.* Third; *n.* a third person; a mediator; an arbitrator; an umpire. *—salása, n.* Trinity. *—náma,* an award by arbitration; or by a jury.

Sálisí, *n.* Meditation; arbitration.

Salmá, *n.* A band of embroidery.

Salná, *v.* To be perforated or pierced; to pierce; to prick; to enter (into).

Saloná, *a.* [Literally-] Salted; seasoned; tasty; beautifuly/handsome (i.e. *Saloná sajan:* handsome/beautiful lover).

Sálús, *n.* The Trinity.

Samá, *n.* Time; season; plenty; abundance; opportunity; concord; harmony.

Samajh/Samajh-Bújh

Samajh-dár, *adj.* One who understands; a wise one.

Samajh-dárí , *n.* Wisdom;

Samajhná, *v.* To understand; to comprehend; to assess; to perceive; to grasp; to consider.

Samáchár, *n.* News; message. Information. *—patra,* n. A newspaper; a journal.

Samad, *a.* High; exalted; eternal; *n.* God; Lord.

Samádh, Samádhi, *n.* Deep meditation; inward concentration of engry and faculties; [Also], the last resting place of a venerated one; a burial place of a holy person; sepulchre; grave that is turned into a place og homage and worship; a shrine.

Samádhán, *n.* Explanation; solution (to a problem); resolution (of a doubt).

Sámagrí, *n.* Stock; effects; goods; chattles; necessaries; apparatus; retinue *(sámán).*

Samáj, *n.* Assembly; congregation; society; company; association; party; community.

Samájat, *n.* Deformity turpitude; entreaty; solicitation; adulation; *a.* deformed; filthy; base.

Samajh, *n.* Understanding; comprehension. *—ná, páná, jáná,* v. To understand, to grasp the gist of; to absorb the fact; to comprehend. *—bújh,* n. Intelligence to comprehend. *—dár,* a. Careful; thoughtful; knowledgeable; *—dárí,* n. Intelligence; maturity; wisdom.

Samjháná, *v.* To cause to know or understand; to explain (to); to apologise; to admonish; to punish.

Samak, *n.* A fish; the fish on which the earth is supposed to rest; the sign Pisces of the Zodiac.

Samán, *adj.* at par; uniform; level.*—tá,* n. Equality; uniformity; state of being at level. Like; similar; resembling; equal.

Sámán, *n.* Furniture; goods and chattels; personal effects; things; tools; preparations. *be sar o—,* destitute, indigent; helpless.

Samáná, *v.* To fit in; to be contained in.

Samand, *n.* A horse of noble breed; a steed; a courser.

Samanvay, *n.* Conjunction; coordination; sequence; synthesis; union.

Sámánya, *adj.* General; common; commonly available; easily accessible; ordinary. *rúp se.* adj. Commonly; ordinarily; easily.

Samápit, Samápt, Samáptí, *n.* Finish; termination; inclusion; perfection; cessation; *a.* completed; ended; terminated; concluded.

Samar, *n.* War; battle; conflict.

Samarpaṇ, *n.* Dedication; offering; handing over. *Atma—,* v. Surrender; giving one's self up (to the authorities).

Samarpit, *adj.* Dedicated; committed to.

Sámarth, Sámarthya, *n.* Power; strength; ability; capacity; fitness.

Samás, *n.* Compounding of words; collection; combination; composition; abbreviation; summary. *Smast-pad,* n. Compound-word.

Samasta, Samast, *a.* Connected; com posed; compound; all; whole; entire; *n.* a whole.

Samasyá, *n.* A problem; a difficulty. —*púrtí,* n. Resolution to the problem.

Samatá , *n.* Equality; similarity.

Samaya, Samai, *n.* Time; season; opportunity. —*pákar,* adv. As soon as the time allows. —*smaya/samai par,* adv. From time to time; occasionally. —*smaya kí bát,* adv. A matter of chance; (it) does happen some times.

Sam̲ban̲dh, *n.* Relationship; Union; affinity. —*men,* adv. In connection with; about.

Sám̲bar, *n.* A kind of deer.

Sam̲bhálná, *v.* To support; to sustain; to take care of; to check; to restrain.

Samdhí, *n.* Relationship between the parents of a husband and wife; father of a bride or bridegroom. *(Fem. Samdhin).*

Sameṭná, *v.* To finish; to contract; to compress; to fold; to amass.

Sam̲hár, *n.* Killing; annihilation; massacre; slaughter. *Nar—,* Genocide.

Sam̲hitá, *n.* A code. —*Áchár—,* a. A code of conduct.

Samíp, *a.* Near; close to; at hand.

Sam̲mat, Sam̲mati, *n.* Consent; assent; opinion; advice.

Sámná, *n.* Confrontation; contest; frontage.

Samápt/Samápat, *adv.* Concluded; finished; terminated; over Ended.

Samápti, *n.* Conclusion; termination; the end; finish

Samarth/Samrath, *adj.* Competent; capable; trained for, equipped with; able and willing to.

Sámná, *n.* Confrontation; competition; encounter.

Sámne, *a.* In front; of; in the presence of; opposite; against.

Sam̲padá, *n.* Wealth; chattels; accumulated property; opulence; propserity.

Sam̲pat, Sam̲patti, *n.* Riches; wealth; opulence; affluence.

Sam̲sthá, *n.* Institution; organization; concern; establishment.

Sam-tal, *adj.* Level; uniform surface.

Samúchá, *a.* All; whole; complete; entire.

Samudra, *n.* Sea; ocean.

Samúh, *n.* Collection; multitude; assemblage; heap.

Sam̲wád, *n.* Conversation; news; information; story.

Sam̲vat, *n.* A year; an era; an epoch.

San, *n.* Year; age.

Sán, *n.* Whetstone; grindstone.

San'at, *n.* Work; craft; handicraft; art. *ahl-i—*, an artist; an artisan.

Sanad, *n.* Certificate; diploma; degree; any deed; warrant; order or other document signed by one in authority; signature; support. *—i-kárguzárí,* certificate of service. *—mu'áfí,* a rentfree grant.

Sanam, *n.* A lover; a mistress; a sweetheart; an object of worship. *—kháná,* n. The dwelling place of one's lover, etc.

Sánaná, *v.* To knead; to mash; to mix up (as flour; dough, etc.); to rule; to smear; to stain.

Sanátan, *a.* Eternal; primeval; existing from time immemorial; prehistoric.

Sá<u>n</u>chá, *n.* A mould; matrix.

Sa<u>n</u>chay, *n.* Collection; accumulation; hoarding*—karná,* To collect; to hoard, & c.

Sanchálan, *n.* Direction (of a business, organisation, or of ameeting, conference etc.); operation (of an instrument, machine, vehicle etc.). Hence, *Sanchálak,* a. Operator(s); director(s); conductor(s).

Sa<u>n</u>chár, *n.* Communication; transmission; movement. *—sádhan,* a. Means of communication. *—vyavasthá,* n. Cummunication system.

Sá<u>n</u>ḍ, Sá<u>n</u>ṛ *n.* A bull; a stallion; a stud horse; animal kept at stud.

Sá<u>n</u>ḍá, *n.* A species of sand lizard (commonly called *úsar sá<u>n</u>ḍá),* the oil extracted from it is believed to cure reheumatism; gout; &c.

Sandal, *n.* Sandal tree and its wood, renowned for its cool, refreshing fragrance.

Sandarbh, *n.* Reference; context; allusion —n. A reference work (like a dictionary, or encyclopaedia). —a. Torn out of context.

Sanḍás, *n.* Latrine; watercloset; sink; sever.

Sandesh, *n.* Message; communique; news; tidings; information.

Sa<u>n</u>dhán, *n.* Marketing a target; aim (of a hit, with a weapon).

Sa<u>n</u>dhi, *n.* Joint; junction; compound.

Sa<u>n</u>dhyá, *n.* Evening; twilight; dusk; eventide; a time-joint of the day when the day and night meet. *—van<u>n</u>dan,* n. Evening prayers; chanting in temples and congregations at evening time.

Sá<u>n</u>ḍní, *n.* A female camel (for riding); a dromedary. *—sawár,* a camel-rider.

Sa<u>n</u>ḍsi, Sansi, Sa<u>n</u>ṛsí, *n.* A pair of

pincers; stud horse; animal kept at stud. tongs. or nippers; forceps;

Saṇdúq, *n.* A box; chest; trunk. *—cha,* a small box; a casket.

Saṉg, *n.* A stone; weight. *—i-aswad,* the black stone, in the K'aba, at Mecca. *—dilí,* hard-heartedness; want of feeling or sympathy. *—i-pusht or post,* a tortoise; a turtle. *—i-maqnátís,* a magne. *—sár karná,* to stone to death.

Saṉg, *n.* Joining; meeting; confluence; friendship; intercourse; a caravan; *adv.* in company, together; collectively.

Sáṉg, Swáṉg, *n.* Imitation; mimicry; disguise; a part of character in a play. *—bharná, v.* to play the fool; to sham.

Saṉgam, *n.* Meeting; contact; confluence of rivers; junction; friendship; intercourse.

Saṉgat, *n.* Company; society; friendship; assembly.

Saṉhár/ Saṉghár, *n.* Killing(s); massacre; destruction; slaughter.

Saṉgín, *a.* Stony; weighty; heavy; severe; *n.* a bayonet.

Saṉgrah, *n.* Collection; compilation; accumulation; abridgement; seizing.

Saṉgrám, *n.* War; battle; contest. *—bhúmi,* battle-field.

Saṉgtará, *n.* A kind of orange.

Sání, *a.* Second; *n.* a second; an equal; a match.

Sáni', *n.* Creator (God); Maker.

Saníchar, *n.* The planet Saturn; Saturday; *(Met.)* bad luck; poverty; a miser; a voracious eater; a glutton.

Sánihá, *n.* Occurrence; event.

Sanjáb, *n.* The grey squirrel; the ermine.

Sanjáf, *n.* The hem or border of a garment.

Sáṉjh, Saṉjhá, *n.* Evening; dusk; twilight; eventide.

Saṉjídagí, *n.* Gravity; solemnity; composure; weight.

Saṉjog, *n.* Junction; adherence; chance; opportunity.

Saṉjukt, Saṉyukt, *a.* Joint; connected; united.

Saṉkalp, *n.* Volition; wish; vow; charitable donation; a deed of gift in fulfilment of a vow.

Saṉkar, *a.* Hybrid; cross-breed; intergrade. *Varṇa—,* a. A cross bred entity; a bastard; child of marriage across the (social, or religious) barriers.

Saṉkaṭ, *n.* Crisis; emergency; danger; hazard. *—kál,* a crisis period; a state of emergency.

Sankh, Shankh, *n.* A conch shell; ten or a hundred billions.

Sankhíyá, *n.* Arsenie.

Sankhyá, *n.* A number; a numeral reckoning of a sun.

Sánkhya, *n.* A school of Hindu Philosophy; one of the six such schools.

Sankoch, *n.* Shyness; bashfulness; modesty; respect.

Sankrántí, Sankránt, The Sun's entering into a new sign; a Hindu festival.

Sankshep, *n.* A summary; a precis; abridgement; abbreviation.

Sankshepaṇ, *v.* The act of abridgement; making a summary; condensation of a work, or statement.

Sanmán, *n.* Respect; esteem; regard; reverence. *—í, a.* respectful; polite; civil; *n.* a polite man.

Sanmukh, *a.* and *prep.* Facing; confronting; face to face; opposite (to); in the presence of; before.

Sán-ná, *v.* To knead; to mash; to mix up (as flour; doubh, &c.); to rule; to smear; to stain.

Sannátá, *n.* Stillness; silence; quietude. *Sannáte men áná,* v. To be dumb-founded; to be stunned; to be stupefied.

Sannipát, *n.* Meeting; union; contract; arrival; a disease in which there is a feeling of chilliness in the whole body.

Sanobar, *n.* The pine-tree; the fire-tree; any coniferous or cone-bearing tree.

Sánp, *n.* [See *Sarp*].

Sáns, *n.* Breath; breathing; respiration. *Ultí—lená,* v. To draw a breath in; to gasp. *Thandí —bharná,* prov. To heave a sigh; to gash, or to pant. *—ká rog,* n. Asthma. [Also see *Shwás*].

Sansá, *n.* [See *Sanshay*].

Sansanáná, *v.* To sound; to resound; to whistle (as a bullet); to whiz; to hiss; to thrill (with enjoyment, &c.); to be excited; to faint.

Sansár, *n.* Transmigration; the world; the universe; mankind; worldly affairs. *—rúpí, a.* mundane; worldly; secular.

Sansárí, *a.* Worldly; mundane; engaged in worldly or secular occupations; *n.* a man; a worldly man; a man of busíness.

Sánsat, *n.* Punishment; pain.

Sanshay, *n.* Doubt; misgiving; anxiety; apprehension; suspicion; uncertainty; hesitation; mistrust; apprehension.*—vád,* n. Scepticism

Sanskár, *n.* Education; refinement; idea; form; design; a santifying or purificatory rite; investiture with the sacred thread.

Sanskrit, *n.* Language formed by accurate grammatical rules; the sacred and classical language of the Hindus; *a.* carefully or accurately formed; perfect; consecrated; sanctitied.

Sanskriti, *n.* Culture; refinement innermost qualities of a human being, or a community; Fundamental value system of a society.

Sant, *n.* A saint; a devotee; *a.* virtuous; pious; devout.

Santáp, *n.* Sorrow; affliction; distress; intense heat; inflamation.

Santosh, *n.* Contentment; satisfaction; gratification; happiness.

Santushṭatá, *n.* Contentment; consolation.

Sanwat, *n.* Story; year; an era; an epoch; the era of Vikramaditya (dating from about 27 B.C.).

Sanwárṇá, *v.* To be prepared; to be dressed; to be decked; or decorated; to be arranged.

Sanyam, *n.* Restraint; control; check moderation; temperance; sobriety.

Sanyás, *n.* Relinquishment; abandonment of worldly attachments; profession of asceticism; non-attachment.

Sanyásí, *n.* One who has abandoned all worldly possessions and affections; an ascetic; a devotee; a religious mendicant.

Sanyog, Sanjog, *n.* Coincidence; chance; accident. *Also* Mixture; coalition; combination; union, etc.

Sapaṛná, *v.* To be caught or taken; to be involved; to be finished.

Sapáṭ, *a.* Level; even; smooth; plain.

Sapáṭá, *n.* Leap; spring; jump; bound.

Saperá, *n.* A snake-charmer; a snake-catcher.

Saphal, *n.* Fruitful; productive; profitable; successful; advantageous; useful. *—tá, n.* fruitfulness; success; productiveness; utility; success.

Sapṛáná, *v.* To involve; to catch; to arrest; to finish; to consume.

Sapta, *a.* Seven.

Saptáh, *n.* Seven days; a week.

Sapúran, *n.* [See *Sampúrn*].

Sapút, Supút, *n.* A tractable or dutiful son; a good or worthy son.

Sáq, *n.* The leg; the shank; trunk (of a tree); shaft; stalk (of a herb).

Saqálat, *n.* Weight; heaviness; gravity; indigestion.

Sáqí, *n.* One who pours wine; a barmaid; a cup-bearer; a page.

Sáqib, *a.* Shining; glistening; famous.

Saqíl, *a.* Heavy; weighty; cumberous; slow; indigestible.

Saqqá, *n.* A water-carrier.

Sar, *n.* A pond; a pool. *Amrit—,* a. (literally) A pool of nectar. Also a proper name for a city in Punjab.

Sar, *n.* Head; chief; leader; top; pinnacle; face. *—anjám,* a. Completion; accomplishment; arrangement. *—kash,* a. Mischief-monger; impudent; rebellious. *—ganá,* a. Leader of the gang; the ring-leader. *—garmí,* n. Hectic activity; passionate effort; enthusiasm. *—guzasht,* n. Life-story; narrative of events one has lived through. *—goshí,* n. Whisper(s); discreet complaint; whispering campaign. *—zamín,* n. Country; territory. *—zor,* a. Impudent; rebellious; insolent. *—táj,* a. Crown; the best (amongst); chief. *—dard,* n. (literally) Headache; trouble; problem. *-parast,* a. Patron; supporter. *—faroz,* a. Honoured; arrogant. *—farosh,* a. Intrepid; ready and willing to be beheaded, i.e. to make ultimate sacrifice. *—shár,* a Full to the brim; bubbling; buoyant. *—o-sámán,* n. Bag and baggage; all of one's worldly goods. *—sabz,* a. Verdant; green; prosperous. *—karná,* v. To conquer; to overcome; to subdue. *—honá,* adv. To be vanquished; to be subdued. *—marhná,* adv. To impose; to dump on.

Saráchá, *n.* A single-poled tent; a small house; a small room or apartment in a house.

Sarad, *n.* [See *Sharad*].

Sarae, *n.* Inn; a wayside rest-house for travellers.

Saráf, Sarráf, *n.* A money-changer; a bullion-dealer; (proverbially) a cheat; a penny-pincher.

saráfá, Sarráfá, *n.* Bullion market; jewellery market.

Saraghá, *n.* A bee.

Saráhná, *n.* Eulogy; praise; enconium; praise. (also as a verb) To praise; to eulogise; to applaud; to approve; to commend.

Saṛak, *n.* Road; way; path; street; highway; thoroughfare.

Sarakná, *v.* To be moved; to stir; to be set aside, to slide.

Saral, *a.* Easy; simple; straight; direct; straight-forward. *—sangít,* a. Light music.

Sara<u>n</u>jám, *n.* Accomplishment; arrangement; preparation

Saráp, *n.* [See *Shráp*].

Saras, *a.* Interesting; juicy; delicious; tasteful; relishable.

Sáras, *n.* A stork; a bird specie.

Sarb, *a.* [see *Sarv*].

Sarbaráh, *n.* Manager; steward; agent. —*kár,* expert or skilled in business matters.

Sarbas, *n.* [See *Sarvaswa*].

Sar-chashma, *n.* Source; spring; fountain.

Sard, *a.* Cold; damp; moist; humid; chilly. —*mizáj,* cold-hearted; apathetic; unsympathetic. —*garm,* hot and cold; changeable; fickle. —*í, n.* cold; coldness; dampness; chilliness; a chill; a cold; a catarrh.

Sardábá, *n.* A cold bath; a place where water is kept cool; a grotto; a cool room for summer.

Sardár, *n.* A chief; a headman; a commander. —*í,* headship; chiefship; lordship; domination; sway.

Saresh, *n.* Glue; an adhesive.

Sardí, *n.* Cold. —*ká mausam,* a. Cold weather.

Sarf, *n.* Extravagance; prodigality.

Sarfarází, *n.* Distinction; exaltation.

Sarganá, *a.* great; large; *a.* a great personage; one equal to a chief.

Sargin, *n.* Cow-dung.

Sarguzasht, *n.* An event; accident; one's owntele of woe.

Sarhadd, *n.* Boundary; frontier.

Sarhang, *n.* A captain; a chief; a foot soldier.

Sarír, *n.* [See *Sharír*].

Sariqá, *n.* Stealing; robbery.

sarishtá, *n.* Custom; usage; office. —*dár,* the chief under the native office in a court.

Sarkaṇḍá, *n.* A reed used in making screens.

Sarkárí, *a.* Of or belonging to the Government or to any superior authority; Government; state; official.

Sar-kash, *a.* Disobedient; rebellious.

Sarmá, *n.* Winter; cold season.

Sarmáyá, *n.* Stock; capital; fund.

Sarná, *v.* To rot; to decay.

Sarnám, *a.* Well-known; famous; distinguished.

Saro, *n.* The cypress tree; the cedar.

Sarod, *n.* A string musical instrument, used in classical Indian music systems.

Saroj, *n.* Lotus; (literally) a flower that rises in a pond.

Sarovar, *n.* A pond; a lake; a large pool of water.

Sarp, Sánp, *n.* A snake; a serpent; (idiomatically) a treacherous being: *Ástín ká sánp,* n. A serpent hiding under one's sleeve.

Sarpaṭ, *n.* Galloping hard; full gallop. *—phenkná, (ghorá),* to speed a horse.

Sarráf, *n.* A money-changer; a banker; an assayer.

Sarsám, *n.* Delirium; frenzy.

Sarsaráhaṭ, *n.* Creeping sensation.

Sarshár, *a.* Brimful; intoxicated; full.

Sarson, *n.* A species of mustard seed.

Sarúp, *n.* [See *Swarúp*].

Sarv, *a.* All; the whole; complete; full. *—vyápak.* a. All pervading; omnipresent. *—shaktimán,* a. All powerful; almighty. *—kálín,* a. Of all times. *—gya,* a. One who knows it all; all knowing. *—darshí,* a All seeing. *—dalíy,* a Pertaining to all parties. *—deshíy,* n. Cosmopolitan. *—nám,* Pronoun. *—násh,* n. Holocault; devastation. *—shreshṭh,* a. Best of all. *—sammat,* a. Unanimous. *—sulabh,* a. Accessible to all. *—mánya,* a. Acceptable to all . *—hit,* a. General welfare; good of all; common good.

Sárvabhaum, *adj.* Pertaining to the whole world; universal; worldwide.

Sárva-janik, *adj.* Public; open to public; for all men and women.

Sarvadá, *a.* Always; at all times.

Sarvaswa, *n.* Entire being; all property; everything.

Sarvatra, *a.* Everywhere; in all places.

Sás, *n.* Mother-in-law.

Sasá, *n.* A hare.

Sastá, *a.* Easily procured; cheap; low-priced.

Sasur, *n.* [See *Shwasur*].

Sustáná, *v.* To rest; to lie down, to relax.

Sat, Sát, *a.* Seven. *—koná,* heptagonal.*—khána,* seven-storied. *—manzilá,* seven-storied.

Satah, *n.* Surface; plane; layer; level. *—i-hastí,* Surface of the world.

Satáná, *v.* To pain; to torment; to oppress; to torture; to persecute; to tease; to vex; to molest; to annoy.

Satar, *n.* Line; row; rank; series.

Sáth, *pre,* and *adv.* In the company (of); along (with); with; together; towards. *—dená, v.* to take part (in); to co-operate (with); to help; to assist.

Sáṭh, *n.* A number; sixty.—*á,* adj. Sixty-years old dodderer.—*á so páṭhá,* prov. One suffering from dementia brought on by old age.

Saṭhiyáná, *v.* To be turned of sixty years; to be superannuated; to become decrepit or doting, to go senile.

Satí, *a.* Virtuous; chaste; faithful; *n.* a virtuous wife; the faithful wife who burns herself with her husband's corpse. —*honá,* to burn alive on the funeral pile; *(Met.)* to endure many hardships.

Sattar, *n.* A number, seventy.—*ká dashak,* adj. The decade of 70s.—*chúhe khá ke billi Hajj ko chali,* Prov. Having lived the life of absolute sin, one going in search of salvation.

Sattár, *a.* Concealing; covering; *n.* an epithet of the Deity. —*ul'aiyúb,* screener of short-comings.

Satún, *n.* A pillar; a column; a prop.

Satv, Sat, *n.* Essence; true nature; sap; juice; spirit; goodness; virtue; extract.

Satya, *n.* Truth; fact; real; reality; honest. —*vádí,* a. One who always speaks the truth. —*vrat,* a. One who is pledged to speaking the truth.

Satyánásh, *n.* Destruction; ruin; perdition; annihilation.

Sau, *a.* One hundred; cent. —*biswe,* in all probability; certainly. —*par sau,* hundred percent. —*guná,* a hundred-fold.

Saudá, *n.* Goods; wares; trade; purchase; bargain. —*patná, v.* a bargain to be struck; a contract to be made.

Saudá, *n.* The black bile, (one of the four humours of the body); melancholy; madness; love; ambition.

Saudágar, *n.* Merchant; trader; shop-keeper. —*í. n.* merchandise; trade; commerce; business of a merchant; *a.* mercantile; commercial.

Saugandh, *n.* An oath; a pledge. Sworn commitment.

Saugát, *n.* A gift; a present; a curiosity; a rarity; an offering.

Saulat, *n.* Impetuosity; violence; fury.

Saunf, *n.* Aniseed.

Saunpná, *v.* To deliver; to hand over; to give in charge.

Saur, *adj.* Solar; pertaining to the Sun; —*mandal,* n. The solar system; the part of the university that is lit and affected by the Sun.

Saut, *n.* A co-wife; a rival wife.

Sautelá, *n.* Belonging to a cowife; born of one and the same father by different mothers.*(in comps.),* half-, step-, as:—*báp,* step-father. &c.

Sávadhán, *a.* Attentive; heedful; careful; cautious; diligent. —*í, n.* attention; carefulness; circumspection; prudence.

Sávan, *n.* The fifth month of the Hindu calender, symbolic of the arrival of high spring, when trees are in full foliage, the birds are courting and offering their music to nature and the lovers are in a swing. Hundreds of folk songs all over India are sung in praise of this period in the year.

Sawá, *a.* One and a quarter more.

Sawáb, *n.* Requital; or reward (esp of obedience to God); reward of virtue in the life to come; virtuous or pious deed.

Sawábit, *n. (Plur. of Sábit).* The fixed stars (as opposed to *saiyárá,* planets).

Sawád, *n.* [See *Swád*].

Sawál, *n.* Question; quest; query; issue in consideration; problem; petition; solicitation.

Sawáneh, *n. (Plur. of Sáníh).* Occurrences; incidents; events; accidents. —*nigár,* a news-reporter; an intelligencer. —*'umri,* the incidents of one's life; a biography.

Sawár, *n.* A rider; a horseman; a cavalryman; a trooper; *a.* mounted; riding on horseback. —*í,* carriage; conveyance.

Sawerá, *n.* Early morning; dawn; daybreak.

Sáyá, *n.* Shadow; shade; shelter; protection; apparition; influence (of an evil spirit); a petticoat; a skirt. —*ban, n.* canopy; verandah; sunshade; parasol; umbrella; a thatched roof. —*dár,* shady.

Sayáná, *a.* Grown-up; adolescent; arrived at years of discretion; sagacious; clever; cunning; artful; sly; *n.* a wise man; prudent; mature an exorcist.

Sáz, *a.* and *n.* Making; preparing; effecting; *n.* maker; counterfeiter; *(used as last member of comps.),* as: gharí—, watch-maker, &c. *n.* accoutrements; harness; concord; harmony; musical instrument. *be—o-samán,* unprovided.

Sazá, *n.* Punishment; chastisement. —*dená,* to inflict punishment. —*yáfta,* an old offender.

Sazáwal, *n.* A revenue collector; a superintendent.

Sazáwár, *n.* Worthy; excellent; deserving; meritorious.

Sázindá, *n.* A maker; a musician.

Sázish, *n.* Confederacy; league; conspiracy; plot.

Se, *pre.* From; out of; of; with; along with; concerning by; by way of; by reason of; through; on account of; as regards; according to; since; than making the comparative degree).

Seb, *n.* An apple; *(Poet.)* a chin—*i-gabgab,* the chin.

sehan, *n.* Courtyard; a squarish area in from of one's home.

Sehrá, *n.* A chaplet.

Sej, *n.* A bed; couch. —*lagáná,* to prepare a bed. —*suhág,* the nuptial bed.

Semal, *n.* The silk cotton tree.

Sená, *n.* An army; body of troops. —*pati,* n. A leader of the troops; a general; a military chief.

Se<u>n</u>dh, *n.* A hole made in a wall by the thieves.

Se<u>n</u>dhá, *n.* White rock-salt.

Se<u>n</u>dhí, *n.* Toddy; palmwine.

Se<u>n</u>dur, *n.* Vermillion; red lead.

Se<u>n</u>kná, *v.* To warm; to heat; to parch; to take.

Se<u>n</u>tmet, *a.* Gratis; free of cost.

Ser, *n.* A weight of 16 chhatáks (almost 90% of a kilogram).

Seṭh, *n.* A banker; a money-broker; a millionaire; a great merchant.

Setu, *n.* A bridge.

Sevá, *n.* Service; worship; bondage. *Sewak,* a servant; a follower; a subject.

Sewaíyá<u>n</u>, *n.* Vermicelli; macaroni.

Sewatí, *n.* A white rose. *(gul-i-nasrin);* the China rose.

Shab, *n.* Night. —*básh,* one who stays all night; a night lodger. —*i-barát,* a Mohamedan festival on the the fourteenth day of *shábán.* —*i-máh,* moonlight night. —*nam,* dew. —*o-roz,* always; day and night —*táb,* a firefly *(jugnú).*

Shabáb, *n.* Youth; prime of life; best of bloom.

Shabáhat, *n.* Similarity; resemblance; likeness; similitude.

Shabán, *n.* A shepherd; a pastor.

Shábásh, *intj.* Bravo ! Well done ! —*í, n.* praise; applause.

Shabda, Sabad, *n.* A word; a term; sound (noise). —*kosh,* n. A dictionary; a lexicon; a glossary. —*chayan,* n. Choice of words; diction. —*jál,* n. Jugglery of words; verbosity. —*bhed.* n. Distinction between similar-sounding words. —*rachná,* v. Word-formation. —*rúp,* n. The grammatical status of a word. —*vír,* a. One blessed with a gift of the gab; a past master in mere talk; an all-talk-and-do-nothing person. *—hín,* a. Speechless; mute; silent.

Shabíb, *n.* The like (of); resemblance; image; portrait.

Shabína, *a.* Nightly; nocturnal; last night's state.

Shád, *a.* Happy; glad; delighted. *—ábí,* moisture; freshness; verdure. *dil—,* cheerful; happy.

Shaḍ, *adj.* Six

Shadd, *n.* Intensifying; emphasizing. *—o-madd,* emphasis; stress; severity; force.

Shádí, *n.* Pleasure; delight; joy; marriage; wedding. *—i-marg,* death from joy; an easy death.

Shadíd, *a.* Violent; intense; severe; rigorous; arduous; grievous; grave.

Shádiyána, *n.* Music and singing at marriage. *—bajáná,* to pay festive music; to rejoice.

Shaḍyantra, *n.* Conspiracy; plot; intrigue. *—kárí,* a. Plotter(s), conspirator(s); one(s) involved in intrigue.

Sháer, *n.* A poet; a versifier. *—í,* n. Poetry; poetic works; an anthology.

Shafí'at, *n.* Intercession; recommendation.

Shafaq, *n.* Fear; affection; evening; twilight.

Shafaqat, *n.* Affection; kindness; pity.

Shaffáf, *n.* Transparent; brilliant.

Sháfí, *n.* Intercessor; *a.* health-giving; sanitary.

Shafíq, *a.* Affectionate; merciful; a kind friend.

Shaftálú, *n.* A peach.

Shágird, *n.* Pupil; disciple; follower; scholar; student.

Shagl, *n.* Business; occupation; employment; assessment; pastime.

Shagun, *n.* An augury; an omen; a presage; a prognostication. [*ap-shagun:* A bad omen; something that does not augur well].

Sháh, *n.* King; prince; monarch; a title assumed by *faqírs; a.* royal; noble; excellent; the longest; a largest; or best of its kind; *(used as first member of compounds),* as:*—báz,* a royal falcon. *—balút,* the oak; the chestnut. *—ráh,* main road; the highway. *—zádá,* a prince. *—námá,* a celebrated epic poem containing a history of the Kings of Persia (written by Firdausi about the year of Christ 1000).

Shahádat, *n.* Evidence; testimony; witness; martyrdom. *—i-táríri,* written or documentary evidence. *—i-zanní,* presumptive evidence. *roz-i—,* the day of martyrdom (of Husain); the tenth of Mohurrum.

Shahámat, *n.* Generosity; bravery.

Sháhanshāh, *n.* Emperor; a great king.

Shahad, *n.* Honey; anything very sweet. *—kí makkhí,* a bee.

Sháháná, *adj.* Princely; royal; king-like.*—chál-dhál,* n. A royal gait. *—andáz,* n. Royal Posture.

Sháhí, *adj.* Royal; regal; majestic; luxurious; top quality. *—darbár,* n. Royal court. *—mahal* n. Royal palace. *—andáz,* n. Royal mannerism(s), &c.

Shahíd, *n.* A martyr.

Sháhid, *n.* A witness. *—i-hál,* an eye-witness; a witness of facts.

Sháhín, *n.* A royal falcon.

Shahnái, *n.* A musical pipe.

Shahr, *n.* A city; a town. *—badr,* banishment; exile. *—panáh,* rampart. *—í,* a citizen.

Shahtút, *n.* Mulberry.

Shai, *n.* An object; a thing; an affair.

Shaidá, *a.* Mad; insane; *a.* deeply in love.

Shaikh, *n.* A venerable old man; a head or chief of a tribe or village; a doctor of religion and law; a title taken by the descendants of the prophet.

Shail, *n.* Hill; mountain. *—ajá,* n. Daughter of the mountain; an epithet of *Párvatí,* Lord Shiva's consort.

Sháiq, *a.* Fond; desirous; zealous.

Shá'ir, *n.* A poet.

Sháistá/ Sháyastá, Polite; courteous; well-bread; gentle; decent; worthy. —worthy. *—miizáj,* adj. Affable; mild; good-tempered.

Shaitán, *n.* The evil; satan; an evil spirit.

Shajar, *n.* A tree; a plant; a shrub. *—a, n.* a genealogical tree.

Shak, Shaq, *n.* Doubt; suspicion; suspense.

Shákáhárí, *a.* A vegetarian; one who does not eat meat, fish, game or poultry.

Shakar, Shakkar, *n.* Sugar. *—qand,* the sweet-potato. *—maqát,* sweet-spoken; sweet-tongued.

Shákh, *n.* A bough; a branch (of a tree); a twig; a stalk.

Shakhs, *n.* A person; individual; being. *—iyat, n.* individuality; personality.

Shakíl, *a.* Handsome; comely; well-formed.

Shákir, *a.* Thankful; grateful; content.

Shakkí, *a.* Suspicious; sceptical; doubtful.

Shakl, Shakal, *n.* Appearance; form; figure; image; effigy; shape; mode; a diagram; a proposition. —*banáná, v.* to make a likeness or figure (of); to give shape to. *ham*—, similar; like.

Shakti, *n.* Power; strength; energy; authority. —*Shálí,* a. Powerful; strong, etc. —*mán, a.* powerful. —*hín,* powerless.

Shakuni, *n.* A hen-sparrow; a villanous character in the Hindu epic, *Mahábhárata.*

Shálá, *n.* A house; a hall; a place *(used in comps.)* as; *páṭh*—, a school; a reading-room, &c., &c.

Shalabh, *n.* A locust; a grasshopper.

Shalgam, *n.* A turnip.

Shalwár, *n.* Punjabi trousers, commonly worn by women, but also by a lot of men, especially by Muslim men, in Punjab.

Shám, *n.* Evening.

Shama', *n.* A lamp; a candle. —*dán,* a candle-stick.

Shaman, *n.* An idolator; an idol; an idol-temple.

Shámat, *n.* Misfortune; ill luck; adversity. —*i-a'mál,* evil days. —*ká márá, a.* unfortunate.

Shámil, *a.* Communicating (with); included (in); blended (with); associated; point; living together; *n.* compriser; confederate; member; *adv.* together; jointly; *pre.* with; along with; in the company of.

Shámilát, *n.* Affairs in common; partnership; land held in common; a co-parcenary estate.

Shámiyáná, *n.* A pavilion; a canopy; a marquee.

Shams, *n.* The sun. —*ul-'ulamá,* the title given by the Government to the learned *moulvies.* —*í,* solar.

Shamsher, *n.* A sword. —*zan,* a swordsman.

Shán, *n.* State; condition; pomp; rank; dignity; grandeur; glory; lustre; glory. —*dár,* glorious; pompous; splendid.

Sháná, *n.* A comb; the shoulder.

Shangarf, *n.* Vermilion; cinnabar.

Shunídá, *a.* That what is heard.

Shanká, *n.* Doubt; suspicion; mistrust. —*kul,* a. One perturbed by doubt; suspicious. —*janak,* a. Source of doubt; something causing a doubt. —*nivárаṇ,* adv. Allaying doubts; removal of suspicion; clarifying the situation. —*samádhán,* adv. Demolition of soubts; resolution of any suspicion(s). —*spad,* a. Questionable; begging critical examination.—*lu,* a. Suspicious; one having a doubt.

Shankar, *n.* Name of Lord Shiva, the annihilator of the Universe, the consort of *Párvatí.* Also the name of a renowned Indian thinker-philosopher who lived and worked in the last quarter of the eighth and first quarter of the ninth century India and who waged a very successful campaign for the revival of *Bráhmanism* in the face of rampant rise of *Buddhism.* Hence his more popular name *Shankarácharya,* meaning Shankara, the *guru.*

Shankh, *n.* A conch shell. (in mathematics) a number equal to 'a thousand billion. —*ákár,* a. Conch-shaped; conchate. —*nád,* n. Blowing a conch as a trumpet; a battle cry (in ancient India, commencement of battle was announced by blowing the conch in the battle-field.

Shankhiní, *a.* One of the four major categories of women according to *Kámasútra.*

Shanku, *n.* Cone.

Shánti, *n.* Peace; calm; still; silent; quiet; tranquil; unperturbed. —*karná,* v. To pacify. —*rahná,* v. To keep one's head. —*aur vyavasthá,* n. Law and Order. —*kál.* n. peace time. —*páṭh,* v. Recitation of Vedic peace Hymn. —*priya,* a. Peace-loving. —*vártá,* n. Peace-talk. —*sandhi,* n. Peace-treaty.

Shapath, *n.* An oath; Swearing; a pleadge. —*grahaṇ karná,* v. To take an oath. —*diláná,* v. To in administer an oath. —*bhang karná,* c- v. To breach an oath.

Shaqáiq, *n. (Plur. of Shuqúq).* Cracks; fissures; the tulip.

Shaqq, *n.* The half of a thing; difficulty; hardship; labour; weariness; a split; a crack.

Sháqúl, *n.* A plummet.

Shar, *n.* Evil; wrongdoing; badness; wickedness; viciousness. —*uṭháná, v.* to raise a commotion or disturbance; to cause a breach of peace.

Shar, *n.* Arrow; missile; dart. —*sandhán,* adv. Aiming of an arrow; focusing on a target.

Shár, *n.* A water-fall.

Sharáb, *n.* (Alcoholic) drink; wine; intoxicating liquid; spirituous liquor. —*i-tahúr,* nectar. —*khána,* a tavern.

Sharábor, *n.* Wet through;

dripping wet; drenched.

Sharad, *n.* Autumn. —*Púrṇimá,* n. Night of the full moon in the month of *Áshwin.*

Sharáfat, *n.* Nobility; politeness.

Sharáit, *n. (Plur. of Shart).* Conditions; stipulations; agreements; signs.

Shárak, *n.* A starling; a maina.

Sharákat, *n.* Partnership; confederacy.

Sharaṇ, *n.* Refuge; asylum; shelter; protection. —*ágat,* one who comes for protection; a refugee.

Shárang, *a.* A peacock; a deer.

Sharar, Sharára, *n.* Sparks of fire; malice.

Sharárat, *n.* Wickedness; vice; villainy; mischief.

Sharbat, *n.* A draught (of water, &c.); drink; beverage; portion.

Sharah, *n.* Explanation; commentary; annotation; rate; allowance; pay; table of rates. —*lagán,* rent rate.

Sharí'at, *n.* The religious law of Muslims; ordinance; statute.

Sharíf, *a.* Noble; of high rank; exalted; eminent; high-born. —*un-nafs,* noble of soul.

Sharík, *n.* A co-sharer; a partner; a partaker (with); a colleague; a comrade; an ally; a member of a community; *a.* joined; united. —*rahná,* to live together.

Sharír, *n.* Body; physique; (sometimes) corpse.

Sharír, *a.* Naughty; mischievous; wicked; bad.

Sharm, *n.* Shame; modesty; sense of honour; bashfulness. —*áná,* v. To be bashful; to be shy; to blush; to hesitate (out of sense of honour). —*nák,* a. Shameful; an unworthy (deed). —*indá/ sár,* a. (To be) ashamed; to feel shy.

Shart, *n.* Condition; stipulation; term; agreement. —*lagáná, v.* to stipulate; to bargain; to bind by contract; to bet.

Shásak, *n.* Ruler; governor.

Shash, *a.* Six.

Shashak, *n.* A hare; a rabbit.

Shashi, *n.* The moon.

Shast, Shist, *n.* Aim; the sight (of a gun, &c.); a planet able; a large fishing-hook. —*patrí,* a plane-table survey.

Shashṭa-dashi, *adj.* sixteenth

Shashṭi, *adj.* Sixth

Shástr, *n.* Scriptures; a discursive treatise on a scientific, or religious subject; a science; a discipline; literature of knowledge. —*charchá,* n. Study, or discussion of *Shástras.*

—*gyán,* n. Knowledge of *S.* —*varjit,* a. Forbidden by *S.* —*vidhán,* n. Prescription of the S. —*vimukh,* a. Profane; contrary to the authority of the *S.* —*siddh,* a. Proved by the *S:* in accordance with the *S.*

Shastr, *n.* Weapon; arms; a sword, etc. —*ábhyás,* n. Weapons practice; a military drill. —*dhárí,* a. one who carries weapon(s); an armed person.

Shat, *a.* One hundred. —*prati-shat,* a Hundred-per-cent. —*shah,* adv. Fully; completely; hundreds; —*shat,* adj. Hundreds

Shaṭh, *n.* Villain; wicked; vicious; deceitful; unprincipled.

Sháṭhya, *n.* Villainous behaviour; wickedness; punishable conduct.

Shátir, *a.* Astute; cunning; sly.

Shatranj, *n.* Chess; a board-game. —*í,* a. Chequered pattern. —*bázi,* adv. Clever moves; sly action; cheating. —*chál,* n. Strategically clever move; well thought out action; out-flanking the rival.

Shatru, *n.* An enemy; a foe; an oppanant. —*tá,* n. Enmity; animosity; rivalry; opposition.

Shauch, *n.* Duty of cleaning; purification. —*ádi,* n. Morning duties (toilet, brushing one's teeth and bathing etc.)

Shauhar, *n.* A husband.

Shauq, *n.* Inclination; fondness; desire; love. —*se,* gladly. —*ín,* fond of; eager.

Sha'úr, *n.* Knowledge; wisdom; sense; sagacity; good management. —*dár,* mannerly; well-bred; wise; intelligent.

Sháyá, *a.* Published; revealed; apparent; manifest. —*honá,* to be spread abroad; to be propagated.

Sháyad, *adv.* Perhaps; perchance; it may be.

Shayan, *n.* A bed; a couch; sleeping.

Sháyán, *a.* Legal; lawful; allowed; proper; fit; worthy. —*honá,* to suit; to become; to be fit.

Shayátín, *n. (Plur. of Shaitán).* Demons.

Shayyá, *n.* A (comfortable) bed. —*grih,* n. A bed-chamber. —*grast,* a. bed-ridden.

Shάzz, *a.* Rare; scare; unusual; —*nádir, adv.* seldom; rarely.

Sheftá, *a.* Distracted (with love); infatuated; enamoured; deeply in love.

Shekhar, *a.* One on top; one placed on the peak; one located on the crest. *Chandra*—, (Literally-) the one with the Moon in his crest/ crown; and epithet for Lord Shiva.

Shekhí, *n.* Bragging; boasting; vaunting.

Sher, *n.* A lion; a tiger; *(Met.)* a lion-hearted or very brave man. *—i-gardún, n.* the sun; the sign Leo (lion).

Shernі́, *n.* A lioness; a tigress.

Shewá, *n.* Business; profession; custom; habit; way; manner.

Shi'a, *n.* A party or sect of Mohammadans who follow Ali and assert that he was the rightful Imán after Mohammad; a follower of the sect of Ali.

Shibáb, *n.* [See *Shabáb*].

Shiddat, *n.* Strength; force; vehemence; violence; severity; difficulty; adversity; trouble; intensity.

Shifá, *n.* Recovery from sickness; convalescence; cure; remedy.

Shigáf, *n.* Split; rent; fissure; crack.

Shíghra, *adv.* Quickly; hurriedly; in haste; in a hurry; fast.

Shíghratá, *adv.* Hurry; haste; quickness; rapidity; speed, etc.

Shigúfa, *n.* Bud; blossom; flower; *(colloq).* a fabrication. *—láná,* to bud; to blossom; to produce something new and wonderful.

Shiguftá, *a.* Expanded; blown (as a flower(; blooming; flourishing.

Shiguftagí, Shuguftagí, *n.* Expanding of a flower; blooming; delight; pleasure; astonishment.

Shikam, *n.* Belly; stomach. *—banda, n.* an epicure; a glutton. *—ser, a.* full; satiated; glutted.

Shikan, *a.* and *n.* Breaking; crushing; overthrowing; *n.* shrinking; shrivelling; a curl; a ply; a fold; a plait; a furrow; a wrinkle. *But–,* adj. idol-breaker(s) [often reference to Muslims]; Reformist Hindu(s) [often a reference to *Arya-samájis*].

Shikanjá, *n.* A bookbinder's press; a clamp; stocks (for the legs); pain; torture; grip.

Shikár, *n.* Hunting; the chase; prey; game; plunder; booty; spoil. *—báz, n.* a sportsman; a hunter.

Shikárí, *n.* Of or belonging to the chase; relating to hunting; *n.* a hunter; a sportsman; a fowler; an angler.

Shikast, *n.* Breakage; fracture; breach; defeat; loss; *a.* broken; odd; uneven.

Shikastá, *a.* Broken; defeated; bankrupt; sick; wounded. *—gí,* breakage; fracture; defeat.

Shikáyat, *n.* Complaint; accusation.

Shikeb, *n.* Patience; endurance; long-suffering.

Shikhanḍí, *n.* A eunuch; an impotent man; a character from the epic *Mahábhárata* who challenged the authority and bravery of his commander-in-chief on the battlefield.

Shikhar, *n.* Peak; crest (of a mountain); point; summit. —*vártá,* n. A meeting, or conference of top leaders.

Shiksha, *n.* Teaching; instruction; education; training; admonition.

Shíl, *n.* Nature; disposition; steady observance of moral codes; modesty. *Pa<u>n</u>ch–,* n. Five principles governing one's conduct, part of the Buddhist thought; also the principles governing state-conduct of foreign policy and mutual relationship, established by the leaders of the Non-Alligned Movement.

Shilá, *n.* A rock; a slab; A solid and stable establishment.

Shilp, *n.* Craft; architecture. —*kalá,* n. technology; craft. —*kár,* n. Craftsman; an architect. —*shálá,* n. A workshop; a studio; a place where crafts are taught.

Shimál, Shumál, *n.* The North. —*Janúb,* n. (literally-) the North-South; (Proverbially-) The Rich Nations (of the Northern hemisphere) and the Poor Nations (of the Southern hemisphere).

Shinákht, *n.* Acquaintance; understanding; identity; recognition.

Shinásái, *n.* Acquaintance; knowledge.

Shír, [A corruption of Sanskrit word *Kshír*], Milk; (also commonly used for-) rice-pudding; *Khír*). —*ságar,* n. The legendary 'Ocean of Milk' where Lord vishnu rest on his bed (made by the coiled *Shesh-nág,* the great thousand-headed serpent).

Shirázá, *n.* The stitching of the back of a book. —*bandí,* the binding of a book.

Shírází, *adj.* Of *Shíráz,* modern Persepolis; originating from *Shíráz;* humble and cultured. *D; áwat-i-Shírází,* adj. Poor-man's feast.

Shírín, *a.* Sweet; pleasant; gentle. —*zabání,* sweetness of speech; eloquence. —*í,* sweet-meat.

Shirk, *n.* Polytheism; paganism; belief in the plurality of gods; partnership.

Shírsh, *n.* Peak; pinnacle; top; highest position; head. —*ásan,* n. A yogic posture, standing upright on one's head with feet up in the air. [This position is supposed to improve one's spinal balance and blood circulation to the brain.

Shísh, *n.* Head; top; peak. —*jhukáná,* v. To offer respects/ veneration by bowing ones head before.

Shísha, *n.* Glass; glass-ware; a looking-glass; a mirror. *shísh mahal,* crystal palace.

Shíshí, *n.* A small bottle; a phil. —*sunghánú, v.* to administer chloroform, &c.

Shishy(a) *n.* Pupil; disciple; apprentice. —*á.* n. A female pupil, etc. *Guru —parampará,* n. Tradition of Teacher-disciple relationship.

Shít, *a.* Cold; cool; chilly; frigid; *n.* coldness; frigidity; the cold season; winter. —*jvar,* ague. —*agar,* n. Cold-storage. —*kál,* n. Cold season. —*oshn,* adj. Temperate weather condition(s). —*pradhán,* adj. Mainly, primarily, or prevalently cold. —*yuddha,* n. Cold-war.

Shitáb, *a.* Hasty; quick; speedy. —*i,* quickness; haste; celerity; speed; fleetness; rapidity.

Shítalá, *n.* Name of female deity among the Hindus; *also* a popular name for Small pox.

Shithil, *adj.* Loose; slack; loosened; weak; relaxed; tired. —*tá,* n. the state of being weak, or relaxed; loose, &c.

Shlok, *n.* A verse in Sankrit composition; a couplet, or stanza in poetry.

Shmsán, Shamshán *n.* A crenation ground; burial-ground.

Shob, *n.* Washing; a wash; ablution.

Shobhá, *n.* Ornament; decoration; grace; comeliness; radiance. brilliance. *Shobhá-e-mán,* a. Graceful looking; set in grandeur.

Shoḍash, *adj.* Sixteen. —*shringár,* n. Sixteen (all possible) ways of body adornment (according to Hindu tradition).

Shoḍashí, *adj.* A girl of sixteen years of age; one ripe and mature for woman-hood; a young lady in prime of youth; nubile; fresh for passion-play.

Shodh, *n.* Research; enquiry; findingout.

Shohdá, *a.* A person of bad character; a profligate; a scoundrel.

Shok, *n.* Sadness; mourning; feeling of sorrow; gloom. —*manáná,* To lay a wake to mourn some one. —*gít,* n. An elege; dirge. —*wihwal,* a. Overwhelmed by grief, or sorrow. —*sabhá,* n. A condolence meeting.

Shoḳh, *a.* Bright (as colour, &c.); gay; sprightly; buxom; brisk; humorous; mischievous; sancy; insolent; presumptuous; wanton. —*mizádj,* of a gay disposition.

Shoḳhí, *n.* Playfulness; mischief; coquetry; impudence.

Sholá, *n.* Flame; blaze; light; flash.

Shoṇit, *a.* Red; purple; blood.

Shor, *n.* Noise; cry; outcry; clamour; uproar; tumult; din; renow; celebrity; *a.* mad; salt; brackish; bitter; unlucky. *—bakht, a.* ill-fated; infamous. *—pusht, a.* noisy; refractory; unruly. *—zamín, n.* barren soil; unfertile land.

Shorá, *a.* Barren (ground); marshy; *n.* barren soil; saltpetre; nitrate of potash. *shore ka tezáb, n.* nitric acid.

Shorbá, *n.* Soup; broth; grawy.

Shoríyat, *n.* Saltness; brackishness.

Shoshá, *n.* An ingot (of gold or silver); a bar (of iron, &c.); a chief; a particle; a piece; filth; rubbish.

Shoshaṇ, *n.* Exploitation; taking advantage of; extracting most than can be (unscrupulously).

Shráddh, *n.* A Hindu ceremony in honour of the departed spirits of deceased relatives.

Shraddhá, *n.* Veneration; honour; faith; respect; belief.

Shram, *n.* Fatigue; weariness; exertion; toil; labour.

Shráp, *n.* Curse; malediction; imprecation.

Shreṇí, *n.* Line; range; row; multitude.

Shreshṭh, *a.* Best; most excellent; pre-eminent; senior.

Shrí, *n.* Prosperity; wealth; beauty; light; intellect. *—mán, a.* prosperous; famous; wealthy. also used as a title in place of 'Mr.'. Hence, *—mán,* n. Sir (as a title). *—matí,* n. Madam (as a title).

Shrigál, *n.* Jackal; a carnivore who always scavenges on others' kill; [*proverbially*] a coward.

Shu'ala', [See *Sholá*].

Shu'ará, *n.* [Plural of *Sháir/Sháyar*] Poets.

Shubahá, *n.* Doubt; uncertainty; scruple; defect; flaw.

Shubh, *a.* Bright; beautiful; fortunate; good; eminent; happy; *n.* happiness; prosperity; welfare. *—chintak, n.* well-wisher. *—lagn,* an auspicious moment.

Shuchi, *n.* Bright; clean; pure; virtuous; pious; faultless; a name given to heavenly bodies like the Sun, the Moon etc.

Shuchit, *adj.* Cleansed; purified; pure.

Shuchitá, *n.* Quality of purity; flawlessness, etc.

Shudá, *a.* Past; gone; having become. *—gum-shudá,* a. Lost; misplaced.

Shudbud, *n.* Imperfect knowledge; circumstances; *adv.* indifferently.

Shuddh, *a.* Pure; cleansed; untarnished; un-polluted; clear.

Shuddhi, *n.* Purity; purification; innocence; truth; acquittal; retaliation. *—patr,* list of errata (in a book).

Shuddhíkaraṇ, *v.* Purification; cleansing; refinement; rectification; correction; setting right.

Shufa', *n.* The right of obtaining possession of a piece of land; the right of pre-emption. *haqq-i—,* the right of pre-emption in favour of a person whose land is contiguous to a piece of ground offered for sale.

Shuhdá, *n.* [See *Shohdá*].

Shuhrat, *n.* Fame; renown; celebrity; notoriety; rumour. *—áfáq,* renowned; of world-wide reputation.

Shujá', *n.* Brave; bold; daring; courageous; intrepid; undaunted.

Shujá'at, *n.* Bravery; courage; valour.

Shuk, *n.* A parrot.

Shúkar, *n.* A hog; wild boar; a pig.

Shukla, *n.* White colour; whiteness; name of a sect of Brahmans; *a.* white; bright; clean; pure. *—paksh,* the light half of the month (the fortnight of the moon's increase).

Shukr, *n.* Thanks; gratitude; thanksgiving. *—karná,* to return thanks (for); to be grateful (for). *—guzár,* thankful; grateful. *—i-niamat,* an acknowledgment of a favour, &c.

Shukr(a), *a.* Bright; resplendent; *n.* the planet Venus.

Shukrwár, *n.* Friday; fifth day of the week.

Shúl, *n.* A thorn; a piercing instrument; a dart; the point of a spear. *Tri—,* n. A Trident.

Shúm, *n.* Niggard; vile; inauspicious; *n.* a miser. *—bakht,* unfortunate; wretched.

Shumá, *pre.* You.

Shumál, *n.* [See *Shimál*]

Shumár, *n.* Number; amount; counting; assessment; calculation. *be—,* incalculable, innummerable.

Shúnya, *n.* Zero; cipher; vacuum; space; emptiness.

Shuqqá, *n.* A royal order; a letter.

Shurafá, *n. (Plur. of Sharíf).* Nobles; grandees.

Shurú', *n.* Commencement; beginning. *—se; ab initio;* from the beginning. *—karná, v.* to enter upon; to start; to begin; to lead off; to establish; to institute.

Shushk, *a.* Dry/ dried; withered; parched; arid; emaciated; tedious; barren; without potential. —*vyavahár,* n. Indifferent behaviour; encounter without any feeling.

Shustá, *n.* Washed; cleaned; neat. —*zabán,* pure language.

Shutr, Shutur, *n.* A camel. —*i-be mihár,* uncontrolled; refractory; wild. —*dili,* timidity. —*gáo.* the camelopard or giraffe. —*murg.* an ostrich.

Shwasan/ Shwás, *n.* Breath; respiration; life. —*kriyá,* n. The process of breathing. —*rog,* Respiratory diseases (like asthma).

Shwasur, *n.* Father-in-law.

Shyám, *a.* Black; dark; also a nickname for Krishna (for reasons of his darker skin). —*á,* n. A nickname for *Koel,* the singing black bird that appears in the grovers in summer.

Siddh, *a.* Accomplished; completed; perfected; per-formed; realized; gained; proved; valid; sound; adjudicated; decided; made up; connected; endowed with supernatural powers; eminent; celebrated; *n.* an inspired sage; a seer; a holy personage. *swayam—,* a. Self-evident; proof in itself; not subject to any outsider proof. —*ánt,* an established truth; conclusion; reliable doctrine; a principle.

Sídhá, Sídhí, *a.* Straight; direct; opp-opposite; facing; up-right; erect; right, proper; easy; straightforward; honest; gentie; right (hand); *n.* undressed victuals; provisions; forage. —*banáná, v.* to correct; to put right; to regulate; to tame; to train. —*ráh se phirná,* to deviate from the straight path; to go astray, *sidhi sun-áná,* to speak plainly (to); to abuse roundly or in set terms.

Sidhárná, *v.* To set out; to set off; to depart; to die.

Sidq, *n.* Truth; sincerity. —*o-kizb,* truth and false.

Sifárat, *n.* Making peace (between). pacifying; mediation; writing of a book.

Sifárísh, *n.* Recommendation; intercession; commendation. —*náma,* a letter of recommendation or introduction.

Sifat, *a.* Qualification; description; an adjective; a quality; attribute; praise.

Sifar, *n.* A cypher; a zero.

Siflá, *a.* Low; mean; ignoble; base; mean; *n.* a low or base man. —*dán,* a cup or plate to throw scraps, &c., on.

Sih, *a.* Three. —*chaṉd,* three-fold. —*máhí,* quarterly. —*pahar,* afternoon.

Sihará, *n.* Wreath; a garland.

Sihat, Sehat, n. Health; soundness of body; accuracy; correctness; validity; integrity. —*baḳhsh,* healthgiving; sanitary. —*páná,* to be restored to health; to recover (from sickness); to get well. —*náma,* a certificate of health; a list of correction; corrigenda.

Sihr, *n.* Enchantment. —*báz,* sorcere.

Sijdá, Sajdá, *n.* Stooping so as to touch the ground with the forehead in adoration (esp. to God); Prostration.

Sikh, *n.* A disciple; a follower of Gurn Nanak.

Síkh, *n.* Advice; admonishment; counsel; instruction; learning; lesson; sermon; teaching; training. [Also see *Shikshá*].

Síkh, *n.* A skewer; a spit.

Síkhná, *v.* To learn; to study; to train for; to acquire knowledge; to master.

Sikká, *n.* A stamp; a seal; a signet; a coining dye; a stamping coin; a rupee. —*baiṭháná,* to establish one's rule or authority. —*bánáná,* to coin money.

Sikoṛná, *v.* To cause to shrink, etc.

Sikuṛan, *n.* Shrinkage; wrinkle(s); shrivelling.

Sikuṛná, *v.* To shrink; to tighten up; to contract; to draw up; to shrivel; to wrinkle.

Sil, *n.* A curry stone.

Sílá, *a.* Damp; moist; humid; moist.

Silah, *n.* A weapon; arm. —*posh,* armed. —*bardár,* an armour-bearer. —*ḳhána,* armoury.

Silli, *n.* A whetstone; a slab.

Silsilá, *n.* Chain; series; succession; genealogy; connection. —*wár,* linked together; serial; consecutive; in a line or series; *seriatim,* adj. in the chain (of); systematically.

Sím, *n.* Silver. —*áb,* quicksilver; mercury. —*andúd,* silver-plated. —*tan, a.* fair.

Símá, *n.* Limit; boundary; frontier.

Simaran, *n.* [See *Smaraṇ*].

Simṭan, *n.* A griffin; an eagle

Símurg, *n.* A griffin; an eagle.

Sin, *n.* Crease; wrinkle.

Sin, *n.* Age. —*i-bulúg, sin-i-tamíz,* years of discretion. —*rasídá,* old. *kam*—, a. young; of lesser age.

Síná, *n.* The breast; bosom; chest. —*ubhár kar chalná,* to walk with the chest stuck out; to walk pompously. —*afgár,* grieved in heart; afilicted— *ba sina,* descending from father to son. —*bía,* stethoseope. —*zor,* stubborn; obstinate.

Sína', *v.* To sew; to stitch; to darn.

Sinchái, *n.* Irrigation; watering (a plant, or a field).

Sínchaná, *v.* To irrigate; to water.

Sindúr, *n.* Vermillion.

Síng, Singh, *n.* A horn.

Singár, *n.* Decoration; embellishment. —*áiná,* toilet glass. —*dán,* dressing table. —*mez,* toilet able.

Sinh, Singh, *n.* A lion; the sign Leo (burj *Asad*).

Singháṛá, *n.* Water chestnut.

Singhásan, *n.* Throne; royal seat.

Singhní, *n. f.* Lioness.

Sípí, *n.* An oyster-shell.

Sipah, Sipáh, *n.* An army; soldiers. —*dár,* commander of an army. —*sálár,* a general.

Sipáhí, *n.* A soldier.

Sir, *n.* [See *Sar*].

Siṛá, *n.* Top; beginning; extremity.

Sirát, *n.* Road; way. —*ul-mustaqín,* the right way.

Sírat, *n.* Nature; disposition; temperament; quality; name.

Sirâyat, *n.* Contagion; infection; penetration; pestilence; plague.

Síṛhí, *n.* A staircase; a ladder.

Sirí, *adj.* Mad; lunatic; insane.

Sirísh, [See *Saresh*].

Sirká, *n.* Vinegar.

Sís, *n.* [See *Shísh*].

Sít, *n.* Cold; chill. —*kál,* winter time.

Sitáish, *n.* Praise; eulogy; benediction; returning thanks.

Sítalá, *n.* a name for the female deity, *Durgá* in her calmer countenance; also a euphemism for an attack of small-pox.

Sitam, *n.* Tyranny; oppression; injury. —*rasídá,* oppressed; injured. —*gár,* tyrant; oppressor.

Sitár, *n.* A well-known Indian musical instrument; less-educated Westerners call it a 'funny guitar'.

Sitárá, *n.* A star; fate; destiny. —*chamakná,* good luck to come.

Síṭí, *n.* A whistle. —*bajáná,* v. To whistle.

Sitúdá, *a.* Praise; eulogised; laudable. —*sifat,*-of laudable qualities.

Sitún, *n.* Pillar; column.

Siwá, *a.* More; besides; over and above; except; save.

Siyáh, *a.* Black; dark. *—baḳht,* unfortunate; unlucky. *—fám,* of a black colour. *—gosh,* a lynx. *—posh,* dressed in mourning.

Siyáhat, *n.* Voyage; travel.

Siyáhí, *n.* Ink; blackness.*—potaná,* v. To malign; to wipe out; to darken.

Siyár, *n.* A jackal.

Siyáq, *n.* Arithmetic.

Siyásat, *n.* Politics; conduct (of affairs); administration; jurisdiction; punishment; torture; pain; agony.

Slok, *n.* [See *Shlok*].

Smaraṇ, *n.* Remembrance; recollection; memory; counting (one's) beads; regretting. *—diláná,* to remind (of); to put one in remembrance (of).

Smrití, *n.* Recollection; memory; a code or body of laws, such as that compiled by Manu.

Snán, *n.* Bathing; washing ablution; cleansing.

Sneh, *n.* Love; kindness; affection. friendship.

So, *prep.* Therefore; hence.

Soch, *n.* Thought; reflection; meditation; imagination; idea; attention; anxiety; sorrow; grief; penitence.

Sog, *n.* Affliction; sorrow; grief. *—karná,* to put on mourning.

Soház, *n.* Symbol of marital bliss; a husband; vermillion worn in the parting of a Hindu woman's hair (as a marker of her being happily married).

Sohágá, *n.* Borax.

Sohan, *a.* Pleasing; beautiful; handsome; *n.* a friend; a lover.

Sokhná, *v.* To absorb; to soak up.

Soḳhtá, *a.* Burnt; scorched. *—ján,* grieved; heart sore. *—ní,* fit to be burnt. *—ní qurbání,* burnt offering.

Som, *n.* The moon. *—wár,* Monday.

Soná, *v.* To sleep; to lie down; to die; to fall asleep.

Soná, *n.* Gold; riches; wealth-bullion, *sone ká pání,* gilding. *—ká warq,* gold leaf.

Sonahrá, [See *Sunahrá*].

So<u>n</u>th, *n.* Dry ginger; a spicey and sour dip.

Sosan, *n.* Lily.

Sotá, *n.* Stream; fountain; spring.

Soz, *n.* Burning; pathos (in poetry) inflaming *(used as last member of compounds,* as; *jigar—,* heart-burning); *n.* burning; heat; inflammation; passion; affection. *—khwán,* one who chants a dirge. *—nák,* burning; ardent; painful.

Sparsh, *n.* Touch; contact.

Spashṭ, *a.* Clear; distinct; manifest; evident; easy. *—rúp se,* adv. Clearly; categorically; evidently, etc. *—vádí,* a. Outspoken; one who calls a spade a spade; frank.

Srashṭá, *n.* The Creator; God Almighty.

Srishṭí, *n.* Creation; universe.

Srot, *n.* Source; spring (of water); orgin (of information, etc.).

Star, *n.* Standard; level; layer; grade.

Sthán, *n.* Place.

Sthápit, *n.* Firm; established.

Stháyí, *a.* Permanent; stable; lasting; durable; steady.

Sthir, *a.* Constant; firm. *—chitt,* sedate; steady.

Sthúl, *a.* Plump; fat; bulky; thick; massive; rough; crude; gross. *—buddhi,* a. nitwit; short-brained.

Stúp, *n.* A (Buddhist) monument (generally a pyramidal, or dome-like structure, usually erected over the sacred relics of Buddha himself or on spots consecrated as the scenes of his acts).

Stuti, *n.* Commendation; praise; eulogy.

Suárath, *n.* [See *Swárth*].

Súá, *n.* A parrot; a packing needle.

Sub, *n.* Short for *Subah: morning.* Used as a prefix for words and phrases relating to morning time. Example: *Sub-ba-ḳhair,* Morning of well-being; good morning.

Súbá, *n.* A province. *—dár,* governor of a province; a native military officer.

Subah, *n.* Morning; dawn; day-break; beginning of. *Subah-i-hayát,* a. Dawn of life. &c.

Subaran, Subarn, *n.* [See *Swarn*].

Subhán, *a.* Magnifying; glorifying. *—alláh,* far be it from God ! Holy God ! Good God ! Bravo ! Well done ! *haq—hú* God the Most Holy.

Subháshit, *n.* A maxim; a quotable quote; a statement well-made.

Subhítá, *n.* Time; leisure; convenience.

Subuk, *n.* Light; frivolous; trifling; debased; delicate. *—mizáj,* fickle-munded; irresolute.

Subút, *n.* Proof; testimony; permanence. *—i-badíhi, —i-bádi-nazar,* a *prima facie* evidence. *—i-lissání,* oral testimony.

Súd, *n.* Interest; profit; gain. *—ḳhor,* A usurer. *—dar—,* compound interest. *—honá,* to be benefited.

Sudh/ Sudhi, *n.* Memory; awareness; consciousness; sensation; care; notice. *—lená,* v. To ask for the well-being; to enquire about; to take care of. *—budh,* n.

senses; consciousness. *Be—*, adj. Unaware; senseless; unconscious.

Sudhí, *n.* [See *Sudh*].

Sudhár, *n.* Reform; uplift; repair; amendment; correction; modification; improvement. *—vád,* n. Reformation movement. *—vádí,* a. Reformist.

Sudhárná, *v.* To reform; to correct; to mend.

Súfí, *a.* Wise; intelligent; pious; devout; a deist; a free-thinker or pantheist; a Muslim mystic.

Sufúf, *n.* Powder; fine dust.

Sugan̲dh, *n.* Scent; odour; perfume. it, a. fragrant; perfumed; odoriferous.

Suhág, *n.* Good fortune; overture. *—utarná,* to become a widow. *—an,* a woman whose husband is alive.

Suháwáná, *a.* Agreeable; pleasing; handsome.

Suí, *n.* Needle; the hands of a watch or clock.

Sújá, *n.* A borer; an awl; a gimlet.

Sujan, *a.* [See *Sajjan*].

Sújan, *n.* Inflammation; swelling.

Suján, *adj.* Intelligent; discerning; one who profits from experience; wise.

Sujúd, *n.* Adoration.

Sukaṛná, *v.* To shrink; to draw in; to be contracted.

Sukh, *n.* Ease; rest; happiness; comfort; tranquility.

Súkhá, *a.* Dry; parched; withered; *n.* draught. *—tálná, v.* to send away empty.

Sukhan, *n.* Speech; language; discourse; eloquence; poetry. *—var,* n. Practitioner(s) of speech; poet(s); eloquent one(s). *—chín,* n. Literary Critic(s); hair-splitter(s); hypocrite(s).

Sukkan, *n.* A rudder; a helm.

Sukumár, *a.* Young; delicate; tender; soft.

Sukúnat, *n.* Habitation; dwelling; tranquillity.

Sukút, *n.* Silence; quietness; calmness.

Súl, *n.* [see *Shúl*].

Sulah, *n.* Peace; reconciliation; truce; compromise; treaty. *—i-chand-rozá,* a. A temporary truce; an armistice. *—shikaní,* n. Breach of ceasefire. *—karná,* v. To strike a deal; to come to terms (with); to make peace. *—námá,* n. A deed of compromise; a treaty-document.

Sulajhná, *v.* To be unravelled.

Sulb, *n.* The backbone.

Sulgáná, *v.* To kindle; to light; to incite; to inflame.

Súlí, Gallows; hanging platform; impaling stake; gibbet.

Sultán, *n.* An emperor; a king; a ruler; a sovereign.

Sulúk, *n.* Treatment; conduct; manner.

Sum, *n.* A hoof.

Súná, *a.* Void; empty; desolate.

Sunár, *n.* A goldsmith.

Súnḍ, *n.* Proboscis of an elephant trunk.

Sundar, *a.* Handsome; fair; beautiful. —*tá,* handsomeness; beauty.

Súnghná, *v.* To smell.

Sunn, *adj.* Numb; without sensation; paralysed.

Sun-ná, *v.* To hear; to listen; to pay attention to.

Sunnat, *n.* A religious ceremony; an ordinance of religion; circumcision.

Súns, *n.* Porpoise.

Sunsán, *adj.* Deserted; lonely; derelict.

Supárí, *n.* Betel nut.

Supurd, *n.* Charge; commitment; trust; delivering or giving over.

Súq, *n.* A market.

Sur, *n.* Tone; note; melody; tone.

Surá, *n.* An intoxicating drink; a wine; liquor. —*sundarí,* prov. Drink and dames (as a indulgence).

Súrág, *n.* Track; sign; footstep; clue; mark.

Suráhí, *n.* Goblet; jug. —*dár gardan,* a. long and beautiful neck.

Súraj, *n.* [See *Súrya*].

Súrákh, *n.* Hole; passage; in-let. —*dár,* perforated; porous.

Suramya, *adj.* Enchanting; heart-warming; Beautiful [often refers to scenery].

Surang, *n.* A subterraneous passage; a mine; *a.* light-bay or chestnut (a horse).

Surat, *n.* Remembrance; memory. —*bisarná,* to lose the recollection of. —*karná, v.* to call to mind.

Súrat, *n.* Form; shape; face; figure; appearance.

Surkh, *a.* Red. —*rú,* Honorable.

Surmá, *n.* Collyrium; antimony.

Súrmá, *n.* Brave; bold.

Surúr, *n.* Slight intoxication; pleasure; delight; cheerfulness.

Súrya, *n.* The sun. —*vanshí,* a. Of sc dynasty. —*mukhí,* n. Sunflower, name flower.

Su-samáchár, *a.* Good news; tidings; (proverbially) the Gospel.

Susar, *n.* [See *Shwasur*].

Susrí, *n.* Mother-in-law; a term of abuse.

Sust, *a.* Lazy; slow. —*chál,* adv. Slow-mover; one dragging his/her feet.

Sustáná, *v.* To rest; to take repose.

Sút, *n.* Thread; yarn; a line; stamen; fibre; tendril.

Sut, *n.* An son.

Sutá, *n.* A daughter.

Sutárí, *n.* An awl.

Suthrá, *a.* Neat; tidy; clean; excellent.

Sutlí, *n.* Threat string.

Sútná, *v.* To strip the leaves of a branch; to drain; to rub.

Sútr, *n.* (Literally) A thread; yarn; fibre; (proverbially source; aphorism of philosophy, or grammar etc.). —*dhár,* n. The stage manager (in a play or other kind of performance); master of ceremonies. —*pát,* n. Commencement; beginning; initiation.

Sutún, *n.* A pillar; a column.

Swád, *n.* Taste; relish; flavour; pleasure. —*isht,* a. Tasty; delicious; flavoursome.

Swadesh, *a.* Native land; country of one's origins; homeland; motherland.

Swadeshí, *a.* Indigenous; originating in one's own country; native.

Swádhín, *a.* Independent; free; self-governing; self-ruled.

Swáhá, *a.* Burnt to ashes; wasted; destroyed.

Swámí, *n.* Master; owner; proprietor; lord; husband. Also a venerative title for learned and preaching *yogis.*

Swapna, *n.* Dream; visions; ambition. *Divá*—, n. Day-dream. *Duh*—, n. Nightmare. —*dosh,* n. Involuntary erection and ejaculation (in the middle of sleep).

Swar, *n.* Sound (in *Gram.*) the vowel points.

Swarg, *n.* Heaven; paradise. —*ik,* a. Heavenly. —*íya,* a. One who has gone to heaven; late; deceased.

Swarglok, *n.* Heaven; Paradise.

Swarṇ, *n.* Gold. —*im,* a Golden.

Swárath, *n.* [See *Swárth*].

Swárth, *n.* Selfishness; self-interest; ulterior motive; aim; personal objective. —*í,* a. Selfish; self-gratifying.

Swarúp, *n.* Form; shape; nature; character.

Swás, *n.* [See *Shwás*].

Swasth, *a.* Healthy; in good health; in good condition; lively; normal.

Swásthya, *n.* Health; condition; well-being.

Swatantr, *a.* Independent; unrestrained; autonomous; not under any duress; self-governing. —*atá,* n. Freedom; Independence, etc. —*atá ándolan,* n. Freedom movement. —*atá senání,* n. Freedom fighter. —*lekhan,* v. Freelance writing.

Swayam, *adv.* By oneself; of one's own accord; personally; automatically.

Syáhí, *n.* [See *Siyáhí*].

Syáná, *a.* [See *Sayáná*].

❃❃❃❃❃❃❃❃❃❃❃❃❃❃❃❃❃❃❃❃

तप से राजसत्ता मिलती है, और
राजसत्ता से नरक की राह!

Tap sé ráj-sattá milti hai, aur
ráj-sattá sé narak kí ráh!

(Hard work will grant you power; but power will lead you straight to hell!)

❃❃❃❃❃❃❃❃❃❃❃❃❃❃❃❃❃❃❃❃

T, t, sounds like (त) in Hindi and (ت and ط) in Urdu. With a dot (.) at the bottom, it will also represent (ट) sound in Hindi and (ٹ) in Urdu. When suffixed by an 'h' it represents the aspirated sound of (थ) in Hindi and of (تھ) in Urdu. When used enjoined with a dot at the bottom, it would sound like (ठ) in Hindi and (ٹھ) in Urdu.

Tá, *adv.* To; until; as long as; whilst; in order (that); to the end (that). —*tá zíst,* while life remains. —*chunín,* hitherto; thus far. —*ki,* so that; until; so long. —*ba maqdúr,* to the extent of (one's) power; as much as possible. —*ham,* yet neverthe-less.

Taálá, *n.* The Most High; the Supreme Being; hence, *Alláh Taálá.*

Ta'ám, *n.* Food; victuals; eating.

Ta'b, *n.* Toil; weariness; labour; fatigue.

Táb, *n.* Endurance; ability; power; splendour; lustre; brilliance; twist; contortion. —*dár,* warm; burning; shining. —*dán,* an opening in a wall; a window. —*rahná,* to be able to bear. —*istán,* hot weather; summer. —*láná,* to muster strength or courage, &c., (for).

Tab, *adv.* Then; at that time; afterwards. —*hí se,* thence; thenceforth. —*hí to,* then indeed. —*se,* thence; since that time.

Taba', *n.* Print; impression; edition (of a book); nature; genius; temperament. —*zád,* original; invented. —*í,* natural; constitutional; physical; *'ilmi—,* natural science; physics.

Tabaddal, *n.* Change; exchange.

Tabádlá, *n.* Transfer; exchange.

Tabáh, *a.* Ruined; destroyed; spoiled; object. —*hál,* in a depolorable condition. —*i,* destruction; perdition; ruin; wretchedness.

Tába'in, *n.* (*Plur. of Tábe'*). Followers; dependents; companions.

Tabakh , *a.* Cooking.

Tablá, *n.* A pair of drums, traditionally played as accompaniment to all musical performances in India, and now it is gaining ever-growing popularity abroad as well.

Tabáq, *n.* A dish; a tray; a basin, (*tasht, síní).*

Tabar, *n.* An axe; a hatchet.—*zan,* a wood-cutter.

Tabarruk, *n.* A sacred relic; blessing; benediction.

Tabarzad, *n.* Conserve of roses (*gulqand);* sugar-candy.

Tabáshír, *n.* Bamboo pith; the sugar of the bamboo; mann; (*banslochan).*

Tabbáḳh, *n.* A cook.

Tabdíl, *n.* Change; alteration; transposition; transformation. —*i-makán,* migration.—*i-nájáiz,* falsification; an unlawful change or alternation.

Tabelá, *a.* A stable; a stall.

Tábe, *a.* Department; subordinate; submission; subjugated.—*dár, n.* slave.

Tabíb, *n.* Doctor; physician; medical practitioner.

Tábír, *n.* Interpretation; translation; explanation.—*go,* an interpretor of dreams.

Tabíyat, *n.* Nature; disposition; temperament.—*'alil honá,* to be indisposed.—*lagná,* to take interest in.—*na lagná,* to be disinclined towards.

Tabl, Tabal, *n.* A large drum. —*báz, a.* drummer. [Also see *Tablá*].

Tabáq, *n.* Stage; shelf; rack.

Tábút, *n.* A bier; a coffin; a model of the tomb of Hussain carried in the Moharrum procession.

Ta'dád, *n.* Enumeration; number; amount; sum; extent.

Tadáruk, *a.* Punishment; penalty; remedy; precaution.

Tadbír, *n.* Opinion; judgement; Device; order; management.—*i-fásid,* a plot; conspiracy.—*i-saltan̉at,* politics.

Ta'ddi, *n.* Oppression; injustice; tyranny.

Tadfín, *n.* Burial; interment; sepulchre.

Tádíb, *n.* Discipline; punishment; admonition; correction.—*kháná,* reformatory; house of correction.

Tadríj, *n.* Gradation; scale, *bá—,* gradually; by degrees.

Tadrís, *n.* Instruction; lecturing.

Tafakkur, *n.* Reflection; cogitation; meditation; anxiety.

Tafrík, *n.* Separation; analysis; subtraction; distinction; interval; classification.

Tafáwat, *n.* Distance; interval; difference; division.

Ta'ffun, *n.* Stink; fetidness.

Tafríh, *n.* Rejoicing; jubilation; gladness; amusement; pastime. —*taba',* cheerfulness.

Tafriqá, *n.* Dissension; discord; disunion. —*dálná,* to sow dissension; to forment quarrels.

Tafsíl, *n.* Particulars; details; analysis; explanation. —*wár,* in full details; minutely.

Tafsír, *n.* Explanation; exposition; commentary; paraphrase.

Taftísh, *n.* Enquiry; investigation; search.

Tafzíl, *n.* Excellence; pre-eminence; superiority.

Tágá, *n.* (Colloquial for *Dhágá* meaning—) A thread; a fibre.

Tagaiyur, *n.* (*Plur. Tagaiyurát*). Charge; revolution; alteration.

Tagallub, *n.* Cheating; embezzlement; misappropriation; fund.

Tagṛá, *a.* Stout; strong; muscular; able-bodies.

Tah, *n.* Fold; plait; layer; stratum; basis; the bottom. *—o-bálá,* upside down; topsy turvy.

Tahaiyur, *n.* Wonder; amazement.

Tahajjí, *n.* Spelling. *hurúf-i—,* the letters of an alphabet.

Ṭahal, *n.* Service; duty; work.

Ṭahalná, *v.* To walk to and fro; to take an airing.

Táham, *adv.* Still; yet; nevertheless; notwithstanding.

Tahammul, *n.* Patience; endurance; fortitude; forbearance.

Tahárat, *n.* Purity; cleanliness; sanctity; ablution.

Taharruk, *n.* Motion; movement.

Taháshá, *n.* Care; fear; awe; dread be—, fearlessly.

Tahassur, *n.* Regret; condolence; grief.

Tahattuk, *n.* Infamy; dishonour; disgrace; ignominy; altercation; quarrelling.

Tahband, *n.* A cloth worn round the waist and passing between the legs.

Táhir, *a.* Clean; pure; virtuous; chaste.

Táhirí, Taharí, *n.* A Kashmírí savoury dish, made from best quality rice, mixed with chopped up potatoes and other vegetables, or chunky pieces of meat, judiciously garnished with butter and spices... and the whole concoction steam-cooked. [*Biriyání* beats a hasty retreat when *Tahari* is served.

Tahlíl, *n.* Solubility; solution; digestion; assimilation.

Ṭahaluá, *n.* A drudge; a menial servant; an odd-job man.

Tahniyat, *n.* Congratulation; compliment.

Tahqíq, *n.* (*Plur. Tahqiqát*). Enquiry; investigation; truth; certainty; a authentic; verified.

Tahqír, *n.* Contempt; scorn; disclaim; neglect.

Tahríf, *n.* Altering (words from their proper meanings); transposition of a word or letter; clerical error; deliberate alteration of word so as to change its meanings.

Tahrík, *n.* Motion; movement; incitement; instigation; temptation.

Tahrír, *n.* Setting at liberty; writing; a written statement; fee for writing.

Tahsil, *n.* Gain; acquisition; a sub-district; office or court of a *Tahsildár.* *—dár,* a sub-collector of revenue.

Tahsín, *n.* Applause; approbation; cheers. *—i-akhláq,* refinement; good breeding.

Taht, *n.* Lower part; depth; subjection; possession; control. *prep.* and *adv.* beneath; under; in subjection (to). *—í-hukúmat,* jurisdiction. *—us-sará,* the nether or infernal regions.

Tahwíl, *n.* change; transfer; trust; cash; capital; a treasury. *—dár,* cashier; treasurer.

Tahzíb, *n.* Civilization; refinement; politeness; correction; amendment. *—yáfta,* refined; polished; educated; civilized.

Táíd, *n.* Corroboration; support aid; succour.

Ta'inát, *n.* Appointment; service; duty; a garrison.

Taintálís, *n.* Forty-three.

Taintîs, *adj.* Thirty-three.

Táir, *a.* Flying; *n.* a bird; a winged creature.

Tairák, *n.* A swimmer.

Tairná, *v.* To swim; to float.

Taish, *n.* Anger; wrath; rage; passion.

Taiyár, *a.* Ready; prepared; complete; plump; ripe; (fruit).

Taiyárí, *n.* Readiness; promptitude; pomp; plumpness.

Táj, *n.* A crown. *—poshí,* v. Installation on the throne. *—mahal,* n. World famous white marble monument/shrine built by a Mughal emperor Sháh-Jahán, near Agra, in memory of his beloved wife, Mumtaz Mahal.

Tajallí, *n.* Brilliance; lustre; radiance; brightness.

Tajammul: *n.* Dignity; pomp; parade; retinue.

Tajammulát, *n.* Household furnitures; moveables; articles of luxury.

Tajarubá/ Tajurbá, *n.* Experiment; experience; maturity. *—át,* n. Plural of—, *dár,* adj. Experienced; mature; wellversed in—.

Tajassus, In. Spying; espionage; exploring; search; investigation.

Tajáwuz, *n.* Transgression; violence; outrage.

Tajhíz-o-takfín, *n.* Burial; interment.

Tájíl, *n.* Haste; speed; celerity; rapidity; fleetness; agility.

Tájir, *n.* A merchant; a trader.

Ta'jjub, *n.* Surprise; wonder; astonishment. *—karná, v.* to wonder at; to be astonished at.

Tajná, *v.* To abandon; to for-sake; to desert; to quit.

Tajurbá(t), *n.* Experience(s); experiment(s). *—kár,* a. A person with experience.

Tajwíz, *n.* A scheme; a proposal; a method; a suggestion.

Tak, *adv.* Till; up to; towards; while.

Ták, *n.* A vine; a creeper.

Ṭaká, *n.* A copper coin equal to one pice (not in use now); money; wealth; riches.

Takabbur, *n.* Pride; haughtiness; arrogance; grandeur.

Takalluf, *n.* Attention; industry; trouble; extravagance; strict observance of etiquette; ceremonies and formalities; insincerity.

Takallum, *n.* Speaking; speech; conversation.

Taḳhaiyul, *n.* Imagination; fancy; supposition; suspicion.

Taḳhallus, *n.* A poet's *nom de plume;* poetic name.

Taḳhfif, *n.* Abridgment; curtailment; diminution; decrease; alleviation; mitigation; relief.

Táḳhír, *n.* Delay; impediment; procrastination; postponement.

Taḳhliyá, *n.* Evacuation; private place or room; manumission (of a slave); divorce (of a wife).

Taḳhmíná, *n.* Guess; conjecture; valuation; estimate.

Ṭaḳhná, *n.* The ankle joint; the ankle.

Taḳht, *n.* A throne; a chair of state; bench; sofa; platform. *—se utárná,* to dethrone. *—gáh,* royal residence; seat of government; capital. *—nashíní,* installation; coronation. *—yá takhtá,* a throne or a bier; victory or death.

Tákht, *n.* Attack; inroad; incursion; invasion. *—o-táráj karná,* to attack and plunder; to sack.

Taḳhtá, *n.* A plank; board; deck; bench; a sheet of paper.

Taḳhtí, *n.* A small plank; a small board used as a tablet for beginners to write on (rarely seen the se days); a signet of stone; a tablet.

Tákíd, *n.* Stress; strict super intendence. *—an,* emphatically; urgently.

Takiyá, *n.* A pillow; a faqir's stand; a support.

Ṭakkar, *n.* Knocking against;

shock; butting; collision. *—khánā,* to be dashed against anything; a stumble.

Taklá, *n.* A spindle.

Taklíf, *n.* Trouble; difficulty; distress; hardship. *—uṭhánā,* to suffer; to take the trouble. *—pahuṉchánā,* to inflict pain; to cause distress.

Takmíl, *n.* Perfection; completion; accomplishment. *—i-tamassuk,* execution of a bond.

Tákná, *v.* To look at; to watch; to look steadfastly; to store.

Ṭakráná, *v.* To dash together; to butt; to knock against; to grope in the dark.

Takrár, *n.* Dispute; wrangle; contention; repetition.

Takrím, *n.* Honor; respect.

Ṭaksál, *n.* A mint. *—í,* a coiner.

Takzíb, *n.* Accusation of falsehood; giving (one) the lie.

Tal, *n.* Surface; bottom; *prep.* under; beneath. *—chhaṭ* sediment; leavings.

Tál, *n.* Pond; tank; pool; time (in music) *—be-tál,* out of time; inopportune.

Tál, *n.* A heap; stack.

Ṭál-maṭol, *n.* Evasion; putting off; postponement.

Tálá, *n.* A lock; a device used to restrain unauthorised opening of or entry into secured spaces, i.e. Cupboards, rooms and houses etc. *—toṛná,* to break open a lock.

Taálá, *adj.* The Most High Revised entry.

T'álá, *adj.* Most High (of station). *Alláh—,* n. God Almighty.

Talab, *n.* Wish; desire; demand; sending for; summous; pay; wages salary; *a.* seeking; requiring; desiring; *n.* seeker; desirer (*used as last member of compounds),* as. *—talab,* fond of ease; a lover of ease, &c., &c.

Táláb, *n.* Pond; tank.

Talabána, *n.* Fees to process-servers.

Talaf, *n.* Ruin; destruction; loss; waste.

Talaffuz, *n.* Pronunciation; utterance; expression.

Talmíz, *n. (Plur)* Scholars; pupils.

Taláq, *n.* Divorce.

Talásh, *n.* Search; investigation; inquiry.

Talattuf, *n.* Kindness; favour; obligation.

Talátum, *n.* Dashing or buffeting of waves.

Tálavya, *a.* Palatal sounds (in a language); sounds produced by the tongue touching the palate, sounds like 't' and 'd'.

Taláwat, *n.* Grace; beauty; elegance.

Tálíl, *n.* A key; a device that opens the lock, or secured spaces.

Tálib, *n.* Seeker; candidate; petitioner; asking; requesting. —*i-'ilm,* a student; a scholar.

Tálíf, *n.* Compilation; collection; composition; joining; uniting.

Ta'lím, *n.* Teaching; instruction; tuition.

Talkh, *n.* Bitter; unpalatable; sorrowful; acrimonious. —*mizáj, a.* ill-tempered; irascible.

Ṭal-jáná, *v.* To pass off; to blow over; to move away; to be averted.

Ṭallebáz, *adj.* Evasive; given to evasiveness; one who tries to put off things or tasks.

Ṭalná, *v.* To be averted; to be postponed; to slip to slink away; to make off; to get out of the way.

Ta'lluq, *n. (Plur. Ta'lluqat.)* Pertaining to; dependent on; connection; relation; concern; reference; property; possession. —*á. n.* possession of land); estate; manor; division of a province, —*dár,* a landholder; possession of an estate; feoffee.

Talqín, *n.* Teaching; instruction; funeral ceremonies; burial service.

Tálú, *n.* Palate; the ceiling of the vocal cavity.

Talwá, *n.* Sole of the foot; heel. —*sahláná,* to flatter.

Talwár, *n.* A sword; sabre; scimitar.

Tam, *n.* Darkness; gloom; (proverbially) ignorance.

Tama', *n.* Avarice; greed; covetousness; ardent desire. —*dená, v.* to tempt; to allure; to bribe.

Tamáchá, *n.* A heavy slap (Across the face).

Tamám, *n.* Complete; perfect; whole; full; total; *n.* the whole; conclusion; end.

Tamanchá, *n.* A pistol; a revolver.

Tamanná, *n.* Wish; desire; inclination; request; petition.

Tamas, *n.* The third of the three *gunas* incidental to creation, or the state of humanity.

Tamáshá, *n.* Entertainment; exhibition; show; sport; pleasure; any thing strange or curious. —*bin,* sight-seer; epicure. —*karná,* to make sport or fun (of).

Tamassuk, *n.* An obligation; bond; promissory note; note of hand; receipt.

Tamawwal, *n.* Riches; wealth.

Támbá, *n.* Copper.

Tambákú, *n.* Tobacco.

Tambíh, *n.* Rebuke; censure; admonition; correction.

Tambú, *n.* Tent; pavilion; canopy.

Támbúl, *n.* Betel; betal leaf, commonly known as *Pán* [leavened with a fine layer of lime paste, catechu *Terra japonica and* sprinkled with chippings of betel nut, and chewed slowly, all over India].

Tamgá, *n.* A medal; seal; royal grant or charter.

Tamhíd, *n.* Preface; introduction; arrangement; management; confirmation. *—en bándhná,* to frame vain suppositions beforehand; to make lame excuses.

Tamil, *n.* The oldest of the four major languages, belonging to the Dravidian family, spoken and written in South India. *—náḍu,* n. A state in the South India, covering most of the Eastern seaboard and almost touching the island of Sri Lanka. *Tamils,* n. Refers to the Tamil-speaking refugees who have flooded to the countries of the West as refugees in the wake of the internecine strife in Sri Lanka. In the popular psyche, the word has become synonimous to 'these poor sods'.

Támíl, *n.* Carrying out; implementation (of an order, or a law etc.); service (of a summons, etc.).

Ta'mír, *n.* Building; construction; erection; repairing.

Tamíz, *n.* Discretion; discernment; judgment; sense. *—dár,* discreet; sensible; well-be-haved.

Tamjíd, *n.* Glorification of God.

Tamkanat, *n.* Dignity; majesty; authority.

Tamlík, *n.* Possessorship; ownership; possession; appointing; master or ossessor. *—námá, n.* a deed of transfer.

Támmul, *n.* Consideration; deliberation; hesitation; reflection. *—karná,* to consider; to reflect.

Tamr, *n.* A rie date. *—i-Hindi, n.* tamarind.

Támr, *n.* Coer. *—patta,* n. A copper plate (used in ancient times to convey official, or royal commands, or to issue inscriptions and edicts etc.) *—pátr,* n. Copperware.

Tamsíl, *n.* Comparison; resemblance; example; fable; allegory. *—an,* for example; allegorically; comparatively.

Ṭamṭamáhaṭ, *n.* Flush; glow; blush.

Ṭamṭamáná, *v.* To become red (in the face); to flush or blush; to twinkle; to flash.

Ta'na, *n.* Blame; reproach; censure; taunt; disgrace.

Tan, *n.* Body. —*man,* prov. Body and Soul. —*kí pyás,* a. Bodily desire. —*kí tapan* n. Need for physical gratification [a reference to 'horizontal refreshment']. —*badan kí sudh ná rahná,* adv. To transcend one's physical being; to be beside one's self. —*badan men ág lagná,* adv. To be outraged.

Taná, *n.* Trunk; stalk; stem; a spider's web.

Tanabbub, *n.* Advice; admonition; bashfulness; modesty.

Tanaffur, *n.* Avoiding; shuning; aversion; disgust.

Tanaffus, *n.* Breathing; respiration; sighing deeply.

Tánaná, *v.* To stretch; to spread; to tighten; to erect; to brandish (a sword, or a stick, in a threatening manner).

Tanásul, *n.* Similarity; resemblance; proportion.

Tanassul, *n.* Pedigree; genealogy.

Tanáwal, *n.* Taking meat and drink; eating.

Tanáza', *n.* Dispute; contest.

Tanazzul, *n.* Descent; decline; decay; falling off; diminution.

Tanazzulí, *n.* Decline; demotion; downward trend or move.

Tandul, *n.* Rice.

Tandúr, *n.* A clay oven used all over Northern India and many countries of the Middle-East and Central Asia to cook and bake in.

Tang, *a.* Tight; narrow; contracted; scarce; poor; sad; *n.* a horse-bet. —*chashm,* moiserly. —*dast,* poor; penniless. —*hál,* straitened in circumstances.

Ṭáng, *n.* A leg.

Ṭángá, *n.* A small two-wheeled carriage.

Ṭángan, *n.* A pony.

Tangí, *n.* Poverty; narrowness; difficulty.

Tanhá, *a.* Alone; solitary. —*í,* loneliness; solitude.

Tanik, *a.* Little bit; slight. —*achchhá,* a. A cut above; somewhat better.

Ṭánká, *n.* Stitch.

Ṭankan, *n.* Typing; minting. —*karná,* v. To type; to undertake typesetting.

Tankhwáh, *n.* Pay; salary; wages.

Ṭánkná, *v.* To stitch; to cobble; to append; to make a note of.

Tanmay, *a.* Identified with; fully engrossed in; totally absrbed into.

Tánpúrá, *n.* (Also called *Tambúrá)* A time-keeping

stringed instrument, used as an accompaniment in Classical Indian Musical performances.

Tanqíh, *n.* Cleansing deciding a dispute.

Tansíkh, *n.* Repeal; aborogation; quashing; cancellation; revocation; annulment.

Tánt, *n.* Catgut; sinews.

Tantr, *n.* A system; a technique.

Tantragya, *n.* One who knows *Tantar;* a technician; a wizard.

Tántragya, *n.* One who knows *Tantar;* a technician; a wizard.

Tántrik, *a.* A practitioner of *Tant:* pertaining to *Tantr.*

Tantu, *n.* A thread; a fibre; a filament; tendril; cord or string (of a musical instrument. —*may,* a. Fibrous).

Tanvangí, *a.* Tenuous; slim; delicate; of a fragile frame; slender.

Tanz, *n.* Taunt; sarcasm; joking.

Tanzîm, *n.* Arrangement; discipline; organization; party; regiment; regimentation.

Táo, *n.* A sheet of paper; passion; rage. —*táoná,* to stroke the whiskers; to heat.

Táp/ Tap, *n.* Heat; warmth; fever. —tillí, enlargement of the spleen—*í-diqq,* hectic fever. —*i-larza,* ague.

Ṭáp, *n.* Hoof of a horse; sound of a horse's hoofs.

Ṭápá, *n.* A hen-coop.

Tapák, *n.* Affection; love; esteem; cordiality.

Tapáná, *v.* To heat; to warm.

Tapasyá, *n.* Penance; self-imposed hardship in pursuit of a material or divine goal; self mortification; ascetic effort.

Tapish, *n.* Heat; warmth; affliction.

Ṭapkáná, *v.* To cause; to drip; to distil.

Tapt, *a.* Heated; warmed up; afflicted; Feverish; angry.

Ṭápú, *n.* An island.

Táq, *n.* A niche; a shelf; a window; *a.* odd; *bálá-i—,* apart; aside; aloof.

Taqaddus, *n.* Being pure and holy.

Taqallub, *n.* Conversion; change; transmutation.

Taqalluf, *n.* Formality; meticulous observance of propriety or etiquette. —*karná,* adv. To be formal; to stand on ceremony.

Taqarrub, *n.* Access; nearness.

Taqarrur, *n.* Confirmation; appointment. —*í,* appointment. *parwáná-i—,* appointment letter.

Táqat, *n.* Strength; power; force —*war,* powerful; strong.

Taqáwi, *n.* Assisting; advancing money to cultivators for digging wells and purchasing imple-ments etc.

Taqáza, *n.* Demand; pressing the settlement of a claim; requisition; exigence. *—i-sinn,* the requirements or natural tendencies or natural tendencies of different ages. 'indal—, on demand.

Taqdír, *n.* Destiny; fate; divine decree.

Taqdís, *n.* Sanctification; purity.

Taqí, *a.* God-fearing; pious; de-vout.

Taqlíd, *n.* Imitation; mimicing; mimicry; feigning; counter-feiting.

Ta'qqub, *n.* Pursuing; tracking; punishment; chastisement.

Taqríb, *n.* Approximation; ap-proach; access; recommenda-tion; conjuncture; festival. *—adv.* nearly; approximately.

Taqrír, *n.* Discourse; speech; declaration; recital; narration; account; detail; confession.

Taqsím, *n.* Division; distribution; allotment; partition.

Taqsír, *n.* Fault; offence; crime; error; guilt.

Taqwá, *a.* Fear of a God; piety; abstinence.

Taqwím, *n.* Regulating; fixing; estimating; symmetry; almanac; calendar.

Taqwiyat, *n.* Strength; support; confidence; trust; confirmation.

Tar, *a.* Moist; damp; wet; fresh; tender. *—ba—,* saturated, soaked; quite wet.

Tár, *n.* Thread; string; wire; continuation; series; electric telegraph; telegram. *—i-'an-kabút,* cobwed.

Táṛ, *n.* The palmyra tree.

Táṛ, *n.* Understanding; apprehen-sion; intelligence.

Tárá, *n.* A star; a planet; pupil of the eye. *—manḍal,* the starry region; firmament.

Taraddud, *n.* Anxiety; hesitation; anzious consideration; exertion; endeavour.

Taraf, *n.* Direction; quarter; end; limit; side *prep.* towards, *—dári,* partiality; bias.

Tarah, *n.* Manner; mode; sort; description; state; condition; plain; air. *—dár,* graceful; beautiful. *—dená,* to overlook; to turn a deaf ear (to).

Tarái, *n.* Lands lying on the bank of a river; marsh; swamp; a river basin.

Taṛak, Tárak, *n.* Saviour; preserver; redeemer.

Ṭarakná, *v.* To slip away; to slink off; to go slowly.

Taṛakná, *v.* To crack; to split.

Táraṇ, *n.* Salvation; saviour.

Taráná, *n.* A rhythmic mucal composition which often enjoys a high degree of audience participation.

Tarang, *n.* Wave; fancy; whim; caprice.

Tarannum, *n.* Song; modulation.

Taṛapná, *v.* To flutter; to palpitate; to quiver; to be violently agitated; to rise.

Taraqqí, *n.* Progress; advancement; promotion; improvement; increment.

Taráshná, *n.* To cut; to shave; to shape; to form; to chip; to trim.

Tarasná, *v.* To long for; to crave; to desire eagerly; to entreat; to implore.

Tarázú, *n.* A scale; a balance.

Tarbiyat, *n.* Education; instruction; rearing; correction. —*pizír,* decile; tractable.

Tarbúz, *n.* A water-melon.

Tardíd, *n.* Refutation; rebutment; reversal (of a decree); repeal.

Targíb, *n.* Incitement; stimulation; instigation; temptation; inducement.

Ta'ríf, *n.* Praise; eulogy; explanation; definition.

Tárik, *n.* Deserter. —*ud-duniyá, a.* abandoning the world; *n.* a hermit; an ascetic.

Táríḳh, *n.* Date; day; era; epoch; history.

Táríkí, *n.* Darkness; obscurity; gloom.

Taríqa, *n.* Way; path; manner; mode; custom; rite.

Tarjaní, *n.* The forefinger; the trigger finger.

Tarjíh, *n.* Superiority; excellence; pre-emience; preference.

Tarjumá, *n.* Translation; interpretation.

Tark, *n.* Logical statement; rationale; argument; point-of-view. —*shástr,* n. Logic, the science of-.

Taṛká, *n.* Dawn; daybreak.

Ṭarkáná, *v.* To put off; to avoid; to evade; to dispose off summarily.

Tarráná, *v.* To croak. To grumble; to haughty.

Tarkárí, *n.* Vegetable.

Tarkash, *n.* A quiver.

Tarkíb, *n.* Composition; formation; mode; arrangement; plan; structure; means.

Tarmím, *n.* Rectification; amendment; revision.

Tárpín, *n. (Corr. from the Eng.)* Turpentine.

Tarqím, *n.* Writing; noting.

Tarrár, *n.* Pick-pocket; cutpurse; *a.* sharp-tongued; eloquent.

Tars, *n.* Fear; terror; alarm; pity; compassion.

Tarsíl, *n.* Sending; dispatch.

Ṭarr-ṭarr, *n.* A croak; a deep hoarse sound; angry or discontented prattle.

Ṭar-ṭaráná, *v.* To prattle angrily; to blab; to clatter; to make noises to express discontent.

Tartíb, *n.* Arrangement; order; system; method; manner.

Taru, Tarwar, *n.* A tree; a shrub.

Taruṇ, *a.* Young; youthful.

Taruṇí, *a.* A young female; a youthful beauty.

Tarz, *n.* Form; fashion; manner; way; mode; style. *—i-kalám,* idiom; diction; phraseology.

Tasadduq, *n.* Almsgiving; charity sacrifice; devotion.

Tasallí, *n.* Consolation; solace; comfort; contentment.

Tasalsul, *n.* Series; succession; sequence; chain.

Tasaníf, *n. (Plur. of Tasníf).* Work; books; literary productions.

Tasarruf, *n.* Application; possession; outlay; expenditure; extravagance.

Tasáwí, *n.* Equality; similarity; likeness; similitude.

Tasawwar, *n.* Imagination; fancy; idea; reflection; conception.

Tasbíh, *n.* A rosary; a string of beads; praising God.

Tasdí'a, *n.* Trouble; affliction; sorrow.

Tasdíq, *n.* Verification; attestation.

Tasfiyá, *n.* Cleansing; purifying; adjustment; settlement.

Tásh, *n.* Playing Cards.

Tasfiyá, *n.* Cleansing; purifying; adjustment; settlement.

Tásh, *n.* Playing Cards.

Tashaffí, *n.* Consolation; comfort.

Tashannuj, *n.* Convulsion; violent agitation.

Tashbíh, *n.* Simile; metaphor; comparison; similitude; allegory.

Tash-hír, *n.* Proclamation; publication; notification; public exposure.

Tashíh, *n.* Correction; rectification.

Tashḳhís, *n.* Ascertainment; diagnosis; specification; assessment.

Tashríf, *n.* Honouring; ennobling; (in address) your honour; your worship.

Tashríh, *n.* Explanation; dissecting; anatomy. —*dán,* an anatomist.

Ta'shshuq, *n.* Love; affection.

Tashtarí, *n.* Saucer; plate; dish (as a utencil); a flat-ish recptacle in which food etc. can be served.

Tásír, *n.* *(Plur. Tásirát).* Impression; effect; operation; influence; inherent quality of [often of medicines and foods].

Tasḳhír, *n.* Subduing; conquering; subjugation; capture; imprisoning.

Taskín, *n.* Consolation; ease; soothing. —*bakhsh,* consolatory; comforting.

Taslíb, *n.* Crucifixion.

Taslím, *n.* Greeting salutation; homage; acceptance.

Taslís, *n.* Dividing into three parts; a traid; the Trinity.

Tasmá, *n.* Shoe-lace; a string with which one tightens and ties up footwear, or even corsettes, a kind if strap.

Tasníf, *n.* Compilation; composition.

Tasríf, *n.* Turning; (in *Gram.*) conjugation; inflection.

T'assub, *n.* Bigotry; prejudice (for, or against); zeal (in favour of a party; or a cause); religious persecution.

Tássuf, *n.* Regret; grief; lamenting.

Taswír, *n.* *(Plur. Taswírát),* picture; portrait; photograph.

Taṭ, *n.* A bank; a coast; a shore.

Ṭaṭ, *n.* Sackcloth; sacking; gunny. —*ulatná,* to become bankrupt or insolvent.

Taṭasth, *a.* Neutral; objective; indifferent; one who does not take sides.

Tathágat, *n.* A proper name for the *Gautama, the Buddha.*

Tathya, *n.* Fact; material truth; reality. —*tah.* Adv. Factually; as a matter of fact.

T'atíl, *n.* Vacation; holiday; abandonment.

Tatimma, *n.* Supplement; appendix; complement; remainder. —*i-khatt,* ostscrit.

Tatkál, *adv.* Instantly; forthwith; immediately; there and then; without delay. —*ik,* adj. Contemporaneous; of immediate concern. —*ín,* adj. Contemporary; current.

Ṭaṭolná, *n.* To touch; to feel; to grope.

Tatpar, *a.* Ready; devoted; at one's bidding.

Ṭaṭṭí, *n.* A framework of bamboo; bamboo trellis-work; a privy; a latrine. —*lagáná, v.* to screen; to enclose.

Ṭaṭṭi, *n.* Human excreta; human faeces; also the name given to the enclosure where one disposes of this discharge i.e. toilet, or a WC.

Ṭaṭṭú, *n.* A beast of burden; a pony; an animal which is cross-bred between a horse and a donkey; (proverbially) a reasonably good-looking but thick-headed creature.

Tattv, *n.* Element(s); essence(s); substance(s); factors(s); final result(s) the Ultimate Truth. —*gyání,* a. One(s) who has (have) realised the Truth. —*nishth,* a. One(s) immersed in the Truth

Taṭ-vartí, *a.* Littoral; riverian; coastal; located on or near the bank.

Taubá, *n.* Repentance; penitence; abjuring; recantation.

Taufíq, *n.* Divine guidance; grace or favour; the completion of ones wishes; prosperity; means; ability.

Tauhíd, *n.* Declaring God to be one alone; believing in the unity of God; unitarianism.

Tauhín, *n.* Disgrace; dishonour; defamation.

Taulíd, *n.* Generation; birth.

Tauliyá, *n.* Towel.

Taulná, *v.* To weigh; to balance; *nazron̲ men̲*—, to estimate the worth of any one.

Tauq, *n.* Collar; necklace; yoke. —*i-zanjír,* to imprison. —*o-zanjír,* fetters and manacles.

Tauqír, *n.* Honor; respect.

Taur, *n.* Condition; state; manner; mode.

Táús, *n.* Peacock. *Takht-i*—, n. The peacock throne.

Tausíf, *n.* Qualifying description; commendation.

Tawáf, *n.* Going round; circumambulating; pilgrimage.

Tawáif, [See *Tawáyaf*].

Tawajjuh, *n.* Attention; consideration; regard; favour; kindness.

Tawakkul, *n.* Trust in God; reliance; faith.

Tawallud, *n.* Birth, *a.* born.

Táwán, *n.* Penalty; compensation; damages; atonement.

Tawánái, *n.* Power; strength.

Tawan̲gar, *a.* Rich; wealthy; opulent.

Tawaqqu', *n.* Hope; expectation; reliance.

Tawaqquf, *n.* Delay; cessation; suspension; tediousness; pause.

Tawáríkh, *n.* Dates; histories; chronicles.

Tawáyaf, *n.* A prostitute; a dancing girl; a *nautch-girl.*

Tawáz'a, *n.* Hospitality; humility; entertainment. *—i-shirázi,* simple fare.

T'awelá, *n.* A stable; a stall.

Tawíl, *a.* Long; tall.

T'awíz, *n.* An amulet.

Tázá, *a.* Fresh; new; green; tender; young. *—wárid,* new-comer.

Tázagí, *n.* Freshness; plumpness; tenderness; greenness.

T'azím, *n.* Reproof; censure; reprimand.

T'azírát, *n. Plur.* Reproofs. *—i-Hind,* the Indian Penal Code.

Táziyan, *n.* A model of the tomb of Hasan and Husain which is thrown into the river at the Muharram.

Táziyáná, *n.* Whip; scourge.

T'aziatnámá, *n.* A letter of condolence.

Tazkír, *n.* Masculine gender.

Tazkirá, *n.* [From Zikr], A mention; bringing up the reference of; memoire; reminiscence.

Tazkirát, *n.* Memory; memorandum. *—ul-mashhúr,* memoirs of eminent men.

Teg, *n.* Sword; scimitar; cutlass; sabre.

Teís, *n.* Sword; scimitar; cutlass; sabre.

Teís, *n.* Twenty-three.

Tej, *n.* Power; wrath; splendour; aura.

Ṭekan, *n.* Prop; pillar; suport.

Tel, *n.* Oil.

Te<u>n</u>duá, *n.* Leopard.

Ṭe<u>n</u>ṭ, *n.* A fold in one's loin-cloth; a hiding-place for one's valuables. A pupilary bulge of the eye.

Ṭe<u>n</u>ṭuá, *n.* The throttle; the throat. *—dabáná,* v. To throttle some one; to curb someone's right to free speech.

Teohár, *n.* A festival; a holiday.

Teorí, *n.* Frown; scowl. *—charháná, v.* to knit the brows.

Terá, *pro.* Thy; thine.

Terah, *n.* Thirteen.

Ṭeṛhá, *a.* Crooked; bent.

Teshá, *n.* A kind of axe used by carpenters; an adze.

Tetís/ Tai<u>n</u>tís, *n.* Thirty-three.

Tez, *a.* Acute; sharp; swift; violent;

quick; rapid; highpriced; clever; dear. *—áb,* nitric acid. *—fahm,* intelligent.

Ṭhag, *n.* A robber; a strangler; a highwayman; a cheat. *—bidyá,* swindling, *—ná,* to cheat; to deceive.

Tháh, *n.* Bottom; depth; ford.

Ṭhahákâ, *n.* An explosive laughter; Loud joyous laughter.

Ṭhaharná, *v.* To stop; to stay; to rest.

Ṭhahráná, *v.* To fix; to settle; to appoint; to cause to stand.

Thailá, *n.* A large bag.

Thailí, *n.* A small bag; a purse.

Thakan, Thakán, *n.* Fatigue, tiredness; boredom [Getting tired of something not for lack of energy, but changing mental disposition].

Thakká, *a.* Coagulated; congealed; *n.* a lump; a clot.

Thakná, *v.* To be wearied; to get tired; to be dull.

Ṭhákur, *n.* Lord; master, idol of a deity (installed in a place of worship), a caste name for the second caste-group amongst the Hindus, called *Kshatriya.* *—dwara,* n. A temple (literally meaning 'the gateway to the Lord'. *ṭhakurar,* n. Supremacy, arrogance of nobility; haughtiness. *ṭhakur-suhati,* n. Flattery; likeable talk; sycohancy.

Thál, *n.* A large flat plate of metal; the trench dug round a tree. *—í,* n. Small one of the 'that'.

Thamb, *n.* Post; column; pillar; support.

Thámná, *v.* To hold; to stop; to pull up a (horse).

Than, *n.* Udder; breast.

Tháná, *n.* A police station. *—dár,* a police office.

Ṭhánaná, *v.* To fix in one's mind; to determine; to make up one's mind about.

Ṭhaṉḍ, *n.* Cold; coldness. *—á, a.* cool; cold; dead; dull. *kalejá —honá,* to be satisfied.

Ṭhanḍáí, *n.* Refreshing or cooling things; refrigerant. Also a nickname for a drink made of ground hemp *(Bháng)* almonds, cardamom, sugar and milk.

Ṭhan-ṭhan, *n.* Clink; metallic ringing sound; jingle of coins [indicating 'plenty of money']. *—gopál,* prov. One who has nothing; an absolute pauper.

Thapeṛá, *n.* A slap; a box.

Ṭhappá, *n.* Seal; stamp; die; matrix; mould; impression. *—lagáná,* v. To brand; to mark with one's own seal.

Thappaṛ, *n.* A heavy slap.

Ṭharrá, *n.* Country liquor; illicit brew; poor quality, corrosive kind of alcoholic drink; hooch.

Thartharáná, *v.* To shiver; to quiver; to tremble.

Ṭháṭ, *n.* Pomp, show; dignity; fashion.

Ṭhaṭherá, *n.* A maker of hardwar or metal pots.

Ṭhaṭholí, *n.* Fun; jest; sport.

Ṭhaṭṭhá, *n.* Fun jocularity; hillarity; derision; jest. *—uráná,* v. To poke fun at some one; to deride some one. *Ṭhaṭṭhe-báz,* a. One who indulges in-.

Ṭheká, *n.* Contract; hire; fare; plug; cork. *—bandí,* a farm held on lease. *Sharáb ká—,* a A shop or mart licensed to sell liquor and other alcoholic drinks.

Ṭhe<u>n</u>gá, *n.* [Literally] Up-thrust thumb; zilch; nothing; a non-result. *—dikháná,* prov. To swallow all the in-puts and show no results; to cheat someone of their effort, inputs, investment, etc.

Ṭheṭh, *a.* Pure; genuine; good; unmixed.

Ṭhík, *a.* Accurate; right; correct; proper; reasonable; true. *—áná,* *v.* to fit; to suit. *—karná,* to adjust; to put to right. *—waqt,* point of time; nick of time.

Ṭhikáná, *n.* Residence; place; station; whereabout; source; origin.

Ṭhíngá, *adj.* Dwarf; diminutive short in height.

Ṭhí<u>n</u>gná, *adj.* [See *Thí<u>n</u>gá*].

Thirak/ Thirakan, *n.* Movement of body parts in keeping with the rhy thm; rhythmic vibration; choreographed dance movement.

Thirakná, *v.* To move in a rhythmic manner; to vibrate nimbly with musical rhythm.

Thirtá, [A corruption of Sanskrit word *Sthirtá.* [Please see under 'S'].

Ṭhiṭhurná, *v.* To be numbed; to be chilled.

Thobṛá, *n.* The snout of an animal; an unlikeable face. *—phuláná,* v. To sulk; to go into a depressive mood.

Thok, *n.* Heap; mass; body; sum. *—dár,* a wholesale dealer.

Ṭhokáí/ Ṭhukáí, *n.* Beating; roundly thrashing; physical punishment; harsh treatment.

Ṭhokar, *n.* A kick; stumble; a stroke.

Ṭhokná, *v.* To hammer in; to beat; to drive in; to impose with force. *Thok-Bajá kar dekhná,* v. To examine something thoroughly, minutely.

Thopná, *v.* To impose; to thrust upon; to implant; to plaster.

Thoṛá, *a.* Little; small; few; some; *adv.* a little; by degrees.

Ṭhos, *a.* Hard; solid.

Thothá, *adj.* Hollow; empty; worthless; unsubstantial. *—chaná bąje ghaná,* prov. An empty vessel makes much noise.

Thúk, *n.* Spittle. *—lagáná, v.* to defeat; to overcome; to cheat; to fool.

Ṭhumakná, *a.* To strut; to walk with grace and dignified pace.

Ṭhumrí, *n.* A highly popular form of light classical music in India which obtains its delicacy and appeal by judicious mixing of the *rágas.*

Ṭhú<u>n</u>sná, *v.* To press down hard; to stuff; to drive in.

Ṭhú<u>n</u>ṭh, *n.* A stump; a leafless branch of or branchless trunk of a tree.

Thúthaṇ, *n.* The mouth; snout.

Tibábat, *n.* The practice of medicine.

Tibb, *n.* Medical treatment.

Ṭiḍḍá, *n.* A grass-hopper.

Ṭiḍḍí, *n.* Locust.

Tifl, *n. (Plur. Tiflán).* A child; an infant. *—i-shírkhwár,* a suckling child. *—íyat, tifúliyat,* infancy; childhood.

Tiguṇá, *a.* Triple; threefold.

Tihái, *adj.* Third portion of; one-third of *n.* a sound-beat, or a stroke, in tabla-playing.

Tihál, *n.* The spleen.

Tihattar, *n.* Seventy-three.

Tihrá, *adj.* Three-fold; three times; multiple of—.

Tíj/ Tíjá, *n.* The third day of the hunar fortnight.

Tíjárat, *n.* Commerce; trade. *—gáh-i-'álí,* emporum. *—i,* mercantile; commercial.

Tijárí, *n.* Tertain fever or ague.

Ṭíká, *n.* Commentary; elaboration; explanation (of a complex text). *—kár,* a. One(s) writing a commentary, ordoing the annotation. *(also)* A vermilion mark, or sandalpaste mark Hindus make on their forehead as a part of their prayer ritual, whether during the visit to a temple, or prayers at home.

Ṭíká, *n.* Vaccination; inoculation; a mark made on the forehead by Hindus.

Ṭikaṭ, *n. (Corr. from the Eng.).* Ticket; stamp; passport.

Ṭikiyá, *n.* A pill; a small cake; a tablet.

Ṭikaná, *v.* To stay; to put up with; to lodge.

Ṭikṛí, *n.* A patch of land yielding poor crops.

Ṭikṭikí, *n.* A state. *—bándh kar dekhná,* v. To focus at an object; to stare without a wink.

Til, *n.* The sesamum plant, or its seed; oil-seed; a mole or black sot on the face; the pupil of the eye. *til-til-ká hisáb,* an exact account.

Ṭílá, *n.* A rising; ground; an eminence; a ridge; a hillock.

Tilak, *n.* A short-sleeved robe; a gown; a robe of honour.

Tiláwat, *n.* Reading; meditation.

Tillá, *n.* Gold; drawn gold; goldlace or braid; ointment; salve.

Tillí, *n.* The spleem.

Tilmíz, *n.* A scholar; a student; a pupil.

Timár, *n.* Care; attendance (on the sick); sickness.

Timir, *n.* Darkness; obscurity; blindness.

Tín, *a.* Three. *—pánch, n.* (lit); three and five; dispute; contention; tricks; dodges. *—pánch karná,* to quarrel; to practise tricks (upon). *—raqmí, qánún,* (in Arith.) the rule of three. *—terah,* dispersed; scattered.

Tinká, *n.* Grass; straw; a blade of grass; a particle; a bit or scrap (of paper), &c.

Ṭíp, *n.* Note of hand; cheque; the act of pressing; compressing; check; raising the voice in singing.

Ṭipká, *n.* A drop; a stain; a blot.

Ṭípná, *v.* To press; compress; to squeeze; to pocket (money); to note down.

Ṭippá, *n.* A rebound; a bounce.

Ṭippaṇ, *n.* Annotation; commentary.

Ṭippaṇí, *n.* A note; annotation; comment; observation; critical remark.

Tippas, *n.* Manipulation; contrivance; manoeuvre to achieve an end. *—bhiṛáná/ laṛáná,* v. To manipulate; to manoeuvre.

Tír, *n.* An arrow; a beam; a mast; the planet Mercury. *—andáz, n.* a bowman; an archer.

Tirásí, *n.* Eighty-three.

Tiránnave, *n.* Ninety-three.

Tirbení, *n.* [See *Triveṇí*].

Tirchhá, *a.* Crooked; crosswise;

bent; perverse. —*dekhná,* to squint. —*laqná,* to strike obliquely.

Tirkhá, *n.* [See *Trishá*].

Tirpaṇ/Tirepan/Trepan, *n.* Fifty-three.

Tirsúl, *n.* [See *Trishúl*].

Tírth, *n.* A place of pilgrimage; a sacred place. —*yátrá, n.* Pilgrimage; journey to the holy places. —*ráj,* n. An epithet of *Prayág,* (the modern city of Allahabad) considered to be the most important of Hindu places of pilgrimage.

Tírtha<u>n</u>kar, *n.* Twenty-four leading preceptors of Jainism, last of whom was Lord *Mahávíra.*

Tiryá, *n.* Woman, —*charitr,* women's wiles. —*ráj,* petticoat government.

Tiryáq, *n.* An antidote (for poisons, snake-bites. &c.), bezoar stone; a sovereign remedy.

Tís, *n.* Thirty. —*guṇá,* adj. Thirty-folds; multiple of thirty.

Ṭís, *n.* Smarting pain; acute throbbing pain; lingering (mental) agony.

Tishná, *n.* [See *Trishṇá*].

Tiswá<u>n</u>, *adj.* Thirtieth.

Títar, *n.* Partridge.

Titar-bitar, *a.* Dispersed; scattered.

Tithi, *n.* Date; an auspicious day and date fixed for a particular ceremony or deed. *Puṇya-tithi,* a. Death-anniversary. —*vár nirváh,* v. To keep a date/ appointment.

Tiwárí, *n.* (country version of the caste-name *Trivedi*)/ A class of Brahmans who are entitled to read three Vedas.

Ṭoh, *n.* Intelligence; secret information; (from the enemy's side) reconnaissance. —*lená,* v. To gather intelligence (from the enemy camp); to reconnotre.

Ṭokná, *v.* To question; to interrogate; to stop; to check; to hinder.

Ṭokrá, *n.* A large basket.

Ṭokrí, *n.* A small basket.

Tol, *n.* Weight. —*ná,* to weigh.

Tolá, *n.* A weight of 12 or 16 *máshás,* the jeweller's weight being 12 *máshás,* or nearly 210 grains Troy.

Toná, *n.* Charm; spell; enchantment. —*báz,* charmer; enchanter.

To<u>n</u>dí, *n.* Navel.

Ṭo<u>n</u>ṭí, *n.* A spout.

Ṭop, *n.* A cannon gun; an artillery

piece. —*ḳháná,* n. A gun battery. —*andáz,* a. An artillery man; a gunner.

Ṭop, Ṭopí, *n.* Hat; helmet; cap.

Toṛá, *n.* Break; interruption; want; scarcity; a bag containing one thousand rupees; the match of a gun; a gold or silver chain for the neck. —*dár bandúq,* a matchlock; a gun of great range and destructive power.

Toṛná, *v.* To break; to burst; to crack; to sever; to destroy; to infringe; to violate; to pluck or gather (fruit); to change money; to interrupt or discontinue.

Toshak, *n.* Bedding; mattress; quilt.

Tosdán, *n.* A cartridge-bag.

Toshá, *n.* Provision for a journey; supplies. —*ḳhána,* a wardrobe; a store-room; *'aqibat ká—,* good deeds.

Totá, *n.* A Parrot. —*chashm,* a. Perfidious; a turncoat; a cheat.

Ṭoṭá, *n.* Loss; deficiency.

Ṭoṭká, *n.* A charm; spell.

Totlá, *n.* A stammerer; a stutterer.

Tráṇ, *n.* Safety; salvation; deliverance.

Trás, *n.* Pain; torture; suffering. *Trast,* adj. Tortured; in pain; in panic; horrified.

Trásadí, *n.* Tragedy; something with a sad Ending.

Tretá, *n.* Proper name of the second Hindu *Yuga.* [Four parts of a Hindu eon *Sat, Tretá, Dwápar* and *Kali,* the four Yugas].

Tri, *adj.* Three, suffix indicating multiples of—; *Tri-ráshik,* n. The rule of three (in *Arith.*).

Trikál, *n.* Three aspects of time —past, present and future. *Trikál-darshí,* adj. One who can see and witness happenings of all times; God himself. *Trikál-gyání,* adj. One who knows of all happenings of all times.

Trikál, *n.* The past, present and future.

Trikoṇ, *n.* A triangle.

Trilok, *n.* Three worlds; three levels of existence—Upper world [heaven], this world and the nether-world [hell]. *-gámí,* adj. One who can go to and traverse all three worlds; an epithet of God. *-i,* adj. Of the three worlds. —*i-náth,* n. The master of all the three worlds; an epithet of God Almighty. *-wásí,* adj. Omnipresent; an epithet of God.

Tripta, *n.* Satisfied; contended; satiated.

Trishit, *n.* Thirsty; pining for.

Trishṇá, *n.* Thirst; desire; longing; craving; greed for.

Trishúl, *n.* Trident; a three-pronged lance [associated with Lord *Shiva*].

Triveṇí, *n.* The confluence (at *Prayág,* i.e. Allahabad) of the three sacred rivers, the Gangá, the Yamuná and Saraswati.

Tufail, *adv.* By means of; through the agency of.

Túfán, *n.* Deluge; flood; storm; tempest; cyclone; calamity; ruin.

Tugyání, *a.* Overflowing; flood; inundation.

Tuhfá, *n.* A present; gift; rarity; curiosity.

Tuhmat, *n.* False accusation; calumny; slander.

Ṭukaṛ, *n.* (An allomorph for the word *Tukrá*) piece. [Used as a *prefix*-] *—ḳhor/toṛ,* adj. A sponger; one thriving on leftovers of his/her patron; dependent on the mercy of a master.

Ṭukṛá, *n.* A piece; bit; fragment; morsel; scrap.

Ṭukaṛí, *n.* A detachment (of armed soldiers); a group; a stone slab; a bit piece.

Tuḳhm, *n.* Seed. *—páshí,* sowing. *—ṛez,* a sower.

Túl, *n.* Length; extent.

Tulá, *n.* A blance; a pair of scales; the sign Libra.

Tulabá, *n. (Plur. of Tálib).* Students; scholars; pupils.

Tulsí, *n.* The sacred basil shrub.

Tú, *pron.* You (singular); Thou (in old English).

Trum, *pron.* You (Common use today for juniors as well as familiar multiples).

Tuman, *n.* Crowed; multitude; troop.

Túmár, *n.* Crowd; multitude; tropp.

Túmár, *n.* A heap; a roll of papers; a book; a volume.

Tumhárá, *a.* Yours (masculine & neutral) *Tumhárí,* a. Yours (feminine) *Tumháre,* a. Yours (Plural).

Tunak, Tunuk, *a.* Delicate; weak; fragile; thin. *—mizaj,* week-minded; whimsical.

Túr, *n.* Mount Sinai.

Turáb, *n.* Earth.

Tura<u>ng</u>, *n.* A horse.

Tura<u>nj</u>, *n.* Citron; orange; lemon.

Turant, *adv.* Instantly; at once; immediately.

Turb, *n.* Radish.

Turbat, *n.* Tomb; sepulchre.

Turhí, *n.* A trumpet; a clarion; a bugle.

Turrá, *n.* Curl; ringlet; forelock; tuft; crest; border; fringe; tassel.

Tursh, *a.* Sour; acid; tart.

Tushár, *n.* Fog; haze; mist; frost; blight; cold; chill; fog; dew.

Tút, *n.* [Proper name *Shahtút*] Mulberry, a semiwild, sweet fruit; name of a frui-bearing tree.

Ṭúṭá, *a.* Broken; smashed; decayed; *n.* loss; failure; deficiency.

Tutláná, *v.* To stutter; to stammer.

Tútiyá, *n.* Blue vitriol; copper sulphate. [Also commonly known as *Nílá thothá*].

Tutláná, *v.* To sutter; to stammer.

Tútná, *v.* To be broken to burst; to crack; to snap; to be impoverished; to rush upon.

Tuzuk, *n.* Ordinance; status; law; pomp; dignity.

Twachá, *n.* Skin; complexion. *—lipi,* a. Short hand.

Twará, *n.* Haste; quickness; urgency.

Twaraṇ, *n.* Acceleration; speed.

Twarit, *adj.* Quick; swift. *—rúp se,* adv. Fast; swiftly; urgently; quickly.

Tyág, *n.* abandonment; relinquishment; renunciation; divorce; abdication; sacrifice. *—patr,* n. Resignation; a letter of divorce. *—ná,* v. To give up; to sacrifice; to renounce. *—í,* adj. One who gives up, or renounces. &c.

Tyon, Tyún, *adv.* So; thus; in like manner; then. *—hí,* at that very moment.

U, u, is a vowel equivalent of (उ) in Hindi and (اُ) in Urdu. If functions as a full letter in its own right, but also grants a tonal value to the preceding consonant, which is represented by (ु) symbol in Hindi and (ُو) in Urdu. When used with a forward slash (́) on top, this assumes a longer vowel sound of (ऊ) in Hindi and (اُو) in Urdu, or vowel tone of (ू) in Hindi and *Pésh,* in Urdu.

Ubál, *n.* Ebullition; boiling; burst of passion.

Ubálná, *n.* To boil; to bubble up; to swell; to overflow; to be flooded; to be inundated; to rise.

Ubarná,*v.*To be out of trouble; to be rid of a nasty/ difficult situation; to be salvaged.

Ubasná, *n.*to become fetid; to rot; to putrefy; to ferment; to become state.

Ubhar, *n.* Rising; swelling; prominence; developing;

Ubharná, v. To emerge; to protrude; to project outward; to bulge out.

Ubhárná,*v.*To rouse; to incite; to in-tigate; to persuade; to raise up.

Ubṭan, *n.* A cosmetic paste, prepared by mixing gram-flour,fine oil or butter, milk and lemon-juice, perhaps a touch of fragrance, rubbed over the body parts for cleansing and softening of the skin.

'Ubúr, *n.*Crossing; passing.—*i-dárya-i-shor,* transporation beyond the sea.

Uchakká, *n.* A thief; a picl-procket; a swindler.

Ucháṭ,*a.* Weary; tired; displeased; downcast.

Uchaṭná, *v.* To rebound; to spring back; to slip away; to be weary (of); to be separated; to be severed.

Uchcháraṇ, *n.* Pronunciation; utterance.

Uchhalná, *v.* To leap over; to jump; to spring up; to bound.

Uchhálná, *v.* To throw up a thing (as a ball) and catch it.

Uchit, *a.* Proper; becoming; fit; suitable.

Uchchhriṉkhal, *a.* Mischievous; haughty; troublesome; unrestrained; indisciplined; impertinent; disorderly. —*tá,* n. State of, or habit of mischief, indiscipline, or haughtiness, etc.

'Úd, *n.* The wood aloes. —*soz,* a censer in which to burn aloes wood.

Údá, *a.* Purple colour.

Udai, *n.* Rising of the sun.

Udás, *a.* Sad; dejected; gloomy; full of pathos; droopy (plants and vegetation).

Udásín, *a.* Indifferent; non-chalant; disinterested; without care.

Uday, *n.* Rise; dawning; ascent over the horizon.

Udayáchal, *n.* [Uday+achal] The mythical mountain from behind which the sun rises every morning. Also known as *Udaygiri.*

Uddanḍ, *a.* Insolent; impertinent; rude; rebellious. *—atá,* n. The state/mood of insolence; impertience, etc.

Uddípan, *n.* Stimulation; excitement, *Uddipak,* a. Stimulating; stimulant, &c.

Uddhat, *a.* Haughty; ill-behaved; boorish; impudent.

Udghosh, *n.* Proclamation; announcement. *—aná,* Declaration; proclamation etc. —adk, n. Ones who make declaration, etc. *—it,* a. What has been declared, proclaimed, announced etc.

Údham, *n.* Disturbance; noise uproar; tumult. *—macháná, v.* to create a stir; to make a great noise.

Udhar, *adv.* Thither; on that way or side.

Udhár, *n.* Loan; debt. *—dená,* to lend; to give on credit. *—lená, v.* to borrow or buy on credit.

Uddhár, *n.* Salvation; deliverance.

Uddharaṇ, *n.* Quotation; verbatim reproduction of some one's statement; citation; extract.

Udheṛná, *v.* To undo; to unravel; to strip off.

'Udúl, *n.* Disobeying; declining; insubordination. *—i-hukmi,* diobedience of orders; evasion of a sentence of process.

Udyam, *n.* Enterprise; venture; diligence; exertion; effort.

Udyán, *n.* Garden; a place of greenery; a place of horticultural activity.

Udyog, *n.* Industry; labour; effort.

Ufaq, *n.* The horizon

Uftádá, *a.* Lying; fallen; waste; *n.* uncultivated land.

Ugalná, *v.* To spit out; to vomit; to throw, *ugáldán,* a spittoon *(píkdán).*

Ugháṛná, *v.* To unveil; to uncover; to open.

Ugná, *v.* To grow; to spring; to shoot; to spring up; to sprout; to rise; to set in; to dawn. *ugte hí jal jáná,* to be withered or blasted at its birth; to be nipped in the bud.

Ugr, *a.* Uiolent; fierce; wrathful; radical; sharp. —*vád,* n. Radicalism; extrememism. —*vádí,* a. Radicalist; extremist.

'Udha, *n.* Rank; dignity; office; business; employment; post; duty. —*dár,* an officer.

Ujágar, *a.* Famous; splendid; celebrated.

Ujala, *n.* Famous; splendid; celebrated, well-lit.

Ujálá, *n.* Light; brightness; splendour.

Ujáṛ, *a.* Desolate; demolished; runied; deserted.

Ujjal, Ujal, *a.* White; shining; bright; clean; pure.

Ujjwal, *a.* Bright; splendid; clear; radiant.

'Ujlat, *n.* Rapidity; haste; speed; velocity.

Ujr, *n.* Wages; hire; remuneration; compensation; reward. —*dená,* to remunerate; to reward; to bestow a reward; to bestow a reward for one's good deeds or to punish him for his evil actions.

Ujrat, *n.* Wages; hire; renumeration.

Úkh, *n.* Sugarcane.

Ukháṛná, *v.* To eradicate; to root up; to pluck.

Uksáná, *v.* To incite; to instigate; to provoke; to raise; to fan; to blow; to stir up; to rouse.

Uksáv, *n.* Stimulation; incitement; instigation.

Ukt, *a.* Afore-mentioned; preceding; stated before; hereabove.

Uktáná, *v.* To be tired of; to be disgusted.

Ukti, *n.* Popular saying; dictum; a proverbial utterance often used in day-to-day speech.

Ulachná, *v.* To throw out; to pour off (water); to drain.

Ulahná, *n.* A complaint; reproach.

Úl-jalúl, *a.* Meaningless; slob; absurd; useless; nick-knack articles; disjointed (talk); irrelevant utterances.

Ulajhná, *v.* To be entangled; to be embroiled.

'Ulamá, *n. (Plur. of 'Álim).* The learned; doctors of law and religion.

Ulaṭná, *v.* To upset; to overturn; to capsize; to turn upside down; to revcerse; to invert.

Ulfat, *n.* Affection; attachment; familiarity; affection; friendship.

Uljháná, v. To entangle; to involve; to embroil.

Ulká, *n.* A falling star; a meteor; flame; firebrand. —*pát,* v. The falling of a meteor; a disaster striking; something that causes devatation.

Ullanghan, *n.* Violation; breach (of an order or instruction); contravention.

Ullekh, *n.* Mention; reference; citation; quotation.

Ullú, *n.* An owl; an idiot; a fool; (in Hindu mythology) the mount of goddess Lakshmi, the goddess of wealth [hinting that wealth often lands with fools who don't know what to do with it]. *—ká, paṭṭhá,* a. swear-phrase, implying some one to be an absolute dullard. *—banáná,* v. To befool; to make a food of; to dupe. *—bolná,* v. (for a place) to be absolutely deserted. *—sídhá karná,* v. To serve one's own ends; to jockey for a favourable position.

Ulṭa, *a.* Contrary; reverse. *—pultá,* topsy-turvy. *—dhará bá<u>n</u>dhná, v.* to bring a cross or counter-action.

Ulṭi, *a. (Same as ulṭá). —sá<u>n</u>s lená, to breathe convulsively. —rít,* improper or unlawful manner.

Ulúhíyat, *n.* Divinity; Godhead.

'Ulúm, *n. (Plur. of 'Ilm).* Sciences. *—o-funún,* arts and scinences.

Uma<u>n</u>ḍná, *v.* To heave; to swell; to surge; to overflow; to rise; to gather thick.

Umaṇg, *n.* Aspiration; gusto; zeal.

Umará, *n. (Plur. of Amír).* Nobles; grandees.

Umaṛná, *v.* To surge; to flood; to overflow; to burst; to gust; to gather thick.

Umas, *n.* Sultriness; sultry weather; stuffy climate; feeling stuffy; kind of weather that urges you to undress.

'Umdá, *a.* Fine; nice; excellent.

Ummat, *n.* Sect; people; nation; religion.

Ummed, *n.* Hope; expectation; prospect; trust. *—wár,* hopeful; expectant; candidate; *n.* an apprentice.

'Umr, *n.* Age; lifetime. *—rasída,* advanced in years; superannuated.

'Umuq, *n.* Depth; profundity.

Umúr, *n.* Matters; affairs.

Ún, *n.* Wool.

Ú<u>n</u>chá, *a.* High; lofty; tall; steep, loud. *—níchá,* uneven; rough; the ups and downs. *—í, n.* height; loftiness; eminence.

U<u>n</u>ḍelna, *v.* To pour out.

Ú<u>n</u>ghná, *v.* To doze; to nod; to droop.

U<u>n</u>glí, *n.* Finger; toe. *—chatkáná,* to crack the fingers. *—pe* *nacháná,* to make a fool (of); to ridicule.

Unhen, *pro.* Them.

Unmád, *n.* Insanity; hysteria; state of intoxication; mania; lunacy; rabidity.

Unmatt, *a.* Wild; crazy; intoxicated; crazy; delirious.

Unnat, *a.* Elevated; developed; of high status; improved. *—i,* n. Progress; improvement; betterment; development.

'Uns, *n.* Love; friendship.

'Unsar, *n.* Primary elements.

Únṭ, *n.* A camel.

Upaban, [See *Upavan*].

Upadesh, *n.* Counsel; advice; admonition.

Upadrav, *n.* Tumult; out rage; injustice.

Upáe, *n.* Plan; contrivance; remedy; means.

Upálambh, *n.* [See *Ulahna*].

Upamá, *n.* Comparison; simile; likeness; resemblance.

Úpar, *pre.* Above; on; upon; over; outside; upward. *—tale.* one over the other.

Upáṛná, *v.* To root up; to extirpate.

Upás, [See *Upavás*].

Upasthit, *a.* Present; ready; impending; near.

Upavan, *n.* Small forest; grove; garden.

Upavás, *n.* Hunger; hunger-strike; fast. *—karná,* v. To fast; to undertake a hunger strike. *—í,* n. Hunger-striker; one undertaking fasting.

Upasthit, *a.* Present; available; in attendance. *—I,* n. Presence; attendance; state of availability.

Upekshá, *n.* Negligence; neglect; indifference; disregard. *—karná,* v. To ignore; to dis-regard; to show no respect for; to place no value upon.

Uphán, *n.* Effervescence; ebullience; ebullition.

Up-hár, *n.* A gift; a present; a gratuity.

Up-hás, *n.* Derision; mockery; ridicule.

Upjáú, *a.* Fertile; fruit-bearing productive.

Upkár, *n.* Kindness; favour; benevolence.

Upkar, *n.* Beneficence; benefaction; a good deed; a favour bestowed without expectation of a return or reward. *—í,* a. One who performs deeds of benefaction, etc.

Uplá/ Uple, *n.* Dung-cake(s), commonly made and used as domestic fuel all over the rural India.

Up-nám, *n.* Nom de plume; nick-name; alias; also-known-as (a.k.a.).

Uptan, *n.* [See *Ubtan*].

'Uqáb, *n.* An eagle.

Up-van,*n.* Garden; park; parkland.

Up-wás, *n.* Fast; abstinence from partaking food. *—í,* a. One observing the fast.

Up-yog, *n.* Use; utilisation; meaningful exploitation. *—í,* a. Useful; worthy of being put to use; deserving to be meaning-fully exploited.

Up-yukt, *a.* Proper; suitable; appropriate.

Ur, *n.* Heart.

Urán, *n.* Flying; flight; leap.

Uṛáká, *n.* Flyer; one who flies. Pilot. *Adj.* Swift.

Uṛáu, *a.* A spendthrift; an extrava-gant person.

Urdú, *n.* An army; a camp; a market. *—í-mu'alla kí zabán,* the court language.

Úrdhw, *a.* Vertical; upward. *—gati, n.* Upward mobility; emancipation; salvation. *—gámí,* One upwardly mobile; one attaining success. *—drishṭi,* n. Ambitious; looking beyond the visible world. *—lok,* n. The heaven; other world. *—bindu,* n. Zenith.

'Urf, *a.* Known; alias.

Uriṇ, *a.* Debt-free; relieved of obligation.*—honá,* v. To be relieved of debt; to discharge the debt.

Úrjá,*n.* Energy; vigour and vitality.

Uṛna, *v.* To fly; to soar.

'Urúj, *n.* Ascension; exaltation; rising; zenith.

'Urús, *n.* A bride.

Uryán, *a.* Naked; bare.

Úsar, *a.* Barren, or fallow land. *—kí khetí,* a. (literally) tilling a barren land; (implicity) wasting one's labour; undertaking an impossible task.

Usárá, *n.* A porch; a portico; a verandah.

Use, *pro.* Him; to him.

Uskáná, Uskáná, *v.* Colloquial usage: see *Uksáná*] To incite; to instigate; to light a candle.

Uslúb, Aslúb, *n.* Form, figure; manner; method; way*—dár, a.* symmetrical. *khush—*, elegant; well-formed.

Ustád, *n.* A master; an adept; an expert; a tutor; a teacher.*—í,* sill; expertness dexterity; genius.

Usturá, Ustará, *n.* A razor.

Ustukhwán, *n.* A bone.

Ustuwár, *a* Strong; firm; powerful; stable.

Usúl, *n.* Doctrines; principles.

Utár, *n.* Descent;fall; subsiding; slope; ferry. —*ḍalna,* to pull down. —*jáná, v.* to beocme faded; to be emaciated; to be growing old; to be dislocated.

Utarná, *v.* To come down; to descend; to alight; to disembark; to dismount; to alight; to be lowered; to be degraded; to be deposed; to decrease; to subside; to abate; to fade; to halt; to encamp; to be displaced or dislocated (a bone).

Utárná, *v.* To bring down; to take off; to cut off; to land; to transport.

Utárú, *a.* Ready for; bent upon; inclining.

Uṭhán, *n.* Rise; ascent; height; top; summit.

Uṭháná, *v.* To bear; to undertake; to squander; to raise; to lift; to abolish.

Uthlá, *a.* Shallow; fordable.

Uṭhná, *v.* To rise up; to get up; to awake; to be abolished.

Utkaṉṭha, *n.* Curiosity; anxiety; craving; arḍour. *Utkaṉṭhit*, a. Curious; one who is subject to anxiety, craving etc.

Utkal, *n.* Ancient name for the province now known as *Orissa.*

Utkaṭ, *a.* Excessive; intense; keen.

Utrkrishṭ, *a.* Excellent; eminent; outstanding; superior.

Utná, *v.* That much; as much as that.

Utpann, *a* Born, produced; n. origin; creation; birth.

Utpát, *n.* Mischief; nuisance; confusion; riot. —*í,* a. One(s) who create mischief, etc.

Utráí, *n.*Price paid for ferrying or crossing a river.

Utran, *n.* Cast-off clothes; second hand clothes.

Utráná, *v.* To float; to swim.

Utsáh, *n.* Enthusiasm, zeal; high spirits. —*í,* a. Enthusiastic; zealous. —*vardhak,* a. Encouraging.

Utsuk, *a.* Eager; curious; anxious; keen. —*tá*, n. Eagerness; curiosity, etc.

Uttál, *a.* High; violent; plentiful.

Uttam, *a.* The best; excellent; good quality; high grade.

Uttar, *n.* North; wnswer; reply; *a.* Later.

Uttarákhaṉḍ, *n.* The northern hilly verdure part of India lying in close proximity of the Himalayas, containing the sources of most norther rivers as well as many holy places of the Hindus and Sikhs; now a state of India by the same name.

Uttarádhikár, *n.* Inheritance; succession; right of succession.

Uttarayaṇ, *n.* The summer solstice when the sun is in the north of the equator.

Uttarottar, *a & adv.*, Progressive; successive; one after the other.

Uttardáyí, *a.* Answerable; responsible; accountable.

Uttardáyitv, *n.* Responsibility; accountability.

Uttar-vartí, *a* Northern; subsequent; later.

Uttejaná, *n.* Stimulation; excitement; provocation. *Uttejak,* a. Provocative; exciting; stimulating.

'Uzr, *n.* Excuse; apology; plea; pretext; objection. *—dárí,* cross demand. *—ke qábil,* excusable; pardonable; objectionable. *—i qaqí,* a valid objection. *— taslím karná,* to accept an apology.

V, v & W, w Both of these letters represent the same consonant in Hindi (व) and Urdu (و). Subtle difference between the two sounds in Hindi and Urdu is that words spelt with 'V' would carry greater emphasis on the consonant (व) or (و) while words spelt with 'W' will tend to emphasize two vovel sounds, i.e. 'u' and 'a' in quick succession, almot bridging the two sounds, as if some old fat soul grunting while getting out of a deep pile sofa: "Oo-ah". Therefore, though we have listed words spelt with each of these letters separately, one section after the other, you should not be surprised to see same words(s) listed in both lists. For the Hindi speakers, in phonetic terms, **V** and **W** are interchangable.

Va, *conj.* And; in addition to.

Vách, Vák, *n.* Speech; language; talking; tongue; expression; pharse.

Váchál, *a./n.* Talkative; chattering; gabby; outspoken.

Vachan, *n.* Utterance; speech; talk; a quotation. *—dená,* v. To make a promise. *—toṛná,* v. To break a promise. *—nibháná,* v. To keep a promise.

Vád, *n.* An 'ism'; a discussion; a law suit; a theory. *—vivád,* a. A debate; a discussion; an exchange of views between opposing 'camps'.

Vádá, *n.* A promise; a commitment; a solemn word.

Vádak, *n.* An instrumentalist; one who plays a musical instrument.

Vadh, *n.* Killing; murder. *—sthal,* a. Place of slaughter; the spot where killing takes place.

Vadhú, *n.* A bridge; a wife.

Vádí, *n.* Speaking; saying; a speaker; a declarant. *—pratirádi.* plaintiff and defendant.

Vádya, *n.* Musical instrument. *—vrind,* n. Orchestra. *—sangít,* a. Instrumental music.

Vafá, *n.* Fiderlity; loyalty.

Vafát, *n.* Death; demise. *—páná,* v. To die; to depart from the mortal life.

Váhak, *n.* A carrier; vehicle; bearer; porter.

Vaham, *n.* [Sanskrit *Bhram*] Doubt; suspicion; illusion; false notion; superstition.

Váhan, *n.* A carrier; a vehicle; a conveyance; a beast of burden.

Vahashat, *n.* Savagery; madness; terror.

Vahashí, *n.* Animal(s); savage; barbarous; mad.

Váhiyát, *a.* Ridiculous; nonsense; meaningless; foolish; useless.

Vaibhav, *n.* Grandeur; glory; magnificence; wealth; prosperity; riches.

Vaidh, *a.* Legal; legitimate; valid; tenable.

Vaidik, *a.* Sacriptual; sacred; relating to or knowing the Vedas; *n.* a Brahman versed in Vedas.

Vaidya, *n.* An Ayurvedic physician. *—ak*, n. The science of practising medicine.

Vaimanasya, *n.* Rancour; malice; hostility, enmity.

Vair, *n.* Animosity; enmity; hostility.

Vairágya, *n.* (an attitude of) renunciation of, or detachment from, the worldly affairs.

Vaishnav, *n./a.* A devotee of Lord Vishnu.

Vaishya, *n.* A caste group amongst Hindus; the third caste group, i.e. the trading class.

Vajah, *n.* Reason; cause; excuse.

Vájib, *n.* Reasonable; proper; incumbent; rightful.

Vajr, *n.* Thunderbolt; lightning; a fatal weapon. *—hriday*, a. Cruel; barbarous; un-feeling.

Vajúd, *n.* Existence; presence; being.

Vak, *n.* A heron; a crane. *—vritti,* n. Pretence; firing bullets from behind the bibles.

Vakíl, *n.* An advocate; a lawyer; a pleader. *Vakálat,* n. Advocacy; plea; practice of law.

Vakf, *n.* Charitable trust; an endowment.

Vakr, *a.* Curved; oblique; cunning. *—gati,* n. Zig-zag motion; crooked. *—buddhi,* a Dishonest; twisted mind. *—drishti*, a. oblique glance; an angry look; a frown; a scowl.

Vaktá, *n.* A speaker; a person delivering a speech, *Pra*—, n. A spokes-person.

Vaktavya, *n.* statement; something worth stating.

Vákya, *n.* A sentence. (grammar); an arrangement of words which contains a comprehensible, meaningful statement. *—khand*, n. A clause. *—rachná,* n. Syntax.

Vallabh, *n.* A husband; a lover.

Vám, *a.* Left; sinistral; reverse; contrary; adverse; preverse. *—márg,* n. Leftism; left-wing; radical philosophy. [Amercans call it communism; British, out of their sophistication, declare it to be 'socialism'].

Vámá, *n.* A woman (owing to the Hindu tradition of women staying on the left side of their husbands, on all ceremonial occasions).

Vaman, *n.* Vomit; puke.

Váman, *n.* A dwarf; a person of very short height; a pygmy; a proper name for one of Lord Vishnu's incarnations.

Van, *n.* Wood; forest; jungle. —*char / chárí,* a. Ones who dwell in the forest; animals of the jungle. —*vidyá,* n. Science of forestry.

Vánar, *n.* A monkey; an ape; (teasingly—) monkeyish i.e. mischievous. —*sená,* n. (literally) an army of monkeys as referred to in the epic *Rámáyan;* proverbially, it implies a noisy, disorderly mob.

Vanaspati, *n.* Vegetation; legumes.

Vanchana, *n.* Deception; irony; humbug; imposture.

Vánchha, *n.* Desire; wish; longing.

Vanchit, *a.* Deprived; cheated out of; tricked.

Vandan, / Vandaná, *n.* Deferential salutatioin; obeisance; worship.

Vandhyá, *a.* Barren; unfertile; unproductive. —*sut,* a. An impossible phenomenon; imaginary product.

Vaṇ, *n.* Sppech; voice; *Saraswati*— the goddess of learning and fine arts. —*vilás,* n. Word-games; indulgence in matters linguistic, the aim of which could be to improve speech-patterns, and the use of language for all purposes.

Vaṇij, *n.* Trade; commerce; buying and selling activity.

Vaṇik, *n.* A trader; a business person; a dealer. —*vritti,* n. The attitude of mind where one always seeks a return on any inputs into a situation. [In common parlance, we call it *Baniyágíri*].

Vansh, *n.* Dynasty; lineage; clan; stock; family. —*gat,* a. Dynastic; pertaining to lineage. —*aj/ dhar,* a. A descendant; a progeny. —*tálika,* n. Genealogy; genealogical chart. —*násh,* n. The end or examination of a family. —Ianukram, n. Family succession; order of succession. —*anugat,* a. Hereditary; obtained through lineal heritance.

Vápas, *a.* Return; taking or giving back; reversal.

Vaquat, Vuqat, *n.* Value; worth.

Var, *n.* A bride groom. *a* . Good; excellent; beautiful.

Vár, *n.* Attack; assault; a stroke; a blow; also a day of the week, i.e. *Somvár, Mangalvár, etc.*

Váráṇasí, *n.* The holy city of Benaras [also known as city of Lord *Shiva*].

Várá-nyárá, A settlement; a

decisive culmination; an outcome of adversarial combat.

Varásat, *n.* [See *Virásat*].

Varchaswa, *n* Excellence; impression; aura; supremacy over one's peers.

Vardán, *n.* A boon; fulfilment of an intense wish; gift.

Várdát, *n.* An incident; a mishap; an unfortunate event.

Vardí, *n.* A uniform.

Varg, *n.* Square; a class; a category; a group.

Váris, *n.* An heir; a successor.

Varishṭh, *a.* Senior; best; most preferable.

Varṇ, *n.* A caste; a colour; a dye. —*sankar, a.* A cross breed; hybrid.

Varṇan, *n.* Description; narration; commantary.

Varsh, *n.* A year (also a prefix marking land/territory; i,e, *Bháratvarsh*). *Prati*—, adv. Annually; per annum.

Varshá, *n.* Rain. —*kál,* n. Rainy season.

Vártá, *n.* Talk; talks; discussion; negotiation. —*láp*, n. Dialogue.

Vartmán, *n.* Present time; existing; current.

Vartaní, *n.* Spelling.

Vás, *n.* Habitation; dwelling; residence; (also means—) fragrance; aroma.

Vasá, *n.* Fat; fats; oils.

Vasantí, *n.* The spring (season); also the name of a *rág* in Indian Classical Music. —*Panchamí,* n. A very popular Hindu Festival which is celebrated on the fifth day of the moonlit fortnight of the month of *Mágh.* [This whole season is marked by a profusion of light yellow, sringy sort of colour in costumes and all other visibles of life].

Vash, *n.* Control; power; subjugation.

Váshp, *n.* Steam; vapour.

Vasílá, *n.* Source of living; means; support.

Vásit, *a.* Perfumed; scented; famous; populous.

Vásná, *n.* Passion; intense sexual desire.

Vastu, *n.* An article; a thing; an object; a substance; material; content. —*gyán,* n. Knowledge of the essentials. —vinimay, n. exchange of things/essentials; barter system. —*sthiti,* n. The real position.

Vástu, *n.* Architecture; the science of house-building. —*vidyá*/-*shástr*, n. Ancient hindu treatise on the art and science of house building.

Vasúl, *n.* Realised; collected. —*karmá*, v. To collect; to realise.

Vasundhara, *n.* The earth.

Vaṭ, *n.* A banyan tree.

Vát, *n.* A road; path; way.

Vatan, *n.* Homeland; native country. —*parast*, a. Patriot. —*farosh*, a. One who sells his/her country, i.e. a traitor. —*í,* of one's home-country; a compatriot.

Vaṭí, *n.* A pill; a tablet.

Váṭiká, *n.* A small garden.

Vats, *n.* Offspring; progeny; used as a vocative address for a son, or a junior.

Vatsal, *a.* Affectionate; tender; darling.

Vatsar, *n.* A year.

Vayas, *n.* Age; lifetime.

Váydá, *n.* [See *Vádá*].

Váyu, *n.* Air; wind; windy humour; the god of wind (according to Hindu mythology. —*márg,* n. Airways. —*yán*, n. Aircraft(s). —*sená,* n. Air force. —*sevá,* a. Airlines.

Vazan, *n.* Weight; importance; the measure of a metre in poetry. —*dár*, a. Weighty; heavy; important.

Vazárat, *n.* Ministry; ministership.

Vazífá, *n.* Scholarship; stipend; a grant (to defray the costs of study).

Vazír, *n.* A minister (in administration, of state). —*i-ázam,* a. Prime Minister.

Ved, *n.* The most ancient and sacred scriptures of the Hindus. (They are four in number: *Yajus, Rig, Atharva and Sáma).*

Vedánt, *n.* System of philosophy based particularly on the Upanishads.

Veg, *n.* Speed; velocity; momentum. —*ván*, speedy; swift.

Vesh, *n.* Costume; dress; external appearance; guise.

Veshyá, *n.* A prostitute; a woman of easy virtue; a swear-word in polite society towards a promiscuous lady. —*gaman*, v. The act of going to prostitutes (for gratification). —*gámí*, a. One who goes to prostitutes. —*vritti,* n. The profession of —. *Veshyálay*, n. A brothel; a place from where they ply their trade.

Vetan, *n.* Salary; wages; pay; remuneration. —*bhogí,* a. One depdendant on wages; a salaried worker.

Vibhág, *n.* Department; section; division (of a bigger establishment/organization).

Vibhájan, *n.* Division of assets; partition of territory.

Vibhakt, *a.* Divided; partitioned; separated.

Víbhats, *adj.* Frightening; macabre; repulsive.

Vibhíshaṇ, *n.* A proper name; name of the defecting younger brother of King *Rávana* of Lanka, the main adversary of the hero *Ráma;* A Quizling character.

Vibhíshiká, *n.* Horror; terror; calamitous happening.

Vichár, *n.* Thinking; thoughts; idea(s); view(s); opinion(s); observation(s). *—goshṭhí,* n. A seminar. *—shakti,* n. Reasoning faculty. *—shíl,* a. Thoughtful; reflective; contemplative.

Vidá, *n.* Taking leave; farewell; adieu; a woman's departure from her parents' home after wedding.

Vidhán, *n.* Legislation; rule; regulation; disposition; manner.

Vidharm, *n.* Heresy; a religion other than one's own; a nonconformist religion.

Vidhawá, *n.* A widow; a woman with her husband dead.

Vidhur, *n.* A widower.

Vidroh, *n.* Uprising; revolt; rebellion; mutiny; insurrection.

Vidúshak, *n.* Jester; buffoon; the jocose companion and confiential friend of the hero in a traditional Indian play; clown; a joker; one who puts up a comic show of mirth and laughter; a mimic.

Vidyá, *n.* Learning; knowledge; education; science; discipline; skill. *—hín,* a Illiterate; stupid. *—rthí,* n. A student; a learner; a trainee.

Vighn, *n.* A obstacle; an intrusion; an interruption; meddling; obstruction.

Vigyán, *n.* Science; systematic knowledge; rational understanding of subjects we study.

Vikár, *n.* Flaw; fault; deformation; defilement; disorder.

Vikás, *n.* Evolution; development; growth; bloom progress; advancement; forward movement.

Vikhyát, *a* Famous; renowned; well-known; reputed; celebrated.

Vikiraṇ, *n.* Radiation; diffusion.

Vikram, *n.* Name of a celebrated Hindu empoeror of 7th century India under whom a vast profusion of arts and learning took place. A time-marker, *Vikarmí Samvat,* was started to remember him.

Vikrit, *a.* Deformed; mutilated; distorted; perverted; disordered; strained, etc.

Vikriti, *n.* Deformation; mutiliation; defect; morbidity; deviation, etc.

Vikshipt, *a.* Mad; crazy; bewildered; insane; perplexed.

Vilakshaṇ, *a.* Queer; strange; peculiar; wonderful; remarkable; exceptional; extra-ordinary; fantastic; prodigious; precocious.

Vilamb, *n.* Delay; procrastination; lag; tardiness.

Viláp, *n.* Lamentation; wailing; crying in memory of the departing/departed soul):

Vilás, *n.* Enjoyment; luxury; amorous plays; wantonness; lust. —*í,* a. Aman who loves luxury; a lustful man. —*iní,* a. A lustful woman; a lady seeking pleasure.

Viláyat, *n.* (Hindi version of the Enlish colloquialism; *Blighty*). England; Europe; foreign land.

Vilay, *n.* Merger; dissolution; submersion.

Vimal, *a.* Clear; clean; free from dirt or dust; spotless; flawless; pure.

Vimán, *n.* An aeroplane(s); aircraft(s); airliner(s).

Vimarsh, *n.* Consultation; consideration; reflection, deliberation. *Vichár*—, n. Coference; exchange of opinions.

Vimukh, *a.* Indifferent One(s) with a sense of aversion; disinclined.

Viṇa, n. A south Indian lute with a large gourd at either end. —*páṇiní/vádiní,* n. A name for goddess Saraswati.

Vinásh, *n.* Destruction; devastation; disaster; ruin; week.

Vinásh, *n.* Destruction; annihilation; ruination. —*kárí,* adj. One causing destruction; one responsible for annihilation; one bringing ruination.

Vináshak, *adj.* Destroyer; one causing annihilation.

Vinay, *n.* Entreaty; obeisance; affability.

Vináyak, *n.* A remover of obstacles; a name for Lord *Ganesha,* a prime Hindu deity.

Vinimay, *n.* Humour; amusement; recreation; skit; jest.

Vipaksh, *n.* Opposition; adversary.

Vipann, *a.* Distressed; destitute; fallen into a calamity; crisis-ridden poor; one without means or resources. —*tá,* n. Poverty; state of poverty.

Viparít, *a.* Opposite/opposed; contrary; reverse; against.

Viparyay, *n.* Metathesis; reversal; transportation.

Viparyáy, *n.* Antonym; antidote.

Viphal, *n.* Unsuccessful; Failed/ failure; inefficacious; fruitless; futility.

Vipr, *n.* A Brahman, a member of the highest caste amongst the Hindus.

Viplau, *n.* Insurrection; insurgency; revolt.

Vír, *a.* Heroic; brave; valiant; gallant. *—kávy*, n. Heroic poetry; poetry eulogising brave deeds. *—gati*, a. Heroic death; demise on the battlefield. *—gáthá,* n. A saga of heroic deeds. *—pújá*, n. Hero-worship. *—hriday*, n. Stout heart(s).

Virah, *n.* Parting from the loved one(s); separation from the dears one(s).

Virájmán, *a.* (Regally) seated; sitting (word used deferentially); gracing by one's presence; appearing splendid.

Virakt, *a.* detached (from wordly attachments and affairs); disaffected; disengaged, indifferent.

Viral/ Virla, *a.* Thin; sparse; rare; scarce.

Viraṭ, *a.* Gigantic; collossal; enormous; huge. *—rúp,* n. A reference to Lord Krishna revealing his Universal form to his disciple Arjuna, in the middle of the battlefield, when he was confused by the perceived differences between the Creator and the beings. [*Bhagavadgítá*].

Virodh, *ń.* Opposition; antagonism; hostility; resistance; objection; antimony; protest; contradiction.

Viráná, *n.* Desolate place; deserted area; derelict place.

Virásat, *n.* Legacy; inheritance.

Vírya, *n.* Semem; potency; manly vigour; heroism. *—pát*, discharge of semen. *—hín*, a Impotent.

Visarjan, v. Relinquishing; dispersal; abandonment; renunciation of (the body; or of desires); sending away; consigning to water [often rivers, holy ponds, or to the ocean] or to sacred fires [of the worshipful images at the end of a festival, like *Ganesh-Pújá,* or *Kálí Pújá. Asthí—*, v. Consigning of cremated remains of a human body to the perceived holy waters.

Vish, *n.* Poison; venom. *—kanyá*, n. A girl/woman so impregnated with poison in her system that any man copulating with her, or even kissing her, would perish. (An ancient instrument of covert warfare in India). *—vaman,* v. Vituperative/ virulent utterance against someone. *—ke bíj boná,* v. To sow the seeds of disharmony. —*gholná*, v. To cause a quarrel.

Vishád, *n.* Gloom; somebreness; melancholy; despondency. —*púrṇa*, a. melancholic; sombre; gloomy.

Vishál, *n.* Huge; large; big spacious; grand; extensive; vast; great; gigantic; colossal.

Visham, *a.* Odd; heterogenous; incongruous; uneven; rough; dissimilar; disagreeable.

Vishay, *n.* Subject; topic; matter; content; sensual/sexual pleasure. —*lolup*, a. Lecherous; sexually indulgent.

Vishay-bhog, *n.* Passionate dalliance; enjoying a sexual encounter.

Vishayì, *adj.* Indulgent [in sexual dalliance].

Vishesh, *a.* Special; specific; particular; distinctive.

Visheshaṇ, *n.* An adjective; attribute; epithet.

Vishishṭ, *n.* Special; specific; particular; prominent; characteristic; typical.

Vishṇu, *n.* The second member of the Divine Hindu trinity, one credited with, and responsible for, the maintenance of this creation, one who feeds, one who nurtures. This deity is credited with more incarnations than any other, in Hindu mythological literature.

Vishrám, *n.* Rest; repose; relaxation. —*grih,* a. Rest House. —*kal,* a. Rest period; an interval.

Vishṭha, *n.* Faeces; excreta; nightsoil.

Vishuddh, *a.* Pure; chaste; virtuous; genuine; unmixed; unadulterated.

Vishwa, *n.* The world; Universe. —*kosh,* n. An encyclopaedia. —*prasiddh,* a. World renowned.

Vishwás, *n.* Assurance; belief; confidence; trust; faith; reliance. —*ghát,* n. Breach of faith; betrayal of trust; treachery; treason. —*yogya,* adj. Dependable; reliable; trustworthy.

Vishwa-vidyálay, *n.* A university. —*parisar,* n. University campus.

Vismay, *n.* Surprise; wonder; astonishment; amazement.

Visphoṭ, *n.* An explosion; a blast; a burst; a crack. —*ak,* a. Explosive.

Vistár, *n.* Expansion; elaboration; spread; extent; span; extension.

Vitrishṇa, *n.* Repugnance; repulsion; revulsion.

Vitt, *n.* Finance; wealth.

Vivád, *n.* A dispute; a controversy; an argument; a discussion; litigation.

Viváh, *n.* Marriage; wedding; matrimony; nuptials.

Vivash, *a.* Under duress; compelled; obliged (to do or say something); helpless; disabled. [Colloquially spoken as *Be-bas*].

Vivechan, *n.* Critical appraisal; evaluation; critical examination; analytical study; investigation; discrimination.

Vivek, *n.* Reason; discretion; judgement; sense of right and wrong; wisdom.

Vividh, *a.* Varied; various; different; diverse; miscellaneous.

Viyog, *n.* Separation; disunion; bereavement.

Vriddh, *n.* Old; elderly; aged; mature; Vriddhi, *a.* Increase; increment; rise; growth; progress; enhancement; augmentation; magnification.

Vrihaspati, *n.* (According to Hindu mythology) the name of the preceptor of all heavenly beings; an epithet for a *guru*; the largest planet in the solar system, called Jupiter. —*vár*, n. Thursday.

Vriksh, *n.* Tree(s).

Vrish, *n.* A bull; a sign in the zodiac—*Taurus*.

Vrishchik, *n.* A scorpion; the eighth sign in the zodiac, *Scorpio*.

Vrishṭi, *n.* Rain.

Vrithá, *a.* In vain; without purpose; ineffective.

Vritt, *n.* Circle; ring; account; record; news; verse.

Vritti, *n.* Instinct; mentality; profession; vocation; function; stipend.

Vyabhichár, *n.* Fornication; lewdness; wenching; debauchery; adultery.

Vyádhi, *n.* A disease; an ailment; a malady. —*grast*, a. One afflicted with disease.

Yyáj, *n.* [See *Byáj*].

Vyákaraṇ, *n.* Grammer. —*siddh*, a. Grammatically correct.

Vyákhyá, *n.* Commentary; explanation; interpretation; elaboration; annotation.

Vyákhyán, *n.* Speech; lecture; oration; exposition; elaboration.

Vyakti, *n.* A person; an individual; a subject. —*gat*, a. Private; confidential; pertaining to an individual.

Vyaktitva, *n.* Personality, individuality. —*hin*, One devoid of personality, etc.

Vyangya, *n.* Sarcasm; Irony; suggestion; innuendo; caricature.

Vyanjan, *n.* A consonant; rich food (dish); dainties.

Vyápár, *n.* Trade; business; traffic. —*sambandhí,* a. Pertaining to trade; mercantile. —*í,* a. A trader; a businessman; a wheeler-dealer.

Vyápt, *a.* Spread; pervaded; permeated; extended.

Vyarth, *a.* Useless; fruitless; futile; ineffective; unprofitable.

Vyasan, *n.* Vice; addition; an (antisocial) habit.

Vyast, *n.* A Busy; occupied; tiedup; engaged (not betrothal-way).

Vyatha, *n.* Pain; agony; anguish.

Vyatít, *a.* Passed; past; bygone.

Vyavadhán, *n.* Hindrance; interruption.

Vyavahár, *n.* Behaviour; dealings; treatment; transaction; practice; usage; use; application. —*kushal,* a. Tactful; worldlywise; circumspect.

Vyavasáy, *n.* Profession; vocation; calling; occupation; practice.

Vyavasthá, *n.* Management; order; system; arrangement. —*pak,* a. Manager; One who organises; one responsible for arranging.

Vyáyám, *n.* Exercise; a work-out; gynastics. —*shala,* n. A gymnasium.

Vyom, *n.* Sky; the dome of universe. —*gangá,* n. The milky way. —*chárí,* n. Sky-faring, i.e. birds, bees and aeroplanes.

Vyúh, *n.* A military array; a strategic placement of soldiers and weapons. —*rachná,* n. To organise the strategic disposition of men and armour in the battlefield.

वहम का इलाज हकीम लुकमान्
के पास भी नहीं था।

Waham/Vaham ká ilaj
hakím lukmán ké páss bhí
nahín thá.

(Even the divinity could not cure
the disease called suspicion.)

W, w, please see the introduction to section 'V'

Wá, *conj.* And; too; also; with; in company with.

Wabá, *n.* Plague; pestilence; epidemic; disease; a major problem.

Wabál, *n.* Misfortune; curse; divine vengeance.

Wábastá, *adj.* Connected; concerning; attached; joined; related; dependant. *—gán,* n. Domestics; relations; adherents.

Wádá, *n.* A promise; an agreement; a vow.

Wádí, *n.* Valley; vale.

Wadúd, *a.* Beloved; friend; an epithet of God.

Wafá, *n.* Performance of a promise; Faithfulness; fidelity; sincerity. *—Dár,* adj. Faithful; loyal. *Be*-adj. Disloyal; treacherous; insincere.

Wafád, *n.* Defence; security.

Wafát, *n.* Death; demise; decease.

Waghaira, *adj.* Et cetera; and others; and so forth.

Wáhid, *adj.* One individual; single; sole; unique; an epithet of God.

Wáhiyát, *adj.* Nonsense; absurb; obscene.

Waham, *n.* Illusion; conjecture; gues; suspicion; doubt; fear; superstition.

Wahshat, *n.* A Desert; grief; horrow; loneliness.

Wahashí, *n.* Wild; untamed; barbarous; fierce; cruel.

Wáiz, *n.* A preacher; a teacher; An advisor; a preceptor; one who delivers sermons; a wise man.

Wajd, *n.* Ecstasy; rapture; religious frenzy.

Wajah, *n.* Cause; reason; justification; Motive.

Wájib, *adv.* Fair; justifiable; correct; proper; deserving; reasonable.

Wakálat, *n.* Pleading; advocacy; practice at the Bar. *—námá,* n. Power of attorney; a legal proxy.

Wakíl; *n* An attorney; an advocate; a lawyer; a pleader.

Waláyat, *n.* Foreign country; (*colloquially*) England; Europe. *—í,* adj. Foreign-made; imported; (*colloquially*) high quality.

Wald, *n.* A son; an offspring; an heir. *Lá—,* adj. Without an offspring; heirless. *—iyat,* n. Descent; parentage; genealogy.

Wálid, *n.* Father; parent. *—á,* n. Mother. *—Ain,* n. pl. Parents.

Wápas, *adv.* Return(ed); back; afterwards. *—karná/dená,* v. To return; to bring back. *—lená,* v. To retrieve; to reposses; to accept back.

Waqf, *n.* A legacy; a trust; an endowment for a religious or social purpose.

Waqfá, *n.* Gap; interval; distance or Time-gap in between; delay; pause; Respite; postponement.

Wáqe'á, *n.* Event; happening; incident; accident; news.

Wáqif, *adj.* One who knows; acquainted with; familiar with; versed in; conversant with; aware of. *Wáqfiyat,* n. Knowledge of; information on; experience of.

Waqt, *n.* Time; season; period; term.

Wár, *n.* Blow; attack; knock; assault.

Wardí, *n.* A uniform; a prescribed form of clothing (as in the police, armed forces, major corporations, etc.).

Wargaláná, *v.* Event; occurance; incident.

Wáridát, *n.* Event; occurance; incident.

Wáris, *n.* Heir; legatee; a master; an owner.

Warq, *n.* A sheet; a leaf; a slice.

Warsá/ Wirsá, *n.* Heritage; inheritance; Bequest; tradition.

Warzish, *n.* Exercise; practice; usage.

Wasíh, *adj.* Vast; roomy; spacious; large; extensive.

Wasílá, *n.* Means; cause; intervention; Affinity.

Wasíyat, *n.* Last will and testament; legacy; bequest; mandate.

Wasl, *n.* Union; conjunction; meeting (of lovers).

Wáste, *n.* For; for the sake of; in behalf of; on account of.

Watan, *n.* Native country; country of origin; country of birth; motherland.

Wázeh, *adj.* Clear; evident; obvious; manifest.

Wazífá, *n.* Salary; stipend; remuneration; scholarship.

Wazír, *n.* A minister of state; a vizier; A piece on the chessboard; a knave In playing cards. *i-ázam,* n./adj. The Prime Minister; a premier. *Wazárat,* n. Ministry; council of ministers.

Wazn/ Wazan, *n.* Weight; measure; clout.

Wazú, *n.* Ablution before prayers (in Islam); ritual purification.

Wír/ Wíráná, *adj.* Waste; deserted; desolate; ruined; derelict; devastated; depopulated.

Wisál, *n.* Interview; rendezvous; union.

Woh, *Pron.* He; she; it; that.

Wujud, *n.* Existence; being; life; body.

Wusúl, *n.* Receipt; collection; realization.

X, x, is redundant in terms of transliterating any standard Hindi or Urdu words. Therefore, we have compiled no words under this heading. Hindi and Urdu vocabulary can well manage its repertoire of compound letters by combining other letters of the Roman alphabet.

Y, y, is used to denote letter (य) in Hindi and letter (ی) in Urdu. It serves no vowel function in our scheme of transliteration.

Yá, *conj.* Or; either.

Yáb, *adv.* Obtaining; ginding; getting. *Das-i—*, Obtained; found. *Kám—*, Successful. *Ná—*, Scarce, rare, perhaps unobtainable.

Yáchak, *n.* A beggar, one who begs, a mendicant. *Yáchiká,* n. Appeal, plea, request.

Yád, *n.* Memory; recollection; remembrance; recognition. —*dásht,* n. Retentive memory; memory bank. —*Diláná,* v. To remind; to job one's memory; emphasise. —*gár,* n. memorial; a keepsake. —*karná,* To remember, to recall, to commit to memory. —*rakhná,* v. To retain in memory; to bear in mind.

Yadá, *adv.* When; where. —*kadá,* adv. Occasionally; sometimes; on and off.

Yadi, *conj.* Even if, although, though.

Yahán, *adv.* Here; hither; in this place. —*tak,* adv. Thus far; so far; as far as this; so much so; to such an extent; hitherto. —*kahín,* adv. Hereabouts; somewhere, within proximity.

Yahín, *adv.* Right here; this very fire.

Yagyopavít, *n.* The scared thread, worn by caste Hindu males, upon achieving puberty; ceremonially worn thread to mark one's age of responsibility for one's own deed.

Yahúdí, *n.* The Jew.

Yajmán, *n.* A priest's client (in matters of rituals and sacrifices);

Yak, *n.* (in Persian and Urdu-) One, single, a, an. —*á-yak,* adv. All at once; suddenly; out of the blue. —*ján,* adj. Close; bosom friends; inseparables. —*musht* adj. All in one go; in a single instalment; in total. —*sálá* adj. Yearling; a year old; once a year. —*sán* adj; uniform; plain; level. —*tarfá* adv. One-sided; unilaternal.

Yaḳh, *n.* Ice. adj. Frozen; extremely cold.

Yakká, *n.* A one-horse cart; an ace (in playing card).

Yakrit, *n.* Liver.—*íya,* adj. Pertaining to liver. —*róg,* n. Diseases of the liver.

Yakshmá, *n.* Tuberculosis. —*grast,* adj. One affected by tuberculosis; tubercular.

Yam, *n.* The deity or demi-god of death in Hindu pantheon. Also, restraint of passions. —*dút,* A messenger of death. —*lók,* the nether-world; the afterworld.

Yán, *n.* A vehicle. *bhojan*—, n. A restaurnant car (on a train). *Jal*—, n. A ship; a sea-going vessel. *Váyu*—n. An aeroplane. *Antariksh*—, n. Space vehicle; spacecraft.

Yantra, *n.* Machine; an instrument; a talisman; a mystical diagram. —*chálit,* adj. Mechanised. —*nirmit,* adj. Machine-made. —*gya,* n. Engineer; one Who knows machines.

Yaqín, *n.* Certainty; assurance; belief; true Faith. —*an,* adv. Truly; certainly; absolutely; undoubtedly.

Yáqút, *n.* Ruby (precious stone).

Yár, *n.* A friend; a companion; a mate; a paramour; a lover. —*bash,* adj. Friendly; cordial; merry; jolly.

Yarqán, *n.* The yellow fever; jaundice.

Yás, *n.* Depression, Despair; fear. *Mahvi*—, adj. Depressed; under a spell of despair.

Yash, *n.* Fame; reputation; credibility; praise; honour.

Yátaná, *n.* Torture; torment; harassment.

Yathásambhav, *adv.* Whatever is possible; as far as within one's power.

Yathháshakti, *adv.* As far as possible; as much as one can.

Yathárth, *adv.* Factually, exactly as is; right; proper; exact.

Yati, *n.* A pause; check; an ascetic; anchoret. —*gati,* n. pausing and pacing (in metrical writing).

Yatím, *n.* Orphan; without father; one without help or support. —*kháná,* n. An orphanage.

Yatn, *n.* Effort; try; energy; remedy.

Yátrá, *n.* A journey; travel; wayfaring; Pilgrimage; a street-play tradition in Bengal. —*vrittánt,* n. A Travelogue; narrative of a journey.

Yátrí, *n.* Traveller; passenger; wayfarer; A pilgrim; a tourist.

Yaum, *n.* A day. —*i-ázádí,* adj. The Independence Day.

Yaun, *n.* Sex; sexual; vaginal. —*sambandh,* n. Sexual relations. —*tripti,* n. Sexual gratification. —*varjaná,* n. Sexual inhibition. —*vikriti,* n. Sexual perversion.

Yauvan, *n.* Youth; youthful spirit;

Yav, *n.* Barley.

Yavan, *n.* A Greek; a foreigner; an alien.

Yavaniká, *n.* Curtain (on the stage); drop scene.

Yé, *adj.* These; they.

Yéh, *adj.* This; it; the; he; she.

Yoddhá, *n.* A Warrior; a combatant.

Yog, *n.* Addition; a system of Hindu philosophy (aimed at bringing body and mind together); a discipline of bodily exercises; asceticism. —*í,* n. Practitioner of the aforementioned.

Yógya, *adj.* Qualified; skilled; able; deserving; capable; competent; worthy; eligible; suitable; meritorious.

Yojan, *n.* A measure of distance (in ancient India) roughly equal to eight miles, or 12 kilometres.

Yojaná, *n.* Plan; scheme; arrangement; Disposition.

Yoni, *n.* Vagina; female procreative organ; the form of existence or station fixed at birth, as a reward or punishment for one's own deeds (according to Hindu philosophy of reincarnation).

Yorúp, *n.* Europe. —*íya,* n. European.

Yuddh, *n.* War; combat; battle; fight. *Malla-yuddh,* n. Wrestling. *Mushti*—, n. Boxing; combat with fists. *Vák*—n. Combat of words.

Yug, *n.* An age; an epoch; an aeon.

Yugánt, *n.* End of an era. Final destruction at the end of an aeon. —*kárí,* adj. Epoch making; revolutionary.

Yukt, *adj.* United; combined; fitted with; Equipped with.

Yukti, *n.* A device; a means; a tactic; a Manoevre; a rationale. —*sangat,* adj. Logical; rational; soundly arguable.

Yuvá, *n.* Young (man and/or woman).

Yuvak, *n.* Young (male).

Yuvatí, *n.* Young (female).

✻✻✻✻✻✻✻✻✻✻✻✻✻✻✻✻✻✻✻✻

ज़रूरत ईजाद की माँ होती है।

Zaroorat íjád kí mán hotí hai.

(Necessity is the mother of invention.)

✻✻✻✻✻✻✻✻✻✻✻✻✻✻✻✻✻✻✻✻

Z, z, is used for representing the imported-from persian sound of (ज़) in Hindi and (ض ز ظ ژ) all four sounds of Urdu alphabet.

Zá, *adj.* Born; descended.

Zabán, *n.* The tongue; speech; language; dialect. —*band honá,* v. To be stricken dumb; to develop locked jaw. —*chaláná,* v. To use foul language; to talk too much. —*daráz,* adj. Saucy. —*kám míithá,* adj. Sweet-talker; honey-tongued.

Zabah, *n.* Slaughter; sacrifice.

Zabar, *adj.* Above; high; superior. —*dast,* adj. Powerful; strong; oppressive. —*dastí,* adv. By force; by violent means.

Zábitá, *adj.* Universal rule; established practice; law; ordinance; procedure. —*i-adálat,* n. Legal procedure. *Hasb-i*—. adv. Through proper channel; according to rules. *Bá*—adv. Formal; regular; duly.

Zabt, *n.* Check; restraint; possession; regulation; confiscation.

Zabún, *adj.* Bad; vicious; wicked.

Zachchá, *n.* A lying-in woman.

Żád, Zádá, *adj.* Born of; son of; descendant of. *Adam*—, adj. born of Adam, the original human; of human race. *Sháh*—, adj. Born of ruler; a prince.

Zadá, *adj.* Struck by; oppressed from; adversely affected by.

Záed, *adj.* Superfluous; in excess; redundant.

Záeqá, *n.* Taste; relish; flavour.

Zafar, *adj.* Triumph; victory. —*námá,* A eulogy or congratulatory message written to mark someone's victory.

Záfrán, *n.* Saffron; world's most expensive spice; a vibrant orange colour.

Zahmat, *n.* Trouble; botheration; pain.

Zahan, *n.* Brain; intelligence.

Zahar/ Zahr, *n.* Poison, venom, bitterness (of words and temperament). —*ílá,* —*ílí,* adj. Poisonous; venomous; bitter; hurtful (words); toxic.

Záhid, *n.* A hermit; an ascetic; a preacher.

Zahín, *adj.* Brainy; sagacious; clever; intelligent; ingenious; sharp.

Záhir, *adj.* Clear; visible; outward; external; apparent; open; plan; manifest; conspicuous.

Zahrílá, *adj.* Poisonous; venomous; toxic.

Záiká/Záyká, *n.* Taste. **Záykedár,** *adj.* Tasty; delicious; appetising.

Zakát, *n.* Alms; charitable gifts.

Zaḳhm, *n.* Wound; scar; sore; cut. —*pakná,* adv. To suppurate. —*í-qárí,* adj. Mortal wound.

Zalíl, *adj.* Abject; mean; disgraced; submissive.

Zálim, *n.* A tyrant; an oppressor; a tyranical person; an oppressive person.

Zalzalá, *n.* Earthquake; a revolutionary event.

Zamáná, *n.* Time; season; period. —*sáz,* adj. One who moves with the times; one who goes with the fashion of the day; trendy. —*sází,* n. Attitude of moving with the times; flowing with the tide.

Zamánat, *n.* Bail; surety; security.

Zamín, *n.* The earth; ground; land; soil; terra firma; background. —*dár,* n. A landlord.

Zámin, *adj.* One who gives Bail; one who offers surety on your behalf.

Zamír, *n.* Conscience; heart; mind; ideal.

Zan, *n.* (Persian) Woman. —*áná,* n. Women's quarters in a household; public facilities, like toilets waiting-rooms and trains etc. reserved for women only.

Zanaḳha, *n.* A eunuch; a sexual deviant.

Za<u>n</u>g/Za<u>n</u>gár, *n.* Rust.

Za<u>n</u>jír, *n.* Chain; fetters.

Zánú, *n.* Knee; lap; thing.

Zar, *n.* (Persian) Money; wealth; Proserity.

Zár, *n.* Lamentation; wailing; desire; wish. —*zár róná,* adv. Shedding floods of tears.

Zaráfat, *n.* Wit; humour; jest.—*an,* adv. In jest; by way of a joke.

Zarar, *n.* Harm; injury; defect.

Zarb, *n.* Blow; stroke; (in arithmatic) Multiplication.

Zard, *adj.* yellow. —*á,* a yellowish, edible tobacco powder. consumed all over north India and Pakistan. —*chób,* n. Turmeric.

Zardí, *n.* Egg yoke.

Zarí, *n.* Gold brocade; embroidery done with gold and siler threads.

Zaríf, *adj.* Witty; clever; one who is good at repartee.

Zariyá, *n.* Means; a way; a method; an Instrument.

Zarrá, *n.* An atom; a particle; a spec of Dut; a jot.

Zarúr, *adv.* Essentially; expedietially; Required; of course. —*i,* adj. Essential; needed; necessary; urgent,—*at,* n. Need; requirement.

Zát, *n.* [a corruption of Sanskrit *Játi*] Caste; essence; origin; sort; kind. *Bad—*, adj. Low-born; born of lower caste parentage; a person of baser nature. *Be—*, adj. An outcaste; one who has been expelled from the caste brotherhood.

Zátí, *adj.* Personal; individual. *—taur par,* Adv. Personally; individually.

Zauq, *n.* Fall from grace; declination; decay; failure; humiliation.

Záviyá, *n.* Angle; a point of view; a corner. *—nashín,* adj. & n. One who has a fixed view; one set in a corner; a hermit.

Zebáish, *n.* Ornament; adornment; elegance.

Zer, *n.* Under; law; down; *adj.* Lower; inferior. *N.* The Persian and Urdu vowel point ( ).

Zewar, *n.* Jewellery; ornaments; jewels. *Adj.* Decorus; enhancing the qualities of—.

Zidd, *n.* obstinacy; stubbornness; contrariness; Perverseness; steadfastness. *—í,* adj. Obstinate; stubborn.

Zikr, *n.* Recollection; remembrance; mention; talk of; reference to.

Zilá, *n.* District; Division. *—dhísh,* n. The district magistrate.

Zillat, *n.* Humiliation; dishonour; baseness; insult.

Zimmá, *n.* Responsibility; Trust.

Zín, *n.* Saddle. *—kasna,* v. To saddle a horse. *—sáz,* n. A saddler.

Ziná, *n.* Adultery; illegitimate sexual relations. *—bil-zabr,* n. Rape; sexual intercourse without consent.

Zíná, *n.* A staircase; a flight of steps.

Zínat, *n.* Beauty; decoration; elegance.

Zindá, *adj.* Alive; living. *—gí,* n. Life; existence. *—dil,* adj. Lively; joyous; full of life.

Zindagí, *n.* Life; *—bhar,* adv. Lifelong; life time.

Zindán, *n.* A prison; a jail.

Zírá, *n.* Cummin seed; a spice.

Zirah, *n.* Armour. *—bakhtar,* n. Protective armour.

Zíst, *n.* Life; existence; being.

Ziyádah, *adj.* More; too much;excessive.

Ziyárat, *n.* Pilgrimage to Mecca, a holy place of the Muslims.

Zor, *n.* Strength; power; energy; vigour; force. *—áwar,* adj. Powerful; strong.

Zuhrá, *n.* Venus; ebauty. *—badan,* adj. As beautiful as venus.

Zukám, *n.* Common cold; runny nose.

Zuleikhá, *n.* A Quranic/Muslim proper name. [proverbially] *adj.* One exceptionally beautiful.

Zult, *n.* Curl; ringlet; lock of hair.

Zulum, *n.* Torture; oppression; tyranny. *—í,* adj. Oppressor; torturer.

Zulmat, *n.* Darkeness; gloom.

Zunnár, *n.* The Urdu-Persian name for the Hindu sacred thread called *Janeú.*

WORD INDEX

A : Page 1 - 44

B : Page 45 - 82

Áá : Parker Éé : Education Íí : Eager Úú : Cooper

D : Page 105 - 122

E : Page 123 - 123

F : Page 125 - 131

G : Page 133 - 152

I : Page 169 - 179

N : Page 281 - 301

O : Page 303 - 304

P : Page 305 - 333

R : Page 345 - 362

T : Page 405 - 428

W : Page 449 - 450